# The Teaching Experience

# The Teaching Experience

## *An Introduction to Reflective Practice*

**Michael L. Henniger**
*Western Washington University*

PEARSON

Merrill
Prentice Hall

Upper Saddle River, New Jersey
Columbus, Ohio

**Library of Congress Cataloging-in-Publication Data**

Henniger, Michael L.
   The teaching experience : an introduction to reflective practice / Michael L. Henniger.
     p. cm.
   Includes bibliographical references (p.) and indexes.
   ISBN 0-13-022521-5
   1. Teaching. 2. Teacher effectiveness. 3. Reflection (Philosophy) I. Title.
   LB1025.3.H46 2004
   371.102-dc22

                                                     2003058016

**Vice President and Executive Publisher:** Jeffery W. Johnston
**Executive Editor:** Debra A. Stollenwerk
**Editorial Assistant:** Mary Morrill
**Development Editor:** Kimberly J. Lundy
**Production Editor:** Linda Hillis Bayma
**Design Coordinator:** Diane C. Lorenzo
**Photo Coordinator:** Valerie Schultz
**Text and Cover Designer:** Ali Mohrman
**Cover Photo:** Getty
**Production Manager:** Pamela D. Bennett
**Director of Marketing:** Ann Castel Davis
**Marketing Manager:** Darcy Betts Prybella
**Marketing Coordinator:** Tyra Poole

This book was set in Berkeley Book by Carlisle Communications, Ltd. It was printed and bound by Courier Kendallville, Inc. The cover was printed by Phoenix Color Corp.

**Photo Credits:** Photo credits appear on page 409, which constitutes a continuation of the copyright page.

Pearson Education Ltd.
Pearson Education Singapore Pte. Ltd.
Pearson Education Canada, Ltd.
Pearson Education—Japan

Pearson Education Australia Pty. Limited
Pearson Education North Asia Ltd.
Pearson Educación de Mexico, S.A. de C.V.
Pearson Education Malaysia Pte. Ltd.

10 9 8 7 6 5 4 3 2 1
ISBN: 0-13-022521-5

# Preface

Every term, college students enter courses in teacher education to explore the possibilities and problems associated with becoming a teacher. These thoughtful, inquisitive, and energetic individuals are eager to learn more about students, teachers, and schools. They bring with them their own past schooling experiences, preconceptions about teaching and learning (some accurate and some not), and a strong desire to have an impact on their world. While there are those who have already made a commitment to the profession, most are exploring the roles and responsibilities to see if there is a good match. What these students need is a clear understanding of teaching as a profession, a rich knowledge base, opportunities to learn about both the joys and difficulties teachers encounter on a daily basis, and the encouragement to stop and reflect on schooling issues both individually and with others.

This text was written to assist prospective teachers in this process of exploration and reflection. Through the use of an engaging writing style that speaks directly to individual readers, those considering teaching as a career are continually challenged to think critically and deeply about the abilities and attitudes of exemplary educators and compare them with their own. The content of each chapter, coupled with captivating special features, provides a thorough and engaging overview of the teaching profession.

## Conceptual Framework: The Process of Reflective Practice

Through opportunities to reflect on their own past learning experiences, read about the realities of schooling, and discuss critical issues with others, prospective teachers are led on a reflective journey that culminates in deeper insights into the teaching profession. This process of reflection directly influences all aspects of teaching and learning, including professionalism, decision making, and accountability.

To be good decision makers, new teachers need to learn the complex process of reflection. This text is designed to help prospective teachers engage in active reflection as they study the decision-making steps needed for effective teaching and learning. This process involves the following:

- *Experience.* This component of the reflective process involves considering one's own life experiences; knowing one's own beliefs, assumptions, or preconceived ideas; and understanding how these experiences, beliefs, and assumptions inform effective teaching. Many of the special features developed for this text and described later in this preface support this aspect of reflection by providing opportunities for consideration of experiences, beliefs, and assumptions.

- *Research.*   Knowledge must inform classroom practice. In this phase of the reflective process, the teacher gathers good information, acquiring knowledge of the student, the content to be taught, the underlying theory and research, and the context or situation. This text provides a wealth of current and relevant information to those considering teaching. Prospective teachers can use this information as a starting point for good reflection.

- *Discussion.*   This component of the reflective process engages the teacher in active consideration of life experiences, beliefs, assumptions, and knowledge, whether with others by discussion or through a vehicle such as journaling. Once again, there are special features included in this text which provide prospective teachers with the content and the questions they need to reflect with others on a diverse array of topics.

- *Implementation.*   In this phase of the process, teachers carry all their understanding and consideration of experiences, beliefs, assumptions, and knowledge into their classroom practice. That is, their experiences, their research, and their discussion all inform their decision making in the classroom. There are several features included in this text that give prospective teachers the opportunity to make decisions informed by reflection.

The process of reflective practice is reinforced throughout the core text and text activities. In each chapter, readers encounter a rich assortment of reflection strategies and are encouraged to begin developing them into habits as they prepare for the day when they will be responsible for making the many difficult decisions required of all classroom teachers.

## Organization of the Text

This text is organized into four major sections that guide students through an introduction to reflection and to teaching as a profession, introduce them to foundational and timely concepts and topics in education, and encourage them to consider their choice of teaching as a career as well as the influences and characteristics that will help them become successful reflective practitioners.

### Part 1   *What Is Today's Context for Reflective Practice?*

In Chapters 1 to 5, prospective teachers are introduced to students, teachers, school settings, and issues of teacher professionalism. Chapter 1 identifies the benefits and challenges of teaching and helps the reader begin the process of determining if teaching is a good career choice. Chapter 2 focuses on the growing diversity among students in American classrooms and describes effective strategies for dealing with the differences that exist. Chapter 3 introduces the reader to the roles and characteristics of effective teachers. Chapter 4 describes the ways in which schools are typically organized and provides information on alternative forms of schooling. Chapter 5 describes the growing professional nature of teaching and the efforts being made to enhance the image of education.

### Part 2   *What Is Reflective Classroom Practice?*

Chapters 6 to 9 are designed to help the reader develop a deeper understanding of the essential elements of effective classroom teaching. Chapter 6 assists prospective teachers in understanding students and the many different ways in which they learn. Chapter 7 identifies the curriculum that is being taught in schools and how it has changed over time. Chapter 8 describes the elements of effective instruction, including an introduction to classroom management and discipline. Chapter 9 helps the reader understand the many issues surrounding the use of computers and other instructional technologies in today's schools.

### Part 3   *What Are the Foundations for Reflective Teaching?*

This section comprises Chapters 10 to 14, which provide prospective teachers with information about the historical, philosophical, and societal issues that influence teaching and learning. Chapter 10 addresses the history of American education and describes how this past has influenced current educational practice. Chapter 11 broadly defines philosophical study and describes several educational philosophies that influence teaching and learning today. Chapter 12 identifies the many ways in which American society influences student behaviors and how schools are responding to these issues. Chapter 13 describes the legal rights and responsibilities of teachers and students and summarizes key legislation and court cases influencing schooling. Chapter 14 provides prospective teachers with a framework for understanding the many levels of school governance and identifies both traditional and more recent efforts being used to finance schooling.

## Part 4 *How Do I Grow as a Reflective Practitioner?*

In this final section, the reader is reminded of the importance of viewing teaching as a profession that requires lifelong learning and continued growth as a reflective educator. Chapter 15 describes what teachers can expect during their first years in the classroom and encourages prospective teachers to continue learning and growing throughout their careers.

## Chapter Features

With a reader-friendly writing style and frequent opportunities for reflection, the text draws readers in and encourages them to personalize the concepts and examples as they develop a clear understanding of all aspects of teaching as a career. Throughout each chapter, these reflective features reinforce the content, examine contentious topics, and challenge students to explore how their own ideas and beliefs inform their teaching practice.

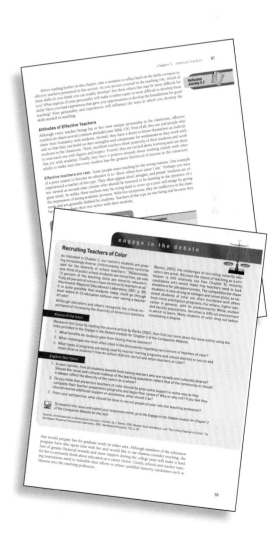

**Focus Questions and Chapter Scenario.** These chapter opener sections introduce chapter content in a meaningful and personalized manner. *Focus Questions* provide the framework around which the chapter and end-of-chapter sections are built.

**Reflective Journey.** This feature encourages prospective teachers to stop at key points within the main chapter narrative and think carefully about the issues being presented. Each reflective journey uses a series of thought-provoking questions embedded directly in the text to help teacher education students develop deeper insights into the issues and concepts being discussed. Students are invited to submit their responses to their instructor through the online journal on the Companion Website for this text.

**Engage in the Debate.** Prospective teachers have the opportunity to spend additional time investigating current issues that affect teaching and learning. Each issue has been chosen because of its direct impact on schooling and its potential for controversy. Those concerned with American education often have very different views on the possible benefits and problems associated with each issue. After presenting some of the key elements of the debate, readers are guided to *Research the Issue* by reading primary source materials and conducting online research using sources available on the Companion Website. *Explore Your Views* questions provide students the opportunity to articulate their own informed positions.

**Explore Your Beliefs.** This feature is designed to help prospective teachers begin to identify and analyze the beliefs about teaching and learning they currently hold. Because each student has experienced both good and bad teaching as part of their own preK–12 education, they bring many preconceived notions about schooling to any discussion of American education. Students are invited to *React and Reflect* to help bring these beliefs to the conscious level where they can be either validated or modified based on new knowledge. The Companion Website provides additional resources for exploring these topics in greater depth before students submit their responses online.

**Reflect on Diversity.** Issues related to race, poverty, exceptionality, gender, and religion are all addressed as important aspects of diversity, allowing students to develop a deeper understanding of diversity issues in schools. Through information and stories, prospective teachers are encouraged to think carefully about the similarities and differences that will exist in their classrooms and the impact they will have on teaching and learning. Readers are directed to the Companion Website to find further information on the topics presented and to respond to the *Explore and Reflect* questions online.

**Views from the Classroom.** The real world of teaching is a roller-coaster combination of joyful interchanges and difficult struggles. This feature gives readers the opportunity to hear directly from teachers in the field about what this experience is really like. Teachers at all levels express in their own words why they chose teaching as a career and what makes it worth all the effort it takes to be successful. These practicing teachers have given generously of their time and effort to share with teacher education students the realities of teaching. (Chapters 1, 2, 3, 5, 6, 8, 10, 11, 12, 15)

**Master Teacher Series.** These features and ABC News videos comprise a six-part *Nightline* documentary that follows a year in the life of a master teacher in an economically challenged school who has accepted the challenge of working with a class who failed the state's English language arts exam. Each feature provides a synopsis of the segment, along with thought-provoking questions that challenge readers to consider the real-life experiences of this teacher and her students. Students are invited to submit their responses online via the Companion Website. (Chapters 1, 3, 8, 10, 11, 15)

**Education in the News.** Video segments from ABC News programs such as *Nightline, 20/20,* and *World News Tonight* present current and controversial issues in education. Each in-text feature corresponds with footage available in the companion ABC News/Prentice Hall Video Library and presents a summary of the clip, along with reflective activities that allow the student to further explore the issue and discuss how such issues affect teachers, students, and schools today. Students are invited to submit responses to the activities online via the Companion Website. (Chapters 2, 4, 5, 6, 7, 9, 12, 13, 14)

# End-of-Chapter Features

The end-of-chapter features are designed to provide students additional opportunities to assess their knowledge of chapter topics and to develop as a professional by applying and exploring chapter concepts.

**Summary.** Each chapter concludes with a summary that provides a concise recap of the chapter topics and relates them to Praxis topics covered within each chapter section.

**Key Terms.** This listing of important terms and concepts covered in the chapter is a useful review and study tool.

**Reflective Journey: Online Journal.** Questions presented throughout the text of the chapter can be used as a starting point for online journal entries via the Companion Website, allowing readers to document personal and professional growth over the course of their career.

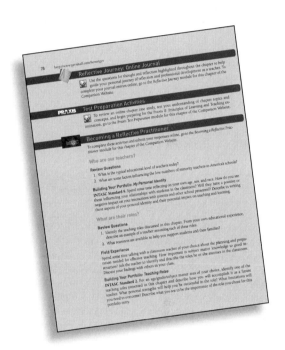

**Praxis Test Preparation Activities.** Online case histories and corresponding short-answer questions are formatted to connect chapter content with relevant sections of the Praxis II Principles of Learning and Teaching exam. Students can review the cases, submit their answers, and receive immediate feedback in this module of the Companion Website. In addition to being a valuable preparation activity, the exercises provide additional insight and practice in a real-world decision-making process.

**Becoming a Reflective Practitioner.** Each section is organized under the same focus questions as the chapter content, providing students with an opportunity to focus their exploration and review on each section. Each section includes three to five review questions and an INTASC-aligned portfolio activity; selected sections also include a field experience activity. The activities in each section are linked to the Companion Website for this text and can be completed online.

- *Review Questions.* Discussion and assessment questions for each major section of the chapter provide opportunities for students to discuss with each other some of the key issues raised.

- *Field Experience.* Suggested field experiences introduce students to the profession from many perspectives, providing suggestions for classroom observations of teaching and learning, interviews with teachers and administrators, and interactions with peers. Questions provide opportunities for reflection and allow students to gain additional insights into the classroom.

- *Building Your Portfolio.* Portfolio-building activities are provided for each major section of the chapter, encouraging readers to create portfolio entries that can be used as a beginning assessment of their understandings and beliefs regarding teaching and learning.

**Suggested Readings.** Additional readings support and enhance concepts and topics presented in the chapter.

## Supplemental Materials for Instructors

For those who adopt this textbook, there are several types of supplemental materials available that expand upon the content of the text and assist both students and professors in gaining greater insights into teaching as a profession.

**Instructor's Manual and Multimedia Guide.** Available on request, this supplement includes: suggestions for teaching the content of each chapter; ideas for using the companion ABC News/ Prentice Hall Video Libraries, PowerPoint slides, and Companion Website available for this text; and test items for each chapter.

**Test Bank.** The multiple choice and critical thinking questions for each chapter are available in both printed and electronic format. The PC and Macintosh-compatible electronic test bank is available on CD and allows instructors to create customized exams on a personal computer.

**ABC News/Prentice Hall Video Libraries.** Free to instructors who adopt this text, these ABC News videos feature 15 thought-provoking video segments that are tied to the content of specific chapters of the text. Two libraries are offered:

- The *Master Teacher Series* consists of 6 video segments of an ABC News series that follows a teacher through a year with her students.
- The *Education in the News* video clips feature 9 ABC News reports covering issues and challenges that face today's teachers, students, and schools.

**PowerPoint® and Acetate Transparencies.** Designed as an instructional tool, the transparencies can be used to present and elaborate on chapter content. They are available on the Companion Website and as acetates.

## Web-Based Supplements: The Prentice Hall Companion Website

The Companion Website for this text can be found at **http://www.prenhall.com/henniger.** The Companion Website is a truly integrated Web-based technology resource that provides support for and builds upon the focus of the text. Technology is a constantly growing and changing aspect of our field that is creating a need for content and resources. To address this emerging need, Prentice Hall has developed Companion Websites—online learning environments for students and professors alike—to support our textbooks. The Companion Website for this text builds on and enhances what the textbook already offers. For this reason, the content for each user-friendly website is organized by chapter and provides the professor and student with a variety of meaningful resources.

### For the Instructor

Every Companion Website integrates **Syllabus Manager**™, an online syllabus creation and management utility.

- **Syllabus Manager**™ provides you, the instructor, with an easy, step-by-step process to create and revise syllabi, with direct links into Companion Website and other online content without having to learn HTML.
- Students may logon to your syllabus during any study session. All they need to know is the web address for the Companion Website and the password you've assigned to your syllabus.
- After you have created a syllabus using **Syllabus Manager**™, students may enter the syllabus for their course section from any point in the Companion Website.
- Clicking on a date, the student is shown the list of activities for the assignment. The activities for each assignment are linked directly to actual content, saving time for students.

- Adding assignments involves clicking on the desired due date, then filling in the details of the assignment—name of the assignment, instructions, and whether it is a one-time or repeating assignment.
- In addition, links to other activities can be created easily. If the activity is online, a URL can be entered in the space provided, and it will be linked automatically in the final syllabus.
- Your completed syllabus is hosted on our servers, allowing convenient updates from any computer on the Internet. Changes you make to your syllabus are immediately available to your students at their next logon.

## For the Student

This Web-based resource allows the reader to gather more information on specific topics identified in the text and respond online to questions presented in several features within the text. Each module has been created to help students connect to the chapter content by providing resources for investigating chapter topics along with opportunities to interact with peers and instructors.

**Chapter Objectives** — outline key concepts from the text.

**Self-Assessment** — with hints and automatic grading, provides students the opportunity to test their knowledge of concepts discussed within the chapter.

**Reflective Journey** — allows students to submit online journal entries based on reflective questions throughout the chapter text, as indicated by numbered margin notes.

**Reflecting with Others** — provides students with expanded questions related to chapter topics and issues, designed to promote reflection and group discussion. Participants can submit their responses via e-mail for viewing by the instructor or members of student discussion groups.

**Engage in the Debate** — links to online research sources and primary source material, along with an opportunity for students to submit responses online.

**Explore Your Beliefs** — includes reflection questions and online resources that encourage exploration of challenging issues and ideas.

**Reflect on Diversity** — incorporates questions for reflection and opportunities for additional online exploration of concepts, ideas, and experiences related to diversity in the classroom.

**Education in the News** — connects to the critical thinking questions presented within the text feature of the same name. (Chapters 2, 4, 5, 6, 7, 9, 12, 13, 14)

**Master Teacher Series** — connects to the thought-provoking questions for deeper understanding posed within the text feature of the same name. (Chapters 1, 3, 8, 10, 11, 15)

**Becoming a Reflective Practitioner** — organized according to the chapter focus questions and major chapter sections, the three component modules provide opportunities for reviewing chapter content, building portfolio artifacts, and reflecting on field experiences.

- *Review Questions* — students can submit responses to review questions for each major section of the text and share them with study groups, fellow students, or instructors.
- *Building Your Portfolio* — allows students to begin building a reflective professional portfolio by using projects and activities linked to chapter content and the INTASC standards.
- *Field Experience* — provides the opportunity for students to submit thoughtful observations and insights gained from suggested field experiences outlined in the text.

**Praxis Test Preparation** — students can prepare for the Praxis II: Principles of Learning and Teaching exam through case histories, critical thinking, and self-assessment questions. Students can review case histories, then respond to related short-answer questions and receive immediate feedback. Multiple-choice questions with immediate feedback test students' knowledge of chapter-related Praxis II topics.

**Web Destinations** — include links to websites where students can learn more about the teaching profession by researching issues, learning more about professional standards such as INTASC and NPBTS, exploring teacher organizations, and finding out more about the Praxis tests.

**Message Board** — a virtual bulletin board that allows users to post or respond to questions or comments from a national audience.

## Online Courses

Online courses for this text are available in two different formats: Blackboard (locally hosted by your school) and CourseCompass (nationally hosted by Prentice Hall).

## Acknowledgments

Without question, this is the most complex writing project I have ever undertaken. It would never have been completed without the assistance of a great many people. I am truly indebted to the following staff at Merrill/Prentice Hall: executive editor Debbie Stollenwerk; development editors Kimberly Lundy and Heather Doyle Fraser; editorial assistant Mary Morrill; and production editor Linda Bayma. The support and assistance I received throughout this endeavor has been truly remarkable. I gratefully thank each and every person who has assisted me with this process.

I am also indebted to the reviewers of this text who have helped me take my initial thoughts and revise and reorganize them into their present form. Their thoughtful commentary and helpful suggestions are much appreciated. Many thanks to Dwight Allen, Old Dominion University; Judy Arnold, Lincoln Memorial University; Les Bolt, James Madison University; Karen Bosh, Virginia Wesleyan University; Mary Lou Brotherson, NOVA Southeastern University; Charles Carroll, Lake City Community College; Jeri Carroll, Wichita State University; Jennifer Deets, University of Central Florida; Kathy Finkle, Black Hills State University; Elizabeth Gensante, Saint Francis University; Patricia Jo Gibson, University of North Carolina–Charlotte; Suzanne Gulledge, University of North Carolina–Chapel Hill; Hall E. Jenkins II, Mississippi University for Women; William R. Martin, George Mason University; Sara McNeil, University of Houston; Steven Oates, Northern Michigan University; Terry Rainey, MacMurray College; and Christina Ramirez-Smith, Christopher Newport University.

It is also important for me to recognize the contributions made by my family as I struggled through the many ups and downs of a major book-writing project. A very special and heartfelt thank-you goes to my wife Lisa, who has supported me in so many ways through this very busy time. With four children at home (two currently under the age of 5), she still found the time to be consistently encouraging to me during those periods when I was feeling overwhelmed. Thank you, Lisa, for your love, encouragement, and flexibility during these four long years of book writing.

# Educator Learning Center:
# An Invaluable Online Resource

Merrill Education and the Association for Supervision and Curriculum Development (ASCD) invite you to take advantage of a new online resource, one that provides access to the top research and proven strategies associated with ASCD and Merrill—the Educator Learning Center. At **www. EducatorLearningCenter.com** you will find resources that will enhance your students' understanding of course topics and of current educational issues, in addition to being invaluable for further research.

## How the Educator Learning Center will help your students become better teachers

With the combined resources of Merrill Education and ASCD, you and your students will find a wealth of tools and materials to better prepare them for the classroom.

### Research

- More than 600 articles from the ASCD journal *Educational Leadership* discuss everyday issues faced by practicing teachers.
- A direct link on the site to Research Navigator™ gives students access to many of the leading education journals, as well as extensive content detailing the research process.
- Excerpts from Merrill Education texts give your students insights on important topics of instructional methods, diverse populations, assessment, classroom management, technology, and refining classroom practice.

### Classroom Practice

- Hundreds of lesson plans and teaching strategies are categorized by content area and age range.
- Case studies and classroom video footage provide virtual field experience for student reflection.
- Computer simulations and other electronic tools keep your students abreast of today's classrooms and current technologies.

## Look into the value of Educator Learning Center yourself

Preview the value of this educational environment by visiting **www.EducatorLearningCenter.com** and clicking on "Demo." For a free 4-month subscription to the Educator Learning Center in conjunction with this text, simply contact your Merrill/Prentice Hall sales representative.

# Brief Contents

# Contents

Note: Every effort has been made to provide accurate and current Internet information in this book. However, the Internet and information posted on it are constantly changing, so it is inevitable that some of the Internet addresses listed in this textbook will change.

# Special Features

#  ABC News/Prentice Hall Video Libraries

Two ABC News/Prentice Hall Video Libraries (the *Master Teacher Series* and *Education in the News*) were created for use with *The Teaching Experience: An Introduction to Reflective Practice.* Both relate and expand upon topics discussed in the text, providing readers with a deeper understanding of issues in education and the realities of teaching. The segments described below are available to accompany this text.

## Master Teacher Series

The ABC News *Master Teacher Series* video segments comprise a six-part *Nightline* special report following a year in the life of Lesley-Diann Jones, a master teacher at PS 27 in the Red Hook area of Brooklyn, New York, who has accepted the challenge of working with a class of fourth-grade students who failed the state's English language arts exam. She faces many challenges associated with preparing students for high-stakes testing while dealing with the realities of poverty, crime, and the pressures associated with proficiency tests. *Master Teacher Series* segments appear in Chapters 1, 3, 8, 10, 11, and 15 of the text and provide a synopsis of the episode along with activities and questions that encourage students to explore Ms. Jones's experience and her teaching style, along with their own experiences and expectations as teachers.

### Segment I: The Challenges of Teaching

In the first segment, the viewer is introduced to Lesley-Diann Jones, the school, the community, and the students who are in her fourth-grade classroom because they have failed the state tests. The viewer is introduced to some of the challenges Ms. Jones faces within her classroom and the community. She immediately accepts the challenges and the students, using several innovative strategies for teaching, classroom management, and establishing contacts with parents.

*Chapter 1, page 13*

### Segment II: Challenging the Students; Challenging Students

In the second segment of the series, Ms. Jones works with the students to help them overcome their lack of self-confidence and to increase their test-taking skills. She faces challenges presented by language barriers, absenteeism, and a lack of parental involvement. All the while, Ms. Jones continues to work with the students to increase their test-taking skills so that they might pass the state tests.

*Chapter 3, page 62*

### Segment III: The Pressure of the Big Test: Never Give Up

Ms. Jones continues to work on the test-taking abilities of the students in her challenging task at PS 27. She is feeling more in control of her class, although one student continues to struggle with behavioral problems. She also worries about how the students are coping with her tough assignments and about whether she has prepared them adequately. When the test is over, more problems arise.

*Chapter 8, page 177*

## Segment IV: When Teaching Is Only Part of the Job

In this segment, Ms. Jones continues to work with the students and parents in difficult situations. Despite these incidents, there are good days and successes. Her students' language skills are improving, and a few are reading at nearly sixth-grade level. Ms. Jones also focuses her attention outside of the classroom on family situations that affect the attendance and performance of her students.

*Chapter 10, page 235*

## Segment V: The Master Teacher and Her Classroom Full of Trouble

Some of the students continue to struggle with difficult home and life situations in addition to the pressures of the proficiency tests. Many students are suffering tremendous anxiety about the upcoming reading exam, and some have already failed to pass the state language arts exam. Some students have difficulty getting through the test due to their feelings of fear and anxiety—they fear they will not pass, yet many have resigned themselves to believing that they are destined to fail again.

*Chapter 11, page 263*

## Segment VI: When the Test Seems to Be All That Matters

Ms. Jones's challenge, and that of her students, was to prepare them to pass the standardized tests imposed by New York State and New York City. Most of the students failed. Ms. Jones faces questions from herself and others about her teaching methods and about how much time she devoted to social skills and the students' home lives. She must break difficult news to many of her students and face comparisons with the outcomes realized by other teachers in similar classrooms.

*Chapter 15, page 366*

 **Education in the News**

These ABC News video segments and the corresponding activities challenge students to explore chapter topics through news reports on controversial educational issues. *Education in the News* features in Chapters 2, 4, 5, 6, 7, 9, 12, 13, and 14 of the text offer a short summary of each episode and ask students to think about and respond to questions relating to the video and chapter content. The following video segments are available to accompany this text.

### The Controversy Over Bilingual Education

This segment follows up with California students and teachers two years after passage of Proposition 227, which ended California's 22-year program of bilingual education in the public schools. Educators, students, and critics from both sides of the bilingual debate discuss the progress and test results following the transition to English-only instruction.

*Chapter 2, page 41*

### The Power of the Neighborhood School

For 30 years, most elementary school students in the predominately African American town of Delray Beach, Florida, were bused to predominately white, higher income neighborhoods in Palm Beach County. In response to high dropout rates and alienation, Delray Beach created a new community school focused on neighborhood involvement and a feeling of community. This report explores the Village Academy and issues it has raised regarding segregation, economics, and equality in public school education.

*Chapter 4, page 97*

### Teacher Competency

All across America, teachers are taking and sometimes failing evaluation tests. What is the problem? What is the answer? This segment examines issues related to the teacher evaluation and competency debates: the difficulty of terminating contracted and/or tenured teachers, the qualifications of today's teachers, teachers' perceptions of preparedness of teaching to high standards, teacher testing, and class size.

*Chapter 5, page 118*

### Too Much Homework?

The amount of homework assigned to students has reached an all-time high. This video segment examines the concerns of parents, students, and some experts who believe that homework causes children too much stress, inhibits their participation in extracurricular and family activities, and may have little impact on achievement.

*Chapter 6, page 134*

## God and Evolution in Kansas Classrooms

This news clip focuses on the controversy surrounding the decision by the Kansas State Board of Education to drop the teaching of evolution from the high school science curriculum. School and political officials, scientists, and religious leaders debate the teaching of evolution in public schools.

*Chapter 7, page 165*

## Computers in the Classroom

In an effort to transform education and raise achievement, schools in the United States have spent over $50 billion for computers in classrooms. The Internet connects people around the world and can provide a valuable research tool, and many educational and administrative software tools are available, but will computers in classrooms really make a difference in education?

*Chapter 9, page 206*

## Action, Reaction, and Zero Tolerance

Schools across the country have adopted zero-tolerance policies. Featured are discussions with students, families, and school and law enforcement representatives regarding the cases of two students, 8-year-old Hamadi Alstead of Irvington, New Jersey, who was suspended after playing cowboys and Indians using a gun made of paper, and high school sophomore Ryan Scofiald, of Loudoun County, Virginia, who was refused in his request to carry a cardboard sword as part of his school mascot costume, both due to zero tolerance policies adopted by their schools.

*Chapter 12, page 286*

## Transgender Teacher

This video segment features David Warfield, a California high school teacher and transsexual who underwent gender reassignment surgery. David lost his job at Center High School in Sacramento after requesting to return as a woman after the summer break. The segment presents some of the major education and legal issues associated with the employment of a teacher who undergoes a medical transformation from male to female.

*Chapter 13, page 305*

## One Last Chance

This segment introduces viewers to the School for Educational Evolution and Development (SEED). SEED is a unique charter school in Washington, DC: It is an urban boarding school for students in grades 7–12. Started in 1997 by two entrepreneurs, SEED provides students with what their communities often do not: high expectations, esteem for education, adult supervision, plenty of extra assistance, three meals a day, and a clean, safe place to live.

*Chapter 14, page 329*

# AN INVITATION TO THE READER

## Becoming a Reflective Practitioner

Teaching is an incredibly complex and challenging profession at all grade levels. Those who enter must be well prepared for both the difficult issues and the great joys that can be found there. This book was written to provide you, the reader, with a thoughtful exploration of teaching's complexities. The process of considering your own past learning experiences, reading about the realities of schooling, and discussing critical issues with others will lead you on a reflective journey that culminates in deeper insights into the teaching profession. This process of reflection directly influences all aspects of teaching and learning, including professionalism, decision making, and accountability.

There are many factors that contribute to the complexities of schooling. At its core, however, teaching is challenging because educators are constantly required to make difficult decisions about what to do and say as they interact with students, parents, and other adults. Decisions must be made throughout the school day about issues such as strengthening student relationships, dealing with discipline problems, presenting a new concept, talking to parents, and relating to other school personnel. Unfortunately, there are no formulas for making these decisions. Because every student, parent, colleague, and situation is unique, teachers must thoughtfully consider appropriate responses to each new set of circumstances.

To be good decision makers, teachers need to learn the complex process of reflection. While on the surface this may appear to be a relatively easy exercise, reflection is actually a complex activity. In *How We Think,* John Dewey described it as "the active, persistent, and careful consideration of any belief or supposed form of knowledge in light of the grounds that support it" (1993, p. 9). The reflective process involves the following:

- *Experience.* It is critical for teachers to regularly stop and take the time that is needed to consider and understand how one's own life experiences, beliefs, assumptions and preconceived ideas can inform teaching. Many of the special features developed for this text support this aspect of reflection by providing opportunities for consideration of experience, beliefs, and assumptions.

- *Research.* Knowledge must inform classroom practice. Knowledge of the student, the content to be taught, the underlying theory and research, and the context or situation provides an effective framework from which the reader can then begin to think about appropriate responses. This text provides a wealth of current and relevant information and activities to support this aspect of the reflective process for those considering teaching. Prospective teachers can use this information as a starting point for good reflection.

- *Discussion.* Considering issues, experiences, beliefs, and knowledge by either talking with others or by using a vehicle such as journaling is another important aspect of reflection. The social learning that occurs when important issues are discussed in groups and the understanding that is gained through journaling are difficult to develop in other contexts. Once again, there are special features included in this text that provide prospective teachers with opportunities to develop this aspect of reflection on a diverse array of topics.

- *Implementation.* In this phase of the process, teachers carry all their understanding and consideration of experience, beliefs, assumptions, and knowledge into their classroom practice. That is, their experience, their research, and their discussion all inform their decision making in the classroom. There are multiple features included in this text that give prospective teachers the opportunity to make decisions informed by reflection.

This text is designed to help prospective teachers engage in active reflection as they study the decision-making steps needed for effective teaching and learning. Each chapter presents a rich assortment of reflection strategies and opportunities for you to begin developing them into habits as you prepare for the many difficult decisions required of all classroom teachers.

Best of luck,
Michael Henniger

# part 1

## What Is Today's Context for Reflective Practice?

# chapter 1

## Choosing to Teach

You are embarking on an important journey that will eventually lead to the choice of a career. Throughout this text and as part of any teacher education courses you are taking, you should begin to carefully consider what it means to be a teacher and whether teaching is the career for you. This first chapter is designed to help you begin the process of reflecting on what it means to be a teacher and how your goals, knowledge, beliefs, and experiences affect your life as a teacher. It contains four sections, each with an organizing question that will guide your thinking.

## Focus Questions

◀ What is teaching really like?

◀ What are the benefits of being a teacher?

◀ How significant are the challenges?

◀ Should I become a teacher?

Mrs. Henderson was the greatest teacher ever. She knew every one of her sixth-grade students so well, spent extra time coming to soccer matches and concerts, and always seemed to know when a kind word and a friendly pat on the shoulder were needed. She truly enjoyed teaching and seemed to make every subject come alive for us. We loved her!

Mr. Blankenship was the pickiest teacher I have ever had. He insisted on perfectly organized proofs for geometry and logical descriptions of the work that went into the solving of algebraic equations. Mr. Blankenship had very high expectations for each of us and kept pushing me and others to excel. At the time, I wasn't sure I liked him. Looking back, however, I realize that he always wanted the best for each of us, and his persistent demands have made me a more organized learner and greatly improved my proficiency in mathematics. I'm actually thinking about majoring in either math or science when I go to college!

Mr. Palmer was the absolute worst teacher I've ever had! He never seemed to enjoy teaching any of the topics in his fourth-grade classroom. He was forever telling unrelated stories about his family or complaining about the low salaries and benefits for teachers. I think he was just putting in his time until retirement and making life miserable for students along the way. Mr. Palmer's tests were the worst. He seldom taught us anything of value and then tried to put the blame on his students by giving impossibly hard tests to "prove" that students were just getting worse every year. What a waste!

One of the interesting aspects of teaching is that we all come to the role having had a wealth of experiences in the classroom where we encountered both excellence and ineptitude. As in the above hypothetical situations, we became better educated and more fully functioning individuals following our quality interactions with some teachers, whereas our frustration, anger, and boredom multiplied from repeated exchanges with others.

This book was written so that you, the reader, can reflect on your choice of teaching as a potential career. While using this text as part of a college or university class, try on the role of teacher and see how well it fits. Do you have the motivation and interest it takes to become an excellent teacher? Can you see yourself working to develop the skills needed for competence in the classroom? Do you find schools comfortable and exciting places to be? Would the bureaucracy and paperwork be manageable or overwhelming? As you respond to these and many other questions, both individually and through discussions with others, you should begin to see a pattern emerge that will help you decide if teaching is the profession for you.

## What is teaching really like?

Many people tend to oversimplify the act of teaching. How difficult can it be, they hypothesize, to know something and then share that understanding with others? If, for example, you understand the process of solving algebraic equations, shouldn't it be possible for you to teach this process to others? This relatively straightforward task becomes far more complex, however, when a variety of other factors are considered. To effectively teach algebraic equations, you need to have a strong conceptual understanding of mathematics in general and algebraic theory in particular. A good teacher would then need to be able to transform this deep knowledge of the discipline into teaching and learning activities that are understandable and motivating to students. Effective educators are also prepared to work with students of varying abilities and those who bring with them a host of emotional and social needs that must be addressed along the way.

Teaching is further complicated by the fact that it is far more than a sharing of knowledge. William Ayers (2001) states it this way:

> Before I stepped into my first classroom as a teacher, I thought teaching was mainly instruction, partly performing, certainly being in the front and at the center of classroom life. Later, with much chaos and some pain, I learned that this is the least of it—teaching includes a more splendorous range of actions. Teaching is instructing, advising, counseling, modeling, coaching, disciplining, prodding, preaching, persuading, proselytizing, listening, interacting, nursing, and inspiring. Teachers must be experts and generalists, psychologists and cops, rabbis and priests, judges and gurus. (p. 4)

But to identify teaching as a complex and challenging profession is only a beginning point for understanding what it is really like in the classroom (see Table 1.1). The discussion that follows will help clarify some important aspects of teaching in America's schools. Consider each of these components carefully so that you can begin to decide how well teaching meshes with your career goals and life expectations.

### The Independence and Interconnectedness of Teaching

The regulation of teaching by local, state, and federal agencies has changed dramatically within the last 50 years. The rules that govern what takes place in the classroom have grown exponentially in that time (see Chapter 14 for more information). Such things as the length of time spent on specific subjects, the textbooks being used for instruction, requirements for being promoted to the next grade, and guidelines for teacher interactions with students are all regulated by various governing bodies.

Despite the growing number of constraints, however, most teachers find that they have considerable independence once the doors to the classroom are closed. For most of the school day, the teacher has primary responsibility for making decisions about such things as the order and empha-

| TABLE 1.1   What Is Teaching Really Like? | |
|---|---|
| **Components of Teaching** | **Comments** |
| Challenging work | Although many people tend to think of teaching as an easy job that nearly anyone can do, it is actually a very challenging task that requires considerable effort and skill. |
| Independence and interconnectedness | Teachers spend much of their time working independently with their students. To be successful, however, it is also important to stay connected with other teachers, school staff, and parents. |
| An art | Teachers are like artists as they think about the content to be taught, consider the needs and interests of students, and creatively teach in the classroom. |
| A science | By understanding the research on effective teaching and developing the needed knowledge and skills, teachers can strengthen their effectiveness as educators. |
| Lifelong learning | Teaching is a career that can never be totally mastered. The best educators continue to gain knowledge and refine skills throughout their years in the classroom. |

sis placed on each subject or topic, the specific methods of instruction, and evaluation techniques used to assess student learning. The general workday of teachers is also quite flexible. Some come to school early in the morning to plan and prepare for teaching, while others stay late. Still others take work home with them in the evenings or spend time on weekends on school-related work. The flexibility and autonomy of teaching are characteristics that often attract people to the profession.

Take a moment now to reflect on both the independence and interconnectedness of teaching. How do you think you would feel about the independence that teachers experience? Do you think you would be comfortable and confident being on your own for much of the school day, with all of the responsibility for a classroom full of students? In addition, do you see yourself as the type of person who can also build strong working relationships with parents, other teachers, administrators, and community members? Continue to think about these issues as you read further in this text and discuss the topics with others.

**Reflective Journey 1.1**

## The Art of Teaching

Another way to get to know what teaching is really like is to learn about how others described it. In broad terms, the education profession has been portrayed by different writers as either an art or a science. Those who think of **teaching as an art** see the educative process as something that cannot be easily defined or described because it changes daily based on the needs and interests of the students and the circumstances within the classroom. Good teachers, they propose, craft a lesson much as an artist takes a lump of clay and molds it into a work of art. By adding a little here, making modifications there, and using the tools of the trade to intuitively shape and form classroom activities, a creative interchange occurs between teacher and students that leads to inspired learning.

Banner and Cannon (1997) describe this creative interchange as follows:

> While pedagogical expertise and technical knowledge are essential to it, ultimately teaching is a creative act: it makes something fresh from existing knowledge in spontaneous, improvised efforts of mind and spirit, disciplined by education and experience. Thus, unlike a technology, in which correct application produces predictable and uniform results, teaching yields infinite surprises—infinite delights—from one moment to the next. What method can supply to teaching we know or can learn; what art can furnish out of our own selves we must imagine—and then practice. (p. 3)

Those who view teaching as an art see education as a very complicated and challenging profession that is continually changing. They believe that there is no "formula" for teaching that can be mastered and then applied in all circumstances to all students. Rather, as educators interact with students and plan for the curriculum, they must continually rethink, reframe, and reconfigure the content and process of teaching. Although this approach makes teaching far more difficult, it also means that the rewards are great for those who continue to work at improving what they do. What are your thoughts about this view of teaching? Do you see yourself as a person who would enjoy the creative aspects of teaching?

**Reflective Journey 1.2**

## The Science of Teaching

In addition to those who emphasize the art of teaching, many think of **teaching as a science.** Those who take this stance believe that good teachers begin with a deep knowledge of the subject matter being taught and a clear understanding of teaching and learning. This is generally referred to as the **knowledge base** of teaching (see Table 1.2). In addition, they have mastered the strategies needed to be successful in interactions with students. The skills needed for effective instruction can be observed, categorized, studied, and practiced by those who want to become ef-

### TABLE 1.2   The Knowledge Base of Teaching

| Area of Knowledge | Description |
|---|---|
| Content knowledge | An in-depth knowledge of the subject(s) taught |
| General teaching knowledge | Understanding the broad principles of classroom management and organization needed for good teaching |
| Curriculum knowledge | Knowledge of the organization and sequencing of the subject(s) taught |
| Pedagogical content knowledge | Knowing how to present content to students of diverse interests and abilities so that effective learning can take place |
| Knowledge of learners | Understanding child development and its applications to teaching and learning |
| Knowledge of educational contexts | Knowing the impact of classroom atmosphere, school climate, and community setting on student learning |
| Knowledge of history and philosophy of education | Understanding the history and philosophy of education and their impact on teaching and learning |

*Source:* "Knowledge and Teaching: Foundations of the New Reform" by L. Shulman, 1987, *Harvard Educational Review, 57*(1), pp. 1–22.

fective teachers. When teachers combine a deep knowledge of subject matter, teaching, and instruction with the use of effective teaching skills, quality learning takes place.

Marzano, Pickering, and Pollock (2001), after a thorough review of the research literature on instructional strategies, have identified several key teaching techniques that all effective teachers display. They include helping students identify similarities and differences, providing guidance in summarizing and note-taking, reinforcing student effort, providing effective homework assignments and time in class to practice what is being learned, helping students generate mental pictures and graphic representations of content, establishing clear goals for students and providing feedback on meeting those goals, assisting students in applying knowledge by guiding them in generating and testing hypotheses, and helping students apply what they already know to the current learning situation. These research-based options are discussed in more detail in Chapter 8.

An important national effort to clearly define what all new teachers should know and be able to do is described in the standards developed by the Interstate New Teacher Assessment and Support Consortium (INTASC). For each of the 10 broad INTASC standards (see Figure 1.1), the knowledge, dispositions, and performances that all beginning teachers should have regardless of

**Figure 1.1**   INTASC Standards

**Standard #1:** The teacher understands the central concepts, tools of inquiry, and structures of the discipline(s) he or she teaches and can create learning experiences that make these aspects of subject matter meaningful for students.

**Standard #2:** The teacher understands how children learn and develop and can provide learning opportunities that support their intellectual, social, and personal development.

**Standard #3:** The teacher understands how students differ in their approaches to learning and creates instructional opportunities that are adapted to diverse learners.

**Standard #4:** The teacher understands and uses a variety of instructional strategies to encourage students' development of critical thinking, problem solving, and performance skills.

**Standard #5:** The teacher uses an understanding of individual and group motivation and behavior to create a learning environment that encourages positive social interaction, active engagement in learning, and self-motivation.

**Standard #6:** The teacher uses knowledge of effective verbal, nonverbal, and media communication techniques to foster active inquiry, collaboration, and supportive interaction in the classroom.

**Standard #7:** The teacher plans instruction based upon knowledge of subject matter, students, the community, and curriculum goals.

**Standard #8:** The teacher understands and uses formal and informal assessment strategies to evaluate and ensure the continuous intellectual, social, and physical development of the learner.

**Standard #9:** The teacher is a reflective practitioner who continually evaluates the effects of his/her choices and actions on others (students, parents, and other professionals in the learning community) and who actively seeks out opportunities to grow professionally.

**Standard #10:** The teacher fosters relationships with school colleagues, parents, and agencies in the larger community to support students' learning and well-being.

*Source:* From *Model Standards for Beginning Teacher Licensing and Development,* by Interstate New Teacher Assessment and Support Consortium, 1992. Retrieved March 12, 2003, from http://www.ccsso.org/intascst.html. Reprinted with permission.

their specialty area have been identified. Most teacher preparation programs are specifically aligned to these standards.

To ensure that INTASC standards are being met, many states have begun to require all teacher candidates to successfully pass a standardized test to assess their understanding of the subjects they will teach and knowledge of teaching and learning. One exam that is commonly used for these purposes is the Praxis II. The first part of this exam tests the subject matter knowledge of the teacher candidate. For example, mathematics teacher candidates take an exam to assess mathematics content knowledge, English teacher candidates take the English content test, and prospective elementary teachers complete a multiple subjects exam. In addition, the Praxis II assesses candidate knowledge of teaching and learning. This Principles of Learning and Teaching component (see Table 1.3) covers four broad topics: (1) organizing content knowledge for student learning, (2) creating an environment for student learning, (3) teaching for student learning, and (4) teacher professionalism (Educational Testing Service, 2002).

### Teaching as Lifelong Learning

Another important characteristic of the education profession is that it requires continued learning and growth on the part of teachers. Even though you have developed insights about teaching just by being a part of the educational system for many years and will learn a great deal more by the time you receive teacher certification, mastering the art and science of teaching is a never-ending process. Education is a very complex profession that requires continued learning.

One of the main reasons that teachers must continue to grow and learn is that no two students and no two teaching situations are ever identical. You will need to begin again to reconstruct the ingredients for effective teaching each time you start working with a group of students. As Parker Palmer (1998) states in his book, *The Courage to Teach:*

**TABLE 1.3   Praxis II—Principles of Learning and Teaching Test**

| Topic | Components |
|---|---|
| I. Students as learners | a. Student Development and the Learning Process<br>b. Students as Diverse Learners<br>c. Student Motivation and the Learning Environment |
| II. Instruction and Assessment | a. Instructional Strategies<br>b. Planning Instruction<br>c. Assessment Strategies |
| III. Communication Techniques | a. Effective Verbal and Nonverbal Communication<br>b. Effect of Culture and Gender on Communication<br>c. Questioning Strategies to Stimulate Discussion |
| IV. Profession and Community | a. The Reflective Practitioner<br>b. The Larger Community |

*Source: Principles of Learning and Teaching: Test at a Glance* by Educational Testing Service, 2003. Retrieved February 23, 2003, from http://www.ets.org/praxis/taags/prx0522.html

I have taught thousands of students, attended many seminars on teaching, watched others teach, read about teaching, and reflected on my own experience. My stockpile of methods is substantial. But when I walk into a new class, it is as if I am starting over. My problems are perennial, familiar to all teachers. Still, they take me by surprise, and my responses to them—though outwardly smoother with each year—feel almost as fumbling as they did when I was a novice. (p. 9)

*Teachers continue to learn in a variety of ways.*

While this notion of beginning again with each new group of students and never really perfecting the act of teaching may seem daunting at first glance, it is also a major reason why educators find their work so rewarding and fulfilling. Each day is filled with new possibilities, unique interactions with students, and formidable challenges that must be met. The best teachers are always thinking, anticipating, feeling, and acting to meet the many demands of the job. If you seek a work environment that is always changing and continually challenges you to try harder, one that requires you to think more creatively, and one that needs people who care deeply about each new student, then teaching may be just the career for you.

Learning to teach, then, can be viewed as a lifelong process that consists of four main phases (see Table 1.4). You may be surprised to know that you have already completed the first phase based on earlier **experiences as a learner** in elementary through high school classrooms. These experiences have given you many opportunities to learn about both positive and

| TABLE 1.4   Phases in Learning to Teach | |
| --- | --- |
| **Phase** | **Description** |
| Experiences as a learner | Your own experiences in elementary through high school classrooms have allowed you to observe and informally learn about teaching. |
| Initial teacher certification | You will need to take courses in subject matter content, teacher education, and classroom applications to receive an initial teaching certificate. |
| Teacher induction | The first few years in the classroom you will be learning "on the job" as you work with students and receive guidance from mentor teachers and others. |
| Continuing professional development | Course work, degrees, advanced certification, and both individual and group reflections will help you continue to grow as an educator throughout your career. |

negative teaching. While providing you with good insights into becoming an effective educator, your observations and participation in these settings have more than likely led to misperceptions as well (Feiman-Nemser, 1999). You will need to begin now to think carefully about the ideas you have developed about teaching and learning from your own experiences and be sure that you are approaching teaching with accurate perceptions of what it takes to be an effective educator.

The second phase in learning to teach is the one you are just beginning. **Initial teacher certification** through colleges and universities requires a minimum of a bachelor's degree and typically includes course work in the subject matter to be taught, teacher education courses, and several experiences working in public school classrooms. The last component of most programs is called the *internship* or *student teaching* experience where you will spend up to a full year in a classroom developing skills as an educator.

Once you complete initial teacher certification, it will be time to find that first teaching job and begin working with students. But the task of learning about teaching is far from complete. In many ways, it has just begun. The first few years in the classroom are often referred to as the period of **teacher induction.** During this time, new teachers are spending long hours in on-the-job training as they refine their knowledge and skills in teaching. For this induction period, most teachers are assigned an experienced educator who serves as their **mentor.** The mentor, along with other colleagues, provides guidance and support regarding all aspects of the teaching role. More information on teacher induction and mentoring can be found in Chapter 15.

After this period of teacher induction, most teachers are beginning to feel like they can breathe a little easier. Although much remains to be learned, they believe that the hardest part is behind them and that life can begin to settle down a bit. During this phase of **continuing professional development,** many opportunities for additional learning take place. In most states, the initial teacher certification is only good for a few years, after which it must be replaced with a permanent or more advanced teaching credential. This typically requires teachers to engage in further formal and informal learning experiences. Many teachers combine the work needed for a permanent teaching credential with a master's degree to add to their knowledge of teaching and learning.

## explore your beliefs

## Teachers Are Born, Not Made

Amy is bright, funny, enjoys being around students, and has a love of learning. She is a natural teacher. As a college senior with no teacher preparation, Amy could walk into any classroom today and know what to do and say to be successful in teaching students.

As with Amy's advocate above, a common assumption held by many people is that someone with strong academic skills and an ability to relate well with others needs very little further preparation to be a teacher. The phrase "teachers are born, not made" effectively summarizes this point of view. Those with this perspective feel that the need for formal teacher preparation is minimal and can be accomplished very quickly and easily when candidates for

the profession have the needed academic and interpersonal skills.

Teach for America (TFA) is one current example of a program grounded in these beliefs. Each year, the Teach for America program accepts up to 1,000 college graduates nationwide, puts them through an intensive 5-week summer training program, and then places these new teachers in urban and rural settings where it is typically difficult to find certified teachers.

Promotional materials state:

We're looking for goal-oriented individuals who will relentlessly pursue results. Our ideal candidates demonstrate leadership ability, strong critical thinking skills and a record of outstanding achievement in past endeavors, whether in academics, extracurricular activities, or work experience. We're searching for individuals who reflect thoughtfully on past experiences, maintain a sense of perspective in the face of challenges, operate with a positive attitude and a sense of realism, and demonstrate self-awareness and sensitivity to others. If you possess these characteristics, we hope you'll become part of our force for change. (Teach for America, 2002)

Despite strong personal qualifications and a desire to be of service through teaching, many TFA teachers find they are unprepared for the challenges of the classroom. One Yale University graduate had this to say about her Teach for America experience:

> I—perhaps like most TFAers—harbored dreams of liberating my students from public school mediocrity and offering them as good an education as I had received. But I was not ready. . . . As bad as it was for me, it was worse for the students. Many of mine . . . took long steps on the path toward dropping out. . . . I was not a successful

teacher and the loss to the students was real and large. (Schorr, 1993, pp. 317–318)

Despite the fact that the Teach for America program recruits applicants with strong academic credentials and effective interpersonal skills, many TFA teachers end up becoming frustrated and leave the profession. The research evidence suggests that a high proportion of these teachers leave during the first 2 years, with departure rates nearly three times the national average (Darling-Hammond, 2000).

Other studies of teachers admitted to the classroom with less than full preparation (including options other than TFA) find that these teachers have greater difficulties in planning, teaching, assessing, and managing classroom activities (Darling-Hammond, 2000). Further evidence indicates that students also suffer when teachers have received inadequate training before entering the classroom. For example, a Texas study found that students in districts where lower percentages of teachers had completed traditional teacher certification programs were less likely to pass the mandated state achievement tests (Fuller, 1999).

### React and Reflect

1. What is your reaction to the statement "teachers are born, not made"? How important do you believe it is to exhibit the kind of personal qualities discussed here? How important is it to undergo extensive training?

2. Think of one or more incidences in which you taught people a new skill or explained an idea your audience did not understand. Did you succeed? Did you have any difficulties? How did you decide what method to use—did you follow the example of another person, seek guidance from someone else, or do it with no preparation? How would you prepare to teach a skill or subject that you do not currently possess?

3. What do your responses to the preceding questions tell you about your potential success in a traditional teacher preparation program and as a future educator?

### Resources

Darling-Hammond, L. (2000). How teacher education matters. *Journal of Teacher Education, 51*(3), 166–173.

Fuller, E. (1999). *Does teacher certification matter? A comparison of TAAS performance in 1997 between schools with low and high percentages of certified teachers.* Austin: Charles A. Dana Center, University of Texas at Austin.

Schorr, J. (1993). Class action: What Clinton's National Service Program could learn from "Teach for America." *Phi Delta Kappan, 74*(4), 315–318.

Teach for America. (2002). Who we are looking for. Retrieved June 3, 2002, from http://www.teachforamerica.org/tfa/why/who.html

 *To explore this topic further and submit your reactions and reflections online, go to the Explore Your Beliefs module for Chapter 1 of the Companion Website for this text.*

# What are the benefits of being a teacher?

Teaching is a very personal activity that attracts people to it for a variety of reasons. Some love the content and want to share that excitement with their students. Others have a passion for working with students and want to do all they can to assist in their growth and development. Most people find that a combination of reasons attracted them to, and keep them in, the teaching profession.

## The Joy of Teaching

The transmission of knowledge to a new generation of students is a time-honored component of education at all levels. All teachers should see this as a significant aspect of their responsibilities in the classroom. For many, this also becomes a major reason for the excitement they experience throughout each school day. For example, a recent survey of new teachers by Public Agenda, a nonprofit public opinion organization based in New York City (Farkas, Johnson, & Foleno, 2000), found that 96% of all educators surveyed indicated that teaching is work they love to do.

This love of teaching is generally seen as consisting of two main components. The first is a *passion for the subject matter* being taught. Many middle school and secondary school teachers are attracted to those levels because of the excitement they feel as they think about and discuss with others the specific subjects they teach. Although elementary teachers are generalists in the sense that they are responsible for all subjects, many educators at this level are also attracted to the profession because of their enthusiasm for the subjects they teach.

Another component of this love of teaching is the *delight found in teaching others*. Many teachers find that the subject matter itself, while interesting, provides less excitement and challenge than does assisting others in understanding and applying new knowledge. They talk about the pleasure they experience when they see students' faces light up as they finally make the connections that are needed for understanding new concepts. These teachers experience a deep satisfaction from facilitating the learning process that makes all the struggles and effort worthwhile.

**Reflective Journey 1.3**

Take a moment now to reflect on how you would feel about teaching subject matter and working with students at the grade level of your choice. Do you see yourself getting excited about the subjects you would teach? What evidence do you have from prior experiences to verify your response? How would you feel about the relationships you would have with students? Are you the type who genuinely enjoys being with students and assisting them in their growth and development? While you may need more information and further experiences in the classroom before you can answer these questions accurately, your responses will help you determine if teaching is the career for you.

## Personal Growth

Personal growth can come from a number of different sources. For a teacher, one option for growth is the need to continually know more about students and the content being shared. But another form of personal growth for teachers comes from knowing oneself. Parker Palmer (1998) makes the case for the importance of knowing oneself as a teacher when he writes:

> After three decades of trying to learn my craft, every class comes down to this: my students and I, face to face, engaged in an ancient and exacting exchange called education. The techniques I have mastered do not disappear, but neither do they suffice. Face to face with my students, only one resource is at my immediate command: my identity, my selfhood, my sense of this "I" who teaches—without which I have no sense of the "Thou" who learns. . . . In every class I teach, my ability to connect with my students, and to connect them with the subject, depends less on the methods I use than on the degree to which I know and trust my selfhood—and am willing to make it available and vulnerable in the service of learning. (p. 6)

Personal understanding and growth are not only necessary prerequisites to good teaching and learning, they are also rewarding for teachers themselves. The challenge to grow and change as an individual is part of the excitement that draws people to continue to put in the long hours

# MASTER TEACHER SERIES

## Segment I: The Challenges of Teaching

*The* Master Teacher Series *comprises a 6-segment* Nightline *special report following a year in the life of a master teacher, Lesley-Diann Jones, a teacher in the New York City Public Schools. The six segments of the series are placed periodically throughout the text and follow Ms. Jones, a teacher of 10 years who has accepted the challenge of working with a class of fourth-grade students who failed the state's English language arts exam. She is a successful teacher: All but two of her previous year's students passed the state exams. She has two degrees and could easily move to the suburban schools, but she has chosen to stay in the city schools and to accept this position. Her challenge is to not only prepare them for the state's test, but to also prepare them to rejoin their class in the sixth grade at the end of the year. The students all live in the Red Hook area, commonly called the Red Hook Projects, one of New York's toughest neighborhoods.*

In the first segment of the *Master Teacher Series*, the viewer is introduced to Lesley-Diann Jones, the school (PS 27), the community (Red Hook, Brooklyn), and the students who are in her fourth-grade classroom. The students are in this class because they have failed the state tests and therefore are all repeating fourth grade. Ms. Jones faces several challenges briefly defined in this first segment. Ms. Jones immediately takes charge and accepts the challenges and the students, enlisting the help of the parents from the first day. She uses several innovative teaching strategies to teach reading and language arts and for the management of the classroom.

### For Deeper Understanding

1. Why do you think Ms. Jones accepted this assignment?
2. In the chapter, we have discussed that each day as a teacher is filled with "new possibilities, unique interactions with students, and formidable challenges that must be met." What did Ms. Jones know about her students before the first day of school? What did she find out about them within the first few days? What problems and challenges did Ms. Jones encounter in this new assignment?
3. Why have states set qualifying exams for students as young as fourth graders and for teachers?
4. How do the lives of these students compare to the life of Ms. Jones? To your life?
5. What kind of support did Ms. Jones expect to have? What kind of support did she have?

 *To submit your responses online, go to the Master Teacher Series module for Chapter 1 of the Companion Website.*

and endure the many frustrations that accompany meaningful teaching. Can you see yourself engaging in this process of personal growth as a future teacher?

## Serving Students, Families, and Community

Many educators find that another major benefit of teaching is that it provides numerous opportunities to serve students, their families, and the broader community that go well beyond the sharing of content knowledge described above. David Hansen, in his book *Exploring the Moral Heart of Teaching* (2001) and an earlier work titled *The Call to Teach* (1995), makes a strong case for teaching being viewed as a **vocation** or calling. This level of service implies a deep commitment to students, families, and community that influences all other aspects of the teaching/learning process:

The Latin root of vocation, *vocare,* means "to call". It denotes a summons or bidding to be of service. It has been used to describe both secular and religious commitments. For example,

*Serving students has many rewards.*

some persons have felt called or "inspired" by divine purposes to join a religious order and to serve faithfully a given community. They have become ministers, nuns, priests, rabbis, missionaries, or pastors. Others have felt impelled to serve not divine purposes but rather human ones. They have felt called to human society with its manifold needs and possibilities. Many nurses, doctors, politicians, lawyers, and teachers have felt the kind of magnetic pull toward a life of service exemplified in the idea of vocation. (Hansen, 1995, p. 1)

As American society continues to grow more complex, fast paced, and impersonal, difficult social issues abound. Drug and alcohol abuse, violence, poverty, discrimination, and child abuse and neglect are among the many challenges that students, families, and communities face (see Chapters 2 and 12 for more information). Add to these the challenges that come from the normal stresses of growing into adulthood and it becomes increasingly clear that viewing teaching as an opportunity to serve the human and personal needs of students and others is essential (see Figure 1.2). Teachers often find themselves plunged into the midst of these difficult issues, and they must make every effort to do what they can to interact with students and others in caring ways.

## Schedule and Job Benefits

Although not as altruistic as the call to serve students and their families, the schedule and job benefits of teachers are often considered important pluses for the profession. The flexibility and security of teaching are viewed as positives that help compensate for some of the frustrations that are also associated with working in school settings.

**Figure 1.2**    Serving Students

> Brenda Morrow, a third-grade teacher in El Paso, Texas, describes three of the many students she has taught and her commitment to serving these students and their families:
>
> For Rika, who spoke little English after only six months in this country, at first too timid to try, won an Honorable Mention in a citywide poetry contest—in English. For her triumphant smile of accomplishment, I teach.
>
> For Sean, who always knew he could do anything, who had a supportive and loving family, who, now in his second year at a prestigious university, has his eyes set upon a Senate seat or the Oval Office. For Sean, I teach.
>
> For Jerry, who, after his father was brutally murdered, found the classroom the haven of peace and safety that a small boy craves when his childhood has forever been robbed by the wickedness of the world. For Jerry, I teach.

*Source: A Passion for Teaching* (p. 103) by S. Levine (Ed.), 1999, Alexandria, VA: Association for Supervision and Curriculum Development.

**Schedule.**  Without question, quality teaching takes hard work and numerous hours of planning, preparation, and assessment. Although this leads to long workdays, especially during the first few years of teaching, many educators appreciate the fact that they have considerable flexibility in completing their tasks. Beyond a minimum number of hours that teachers are contracted to be in the school building each day, they can work at a time and place of their choosing. Some teachers arrive early in the morning to prepare, while others choose to stay in their classrooms after the students have left to complete their preparations for the following day. Still other teachers find that getting away from the school setting and working from the comfort of their own homes is a more relaxing and productive option. This flexibility, which helps satisfy the individual work preferences of educators, also enables many teachers to blend work and family responsibilities more effectively.

Another aspect of the teacher's schedule that is important to consider is the summer vacation time. Although some schools are moving to a year-round schooling format (see Chapter 4), the period from mid-June through mid-August is still considered a time away from the classroom for most teachers. It allows for a change of pace from the rigors of classroom teaching and time to engage in other activities. Some take this opportunity to slow down, become reenergized, and engage in their favorite hobbies and activities. Others feel the need to supplement their income through additional work experiences. Still others use the time to take course work through their local colleges or universities to increase their knowledge and understanding of teaching and learning. Once again, the teaching schedule allows considerable flexibility in determining how to make use of a substantial portion of time during the calendar year. How important is this option in your future?

**Job benefits.**  Although improvements have been made in teacher salaries during the last several years, most educators find that they are below the income levels found in comparable positions (see Table 1.5). Despite the low salaries, most teachers find at least three other job benefits attractive. One is the *health and dental care benefits* that teachers receive as part of their contractual agreements. Quality health and dental coverage is generally available to teachers at an affordable cost. Another valuable benefit is a strong *retirement plan*. In most states, the teachers' contributions to this plan are matched with monies from the state to provide a secure and generous retirement payment that can begin as early as age 50 with a minimum number of years of service. A third benefit associated with teaching is *job security*. Whereas economic downturns may influence future pay increases and the costs of health and dental care benefits, once a teacher is tenured (see Chapter 13) there is a high level of job security in teaching as compared with other occupations.

**TABLE 1.5   Teacher Salaries Compared with Other Occupations**

| Occupation | Average Annual Salary |
|---|---|
| Full professor | $84,007 |
| Attorney | $82,712 |
| Engineer | $74,920 |
| Programmer/analyst | $71,155 |
| Buyer | $57,928 |
| Accountant | $52,664 |
| Assistant professor | $45,147 |
| Teacher | $43,250 |

*Source:* From *Survey & Analysis of Teacher Salary Trends 2001,* by Nelson, F. H., Drown, R., & Gould, J. (2002). Washington, DC: American Federation of Teachers, AFL-CIO. Reprinted with permission.

## How significant are the challenges?

As you begin to think seriously about teaching as a career, it is important to be aware of more than just the benefits that come from working in the classroom. It is also necessary to understand the potential difficulties you will face. By discussing the issues that make teaching more complex, you can develop a more balanced perspective on the realities of the teaching profession. This perspective should then help you make the best personal decision about the potential that teaching may have as a future career option. Each of the issues discussed below is addressed in more detail in Chapters 2, 5, and 12.

### Diverse Student Population

Without question, one of the challenges you will face if you choose to teach is the diversity of students found in virtually every school across the nation. This diversity can be categorized into four main areas: cultural, racial, and ethnic diversity; family diversity; diverse student abilities; and diversity due to gender. The very real differences that can be found among each of these groups of students has important implications for teaching and makes your work in the classroom both more rewarding and more complicated (see Chapter 2 for more details).

Take, for example, the fifth-grade classroom of Sandra Thornton. In terms of diversity, Sandra's class is fairly typical for her school. Of the 27 students, 4 are Hispanic, 3 are African American, 2 are of Asian descent, and 18 students are Caucasian. Fourteen live in families with two parents, 12 come from families where the biological parents have divorced (with 9 of these parents having remarried), and 1 student lives in a family situation that includes two female parents. Furthermore, 5 of the families live at or below the poverty level, 19 families are considered middle class, and 3 would be classified as upper middle class in terms of income. Sandra's students are divided fairly evenly by sex, with 15 boys and 12 girls. The teaching challenges she faces are further complicated by the ability levels of students placed in her classroom. Two students with special needs and 4 that have been classified as gifted are part of the mix that Sandra must plan for every day. See if you can imagine yourself in Sandra's classroom facing both the challenges and opportunities of her diverse group of students. How does it feel?

The rich diversity of a classroom like Sandra's provides many opportunities for exciting interactions between the teacher and students. At the same time, however, the complexities of planning for and teaching a group with this level of diversity are challenging. To take just one small example, Sandra plans six separate sets of activities for the mathematics curriculum she is required to teach. In addition to the primary activities planned for the majority of the class, individual plans must be made for each of the students with special needs and enrichment activities provided for those students who are moving more quickly in their development of mathematical concepts.

*There is growing diversity within American schools.*

### Complexities of Students' Lives

In addition to the growing diversity of students and families, many societal factors contribute to the complexities of students' lives today and make teaching a more challenging profession (see Chapter 12 for more information). These factors include poverty, teen pregnancy, AIDS/HIV, child abuse and neglect, suicide, violence, alcohol and drug abuse, and school dropouts. These are all

# The Road to Homelessness

Here, in the words of a homeless parent, is the story of one family's experience in moving from a relatively comfortable life situation to one of hardship and strife:

> Canton is my hometown. I graduated from the practical nurse program of the Canton City Schools System. I have worked for the past fifteen years as an LPN, including the past eight years at the Pines Nursing Center. I married and have two children—Aaron, who is eighteen, and Jasmine, who is nine. When my husband and I were together, we made decent money.
>
> Everything began to unravel last summer. My husband and I separated. At the same time, I began missing work due to illness. Eventually, I had to take a leave of absence. It took all summer for my physician to diagnose me with a very serious heart condition. This diagnosis couldn't have come at a worse time. I had just switched employers—one that provided better health insurance. But the diagnosis occurred when I was between coverage, and so I had no means to pay my huge health care expenses. With my husband gone and my physician having instructed me to stop working, I had no way to pay the rent for our apartment. Jasmine and I were evicted in October.
>
> We moved in with my sister. That arrangement lasted only a week and a half, because she had to move as well. Then, we were really in a jam. A friend as-

sisted me in locating the YWCA of Canton Homeless Shelter, where Jasmine and I have been staying since November. We live together in a single room. We've managed to hold onto our clothes and some personal belongings, but all of our furniture and house wares are long gone.

> The hardest part of being homeless is the waiting time to return to our own home. Jasmine and I desperately want stability, and we just can't seem to get there. We have applied for subsidized housing in Canton. We understand that we have been approved, but something is holding it up. We don't understand it at all.
>
> Jasmine has changed schools during this period, and that has been a big thing for her. She misses her old friends and teachers. I relocated Jasmine from her prior school to her current school because it was close to my sister's apartment. I thought we were going to be living with my sister permanently, and it seemed to make sense that her school be close to home, since I didn't have a car to transport her to her old school.
>
> We've been lucky. Jasmine has been able to remain in her elementary school throughout this ordeal. I don't know what we would do if she had to stay at the shelter all day. School gives her something to do and keeps her mind off of the stress in our lives right now. I dread if we are still homeless in the summer.

### Explore and Reflect

Learn more about homelessness in this country and read the story from Lois and others in the "Personal Experiences of Homelessness" section of the National Coalition for the Homeless website at **http://www.nationalhomeless.org** and by using the links provided on the Companion Website.

1. Explore the resources available to the homeless residents of your community by making a list of the local agencies that assist homeless individuals, children, and families.

2. If you were Jasmine's teacher, how would you feel about helping her through this difficult time in her life? As a teacher, what experiences, support, or resources would you draw on that might make you more effective in this situation?

*To explore this topic further and submit your reflections online, go to the Reflect on Diversity module for Chapter 1 of the Companion Website for this text.*

*Source:* Ferguson, L. (2001). *Oral Testimony of Lois Ferguson on Behalf of the National Coalition for the Homeless Regarding FY 2002 Appropriations for Homeless Programs Within the U.S. Departments of Health and Human Services, Education, and Labor Before the United States House of Representatives Committee on Appropriations Subcommittee on Labor, Health and Human Services, Education, and Related Agencies March 20, 2001.* Retrieved March 25, 2002, from http://www.nationalhomeless.org/experiences/lois.html

powerful issues that impact teaching and learning in virtually every classroom in America. Teachers cannot be expected to solve these complex problems on their own, but they need to be aware of the extent of the problems and contribute time and energy when possible in an effort to help students and their families find solutions.

The students in Jim Masterson's high school chemistry classes exemplify the many complex issues that students face. Four seniors were recently arrested outside the high school gym during a basketball game for substance abuse. Three were caught drinking beer and the fourth was smoking marijuana. A junior in one of his classes tried to commit suicide and needs to be watched carefully for any signs that might indicate another attempt is imminent. Jim also reported one suspected case of child abuse early in the school year when a sophomore student came to class with unexplained bruising on his arms and face. In addition, one of his students is an unmarried teen mother. The father is also a member of the same chemistry class. Can you imagine yourself feeling good about working in this setting?

Although it should be clear that Jim cannot expect to fully resolve any of these difficult issues on his own, he can work to support and encourage students as opportunities arise. For example, he made a point to work harder to understand and relate to the student who had tried to commit suicide. Jim found that she was frustrated with her chemistry assignments and needed additional help in completing them. He suggested an after-school tutoring session with two other classmates and the student agreed. Jim checks in with her regularly to see if there is anything else he can do to help her feel better about her academic accomplishments. The extra attention has helped her open up a bit more and she is starting to share with her tutors some of the frustrations she has had in her home life.

## Increasing Societal Expectations

Another challenge facing teachers today is the increasing number of expectations being placed on them by community, state, and federal groups. In addition to the expectation that teachers assist students in dealing with the kinds of social forces described above, four other pressures are adding new challenges to working with students. The first of these challenges is brought about because of the effort to *include students with special needs in the classroom.* The passage of several pieces of federal legislation during the past 30 years has led to growing numbers of students with special needs being included in regular education classrooms. Although there are many benefits to this approach for teachers and all students, it also brings new challenges. For example, despite the fact that most teachers have had only limited training in working with students with special needs, they are expected to plan activities for them when they are in the regular classroom.

Another pressure that teachers face is the pressure to *increase graduation rates.* Teachers at all levels are being encouraged to do everything they can to keep students in school through graduation from high school. Despite the fact that graduation rates have increased significantly during the past 50 years (see Table 1.6), the pressure is on to help every student receive a high school diploma. What this means is that some students who would have opted out of formal education in the past to join the workforce are now expected to stay in school. Many of these students are more difficult to teach, and they challenge educators in a variety of ways.

A third expectation that may increase teacher stress comes from an *expansion of the teaching role.* For a variety of reasons, many teachers today are expected to teach an expanded curriculum. At the elementary level, for example, the social issues referred to above have made it necessary for teachers and schools to take the lead in educating students in new ways. Some examples of this are sex education units, discussions about the problems of drug use, helping students develop strong self-esteem, and the implementation of violence prevention programs.

A final pressure that teachers face today is to help students *develop greater proficiency in basic skills.* At the same time that teachers are expected to do everything they can to keep students in school, they are asked to help them develop stronger skills in core curriculum areas such as sci-

**TABLE 1.6  High School Completion Rates**

| Year | Percentage of Students Who Graduated |
| --- | --- |
| 1910 | 13.5 |
| 1940 | 38 |
| 1970 | 55 |
| 1988 | 86 |
| 1994 | 88 |
| 1999 | 90 |

Sources: *High School Dropouts: How Much of a Crisis?*, by M. McLaughlin, 1990, Washington, DC: The Heritage Foundation; and *Kids Count Data Book,* by Annie E. Casey Foundation, 2002, Baltimore, MD: Author.

ence, mathematics, social studies, and literacy. Individual state governments and the legislative branch of the federal government are consistently mandating higher standards that students must meet to move through the educational system. In many states, students who fail to meet targeted levels of achievement are forced to take summer school programs or are retained in a grade so that they can have additional time to develop the needed skills. Teacher and school performance ratings are also being tied to the success rates of students as measured on tests of basic skills.

## Occupational Status

Another challenge you will face if you choose to enter teaching relates to the attitudes of others toward education as a profession. Unfortunately, many people still view teaching as a rather easy job that requires only minimal academic preparation and limited skills in working with people. Those who have not experienced the challenges of the classroom often fail to see the true complexities of teaching. This fairly common attitude can be summarized in the often-heard phrase "those who can't, teach." The assumption inherent in this statement is that people who enter the teaching profession would probably be unsuccessful in other occupations and therefore choose the "easy" task of teaching.

Ayers (2001) provides three indicators of the low status of teaching as a career. One that has already been mentioned is the issue of *salary*. The relatively low pay of teachers may well reflect the general attitude of society toward the education profession. A second indicator is the *high percentage of women* in the profession. Because men have historically dominated virtually every high-status occupation, teaching was one of a limited number of alternatives open to women. The third indicator of the low occupational status of teachers is the attempts by many to *make curriculum materials "teacher-proof."* By providing a teacher's guide with step-by-step directions and frequently even the words teachers should use in instruction, many publishers are implying that educators lack the skills needed to design lessons and activities on their own.

## Lack of Support

A final challenge that faces many teachers entering the profession is the low level of economic and emotional support they receive as educators. Economic support for teaching covers such things as money to purchase teaching materials, equipment, and supplies used in the classroom. For example, the costs associated with a textbook series to teach a single high school subject such as biology can run several thousand dollars. Not surprisingly, it is difficult for school districts to continually update these books and, consequently, teachers must often make do with materials

# Male Elementary Teachers

Current national statistics indicate that approximately 75% of all teachers today are women (National Education Association, 2001). Men are definitely in the minority, especially in elementary schools, where only about 14% are male (Peyton, 2000). Many men avoid teaching altogether because of the low wages and the difficulties of supporting a family on a teaching salary. Those who do choose to teach tend to gravitate to the middle and high school levels so that they can teach specific subject matter content.

In addition to the desire to teach only one or two subjects, others avoid elementary teaching because of role stereotyping. "Maybe that's why men are not at the lower levels: some view it, wrongly, as a form of baby-sitting" (Anderson, 2002, p. 1). Others feel that society in general thinks that men who want to work with younger children are "strange" and worry about being accused of child molestation. Some men also find it easier to relate to older students or want to be able to coach so that they can supplement their income (Peyton, 2000).

Despite the low numbers of male teachers, many people believe that it is beneficial to have men in the elementary classroom. These teachers can serve as role models for children from single-parent families who have fewer interactions with men. Boys, especially, may relate better to male teachers and be more successful in the classroom as a result (Anderson, 2002).

## Research the Issue

Research this topic by linking to the online source articles by Anderson (2002) and Peyton (2000) and explore the information provided at the additional sites listed on the Companion Website for this text.

1. From your research, make a list of the benefits of having male teachers for younger students. What problems do male teachers face that make it difficult for them to consider teaching at the elementary level?

2. What are some of the programs or efforts being made to recruit more males as elementary school teachers?

## Explore Your Views

1. What do you consider to be the benefits of having male teachers in elementary schools? Do you think that the presence of male teachers has a significant impact on young students?

2. Should teacher training programs and school districts make a concerted effort to recruit more men to teach at the elementary level? Why or why not? Do the benefits of attracting and retaining more male elementary-level teachers outweigh the costs involved in implementing recruitment or support programs?

 *To research this issue and submit your responses online, go to the Engage in the Debate module for Chapter 1 of the Companion Website for this text.*

*Sources:* "Male Teachers in Minority at Elementary Level," by H. Anderson, 2002, *Metro West Daily News*, April 9, 2002. Retrieved October 10, 2002, from http://www.metrowestdailynews.com/news/local_regional/classroom20409002.htm; "Male Elementary School Teachers Are Uncommon, But Sought After," by C. Peyton, 2000, *Corpus Christi Caller-Times*, July 16, 2000. Retrieved September 9, 2002, from http://www.caller2.com/2000/july/16/today/national/4876.html; and "Rankings and Estimates," by National Education Association, 2001. Retrieved March 12, 2003, from http://www.nea.org/edstats/images/02rankings.pdf

that are out of date. Equipment for use in the classroom, ranging from such things as computers and high-power microscopes to maps, is often in short supply due to limited budgets for these items. Even regular consumable materials such as test tubes, petri dishes, and chemical supplies for science laboratories may be difficult to purchase in some schools facing tight financial constraints. Teachers often find it necessary to dip into their own pockets for the money needed to support the many interesting projects they want to bring into the classroom. As one first-year teacher put it: "The students are so needy. And, there's no budget. I had to do everything without money and beg, borrow, or steal" (DePaul, 1998, p. 3).

In addition to the low level of economic support for materials and supplies, most teachers find that it can be lonely in the classroom, with few opportunities to discuss successes and problems with others. Although other teachers and administrators are well meaning and would truly like to spend time assisting you and others with the difficult tasks that will help you grow into strong teachers, the realities of teaching are such that there is little time to engage in this kind of support and encouragement. One first-year teacher, when asked if she felt isolated, responded: "Not physically, but certainly mentally. Sure, the other teachers are nice. But they didn't seem to want to get to know me or make sure everything was going OK" (Boss, 2001a, p. 3).

As you reflect on the challenges described in this section, what are your initial reactions? Do you get energized or discouraged? Would you envision yourself getting up each day excited about the prospects of facing complex intellectual and social issues or does this scenario make you feel overwhelmed? Continue to reflect on these issues as you read more about these topics in future chapters. If you consistently respond to these challenges without becoming overwhelmed or discouraged, then teaching is more likely to be a fulfilling profession for you.

**Reflective Journey 1.4**

## Should I become a teacher?

As indicated earlier in this chapter, people choose the teaching profession for many different reasons. Despite the significant challenges that every teacher must face, the benefits make it a very attractive option for many people. Sharon Draper, the 1997 National Teacher of the Year, wrote in a letter to prospective new teachers:

> As you consider teaching as a career, I'd like to offer my own personal response to teaching as a profession. My students often ask me, "Why are you a teacher?" implying that teaching is a terrible career choice. I tell them in response, "I teach because I need you as much as you need me. I teach because once upon a time a teacher made a difference in my life, so I am here to make a difference for you." . . . I never wavered in my desires and determination to become not just a teacher, but a really good teacher who made memories in the minds of children. . . . I continued to try to make a difference—one child at a time. For our greatest accomplishments in education are not the plaques and awards, but the smiles and hugs and memories of children touched today and somehow influenced tomorrow. (Council of Chief State School Officers, 2002, p. 3)

Sharon Draper's passion and commitment to teaching are clearly evident in the above letter. Not all who enter the profession, however, find this level of fulfillment. And because teacher preparation is a long and arduous task, you should make every effort to determine as early as possible whether or not teaching is the career path for you. While some people "just know" from a very early age that teaching is where they are called to be, most future educators need to spend a significant amount of time and energy thoughtfully considering life in the classroom before they can make the right decision about teaching as a career. You should begin this process of reflection now and continue to revisit these issues at intervals throughout your teacher preparation program.

### Reflect on Your Personal Skills and Attitudes

One important strategy that you can use to determine if teaching is a good career option is to carefully consider the skills and attitudes that you bring to the profession and the impact these personal characteristics may have on your potential effectiveness as a teacher. You may want to organize your thinking by considering four broad categories of skills and attitudes that can have a far-reaching influence on your success as a future teacher (see Table 1.7). The first of these is your *people skills*. Because teaching is about working with people, you will need the ability to establish and maintain strong relationships with others. A second broad category is your *organizational skills*. Teachers need to think carefully about the ways in which they organize and present the concepts to be learned in their classrooms. In addition, effective organizational skills

**TABLE 1.7**   Skills and Attitudes Influencing Teaching

| Skills and Attitudes | Examples |
|---|---|
| People skills | Seeing the perspectives of others<br>Remaining calm in emotional situations<br>Getting along with others<br>Looking for the best in others |
| Organizational skills | Giving clear directions<br>Anticipating steps to accomplish tasks<br>Managing time efficiently<br>Keeping effective records |
| Intellectual and linguistic skills | Understanding the subject(s) to be taught<br>Using effective verbal communications<br>Using effective written communications |
| Attitudes toward learning | Seeing self as a lifelong learner<br>Getting excited about learning<br>Wanting to share the excitement of<br>learning with others |

are needed in such areas as planning the school day, providing equitable interactions with all students, and developing meaningful assessments of student progress. Third, you will need strong *intellectual and linguistic skills* to understand and effectively communicate the concepts to be shared with students. Finally, *attitudes toward learning* are important to your success as a future teacher. If you are excited about learning, are able to share that enthusiasm with students, and expect that all students can learn, teaching becomes a much more productive enterprise.

**Reflective Journey 1.5**

While this issue is fresh in your mind, consider taking a few moments to make a list of the skills and attitudes you would bring to the teaching profession. As you reflect on the list you created, what impact do you think each of these items might have on the ways in which you teach? You may also want to discuss your skills and attitudes with classmates or a current teacher to gain further insights about their potential impact on your role as a teacher.

## Think About Your Motives for Considering a Teaching Career

Once you have thought through your personal strengths and limitations and their potential impact on a career in teaching, another strategy that you can use to gather further information is to think about the motives you have for considering the education profession. A decision about a career is a complicated one that is seldom based on a single motive, but rather is a mix of factors that come together to guide one's choice. As you read through this section, try to make sense of your own motives for considering teaching as a career. If you are approaching education for the right reasons, it is much more likely that you will find the profession a satisfying one and students will learn and grow from their interactions with you.

The positive reasons for entering teaching closely parallel the benefits of being an educator described in an earlier section of this chapter. They include the pleasure of being around students of a specific age, sharing a love of subject matter with students, the excitement and challenges of teaching, and making a difference in students' lives (see Table 1.8). All four of these motives are important for successful teaching. It is difficult to imagine, for example, that a person could be successful in the classroom without getting significant pleasure from the many daily interactions a teacher has with students. Similarly, if you don't get excited by the content you teach, each day would be hard

**TABLE 1.8   Why Teachers Enter the Profession**

| Reason | 1971 | 1976 | 1981 | 1986 | 1991 | 1996 |
|---|---|---|---|---|---|---|
| Desire to work with young people | 71.8% | 71.4% | 69.6% | 65.6% | 65.9% | 68.1% |
| Value or significance of education in society | 37.1 | 34.3 | 40.2 | 37.2 | 37.2 | 41.9 |
| Interest in subject-matter field | 34.5 | 38.3 | 44.1 | 37.1 | 33.6 | 36.5 |
| Influence of a teacher in elementary or secondary school | 17.9 | 20.6 | 25.4 | 25.4 | 26.8 | 30.5 |
| Never really considered anything else | 17.4 | 17.4 | 20.3 | 21.0 | 23.8 | 19.3 |
| Influence of family | 20.5 | 18.4 | 21.5 | 22.9 | 22.7 | 19.3 |
| Long summer vacation | 14.4 | 19.1 | 21.5 | 21.3 | 20.7 | 20.3 |
| Job security | 16.2 | 17.4 | 20.6 | 19.4 | 16.7 | 18.1 |
| Opportunity for a lifetime of self-growth | 21.4 | 17.4 | 13.1 | 9.7 | 7.9 | 10.9 |

*Source:* From National Education Association, *Status of the American Public School Teacher 1995–96,* Table 47, p. 59. ©1997 NEA, Washington, D.C. All rights reserved. Reprinted with permission.

to endure rather than a stimulating experience. What does vary from one teacher to the next, however, is the relative strength of each of these motives. Some may see assisting students in their growth and development as the most important reason to teach, whereas others may find a shared love of learning to be a highly motivating reason to teach. Although your experiences in the classroom are probably limited at this point, which of these motives do you think would be at the top of your list?

## Try on the Role

One final strategy you can use to help answer the question of whether or not to become a teacher is to do your best to understand and experience as many aspects of the role as possible. You can see how well teaching suits your interests and skills by thinking carefully and deeply about different aspects of working in the classroom, reading and learning more about education, talking with others, and spending time in classrooms and schools. As you try on the role, you will be able to make the best possible decision about teaching as a future career. Each chapter of this text is organized to help you in this process of reflection. Several features have been incorporated into the body of the chapter, with additional opportunities for deliberation found at the end.

*Working with students can help you decide about teaching as a career.*

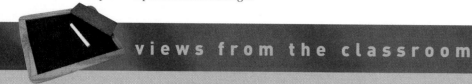

## views from the classroom

### Answering the Call to Teach

**Molly K. George**
**Devonshire Project Adventure Elementary School**
**Columbus, Ohio**

Most of my colleagues have always known that they wanted to be teachers. They always loved the feeling of chalk dust and the smell of pencil shavings. But I didn't. I wanted to be a doctor, or a veterinarian, or an astronaut, or run a Fortune 500 business. I wanted to be anything but a teacher. It wasn't until the end of my sophomore year of college that I realized I needed to be in the classroom.

The signs were all there, but I ignored them for years. I've always loved red pens. Friends came to me when they needed someone to proof papers or critique speeches. Both of my parents started their careers in education.

So why did it take me so long to realize this was my "calling"? I guess it was denial. But the first time I walked into the classroom to do field experience, I knew. Suddenly I was one of "them." I was teaching, and correcting, and laughing, and loving every minute of it. So began my life as a teacher.

## Summary

In this chapter, four organizing questions were used to help you think carefully about teaching as a future career:

### What is teaching really like?

Teaching is much more complex than most people believe it to be. It is a combination of the following:

- Independence and interconnectedness (Praxis II, topic IVa)
- An art
- A science (Praxis II, topic II)
- Lifelong learning

### What are the benefits of being a teacher?

Many positive benefits accrue from a career in teaching:

- The joy of teaching
- Personal growth
- Serving students, families, and community
- Schedule and job benefits

### How significant are the challenges?

Although teaching has many benefits, every educator also faces challenges:

- The diverse student population
- Complexities of students' lives
- Increasing societal expectations
- Occupational status
- Lack of support

## Should I become a teacher?

As you begin to think about the possibility of teaching as a career, it is important to use a variety of strategies to clarify your perspectives:

- Reflect on your personal strengths and limitations
- Think about your motives for considering teaching
- Try on the role

## Key Terms

continuing professional development
experiences as a learner
initial teacher certification
knowledge base
mentor

teaching as a science
teaching as an art
teacher induction
vocation

## Reflective Journey: Online Journal

Use the questions for thought and reflection highlighted throughout the chapter to help guide your personal journey of reflection and professional development as a teacher. To complete your journal entries online, go to the *Reflective Journey* module for this chapter of the Companion Website.

## PRAXIS Test Preparation Activities

To review an online chapter case study, test your understanding of chapter topics and concepts, and begin preparing for the Praxis II: Principles of Learning and Teaching examination, go to the *Praxis Test Preparation* module for this chapter of the Companion Website.

## inTASC Becoming a Reflective Practitioner

To complete these activities and submit your responses online, go to the *Becoming a Reflective Practitioner* module for this chapter of the Companion Website.

## What is teaching really like?

### Review Questions

1. How are teachers both independent and connected with others?
2. What is the knowledge base of teaching?
3. What are the phases in learning to teach?

### Field Experience

Find a teacher who is working at a grade level that may be of interest to you and spend time discussing education with that person. Ask for information on why he or she entered the profession. Also find out what this person sees as the benefits and challenges of teaching. Write a summary of your interview and share with others the insights developed from your discussion. How did the teacher's responses affect your feelings or motivation for becoming a teacher?

**Building Your Portfolio:** *Experiences with Students*

**INTASC Standard 2.** Identify all experiences you have had to date working with students. These experiences need not be in formal educational settings and should include babysitting, summer camps, and past jobs that have allowed you opportunities to interact with preschool through high school students. Give detailed information that includes the approximate dates, kinds of experiences, and the names of any contact people who could help clarify the tasks you performed. Next, review the items you included in your list of experiences. In a separate document, briefly describe something you gained from each experience, and consider how these experiences can contribute to your success as a teacher. Put this document in your portfolio and plan to update it as you engage in new experiences with students.

## What are the benefits of being a teacher?

### Review Questions

1. What are the two components associated with a love of teaching?
2. How would you define vocation?
3. What are the job benefits that most teachers find attractive?

### Field Experience

Talk to four or five adults who do *not* work in school settings. Ask them to identify another occupation or two that they think requires skills comparable to those of teaching. Probe to find out why they feel this way. Also ask these adults to describe their views on the importance of teaching to the greater society. Once you have collected this information, spend some time reflecting on your findings. From your discussions, what other occupations were identified as requiring skills similar to those of teachers? What does this tell you about the status of teaching? How did these adults view the importance of teaching? Discuss what you found with others.

### Building Your Portfolio: *A Case for Teaching*

**INTASC Standard 9.** Based on your current understandings of education, make the strongest/most persuasive case you can for someone else becoming a teacher. What do you see as the potential benefits? How can the problems be minimized? Make sure you include in the rationale your understanding of the importance of teachers to society at large. Revisit your response after you have read the last chapter of this text.

## How significant are the challenges?

### Review Questions

1. Describe the diversity you can expect to find in American schools.
2. What are some of the stresses students face?
3. How are societal expectations for teachers and schools changing?

### Building Your Portfolio: *Special Talents*

**INTASC Standard 9.** One thing that may help you make a decision about teaching as a career is to think about the special talents you possess that would help you meet the challenges of being a teacher. Create a list in which you identify special talents you have and describe how they could be put to use in the classroom. There are many possibilities for this list including athletic skills/experiences, musical and/or artistic talents, writing skills, special aptitudes in subject matter areas, theatrical skills, speaking abilities, and other hobbies or talents.

## Should I become a teacher?

### Review Questions

1. What personal skills and attitudes are important for you to have as a future teacher?
2. Identify the positive reasons teachers cite for entering the profession.

### Building Your Portfolio: *Perceptions of Others*

**INTASC Standard 9.** Select four or five friends and/or family members and ask them for an honest assessment of why they think you should or should not consider teaching as a career. Have them identify specific personality characteristics that they think would enhance your chances of success in the classroom as well as those that may cause you difficulties. Record their responses. Honestly assess yourself in the same manner and record your responses. Carefully consider the responses of your friends and family and compare them with your own responses. Summarize your findings along with any insights you gained into your potential as a future teacher.

## Suggested Readings

Ayers, W. (2001). *To teach: The journey of a teacher* (2nd ed.). New York: Teachers College Press. This book challenges teachers and teachers-to-be to emphasize caring and giving in their relationships with students at the same time that they help develop academic and life skills. The author makes it clear that while excellent teaching is a constant challenge, it can also be one of the most rewarding of professions.

Barone, T. (2001). *Touching eternity: The enduring outcomes of teaching.* New York: Teachers College Press. The author of this book emphasizes the positive long-term impact that good teachers have on their students. A case study of a high school art teacher and his former students is used to help the reader reflect on the importance of highly effective teachers in American society.

Graves, D. (2001). *The energy to teach.* Portsmouth, NH: Heinemann. The basic premise of this book is that quality teaching requires a great deal of energy. While many people enter the profession with a strong commitment to students and a willingness to expend the energy necessary to be successful, many end up feeling worn out. Graves provides encouragement to teachers by helping them understand what they can do to get the energy they need to be successful and what actions or activities they should avoid so that they will not end up physically and emotionally exhausted.

Levine, S. (Ed.). (1999). *A passion for teaching.* Alexandria, VA: Association for Supervision and Curriculum Development. This edited book contains a wealth of stories and poems from master teachers that describe the reasons for their continued passion for teaching. Reading them helps clarify the many positive benefits of the teaching profession.

# chapter 2

## Students Today

Each and every teaching day you will come face to face with one or more groups of exciting, frustrating, and challenging students. They will be both your greatest joy and your biggest challenge. To do your job effectively, you will need to have a deep understanding of both the similarities and differences you will find among your students. Four key questions are presented here to organize your thinking as you begin the process of understanding the students you will teach.

## Focus Questions

◢ What differences among people influence interactions in the classroom?

◢ How do social and cultural differences impact teaching and learning?

◢ What responses should teachers make to differences among students?

◢ What are your attitudes toward student differences?

Kathy Klein teaches seventh-grade social studies and has just finished another rewarding school year. As she reflects on her experiences, Kathy is once again struck by both the joys and challenges of working with the diverse group of students she had in her classes. Out of the many she taught, four stand out in her memory. Quan and her family arrived in the United States from Cambodia 2 years ago. Despite all her hard work, she continues to struggle in her efforts to master the English language. Nonetheless, Quan's quiet attentiveness and willingness to learn made her a pleasure to have in class.

Dennis, on the other hand, was a much more difficult student because of his total lack of interest in the social studies curriculum. Clearly a bright young man, Kathy recently learned that Dennis's mother has been on welfare for several months and is struggling to raise her four children with little support from other family members. Despite Kathy's many efforts to befriend Dennis and get him motivated, he continued to do barely passing work in her class.

Then there was Samuel, who served as an inspiration to the whole school. Paralyzed from the waist down since birth, Samuel was one of the brightest and most upbeat individuals Kathy had the pleasure of teaching. His enthusiasm was infectious and everyone seemed to be a little bit happier and more productive when Samuel and his wheelchair were nearby.

Kathy also remembered with considerable sadness the time when Sherry and her family became homeless and had to sleep in their car. Sherry's grades fell dramatically before the family finally moved to a new state in search of a job. The joys and challenges that come from the diversity found in Kathy's classroom are becoming the norm for all teachers.

As we begin the 21st century, a very visible change that is taking place in America's schools is the growing diversity of students and their families. From rural America to the big city, schools are no longer populated with primarily White, Anglo-Saxon, Christian students of average and above-average abilities. Less than half of today's children come from two-parent homes in which dad earns a wage and mom raises the children (Annie E. Casey Foundation, 2002). Students bring diverse languages, cultural traditions, religions, family support systems, and abilities to the classroom. Although student diversity adds complexities to the teaching role, it also creates an even more exciting teaching and learning environment and provides greater rewards for those who rise to the challenges presented.

## What differences among people influence interactions in the classroom?

**Reflective
Journey 2.1**

Before beginning a discussion of the differences that you will find among students in your future classroom, it is important to take a moment and reflect on the many similarities that also exist. To personalize this issue, think about someone you currently know or have known reasonably well who is of a different race, sex, sexual orientation, or ability. What does this person have in common with you? Construct a list of similarities. Are there things you both like or dislike? Do you share some common values with this person? What shared experiences have you both had? If you think hard, it should be easy to construct a fairly long list of things that you both have in common. This person who is different from you in some significant way is also much the same.

In exactly the same way, the students you will teach have much in common with each other and with you, despite the differences that exist. They have many similar needs, interests, and attitudes. Chapter 6 describes in detail many of the common student characteristics that influence learning. Even though these similarities will vary with each student you teach, it is important to be aware of them while at the same time adapting to the differences you will also find.

In addition to remembering the similarities that all students share, please realize that the information presented here describes in general terms the conditions of different groups of students involved in American schools. Although it is useful to be aware of these averages and percentages, students in your future classrooms will be unique individuals and will seldom neatly fit the national norms being shared here. Your job as a teacher is to balance an understanding of this general information with the more specific knowledge gathered about each of the individual students you teach. The following information then becomes a good starting point for understanding and dealing with students.

### Race

One important difference between people that has had a long-standing impact on interactions in the classroom is race. The U.S. Census Bureau has traditionally identified five main racial groups: Caucasian (White), Hispanic, African American (Black), Asian, and Native American. More recently, these racial categories have been called into question, in part because so many people do not readily "fit" into a single racial category. Despite this blurring of the lines between groups, race continues to be one of the most powerful and destructive forms of social categorization. Lee, Menkart, and Okazawa-Rey (1998) state:

*Teachers work to meet the needs of all students.*

Race is not a biological construct, with clearly definable features and characteristics, as most of us were taught to think. Yet, as it has been constructed in our society, race plays a critical role in many social interactions in general. Racism is pervasive and has an impact on all aspects of society. (p. viii)

A study of population trends indicates that racial diversity in the United States has grown dramatically in the last several decades and is projected to change even more in the years ahead (Forum on Child and Family Statistics, 2002). One reason for these changes is that birth rates vary between subgroups within our country. For example, birth rates for Hispanic women in the United States are about 40% higher than those for African American women (Jacobson, 1998). The second main reason for this growing diversity is the continued immigration of people from around the world to the United States (see Table 2.1). As a nation, we are experiencing the largest influx of immigrants since the early 1900s (Olson, 2000). In addition, whereas earlier immigrant populations came primarily from European countries, larger numbers are now entering the United States from Asia and Central and South America. These families are having a significant impact on diversity in the schools.

Looking more specifically at the racial composition of classrooms (see Figure 2.1), population statistics indicate that the percentage of U.S. children who are White (non-Hispanic) has decreased during the last several decades and will continue to drop in the years ahead (Olson, 2000). In some parts of the country, White students already make up less than 50% of the student population in many schools. While these percentages continue to drop, the large numbers of immigrants and high birth rates of Hispanic families have led to rapid growth in the Hispanic student population. At the same time, growth in the African American student population is less than that for other groups, and their percentage of the total population is estimated to remain relatively constant in the next two decades. Similarly, the percentage of American Indian/Alaska native students should remain relatively constant. Finally, the number of Asian and Pacific Islander students, while small, is expected to grow by 50% by the year 2020.

**TABLE 2.1   Changing Immigrant Populations**

| 1960 | | 1999 | |
|---|---|---|---|
| Italy | 1,256,999 | Mexico | 7,197,329 |
| Germany | 989,815 | Philippines | 1,455,046 |
| Canada | 952,500 | Vietnam | 966,209 |
| Poland | 747,750 | Cuba | 943,424 |
| Soviet Union | 690,598 | China | 842,795 |
| Mexico | 575,902 | India | 838,512 |
| England | 528,205 | El Salvador | 760,972 |
| Ireland | 338,722 | Dominican Republic | 678,986 |
| Austria | 304,507 | Canada | 662,089 |
| Hungary | 245,252 | Korea/South Korea | 610,567 |

Source: *Foreign-Born Populations of the United States: Current Population Survey,* by U.S. Census Bureau, 2002. Retrieved March 13, 2003, from http://www.census.gov/population

**Figure 2.1**   Changing Racial Composition of Schools, by Percentage, 2000–2040

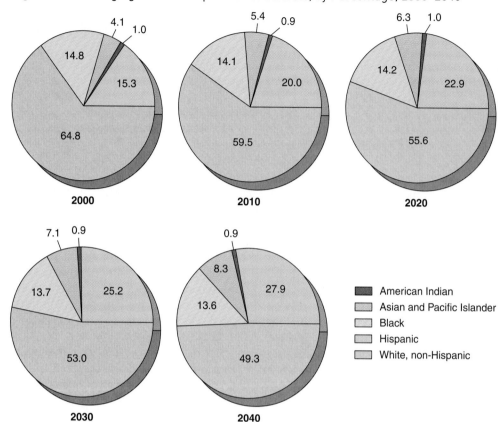

*Note:* Percentages for 2010 and 2030 do not equal 100% due to rounding.
*Source: National Population Projections,* by U.S. Census Bureau, 2003. Retrieved March 13, 2003, from http://www.census.gov/population/www/projections/natproj.html

## Gender

There is little question that male students differ from their female counterparts in many of their emotional, social, and behavioral traits, and that these differences are influenced by society, culture, and education. From kindergarten through high school and beyond, male and female students are very different in terms of temperament, interests, and needs. You will want to understand this aspect of diversity and be prepared to deal with it as you prepare for work in your future classroom.

The women's movement and gender-related federal legislation have clarified the need for schools to treat boys and girls more equitably. Although much progress has been made in this regard, subtle forms of gender bias still exist within American society and the schools. For example, the American Association of University Women (AAUW) published a controversial report in 1992 that described how girls were being shortchanged in American schools. They stated that girls "do not receive equitable amounts of teacher attention, they are less apt than boys to see themselves reflected in the materials they study, and they often are not expected or encouraged to pursue higher-level mathematics and science courses" (p. 147). This report and the research on which it was based led to a renewed emphasis by the schools to provide more equitable educational opportunities for girls.

# Digital Equity

In simple terms, digital equity means all students have adequate access to information and communication technologies for learning and for preparing for the future—regardless of socioeconomic status, physical disability, language, race, gender, or any other characteristics that have been linked with unequal treatment. (Solomon, 2002, p. 18)

With the rapid growth in computer and technology use, the issue of equal access to this important teaching and learning option has become increasingly important. Many students come to school with fewer opportunities to engage in technology use. For example, in families with a household income of less than $30,000, only about 31% have Internet access compared to 78% of households with incomes above $75,000. Similarly, 36% of Black families as compared to 50% of Whites have Internet access (Solomon, 2002).

Schools are becoming increasingly important sites for providing greater digital equity. Unfortunately, injustices continue to exist here as well. Schools in low-income areas, for example, tend to have less money to invest in computers and Internet access and lag behind many wealthier districts in technology use. Most schools have also found it difficult to provide the hardware and software needed for students with disabilities to effectively use computers. Students with limited English proficiency make up another group that has had difficulty receiving equitable technology opportunities. Educators agree that these situations must be remedied, but the challenges to doing so are many.

### Research the Issue

Research the issue of digital equality by reading the source article by G. Solomon, then find out more about the issue online using the links provided on the Companion Website.

1. Which groups of students are reported to be having the fewest opportunities for computer and Internet use?

2. According to your research, what is currently being done to minimize any inequities?

3. What are the most frequently cited challenges to providing digital equality in schools?

### Explore Your Views

1. Review the definition of digital equity given at the beginning of this feature, and consider the results of your research. Based on what you have seen and read, do you think that digital equity is a significant concern? Do you feel that specific measures should be taken to provide equitable access at the classroom, district, state, or federal level? Why or why not? Explain your position.

2. In your opinion, how important is it to provide the same quantity and quality of computer instruction and Internet access to all students across the country? Do you believe that computer and Internet skills are vital for success in learning or as an adult in the working world? In your view, what can schools and individual teachers do to minimize the digital inequities that currently exist?

 *To research this issue and submit your responses online, go to the Engage in the Debate module for Chapter 2 of the Companion Website for this text.*

*Source:* Digital Equity: It's Not Just About Access Anymore by G. Solomon, 2002, *Technology and Learning, 22*(9), pp. 18–26.

Although most of the research and writing to date has focused on educational inequities for girls, concern for boys and their performance is growing (Viadero, 1998). Boys get poorer grades than girls in school, drop out more frequently, and are referred to special education classes more often. Furthermore, boys score considerably lower than girls on national reading tests. School personnel will need to work hard to make sure that boys are more successful in these problem areas.

## Sexual Orientation

Another important and highly controversial difference that exists between people concerns their sexual orientation. While most Americans are **heterosexual, gay** and **lesbian** individuals account for an estimated 4% of the population (Bailey, Magpantay, & Rosenblum, 2001). This percentage may underrepresent the actual size of the gay and lesbian community due to the powerful stigma attached to homosexuality and the tendency of this group to remain silent concerning their sexual orientation.

Teachers and schools are becoming increasingly involved in the issues surrounding sexual orientation for two main reasons. First of all, gay and lesbian students deserve the same opportunities as heterosexual students to learn in an environment that is both safe and supportive. If you choose to teach at the middle school or high school level, you will need to understand the additional stresses that gay and lesbian students face and be prepared to support and encourage them in every way possible as they spend time in your classroom. The second reason that you and others will need to be involved in supporting gay and lesbian students is that you are legally required to do so. The 14th Amendment to the U.S. Constitution requires equal treatment of all people, including gay and lesbian individuals (see Chapter 13 for more information on legal responsibilities).

## Abilities

Another major factor influencing diversity in American schools is the large variance in student abilities. Students with disabilities, normally developing students, and those who are gifted and talented create a mix of abilities and needs that significantly influence the ways in which you will teach. A typical classroom of 25 students, for example, could easily have 3 or 4 students with disabilities and an equal number of students categorized as gifted. As a teacher, one of the significant challenges you will face is to plan lessons and activities that meet the needs of all students' different ability levels in your classroom.

Students with special needs are often categorized as either disabled or gifted. **Students with disabilities** include those with speech and language difficulties, physical-motor handicaps, intellectual impairments, social-emotional problems, and health-related disabilities. **Gifted students** perform exceptionally well in one or more aspects of schooling and need specialized help to meet their potential. It is estimated that 3% to 5% of American students are gifted as determined by standardized intelligence tests (Gollnick & Chinn, 2002).

**Students with disabilities.** As you begin to think about working with students with disabilities, remember that they are people first and only secondarily require special services. As indicated in the earlier discussion of similarities among all people, students with disabilities are more like their peers than they are different from them. Approaching them with this attitude will make it more likely that they will receive the experiences they need for healthy development. For example, Evan is an elementary child with Down syndrome. He has the same needs for positive social interactions with his peers and affirmation from his teacher as any of the other students in his class. Evan also needs appropriate learning opportunities that match his abilities and interests. Although his disability means that learning may require more time and effort than it does for other students, Evan is more similar to his classmates than he is different and should be treated as such.

Historically, the vast majority of children with disabilities were educated in separate classrooms. Those with severe disabilities were frequently placed in institutions where they had little or no contact with more normally developing children (Walther-Thomas, Korinek, McLaughlin, & Williams, 2000). Through the advocacy efforts of parents and concerned others, federal legislation was passed in the 1970s that made it mandatory to include children with disabilities in the regular school classroom whenever possible. This approach, originally referred to as **mainstreaming** and more recently called **inclusion**, means that virtually every classroom will have students with disabilities.

## Sexual Orientation and Hate Crimes

While hate crimes perpetrated against people of color continue to be a major concern, hate crimes against non-heterosexual individuals is another area with significant problems. The Human Rights Campaign (2002) has compiled a list of hate crimes against individuals that have resulted in death or bodily injury. A sampling of actions against gay and lesbian individuals includes:

- *July 31, 1998, Falmouth, Maine.* Brian M., 39, was charged with terrorizing, violating a protective order, and disorderly conduct for allegedly threatening to kill and behead two lesbian neighbors.

- *October 12, 1998, Laramie, Wyoming.* Matthew S., an openly gay 21-year-old University of Wyoming student, was savagely beaten, tortured, tied to a wooden fence in a remote area, and left to die in freezing temperatures.

- *November 6, 1998, Seattle, Washington.* A gay man was severely beaten with rocks and broken bottles in his neighborhood by a gang of youths shouting

"faggot." The victim sustained a broken nose and swollen jaw. When he reported the incident to the police 2 days later, the officer refused to take the report.

- *March 29, 2000, Santa Rosa, California.* Christopher D. was sentenced to 6 months in jail for shooting out the rear window of a woman's car that had gay pride stickers on it.

- *February 8, 2002, Missoula, Montana.* A lesbian couple and their infant son narrowly escaped their burning home alive when it was set ablaze in an attempted homicide.

These are more extreme examples of the prejudices that exist against gay and lesbian individuals, but they point out the need for increasing our awareness and acceptance of people with differing sexual orientations. You will need to provide a classroom setting in which all students can expect to be treated with dignity and have equitable opportunities for quality learning experiences.

### React and Reflect

1. Do you think bias against gay and lesbian students or adults is a significant issue? What makes you feel this way? Have you seen or heard examples of bias?

2. Reflect on your own biases. How would you feel about teaching students who are openly gay or lesbian? Do you think you could effectively work with gay or lesbian parents or teachers?

3. For the grade level you are interested in teaching, what can you do as a classroom teacher to minimize the prejudice against gay and lesbian students?

 *To explore this topic further and submit your reactions and reflections online, go to the Explore Your Beliefs module for Chapter 2 of the Companion Website for this text.*

Source: *Hate Crimes,* by Human Rights Campaign, 2002. Retrieved March 2003 from http://www.hrc.org

Three individual pieces of federal legislation have collectively had a major influence on the inclusion of students with special needs in the regular classroom. The first of these was the *Education for All Handicapped Children Act* (Public Law 94–142) that was passed into law in 1975. The most significant provision of this law was that all students with disabilities were guaranteed a free and appropriate education. In addition, children between the ages of 3 and 18 were to be educated in regular classrooms with students without disabilities whenever possible. This process of mainstreaming or inclusion has gradually led to higher levels of participation by children with disabilities in the regular classroom. In 1990, the U.S. Congress amended Public Law 94–142 and renamed it the *Individuals with Disabilities Education Act* (Public Law 101–476). This law expanded the coverage of the original law from age 18 to age

## Yes I Can!

Sometimes, when people think about students with disabilities the things that stand out in their minds are what these students *can't* do. It is important, however, that as a future teacher you remember that students with disabilities are capable of a great many accomplishments. Each year the Council for Exceptional Children and the Yes I Can Foundation present awards to 35 students with disabilities for their academic, artistic, athletic, community service, and employment achievements. Here are three stories of these highly accomplished students (Ladd, 2002).

Carl Fetzner is the proud father of 18-year-old Laura, who has used a wheelchair and a breathing tube since receiving a spinal cord injury at the age of 3. Laura was given the Yes I Can award for her academic accomplishments. With a grade point average of 3.75, she has demonstrated excellence in all aspects of her high school career. Like other students her age, Laura also engages in many interesting extracurricular experiences, including a recent trip to Myrtle Beach, South Carolina, with her best friend Carrie.

Bob, another Yes I Can award recipient, is an accomplished piano player despite his cerebral palsy. His award was one of several given for the arts. Even more significant than his musical talent is Bob's terrific attitude. At the awards ceremony he said, "I thank God for the talent He has given me" (Ladd, 2002, p. 2).

Caitlin Omness is yet a third recipient of the Yes I Can award for her accomplishments in athletics. Despite having cerebral palsy and using a walker, at age 13 Caitlin is an accomplished horseback rider. Her many trophies attest to her skills in horsemanship.

### Explore and Reflect

Learn more about students with disabilities and link to the "Yes I Can" home page and CEC website using the links provided on the Companion Website for this chapter.

1. Do you know someone with a disability? (If you do not, focus your responses below on one of the stories highlighted on the Yes I Can web page.) What are some of the important accomplishments of this individual? What challenges has this person faced?

2. If you were this student's teacher, what could you do to celebrate the successes of this student in your classroom?

 *To explore this topic further and submit your responses online, go to the Reflect on Diversity module for Chapter 2 of the Companion Website for this text.*

*Source:* "Our 2002 Yes I Can! Award Winners—An Inspiration to All" by W. Ladd, 2002, *CEC Today, 8*(8), 2–3.

21 and modified the categories of disability to include such things as autism and attention deficit disorders (ADD) (see Table 2.2). The third important law influencing students with disabilities is the *Americans with Disabilities Act* (Public Law 101–336), which was also enacted in 1990. This piece of legislation was designed to end discrimination against individuals with disabilities in employment, public services (including education), public accommodations, and transportation. In essence, this law mandates the mainstreaming of people with disabilities into all aspects of American life.

Having students with disabilities in your future classroom will either be something you enjoy or it will be an aspect of teaching you need to constantly monitor. The reason for this is that teachers generally find that they are most attracted to, and work best with, students of specific ability levels. For example, some teachers get very excited about and are most effective when teaching gifted and talented students. Others, however, feel drawn to children with disabilities.

**TABLE 2.2   Students with Disabilities**

| Category | Description |
|---|---|
| Autism | Significantly influences verbal and nonverbal communication and social interaction, making it difficult to learn in traditional ways |
| Deafness/hearing impairment | Difficulty in processing linguistic information through the normal hearing process |
| Deafness-blindness | Having simultaneous hearing and visual impairments |
| Mental retardation | Significant, below-average ability in general intellectual functioning |
| Multiple disabilities | Two or more disabilities, often interrelated |
| Orthopedic impairment | A physical disability that affects walking or other motor function |
| Other health impairments | Chronic or acute health problems that limit strength, vitality, or alertness |
| Emotional disturbances | Social or emotional problems that seriously impact the ability to learn |
| Specific learning disabilities | Basic disorders in the processing of language that significantly influence the ability to listen, think, speak, read, write, spell, or do mathematics |

*Source: Digest of Education Statistics* by the National Center for Education Statistics, 2001, Washington, DC: U.S. Government Printing Office.

Unfortunately, most of us find that we aren't equally well suited to interacting with children of all ability levels. Our personal preferences get in the way.

**Gifted and talented students.** A small, but important percentage of students in American schools can be classified as gifted and talented. These students are often identified early in their schooling for having demonstrated a level of accomplishment well beyond what others of the same age can do. Traditionally, high levels of intellectual functioning have been viewed as the primary form of giftedness. Consequently, standardized intelligence tests were the primary tools used to identify people who are gifted. More recently, however, giftedness has been more broadly defined to include exceptional skills in other areas as well (Heward, 1996).

Unlike students with disabilities, gifted students have limited legal rights under state and federal law (Karnes & Marquardt, 1997). There is no federal legislation, for example, that mandates educational opportunities for gifted students. The *Jacob K. Javits Gifted and Talented Students Act of 1994,* while providing for model programs and projects, does not give gifted students legal rights similar to those for children with disabilities (Karnes & Marquardt, 1997). Approximately 30 states, however, do require that special services be provided to gifted students (National Center for Education Statistics, 2001).

**TABLE 2.3** Gardner's Multiple Intelligences

| Intelligence | Description |
|---|---|
| Linguistic intelligence | The ability to speak or write creatively and with relative ease |
| Logical-mathematical intelligence | Strong reasoning skills and ability to effectively engage in mathematical and scientific inquiry |
| Spatial intelligence | Allows people (such as engineers and sculptors) to form refined mental models of the spatial world around them |
| Musical intelligence | Special talent in singing or playing a musical instrument |
| Bodily kinesthetic intelligence | Intelligence that helps people (like athletes and dancers) solve problems and fashion products using their body or body parts |
| Interpersonal intelligence | A particularly strong ability to understand other people |
| Intrapersonal intelligence | Allows people to be particularly insightful about themselves |
| Naturalistic intelligence | A special ability to recognize differences in the natural world |

Perhaps the best framework for understanding categories of giftedness is the work of Howard Gardner, a faculty member at Harvard University. Gardner (1983) has promoted a view of intelligence or giftedness that he calls his **theory of multiple intelligences** (see Table 2.3). He identifies eight distinctly different intelligences. Using these as a framework for understanding giftedness helps teachers to realize that there are many students with exceptional skills in every classroom. It also clarifies the need to modify instructional strategies to meet the learning styles and gifts of different students.

## How do social and cultural differences impact teaching and learning?

**Reflective Journey 2.2**

Every student brings a unique blend of social and cultural experiences to the classroom. These include an assortment of religious traditions, first-language experiences, family income levels, and family structures. Take a moment to think about your own social and cultural traditions. What is your religious, linguistic, economic, and family history? What aspects of this history are unique? Think about the beliefs and experiences that you have in common with others around you. How do you think that this history will influence your ability to work with students in your classrooms? Continue to reflect on these questions as you read the following sections about the social and cultural backgrounds of students.

| TABLE 2.4   Top Ten Organized Religions in the United States, 2001 | | |
|---|---|---|
| **Religion** | **Estimate of Adult Population** | **Percent of Population** |
| Christianity | 159,030,000 | 76.5 |
| Judaism | 2,831,000 | 1.3 |
| Islam | 1,104,000 | 0.5 |
| Buddhism | 1,082,000 | 0.5 |
| Hinduism | 766,000 | 0.4 |
| Unitarian Universalist | 629,000 | 0.3 |
| Wiccan/Pagan/Druid | 307,000 | 0.1 |
| Spiritualist | 116,000 | — |
| Native American religion | 103,000 | — |
| Baha'i | 84,000 | — |

*Source:* From "Largest Religious Groups in the United States of America" by Adherents.com, 2002. Retrieved March 14, 2003, from http://www.adherents.com/rel_USA.html. Reprinted with permission.

## Religion

From its earliest days, America has been a nation in which Christianity has been the primary form of religious expression (see Table 2.4). Despite its acceptance by an overwhelming majority of the population, however, Christianity itself has a diversity of beliefs and traditions. For example, the beliefs of Mormons, Seventh Day Adventists, and Jehovah's Witnesses differ significantly from protestant groups such as Lutherans, Baptists, and Presbyterians. Knowing about these similarities and differences may be important to you as a future teacher.

In addition to the differences in beliefs that exist within Christianity, a growing number of students have non-Christian religious backgrounds. As greater numbers of immigrants from non-European countries have found their way to the United States, they have brought with them an increasingly diverse set of religious traditions. Among the largest of these are the Buddhist, Muslim, and Hindu religions. According to Diana Eck (2001), "The United States has become the most religiously diverse nation on earth" (p. 4).

Religious beliefs and traditions can potentially impact life in the schools in any number of ways. For example, should Muslim or Jewish public school teachers be allowed to wear head coverings as expected in their religious traditions? If schools acknowledge Christian holidays, what should be their response to the holidays of other religious groups? Should a Sikh student be allowed to wear the

*It is important to respect the religious customs and beliefs of all students.*

*kirpan,* a symbolic knife required of all initiated Sikhs, to school? These and many other dilemmas must be addressed by schools and teachers in the 21st century.

How will you as a future teacher respond to the religious diversity you encounter? The first step is to recognize your initial reaction to people who look and dress differently from yourself:

> After race, the most visible signal of difference is dress, and this is where religious minorities become visible minorities. Many Muslim women wear *hijab,* either a simple head scarf or a full outer garment. A few even wear a face covering called *nikab.* Muslim men may wear a beard, and Sikh men may wear not only a beard but also a turban wrapped around their uncut hair. Jewish men may wear a yarmulke or skullcap. Buddhist monks may wear saffron, maroon, black, brown, or gray robes. (Eck, 2001, p. 297)

For many people, the first response to visible differences is suspicion, fear, or discomfort.

**Reflective Journey 2.3**

You should also reflect on your attitudes toward those whose religious beliefs differ from your own. Can you look beyond these religious differences and work to help each individual within your classroom learn and grow? Would your religious convictions make it difficult for you to work with parents whose beliefs are different from your own? These are not easy questions to answer and may require careful thought as you prepare to enter the teaching profession.

## Language

Just as religious beliefs are growing increasingly diverse within the United States, the languages spoken by students are also becoming more varied. Immigrant families bring with them a variety of languages spoken at home, with Spanish, Chinese, Tagalog (Filipino), Korean, Vietnamese, Arabic, Hindi, and Russian being some of the more common (Banks, 2002). Many students from these immigrant families haven't yet mastered English and are defined by the schools as **limited English-proficient (LEP)** learners. Students whose first language is not English are often placed in **bilingual education** or **English as a Second Language (ESL) programs** for assistance in language learning.

Data from the U.S. Census Bureau (2000) indicate that nearly one in five families speaks a language other than English in the home (see Table 2.5). Most of the children in these settings have limited English proficiency. Considerable differences exist between the estimated 3.5 mil-

**TABLE 2.5   Languages Spoken at Home**

| Language Spoken at Home | Estimate (in millions) |
|---|---|
| English only | 209.86 |
| Spanish | 26.74 |
| Number that speak English less than "very well" | 12.46 |
| Other Indo-European languages | 9.48 |
| Number that speak English less than "very well" | 3.1 |
| Asian and Pacific Islander languages | 6.86 |
| Number that speak English less than "very well" | 3.4 |
| Other languages | 1.8 |
| Number that speak English less than "very well" | 0.53 |

*Source: Census 2000* by the U.S. Census Bureau, 2000, Washington, DC: U.S. Government Printing Office.

lion LEP students in American schools and their English-proficient peers (Garcia, 2000). One difference is that approximately 45% are foreign born. Frequently, parents of LEP students immigrated to the United States when the children were very young. Another difference is that many LEP students have had inadequate preparation for starting school ready to learn. They are less likely than their English-speaking peers to have attended preschool, been read to regularly by parents (who are often non-English speaking), or played extensively with educational games and toys. Finally, many LEP students live in poverty settings where poor nutrition, inadequate health care, and safety concerns are common.

To help students with limited English proficiency become more successful in school, the federal government passed the *Bilingual Education Act of 1968,* which provided money to schools for the operation of bilingual education programs. Further motivation for offering such programs came from the 1974 Supreme Court ruling in *Lau v. Nichols* in which the court held that Chinese-speaking students in San Francisco were being discriminated against because the schools were not helping students deal with their language difficulties.

While states such as California, Texas, Florida, and New York are seeing the greatest influx of LEP students, the growing numbers nationwide mean that you can expect to have several in your future classrooms. This change will impact your teaching in several ways. One example of this is the way in which you communicate with parents. Because of language differences, newsletters sent home to non-English-speaking parents may need to be written in their native language and, similarly, some parent–teacher conferences will require the services of an interpreter. Another challenge you will need to overcome as you work with LEP students is the tendency to focus primarily on low-level repetitive drills rather than on higher level content (Garcia, 2000). In

# EDUCATION IN THE NEWS

## The Controversy Over Bilingual Education

In 1997, California made the decision to teach bilingual children in English only. Parents who want their students taught with a bilingual method can ask for a waiver from English-only instruction. Opponents said that it would not succeed, and many were surprised at its success. In less than 2 years the standardized test scores went up 40%. Students speak English in school, and many still speak Spanish at home. Opponents still say that English-only instruction alone is not responsible for the improvement in standardized test scores. Other variables at work are better teacher training and smaller class size. Bilingual program research still indicates the success of bilingual education.

### Critical Thinking Questions

1. In many communities in the United States, the home language of students and families is different than that of the schools. What problems arise when the home and school languages are different? How might they be overcome?

2. Language is an obvious difference in students, whereas culture, religion, family support systems, and ability are less readily apparent. California has decided to teach in only one language. What would happen if the decision was made to teach to only one culture, one religion, one income level, one gender, to one family system, to one ability? How is this similar to teaching in one language? How is it different?

3. What personal attitudes do you bring to the teaching of students who speak different languages? How might this influence your teaching? What can you do in your classroom to respond equitably to all students?

 *To submit your responses online, go to the Education in the News module for Chapter 2 of the Companion Website.*

addition to being less likely to hold the attention of students, these activities fail to challenge LEP students to build on what they know.

## Family Income

Another difference that exists between students is the amount of income earned by their families. As you might expect, there are great variances in incomes and these differences can have a significant impact on student learning. In general, families with incomes near or below the poverty level are of the most concern to teachers and schools. The highest rates of poverty in the United States are for families with children under the age of 3 (National Center for Children in Poverty, 2002). The estimated 2.1 million children in this category are more likely than their more financially advantaged peers to have increased exposure to a number of risk factors such as inadequate nutrition, environmental toxins, fewer adult interactions due to maternal depression, trauma and abuse, lower quality child care options, and substance abuse by parents. Children who grow up in poverty are more likely to drop out of school, have children out of wedlock, and be unemployed (National Center for Children in Poverty, 2002).

Historically, several family groups have had a higher than average level of poverty (see Table 2.6). One of these is the single-parent family headed by a woman. Children who live with their mothers only are approximately five times more likely to live in poverty than peers with two parents (Dalaker, 2001). This statistic is even higher for Black and Hispanic children, with approximately half of all single-mother families living in poverty. The poverty rate for Black and Hispanic families in general also remains three times higher than the rates for White families. One final poverty statistic concerns Hispanic children living in one-parent families. These children are over two and one-half times more likely to live in poverty than those in two-parent families (Dalaker, 2001).

As a future teacher, you will work with many students who come from low-income families. In addition to limiting the school-related financial burdens of these children and their families, you should work to provide support in whatever ways you can. For example, Venus Jones is a student in Adele Robert's fifth-grade classroom. Venus is from a single-parent family and her mother is currently unemployed. Adele has provided support to the family in several important ways. Last winter, when she overheard Venus talking to a classmate about her younger sister's need for a winter coat, Adele contacted a local community organization that

| **TABLE 2.6    Poverty Statistics, 2000** | |
|---|---|
| **Characteristic** | **Number** |
| **Race** | |
| White | 14,572,000 |
| Black | 7,901 |
| Asian and Pacific Islander | 1,226,000 |
| Hispanic | 7,155,000 |
| **Families** | |
| Total | 6,226,000 |
| Married couple | 2,638,000 |
| Single-parent mothers | 3,099,000 |

*Source: Poverty in the United States: 2000* by J. Dalaker, 2001, Washington, DC: U.S. Census Bureau.

was able to help. In preparation for the upcoming field trip to the city zoo, Adele also made sure that scholarship money was allocated for Venus's zoo entrance fee. Finally, at the parent–teacher conference last month Venus's mom admitted to being discouraged about her unemployment and Adele recommended a community employment service that could assist her in finding a new job. While you will never be able to fully resolve many of the problems faced by low-income students and their families, options are available that can be pursued to assist in meaningful ways.

## Family Structure

Another difference that students bring with them to the classroom is the family unit from which they come. The home living situations of students are becoming increasingly more diverse. By 1995, the traditional two-parent family with one wage earner was in the minority (Annie E. Casey Foundation, 2002). In its place, various other family configurations are becoming more common. For example, the number of *single-parent families* has remained relatively constant during the last several years at approximately 27% (see Table 2.7) (Annie E. Casey Foundation, 2002). Another more common situation is to have *parents who are considerably older or younger than the norm.* A small, but growing number of couples are waiting until later in life to have children. First-time parents who are in their late thirties or early forties are more common today than in the past. Conversely, many young women in their teens continue to have children. The percentage of teen mothers appears to have stabilized at between 5% and 6% (Portner, 1998). Another growing family situation is to have *both parents work.* In homes with two parents, the growing trend is for both parents to work. From 1980 to 1999, the percentages increased from 17% to 32% (Forum on Child and Family Statistics, 2002). Numbers are also growing for families in which *children live with grandparents.* Approximately 2.5 million children in the United States under the age of 18 live with their grandparents (U.S. Census Bureau, 2000). Finally, the numbers of *gay and lesbian families* are increasing. A small, but growing number of gay and lesbian couples in the United States are raising children (Berger, 2000). Teachers can expect to have students in their classrooms living in this family constellation as well.

As a future teacher, you will need to adapt your interactions with families based on the diversity of situations you will encounter. Begin by thinking about your attitudes toward these family units. Do you, for example, have negative reactions to single-parent families or gay/lesbian families? If so, what could you do to change your attitudes or set them aside so that your interactions with the students involved will be positive? How would you change the interactions you have with parents knowing the diversity you will find?

**Reflective Journey 2.4**

| **TABLE 2.7   One- and Two-Parent Families** | | |
|---|---|---|
| **Race** | **Married-Couple Family (%)** | **Single-Parent Family (%)** |
| White | 80.2 | 19.8 |
| Black | 41.9 | 58.1 |
| Native American | 61.2 | 38.8 |
| Asian | 87.9 | 12.1 |
| Hispanic | 71.3 | 28.7 |

*Source:* From *Census 2000* by U.S. Census Bureau, 2000, Washington, DC: U.S. Government Printing Office.

# What responses should teachers make to differences among students?

Teaching a diverse group of students in the same classroom means that you, the teacher, must be thoughtful and creative in the ways in which you interact with students and organize for instruction. While adding to the complexities of teaching, it also brings an excitement to the process that would not be available otherwise. As you read each of the following sections, think about your own willingness to respond to diverse students in these ways (see Table 2.8). If your reactions are positive, this is another good indicator that teaching is a good career choice for you.

## Create a Climate of Acceptance

Good learning takes place in classrooms where *all* students are valued and encouraged to do their best work. To accomplish this, you will need to create a classroom climate in which students feel accepted by both adults and their peers. Glasser (1990) describes this as a **friendly workplace.** In these environments, people are polite to one another and work well together. Diversity in the classroom may make the goal of a friendly workplace more difficult to attain. Just as you can probably identify areas of prejudice in your own thinking and actions, students in your classroom will have similar issues that may lead to negative feelings and problem behaviors.

When necessary, you should plan to take the time to discuss any problem behaviors or negative attitudes that are expressed. Often, this will need to be done individually to avoid embarrassment and potential confrontation. At other times, it may be helpful to discuss these issues as a class. In either case, even though the content of these discussions may not relate to the subject(s) you teach, you will need to work through the concerns and conflicts before addressing the content of your lesson plans.

**TABLE 2.8   Responses to Diversity**

| Response | Description |
| --- | --- |
| Create a climate of acceptance | Create a classroom in which students feel accepted by both adults and their peers. |
| Eliminate gender bias | This deeply rooted bias will need to be addressed personally, with students in your classes, and with parents and community members. |
| Use a variety of instructional techniques | Such strategies as individualized instruction, cooperative learning, and project learning will help you meet the needs and build on the interests of a diverse classroom of students. |
| Implement multicultural education | By making the curriculum more inclusive of different cultural perspectives and contributions, raising the academic achievement of minority students, improving intergroup relations, and helping students understand and deal with social and structural inequities in society, you are engaging in multicultural education. |

## Eliminate Gender Bias

The effort to eliminate gender bias from the schools will require the continued involvement of students, teachers, parents, and administrators during the next several decades. Deeply rooted attitudes such as this one and others discussed in this chapter change slowly and require constant work on everyone's part. As a classroom teacher, your role is multifaceted. Here are some suggestions:

*Girls should be encouraged to excel in science and mathematics.*

- *Identify your own gender bias.* While we all want to think we are without bias, the little things we do often subtly influence both boys and girls in our classrooms.

- *Confront the bias of students.* Many of the students you will teach bring gender bias to the classroom from television viewing, parental attitudes, and life experiences. These attitudes should be identified and discussed in nonthreatening ways.

- *Educate parents and community members.* Many people outside the schools are unaware of the extent of gender bias and its harmful effects. It is important to take the opportunities that are presented to educate others.

- *Select appropriate curriculum materials.* Many instructional materials are sexist and portray women and girls in very stereotypic ways. These options should be avoided when possible.

- *Provide equitable learning opportunities.* Make sure you give both boys and girls equal chances to answer questions and fully participate in classroom activities. Consider videotaping or audiotaping yourself to make sure you are allowing equitable opportunities.

## Use a Variety of Instructional Techniques

It should be obvious that students with diverse abilities have different academic needs that you as the classroom teacher must work to meet. A gifted student, for example, may excel when engaged in individualized learning tasks, whereas other students may require more directed instruction to be successful. A variety of instructional strategies should be considered when working with diverse students. One such strategy is *individualized instruction*. Some students may work best when given instructional activities that are specifically prepared for them and that are different from the assignments given to other students in the class. By modifying the level of difficulty and challenge provided by these tasks, students are more likely to have their academic needs met.

Another instructional strategy to consider is *cooperative learning*. Students are placed in small groups in which each student has a specific role that allows for positive contributions to the group. In this environment, students support one another more effectively in their learning.

A third instructional strategy that can work effectively with many students is called *project learning*. Teachers using this approach allow small groups of students to do in-depth investigations of interesting topics related to the classroom curriculum. For example, a ninth-grade teacher of European history might allow a small group of students to do an in-depth study of the Crusades as a special project. Or a second-grade elementary teacher may encourage a group of interested students to spend time studying spiders during the science unit on insects. Chapter 8 provides more information on these and other teaching strategies.

## Implement Multicultural Education

An educational institution that is meeting the academic and personal needs of diverse students is engaged in **multicultural education.** Banks (2002) has identified two broad goals for multicultural education. The first of these is to improve educational equality for young women and men, students from varying ethnic and cultural groups, and students with special needs. Secondly, multicultural education should help all students (including those who are Caucasian) build the knowledge, skills, and attitudes they need to be successful in a diverse American society.

Teachers and schools should plan on implementing a variety of strategies to meet these goals. Campbell (2000) identifies four main components to multicultural education:

1. *Making the curriculum more inclusive of different cultural perspectives and contributions.* For example, a course on American history should include relevant information and discussion of the contributions of Native Americans, African Americans, and Hispanic people to the time periods being studied.

2. *Raising the academic achievement of minority groups.* Although many large-scale government projects (such as Project Head Start for preschool children) have had limited success in improving the academic performance of minority students, every teacher must commit to helping students grow academically, regardless of race or ethnicity (see Table 2.9).

3. *Improving intergroup relations.* Teachers need to use materials and techniques in their classrooms that break down thinking and actions that are prejudicial, stereotypic, and discriminatory.

4. *Helping students understand and deal with social and structural inequities in society* (such as racism, sexism, and class prejudice). For example, although racism may not be exhibited in your classroom, it is important for students to know that it exists and that strategies are available that can be used to minimize its consequences.

**TABLE 2.9    The Achievement Gap**

| Race | Mathematics—Grade 12 | | Reading—Grade 4 | |
| | Year | Scale Score* | Year | Scale Score* |
|---|---|---|---|---|
| White | 1990 | 301 | 1992 | 225 |
| | 2000 | 308 | 2000 | 226 |
| Black | 1990 | 268 | 1992 | 193 |
| | 2000 | 274 | 2000 | 193 |
| Hispanic | 1990 | 276 | 1992 | 201 |
| | 2000 | 283 | 2000 | 197 |
| Asian/Pacific Islander | 1990 | 311 | 1992 | 214 |
| | 2000 | 319 | 2000 | 232 |
| American Indian | 1996 | 279 | 1992 | 207 |
| | 2000 | 293 | 2000 | 196 |

*Scores on the National Assessment of Educational Progress.

*Source:* From *The Nation's Report Card* by National Center for Education Statistics, 2002. Retrieved December 17, 2002, from http://nces.ed.gov/nationsreportcard

Individually, each of these four approaches has merit in the classroom. It appears, however, that a combination of all four would be the most beneficial in meeting the academic, social, and emotional needs of all students.

To avoid marginalizing the importance of multicultural education, you will need to infuse the curriculum with activities that validate the importance of different racial, cultural, ethnic, gender, and ability groups. This infusion process requires more than simply adding diverse perspectives to the academic content. It also means that teachers need to consistently take the time to work on building intergroup relationships. Discussing current events that have racial, cultural, ethnic, and gender significance is another option that can be worked into many classrooms. Identifying prejudices exhibited in the classroom and then working to break them down is yet another aspect of infusing the curriculum with multicultural issues.

## What are your attitudes toward student differences?

Teaching students from diverse backgrounds is a situation full of stimulation and change. Imagine having a classroom, for example, that includes a student in a wheelchair, two students with learning disabilities, a gifted student, and one Russian, two African American, and three Hispanic students. With the additional diversity that comes from different religious beliefs, languages spoken, income levels, and family structures, it is easy to see that the "typical" classroom of students is full of differences. For teachers who love students and get excited about the challenges each one presents, this kind of diverse classroom provides a wonderfully stimulating set of experiences. Each new day is filled with the promise of struggles, the hope of success, and the joy of connecting with students from all walks of life.

Although student diversity should be viewed primarily as an exciting opportunity, it also presents new challenges to you as a future teacher. The first obstacle is to understand your own personal feelings and attitudes about people who are different from yourself. For example, how do you think you will feel about having diverse cultures in your classroom? Do you have any negative feelings about working with different family configurations (single-parent families, gay parents, etc.) or teaching children with special needs? Are you ready to commit the extra time and

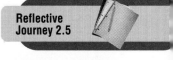

Reflective
Journey 2.5

energy it will take to make diversity a positive experience in your classroom rather than a negative one? These are not easy questions to answer and should be thoughtfully considered both now and throughout your teacher preparation program.

### The Development of Attitudes

As you begin to think about your attitudes toward students and adults who are different from yourself, it is important to understand how these attitudes develop. There are many influential factors, but one of the most important is the *attitudes of parents and family members*. Starting as early as 2½ years of age (Banks, 1993), children develop attitudes about diversity by watching and listening to family members interact with and talk about diverse people.

The *stereotypes of diverse people presented in movies and television* also significantly influence

*Attitudes may influence your interactions with students.*

attitudes. Students spend many hours each day watching movies and television in which diverse people are often portrayed in negative and stereotypic ways. The *attitudes of peers* also shape the values and beliefs of others. Students notice how their peers talk about and interact with those who are different from themselves. They often imitate these interactions in an attempt to be a part of the group.

## Your Attitudes

Are you able to identify attitudes you hold toward people who are different from yourself? If you are like most people, some will be obvious and easy to understand, while others are far more subtle. In this section, you will be given some guidelines to assist you in the process of understanding your personal attitudes toward diversity. Four questions will be presented along with suggested activities to help you respond to each (see Table 2.10). While you should begin now to understand and improve your attitudes toward diverse people, this is an issue that most teachers must continue to address throughout their careers.

The first guiding question that should help you better understand your attitude toward diversity is simply *Who am I as a person?* Throughout this chapter you have been given information on the differences that exist among students. Race, gender, sexual orientation, ability, religion, language, family income, and family structure play major roles in determining who you are as an individual. Take a few minutes to reflect on these aspects of your own personhood. Think about the importance to you of each of these aspects of your life. For example, how important are your religious beliefs to the ways in which you think and interact with others? It may also be useful to jot down some more specific characteristics for each aspect of your life. For example, if you are of average ability, describe academic areas in which you struggle and those in which you excel. As you respond to each of these items, you will begin to develop a better understanding of your personal history and who you are as a person. In turn, this should help you better understand the basis on which you evaluate these characteristics in others. If possible, discuss your thoughts with another person or a small group to help you refine your thinking.

**Reflective Journey 2.6**

**TABLE 2.10   Understanding Your Attitudes Toward Diversity**

| Guiding Question | Description |
|---|---|
| Who am I as a person? | Take time to reflect on your race, gender, sexual orientation, ability, religion, language(s), family income, and family structure to better understand your own background. |
| What kinds of diversity experiences have I had? | Think about the diverse people you have spent time with over the course of your lifetime and their influence on your thinking about diversity. |
| What do I know about diversity? | Consider what you currently know and what you need to learn to be able to understand and work with people from diverse backgrounds. |
| How can I grow and change? | Think about spending additional time with people different from yourself and also making the effort to learn more about others so that you can grow in your understanding and acceptance. |

## One Student Leads a Powerful Lesson

**Tammy Underwood**
**Fulmore Middle School**
**Austin, Texas**

After the tragedy of September 11, 2001, my students really opened up with dialogue about so many issues. One of my classes includes 32 children representing a diverse mix of religious, cultural, and ethnic backgrounds. This class alone includes Islamic, Catholic, Jewish, Hindu, Pagan, Buddhist, Protestant, Agnostic, Atheist, Hispanic, African American, Asian, Middle Eastern, and Anglo children. One of my students is Ojai, a Muslim boy whom I have known for 3 years.

A class discussion was underway about modern day witch-hunts. We were comparing the Salem Witch Trials to current events while doing background for our one-act play, *The Crucible*. During our discussion, Ojai asked for the floor. I found myself sitting and listening to this 13-year-old boy discussing his very personal feelings about the recent ter-rorist attacks. He went from being cautiously informative about what Islam meant to him, to describing how he felt that the highjackers' actions went against his understanding of Islam. Ojai taught the class that day. The lesson I had planned was worthless compared to the door he opened for us. His courage to speak helped prevent us from reacting with fear or suspicion to all Arab, Middle Eastern, or Muslim people.

Sharing and celebrating our differences opens up an exciting world of ideas and understanding in my class. My students and I share the experience of the teaching moment. I did not get that in my own middle school education, and I cherish the ability to teach the value of an amazing mixture of cultures.

A second guiding question to consider is *What kinds of diversity experiences have I had?* Think about the people you have met and spent time with over the course of your lifetime that were different from yourself. Were these experiences that led to positive attitudes or less favorable ones? It may be beneficial to also consider ways in which you could create opportunities for additional meaningful experiences with diverse people. While a deeper understanding can't be accomplished in a brief interaction, doing something like volunteering to tutor an LEP student for a semester may give you important insights into diversity issues. Once you have reflected on the diversity experiences you have had, consider discussing them with another person or small group.

**Reflective Journey 2.7**

A third guiding question that should help you better understand your attitude toward diversity is *What do I know about diversity?* You can add to your knowledge by reading about theoretical perspectives and research results that relate to diverse people. Although there are many resources from which to choose, three books that can add much to your understanding are *Teaching/Learning Anti-Racism* (Derman-Sparks & Phillips, 1997), *The Light in Their Eyes—Creating Multicultural Learning Communities* (Nieto, 1999), and *Collaboration for Inclusive Education* (Walther-Thomas et al., 2000). Consider reading some information from one or more of these books and then writing about what you learn. In addition, you can learn a great deal from reading the stories of people with diverse backgrounds. Two good resources for essays of this type are *Daily Fare: Essays from the Multicultural Experience* (Aguero, 1993) and *The Politics of Reality: Essays in Feminist Theory* (Frye, 1983). Choose two or three essays of interest to you, read them carefully, and then spend some time writing about your reactions to these perspectives.

**Reflective Journey 2.8**

A final question to ask is *How can I grow and change?* As mentioned earlier, we all need to grow in our understanding and acceptance of diverse people. Undoubtedly, the best way to do this is to spend time with diverse people and work hard to understand both the similarities and differences that exist. In addition, you could consider reading about how others have grown and changed in their understandings of diversity. Nieto (1999) provides several essays of this type that give the reader ideas about strategies that may be effective to try.

**Reflective Journey 2.9**

## Summary

In this chapter, four organizing questions were used to guide your thinking about students today:

### What differences among people influence interactions in the classroom?

While it is important to remember that there are many similarities between students, some important differences include these:
- Race (Praxis II, topic Ib)
- Gender (Praxis II, topic Ib)
- Sexual orientation (Praxis II, topic Ib)
- Abilities (Praxis II, topic Ib)

### How do social and cultural differences impact teaching and learning?

Student differences are also related to social and cultural factors:
- Religion (Praxis II, topic Ib)
- Language (Praxis II, topics Ib, IIIa)
- Family income (Praxis II, topics Ib, IIIa)
- Family structure (Praxis II, topic Ib)

### What responses should teachers make to differences among students?

There are several important actions that teachers can take in response to student differences:
- Create a climate of acceptance (Praxis II, topic Ic)
- Eliminate gender bias (Praxis II, topic Ic)
- Use a variety of instructional techniques
- Implement multicultural education (Praxis II, topic IIa)

### What are your attitudes toward student differences?

As you think about your own attitudes toward diversity, it is important to determine the following:
- How attitudes toward diversity develop
- Your own attitudes and how to change them

## Key Terms

| | |
|---|---|
| bilingual education | inclusion |
| English as a Second Language (ESL) programs | lesbian |
| | limited English proficient (LEP) |
| friendly workplace | mainstreaming |
| gay | multicultural education |
| gifted students | students with disabilities |
| heterosexual | theory of multiple intelligences |

## Reflective Journey: Online Journal

Use the questions for thought and reflection highlighted throughout the chapter to help guide your personal journey of reflection and professional development as a teacher. To complete your journal entries online, go to the *Reflective Journey* module for this chapter of the Companion Website.

**Test Preparation Activities**

To review an online chapter case study, test your understanding of chapter topics and concepts, and begin preparing for the Praxis II: Principles of Learning and Teaching examination, go to the *Praxis Test Preparation* module for this chapter of the Companion Website.

 **Becoming a Reflective Practitioner**

To complete these activities and submit your responses online, go to the *Becoming a Reflective Practitioner* module for this chapter of the Companion Website.

## What differences among people influence interactions in the classroom?

### Review Questions

1. Why is the racial composition of American schools changing?

2. What does it mean when a student with disabilities is described as a person first and only secondarily as one with special needs?

3. Describe Gardner's theory of multiple intelligences.

### Field Experience

Spend some time observing a student with special needs in the regular classroom and as this student receives special services. What accommodations does the regular classroom teacher make to involve this student in the learning process? Where does this student receive special services and what are they? Talk to the classroom teacher and the special services provider(s) to learn more about how this student's needs are being met.

### Building Your Portfolio: *Knowledge of Diverse People*

**INTASC Standard 3.** Choose a subgroup of people within American society and spend some time researching characteristics of this group. In what ways are their traditions, family interactions, attitudes, and behaviors similar to ones you have? Identify ways in which this group of people differs from you. Describe the impact the differences you found may have on your feelings toward this group of people and your ability to teach them in your classroom. Include a summary of this information in your portfolio.

## How do social and cultural differences impact teaching and learning?

### Review Questions

1. How is religious diversity influencing teaching and learning in the classroom?

2. In what ways does poverty affect student learning?

3. How does family diversity shape the interactions you will have with students and their families?

### Building Your Portfolio: *Lesson Plan for Diverse Students*

**INTASC Standard 3.** When you begin the process of writing lesson plans, it is important to clearly identify strategies you can use to meet the needs of diverse students (ability, cultural/racial, family, or gender differences). Consider the group of Americans you identified and researched in the previous portfolio activity and create a list of well-described strategies you could use to meet the needs of these students in your classroom. As you continue throughout your career, add additional good examples of this planning to your portfolio.

## What responses should teachers make to differences among students?

### Review Questions

1. Develop a list of five things you can do to create a climate of acceptance in your future classroom.

2. Identify several subtle ways in which gender bias exists in classrooms today.

3. What are the goals of multicultural education?

### Field Experience

Talk to a classroom teacher to get additional perspectives on the impact of diversity on teaching and learning. How does the teacher describe the diversity that exists within his or her classroom? What are the strengths and problems associated with diversity? What does she or he do to meet the needs of diverse learners?

### Building Your Portfolio: *Experiences Working with Diverse Students*

**INTASC Standard 3.** As you begin your teacher preparation program, start the process of documenting the experiences you have with diverse students. Describe what you did, the diverse students you worked with, and the results of your interactions. Review the different types of diversity described in this chapter and create a file for each. Continue to seek out experiences with diverse populations with which you are less familiar or comfortable. Keep a journal or other written record of your interactions to add to this portion of your portfolio.

## What are your attitudes toward student differences?

### Review Questions

1. How are attitudes toward diversity developed?

2. What can you do to improve your attitudes toward diverse students?

### Building Your Portfolio: *Your Diversity Background*

**INTASC Standard 9.** Summarize the diversity experiences you have had as part of your day-to-day life in a family and community. Was your family experience diverse in some way? Describe experiences you had in school with children who were culturally, racially, and ethnically different from yourself. Have you traveled to or lived in another country? Can you speak a second language? Describe how your diversity experiences have influenced your attitudes toward student differences.

## Suggested Readings

American Association of University Women. (1998). *Gender gaps: Where schools still fail our children.* Washington, DC: AAUW Educational Foundation. This report provides a strong rationale for continued efforts to remove gender bias from American education. It reviews research studies as a basis for its conclusions.

Gollnick, D., & Chinn, P. (2002). *Multicultural education in a pluralistic society* (6th ed.). Upper Saddle River, NJ: Merrill/Prentice Hall. This book includes information on dealing with diversity in its many forms. Separate chapters discuss gender issues, ethnic and racial concerns, exceptionality, and language differences. Religion, class, and age as diversity factors are also addressed in other chapters of the text.

Gruwell, E. (1999). *The freedom writers diary.* New York: Broadway Books. This powerful book describes how 150 teens and their beginning teacher (Erin Gruwell) changed their lives despite incredibly difficult circumstances. Through the diary entries of the students and teacher, you learn how they overcome poverty, racism, and injustice to make a difference in the world around them.

Walther-Thomas, C., Korinek, L., McLaughlin, V., & Williams, B. (2000). *Collaboration for inclusive education.* Boston: Allyn and Bacon. This text describes the many issues related to including students with special needs in the regular education classroom.

# chapter 3

## America's Teachers

Teachers, although diverse as a group, share many common characteristics. In this chapter, you will read about both the similarities and differences among America's teachers. As you read and reflect on the chapter content, continue to try on the role of teacher. Can you see yourself among the ranks of teachers working hard to meet the needs of a diverse group of students? The following key questions should help you learn more precisely what teachers are like as a group and how closely you see yourself fitting this role.

## Focus Questions

◢ Who are our teachers?

◢ What are their roles?

◢ What skills and attitudes are characteristic of effective teachers?

◢ Can effective teachers have different styles?

*My mission is to impart knowledge while encouraging the question. I strive to arm the children with the tools necessary for success and then stand back and watch them make the dance their own.*
— Paula Reckley, elementary school teacher

*I will always frame my work around why I chose this career: to better prepare my students for what lies ahead of them and enable them to develop a sense of self-worth, dignity and individuality.*
— Mike Beranek, elementary school teacher

*I want to give them the best that I have to offer—someone to lean on and a brighter future.*
— Peggy Myers, middle school teacher

*The real 'Three R's' of education are respect, rapport, and relationships. I treat my students with the respect they deserve as young men and women, and I nurture in them a respect for themselves that is denied to them by too many facets of our society. I build a rapport with all my students that is based on this respect, along with trust and compassion.*
— Nora Flanagan, high school teacher

Each year, the Disney Learning Partnership honors outstanding American teachers. The chapter opening quotes are from some of the 2001 honorees (Disney Learning Partnership, 2002). They emphasize some of the key elements of their teaching philosophies and highlight how these outstanding teachers interact with their students. Although they take very different approaches to the profession, these award-winning teachers share a commitment to meeting the needs of students and engaging in outstanding instruction in the classroom. In this chapter, you will learn more about the skills and attitudes that all effective educators have in common as well as the differences in style that make each of them unique.

## Who are our teachers?

Schooling consists of many parts, each of which has an important role to play in the overall success of students. The many physical elements of school, such as books, desks, school supplies, teaching materials, school buses, and even the school buildings themselves, significantly impact teaching and learning. Support personnel, such as janitors, cooks, teachers' aides, secretaries, counselors, and principals, also provide many valuable services to students and teachers. As important as these elements are to schooling, they are still far less vital to student success than the teachers themselves who serve in classrooms across America. To a large extent, teachers determine whether or not students learn and grow. Excellent teachers tend to overcome whatever negative circumstances they face and guide students into quality learning experiences. Conversely, even in the best of conditions, poor teachers are seldom capable of fostering good education.

Lewis Solomon, senior vice president and senior scholar at the Milken Family Foundation, had this to say about the importance of excellent teachers in the preface to a recent report (Wenglinsky, 2000):

> The Milken Family Foundation has been studying school reform for over a decade. As we have considered specific reforms as diverse as early childhood education, smaller class sizes, parental involvement, and learning technology, one point became abundantly and unequivocally clear. Unless a child is taught by competent teachers, the impact of other education reforms will be diminished. Simply put, students learn more from "good" teachers than from "bad" teachers under virtually any set of circumstances. (p. 3)

Before looking carefully at the elements of effective teaching, you will first have the opportunity to more clearly understand what teachers are like as a group. In this section, you are going to look at several descriptors of America's teachers. By reviewing this information, you can grow in your understanding of the profession and the people who are essential to its success. As you think about the women and men who serve as educators in America's schools, try to envision yourself working alongside those being described here. Can you see yourself becoming part of the "teaching family" in America's schools?

### Teachers' Ages and Years of Service

Bill Holmgren has been teaching middle school mathematics for 25 years now. He began his career at age 24 and has been going strong ever since. Bill still loves the challenges associated with teaching middle school students. Their enthusiasm and energy help balance the constant struggle he faces in keeping them focused on learning mathematical concepts. Bill's work is never easy or dull, but is always rewarding. Despite his love of teaching, Bill has decided to retire at age 54 when he has completed 30 years in the classroom. At that point, his retirement benefits are maximized and he can move on to other interests with no financial worries. Bill has mixed feelings about this impending change.

National statistics indicate that there are increasing numbers of teachers like Bill in classrooms across the country. Beginning in 1960, the National Education Association (NEA) has regularly conducted surveys to assess the status of American public school teachers. In its most recent survey published in 1997, the NEA found that the average age of teachers is 43, with nearly 70% over the age of 40 and approximately 10% under 30 years of age. This trend toward an older and more experienced workforce has been in progress since the mid-1970s, with approximately 46% of all teachers having more than 20 years of experience, while under 17% have fewer than 5 years in the classroom. In addition, the median years of experience for America's teachers has increased from 8 in 1976 to 15 in 1996 (National Center for Education Statistics [NCES], 2001).

One consequence of a more mature teaching force is that America's schools benefit from having increasingly more experienced educators guiding student learning. A large portion of America's teachers are seasoned veterans who have accumulated a wealth of knowledge and experience in working with students. A second implication of these statistics is that the educational workforce is gradually aging, leading to greater numbers of retirements in the years ahead as teachers complete their classroom careers. This "graying" of the teaching profession is one of the primary reasons for the teacher shortages currently being experienced in many regions of the country. This trend is expected to continue during the next several years, increasing the demand for new teachers at all levels.

## Degrees Earned

Another set of statistics that should further clarify your understanding of America's teachers is the degrees they have earned (see Table 3.1). Most teachers are highly educated, with nearly 55% holding a master's degree and an additional 2% having earned their doctoral degrees (NEA, 1997). Since the early 1960s, dramatic increases have been seen in the numbers of advanced degrees earned by teachers.

Sherrie Jacobs is a good example of this trend. She has been teaching third grade for 8 years now and has decided to enroll in a master's degree program in the fall. The program is designed to assist teachers in developing stronger theoretical and practical knowledge of literacy learning. Sherrie will complete her degree by taking weekend and summer courses that

| TABLE 3.1   Teachers' Highest Degrees Held | | | | | | | | |
|---|---|---|---|---|---|---|---|---|
| **Degree** | **1961** | **1966** | **1971** | **1976** | **1981** | **1986** | **1991** | **1996** |
| Less than bachelor's | 14.6% | 7.0% | 2.9% | 0.9% | 0.4% | 0.3% | 0.6% | 0.3% |
| Bachelor's | 61.9 | 69.6 | 69.6 | 61.6 | 50.1 | 48.3 | 46.3 | 43.6 |
| Master's or specialist degree | 23.1 | 23.2 | 27.1 | 37.1 | 49.3 | 50.7 | 52.6 | 54.5 |
| Doctorate | 0.4 | 0.1 | 0.4 | 0.4 | 0.3 | 0.7 | 0.5 | 1.7 |

*Source:* Adapted from *Digest of Education Statistics,* by National Center for Education Statistics, 2001, Washington, DC: U.S. Government Printing Office.

*Male teachers are important role models.*

blend well with her teaching schedule. Her main motivation for taking on this additional workload is the desire to learn more about teaching reading and language arts to her diverse group of elementary students. Sherrie is looking forward to putting into practice the information she will gather about teaching literacy. Like Sherrie, many of today's teachers are working to develop strong academic credentials to assist them in dealing with the complexities of the classrooms in which they teach.

## Gender

If you haven't already done so, take a careful look at the gender of the students in your college's education classes. Do you find more men or women represented? Unless the program you are in is unusual, you will find more women than men. Women are more likely than men to enter and complete teacher education programs. Recent statistics also support the observation that the number of women teachers continues to grow. Since the early 1960s, the percentage of women engaged in K–12 teaching has gradually increased from just under 70% to currently about three-quarters of the total (NCES, 2001).

Historically, women taught almost exclusively at the elementary level, while the opposite was true for men, who typically taught at the secondary level. Those trends have changed somewhat, with more women found in secondary schools and greater numbers of men teaching in elementary classrooms. In terms of overall numbers, however, there has been a steady increase over the years in the percentage of women teaching in America's schools. The recruitment of more men into teaching, particularly at the elementary level, may be a difficult task, but one that could benefit many students.

## Racial Diversity

In the last chapter, you learned about student diversity and its impact on schooling. The growing number of students of color is one aspect of this diversity. At the same time that the student population is becoming more racially diverse, however, the teaching ranks remain predominantly White. The most recent NEA survey data (1997) indicate that approximately 7% of all teachers are Black, 1% are Native American, 4% are Hispanic, and 1% are Asian/Pacific Islander. Other data suggest that there has been virtually no overall change in minority teacher percentages since 1971 (NCES, 2001).

Despite the efforts of both public schools and colleges to encourage minority teachers, little change has been seen in the numbers of minority teachers finding their way into America's classrooms. Shawna Robinson is a good example of the difficulties that K–12 schools and colleges face in recruiting minority teachers. She is a bright African American student beginning her first year of college. Shawna's prior work in chemistry has already made her a strong contender for a continuing full scholarship in that discipline. She has been approached by the department chair and encouraged to continue her studies in chemistry. Meanwhile, the mathematics department is trying to get Shawna to consider a joint mathematics/technology degree

# Recruiting Teachers of Color

As indicated in Chapter 2, our nation's students are growing increasingly diverse. Unfortunately, the same cannot be said for the diversity of school teachers: "[N]ationwide, one-third of public school students are minorities, yet only 13 percent of the teaching force are minority educators. Fully 40 percent of schools have no minority teachers at all" (Northwest Regional Educational Laboratory, 2001, p. 28). It is quite possible that students today could go through their entire K–12 education without ever seeing a teacher of color.

Although educators and others recognize the critical importance of increasing the diversity of America's teachers (Banks, 2002), the challenges of recruiting minority educators are great. Because the status of teaching as a profession is still relatively low (see Chapter 5), minority candidates who would make fine teachers tend to look elsewhere for job opportunities. The competition for these students is very strong at colleges and universities, so talented students of color are often inundated with offers from more prestigious programs. For others, higher education in general, with its predominantly White student and faculty populations, becomes a difficult environment in which to learn. Many students of color drop out before completing a degree.

### Research the Issue

Research this issue by reading the source article by Banks (2002), then find out more about the issue online using the links provided in the *Engage in the Debate* module for Chapter 3 of the Companion Website.

1. What benefits do students gain from having diverse teachers?
2. What challenges are most often cited in the discussions regarding recruitment of teachers of color?
3. What types of programs are being used by teacher training programs and school districts to recruit and retain diverse students? How do school districts recruit and retain teachers of color?

### Explore Your Views

1. In your opinion, how do students benefit from having teachers who are racially and culturally diverse? Should the racial and cultural makeup of the teaching population reflect that of the community or should it always reflect the diversity of the nation as a whole?
2. Do you think that preservice teachers of color should be given extra support in some way as they complete their teacher preparation programs and begin their careers? Why or why not? If you feel they should receive additional support or assistance, what should it be?
3. From your perspective, what should be done to recruit people of color into the teaching profession?

 *To research this issue and submit your responses online, go to the Engage in the Debate module for Chapter 3 of the Companion Website for this text.*

*Sources: An Introduction to Multicultural Education*, 3rd ed., by J. Banks, 2002, Boston: Allyn and Bacon; and "Recruiting Teachers of Color," by Northwest Regional Educational Laboratory, 2001, *Northwest Education, 7*(2), p. 28.

that would prepare her for graduate study in either area. Although members of the education program have also spent time with her and would like to see Shawna consider teaching, the lure of greater financial rewards and more support during the college years will make it hard for her to seriously think about education as a career choice. Clearly, schools and teacher training institutions need to redouble their efforts to attract qualified minority candidates such as Shawna into the teaching profession.

## Under the Same Sun

Dorothy Epchook is an associate teacher at the village school in Kwethluk, Alaska. Despite her lack of formal training as an educator, she teaches Yup'ik Studies, which consists of instructing students in traditional crafts and skills and helping them reconnect with their native language. Weeks (2001) interviewed her to learn more about her attitudes and the impact she has on student learning:

- *On attitudes:* Dorothy described how she learned about the word *bigotry* from experiences in a Native American boarding school in Oklahoma. "In our culture there was no such thing (term). I was taught never to pass judgment on anybody. Grandfather always said, if you're under the same sun, we're the same" (p. 13).

- *On student learning:* She believed that having a Native American teacher assistant helped students learn more effectively about their culture. Epchook relearned her native language as an adult and assisted her students in learning it as well. In addition, she taught them how to make traditional materials for survival. In addition to being practical, it assisted students in learning more about their heritage. One example of this effort was that she invited a village elder to come to the classroom to show students how to make a *qalu,* a dip net for catching small white fish from the nearby Kuskokwim River.

Dorothy believes that every adult is capable of teaching students in some important ways. "By sharing [my teaching responsibility] with elders, students can learn from the elders how to stand on their own two feet" (p. 14).

### Explore and Reflect

Learn more about integrating unique and diverse social, cultural, and personal experiences into being a good teacher by going to the *Reflect on Diversity* module for Chapter 3 of the Companion Website for this text.

1. Dorothy Epchook is an example of an adult who has not had formal teacher training but is engaged in educating other Native American students about their language and cultural heritage. Regardless of your heritage, are there adults in your past who have educated you in similar ways?

2. Is it important for schools to engage students in activities that help them become more aware of their cultural heritage? Do these activities need to be led by those from minority groups?

 *To explore this topic further and submit your reflections online, go to the Reflect on Diversity module for Chapter 3 of the Companion Website for this text.*

*Source:* "Under the Same Sun," by D. Weeks, 2001, *NW Education, 7*(2), pp. 13–19.

## What are their roles?

Whereas most people not associated with education tend to think of teaching solely in terms of sharing information and skills with future generations, those who have been in the classroom understand that this is only one of several key roles that teachers assume as they work with their students. The best teachers deal with more than just the learning task; they provide support as students struggle with personal and interpersonal issues, guide students and families to resources needed to help resolve conflicts and problems, and serve as role models for their students in virtually all aspects of life.

### Facilitator of Learning

A traditional view of education would have teachers spending most of their classroom time sharing their accumulated wisdom with less knowledgeable students who were expected to internalize this

**TABLE 3.2   Teaching Roles**

| Role | Description |
| --- | --- |
| Facilitator of learning | Help students grow in their knowledge of the world. |
| Supporter of emotional and social development | Assist students in dealing with emotions and interacting with others. |
| Guide to resources | Direct students and their families to resources that help reduce or remove stress. |
| Role model | Use actions and words that show students positive ways of interacting in the world. |

information for future use. This "factory model" of teaching and learning (Glasser, 1990) implies that teachers should serve as dispensers of information and, conversely, that students are rather passive recipients of this content.

Although this model may be appropriate in some educational circumstances, it is being replaced in many classrooms with an approach in which the teacher becomes more of a *facilitator of learning* (see Table 3.2). In this facilitator role, teachers recognize the necessity of students having a significant role in their own learning. Teacher facilitators provide a variety of resources and guide students as they work to build their own understandings of the world. This *constructivist approach to learning* is grounded in the writings of theorists such as John Dewey and Jean Piaget (see Chapter 10) and is gaining acceptance in many K–12 classrooms. For example, Mike Beranek's third-grade classroom is described as follows:

> "Under Construction" yellow tape and flashing hazard signs are part of the empty classroom that students discover the first day of school, as they become active participants helping to construct their learning environment for the year. Mike works hard to assure that students become actively engaged in learning by identifying projects and activities they wish to study. (Disney Learning Partnership, 2002)

The learning that takes place in these settings can be richer and more meaningful to students. A love of learning and a lifelong interest in growing as a person often result when this approach is used.

## Supporter of Emotional and Social Development

A second role that teachers assume in their work with students is that of *support person for social and emotional development*. For a variety of reasons (see Chapter 12 for details), students today encounter stressors that complicate their lives. Because of this stress, teachers are an important source of support to many students in their classrooms as they struggle with complex emotional and social dilemmas. Esmé Codell (1999) describes one such emotionally troubled student in a diary summarizing her first year of fifth-grade teaching:

**September 30**
Shira is Filipino and speaks mostly Tagalog. Sometimes she goes into fetal position under her desk. She has four brothers, named Vincent I, Vincent II, Vincent III, and Vincent IV. (p. 35)

**December 13**

Shira heard "I Saw Mommy Kissing Santa Claus" as I was trying to find something on a cassette. She came out of a fetal position and started to dance in front of the whole class, shaking and everything, with all these Polynesian-like hand movements. All of us watched in utter astonishment. When she finished, we went wild with applause. She did it again and again and again, crying and laughing at the same time. It was the weirdest thing. Then she hugged me. . . . She has not gone into a fetal position since and does not cry as much and is making all sorts of friends, smiling all the time. (pp. 67–68)

As in the preceding narrative, it is often hard to know when and how our supportive actions will benefit students emotionally and socially. Yet, those actions can and do have a very powerful effect. Teachers in schools across America are providing encouragement that is helping students develop both emotionally and socially. Sometimes, students themselves are aware of the impact teachers have had in their lives. Others may not be able to verbalize the results of this support for many years, if at all. But, without question, both students and teachers are often deeply impacted by this important role in the classroom.

## MASTER TEACHER SERIES

### Segment II: Challenging the Students; Challenging Students

In this, the second segment of the series, Ms. Jones works with the students to help them overcome their lack of self-confidence and to increase their test-taking skills. She attempts to enlist the help of the parents through phone calls, home visits, and parent conferences, but many have little time to spend with their children, feeling as though the world is falling in on them as well. When students are asked to serve as translators in parent conferences, false information is conveyed to the parent, unbeknownst to the teacher. Ms. Jones confronts the parent of a child who is chronically absent; Ms. Jones is also challenged by the administrator who complains of her absence from the classroom as well. All the while, Ms. Jones continues to work with the students to increase their test-taking skills in order to pass the state tests.

### For Deeper Understanding

1. What are some of the roles that Ms. Jones has to assume? What are some of her personal strengths that help her with those roles? What types of resources are available to her to assist with the many challenges the students bring?

2. What are some of the skills and personality traits that Ms. Jones has that make her a successful teacher?

3. Consider the chapter discussion regarding the considerable "behind-the-scenes" work that effective teachers complete in planning the classroom environment to allow for positive student learning experiences. From watching the types of experiences that the students had, what were some of the things Ms. Jones had to do to orchestrate each day?

4. What does Ms. Jones's day look like outside of the regular school day?

5. How would you describe Ms. Jones's teaching style?

 *To submit your responses online, go to the Master Teacher Series module for Chapter 3 of the Companion Website.*

## Guide to Resources

Although caring teachers can assist students in dealing with many of their problems and concerns, some problems are too large or complex for teachers to manage on their own. In these circumstances, teachers can still help by knowing—and sharing with students and their families—information about school, community, state, and national resources that are available to meet a variety of needs (Table 3.3). Perhaps this role can best be explained through an example. Assume that Rhonda is a student in your seventh-grade social studies class. She is living in low-rent housing with her mom and boyfriend. You have recently found out that the boyfriend is dealing drugs and has offered "samples" to Rhonda on several different occasions, which she has reluctantly accepted. You have a good relationship with Rhonda and she has confided to you that she is worried that she may become addicted to one of the drugs being used or that she will be permanently harmed by the ones she has taken. This issue is a complex one that you feel needs to be addressed by others more knowledgeable and better trained than you. You will need to be aware of the resources available to support Rhonda through these difficult times.

*Communicating with parents helps them feel valued.*

## Role Model

Another powerful tool that teachers have as they interact with students is the ability to influence others through example. What teachers *do* often has a more powerful impact on students than what they *say*. Genuine excitement about learning, taking extra time to listen and respond to students' problems and concerns, and a demonstration of positive attitudes about diverse students and their families are some examples of ways in which teachers serve as role models for their students. To personalize this aspect of the teacher's role, think back to a teacher from your own schooling experiences that had a significant impact on your life. What did this person do or say that influenced you? Can you remember specific examples of this teacher's behavior or attitudes they conveyed that had an influence on you? Try to remember aspects of this teacher's personality that made him or her attractive to you.

**Reflective Journey 3.1**

| TABLE 3.3   Resources for Students and Families | |
| --- | --- |
| **Resource** | **Description** |
| School resources | The school counselor, librarian, principal, staff specialists, and other teachers may all be potential resources to support students and their families. |
| Community options | Community counselors, service organizations such as those sponsored by United Way, and churches are examples of community resources. |
| State and federal programs | Websites on the Internet, crisis hotlines, and state and federal support agencies are all available for a variety of student and family needs. |

## What skills and attitudes are characteristic of effective teachers?

Peggy Myers is a middle school science teacher honored by the Disney Learning Partnership as an American Teacher Award Honoree for 2001. Her teaching is described as follows:

> Peggy never liked science when she was in school; however, science became her favorite subject when she started teaching. Peggy sees herself as a "salesman" trying to sell curiosity and a love of learning to her students. Using real world examples, connecting new learning to prior learning and integrating other subjects, she strives to have her students personalize and internalize science. Peggy likes to involve her middle school parents by having students demonstrate and explain photographs and charts to their parents at home. (Disney Learning Partnership, 2002)

During the last several decades of the 20th century, educational researchers and theorists worked to identify a core set of skills and attitudes that effective teachers like Peggy possess. In this section, you will begin to learn more about these common characteristics.

### Skills Common to Effective Teachers

After a thorough analysis of current research, Danielson (1996) proposed a broad framework for understanding the key skills needed for effective teaching. She suggests four main skill areas in this framework. Effective teachers (1) engage in quality planning and preparation, (2) prepare a positive classroom environment, (3) use proven instructional techniques, and (4) exhibit professional behavior. Each of these skill areas is described in more detail in the sections that follow. Further information on effective teaching can also be found in Chapter 8.

**Engaging in quality planning and preparation.**  Many people assume that the only real challenge in teaching comes from understanding the content to be taught. They seem to think that once this has been mastered, it is simply a matter of telling others what you know. In reality, subject matter knowledge is only the beginning point of the instructional process. Teachers who possess a thorough understanding of what is to be taught then must spend considerable time and energy in planning the activities, materials, and evaluation elements that are necessary to successfully help others develop new understandings (see Table 3.4). Effective teachers carefully orchestrate the many elements involved into a coherent plan of instruction.

| **TABLE 3.4  Teacher Planning and Preparation** | |
|---|---|
| **Skill** | **Description** |
| Knowledge of content and pedagogy | Teachers know the subjects they teach and the appropriate methods of instruction. |
| Knowledge of students | Teachers know the typical patterns of student learning and development and can apply that knowledge to individual students. |
| Selecting instructional goals | Teachers set appropriate learning expectations for lessons and activities. |
| Knowledge of resources | Teachers can locate the materials and people needed for instruction. |
| Designing instruction | Teachers plan lessons that are organized for effective learning. |
| Assessing student learning | Teachers engage in fair and meaningful evaluation of student learning. |

**Preparing the classroom environment.** Have you ever stopped to reflect on the many behind-the-scenes activities that must take place if a stage play is to be successful? The lighting crew, prop assistants, makeup and costume workers, and special effects crew are just a few of the possible groups that work unobserved to make sure all parts come together to create a smoothly flowing performance. In much the same way, effective teachers do considerable "behind-the-scenes" work in planning the classroom environment in ways that allow for positive student learning experiences (see Table 3.5). For example, Jacob Nelson is preparing to teach his high school American history class about the Civil War. In preparation for this unit of study, he has organized several experiences and activities for students. These include the participation of a local group of Civil War enthusiasts who will come to class in costume to describe key battles and the horrendous loss of human life for both sides in the conflict. Jacob has also located a Black civil rights activist who has agreed to come and discuss the long-term impact of slavery on African Americans today. They are planning to meet at least twice to carefully plan for the discussion of this volatile topic. Jacob has also located three videos on the Civil War

*Teachers carefully plan the use of classroom space.*

that he will review and consider for use and has identified numerous Internet resources that students can explore as they start to collect additional information on topics of interest to them.

**Using proven instructional techniques.** Marilyn Wilson is preparing for an upcoming unit on chemical reactions for her eighth-grade general science class. She is in the process of planning several hands-on experiments in which her students can safely mix different chemicals and note their reactions. As students work in pairs, they will make hypotheses and test them out with their equipment and supplies over the next several classes. Students always seem to enjoy these opportunities to experiment and explore. Marilyn must be sure she has clearly defined the tasks to be accomplished and identified the questions she will use to get her students focusing on the appropriate aspects of the experiments (see Table 3.6). She plans to be available to answer questions as they come up and will give suggestions and hints to help those who are struggling. Instructional strategies like those used by Marilyn in her eighth-grade science classes captivate the interests of students and motivate them to learn.

| TABLE 3.5   Preparing a Positive Classroom Environment | |
|---|---|
| **Skill** | **Description** |
| Creating an environment of respect and rapport | Developing caring teacher–student and peer relationships |
| Establishing a culture for learning | An environment in which learning is valued and meaningful experiences occur |
| Managing classroom procedures | Successful management of classroom routines |
| Managing student behavior | Effectively responding to appropriate and inappropriate student behaviors |
| Organizing physical space | Positive use of classroom space to facilitate learning |

**TABLE 3.6    Proven Instructional Techniques**

| Skill | Description |
|---|---|
| Communicating clearly and accurately | Use of strong verbal and written communication skills |
| Using effective questioning and discussion techniques | Questioning and discussion strategies that expand student understanding and get them actively involved |
| Engaging students in learning | Actively involving students in significant learning |
| Providing feedback to students | Giving students continued information about their progress in learning |
| Being flexible and responsive | Spontaneously modifying lessons based on student needs and interests |

**Exhibiting professional behavior.** Teaching is a complex occupation requiring continued professional growth and responsibilities that go beyond traditional classroom instruction (see Table 3.7). Effective teachers embrace these extra tasks and strive to become true professionals by improving their knowledge and skills in instruction while working to make significant contributions to their school, district and community. For example, Kara Sorenson has been teaching history at the high school level for the past 15 years. In addition to completing her master's degree, Kara has taken numerous workshops and participated in regular professional development activities provided by her school and district. Kara spends long hours thinking about, and planning for, instruction and student evaluation. She also works collaboratively with the school counselor, special education staff, and building administrators to meet the needs of her students. Kara is engaged in the work of being a professional.

**TABLE 3.7    Professional Teaching Behaviors**

| Behavior | Description |
|---|---|
| Reflecting on teaching | Thoughtful consideration of what should be taught and how |
| Maintaining accurate records | Keeping written records to document student learning |
| Communicating with families | Staying in written and verbal contact with families to support student learning |
| Contributing to the school and district | Supporting the smooth functioning of the school and school district |
| Growing as a professional | Taking courses and workshops and talking to others about teaching and learning |
| Showing professionalism | Serving as advocates for students and their families |

Before reading further in this chapter, take a moment to reflect back on the skills common to effective teachers presented in this section. As you picture yourself in the teaching role, which of these skills do you think you can readily develop? Are there others that may be more difficult for you? What aspects of your personality will make it either easier or more difficult to develop these skills? Have you had experiences that gave you opportunities to develop the foundations for good teaching? Your personality and experiences will influence the ways in which you develop the skills needed in teaching.

**Reflective Journey 3.2**

## Attitudes of Effective Teachers

Although every teacher brings his or her own unique personality to the classroom, effective teachers do share several common attitudes (see Table 3.8). First of all, they are real people who share their humanity with students. Second, they have a desire to know themselves as individuals so that they can build on their strengths and compensate for weaknesses as they work with students in the classroom. Third, excellent teachers think positively of their students and work to treat each one with dignity and respect. Fourth, they are excited about learning and can share that joy with students. Finally, they have a positive attitude about working closely with other adults to make sure that every student has the greatest likelihood of success in the classroom.

**Effective teachers are real.**  Some people enter teaching for the wrong reasons. One example of a poor reason to become an educator is to "show others how smart I am." Perhaps you have experienced a teacher of this type. They often appear aloof, arrogant, and proud. Students are often viewed as second-class citizens who should be honored to be learning in the presence of a great mind. In reality, these teachers may be trying hard to cover up a poor self-image by giving the impression of strong academic prowess. With few exceptions, they are ineffective in the classroom and are generally disliked by students. Teachers of this type are not being real because they have failed to share their true selves with their students.

**TABLE 3.8   Attitudes of Effective Teachers**

| Attitude | Description |
| --- | --- |
| Effective teachers are real. | Teachers share their true selves with students. |
| Effective teachers seek self-understanding. | They know their own strengths and limitations, understand what is meaningful to them, are in touch with their emotions, and know their personal likes and dislikes. |
| Effective teachers have positive expectations for students. | Teachers have realistic, yet challenging, expectations for individual students and their learning. |
| Effective teachers care about their students. | They have an attitude of prizing, acceptance, and trust in relation to their students. |
| Effective teachers are excited about learning. | Teachers demonstrate to students their love of learning. |
| Effective teachers are willing to collaborate with other adults. | They see themselves as part of an educational team, take time to maintain and strengthen relationships, and value these relationships. |

Rogers (1969) puts it this way:

> When the facilitator (teacher) is a real person, being what he is, entering into a relationship with the learner without presenting a front or a façade, he is much more likely to be effective. This means that the feelings which he is experiencing are available to him, available to his awareness, that he is able to live these feelings, be them, and able to communicate them if appropriate. It means that he comes into a direct personal encounter with the learner, meeting him on a person-to-person basis. It means that he is *being* himself, not denying himself. (p. 106)

The teachers that Rogers describes are the ones that students enjoy being around and can relate to because of their genuineness. These qualities in a teacher give students the confidence to be real themselves and expect to be understood. This atmosphere of openness and trust is critical for effective learning.

**Self-understanding.**   In the hustle and bustle of life, how often do you go beyond the tasks of the moment to reflect on who you are as a person or why you do the things you do? This introspection takes time and effort and is frequently avoided by many people. The best teachers, however, somehow find time for this important task because it is so critical to success in the classroom. This makes sense when you realize that teachers can only help others learn and grow as individuals when they have first taken the time to do this for themselves. In addition to being discussed here, Chapter 15 provides additional information on seeking self-understanding.

This process of self-awareness for teachers is a lifelong process that consists of four main components. The first component is *knowing your strengths and limitations as a person.* Genetic inheritance and life experiences combine to determine your personal strengths and weaknesses. You come to teaching with a unique mix of both. Through personal reflection and discussion with others, you can determine your strengths and weaknesses and begin to build your teaching style with this information in mind. For example, if one of your strengths as a person is using humor in your interactions with others, you will want to decide how this can be used to your advantage as a future teacher.

A second component of self-understanding consists of *reflecting on what is meaningful to you as a person.* To understand yourself, you must determine the things, activities, and interactions that bring meaning to your life. Jersild (1955), in a classic text on teachers' search for self-understanding, states:

> The search for meaning is not a search for an abstract body of knowledge, or even for a concrete body of knowledge. It is a distinctly personal search. The one who makes it raises intimate personal questions: What really counts, for me? What values am I seeking? What, in my existence as a person, in my relations with others, in my work as a teacher, is of real concern to me, perhaps of ultimate concern to me? (p. 4)

Although this reflection is a difficult task, teachers who expect to guide their students in their search for meaning must first work at coming to grips with this issue themselves.

A third component of self-awareness is *understanding your emotional life.* Without question, interactions between teachers and students evoke many emotions from both parties. For example, how would you react to a student who snickers at a statement you just made as the classroom teacher? How would you feel about a student making a racist or sexist statement aimed at another student? What emotions would you experience if a student were to give you a big hug on the way out the classroom door at the end of the day? Understanding your emotional responses and what triggers them can help you deal with the many emotion-filled situations you will face as a future teacher. It will also give you empathy and understanding as you guide students in managing their own emotions (Greenberg, 1969).

A final component of self-understanding is *knowing your likes and dislikes about people.* Our values, beliefs, experiences, and personality create for each of us a very strong attraction to some students we teach and a definite aversion to others. Greenberg (1969), in a classic text titled *Teaching with Feeling,* tells us:

It is impossible to feel the same way toward all children. Human beings inevitably react
uniquely and specifically to other human beings. . . . Appearances, manners, gestures, ways of
speaking and relating to others, all affect our likes and dislikes. . . . Factors we dislike in
ourselves can influence our dislike for others. (pp. 39–40)

When these personal attitudes toward others are recognized, teachers can work hard to be more
equitable in interactions with students, their families, and other adults associated with the
schools.

**Positive expectations.**  In addition to understanding themselves, teachers need to clearly recognize the attitudes they hold toward students and the significant influence these attitudes have on student learning. Positive attitudes create a climate in which effective schooling can take place, whereas
negative ones lead to destructive relationships and diminished opportunities for learning. Good and
Brophy (2000) describe this attitude in terms of **teacher expectations** for student learning.

Take, for example, Mary who is beginning her third year teaching high school mathematics. Two students in her second-period algebra class highlight the influence of teacher expectations. Mary understood from another teacher that Amy R., who has just transferred into the
class, was a difficult student and would do poor work. Although Amy's performance in class
has been fine so far, Mary is expecting problems from her. Ron, another student in the same
class, has been turning in only about a third of his assignments, often stares out the window as
if he is bored, and got a D grade on the first exam. Mary expects that Ron will continue to be a
low performer in her class.

While Mary's expectations are understandable, the effects of her attitudes may be problem-
atic. Good and Brophy (2000) suggest that one possible effect is that her attitude may become a
**self-fulfilling prophecy.** In the case of Amy R., Mary received erroneous information. The other
teacher had been talking about Amy *D.* rather than Amy *R.* Because Mary expects poor performance, however, she may well find that Amy R. achieves only to the level of her expectations. Research suggests that in many circumstances, the teacher's expectations can either positively or
negatively influence student performance (Brophy, 1983).

**Caring attitude.**  Andy Baumgartner was the 1999 National Teacher of the Year. In an open letter to new teachers, he states:

"How does one sort through the many and confusing descriptors of life as an educator, in order
to plot a successful and rewarding career in teaching?" you ask. I can only relate what I have
observed about my colleagues:
- The effective teacher always considers the needs of his/her students first!
- The truly successful teacher knows and cares about students as individuals and worthy
    members of a school community. (Council of Chief State School Officers, 2002)

Although Mr. Baumgartner's list of ingredients for successful teaching consists of several more elements beyond the two listed here, these two are clearly essential. This attitude of caring and working to meet the needs of students is at the heart of excellent teaching.

Similarly, Rogers (1969) describes the importance of teachers having an attitude of prizing,
acceptance, and trust in relation to their students. He suggests qualities that teachers must possess to facilitate learning in the classroom. One of these qualities is the teacher's attitude toward
students:

There is another attitude which stands out in those who are successful in facilitating learning. I
have observed this attitude. I have experienced it. Yet, it is hard to know what term to put to it
so I shall use several. I think of it as prizing the learner, prizing his feelings, his opinions, his
person. It is a caring for the learner, but a non-possessive caring. It is an acceptance of this other

## Hate Hurts

As much as we might like to think that students today are different from those from previous generations and that they neither experience nor are the initiators of prejudice and hate, such is not the case. Stern-LaRosa and Bettman (2000) cite the following examples of prejudice and hate that range from fairly subtle to more violent. After suffering through many incidents of prejudice, it's hard not to want to hurt others in return:

- A student new to this country had problems speaking English properly. Other students noticed the accent and made fun of him.

- Another student described being punched in the face. Although it was a painful blow, it didn't hurt nearly as much as the words they used. While physical wounds heal, continuing to be called "spic" made this student feel lower in status than others.

- The prejudice of others affects the way recipients feel about people who are different from themselves.

Those who receive prejudice start to react by being prejudiced themselves.

- A student actually spit in another student's sandwich. As negative as this action was, he followed up with a statement like, "I bet you're really hungry now, right? I bet you're really hungry now, black nigger—right? Right?" (p. 10).

- Some students experience so much prejudice that they gradually reach the boiling point. If one more comment is made, or one more negative action is taken, they are likely to explode.

At every grade level, you can expect to encounter elements of prejudice and hate. As a future teacher, it will undoubtedly be necessary for you to intervene when students engage in these actions. These are complex issues that cannot be easily solved.

### React and Reflect

1. Choose one of the above situations to respond to. How would you react if you were the student in this situation? Would your response be any different if it were the 3rd or 33rd time something like this had happened to you?

2. Assume that you are teaching and a student comes to you and describes one of the situations listed above. How would you respond to this student?

3. How can you help students identify prejudicial behavior and work through their attitudes toward people who look, act, speak, or believe differently from themselves?

 *To explore this topic further and submit your reactions and reflections online, go to the Explore Your Beliefs module for Chapter 3 of the Companion Website for this text.*

*Source:* Stern-LaRosa, C., & Bettman, E. (2000). *Hate hurts: How children learn and unlearn prejudice.* New York: Scholastic.

individual as a separate person, having worth in his own right. It is a basic trust—a belief that this other person is somehow fundamentally trustworthy. (p. 109)

Teachers who bring this attitude of prizing, acceptance, and trust to their relationships with students create a climate in which students feel good about themselves. When teachers value students, encourage them as individuals, and expect them to be successful in their efforts, conditions are optimal for learning.

**Excitement for learning.** The principal has just walked into Mark's fourth-grade class to casually observe his teaching. She watches as Mark leads students in a group discussion related to recycling of household materials. Students have brought materials from their trash at home that could potentially be recycled. Mark and his students are talking animatedly about the items exhibited and the ways in which they could be reused or recycled. It is obvious that he feels strongly about this topic and students are responding with enthusiasm. Mark is excited about his teaching and it is contagious.

Mark is demonstrating an attitude toward learning that is critical for teachers at all levels to possess. When teachers get excited about learning, the enthusiasm usually spreads to students and meaningful educational experiences abound. While some may find it difficult to maintain a consistent level of excitement toward learning, the best teachers seem able to do so. And when they get excited, teaching becomes a much more rewarding experience for everyone involved. Memorable teachers are often passionate about their work. Sylvia Ashton-Warner (1963) exemplifies this passion as she responds to her editor's request for a "few cool facts" about her celebrated teaching techniques with young Maori children in New Zealand: "A 'few cool facts' you asked me for. . . . I don't know that there's a cool fact in me, or anything else cool for that matter, on this particular subject. I've got only hot long facts on the matter of Creative Teaching, scorching both the page and me" (p. 23).

**Collaborate with others.**    Although it is true that teachers have considerable autonomy in their work with students, a number of other adults also play important roles in student learning and development. As a future teacher, you will need to work with a long list of other people to maximize student learning and development. This list includes school administrators, counselors, special educators, educational assistants, and parents. The roles will vary in each circumstance, but the attitude effective teachers have in their interactions with this diverse group of adults is one of professional collaboration to best serve the needs of students (see Table 3.9). These professional relationships require effort and a commitment of time by all participants.

**TABLE 3.9    Effective Collaboration**

| Component | Description |
| --- | --- |
| See yourself as part of an educational team. | Effective teachers realize that their students can be most successful when a variety of adults work collaboratively on behalf of students. By taking advantage of the insights and talents of other adults, teachers and others have a much greater chance of positively influencing students' lives. |
| Take time to maintain and strengthen relationships. | Teachers who collaborate with other adults find the time to maintain and strengthen their rapport. The essential ingredient in this process is effective communication through such things as face-to-face contacts, telephone calls, e-mail messages, and written documents. |
| Prize, accept, and trust other adults. | When teachers set aside their own prejudices and preconceived notions and work to understand and value the contributions of other adults, many opportunities for productive collaboration on behalf of students will result. |

## Can effective teachers have different styles?

Good teachers do indeed differ in the ways in which they interact with students. This statement shouldn't be particularly surprising, since every teacher is an individual and brings her or his own unique combination of strengths, weaknesses, and attitudes to the task. Guild and Garger (1998) state:

> When we accept that people really are different, we also must accept that teachers will bring their own unique qualities to the way they teach. We call this "teaching style," and it means we will see teachers' personalities reflected in their professional behavior. We will see differences in the way teachers relate to students. We will see differences in how teachers structure and manage their rooms. We will see differences in the mood and tone that teachers set in their classrooms. We will see differences in the methods and materials teachers use to help students learn. We will see differences in curriculum interests and emphases. We will see differences in expectations for student work and in priorities and strategies for evaluating student learning. (p. 90)

Many different writers and researchers during the last several decades have written about teaching styles. While some have carefully identified and described these styles for better understanding and future research, others have used metaphors to help others grasp the essential differences in teaching styles (see Table 3.10). Some examples from this latter group will be presented here. Goodlad (1984) described teachers using sports metaphors including coach and quarterback to summarize different teaching styles. Rubin (1985) drew on the arts to identify teaching styles that he referred to as artist and actor, whereas Rogers (1969) saw teachers as counselors, and Glasser (1990) likened teachers to managers in business. Although these teaching style metaphors have overlapping characteristics, they help clarify the differences that exist among equally effective teachers.

As you read through the following descriptions, think about teachers you have known and try to identify the styles they exhibited. As you reflect on their abilities and personalities, were

### TABLE 3.10   Teaching Styles

| Style | Description |
|---|---|
| Teacher as coach | Actively involved from outside the learning experience in giving directions, providing instruction, and motivating students to learn |
| Teacher as quarterback | Active member of the learning team working to facilitate learning through personal excitement and example |
| Teacher as artist | Using a deep understanding of the components of learning to create unique lessons and activities that facilitate student learning |
| Teacher as actor | Making learning exciting and meaningful through actions and words |
| Teacher as counselor | Making the support of students' social and emotional development central to teaching |
| Teacher as manager | Creating a supportive learning environment in which students are eager to work individually and in groups |

there differences in the ways in which they approached the challenges of teaching? Think about which style or styles you responded to favorably as a student. Which teaching style or styles do you think were most effective in promoting your learning and development? Did other students prefer different styles? Also consider which style seems appealing to you at this time. What do you like about this description of teaching?

One teaching style that is common in the schools is the **teacher as coach.** A coach knows her sport, makes most of the decisions about plays and players, instructs team members on how to play the game, and exhorts the team to give their all. Coaches control the activities of the participants as they work to ensure victory over their opponents. Many educators have a coaching teaching style in which they exhibit strong content knowledge, make most of the decisions about what is to be taught, share their expertise with students, and encourage students to learn. A charismatic teacher, like a good coach, leads his or her students to greater levels of understanding through direct involvement in the learning process.

Other educators use a style described as **teacher as quarterback.** A quarterback is a member of the team who serves as the key leader on the field of play. He calls the plays and directs the team from within the game itself. Unlike the coach who directs from the sidelines, the quarterback is actively engaged in the sport along with the other players. Teachers using this style view themselves as colearners along with their students and work to facilitate learning through their take-charge attitude, an excitement about learning, and through example. In addition, just as a quarterback sometimes changes the play at the last moment, teachers also adjust their activities to meet the needs and interests of students.

A third teaching style can be identified as the **teacher as artist.** Artists take raw materials and with imagination, skill, and a touch of the unexplainable create an object of beauty. They know the characteristics of the materials used well and can transform them into objects of beauty. Teachers using this style are often hard to analyze because it is difficult for others to see how they took the building blocks for learning and blended them in creative ways into a meaningful experience for students. This "little bit of magic" is difficult to teach others, but is found in abundance in many teachers.

Another important approach to teaching can be described as **teacher as actor.** Actors engage their audiences in two primary ways. Through their words and actions they either entertain or get their audiences to think deeply about complex issues. Similarly, teachers engage their students by entertaining them or by motivating them to reflect on difficult topics. Some people dislike this metaphor because actors are not genuine and real when they play a part, but it should be obvious that teachers are in a sense performers who each day step onto the classroom stage to share with the audience through their actions and words. Part of the time, these performances are designed to help students think deeply about important topics. On other occasions, their role is to entertain in an effort to motivate students to learn. Some teachers are better than others in getting excited about this role and in "hamming it up" a bit with their students. These teachers truly love the opportunity to be in the limelight and can use their time to motivate student learning through their daily performances.

*Role playing is appealing to many teachers.*

The teaching style of some teachers can best be described as the **teacher as counselor.** A counselor is trained to assist others in their social and emotional development. By spending time listening carefully, asking effective questions, and letting others know they care, counselors have a significant impact on healthy development. As discussed earlier in this chapter, an important role that all teachers assume to some degree is supporting students' social and emotional development. Some teachers, however, despite a lack of training, find this aspect of teaching extremely important and make it a high priority in their interactions with students. They enjoy the opportunity to assist students in their social and emotional development and do an excellent job of listening to and guiding students as they struggle with a variety of difficult and stressful issues.

A final teaching style to be identified is the **teacher as manager.** A good manager in business and industry today is considered a person who creates a supportive atmosphere where employees are eager to do their jobs and work as a team for the good of the group. These managers have established a good rapport with employees, get them involved in the decision-making process, and provide them with the support they need to be productive in their work efforts. Teachers who see themselves as managers serve as guides to student growth by preparing an environment that is rich in potential learning possibilities. Managing teachers give students the opportunity to make at least some of the decisions that are relevant to their own learning. In addition, they work to foster positive teacher–student and peer relationships.

Because students come to the classroom with varying learning styles (Guild & Garger, 1998) and diverse needs and interests, schools benefit when they can hire effective teachers with a variety of teaching styles. There is no one style that is the "best." They each have their strengths and are needed in every school.

## views from the classroom

## Together, We Made It Through First Grade

**Lori Price**
**Loveland Elementary School**
**Loveland, Ohio**

As I approach the conclusion of my 17th year of teaching, I am still amazed at the growth I have the opportunity to witness every year. Surrounded by first graders, I have learned to see the world through the eyes of a child once more. I am beginning to once again understand how important it is to see the world as fair and to never lose my place in line. Even more importantly, I have come to understand that you can never predict a child's ability to succeed by his performance during the first month of school.

Last year was my first year teaching first grade. My prior experience had been with older elementary children, and over half of that was in a special education setting. I quickly learned that there were parts of first grade for which nothing could prepare me. One of the first things that became clear is that many of the children had not been away from their parents for that many hours every day. Homesickness was a way of life for a while. I also found that, for a first grader, learning to share one adult with 22 other children was a real adjustment.

For one student, first grade was simply overwhelming. He had a difficult time completing tasks and became more frustrated every day. This frustration led to numerous tantrums and disruptions. There were days when I was so tired from just trying to keep up with his needs—not to mention the needs of the other 22 students—that I didn't know how we would make it until June. I knew, though, that he needed me to have faith in him so he could succeed. He kept working to get good daily behavior reports, and I kept praising even the smallest achievement. Constant communication between school and home quickly became the norm for both his parents and me. Together we made it through the year. As June approached, I began to realize how difficult it was going to be to see the year come to an end.

Looking back to where we began, I can see how much progress was made last year. His second-grade teacher keeps me informed of his progress, and he is doing very well both academically and socially.

Every day when I pass the lunch line outside the cafeteria, he is there to greet me with a huge grin and a hug. Those hugs remind me what it was that drew me to teaching and what it is that keeps me coming back to the classroom every year.

## Summary

In this chapter, four questions were used to clarify your thinking about America's teachers:

### Who are our teachers?

A number of characteristics help define teachers today:
- Teachers' ages
- Years of teaching experience
- Degrees earned
- Gender
- Racial diversity

### What are their roles?

The many roles of teachers today make education a challenging, yet exciting career. These roles include the following:
- Facilitating learning (Praxis II, topics IIa, b)
- Supporting social/emotional development (Praxis II, topics Ia, IIIa)
- Sharing resources for growth and development
- Serving as a role model

### What skills and attitudes are characteristic of effective teachers?

All good teachers share a common set of skills and attitudes, such as these:
- Engaging in quality planning and preparation
- Preparing a positive classroom environment
- Using proven instructional techniques
- Exhibiting professional behavior (Praxis II, topic IVa)
- Being real
- Seeking self-understanding
- Having positive attitudes toward students (Praxis II, topics Ia, b)
- Getting excited about learning
- Collaborating with other adults (Praxis II, topic IVb)

### Can effective teachers have different styles?

Because teachers bring their own personalities to teaching, effective teachers often have very different styles. Metaphors have been used to describe these styles:
- Teacher as coach
- Teacher as quarterback
- Teacher as artist
- Teacher as actor
- Teacher as counselor
- Teacher as manager

## Key Terms

self-fulfilling prophecy
teacher as actor
teacher as artist
teacher as coach

teacher as counselor
teacher as manager
teacher as quarterback
teacher expectations

## Reflective Journey: Online Journal

 Use the questions for thought and reflection highlighted throughout the chapter to help guide your personal journey of reflection and professional development as a teacher. To complete your journal entries online, go to the *Reflective Journey* module for this chapter of the Companion Website.

## PRAXIS  Test Preparation Activities

To review an online chapter case study, test your understanding of chapter topics and concepts, and begin preparing for the Praxis II: Principles of Learning and Teaching examination, go to the *Praxis Test Preparation* module for this chapter of the Companion Website.

## inTASC  Becoming a Reflective Practitioner

To complete these activities and submit your responses online, go to the *Becoming a Reflective Practitioner* module for this chapter of the Companion Website.

### Who are our teachers?

#### Review Questions

1. What is the typical educational level of teachers today?
2. What are some factors influencing the low numbers of minority teachers in America's schools?

#### Building Your Portfolio: *My Personal Identity*

**INTASC Standard 9.** Spend some time reflecting on your own age, sex, and race. How do you see them influencing your relationships with students in the classroom? Will they have a positive or negative impact on your interactions with parents and other school personnel? Describe in writing these aspects of your personal identity and their potential impact on teaching and learning.

### What are their roles?

#### Review Questions

1. Identify the teaching roles discussed in this chapter. From your own educational experience, describe an example of a teacher assuming each of these roles.
2. What resources are available to help you support students and their families?

#### Field Experience

Spend some time talking with a classroom teacher of your choice about the planning and preparation needed for effective teaching. How important is subject matter knowledge to good instruction? Ask the teacher to identify and describe the roles he or she assumes in the classroom. Discuss your findings with others in your class.

#### Building Your Portfolio: *Teaching Roles*

**INTASC Standard 2.** For an age/grade/subject matter area of your choice, identify one of the teaching roles presented in this chapter and describe how you will accomplish it as a future teacher. What personal strengths will help you be successful in the role? What limitations will you need to overcome? Describe what you see to be the importance of the role you chose for this portfolio entry.

## What skills and attitudes are characteristic of effective teachers?

### Review Questions

1. Outline the process of preparing a positive classroom learning environment.
2. What are the behaviors you will need to exhibit to engage in professional teaching?
3. Identify the attitudes of effective teachers.

### Field Experience

Observe a teacher working with students in the classroom. What strategies were used to stimulate student learning? Describe the efforts made to maintain and build teacher–student and peer relationships. Did you see the teacher interact with parents or other school personnel? If not, try to spend time talking with the teacher about these interactions. What do your observations tell you about the skills and attitudes needed for effective teaching?

### Building Your Portfolio: *Positive Attitudes*

**INTASC Standard 9.** Write down in list format the attitudes of effective teachers defined in this chapter. As you reflect on this list, consider adding others of your own choosing. Once your list is complete, write down your own interpretation of how effective you will be in maintaining each of these attitudes as you work with students. Describe any problem areas you see and how you will work to overcome them. Save this list and your responses to it as an entry in your portfolio.

## Can effective teachers have different styles?

### Review Questions

1. Why are metaphors useful in helping others understand differences in teaching styles?
2. How can teachers with different styles be effective?

### Building Your Portfolio: *Teaching Style*

**INTASC Standard 9.** Choose one of the metaphors for teaching style described in this chapter or come up with one of your own (examples: teacher as gardener; teacher as conductor) that you feel describes the teaching style you would like to have. Describe the characteristics of this teaching style and how your personal strengths and limitations would influence your use of this style.

## Suggested Readings

Ashton-Warner, S. (1963). *Teacher*. New York: Bantam. In this classic book a passionate educator describes her methods and shares her love for teaching. Whether or not you agree with her methodology, you will be inspired by the joy she found in teaching and the caring attitude she had toward children. Ashton-Warner's teaching style has been an encouragement to a great many over the years.

Guild, P., & Garger, S. (1998). *Marching to different drummers* (2nd ed.). Alexandria, VA: Association for Supervision and Curriculum Development. This text provides an excellent overview of student diversity due to culture, brain differences, and learning styles. Several chapters also deal with the issues of teaching styles and the importance of finding one's personal style and building on its strengths.

Jersild, A. (1955). *When teachers face themselves*. New York: Teachers College Press. Jersild, in this classic text, describes the importance of teachers' self-understandings in effective education. He makes a strong case for self-understanding being a foundation to effective teaching and learning.

Rogers, C. (1969). *Freedom to learn*. Columbus, OH: Merrill. Rogers, in another classic text, proposes an approach to education in which teachers create an atmosphere where students are free to learn. Teachers do not simply turn students loose to do what they please, but rather carefully create a caring environment in which "significant, self-initiated, experiential learning is possible" (p. 9).

# chapter 4

## Today's Schools

As you consider teaching as a career, it is important to determine which level and type of schooling appeal to you the most. It may be surprising to learn that there are a variety of alternatives from which to choose. By increasing your understanding of these options, you will be able to make the decision that is right for you. Three key questions will guide you to a better understanding of schools and what teaching there would be like.

## Focus Questions

◢ How are schools organized?

◢ What are the alternatives to traditional public schools?

◢ What does schooling look like?

Matiul and Happy immigrated to the United States 4 years ago from Bangladesh and have recently moved to a new community within the state. Matiul has his doctorate in computer science and accepted a good position with a local firm. As the parents of three school-age children, they are looking at different neighborhoods and schools as they prepare to buy a home. With two children in elementary school and one middle school student, they have been given tours of several school buildings and met a variety of teachers and administrators. These visits have left them with a bewildering number of options. Some of the buildings themselves are old and seem poorly maintained; a few are new and attractive. More importantly, the structures of the schools vary, with some elementary schools going through the fifth grade, followed by grades 6 through 8 for middle school. Other schools in a nearby community included the more traditional K–6 elementary with a junior high school for grades 7 through 9. Not only are the schools organized in very different ways, the feelings they came away with after visiting each one also varied. Some had an atmosphere of openness and seemed welcoming to them, while others appeared chaotic and less accommodating. It will be a challenging task to pick the best schools for their children.

There are many parents like Matiul and Happy who struggle with the task of finding the best schools to meet the needs of their children. Statistics indicate that more students than ever before are enrolled in schools that their parents have selected (Holloway, 2001b). As this trend toward increasing educational options for students continues, parents will be faced with even greater challenges in determining the best choices for their children.

Just as parents are seeking the best educational options, you will need to identify which programs, grades, or subject matter areas best fit your personality and interests. As you read through this chapter, reflect on your feelings about each option presented. If possible, spend some time observing and participating in a variety of settings. After reading about and getting involved in several classrooms, most people find some that feel right, others that seem an unlikely match, and a few that are definitely out as possibilities. While this "matchmaking" may take several years to complete, it is important to begin now to identify your place in the educational system.

## How are schools organized?

Although great diversity exists in school organization, American education is often viewed as consisting of four levels: early childhood, elementary, junior high/middle school, and high school (see Figure 4.1). The National Association for the Education of Young Children (NAEYC) has identified early childhood education (ECE) as including children from birth through 8 years of age (Bredekamp & Copple, 1997). Traditional elementary education overlaps with ECE, focusing on

**Figure 4.1**   Typical School Organizations

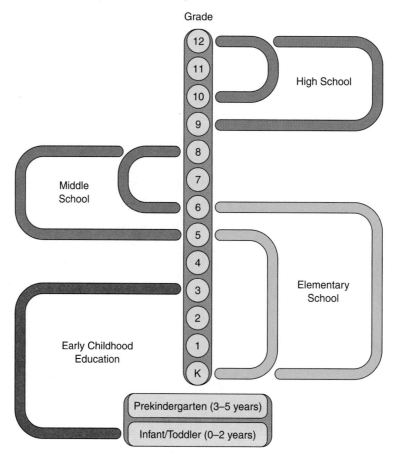

| **TABLE 4.1**   Specialized Education Services | |
| --- | --- |
| **Service** | **Description** |
| Special education | Educational efforts on behalf of students with disabilities, many of which are provided in the regular classroom |
| Bilingual education | Programs designed to help students with limited English proficiency to develop language skills in English |
| Gifted and talented education | Programs for students who are identified as gifted and talented offer educational opportunities to meet their interests and needs |
| Vocational-technical education | Programs at the middle school and high school designed to provide educational experiences that lead more directly to employment following high school rather than to higher education settings |

children from kindergarten through 5th or 6th grade. In most school districts, students move from their elementary experiences to the middle school/junior high school. Middle school is most commonly organized for children in the 5th or 6th through 8th grades, while junior high schools often consist of the 7th through 9th grades. The final level is the senior high school, typically organized to accommodate students in the 9th or 10th through 12th grades.

Four other groupings of specialized educational experiences are commonly found in American schools (see Table 4.1). Special education services are designed for students with special needs and can be found at each of the four educational levels described above. Bilingual education is provided in many school districts to meet the needs of students who come to school with limited English proficiency. Programs for the gifted and talented typically begin during the elementary school years and continue through high school. Vocational-technical education options are generally associated with the senior high school, but may be introduced earlier in some settings.

## Early Childhood Education

Programs in **early childhood education** have shown steady growth during the last several decades. One reason for this increase is the growing number of mothers with young children entering the workforce (Annie E. Casey Foundation, 2002). Another major factor is the recent research evidence that supports the importance of the early years for overall child development (Council of Chief State School Officers, 1999). Early childhood programs can be divided into three subgroups: Infant/toddler programs are typically for children from birth to 2 years of age, prekindergarten options support learning and development for 3- to 5-year-olds, and primary education is for children from 5 through 8 years of age.

**Infant/toddler education.** Programs for infants and toddlers are not yet a common part of public education. Options for children with special needs at this age, however, are becoming more widespread in many communities and are starting to find their way into public school settings. A parent education program for teens combined with infant/toddler care at the high school level is another option that is available in many communities. Maggie Wilson, for example,

| **TABLE 4.2** Enrollment in Prekindergarten Programs | | |
| --- | --- | --- |
| **Year** | **3-Year-Olds (%)** | **4-Year-Olds (%)** |
| 1965 | 4.9 | 16.1 |
| 1975 | 21.5 | 40.5 |
| 1985 | 28.8 | 49.1 |
| 1990 | 32.6 | 56.1 |
| 1995 | 35.9 | 61.6 |
| 1998 | 37.6 | 66.6 |
| 2000 | 39.2 | 68.9 |

*Source:* Adapted from *Digest of Education Statistics,* by National Center for Education Statistics, 2001, Washington, DC: U.S. Government Printing Office.

teaches high school social studies but also spends part of her day teaching a course in child development and coordinating the infant/toddler program offered for teen mothers and fathers. She has seven children in the program, with mothers and fathers spending time each day working with the infants and toddlers as part of the requirements for the course in child development.

**Prekindergarten education.** Children 3 and 4 years of age are increasingly involved in prekindergarten education (see Table 4.2). There are a variety of options such as **preschool** and **day care** that are open to all families. Preschool programs typically operate two or three half days each week and provide play opportunities and enrichment experiences that help prepare children for K–12 education. Day care programs provide services for employed parents who need education and care for their children during the workday and typically offer care from around 7 a.m. until approximately 6 p.m. Other prekindergarten programs are designed to meet the needs of special populations of young children. The **Head Start** program for young children from low-income families is probably the best known of these options. **Special needs preschools** for children with identified handicapping conditions are also growing in numbers due to federal legislation mandating these programs within school districts.

**Primary education.** Until the 1950s, theorists and practitioners alike generally defined early childhood education as teaching children from birth through age 5 (kindergarten). However, the growing popularity of theorists such as Piaget and Erikson (see Chapter 6) in the 1960s and 1970s led to a redefinition of early education. These theorists suggested that children in the primary grades are more like 3- to 5-year-olds in their thinking and learning than older elementary-aged children. This led NAEYC and others to include the primary grades as an important part of ECE. While not all primary teachers approach primary education from an early childhood perspective, those who do emphasize the importance of understanding child development and planning activities that meet the developmental needs and interests of children. Learning through the manipulation of materials and social interactions with peers is also encouraged.

### Elementary Education

Traditional **elementary education,** from colonial times through the early part of the 20th century, consisted of grades 1 through 8. Students completing elementary school then moved directly into 4-year high schools. Three sublevels were common to this traditional elementary school: primary education (grades 1 through 3), the intermediate grades (4 through 6), and upper elementary (grades 7 and 8). This pattern of organization slowly changed at both ends, with kindergarten programs being added to the beginning and the fifth or sixth through eighth grades moving to junior high or middle school buildings.

Teachers in elementary schools typically have what are referred to as **self-contained classrooms.** For the most part, this means they are responsible for teaching all subjects and that students remain in the same classroom for most of the school day. The common exceptions to this self-contained format are the teaching of music, art, and physical education by specialists in areas outside the regular classroom. For example, Josh Anderson's fifth-grade students spend 30 minutes twice each week with the physical education specialist and receive music and art instruction on alternate weeks. Josh is responsible for any additional time spent with these important components of the curriculum.

**Kindergartens.**  Kindergarten programs began in Germany in the middle part of the 19th century under the leadership of Friedrich Froebel (1886). Teachers trained in Froebel's methods brought kindergarten programs to the United States as a private school option. They initially provided children from well-to-do families with a positive educational option prior to entry into the elementary school. Later, kindergartens were also used as a means of helping low-income children gain the experiences they needed to be successful in the elementary school (see Chapter 10 for more information). The popularity of kindergarten education continued to grow, and during the 20th century it slowly became an integral part of most public elementary schools.

**Primary education.**  The first through third grades are an important time for developing basic academic skills that are needed for success in later schooling. The teaching of reading, writing, spelling, arithmetic, science, and social studies forms the core of the curriculum. Typically, students spend an hour or more daily in literacy learning, a similar amount of time in mathematics instruction, and have two or three weekly opportunities for science and social studies learning. Children who successfully master these fundamental skills develop attitudes and expertise that will help them throughout their schooling. Those who fall behind or struggle at this level may well find their future academic progress hindered.

**Intermediate grades.**  The fourth through the fifth or sixth grades are an important time for students. Students spend this time refining the basic academic skills learned during the preceding years and begin to pursue special interests in more depth. Students are becoming more self-aware and learning more about their own personal strengths and limitations. During this time, students also begin to separate emotionally from their families and peer influence grows.

While remaining self-contained, some intermediate classrooms become more specialized when two or more teachers work together to provide instruction for all students involved. For example, Sharon White and Alyssa Franklin, two fifth-grade teachers, are sharing the teaching responsibilities for their respective classes of 25 and 27 students. Sharon teaches both groups mathematics, while Alyssa takes responsibility for all language arts instruction. The teachers have adjoining classrooms and simply switch rooms when it becomes necessary to do so. This option allows them both to teach subjects they enjoy and accommodates their individual strengths. Students and parents both seem to like this approach to instruction.

## Junior High and Middle Schools

Beginning in the early 20th century, the combination of a burgeoning school population and an increasingly complex curriculum led to the growth of new schooling options. **Junior high school** programs for students in grades 7 through 9 appeared in the early part of the 20th

| Year | Middle Schools | Junior High Schools |
|------|----------------|---------------------|
| 1970–1971 | 2,080 | 7,750 |
| 1975–1976 | 3,916 | 7,521 |
| 1980–1981 | 6,003 | 5,890 |
| 1990–1991 | 8,545 | 4,561 |
| 1995–1996 | 10,205 | 3,743 |
| 1997–1998 | 10,944 | 3,599 |

**TABLE 4.3   Public Junior High and Middle Schools**

*Source:* Adapted from *Digest of Education Statistics,* by National Center for Education Statistics, 2001, Washington, DC: U.S. Government Printing Office.

century. By midcentury, they were common in most American school districts. Beginning in the late 1960s, **middle schools** for grades 6 through 8 provided yet another option for schools. They are now the more common bridge between elementary and secondary education. While middle schools continue to grow in number, junior high options continue to decline (see Table 4.3).

**Junior high schools.** Educators at the beginning of the 20th century gave three main reasons for the creation of junior high schools as a transition between elementary and secondary education (Pulliam & Van Patten, 1999):

- Educators desired to extend the academic curriculum of the high school downward into the upper elementary grades (seventh and eighth grades).
- The needs of older elementary students were not being met by the traditional elementary school.
- A new school structure was needed to smooth the transition from childhood to young adulthood.

Another more practical and less student-oriented reason for the movement to junior high school programs was the need to alleviate a school building shortage at the elementary level due to increasing enrollments. Many school districts decided to build new high schools and then use the vacated school buildings to house junior high programs for the seventh through the ninth grades. While this approach was effective in managing the large elementary school enrollments, it did not provide a good rationale for quality programs at the junior high school level.

While some teachers at this level are responsible for teaching a block of courses such as the language arts, junior high schools are usually departmentalized, and teachers typically specialize in one or more subject areas. For example, Bill North spends his day teaching mathematics at the junior high level. He has two integrated mathematics classes, two groups of beginning algebra students, and one geometry class in addition to his planning period. In addition to the core academic subjects of mathematics, social studies, science, and the language arts, junior high school teachers often provide opportunities to explore an assortment of other courses, including such things as business, agriculture, physical education, home economics, and vocational education.

**Middle school programs.**  One very positive feature of the typical middle school program is the effort made to transition students from the self-contained teaching typically found in elementary schools to the departmentalized format they will see in high school. Fifth- and sixth-grade teachers at the middle school level typically spend about half of their day with the same group of students and then have the opportunity to do more departmentalized teaching for the remainder. For example, Tanya Jacobs teaches sixth grade in a middle school and spends her mornings teaching the same group of students an integrated language arts curriculum. Her afternoons are then spent teaching social studies to three classes of sixth graders. Seventh- and eighth-grade teachers in Tanya's building, on the other hand, spend most of their time instructing four or five different groups of students in a more specialized curriculum.

In comparison to traditional junior high schools, middle school programs have tended to place greater emphasis on career counseling, personal counseling, and relevant learning experiences. These emphases have been accused by some of creating a "shallow, fragmented, and unchallenging curricula" (Manzo, 2000, p. 15). Current efforts under way to reform the middle school curriculum emphasize seven key ingredients (Jackson & Davis, 2000):

- A rigorous yet relevant curriculum based on how students at this age learn best
- Instructional methods that help all students achieve high standards and develop into lifelong learners
- Teachers who are well prepared to understand and instruct young adolescents
- A caring community of learners developed through strong adult–student relationships
- Democratic governance of schools through the participation of all staff members
- A safe and healthy school environment that promotes academic performance and personal development
- Parent and community involvement in supporting student learning

## Senior High Schools

For much of their history, **senior high schools** consisted of grades 9 through 12 for those students who were able to continue their education following 8 years at the elementary level. With the addition of junior high schools in the early part of the 20th century, high schools more typically enrolled students in grades 10 through 12. Currently, both organizational structures are found. Districts using a middle school model usually have 4-year high schools, whereas those with junior high programs generally have 3-year high schools.

Initially, high schools were privately supported through parental tuition and served one primary purpose: to prepare students for a college education. It wasn't until the late 1800s that publicly funded high school programs began to appear. Gradually, as a high school education became more available to all, the focus became more comprehensive. Shawn Smith and Jerry Baldwin, good friends who teach at the same high school, are typical of the very different teaching assignments that exist at most high schools. Despite their friendship, they rarely see each other during the school day. Shawn's classroom is in the industrial technology wing where he teaches principles of technology and manufacturing technology. Many of his students will complete their high school degrees and then attend the local community college for more specific vocational-technical preparation. Jerry, on the other hand, teaches science in a separate campus building that houses both the science and mathematics departments. He has three periods of general science and two biology classes each term. Typically, Jerry's students are more likely to go on to a 4-year college after their high school experience. School-wide meetings, which occur infrequently, are generally the only time when Shawn and Jerry see one another at school.

## As Colorful as a Box of Crayolas

In 1994, Erin Gruwell began her first year of teaching at Wilson High School in Long Beach, California. Having student taught there the year before, she was aware of the diversity she would encounter. Erin characterized the students "as colorful as a box of Crayolas" (Gruwell, 1999, p. 4). Sitting side by side in her English classes were Caucasian students from wealthy local families, Hispanic students from the barrio, students of Asian descent, and African American students. Many lived in extreme poverty and experienced violence on a daily basis. Drive-by shootings, gang violence, and family abuse were just some of the challenges they faced. One 14-year-old Hispanic student described in his diary entry the daily experience of walking home from his bus stop. Chased regularly by older African Americans from the neighborhood carrying bats and knives, he decided to buy a gun for protection. Carrying it in his backpack at school, the student felt a sense of anticipation as he prepared for the trip home. When chased again, the student pulled out his gun and waved it menacingly at the others, who quickly dispersed.

As a beginning teacher at Wilson High School, Erin was given a high percentage of at-risk students. They were basically those who other teachers and administrators had labeled as unreachable and who were simply putting in their time until they could leave school and move on to other activities. For example, one of her students was on parole for gang-related activities and was told to either

attend school or pack his bags in preparation for boot camp. The student decided that school would be much easier. Another student in a Latino gang described in a journal entry how several of his "soldiers" were either dying or being sent to prison. It was time to recruit new gang members. The only criterion for admission was the willingness to literally give their lives to the gang. They had to be willing to either "take a bullet or pull the trigger" (Gruwell, 1999, p. 17). This student's motivation to learn in school was being superceded by other more pressing matters.

Despite these seemingly impossible circumstances, Erin Gruwell slowly began to have an impact on her students. By selecting literature such as *Zlata's Diary: A Child's Life in Sarajevo* and *Anne Frank: The Diary of a Young Girl* that related to their experiences in the world and pushing hard to get students to write about the things that were important parts of their lives, she started to motivate these at-risk students to make personal changes and eventually helped them have an impact on the world around them. After reading about the Freedom Riders of the 1960s, who traveled on an integrated bus to the Deep South in an effort to change segregated bus and train travel, Ms. Gruwell's students decided to become Freedom Writers. Through their diary entries, they told their stories and began the process of changing their lives and those of others around them.

### Explore and Reflect

Learn more about the Freedom Writers by reading the source book by Gruwell (1999) and reviewing other online resources provided in the *Reflect on Diversity* module for Chapter 4 of the Companion Website.

1. Imagine yourself beginning your teaching career with a class of students like the ones in Wilson High School described above. Do you think you would welcome the challenges or feel overwhelmed by the complexities of the situation? What makes you think this way?

2. Is Erin Gruwell simply one of a very few exceptional teachers that can reach at-risk students or can larger numbers of teachers be successful in these settings? What makes you feel this way?

3. What can you do to prepare yourself for the diversity you will find in your future classroom? What do you need to know and be able to do in order to be successful in a diverse setting?

 *To explore this topic further and submit your responses online, go to the Reflect on Diversity module for Chapter 4 of the Companion Website for this text.*

*Source: The Freedom Writers Diary*, by E. Gruwell, 1999, New York: Broadway Books.

**TABLE 4.4   High School Reform Efforts**

| Proposal | Description |
|---|---|
| The Paideia proposal | Adler (1982) proposed a more classic high school curriculum based on the Great Books that would allow students virtually no elective course work. |
| *A Nation at Risk* | This influential report (National Commission on Excellence in Education, 1983) suggested that all high school students be required to take 4 years of English, and 3 years each of mathematics, science, and social studies. |
| American high school study | In a proposal parallel to that of the *Nation at Risk* report, this study recommended an increase in the academic core required for graduation from one-half to two-thirds of the total credits. More course work in English, history, science, mathematics, foreign language, and civics was recommended (Boyer, 1983). |

This move to comprehensive high schools has been accompanied by considerable controversy. Critics have been vocal in their concerns over many aspects of high school life. In the 1980s three key reform reports proposed significant modifications in the high school curriculum (see Table 4.4). Despite these concerns over what is being taught in American high schools, most young people attend and successfully complete a secondary education degree. At the same time, however, the number of students who fail to complete a high school education or its equivalent is troublesome. Although the percentage of dropouts has continued to decline, far too many young people still fail to complete what has become the basic level of education necessary to result in reasonably good job opportunities (see Table 4.5).

**TABLE 4.5   Percentage of High School Dropouts, 1960–2000**

| Year | Percentage |
|---|---|
| 1960 | 27.2 |
| 1970 | 15.0 |
| 1980 | 14.1 |
| 1990 | 12.1 |
| 1998 | 11.3 |
| 2000 | 10.9 |

*Source:* Adapted from *Digest of Education Statistics,* by National Center for Education Statistics, 2001, Washington, DC: U.S. Government Printing Office.

**TABLE 4.6**  **Students Receiving Special Education Services**

| Year | Number Served (millions) | Percentage Served (of total enrollment) |
|---|---|---|
| 1976–1977 | 3.69 | 8.33 |
| 1985–1986 | 4.32 | 10.95 |
| 1995–1996 | 5.57 | 12.43 |
| 1997–1998 | 5.90 | 12.8 |
| 1999–2000 | 6.20 | 13.2 |

*Source:* Adapted from *Digest of Education Statistics,* by National Center for Education Statistics, 2001, Washington, DC: U.S. Government Printing Office.

**Reflective Journey 4.1**

Stop for a moment to reflect on the levels of education mentioned in this section. Prekindergarten, elementary, middle school/junior high, and high school teaching are all possibilities for you to consider. At this point, which of these levels holds the greatest appeal for you? What is it about the students at this level that you find most inviting? If you were teaching at this level, which subject or subjects would you enjoy sharing with others? Do any other aspects of working at this level make it more attractive than others?

## Special Education

For much of American history, **special education** services were provided in segregated programs housed away from regular classrooms. Children in these settings were isolated from virtually any contact with their more normally developing peers. Beginning in the 20th century, classes for children with milder disabilities were gradually located in regular public school buildings. While the number of students receiving special education services has increased during the last three decades, segregated special education programs for all levels of disabilities have decreased markedly as greater numbers of children with special needs have been placed in regular education classrooms for part or most of their school day (see Table 4.6).

Marissa Davis is a special education teacher at the middle school level. Her daily routine is typical of many special educators. Marissa begins by working one on one with a variety of students with special needs. For example, she visits and spends time with a seventh-grade student with autism, two eighth-grade students with physical handicaps, and three others who have various learning disabilities. Marissa travels throughout the school building to work with each of the students assigned to her. Sometimes, she takes the student out into the hallway for a brief lesson, while at other times she provides assistance within the regular classroom. In the afternoons, Marissa has her own classroom and small groups of students come in for specialized instruction.

During the past 25 years, the costs of providing programs for children with special needs and the number of students being served have increased dramatically. Federal spending has grown from approximately $100 million in 1975 to $4.9 billion in 2000 (Sack, 2000). For this same time period, state and local allocations have grown proportionately, with each continuing to be several times larger than the federal commitment. The growth in services for students with special needs has been both a blessing to the students and a major problem for the schools. The students themselves appear to benefit from opportunities to interact with peers in educational settings that allow for optimal growth. Schools, on the other hand, struggle to accommodate students with disabilities in the regular classrooms, find it difficult to hire enough qualified staff to work with these students, and scramble to locate the funding needed to implement mandated programs (Sack, 2000).

## Bilingual Education

Traditionally, **bilingual education** was viewed as an opportunity to help students whose native language is other than English to learn a second language. These limited English-proficient (LEP) students were taught for at least a portion of the day in their native language and then moved to strictly English-speaking classes. This approach still exists, but considerable controversy surrounds its necessity and effectiveness. Those opposing bilingual education suggest that students should simply be immersed in English language classrooms and given extra assistance in that setting to master the language. Those who support a more traditional approach

*Students with special needs are included in classrooms whenever possible.*

suggest that this "sink or swim" option is unfair and leads to far greater numbers of students failing and dropping out of school. In June 1998, the state of California became a major proponent of the immersion approach with the passage of Proposition 227. This measure virtually ended the state's traditional bilingual education programs in favor of a 1-year English-immersion option.

With the growing linguistic diversity of students and their families, bilingual education is becoming an increasingly important component of education at all levels within American schools. Educators need to know how to implement quality programs. Montecel and Cortez (2002) have identified these key components of successful bilingual education programs:

- Supportive and informed district and school leadership
- Clear goals for LEP students
- Safe and orderly school climate
- Fully credentialed bilingual teachers
- Parent involvement in bilingual programs

## Gifted Education

Adam is finishing his last term of high school classes and is preparing for college in the fall. He is a hard-working student who is liked by both classmates and teachers. Adam has taken challenging courses in mathematics, the sciences, social studies, and English throughout his schooling and always seems to do well. He has never received an end-of-term grade lower than an A. Adam has always scored within the top 5% on the standardized tests administered by the school district. Some of his elementary and secondary teachers consider him gifted, while others attribute his success to an outstanding work ethic. Depending on the definition used for giftedness and the availability of programs, students like Adam may or may not be involved in **gifted education** programs during their elementary and secondary schooling.

In many ways, gifted and talented students are the "forgotten minority." Without clear legal rights and because of the general emphasis on lower achieving students, they are frequently overlooked. Already overworked teachers often find it difficult to prepare all of the special activities needed to challenge the gifted and talented in their classrooms. To combat

**TABLE 4.7**    Gifted and Talented Programs and Students

| State | Mandated Gifted and Talented Programs (Y or N) | Gifted and Talented as Percentage of State Total |
|---|---|---|
| Alabama | Y | 2.4 |
| Arkansas | Y | 8.0 |
| Florida | Y | 3.5 |
| Hawaii | Y | 11.0 |
| Maryland | N | 12.0 |
| Michigan | N | 14.0 |
| Minnesota | N | 7.2 |
| Missouri | N | 5.0 |
| Nebraska | Y | 10.0 |
| North Dakota | N | 1.0 |
| Ohio | Y | 13.0 |
| Pennsylvania | Y | 4.6 |
| Tennessee | Y | 2.0 |
| Washington | N | 1.5 |
| Wisconsin | Y | 15.0 |

*Source:* Adapted from *Digest of Education Statistics,* by National Center for Education Statistics, 2001, Washington, DC: U.S. Government Printing Office.

this problem, many school districts and states have developed program options to meet the special needs of this student population (see Table 4.7). For example, Kendra James is a teacher of gifted and talented students at the upper elementary and middle school levels for a smaller school district. Students who have been identified as gifted and talented come from all over the district to participate in her program one day a week. Kendra works with fifth graders on Monday, sixth-grade students on Tuesday, and seventh- and eighth-grade students on Wednesday and Thursday, respectively. She plans creative and challenging tasks that stretch each group as they spend a day in her classroom. Last month Kendra's sixth-grade students studied classical architecture and compared what they found to buildings in the local area.

### Vocational-Technical Education

**Vocational-technical education** has been an important option for many students throughout most of the 20th century. With the recent move toward more rigorous academic programs at the high school level, these programs have suffered an image problem. "Leaders of the new school reform movement do not give it [vocational education] high priority. They assume that it is separate from general education, has little educational value, and should be replaced by a predominantly academic curriculum. At best, vocational courses are expected to provide stu-

**TABLE 4.8**   Vocational Education Courses Taken in High School

| Student Characteristics | Average Number of Courses* |
|---|---|
| Male | 4.25 |
| Female | 3.77 |
| White | 3.97 |
| Black | 4.33 |
| Hispanic | 3.97 |
| Asian | 3.15 |
| American Indian | 4.02 |
| Academic track | 2.22 |
| Vocational track | 9.12 |

*The number of courses is measured in Carnegie units, with one unit representing the completion of a 1-year course.

*Source:* Adapted from *Digest of Education Statistics,* by National Center for Education Statistics, 2001, Washington, DC: U.S. Government Printing Office.

dents who are not college bound with minimal training for low-status jobs at entry level" (Catri, 1998, p. 1).

Despite the concern over its status, some middle schools and most high schools offer students the opportunity to participate in vocational-technical education (see Table 4.8). These courses introduce students to career possibilities in business and industry and provide them with initial educational experiences needed for success. Career counseling for vocational-technical job options is also readily available at the high school level. Students at the middle school/junior high school level may have the opportunity for exploratory experiences in vocational-technical education as well. These programs introduce interested students to some of the possibilities available to them. Career guidance and counseling at this level also provide additional information regarding these job opportunities.

After reading about special education, bilingual education, gifted education, and vocational-technical education, spend a few moments thinking about the possibility of working in one of these settings. Have you had the opportunity to observe in or be involved with one of these programs? What do you see as some of the potential benefits and problems of working in specialized educational settings? Can you see yourself preparing for, and then teaching in, one or more of these programs? Why or why not?

**Reflective Journey 4.2**

## What are the alternatives to traditional public schools?

Although the school settings described above are the most common configurations found in schools today, students and their families are experiencing many alternative forms of education. Some of the more prominent options include magnet schools, charter schools, year-round schools, private schools, and alternative schools. Many of these programs are physically and administratively housed in the public schools, others have loose connections to public education, and yet others have no direct relationship. As you read about these various options, see if any are of particular interest to you as a site for your future teaching.

## Charter Schools and Teacher Decision Making

When individual charter schools are given the freedom to make decisions about how education should be run, some interesting options unfold. The Minnesota New Country School is one example.

Gigi Dobosenski is in her first year of teaching at Minnesota New Country School. In addition to the normal challenges of beginning teaching, she's also responsible for developing curriculum, recruiting new staff, evaluating the performance of her peers, serving as an advocate for the school in the community, and engaging in her share of school maintenance (Blair, 2002).

Ms. Dobosenski has taken on these additional roles because she is part owner of the nonprofit organization that was hired to run the charter school. The EdVisions Cooperative for whom she works has authorized her to participate in making most of the decisions that are traditionally made by school administrators.

The Minnesota New Country School, in addition to being a charter school, has taken steps to make teachers responsible for most of the decision making. Instead of having administrators who hire staff, evaluate them, select curriculum materials, and make most of the decisions about what should be taught and how, the teachers themselves are empowered by the school charter with these responsibilities.

### Research the Issue

Research this topic online using the links provided in the *Engage in the Debate* module for this chapter of the Companion Website. Link to the online source article by Blair (2002) and explore the information provided at the additional sites listed.

1. From your research, what are the benefits of getting teachers more involved in decision making?

2. What are some of the ways in which schools are involving teachers in the decision-making processes described?

### Explore Your Views

1. What do you see as potential problems that may occur when teachers get more involved in school-wide decision making?

2. Do you think teachers should be made more responsible for the decision making within schools? Why or why not?

 *To research this issue and submit your responses online, go to the Engage in the Debate module for Chapter 4 of the Companion Website for this text.*

*Source:* "Doing It Their Way: Teachers Make All Decisions at Cooperative Venture," by J. Blair, 2002, *Education Week,* March 27, pp. 1,14,15.

### Magnet Schools

**Magnet schools,** while providing students with a well-rounded education, tend to have specialized curricula. For example, magnet high schools often emphasize mathematics, science, or the arts and attract students from a relatively large geographic area interested in pursuing study in that specialty. During the 1970s, magnet schools became popular options in large urban areas primarily as a tool to reduce "White flight" from the inner city and to serve as a voluntary option to aid in desegregation efforts (Steel & Levine, 1994).

Magnet schools have proven to be a popular option for both students and their families. From just a few schools in the 1970s, their numbers have grown to more than 2,600 elementary and secondary schools serving approximately 1.5 million students (Black, 1996). One reason for their popularity is that parents and students have some control over the school attended. Although waiting lists are often long, the opportunity to choose a school with a specific area of emphasis is attractive to many. Teachers with skills and interests in the magnet school curriculum are also eager to get involved in these programs, making for a strong and motivated faculty.

## Charter Schools

The **charter school** movement began in the 1990s as another option for parents who wanted alternatives to the traditional public schools that could help boost their children's academic achievement. As of November 2001, 38 states had passed legislation allowing for the creation of charter schools (Center for Education Reform, 2001). By freeing up these schools from many of the local and state regulations currently in place and allowing families to choose this educational option, the expectation was that in 3 to 5 years these programs could show results that surpassed those of traditional schools. "The theory behind such changes is that the combined pressures of consumer choice and market competition will force education to shape up, in the same way that international competition spurred U.S. corporations to restructure themselves in the 1980s" (Olson, 2000, p. 24).

The growth in charter schools has been dramatic, with 2 schools operating during the 1992–1993 school year and approximately 2,500 programs in 2000–2001 (Nathan, 2002). One of the main reasons cited for this rapid growth is the desire to have an alternative to traditional programs, which were seen as lacking ingredients that could help students reach their true academic potential (*Education Week,* 2003). The second most common reason for starting a charter school was to better serve special populations of students who are currently underserved.

## Year-Round Schools

Another educational option that is gaining in popularity is the **year-round school** (see Figure 4.2). Districts that move to this model reorganize the academic calendar by breaking up the summer vacation into shorter, more frequent breaks throughout the school year. According to data collected by the National Association for Year-Round Education (2001), currently 3,011 schools operate on a year-round schedule and together they serve a total of more than 2 million students.

Three main reasons are cited for the move to year-round schools (White, 1999). The first is a *concern about student achievement.* Teachers have long been frustrated by the losses in learning that tend to occur over the traditional summer vacation. Younger children, especially, need to relearn at least a portion of what they had mastered in the previous academic year. Year-round schools are seen as a way to eliminate this problem. A second reason frequently cited is the *overcrowding of*

**Figure 4.2**   Sample Year-Round School Calendar

| | |
|---|---|
| *Early July* | School year begins. Students begin classes 2 days after teachers return. |
| *Mid-September* | Fall break, approximately 2 weeks. No school. |
| *October to Mid-December* | Remainder of fall term. |
| *Mid-December to New Year* | Christmas break. |
| *January to Mid-March* | Winter term. |
| *Mid-March to Mid-April* | Spring break. |
| *Mid-April to Late May* | Spring term. |
| *Late May to Early July* | Summer break. |

*Source:* Jefferson County Public Schools, Louisville, Kentucky. Retrieved July 24, 2002, from http://www.jefferson.k12.ky.us/Calendars/45-15cal.pdf

*classrooms.* School districts that are short on classroom space are giving year-round schools a try as one way to alleviate the space crunch. By operating on a staggered, multitrack schedule, schools can accommodate larger numbers of students in the same physical space. Finally, year-round schools give more opportunities to *work with students who fall behind.* Summer school offerings for students who are at risk of failing have extended the school year for many. Rather than promoting students before they are ready, these summer programs (often mandatory) are designed to give these students extra assistance to keep them from falling behind their peers.

### Private Schools

For much of American history, private schools were the most common option available to students and their families, especially at the secondary level. Throughout the 19th and 20th centuries, however, publicly funded education gradually became more plentiful and enrollments in private schools slowly declined. According to data from the National Association of Independent Schools (NAIS), currently about 25% of all schools in the United States are private and approximately 11% of all school-age children attend these schools (NAIS, 2001).

Private schools can be grouped broadly into two categories: those that have religious affiliation and those that do not. By far the largest percentage has religious affiliation. Catholic schools enroll the largest number in this category, with approximately 2.6 million students nationwide (National Catholic Educational Association, 2002). Other religious groups together serve an additional

**e x p l o r e   y o u r   b e l i e f s**

## Single-Sex Schools

Until recently, most single-sex schools were private institutions catering to wealthy parents able to afford what they consider a classic model of excellence in education. Title IX of the Education Amendments of 1972 is the primary reason there are very few publicly funded options. This federal mandate specifically prohibits any institution from receiving government money if the institution discriminates on the basis of sex. The issue is being revisited, however, by state and federal officials and growth may be seen in publicly funded single-sex schools (Davis, 2002).

Before promoting single-sex schools, however, it would make sense to ask about the benefits and drawbacks of this approach. Unfortunately, the limited research results available to date have come to mixed conclusions. Part of the problem is that the studies that do exist "tend to focus on women's colleges, elite private schools, Roman Catholic schools, or single-sex schools in faraway nations" (Viadero, 2002, p. 8).

Some examples of the mixed research results include a study by the American Association of University Women that found no clear evidence that single-sex education was any better that coeducation. Fred Mael, at the American Institutes of Research, on the other hand, found some evidence of academic and social benefits from single-sex schools. A recent study by the Australian Council for Educational Research also found indications of greater academic gains for students in single-sex schools (Viadero, 2002, p. 8).

### React and Reflect

1. Try to imagine yourself in a single-sex school. What do you think your reaction would be?
2. What do you see as the strengths and limitations of single-sex schooling?
3. Do you think single-sex schools would benefit boys or girls or both sexes? Why or why not?
4. Would you support the idea of increasing the numbers of public single-sex schools?

    *To explore this topic further and submit your reactions and reflections online, go to the Explore Your Beliefs module for Chapter 4 of the Companion Website for this text.*

*Sources:* "Department Aims to Promote Single-Sex Schools," by M. Davis, 2002, *Education Week*, May 15, pp. 24, 26; and "Evidence on Single-Sex Schooling Is Mixed," by D. Viadero, 2002, *Education Week*, June 12, p. 8.

1.7 million students. Schools without religious affiliation also en-rolled an estimated 1.7 million students in U.S. elementary and sec-ondary schools in 1999–2000 (NAIS, 2001).

## Alternative Schools

The 1960s and 1970s in America represented a time of awakening civil rights, a questioning of leadership and the status quo, and a period of growing concern for the effectiveness of all public insti-tutions. Schools, as a major public institution, came under fire for being uncaring and rule bound (Raywid, 1994). One attempt made during these years to rethink how schools should operate was the creation of programs that served as alternative places of learning for students who were unsuccessful in traditional settings.

One of the early problems encountered by **alternative schools** was the lack of a clear understanding of their purposes. Were these schools created to meet the needs of special populations of students that had specific educational needs not being met in the regular school system? Or were they in operation to provide alternative strategies for the delivery of instruction? In many cases, these pur-poses overlapped and led to an unclear sense of direction.

*Private schools are a valued option for some students and their families.*

Take a few moments to thoughtfully consider the different al-ternatives to traditional schooling presented in this section. Mag-net schools, charter schools, year-round schools, private schools, and alternative education are all possible settings that you may wish to consider for teaching opportunities. Which of these options do you find intriguing? What is it about them that you find attractive? Can you see yourself being happier and more fulfilled as a teacher in one or more of these options?

**Reflective Journey 4.3**

## What does schooling look like?

A significant decision that you will need to make early in your college career is the choice of an educational level that best fits your interests and talents. The most effective way to make this decision is by spending time observing and participating in schools. Ideally, you should spend several days each in prekindergarten, elementary, middle school, and high school class-rooms before narrowing your efforts to a specific educational level. Because this is such a time-consuming activity, however, it may be useful to first learn as much as you can from a "verbal tour" of four typical schools. Although each of the programs described in the following sub-sections is hypothetical, data from real schools were used in preparing these scenarios.

As you read about each school setting, try placing yourself in that situation as a new teacher. How would you feel about working with students at that level? Think about personal strengths and limitations that might make it easier or more difficult for you to work at this level. Some of the school settings described will be more attractive than others. Once you have narrowed the possibilities, make sure you spend time observing and participating in your preferred settings so that you can continue to refine your interests.

## Brookhaven Head Start Child Care Center

The Brookhaven Head Start Child Care Center has provided quality services to low-income chil-dren and their families for the past 7 years. It is one of eight centers in this community of 75,000 and is part of a growing number of Head Start programs that offer full-day child care for those who participate. Funded through a combination of federal, state, and local housing authority monies, Brookhaven is open from 6:30 A.M. until 6:30 P.M. 49 weeks of the year. Thirty-four 4- and 5-year-old children from low-income families are enrolled.

*Preschool programs can now be found in many elementary schools.*

A Head Start program supervisor for the community oversees the education curriculum and basic child services provided at each of the Head Start centers, including Brookhaven. In addition, the center supervisor coordinates student and family services on site. Three teachers work 40 hours each week planning, preparing, and implementing educational experiences for their students. Each teacher is also responsible for conducting regular home visits with 10 to 12 families. During these contacts, teachers share suggestions with parents about working with their children at home and identify resources to help meet a variety of family needs. An assistant to the center supervisor, four teaching assistants, and a cook are also employed at Brookhaven. Three times each year, the Interfaith Coalition sponsors a health and dental screening program. Children who are found to have medical or dental needs are referred to appropriate community services.

The Brookhaven Center consists of two large rooms that are organized into learning centers. Each center is equipped with toys and materials that children use during free-choice times throughout their school day. The learning centers include art, books, blocks, computers, writing materials, dramatic play materials, manipulatives, and music. Materials in each center are organized on low shelves so that children can easily access them and can readily return materials to their proper places at the end of their play times.

Sue Sandford has been a teacher at Brookhaven for the past 3 years. She has a bachelor's degree in elementary education and is working toward her endorsement in early childhood education. Sue spends 6 hours each day in the classroom working with children in the center (see Figure 4.3). In addition, she sets 2 hours aside for daily planning and the conducting of home

**Figure 4.3**   Sample Daily Schedule, Child Care Center

| | |
|---|---|
| 6:30–8:00 A.M. | Opening/safety checklist/setup/early morning snack/limited center activities |
| 8:00–9:00 A.M. | Learning Center choices |
| 9:00–10:00 A.M. | Cleanup, toileting, snack time, tooth brushing, transition to group time |
| 10:00–11:00 A.M. | Circle time, small-group times (language, math, science, gross motor), cleanup, cooperative group skill development |
| 11:00 A.M.–12:15 P.M. | Learning areas, large- and small-group activities, cleanup |
| 12:15–1:00 P.M. | Hand washing, lunch, cleanup |
| 1:00–2:30 P.M. | Tooth brushing, bathroom, nap preparation, nap time/quiet time |
| 2:30–3:15 P.M. | Outdoor time |
| 3:15–4:45 P.M. | Transition to classroom, Learning Center choices |
| 4:45–5:30 P.M. | Small motor activities, journals |
| 5:30–6:30 P.M. | Cleanup, story, departure |

visits with families participating in the Head Start Center programs. Although the center opens at 6:30 A.M., teachers stagger their times in the classroom and Sue is responsible for children beginning at 12:30 P.M. and remains until the center closes at 6:30 P.M.

## Trentwood Elementary School

Trentwood Elementary is a K–5 school with just over 300 students. It is nestled into a quiet neighborhood of predominantly lower middle class families. Some students are close enough to walk to school, but many ride school buses and begin arriving around 8:30 A.M. for the 8:55 A.M. through 3:30 P.M. school day. The school has 14 classroom teachers, 2 special education teachers, a music specialist, a physical education teacher, and 2 reading specialists. Years of teaching experience vary from 2 to 32, with the average being 18 years in the classroom. In addition, there are 9 part or full-time instructional assistants who provide support for classroom instruction, English as a Second Language (ESL), and special education. Other staff members include the school principal, secretary, school psychologist/student support specialist (two-thirds time), library/media specialist, library assistant, two cooks, two custodians, and a school nurse (1 day a week).

Although most teachers spend considerably more time than the minimum required in their contracts, they are expected to be in the elementary school building between 8:30 A.M. and 4 P.M. daily (see Figure 4.4). Planning lessons, preparing materials for classroom use, evaluating student performance, communicating with parents, and meeting with other teachers generally occur outside the regular school day. Steve Brenner, in his second year of teaching at Trentwood Elementary, is already involved in a number of extracurricular activities at the school. In addition to the biweekly staff meetings called by the school principal, he

# EDUCATION IN THE NEWS

## The Power of the Neighborhood School

The Village Academy, a privately funded community-based elementary school, opened in Delray Beach, Florida, in August 2000 with grades K–2. It is slated to gradually include grades 3–5 by adding one additional grade each year. The intent of this school was to alleviate the pressures of busing and to break the cycle of poverty for low-income minority children by providing them with a high-quality education in their own neighborhood. The expectations for students and teachers in this school are high. Higher demands are put on students' energy and time, 7 A.M. to 7 P.M. Monday through Friday and a half day on Saturday. In addition, students attend summer school for 6 to 8 weeks. Class sizes are kept at 15. As part of community outreach, courses in adult literacy, GED, training, community health center, and other social services are phased in over time.

### Critical Thinking Questions

1. A lot about The Village Academy is attractive, but Jonothan Kozol says it poses very deep, moral questions, challenges the dreams of Martin Luther King, and goes against the decisions represented in *Brown v. the Board of Education,* taking us back to *Plessy v. Ferguson*—separate but equal schools. Do you agree or disagree with this statement? Why? Why not?
2. Whose responsibility is the education of America's children?
3. What is the power of the neighborhood school?
4. Visit the Village Academy web page within the website of the Palm Beach School District to see where it is today. What initiatives has the school undertaken? Is the school reaching its goals? (http://www.palmbeach.k12.fl.us)

 *To submit your responses online, go to the Education in the News module for Chapter 4 of the Companion Website.*

**Figure 4.4**   Sample Elementary Schedule, Grade 3

| | |
|---|---|
| 8:55–9:45 A.M. | Opening, daily oral language, spelling |
| 9:45–10:30 A.M. | Mathematics, PE (Monday, Wednesday) |
| 10:30–10:45 A.M. | Recess |
| 10:45 A.M.–12:00 P.M. | Literacy block |
| 12:00–12:45 P.M. | Lunch |
| 12:45–1:45 P.M. | Sustained silent reading, library (Friday) |
| 1:45–2:45 P.M. | Science, PE (Thursday) |
| 2:45–3:30 P.M. | Social studies, music (Tuesday, Thursday) |

is a member of the professional development committee, which helps plan the in-service training activities that will occur throughout the year. Steve also participates in the technology and literacy study group and meets once a month with fellow teachers to collaborate and plan for these two important parts of the curriculum. In addition, he is involved in individualized education plan (IEP) and multidisciplinary team (MDT) meetings for children with special needs. Finally, Steve organizes an after-school art club that meets for 6 weeks every spring. With the exception of music and physical education, Steve teaches all subjects to his class of 26 eight-year-olds.

## Hoover Middle School

Hoover Middle School is one of the older buildings in the school district, having been built in 1953. It was originally constructed as the high school for a community of approximately 15,000. As the city grew and needs changed, Hoover eventually became a middle school and now houses approximately 650 sixth-, seventh-, and eighth-grade students. The staff includes 28 teachers, 4 special educators, 1 library media specialist, 1 counselor, 2 administrators (principal and assistant principal), 2 certified support staff (a psychologist and a speech and language pathologist), and 15 classified support personnel (instructional assistants, office personnel, custodians, and food service staff).

Although the building is showing signs of wear, the teachers and staff at Hoover are enthusiastic and motivated. They have adopted a "teaming" model and six interdisciplinary teams work cooperatively to teach integrated studies (language arts and social studies), science, and mathematics. Students with special needs are included within each of the six groups and special education teachers are assigned to each grade level to support students with disabilities who have been placed in the regular education classroom.

Teachers at Hoover Middle School are contracted to be in the school from 8:00 A.M. through 3:30 P.M. daily, with lunch breaks and planning periods free from student responsibilities (see Figure 4.5). Each interdisciplinary team meets for 2 hours each week outside the regular school day to jointly plan future activities. Meetings of the entire school staff are held after school on the third Tuesday of each month.

Mary Franklin is in her 12th year of teaching at Hoover. Her teaching responsibilities include language arts, reading, and social studies. Mary is part of the Cypress interdisciplinary team and works with five other science, mathematics, and special education teachers to implement an integrated curriculum for just over 100 seventh-grade students in the school. In addition to her responsibilities in the classroom, Mary has chosen to get involved in several

**Figure 4.5**   Sample Teaching Schedule, Middle School

| | |
|---|---|
| 8:25–9:33 A.M. | Block I (integrated language arts and social studies) |
| 9:37–10:41 A.M. | Block II (integrated language arts and social studies) |
| 10:45–11:49 A.M. | Block III (integrated language arts and social studies) |
| 11:54 A.M.–12:24 P.M. | Lunch |
| 12:29–1:00 P.M. | Block IV (reading) |
| 1:04–2:09 P.M. | Block V (integrated language arts and social studies) |
| 2:13–3:02 P.M. | Planning period (students in enrichment activities) |

extracurricular activities. She is head coach for the track team, assists with girls' basketball, and is part of the faculty group that coordinates the after-school study lab. Mary receives extra pay for each of these assignments and has a supplementary contract with her school district for the delivery of these services.

## Sentinel High School

Constructed in 1966 to meet the growing educational needs of a suburban community, Sentinel is now a large campus housing more than 1,600 students in grades 9 through 12. Sentinel has four full-time administrators, including the school principal, two assistant principals, and an activities and athletics director. The 82 certificated faculty are organized by area of expertise, with 3 in business education, 5 in the career/counseling center, 11 English educators, 3 faculty in family and consumer education, 6 in the fine arts (music, art, and drama), 7 world language educators, 1 library media and technology specialist, 9 mathematics faculty, 5 faculty in physical education, 8 science educators, 7 social studies instructors, 2 technology faculty, 7 staff in the specialized instruction department, and 8 faculty in interdepartmental instructional programs (alternative school, driver education, ESL, drug counseling, and highly capable learners). An additional 38 classified staff support the educational efforts of the school (secretaries, food services staff, custodians, interpreters, and instructional assistants).

Whereas a traditional high school schedule typically consists of the same six or seven 50-minute classes each day, students at Sentinel participate in what is generally referred to as partial block scheduling (see Figure 4.6). In exchange for longer class periods of 1 hour and 50 minutes two days a week, students take only half of their scheduled subjects on those days. For the rest of the week, students follow a more traditional schedule in which all of their subjects are taught.

Jeff Conners is in his eighth year of teaching social studies at Sentinel High School. After receiving his secondary education certification and a bachelor's degree in history, Jeff taught for 5 years at the middle school level before transferring to the high school. Along with the rest of the school staff, he is contracted to be in the school from 7:15 A.M. until 2:45 in the afternoon. Despite being in his second decade of teaching, Jeff still finds it difficult to leave the building before 4:30 P.M. each day. In addition to class preparation, grading, and communicating with parents, he has biweekly meetings with other members of the social studies faculty, is currently serving on the Task Force on Student Violence, and is chairing the school's efforts to revise the parent handbook sent out each year. Jeff currently teaches one period of economics, two U.S. history classes, one period of world history, and a class in government. This semester, the second period is his planning and preparation time.

**Figure 4.6**   Weekly Schedule, Sentinel High School

| Schedule A | Period 1 | Break | Period 3 | Period 5 | | |
|---|---|---|---|---|---|---|
| 1, 3, 5 (Tuesday) | 7:45– 9:35 A.M. | 9:35– 9:55 A.M. | 9:55 A.M.– 12:20 P.M. (includes lunch) | 12:25– 2:15 P.M. | | |
| **Schedule B** | Period 2 | Break | Period 4 | Period 6 | | |
| 2, 4, 6 (Wednesday) | 7:45– 9:35 A.M. | 9:35– 9:55 A.M. | 9:55 A.M.– 12:20 P.M. (includes lunch) | 12:25– 2:15 P.M. | | |
| **Schedule C** | Period 1 | Period 2 | Period 3 | Period 4 | Period 5 | Period 6 |
| Monday, Thursday, Friday | 7:45– 8:39 A.M. | 8:45– 9:44 A.M. | 9:50– 10:44 A.M. | 10:50 A.M.– 12:14 P.M. (includes lunch) | 12:20– 1:14 P.M. | 1:20– 2:15 P.M. |

## Summary

In this chapter, three organizing questions were presented to help you develop a better understanding of schools today:

### How are schools organized?

There are four major levels of schooling and four additional groupings of specialized educational experiences found in most school districts:

- Early childhood education
- Elementary schools
- Junior high and middle schools
- Senior high schools
- Special education (Praxis II, topic Ia)
- Bilingual education (Praxis II, topic Ia)
- Gifted education (Praxis II, topic Ia)
- Vocational-technical education

### What are the alternatives to traditional public schools?

Virtually every school district has a number of alternatives to traditional formats for schools, including these:

- Magnet schools
- Charter schools

- Year-round schools
- Private schools
- Alternative schools

## What does schooling look like?

To give you a better understanding of what schools are actually like, four hypothetical situations were described:

- Brookhaven Head Start Child Care Center
- Trentwood Elementary School
- Hoover Middle School
- Sentinel High School

## Key Terms

| | |
|---|---|
| alternative schools | magnet schools |
| bilingual education | middle schools |
| charter schools | preschool |
| day care | self-contained classrooms |
| early childhood education | senior high schools |
| elementary education | special education |
| gifted education | special needs preschools |
| Head Start | vocational-technical education |
| junior high school | year-round school |

## Reflective Journey: Online Journal

 Use the questions for thought and reflection highlighted throughout the chapter to help guide your personal journey of reflection and professional development as a teacher. To complete your journal entries online, go to the *Reflective Journey* module for this chapter of the Companion Website.

## PRAXIS Test Preparation Activities

To review an online chapter case study, test your understanding of chapter topics and concepts, and begin preparing for the Praxis II: Principles of Learning and Teaching examination, go to the *Praxis Test Preparation* module for this chapter of the Companion Website.

## InTASC Becoming a Reflective Practitioner

To complete these activities and submit your responses online, go to the *Becoming a Reflective Practitioner* module for this chapter of the Companion Website.

## How are schools organized?

### Review Questions

1. What are the student ages and groupings within early childhood education?
2. How is the typical middle school different from a junior high school?
3. What is a comprehensive high school?
4. In what ways do bilingual education programs assist LEP students to learn?

### Field Experience

Select what you currently think to be your *first choice* for a teaching position (elementary, middle school, secondary, special education, etc.) and then spend as much time as you can (two or three full days would be best) in the teaching setting you select. Study students at that level, thinking particularly about how well you see yourself relating to them. Take time to review the materials available for the subject(s) being taught and think about how interesting this content is to you. Pay particular attention to the role of the teacher and how you see yourself fitting into a similar position. Discuss what you find with others.

### Building Your Portfolio: *Special Education*

**INTASC Standard 3.** Whether or not you choose to become a special education teacher, you will need to be aware of the many issues surrounding working with children with special needs. For a level of education that interests you, contact an appropriate school and ask for written information about its special education programs. After reviewing these materials, write a one- or two-page summary of special education efforts in that setting.

## What are the alternatives to traditional public schools?

### Review Questions

1. How is a charter school different from a regular public school?

2. Why are year-round schools becoming more popular?

3. What kinds of students are typically served in an alternative school?

### Field Experience

Choose one of the alternatives to traditional public schools described in this chapter and spend some time in a representative program. What do you like and dislike about this option? What are the strengths and weaknesses for both students and teachers? Can you see yourself teaching in this setting? Discuss what you find with others.

### Building Your Portfolio: *Alternative Education*

**INTASC Standard 4.** Do some research on one of the alternative education options presented in this chapter. This may include spending time in a local program, collecting written materials from local and state options, and doing an Internet search for articles and websites about existing programs. Once you have collected these data, summarize your findings in a short paper describing the strengths and limitations of this form of alternative education.

## What does schooling look like?

### Review Questions

1. What differentiates a child care center from a preschool?

2. What are the major differences between teaching at the elementary and middle school levels?

3. Describe block scheduling at the high school level.

### Building Your Portfolio: *Public School Portrait*

**INTASC Standard 9.** Choose the level of schooling of most interest to you at the current time and make a careful analysis of a public school at that level. In as much detail as possible, describe the physical setting (age of the building, size, location, etc.), the staff (teachers, administrators, specialized staff, support staff, etc.), and the student population (number, diversity of students, economic levels of families, etc.) for inclusion in your portfolio.

## Suggested Readings

Gordon, H. (1999). *The history and growth of vocational education in America.* Boston: Allyn and Bacon. This book details the legislation and theory that has shaped the history and growth of vocational education in the United States.

Henniger, M. (2002). *Teaching young children: An introduction* (2nd ed.). Upper Saddle River, NJ: Merrill/Prentice Hall. This book provides a description of children and families during the early childhood years. It presents an overview of teaching and learning at this level.

Piirto, J. (1999). *Talented children and adults: Their development and education* (2nd ed.). Upper Saddle River, NJ: Merrill/Prentice Hall. This book provides a detailed description of the students who are categorized as gifted and talented and the teaching strategies being used by teachers to assist them in their development.

Turnbull, A., Turnbull, R., Shank, M., Smith, S., & Leal, D. (2002). *Exceptional lives: Special education in today's schools* (3rd ed.). Upper Saddle River, NJ: Merrill/Prentice Hall. This text provides a thorough overview of special education and prepares future teachers for their role in the education of students with special needs.

# chapter 5

## The Teaching Profession

If you choose a career in teaching, you are doing more than just committing to doing your best to educate the students walking through your classroom door. You are entering a profession, with all the rights and responsibilities associated with it. In this chapter, you will learn more about teaching as a profession. Four questions will guide your thinking.

### Focus Questions

- Is teaching a profession?
- What professional organizations exist?
- How is teacher professionalism changing?
- What are my professional responsibilities?

Trina and her
husband Rod, both
teachers in the local
schools, are attending a
neighborhood Christmas party.
The conversation, as it often does in this
kind of social situation, has focused on the latest
developments in people's lives at work. The guests' occupations are varied and include a carpenter, nurse, bank
teller, lawyer, grocery clerk, medical doctor, physical therapist, and a salesman. A rather natural human
tendency in this situation is to mentally compare the benefits, drawbacks, and status of your occupation with
the others being discussed. During the conversation, Marcie, a doctor in general practice, talks about the
growing complexities of childbirth from a physician's perspective. Suzanne describes the back strain she is
getting from standing all day in her job as a grocery clerk. Randy shares some insights on the latest issues in
corporate law, his specialty. David, a bank teller, describes the humorous interactions he has had recently with
people regarding money. At one point in the conversation, someone mentions the upcoming statewide school
testing efforts and both Trina and Rod share their concerns about the school district's overreliance on
standardized tests to assess student progress.

**Reflective
Journey 5.1**

If you were a participant in the above party, how would you compare teaching with the other occupations identified? Based on its importance to society and status among other professions, where do you see education fitting? How do you think others at the party might view Trina and Rod's careers in teaching when compared with the other occupations represented? In all likelihood, both you and they would see teaching as closer in status and benefits to the nurse and bank teller than to the lawyer or doctor.

While very few people deny the critical importance of education to a healthy American society, the professional status of a career in teaching is not as high as it should be. The expression "those who can't, teach" is a highly inaccurate, but widely held sentiment many people believe to be true. Despite the many challenges presented, the common perception is that teaching is a rather easy job that nearly anyone with a little training can do well. For this reason and several others described below, the profession of teaching is still "a work in progress."

## Is teaching a profession?

Before specifically looking at teaching to determine if it is a profession, you should first be aware of the common traits that all professions share. Some writers who have studied this issue identified a list of common characteristics of professions, while others looked at the complexities of the work performed as a means of comparing occupations. Salary and status also add important insights into the professional status of an occupation. This information will give you a starting point for an analysis of teaching as a profession.

### Defining a Profession

Have you ever stopped to wonder what makes an occupation a **profession?** Most people, for example, would consider the practice of medicine an important profession. Fewer, however, would consider bricklaying a professional occupation. Despite the bricklayer's obvious talents and the value of the work performed, bricklayers are usually considered highly skilled laborers rather than professionals. But what factors have led our society to view doctors as part of a profession while talented bricklayers are not? Is it status, salary, professional preparation, or some combination of these and other characteristics? Is it the work they do or the salary they earn? The seemingly simple task of defining a profession is actually a complex one.

**Characteristics of a profession.** Based on their research, observations, and discussions with others, several writers have developed a set of common characteristics for all professions (see Figure 5.1). Although the lists that have been generated are somewhat different, the following are frequently listed as characteristics of a profession (Rowan, 1994; Webb, Metha, & Jordan, 2000). A profession first of all *requires strong intellectual skills.* Members of professions must use their intellectual abilities to investigate issues, problem solve, and effectively communicate their findings to others. A profession also *provides an essential service.* Professions

*Professions provide an essential service.*

**Figure 5.1**   Characteristics of a Profession

*A profession:*

- Requires strong intellectual skills.
- Provides an essential service.
- Requires extensive specialized training.
- Allows autonomy in decision making.
- Emphasizes service to its clients.
- Identifies professional standards of behavior.
- Assumes individuals are responsible for their own actions and decisions.
- Engages in self-governance.

offer services to clients that are vital to their health and well-being. A third characteristic of a profession is that it *requires extensive specialized training.* Several years of education and practical experience with the essential elements of the profession are necessary for entry. A profession also *allows autonomy in decision making.* Professionals are given the freedom to apply their knowledge of the profession to the specific requirements of individual clients in making decisions about what is best for them. A profession also *emphasizes service to its clients.* Professionals dedicate themselves to meeting the needs of the people they serve. They are obligated to always do what is in their clients' best interests. Another characteristic of a profession is that it *identifies standards of behavior.* Professions have developed codes of ethical conduct that clearly identify what is acceptable and unacceptable in interacting with clients. A profession *assumes individuals are responsible for their own actions and decisions.* Members of a profession accept the fact that they are personally responsible for their own behavior in relationship to their clients. Finally, a profession *engages in self-governance.* Professional groups see themselves as responsible for independently monitoring admission, retention, and exclusion from the profession.

**Complexity of work.**   Another approach to assessing the professional status of any occupation is to look at the complexity of the work being performed (Rowan, 1994). The *Dictionary of Occupational Titles,* published by the U.S. Department of Labor (1991), identifies three broad areas that influence work complexity. The first of these is the complexity of *worker functions.* Occupations differ in terms of the interactions that workers have with data, people, and things. Engineers, for example, have highly complex interactions with data, while social workers score most highly in interacting with people, and those employed in the skilled trades such as electricians score highly in interactions with things. A second measure used in comparing occupations is the *general intellectual and linguistic skills* required. Most people would believe, for example, that lawyers need higher levels of reasoning and language skills in their work than grocery clerks. Similarly, an accountant's daily activities would typically require greater abilities in mathematics than would a salesman's. A final difference between occupations is the *specific vocational preparation* needed. Longer periods of training and education indicate a greater degree of complexity in the work of the occupation.

Applying the above rating scales to different occupations gives useful information about the complexity of work required for each. Although no occupation scores at the top in all areas, those that are generally considered professions score highly in most areas. Economists, for example, are typically considered part of a profession and tend to receive high scores in all areas. On the other hand, those occupations that receive low scores in most areas (such as a fast-food worker) are typically thought of as nonprofessional.

**Salary and status.** Although salary and status aren't the sole criteria used to determine professions, they are often viewed as indicators of how others perceive specific occupations. Higher salaries usually accompany professions and reflect the values placed on these occupations by society. For example, the salaries for leaders in business far exceed those earned by bank tellers or laborers. Whereas comparing salaries across occupations is a relatively easy task, occupational status is more difficult to accurately assess. It is often the more subtle statements and interactions that give clues as to the status of an occupation. For example, you might listen intently to the opinions of someone you consider a professional while only partially hearing those of someone you consider nonprofessional.

## explore your beliefs

## Performance Pay for Teachers

One strategy that is being tried in some school districts to motivate teachers to engage in effective instruction is to offer them pay increases for improved student performance. In theory, this monetary payoff would prompt teachers to work harder to assist students in their learning. Teacher performance, as measured by student achievement, is then rewarded through higher salaries.

Performance pay for teachers is a concept that has been talked about for many years, but tried in only a few school districts. Recently, this notion has gained momentum and is being directly connected with attempts to improve student performance as measured through standardized test results. For example, "at the third National Education Summit in 1999, the assembled governors and business leaders resolved to set up a system of 'rewards and consequences' for teachers—'competitive salary structures' that will tie teacher salaries to student achievement and provide salary credit for professional development only when it is standards-based" (Holt, 2001, p. 313).

Although business leaders and many political figures support the concept of performance pay, many educators tend to dislike the approach as being divisive and nonproductive. "Of all the consequences of the standards movement, pay-by-performance will be the most destructive: of education, of teachers' careers, of students' opportunities. The U.S. would be unwise to ignore the lessons of history" (Holt, 2001, p. 316).

### React and Reflect

1. What motivates you to do good work? Make a list of the five most important motivators for you to do good work. Is money an effective tool to stimulate your performance?

2. Consider the comments of Maurice Holt, the author of the source article, that pay for performance would be the most destructive result of the standards movement for education, teachers' careers, and students' opportunities. Do you agree with this statement? What are the positives and negatives of linking student performance on standardized tests to increased salaries for teachers? Is this the best way to measure teacher performance, or do you feel that other factors are more important or effective?

3. Do you think teachers should be given pay increases based on their ability to raise student scores on standardized tests? Why or why not? Should teachers receive reduced pay if their students fail to achieve required test scores?

    *To explore this topic further and submit your reactions and reflections online, go to the Explore Your Beliefs module for Chapter 5 of the Companion Website for this text.*

*Source:* "Performance Pay for Teachers: The Standards Movement's Last Stand?" by M. Holt, 2001, *Phi Delta Kappan, 83*(4), pp. 312–316.

## Teaching as a Profession

Although many good reasons exist for categorizing teaching as a professional occupation, most of those who have studied this issue in more depth would suggest that education has not yet fully achieved that status. Etzioni (1969), for example, called teaching a *semi-profession*. Howsam, Corrigan, Denemark, and Nash (1976) identified teaching as an *emerging profession*. More recently, Goodlad (1990) suggested that teaching should be considered a *not-quite profession*. Whatever it is called and despite its many advances, most would agree that teaching still falls short of its goal of being accepted as a profession.

**Historical perspectives.**  Throughout the history of American education, teaching has slowly but steadily moved toward greater professionalism. In colonial days, teachers had no formal teacher preparation and frequently knew little more than the students they taught. Many viewed education as merely a stepping stone to a better position. Salaries were very low, and often were no better than wages paid for common manual labor (Cubberley, 1934).

By the mid-1800s, teachers began to receive specialized training before entering the classroom. Teacher education institutions referred to as **normal schools** became more common across the United States. Initially, the education received there by future teachers was exclusively in the academic disciplines and provided no instruction regarding the principles of good teaching. The salaries of teachers remained low, exemplifying the low status of education.

Following the Civil War, teacher preparation continued to improve. The growth in numbers of secondary schools led to an increasing demand for teachers with strong academic preparation. In addition, an expansion of the knowledge regarding teaching and learning led to the gradual inclusion of this content in teacher education programs.

The 20th century saw additional progress made toward teacher professionalism. The length of teacher preparation programs slowly moved from 2 to 4 years, and by the 1950s the requirement of at least a 4-year college degree for teaching was common. National professional organizations such as the National Education Association and the American Federation of Teachers grew in size and number. These organizations further promoted rigorous teacher preparation programs, lobbied for better salaries and benefits, and developed guidelines for professional conduct (Pulliam & Van Patten, 1999).

**Arguments for teaching as a profession.**  A strong case can be made for considering teaching a profession. It has many of the characteristics described earlier that are common to all professions and has a high degree of complexity in the work required. One reason for considering teaching a profession is that it *requires strong intellectual skills*. The reasoning, mathematics, and language skills required of teachers compare well to other selected occupations. Particularly in the areas of reasoning and language, teachers need intellectual skills similar to those of other professions. Reformers of teacher education have recognized this need for strong intellectual skills and have helped implement a steady rise in the academic requirements for entering and exiting teacher education programs (National Center for Education Statistics, 2001). Another argument is that *teaching involves complex human interactions*. In research comparisons with other occupations, teachers' human interaction skills are rated as more complex than those of accountants, registered nurses, and secretaries, but somewhat less complex than those of physicians and lawyers (Rowan, 1994). A third rationale for considering teaching to be a profession is that *teaching requires extensive specialized training*. The requirements for teachers have become more complex during the past several decades, making teaching comparable to many other professions in the length of its vocational preparation. It should be obvious that *teaching provides an essential service*. While children learn from a variety of people and circumstances, teachers pass on information that is essential for healthy growth and development. A teacher's specialized training helps make the sharing of this

## The Story of an Incognegro

Amber Musser was an African American student at Harvard University. She saw herself "as a solitary black face in a sea of white, I am an incognegro" (Musser, 2000, p. 1). Using a play on words, Amber saw herself as moving through Harvard incognito, with her true identity hidden or disguised. Despite her many efforts to share her heritage and "blackness" with others, she believed that her peers truly did not recognize or understand her.

Amber's life history is full of stories about her Caribbean heritage and how it was misunderstood by others. In elementary school, for example, the first time she lost a tooth in class everyone crowded around to see what color her blood would be. It was assumed by her peers that it would be much darker than theirs. Amber also talks about one of her first memories of being called *Black*. She responded by indicating that the asphalt was Black, but that her skin color was tan. Amber was beginning to learn that others didn't see things the same way she did.

Race became a conscious issue for her in high school when she moved to a new school. As with all students her age, friendships were critically important to Amber. Luckily, she was able to establish a close friendship with another Black student and in time came to know her Black friends. They all ate lunch together at a table dubbed "Little Africa." But through this experience she also began to realize that because of her Black friends, White students were hesitant to spend time with her. Timid hellos and brief conversations were the extent of Amber's interactions with others in the school. While there was no overt racism, there was also little opportunity for Amber to share her true self with others whose skin color was different from hers. She was moving through her schooling as an incognegro.

### Explore and Reflect

Learn more about life as an African American student by reading the source article by Musser (2000) and reviewing other online resources provided in the *Reflect on Diversity* module for Chapter 5 of the Companion Website.

1. Reflect back on your own school experiences. Do you remember attending classes with students whose skin color was different from yours? Did you get to know any of these students well enough to feel that you knew their true identity or did they pass through your life incognito? What either allowed you to make meaningful connections or got in the way of these needed interactions?

2. What is the role of the teacher in creating opportunities to learn more about the similarities and differences that exist among students? Should this be a part of a professional educator's responsibilities?

 *To explore this topic further and submit your reflections online, go to the Reflect on Diversity module for Chapter 5 of the Companion Website for this text.*

*Source:* "Confessions of an Incognegro," by A. Musser, 2000, *Diversity and Distinction*, Winter 2000, pp. 1–4. Retrieved June 17, 2002, from http://www.hcs.harvard.edu/~dnd/pages/archives/2000/winter/incognegro.html

knowledge both efficient and exciting. Finally, *teaching has identified professional standards of behavior.* Several codes of ethical conduct guide the practicing teacher. The best known example comes from the National Education Association (1975).

**Arguments against teaching as a profession.** Although much progress has been made, more work must be done before educators can truly be considered part of a profession. Several arguments are frequently cited as reasons for considering the teaching profession a work in progress. The first of these is that *teaching requires only moderate specialized training.* Although teacher preparation has grown stronger over time, its length and intellectual rigor still lag behind that of many other professions. The competition for entrance into teacher education programs and later into the teaching ranks has also typically been minimal, leading many to question the qualifications of new teachers. The relatively recent adoption of standardized testing for entrance into, and exit from, teacher training programs is an attempt to remedy this situation (Latham, Gitamer, & Ziomek, 1999).

A second reason often cited for education's lack of professional status is that *teaching allows limited autonomy in decision making.* Although it is true that teachers make many decisions each day that impact the lives of students and their families, they frequently have limited input into the overall directions of teaching and learning. In the medical profession, doctors make independent decisions about medicines and medical procedures based on an understanding of the symptoms and past histories of individual patients. Teachers, on the other hand, must work within the confines of school policies, state regulations, and federal mandates as they work to meet the needs of their students.

In addition, many would suggest that education is still developing as a profession because *teaching has minimal self-governance.* Admission criteria for teacher education programs are typically created and monitored by state education agencies with little input from teachers themselves. Similarly, retention in the teaching ranks is typically based on the observations and evaluations of local school administrators based on school or district policies. Removing ineffective teachers from the classroom is often a very difficult task once tenure has been achieved. Legal proceedings that substantiate grossly inappropriate actions on the part of the teacher are generally the only way in which tenured teachers can be removed.

Finally, full status as a profession eludes education partly because *the salaries and status of teaching remain relatively low.* As indicated in Chapter 3, although teacher salaries have improved, they tend to be lower than those for occupations requiring similar skills and having equivalent levels of responsibility. Both beginning and average salaries for teachers lag behind those of other comparable occupations (see Figure 5.2). In addition, there is evidence that U.S. teachers' salaries lag behind those of educators in other countries (Hoff, 2000). The status of teaching in America is often closely linked to the perceived performance of students (Bracey, 1999). When compared with students in other countries, Americans score lower on several measures of achievement. Because of this, many assume that teachers are doing a less-than-adequate job in the classroom. Consequently, the status of teaching is lowered in the eyes of many.

**Figure 5.2**   Beginning Salaries for Selected Occupations

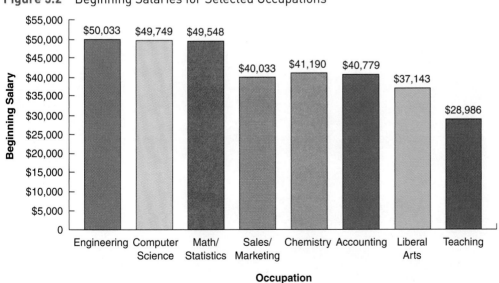

*Source:* From *Survey & Analysis of Teacher Salary Trends 2001,* by Nelson, F. H., Drown, R., & Gould, J. (2002). Washington, D.C.: American Federation of Teachers, AFL-CIO: Reprinted with permission.

**Reflective Journey 5.2**

After reading about the arguments for and against teaching as a profession, how would you describe it? What do you see as the most significant reasons for identifying teachers as professionals? What must yet be done to further the development of the teaching profession? When reflecting on your personality and skills, can you see yourself as a professional educator? Why or why not?

## What professional organizations exist?

Although teaching may lack several characteristics of a true profession, there is no shortage of professional education organizations designed to provide information, leadership, and support to teachers at all levels. There are literally hundreds of different national organizations associated with education. Most hold an annual national meeting where members come to learn more about various aspects of education and to network with others in the field. In addition, many organizations publish materials related to teaching and learning, and spend considerable time and energy advocating at all levels on behalf of students and teachers.

Two professional organizations that you will become familiar with as a teacher are the National Education Association (NEA) and the American Federation of Teachers (AFT). These two organizations strive to improve the professional lives of all teachers. Each organization has two major purposes. One is to serve as a strong teacher union, with collective bargaining, strikes, and sanctions used to better the working conditions of all teachers. The other is to assist in the continuing professional development of all teachers through the sponsorship of local, regional, and national conferences and the development of timely publications on issues related to education.

In addition to membership in either the NEA or AFT, you will want to be aware of and participate in a variety of other professional organizations. Generally, these specialty organizations focus more on identifying and disseminating information on excellence in curriculum and instruction rather than the promotion of better working conditions for teachers. You will probably want to be a member of one or more of the associations that focus on a specific age group (such as middle school), a subject matter area (such as mathematics or physical education), a specialty area (such as gifted education or technology), or of organizations that take a more general approach that appeals to a wide spectrum of educators.

*Professional organizations provide learning opportunities.*

## National Education Association

By far the largest professional organization for teachers, the National Education Association is a complex institution serving more than 2.7 million members (NEA, 2002). Although teachers are the most prominent affiliates of the NEA, administrators, teacher aides, professors, guidance counselors, librarians, and college students are also involved. Operating at the national, state, and local levels, the NEA exerts a powerful influence on teachers and schools.

**Services provided.**   The NEA offers a wealth of services to teachers and others. In addition to publishing numerous books and pamphlets on educational topics, the organization regularly produces *NEA Today, Today's Education,* and the *NEA Research Bulletin* to update members on current issues in education. The NEA also has personnel who give local affiliates and members assistance with their collective bargaining and lobbying efforts. Finally, members can receive benefits such as life and health insurance coverage, credit cards, and mortgages through the national organization.

**Central purpose.**   The National Education Association was founded in 1857 to "elevate the character and advance the interests of the profession of teaching and to promote the cause of education in the United States" (NEA, 2002). To further this goal, the NEA sees itself as a leader in the school reform efforts of the past and present. The association promotes the importance of every student having access to a quality education in a safe and caring setting. The NEA's central purpose has led to active involvement in politics at the local, state, and national levels. Because of its size and the quality of its membership, the NEA has had a significant impact on political campaigns and issues ranging from teacher salaries and benefits to such topics as providing public funds for private schooling.

## American Federation of Teachers

The American Federation of Teachers is somewhat younger and smaller than the NEA. Founded in 1916, the AFT currently has about 1 million members, many of whom are teaching in key urban areas such as Chicago and New York. The organization is affiliated with the AFL-CIO and sees itself as an important part of the American labor movement. The mission statement of the AFT gives as its purpose

> to improve the lives of our members and their families, to give voice to their legitimate
> professional, economic and social aspirations, to strengthen the institutions in which we work,
> to improve the quality of the services we provide, to bring together all members to assist and
> support one another and to promote democracy, human rights and freedom in our union, in our
> nation and throughout the world. (AFT, 2002)

**Union roots.**   Over the years, the AFT has unflinchingly viewed itself as a labor union for teachers and has worked hard to improve their working conditions. Collective bargaining and strikes (when necessary) are used to negotiate increasingly better teacher contracts. Though sometimes accused of being unprofessional and too concerned with issues benefiting teachers, the AFT has been very successful in improving the salaries, benefits, and general working conditions of the teachers it serves.

**Current directions.**   While maintaining its involvement in union activities, the AFT has broadened its focus in recent years to include other interests. It is now very much an advocate for a variety of educational reforms. Examples of current interests include the following: providing quality health care in school settings, improving the status and qualifications of paraprofessionals, identifying world-class standards for schools, involving higher education in raising academic standards, and supporting the National Board for Professional Teaching Standards (AFT, 2002).

| TABLE 5.1 Professional Organizations for Teachers | |
|---|---|
| **Type** | **Examples** |
| Educational level | National Association for the Education of Young Children (birth–age 8)<br>National Middle School Association |
| Subject matter | National Council of Teachers of Mathematics<br>National Council for the Social Studies<br>National Council of Teachers of English |
| Specialty | National Association for Gifted Children<br>Council for Exceptional Children<br>National Association for Multicultural Education |
| Generalist | Association for Supervision and Curriculum Development<br>Phi Delta Kappa International |

## Other Professional Organizations

In addition to the NEA and AFT, four other types of professional organizations are available that you may want to join (see Table 5.1). One group of associations focuses on a specific educational level. Others have a subject matter focus. A third group of organizations has a specialty focus, such as the Council for Exceptional Children and the National Association for Gifted Children. A final type of professional organization can best be categorized as generalist and appeals to a broad range of educators. None of these specialty organizations would be considered a union; instead, they see themselves as groups of educators with common interests who communicate through regularly scheduled conferences and publications.

**Organizations for specific educational levels.** Because there are many common issues associated with teaching at specific grade levels, educators have created a variety of professional organizations to meet their shared needs and interests. For example, early childhood educators who work with prekindergarten and primary children often join the National Association for the Education of Young Children (NAEYC). With more than 100,000 members nationally, NAEYC "exists for the purpose of leading and consolidating the efforts of individuals and groups working to achieve healthy development and constructive education for all young children. Membership is open to all who share a desire to serve and act on behalf of the needs and rights of young children" (NAEYC, 2002). Similar professional organizations exist for elementary, middle school, and high school teachers.

**Subject matter organizations.** Teachers at all educational levels also have interests in specific subject matter areas and find that joining a professional organization with a subject matter focus is useful. For example, if you choose to be an elementary educator and spend a significant part of your school day engaged in reading instruction, the International Reading Association (IRA) would be a good choice for a subject matter specialty organization. As the title suggests, this organization focuses on the many issues surrounding the teaching of reading. The association publishes several journals, including *Reading Teacher* which discusses many issues relevant to the elementary school classroom. Organizations like the IRA are available for every subject matter area taught in the public schools.

**Specialty associations.** If you specialize in some aspect of education, you can also expect to find professional organizations to meet your needs and interests. For example, there are associations for special educators, bilingual teachers, teachers of the gifted and talented, and vocational-technical educators. The Council for Exceptional Children (CEC) exemplifies these associations:

> The Council for Exceptional Children (CEC) is the largest international professional organization dedicated to improving educational outcomes for individuals with exceptionalities, students with disabilities, and/or the gifted. CEC advocates for appropriate governmental policies, sets professional standards, provides continual professional development, advocates for newly and historically underserved individuals with exceptionalities, and helps professionals obtain conditions and resources necessary for effective professional practice. (CEC, 2002)

**Generalist organizations.** Several professional associations appeal to teachers from a broad range of educational settings. For example, you may find an organization such as Phi Delta Kappa (PDK) of interest as a future teacher. Phi Delta Kappa is an honorary society whose members have demonstrated high academic achievement, completed at least 15 semester hours of graduate course work, and shown a commitment to educational service. PDK members receive the *Phi Delta Kappan* journal, which publishes a broad range of articles of interest to a diverse group of teachers. An example of this type of article is the journal's annual national survey of the general public's attitudes toward America's schools.

## How is teacher professionalism changing?

Although teacher professionalism has been growing steadily throughout America's history, recent activities in three areas have led to an even greater emphasis on moving teaching closer to professional status. The first of these areas is the educational reform efforts that began in the mid-1980s. These activities focused national attention on many issues related to professionalism. Higher standards for students in recent years have also had an impact on professionalism. Finally, more rigorous teacher certification standards have helped create better prepared educators for America's classrooms.

### Educational Reform Efforts

You are probably aware of the considerable debate in public and professional circles about the health of the American educational system. Many suggest that it is in crisis and requires major reform in order to remain viable. Others believe that while much can be improved, American education is doing well and the criticisms being leveled against the system are exaggerated. Typically, it is the former position that gets the most publicity both within educational circles and in the popular media.

The most recent efforts to implement major reform in American education began in the early 1980s when President Reagan established the National Commission on Excellence in Education. The commission's 1983 report, *A Nation at Risk: The Imperative for Educational Reform,* identified many serious problems with American education. Citing a "rising tide of mediocrity," the report emphasized the importance of rigorous academic programs, proposed that teacher preparation programs be strengthened, and promoted the introduction of more sophisticated school management procedures.

In addition to the report issued by the National Commission on Excellence in Education, several other writers and researchers added their voices to the call for reform during this same time frame. Responses, although varied, were unified in their strong criticism of the current educational system and their insistence on the need for major change. Educational reform proponents such as John Goodlad (1984), Theodore Sizer (1984), William Glasser (1986), and Ernest Boyer (1983) emphasized the importance of restructuring the ways in which schools are operated and suggested alternatives such as site-based management, improving school climate, identifying teachers as facilitators of learning, encouraging parent participation in education, and implementing school choice. In response to these proposals and the original report from the National

| TABLE 5.2 Education Reform Efforts | |
|---|---|
| **Emphasis** | **Description** |
| Higher standards for students | • Focused efforts to get students to take more rigorous course work<br>• Development of broad standards for core subjects<br>• Increased use of standardized testing |
| More rigorous teacher certification | • Testing requirements for entrance into, and exit from, teacher education programs<br>• Improving the curriculum students in teacher education must take<br>• Mandating continuing education following initial teacher certification |

Commission on Excellence in Education, individual states initiated changes in two major areas (see Table 5.2). They began implementing higher graduation requirements for students and increased their testing of both students and teachers.

## Higher Standards for Students

Initially, you may see little connection between increasing expectations for students in American schools and the issue of professionalism. But consider the impact of higher standards on teachers themselves. As students are expected to learn more and perform at higher levels, the quality of teaching required must also improve. Teachers who are successful in encouraging higher performance in their students are therefore perceived as more competent and professional.

Efforts to increase standards for students have taken three main directions. The first is a focused attempt to get students to take more rigorous course work, particularly at the high school level. In 1987 U.S. Secretary of Education William J. Bennett proposed the creation of a **core curriculum** for all high school students that called for 4 years of English; 3 years each of mathematics, science, and social studies; 2 years of foreign language study; and other requirements that limited the number of electives students could take to approximately a quarter of their total time. Many states responded to this proposal by increasing their requirements for high school graduation.

The second direction taken to increase expectations for students was the development of broad **standards for core subjects** such as mathematics, science, language arts, and social studies (Marzano, 1998). With the support of the federal government, professional organizations such as the National Council of Teachers of Mathematics, the National Association for the Advancement of Science, the National Council of Teachers of English, and the National Council for the Social Studies developed reports that identified the essential knowledge and skills expected from students in each of these areas. These efforts led to a clearer definition of the core competencies needed by all students.

The final direction that has led to higher standards for students is the increased use of **standardized testing** to determine how well students are doing in learning the essential content and skills of each discipline. During the last 20 years, states have passed legislation mandating testing at different grade levels. These data are then used to compare students from year to year in the same state and with others around the nation to see if student performance has increased.

Although these tests have value, the heavy emphasis on standardized testing has been criticized for several reasons (Kohn, 2000). One key problem is the tendency for educators to spend their time teaching students content they will need to be successful on the tests. This "teaching to the test" mentality places too much emphasis on the rote memorization of facts and de-emphasizes problem solving and process-oriented learning. Another issue is the concern that standardized tests fail to accurately assess the diverse student populations served in the schools. They tend to discriminate against females, minorities, and students from lower socioeconomic groups. Finally, Kohn and others are critical of standardized tests because they are not effective in assessing the problem-solving abilities and higher level thinking skills needed by students to be successful in today's world.

## More Rigorous Teacher Certification

Because teacher certification is a state responsibility, the framework for the teacher education program you are entering was largely determined by an education agency in your state. If you were to move to another part of the country, you would encounter at least a few differences between your current state's and your new state's requirements for initial and continuing teacher licensure. Despite these differences, trends indicate that all future teachers are completing more rigorous preparation programs than in the past. Three major changes have been implemented during the last two decades. The first change has been in the *testing requirements* for entrance into, and exit from, teacher education programs (Blair, 2000). Exit exams are common, and some states such as Washington require minimum scores on SAT or ACT tests or other standardized exams as a prerequisite to admission to teacher education programs. In addition, the majority of states now require students completing their teacher preparation programs to have adequate scores on standardized tests such as the Praxis Exam series prior to receiving their teaching certificates.

These standardized tests for entrance into, and exit from, teacher education programs have been criticized for two main reasons. As with standardized exams in general, these tests discriminate against minorities and low-socioeconomic status students and therefore tend to exclude these important groups from the teaching ranks. A second criticism is the low scores required by states for teacher certification. Crosby (1993) stated: "Not only are the majority of the state teacher tests absurdly easy, the scores needed to pass them are astonishingly low. . . . Nonetheless, the failure rates on the tests have been extraordinarily high" (p. 603).

The second major change that has been implemented to strengthen the rigor of teacher preparation programs has been to *improve the curriculum* students must complete. In many states, these changes have included a stronger emphasis on liberal arts as a component of teacher preparation. For example, some states now require a liberal arts major or an academic concentration in addition to the teacher education course work required for certification. Another major modification in teacher preparation has been the implementation of early field experiences to give preservice teachers a variety of opportunities to work with students. These early and regular contacts with students help build the skills and confidence needed to be successful in the student teaching experience and beyond.

*Teachers deserve recognition for their efforts.*

All across America, teachers are taking and sometimes failing evaluation tests. What is the problem? What is the answer? Several issues are examined in this documentary: (1) the difficulty of terminating contracted and/or tenured teachers, (2) qualifications of today's teachers, (3) teachers' perceptions of preparedness of teaching to high standards, (4) teacher testing, and (5) class size.

### Critical Thinking Questions

1. What should be the qualifications for teachers of today's students? Are those qualifications different than they might have been 20 or 40 years ago? Why or why not? This video was produced in 1999. If it were produced today, what issues might be brought to the forefront?

2. What would you expect the two national teacher organizations to say on issues of teacher competence? You can check your predictions at their websites: National Education Association (http://www.nea.org/); American Federation of Teachers (http://www.aft.org/).

3. The No Child Left Behind (NCLB) (http://www.nclb.gov/) legislation addresses issues of teacher competence and connects it to federal funding. Which of the "directives" do you think will make the most difference? The least difference? How will NCLB affect current teachers and prospective new teachers?

 *To submit your responses online, go to the Education in the News module for Chapter 5 of the Companion Website.*

The final effort to strengthen teacher certification programs has focused on *continuing education following initial certification*. During the past two or three decades, states have generally moved away from giving lifetime teaching certificates and instead have implemented a system in which licenses require periodic updating. In most cases, this updating comes in the form of additional college or university credits every few years. For example, in many states teachers receiving credentials in 2002 would be required to take an additional 10 to 15 credits within the next 3 to 5 years to avoid having their certificates expire. Other states require educators to complete a master's degree or a specific plan of further study to receive a permanent teaching credential replacing the initial certificate.

Unfortunately, these efforts to strengthen the rigor of teacher certification programs are coming at a time when states are experiencing shortages in many areas and have begun implementing strategies to put less qualified personnel in K–12 classrooms (Archer, 2000; Bradley, 1998). For example, the use of emergency certificates to meet the demand for teachers in urban areas and for mathematics, science, and special education teachers has grown during the last several years. Although the need for teachers in these areas is undoubtedly great, these efforts fail to support the move toward increased professionalism in teaching.

## What are my professional responsibilities?

Although the above discussion of teaching as a profession is interesting and can lead to lively discussions, it has little real value unless you as an individual begin to see yourself as moving toward greater professionalism throughout your teaching career. You may not have much direct impact on the overall course of teacher professionalism, but you do have ultimate control over your own personal actions. Consider engaging in three categories of behavior that can markedly enhance your own interactions with students and others: personally conducting yourself in a professional manner, participating in continuing professional development, and getting involved in advocacy efforts.

**Figure 5.3** Sample Professionalism Statement

Students are expected to familiarize themselves with, seek clarification of, and adhere to the expectations of university faculty, school principal, and classroom teachers regarding:

1. Conducts self ethically
   1.1 Maintains confidentiality of privileged information
   1.2 Interacts with students in an adult professional manner
   1.3 Displays sensitivity and balance when treating controversial issues

2. Works productively
   2.1 Makes expected contributions to solving student academic/conduct problems
   2.2 Makes expected contributions to maintaining communications with parents
   2.3 Maintains professional manner in dealings with parents, faculty, and others

3. Displays initiative by using a variety of resources
   3.1 Maintains expected teacher hours/schedules
   3.2 Submits plans and other requested information punctually
   3.3 Attends school and department/grade level meetings
   3.4 Adheres to established standards for dress and grooming

4. Initiates personal growth in subject area(s), learning theories, and/or instructional practices; establishes goals for professional improvement
   4.1 Sets goals for learning
   4.2 Solicits and considers suggestions from others
   4.3 Completes any prescribed training or self-study to attain goal
   4.4 Meets university expectations

5. Utilizes knowledge of families and community resources to enhance support for children and families, including those from diverse racial and ethnic groups
   5.1 Demonstrates an awareness of factors such as family structure, lifestyles, culture, and special challenges/stressors that can make an impact on parent participation/involvement
   5.2 Demonstrates awareness of agencies/resources available to support families and knowledge regarding access to such services

*Source:* The professionalism statement of the Woodring College of Education, Western Washington University. Reprinted with permission.

## Conducting Yourself in a Professional Manner

You can begin right now to learn more about teacher professionalism and start engaging in appropriate interactions with others. Find out if your teacher preparation program has created a statement on professional behavior and make sure you understand the implications of such a document. If your institution doesn't have such a document, consider proposing that it be developed and discussion initiated to clarify its implications. Figure 5.3 shows a sample professionalism statement. You can also find and read the codes of professional conduct written by organizations such as the NEA. Make sure that you take time to discuss the implications of these documents with others.

A discussion of issues related to professionalism should be a regular part of your teacher preparation program. For example, seminars associated with field experiences provide excellent opportunities to discuss professional interactions with students, teachers, parents, and other school personnel. Most of your university course work should also address professionalism

*Speaking at a school board meeting requires many skills.*

issues from time to time. When you discuss these issues with peers and others, you will experience many opportunities to grow in your understanding of, and engagement in, professional behavior.

## Continuing Your Professional Development

If you've spent much time in the K–12 schools, you know that there is seldom a dull moment in teaching. New strategies for teaching, changes in the curriculum, and the challenges of unique students are just some of the things that keep life interesting. In responding to these challenges, the best teachers are continually seeking out new information from a variety of sources so that they can do the best job possible in their interactions with students and others.

It may be difficult to imagine at this point in your teacher preparation program, but your quest for knowledge about teaching and learning has only just begun and will continue throughout your career. You can begin now to establish the mind-set needed to be successful in growing as a teacher by first *seeking advice from others you respect*. Teachers you have met, university professors, and classmates are all valuable resources that can assist in your professional development. By beginning now to reach out to others you respect, you will be much more likely to continue this as a future teacher.

You should also consider *getting involved in professional organizations* while you're working on teacher certification as another means of beginning your long-term professional development. Most organizations have student memberships that provide all of the benefits of involvement, but at a lower cost to you. Carefully review the many options available to you, seek the advice of a mentor, and join one or two organizations that will benefit you now and set the stage for further development in the future.

The third thing you should do is *start thinking about future course work* following your initial teacher certification. Although this may be the last thing you want to think about at this point in time, you need to mentally prepare yourself for this important eventuality. Find out what your state requires for continuing certification and then consider how you can most effectively grow through additional university course work. You may want to think about working toward additional teaching endorsements once you get your first teaching job. In some cases, these endorsements strengthen your ability to teach at a given level (i.e., a reading endorsement strengthening your work with primary-aged children), while other endorsements give you the flexibility to teach a completely new subject or grade level (i.e., adding a mathematics endorsement to supplement your science teaching certificate). In many situations, working toward a master's degree also makes good sense. You may wish to talk to a faculty advisor who can give you more information about this option. In any case, begin thinking about some goals for longer term professional development that can be met through future university course work.

## Getting Involved in Advocacy Efforts

Attempts to move teaching closer to professional status will only occur when people associated with education speak out at every opportunity for changes that can make a difference.

# Learning to Teach Comes from Working with Students

Because learning to teach is such a complex process, there are a number of important components to a successful teacher preparation program. It is important to learn as much as you can about the students you will teach, the content of the curriculum, and proven teaching strategies so that you can be successful in the classroom. Although there is little debate about the broad categories of knowledge needed for excellence in teaching, there is considerable controversy over how this knowledge can be acquired. Some would suggest that this learning can come primarily from textbooks and discussions with highly qualified teacher educators. Others would suggest that learning to teach comes primarily from direct experiences with students.

In the early 1900s, most teacher preparation occurred in college and university classrooms where teacher candidates gained content knowledge, strategies for teaching, and information about the students they would teach. At the very end of these programs, students would have a brief "practice teaching" experience before becoming full-time teachers in their own classrooms. More recently, the pendulum has moved in the opposite direction for some teacher candidates. They are taking a much more limited number of college and university classes and instead spending nearly all of their time in the classroom "learning through doing." The theory behind this approach is that teaching can best be learned from the trial and error that comes from actual interactions with students.

Most teacher educators today would suggest that classroom instruction about students, teaching, and learning must be balanced with quality experiences in real schools (National Commission on Teaching and America's Future, 1996). Both are needed for success as a teacher. The task of teaching is just too complex to learn from only one of these options.

## Research the Issue

Research this topic by reading the source article by the National Commission on Teaching and America's Future, then explore it online using the links provided in the *Engage in the Debate* module for Chapter 5 of the Companion Website for this text.

1. What are some of the arguments given in the article for initial transition from the teacher training programs of the early 1900s (predominantly college based) to programs with an increased emphasis on classroom experience?

2. What are some reasons cited for the more recent shift by some programs to a primarily field-based program with limited college course work?

3. What did your research indicate was the most common focus of current teacher training programs: course work, classroom experience, or a blend of the two?

## Explore Your Views

1. In general, what strategies work best for you in learning something like playing a musical instrument for the first time? Can you listen to someone else explain the techniques and then go out and do it, or do you learn most quickly and effectively when you simply explore and experiment on your own? Would a combination of someone explaining strategies and then trying it out under the supervision of a more experienced person work the best? Try to identify one or more specific learning experiences that characterize which of the approaches identified here works best for you. Does this line of thinking have any relevance to learning to teach?

2. Imagine what it would be like to try to learn to teach by being placed in a classroom with a mediocre or poor teacher. Do you think you could develop the skills you would need to be successful? Why or why not?

3. What type of program appeals most to you? Would you prefer to go into a classroom and learn to teach through trial and error, or would you prefer to focus on course work and spend little time with students in the classroom? What do you feel is the right balance for a training program?

 *To research this issue and submit your responses online, go to the Engage in the Debate module for Chapter 5 of the Companion Website for this text.*

*Source: What Matters Most: Teaching for America's Future,* by the National Commission on Teaching and America's Future, 1996, New York: Author.

Again, it is important for you to begin now to **advocate** for positive change. It's often the little things you and others do today that make a difference in the long run. For example, when parents, neighbors, or friends ask you about your future, speak out proudly and intelligently about teaching. Share your thoughts about the value of having quality educational programs and what it will take to make these programs a reality. Be informed so that you can help others know the good things that are happening in classrooms throughout your community. Take the opportunities that present themselves to share with others both the importance of quality teaching and the challenges encountered daily in educational settings. Make sure that you know and can articulate to others the things that need to happen to move teaching closer to professional status.

One other way in which you can serve as an educational advocate is to encourage others to consider teaching as a career. Perhaps you are involved in teacher preparation right now because a teacher or another significant adult encouraged you to consider it as an option. You should now consider it your responsibility to begin noticing other capable individuals who might find teaching a rewarding career. Taking a few minutes to share your perspectives on teaching could help them decide to give it a try. Make it your goal to seek out individuals throughout your career and suggest that they consider teaching as a career.

After reading about your role in becoming a professional, stop and reflect on the implications for your life. How do you feel about your ability to conduct yourself in a professional manner? Are you committed to continuing your professional development? Do you see yourself getting involved as an advocate for teaching and learning?

**Reflective Journey 5.3**

**views from the classroom**

## Simple Goals in a Complex World

**Nancy Raschko**
**Centennial Elementary School**
**Mount Vernon, Washington**

I choose to teach because it is my passion, and because I believe that all children can learn. By that I mean all children can become learners and thinkers. In over 18 years of teaching, my goal has remained the same: To empower students to become engaged, confident, and capable learners and thinkers.

Demands, pressures, curriculum, delivery methods, and students continue to change. Teachers are being asked to do and to know more. Classrooms are more diverse. My students face poverty, English as a second language, and learning disabilities, to name just a few of the cultural, economic, and experiential differences they possess. Demands for increased performance require constant assessment

and reassessment of methods, curriculum, and students. What we do and how we do it makes a difference.

During the 1980s precocious first graders needing an expanded program challenged me. My fourth-grade students in 2003 are still creative and capable, yet myriad issues complicate education for them and for teachers, too. Some of my students have never traveled very far outside of the county. Many of their parents work extremely long hours away from home, and many of the students come from non-English-speaking households. But they can be motivated and excited to learn. As their teacher, I can continue to learn. We never give up, and because of that, each day and each student is exciting and challenging.

## Summary

In this chapter, four questions were identified to help you better understand the issues surrounding teaching as a profession:

### Is teaching a profession?

It is important to know what it means to be a profession and how teaching matches up with these criteria:

- Defining a profession
- Teaching as a profession (Praxis II, topic IVa)

### What professional organizations exist?

Professionals are members of and get involved in a variety of professional organizations:

- National Education Association
- American Federation of Teachers
- Other professional organizations

### How is teacher professionalism changing?

Teaching is growing toward greater professionalism through these means:

- Educational reform efforts
- Higher standards for students
- More rigorous teacher certification

### What are my professional responsibilities?

Your professional responsibilities include the following:

- Conducting yourself in a professional manner (Praxis II, topic IVa)
- Continuing your professional development
- Getting involved in advocacy efforts (Praxis II, topic IVb)

## Key Terms

advocate
core curriculum
normal schools

profession
standardized testing
standards for core subjects

## Reflective Journey: Online Journal

Use the questions for thought and reflection highlighted throughout the chapter to help guide your personal journey of reflection and professional development as a teacher. To complete your journal entries online, go to the *Reflective Journey* module for this chapter of the Companion Website.

## PRAXIS Test Preparation Activities

To review an online chapter case study, test your understanding of chapter topics and concepts, and begin preparing for the Praxis II: Principles of Learning and Teaching examination, go to the *Praxis Test Preparation* module for this chapter of the Companion Website.

## Becoming a Reflective Practitioner

 To complete these activities and submit your responses online, go to the *Becoming a Reflective Practitioner* module for this chapter of the Companion Website.

### Is teaching a profession?

**Review Questions**

1. What are the characteristics of a profession?
2. What arguments are usually given for teaching being considered a profession?
3. In what areas is teaching considered less professional?

**Field Experience**

Review the characteristics of a profession cited in this chapter and then spend time observing a teacher during his or her school day. Look for specific indicators of professional behavior on the part of the teacher. What was said or done that indicated the teacher was part of a profession? Share your insights with others.

**Building Your Portfolio:** *Code of Ethical Behavior*

**INTASC Standard 9.** Go to the website of the National Education Association at http://www.nea.org and search for and review the code of ethics of this organization. What does this document tell you about ethical behavior of teachers and what are its implications for teaching as a profession? Include a copy of this code of ethics in your portfolio along with a brief summary of the key points of the document.

### What professional organizations exist?

**Review Questions**

1. Describe the similarities and differences between the National Education Association and the American Federation of Teachers.
2. In addition to teacher unions, what professional organizations exist and what are their purposes?

**Field Experience**

Attend a local meeting of a professional organization of interest to you. What was the content of the meeting? What did you learn from participating in the meeting? Talk to one or two members after the formal meeting about the benefits of the organization. What did you learn? Share what you learned with others.

**Building Your Portfolio:** *Professional Organization*

**INTASC Standard 9.** Research a professional organization that you think you will want to join as part of your own continuing development as a teacher. Describe the mission and activities of this group. Put literature about this organization into your portfolio. Consider actually joining the organization as a student member.

### How is teacher professionalism changing?

**Review Questions**

1. What efforts have been made to increase the expectations for students in American schools?
2. In what ways has teacher certification become more rigorous?

**Building Your Portfolio:** *Teacher Certification Requirements*

**INTASC Standard 9.** Research the requirements for initial and continuing teacher certification in your state. The Internet website for your state department of education should be a good source of information. What entrance and exit exams, if any, will be required of you? Describe the content knowledge, understandings of students and teaching, and practical experiences in the classroom required by your state for the level at which you want to teach. Will you also be expected to take further college and university courses to receive a permanent teaching certificate? Write up your findings for your portfolio.

## What are my professional responsibilities?

**Review Questions**

1. What can you do to conduct yourself in a professional manner?

2. Describe the strategies you can use to continue your professional development.

3. How can you serve as an advocate for your chosen profession?

**Building Your Portfolio:** *Professional Teaching Responsibilities*

**INTASC Standard 9.** Think back to teachers you have had who you feel were especially professional in their interactions with you and other students. Describe the behaviors they engaged in that made you feel that they were being professional. How can you make sure that you engage in similar activities as a future teacher? Summarize your responses in a brief paper.

## Suggested Readings

Boyer, E. (1983). *High school: A report on secondary education in America.* New York: Harper and Row. In a report to the Carnegie Foundation for the Advancement of Teaching, Boyer recommended strengthening the academic core curriculum in American high schools. His proposal was widely adopted in the 1980s and 1990s.

Glasser, W. (1990). *The quality school: Managing students without coercion.* New York: Harper and Row. Glasser advocates moving away from the current model of teacher-directed learning to experiences that are teacher facilitated. By removing the element of coercion and allowing students to engage in cooperative learning, schools can become stimulating environments for student learning and development.

Goodlad, J. (1984). *A place called school.* New York: Macmillan. This book is a summary of a study entitled "A Study of Schooling" funded by several major foundations. From his research, Goodlad found that improving schooling requires changing many components at the same time: teacher behaviors, administrative interactions, curricula, school organization, and school–community relations. His book, he lays out a plan for accomplishing positive school reform.

Sizer, T. (1984). *Horace's compromise: The dilemma of the American high school.* Boston: Houghton Mifflin. After spending 2 years visiting high schools throughout the United States, Sizer found that good teachers are being hampered in their efforts to engage in quality instruction by the school environments themselves. He proposes several changes that can help high school teachers engage in more effective instruction.

# part 2

## What Is Reflective Classroom Practice?

# chapter 6

## Understanding Student Learning

Because it takes place within the individual, learning is a difficult concept to fully understand. In addition, numerous factors influence how and when a person comes to master a concept or skill. Despite these challenges, understanding student learning is a key element of effective teaching. Four key questions will guide your thinking as you gain additional insights on this topic.

## Focus Questions

◢ Do student needs affect learning?

◢ How does development influence learning?

◢ What is the impact of the environment on student learning?

◢ What is the role of assessment in learning?

Nathan has just finished teaching his third week of integrated language arts classes at Mapleton Middle School. As he reflects on his new students for the year, Nathan is once again amazed at the diversity of abilities, interests, and skills of his seventh-grade students. For example, Shakara surprised him with her exceptional writing skills. She is one of the youngest students in the seventh grade because of an earlier academic promotion. Yet despite the age differences, Shakara has excelled in class and seems well liked by her peers. Abe is another interesting student in one of Nathan's afternoon classes. He has been tested for the gifted and talented program and received one of the highest scores in the school on the exam. Yet, Abe's performance in Nathan's class leaves much to be desired. His written work shows little thought or creativity and two assignments have already been turned in late. It is hard to explain Abe's indifference to school this year. Sharon, yet another one of Nathan's students, has been a pleasant surprise. He just learned that her alcoholic father moved out of state this past summer to be with another woman. Despite the personal stress she undoubtedly faces at home, Sharon has tried hard to complete her assignments and is doing passing work.

Have you noticed that significant differences exist in the ways students learn? Some pick up information quickly and with relative ease, while others seem to struggle mightily to make the same connections. Certain students learn best when they engage in physical manipulation of objects, while others prefer to discuss things verbally with their peers. And while many students seem independently motivated to learn, others need constant feedback from the teacher to get even the simplest tasks accomplished. What causes these and other differences and how do these differences influence the ways in which you will interact with students? This is a complex question that will require in-depth study at some point in your teacher preparation program. You will probably have at least one course that focuses on these issues in greater depth. At this point, however, you will begin by looking at the multifaceted nature of this question.

## Do student needs affect learning?

Kendra is a 16-year-old student in your sophomore biology class. She attended the first parent–teacher conference of the year with both of her upper middle class parents. It was frustrating to hear how Kendra's dad, in particular, seemed to feel that she was never doing work that met his expectations. Perhaps that partially explains her recent near-obsession over her peer relationships. Although most sophomores see friendships with classmates as important, Kendra seems to go to any extreme in the school setting to get approval from them. Her clowning around in class, cigarette smoking during lunch breaks, and new style of dress are indicators of this high need for peer acceptance. Kendra's behavior has you concerned that her academic performance will be far less important to her in the coming months than the need for approval from her peers.

Every student brings personal needs to the classroom that influence how they learn. In some cases, like that of Kendra, these needs may significantly hinder school performance. For others, these personal needs may be less obvious and mainly affect the ability of students to give their best performance in class. In either case, your job as a future classroom teacher will be to understand what those needs are for each student and to develop strategies to help meet them whenever possible. This is another challenging aspect of teaching, but one well worth the effort it takes to successfully manage.

### Basic Human Needs

To live a healthy life, every person needs to have certain basic human needs met. Some, such as food and drink, are necessary for life itself. Others, such as the need for affection and love, are less obvious but still essential to good health. Theorist Abraham Maslow (1968) has identified a categorization scheme for human needs that effectively describes how these needs influence one another. He suggests a hierarchy that graduates from basic needs to higher level ones, as shown in Figure 6.1. The most fundamental needs have priority over those at a higher rank for healthy development. In other words, basic needs such as food and shelter must be satisfied before higher level needs such as being valued by others can be met.

You will come face to face with student needs every day of your teaching career. Sometimes, the needs are short term and caused by unforeseen circumstances such as temporary homelessness. Others will be issues that you and the student must address every day of the school year. For example, the student living in her third foster care home in 6 months may well have belongingness and affection needs that persist over time. In some circumstances, the need is clear and relatively easy to meet. A student who comes to school without breakfast because there is no food in his house presents an example of this type of need. Other needs are far more complex, such as the student with poor self-esteem who continually denigrates others in order to feel better about herself.

You might initially think that the topic of student needs is an interesting one, but not particularly relevant to your role as a teacher. In actuality, it is a vitally important issue that significantly impacts classroom learning. Maslow makes it clear that students who come to the classroom with

**Figure 6.1**   Maslow's Hierarchy of Needs

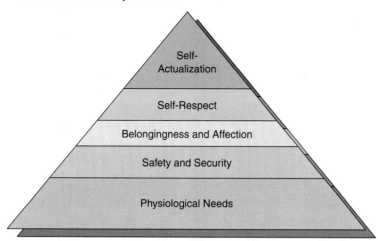

unmet lower level needs are going to struggle academically. If learning is going to take place, it becomes necessary for teachers to assist students in meeting these lower level needs. For example, the elementary school teacher who keeps a box of crackers and some peanut butter available for students who come to school without having had breakfast is helping to meet a lower level need. The secondary teacher who works hard to create a safe, caring classroom atmosphere is assisting students with another important basic need. Once lower level needs are met, the academic learning that takes place in schools helps students meet the higher level needs of self-respect and self-actualization.

## Need for Social Acceptance

Take some time to reflect on your own school experiences. Can you remember one or more students who struggled with being accepted by either their peers or classroom teachers? Students who fit this category tend to be loners or see themselves as rebels. If you remember someone matching this description, was that person successful academically? In most cases, students who find it difficult to feel socially accepted tend to have greater trouble dealing with the academic aspects of schooling. Their energy and efforts are diverted into other areas and little is left for intellectual pursuits. Social acceptance is a second category of student needs that you will want to know more about as a future teacher.

Reflective
Journey 6.1

   Rudolf Dreikurs (Dreikurs, Grunwald, & Pepper, 1971) wrote about this issue and adds further insight into our understanding of the personal needs students bring to the classroom. He suggests that an important need for all students is the desire for social acceptance. For very young children, acceptance by the classroom teacher is the most important. Over time, this need becomes more peer oriented. Older students, while still wanting the approval of their teachers, are often more focused on seeking acceptance from their classmates. When students feel unacceptable to either peers or teachers, they become behavior problems in the classroom (Charles, 2002). They mistakenly choose to engage in problem behaviors while attempting to gain social acceptance. Dreikurs identifies a downward spiral of misbehaviors on the part of students engaged in this struggle for approval: (1) attention seeking, (2) exerting power over others, (3) seeking revenge, and (4) engaging in displays of inadequacy (giving up). Students who choose these options are causing themselves and others difficulty in the classroom. Teachers must work to prevent these problems, where possible, and assist students in developing more appropriate ways of interacting with others. Until their need for social acceptance is met in more positive ways, these students will find it difficult to learn.

*Students need to feel socially accepted.*

## Self-Esteem Needs

Jay is the kind of student who teachers love to have in their classrooms. As a junior in high school he has already distinguished himself academically, socially, and on the athletic fields. Academically, he has taken all of the available higher level mathematics courses, two advanced science classes, 2 years of Japanese language study, and advanced placement English. Socially, Jay has been elected junior class president and is well liked by both classmates and teachers. Jay is also a 2-year letterman in both football and wrestling. As you talk to him, he appears confident, relaxed, and positive about life. Jay is said to have high **self-esteem.** His feelings of self-worth make it much easier for him to succeed in all aspects of school life.

Not all students will have the high level of self-esteem that Jay brings to the classroom. Consider, for instance, Aleetha. Just entering the second grade, she is already showing signs of poor self-esteem. Yesterday, the physical education teacher had a very difficult time getting Aleetha to even try to play the game planned for the day. She complained of not being able to move quickly because of a sore ankle, but an examination by the school nurse showed no signs of an injury. Aleetha was brought to school today by her mom and sobbed uncontrollably as she clung to her on leaving. During an art activity, her hand slipped and caused the paintbrush to skew out of control across the page. Aleetha was furious at herself and just sat and fumed for the rest of the activity. She shows many of the symptoms of low self-esteem and will need extra attention and guidance from her classroom teacher throughout the school year.

Self-esteem of students, especially when it is low, is yet another factor that will influence the interactions you have with students. Stanley Coopersmith (1967) is generally credited with being one of the first to write about the importance of self-esteem in people's lives. He identified the elements needed for the development of positive self-esteem and described the problems that occur when individuals have poor self-perceptions. More recently, Kostelnik, Stein, Whiren, and Soderman (1998) have identified three dimensions to self-esteem: competence, worth, and control. They define *competence* as the belief that you can accomplish tasks and achieve goals. *Worth* can be viewed as the extent to which you like and value yourself. *Control* is the degree to which people feel they can influence the events around them.

You will have many opportunities as a teacher to either positively or negatively influence each of these three dimensions of self-esteem. For example, teachers who have high expectations for their students and clearly communicate confidence in them are building each student's sense of competence. Or, teachers who spend time learning about student interests and genuinely enjoying them as individuals are enhancing their sense of worth. On the other hand, teachers who fail to give students choices about what they do in the classroom and make all their educational decisions for them are negatively influencing their sense of control.

As you might expect from the example of Jay presented earlier, high self-esteem students are generally more confident in their learning abilities and tend to display greater interest and motivation in school (Schunk, 2000). Low self-esteem students, on the other hand, are characterized by feelings of inadequacy, fear of rejection, dependence on others, and loss of control over events (Kostelnik et al., 1998). This confidence level may be affected, however, by the content being

## Twice Exceptional

The behavioral and attitudinal changes occurring with Lisa Greim Everitt's son Mark were baffling. The same student who a few years earlier had been reading articles in *National Geographic* as a 5-year-old was now having significant difficulties in the first and second grades (Fine, 2001).

Rather than being a delight to his teachers as he was in earlier years, Mark had now become a "problem student." Instead of participating in group activities and following teacher directions, Mark began to retreat into his own little world. His refusal to answer questions, even when he clearly knew the answers became a real frustration to his teachers. And despite his exceptional abilities in reading, Mark had significant difficulties in doing even the simplest of writing tasks.

School personnel went so far as to label Mark as "emotionally disturbed." They strongly encouraged his mother to seek out an alternate school setting for him. Unfortunately, there were no local settings that could serve Mark's unique needs. None of the private schools in the area felt that they could help him be successful. And despite his exceptional reading abilities, none of the gifted education programs felt equipped to help Mark deal with his problem behaviors.

Students like Mark are now being called "twice exceptional." He is considered gifted by his school district, but also has been identified as having attention deficit hyperactivity disorder, bipolar disorder, and nonverbal learning disabilities. Programs for students such as Mark are very rare.

Although this story may seem unusual, many gifted students have considerable difficulty adjusting to life in the schools. For example, "Despite Einstein's brilliance, as a schoolboy he had behavioral problems, was a rotten speller, and had trouble expressing himself. His report cards were dismal" (Fine, 2001, p. 39). It seems that many gifted students struggle to be successful in traditional educational settings.

### Explore and Reflect

Learn more about students who are "twice exceptional" by reading the source article by Fine (2001) and reviewing other online resources provided in the *Reflect on Diversity* module for Chapter 6 of the Companion Website for this text.

1. Have you known someone who was "twice exceptional"? How did this person do in school or in life? Were there special services available to assist this person?

2. Even if students aren't viewed as "twice exceptional," what are some of the difficulties that gifted and talented students face in schools? How can schools and teachers better meet the needs of these students?

 *To explore this topic further and submit your responses online, go to the Reflect on Diversity module for Chapter 6 of the Companion Website for this text.*

*Source:* "Research: Diamonds in the Rough," by L. Fine, 2002, *Education Week*, October 24, pp. 38, 39, 41.

learned. Some writers are suggesting that self-esteem may be hierarchical and that while general self-concept can be high (or low), student perceptions of their abilities in specific subject matter areas may vary (Marsh & Shavelson, 1985). So, for example, a student with generally high self-esteem may view himself as only average in his mathematics capabilities.

## Responding to Student Needs

Once you understand the importance of student needs, the next step is to identify those that are influencing classroom learning. This can be accomplished in two main ways (Jones & Jones, 2001). One option is to carefully observe students to determine their needs. By listening to conversations with others and watching what students do and how they interact, you can learn a great deal about needs. The second technique is to directly ask students what they require to be more

**Figure 6.2** Meeting Students' Needs

- Spend extra time with individual students to let them know you care about them.
- Learn about hobbies and interests and give students positive feedback for the extracurricular activities they enjoy.
- Create a classroom environment in which students feel comfortable and can learn without fear of rejection or put-downs.
- Allow students to have choices in learning activities for at least part of the school day.
- Give students responsibilities in the classroom to increase their sense of involvement and control.
- Suggest the student spend some time talking to the school counselor.
- Identify community resources that can help students meet personal needs.

successful in learning. Students are surprisingly good judges, so taking the time to talk to individual students about their needs can be very productive. Figure 6.2 lists some additional ways to meet student needs. A questionnaire addressing these same issues can also be used to collect information on student needs (Jones & Jones, 2001).

It is important to realize that while you can *assist* in meeting many personal student needs, the issues are frequently too difficult or time consuming for the average teacher to resolve on his or her own. Take, for example, the need for safety and security as described by Maslow. It is possible for teachers to take responsibility for meeting these needs while students are in the classroom, but there is very little that teachers can do when students are at home. Similarly, the need for belongingness and affection can be addressed by you as the classroom teacher, but it is probably not possible for a nonfamily member to meet this need completely. John, a third-grade teacher, has discovered this in his classroom. He has six children this year who are in single-parent families headed by moth-

## EDUCATION IN THE NEWS

### Too Much Homework?

Many students—and parents—will attest that the amount of homework has reached an all-time high. In some cases, the amount of homework assigned to students has increased by threefold or more. Now parents, students, and some experts are concerned that homework causes children too much stress, inhibits their participation in extracurricular and family activities, and sometimes has little impact on achievement.

**Critical Thinking Questions**

1. Think back to your own elementary, middle and high school education. How much homework time did you spend on homework each night? Did it affect your ability to be involved in other activities? Do you feel it was helpful, detrimental, or had no effect on your success as a student?

2. Do you think that it is important for all students to have homework every day? Discuss some of your reasons for feeling this way.

3. Think of some of the most exciting or helpful homework assignments you have been given as a student or that you have assigned as a teacher. What components did these assignments possess that made them so effective? What should you, as a teacher, consider about your students' abilities, learning styles, and family lives when creating an effective homework assignment?

 *To submit your responses online, go to the Education in the News module for Chapter 6 of the Companion Website.*

ers. Four of these children seem particularly in need of affection and caring from John as a significant male figure. Despite his many efforts to have positive interactions with each one as regularly as possible, they never seem to be able to get enough personal time from him.

Another factor you must consider in meeting student needs is that every teacher will have different personal limits about getting involved in nonacademic issues. For example, spending some of your lunch break building a stronger relationship with a student may help meet his need for social acceptance but take away important break time for you as a teacher. Or attending a special concert or sporting event would be a very meaningful way to show a student you care about her. But your involvement in this activity would mean a night away from home and missed opportunities for quality time with your own family. You will need to decide just how involved you can be in meeting student needs without resenting it, getting burned out, or having it impact aspects of your personal life.

## How does development influence learning?

Imagine you are preparing for a road trip across the United States. What would you do to prepare for this adventure? You would probably begin by getting out some maps and planning a route to follow, deciding how many miles to travel each day, and determining where to stay at night. The road maps allow you to plan for a successful trip.

In much the same way, an understanding of human learning provides teachers with a "road map" describing in detail the journey of students to physical, emotional, intellectual, and social maturity. By knowing the normal paths that most students follow as they learn and grow, and by understanding the implications of this information for your teaching, you will be more successful in your work in the classroom. Because of the complexities of human behavior, however, there are no simple, universally accepted descriptions of learning for all students in every circumstance.

Two broad perspectives have been defined to describe human learning, one emphasizing the internal factors that influence learning and a second stressing the importance of external factors (see Table 6.1). These two points of view would have very different explanations, for example, of the developmental milestone of learning to walk. Those emphasizing the internal factors would

**TABLE 6.1   Factors Influencing Learning**

| Factor | Described In | Definition |
|---|---|---|
| Internal factors (come from within the individual) | Developmental theories | Movement through predictable stages in development that are determined primarily by heredity |
| | Developmental norms | Typical behaviors that can be expected at a given age and stage of development |
| | Learning styles | Individual's preferred method of learning; varies primarily due to genetics |
| External factors (come from outside the individual) | Learning theories | Learning from the ways in which people and things in the environment respond to one's actions |
| | Social learning theory | Learning that occurs from watching what others do and say |

describe the mental and physical capabilities needed in learning to walk and the internal motivation required to begin the learning process. Those taking this approach suggest that until the child is developmentally ready to learn to walk, little progress will be made in acquiring this skill. The other explanation emphasizes external factors and their importance in learning to walk. According to those holding this view, the availability of equipment such as walkers and the positive encouragement of excited adults are examples of factors outside of the child that provide the motivation and training needed to learn to walk.

Those who focus on the internal factors are emphasizing the importance of *heredity* in human learning. They see genetic programming as the best explanation for the changes that occur and propose **developmental theories** to describe them. In addition, those with this perspective have identified typical patterns of behavior common to specific ages called **developmental norms.** These norms help give teachers and parents information about what can be expected of children at different ages. Finally, those emphasizing internal factors and their influence on learning also suggest that the strategies used by students to actually gather and internalize information about the world will vary between individuals. These **learning styles** are also important for you to understand as you plan lessons and activities for the classroom.

On the other hand, researchers and writers looking at the importance of external factors in learning are suggesting that the *environment* has a significant impact on overall development. These **learning theorists** view factors that are external to the learner as having the primary influence on human growth. Environmental factors are broadly defined from this perspective to include everything from other people and the interactions they have with the learner to such things as books, food, shelter, and community that have either a direct or indirect impact on the learner. So, for example, students who grow up in homes with a wealth of children's books and adults who take the time to read to them often are experiencing an environment that leads to excellent literacy learning.

**Reflective
Journey 6.2**

Although some people believe almost exclusively in the importance of either hereditary or environmental influences, most would suggest that both play a role in human growth and development. Take a moment to reflect on your own past learning experiences. Can you identify situations in which you felt learning was influenced by your level of developmental understanding? Conversely, what can you remember about learning that was significantly influenced by the people, places, and things around you? Do you remember situations in which both internal and external factors influenced your personal growth and development?

## Developmental Theories

One of the first to popularize developmental theories was Jean Jacque Rousseau (1979), whose writings in the mid-16th century ushered in a radically different view of children and development. In his book, *Emilé,* first published in 1762, Rousseau described what he saw as the natural characteristics of children at different ages and the type of education appropriate for each level. For example, he felt young children learned primarily through their senses:

> Since everything that comes into the human mind enters through the gates of sense, man's first reason is a reason of sense-experience. It is this that serves as a foundation for the reason of the intelligence; our first teachers in natural philosophy are our feet, hands, and eyes. To substitute books for these does not teach use of reason, it teaches us to use the reason of others rather than our own; it teaches us to believe much and know little. (Rousseau, 1979, p. 90)

Other noted developmental theorists include Arnold Gesell (Gesell & Ilg, 1949), Sigmund Freud (1920), Jean Piaget (1950), and Erik Erikson (1963). All of these researchers' theories of human development suggest that people pass through a series of predictable stages as they mature. People at the same stage share common characteristics and typically enter and exit the stage at similar ages. Many feel that these developmental stages significantly influence learning (Schunk, 2000). Knowledge of developmental theories can help you understand students' learning needs and plan for more effective instruction. Two key theories will be briefly described here.

## Failure to Learn Is the Student's Fault

In case you haven't already discovered this important fact, you should know that good teachers work very hard to plan for and engage students in quality classroom learning experiences. It takes considerable time and effort to get ready for and then guide quality educational experiences. Despite the efforts that teachers put into their instruction, however, some students are still unsuccessful in learning the content and attitudes being shared. Even though it feels very good to know that many students have learned and grown from your teaching, you will still find yourself frustrated by those who just don't learn.

What causes this failure? If you've invested considerable effort into the learning situation, a rather natural reaction is to assume that it was the student's low level of motivation that led to the lack of success. Although this may be true in some circumstances, there are other important causes for a student's failure to learn. The following examples highlight these possibilities.

> Jason is struggling in Marsha Bailey's 10th-grade history class. He seems to be constantly distracted and unable to concentrate on the discussions in class and has failed to turn in his written assignments for the past 2 weeks. Marsha just learned today of a major change in Jason's life that may well be affecting his work. His dad was diagnosed with terminal cancer and is expected to live only a few more months.

Ahmad Rasheed, a fairly recent immigrant to the United States, teaches high school mathematics. His mathematics colleagues are thoroughly impressed with his knowledge of the subjects he teaches. Students, however, are finding it difficult to learn in his classes. The principal has identified what seem to be two recurring problems. First, despite having been in the United States for the past 8 years, Ahmad's English is still a little difficult to understand and this seems to be affecting student performance. Secondly, his depth of mathematical knowledge makes it hard for Ahmad to explain processes in terms that make sense to his students. They seem bewildered by many of his descriptions of mathematical problem solving.

Ben has recently transferred to Ellen Barsten's third-grade classroom from out of state. He seems to be a bright and motivated student, but is having difficulty with his writing assignments. He doesn't seem to be able to compose a well-conceived sentence or paragraph. After spending some individual time with him during the last 2 days, Ellen realizes that Ben has simply not been taught the skills he needs to be a good writer. Even though others in the class have been given that information, Ellen will need to work with Ben individually to develop his writing skills.

### React and Reflect

1. What is the problem with assuming that failure to learn is basically the student's fault?

2. Think about some times when you received low grades in school. What do you think caused you to do poorly? How did the teacher respond?

3. Do you think it will be important for you to discover the reasons for failure in your future students? Why or why not?

 *To explore this topic further and submit your reactions and reflections online, go to the Explore Your Beliefs module for Chapter 6 of the Companion Website for this text.*

**Psychosocial theory of development.** Erik Erikson (1963) provides a description of human development referred to as a **psychosocial theory.** He identifies stages in a person's psychological growth, each of which is influenced by interactions with the social environment. Erikson suggests that humans pass through a series of eight stages from birth through old age (see Table 6.2). Each of these stages has a major issue that must be addressed and which Erikson refers to as a *psychosocial crisis.* As the person successfully resolves the crisis of the current stage, he or she is better prepared for the challenges of the next developmental period.

Each stage of psychosocial development has applications for teaching. If you intend to teach at the high school level, for example, you would want to pay particular attention to Erikson's fifth

**TABLE 6.2** Stages of Psychosocial Development

| Stage (Age) | Description |
|---|---|
| Stage I: *trust vs. mistrust* (birth–1 year) | Young children are dealing with the trustworthiness of their primary caregivers. When parents and others provide consistent care and meet the child's physical and emotional needs, a sense of trust begins to develop. |
| Stage II: *autonomy vs. shame and doubt* (1–3 years) | Children make initial attempts at doing some things for themselves. Feeding and dressing themselves, for example, help give children a sense of independence. |
| Stage III: *initiative vs. guilt* (3–5 years) | Children develop a sense of initiative by making plans, setting goals, and working hard to accomplish tasks. Parents and teachers must encourage the child's natural curiosity so that initiative will grow. |
| Stage IV: *industry vs. inferiority* (6–12 years) | Children are working on learning the skills necessary for success in society. If they struggle in their mastery of these skills, children start to think of themselves as inferior. |
| Stage V: *identity vs. confusion* (13–19 years) | Young people are working to identify their vocational and professional orientation. If they fail to find this identity, they become confused and directionless. |
| Stage VI: *intimacy vs. isolation* (young adult) | People are seeking a love relationship that will lead them to personal intimacy. Failing that, they become more isolated. |
| Stage VII: *generativity vs. stagnation* (mature adult) | Adults find themselves more involved in helping relationships through parenting, supporting others, and taking on civic responsibilities. |
| Stage VIII: *integrity vs. despair* (older age) | Older adults reflect on their accomplishments. If they can accept the positives and negatives they find, a sense of integrity is found. |

*Source: Childhood and Society,* by E. Erikson, 1963, New York: W. W. Norton.

stage of development. He calls the psychosocial crisis at this stage *identity vs. confusion* and describes it as the adolescent's struggle to find a vocational and professional focus. As a high school teacher, part of your informal interactions with students would probably include information and guidance as they engage in beginning attempts at vocational decision making. For example, you might suggest an advanced chemistry course for a student considering entering the medical profession while encouraging another student to take a foreign language. In addition, you will want to make clear connections between the subject matter you are teaching and real-world occupations that students may enter so that they can begin to make informed decisions about the knowledge and expertise needed for various careers.

**Cognitive-developmental theory.** Over a long and productive career, Jean Piaget created an influential **cognitive-developmental theory** that explains intellectual or cognitive growth. In it he suggests that each person passes through a series of four stages as they grow to matu-

| TABLE 6.3   Stages of Cognitive Development | |
| --- | --- |
| **Stage (Age)** | **Description** |
| Sensorimotor intelligence (birth–2 years) | Children learn about the world through sensory experiences and motor activity. An infant's sucking and shaking of various objects are examples. |
| Preoperational intelligence (2–7 years) | Children begin to use symbolic thinking rather than exclusively learning through sensory and motor interactions with the world. Children make initial attempts at being logical, but are unsuccessful by adult standards. They have difficulty seeing things from any perspective other than their own. |
| Concrete operations (7–12 years) | Children think more logically and systematically, especially when dealing with concrete objects. They recognize that matter doesn't change in quantity or mass when moved or manipulated. There is more ability to see the perspectives of others. |
| Formal operations (13 years on) | This stage marks the beginning of adult thinking. The abstract and logical thought necessary for scientific investigation are possible. |

*Source: The Developmental Psychology of Jean Piaget,* by J. Flavell, 1963, New York: Van Nostrand.

rity (see Table 6.3). These stages occur at approximately the same ages for every person, so knowing about them helps adults understand the ways in which students think and learn. Piaget (1950) suggests that the ways in which people understand the world vary significantly from one stage to the next. At about age 2, children make one of their most significant shifts in thinking:

> It is during the preschool years that the human mind performs its greatest magic: the child is freed from dependence on sensory-perceptual-motor experience as the sole channel of communication with his environment. The evolution of the capacity to deal with experience symbolically represents the key extensor process of the maturing organism. It manifests itself in every medium of expression known to man, and runs the full course from the simplest gestural representations to advanced levels of abstraction. (Biber, 1964, pp. 90–91)

Each of Piaget's four stages of cognitive development has direct implications for teaching. If, for example, your teaching interests are at the primary level in elementary school, you should pay careful attention to Piaget's stage of preoperational development. Rhonda, a first-grade student, exemplifies the characteristics of this stage. She is making good progress in her ability to think symbolically, so the many symbols associated with her mathematics activities (such as the symbolic equation $3 + 2 = 5$) and reading are beginning to make sense to her. Rhonda is still egocentric in her thinking, so it is difficult for her to see things from another's perspective. An example of this occurred yesterday when Rhonda had trouble understanding why her best friend Erika wanted to play with another girl at recess. The incident affected her work efforts for the rest of the day. Rhonda still struggles to take into consideration multiple features of a more complex problem. For the science activity last week, for example, she had difficulty realizing that the items being used on the balance beam varied in both size and density, both of which were factors in determining the weights of these objects.

*Physical and social development are important parts of schooling.*

## Developmental Norms and Teaching

In addition to important developmental theories such as the two described above, researchers over the years have collected considerable information that describes the typical behaviors of children at different ages. These characteristics are often referred to as *developmental norms*. If you understand the typical social, emotional, cognitive, physical, and linguistic abilities of the students you teach, it becomes much easier to plan effective learning experiences for them.

Tanya, a middle school mathematics teacher, took two courses on child development and learning as part of her teacher preparation program. In addition, the district has conducted several workshops during the last few years that have focused on developmental issues and teaching. Because of this training and experience, Tanya understands what typical middle school students can be expected to do and she builds her class activities around this information. For example, she understands that most of her students still find it difficult to grasp abstract mathematical concepts and plans to use some manipulatives called Cuisenaire rods to help her advanced classes visualize some basic algebraic concepts. Similarly, other students are benefiting from some overheads she developed to help them conceptualize fractions and decimals.

## Learning Styles

**Reflective Journey 6.3**

Take a moment to think about your personal learning style preferences. How would you describe your preferred learning environment? Do you study best when you listen to music while curled up in a favorite chair? Is it more effective for you to work alone or in a small group? As you read a chapter in your textbook for an upcoming class, do you find it easier to learn when the material is carefully organized or can you dig out the key information even when the author's writing style is less structured? When a question is asked in class, do you need time to reflect before giving a response or are you quick to answer?

**Figure 6.3**    Learning Styles

> - *Sensory modality preference.* Students vary in terms of their preferred sensory mode for learning. Some choose auditory input, others like visual stimuli, and another group learns best through touching and moving objects in the real world.
> - *Field dependence–independence.* Field-dependent learners tend to think more globally, whereas field-independent thinking is more analytical. Both learning styles have their own strengths and drawbacks in classroom settings.
> - *Categorization style.* This learning style refers to the ways in which learners see objects as similar to others. Different learners choose to categorize objects in terms of their functions, physical attributes, or category.
> - *Cognitive tempo.* Some students respond quickly to questions or information they are given, whereas others choose to reflect on the data before proceeding.

*Source: Learning Theories: An Educational Perspective,* 3rd ed., by D. Schunk, 2000, Upper Saddle River, NJ: Merrill/Prentice Hall.

Your answers to the above questions help identify components of your personal learning style. The ways in which you perceive, organize, process, and remember information are often different from those of the person sitting next to you in class (Schunk, 2000). Various learning styles are presented in Figure 6.3. Your future students will also have varied learning (also called cognitive) styles based on their personalities and preferences. Knowing more about these styles will help you plan more effective learning experiences for all your students.

Information on learning styles is important to your future teaching because it helps explain why students are so very different in the ways they learn. Knowing about these differences allows teachers to plan a variety of experiences to take advantage of these styles. For example, a high school English teacher discussing a medieval play could use overhead transparencies to attract the interest of visual learners, small-group discussions for those who prefer this mode for learning, and sample costumes for those who benefit from kinesthetic experiences.

## What is the impact of the environment on student learning?

Kyla and Roxann are twins with unusual personal histories. Adopted at birth into two very different families, they have recently been reunited through their joint efforts at tracing their family roots. These two sisters find it hard to believe how alike they are in many ways that go well beyond their shared physical characteristics. Tastes in music, food preferences, and similar personality characteristics are just some of the many common traits. Yet, at the same time, their varied adoptive families have led to some significant differences as well. Kyla's adoptive family had three other children, with all four being encouraged by their parents to be involved in intramural and sports activities. They all loved intellectual challenges and spent many evenings engaged in playing board games such as chess and Scrabble and card games like Pinochle. Roxann, on the other hand, was adopted by a couple with no other children and spent more time on her own. She entertained herself by watching television, writing in her journal, or reading quietly in her room. These experiences led each of the twins to very different academic and personal interests. Whereas internal factors shaped the overall development of both Kyla and Roxann, the external settings in which they were raised also had a significant effect.

Learning is a complex process that is difficult to understand. Because it occurs within the minds of individuals who vary greatly in terms of personality, genetic inheritance, and environmental experiences, no one theory can adequately explain its many facets. In the last section, you were given information about the internal factors that influence learning. Here you will learn more about the effect of the environment. Two separate, but interrelated, theories help explain how these external factors impact learning. **Behavioral learning theory** describes how responses made by the environment to actions taken by the learner determine whether or not the acts will occur again in the future. If the responses are positive, then the behaviors are more likely to re-occur. **Social learning theory** emphasizes the importance of learning from the actions of others. When learners see these behaviors being encouraged, it increases the chances that they will also engage in the same activities. Both of these theories provide deeper insights into the learning process.

## Behavioral Learning

John B. Watson was an early 20th-century proponent of behavioral learning theory. He believed that through careful control of the environment, you could guide learning and development in whatever direction desired. One of his most famous quotes summarizes this attitude:

> Give me a dozen healthy infants, well-formed, and my own specified world to bring them up and I'll guarantee to take any one at random and train him to become any type of specialist I might select—doctor, lawyer, merchant-chief, and yes, even beggarman and thief, regardless of his talents, penchants, tendencies, abilities, vocations, and race of his ancestors. (Watson, 1924, p. 5)

By far the best known and most influential behaviorist is B. F. Skinner (1953), whose writings have had a major impact on educational thought and practice (Schunk, 2000). Learning, according to his work, is explained by the impact that environmental events have on people. Rather than viewing internal cognitive structures and developmental stages as factors, behaviorists believe that learning can be described by the positive and negative interactions that the learner has with people and things in the environment (see Table 6.4). So, for example, a parent who is toilet training a child rewards him with candy and praise as external incentives to get the child to use the toilet. Similarly, the elementary teacher who uses behaviorist theory in the classroom rewards students with praise, time for fun activities, and stickers when they engage in behaviors the teacher is working to promote.

Behaviorism assumes that the motivation to learn is external to the individual. That is, the reactions of people or the consequences of events determine whether or not a person will be more or less motivated to learn in the future. For example, Rachel received praise from her teacher and positive feedback from her classmates after her science project was placed on display near the high school office. These experiences will positively motivate her to engage in future science activities.

**TABLE 6.4  Elements of Behavioral Learning Theory**

| Element | Example |
|---|---|
| Positive reinforcement | Spending positive time with students<br>Candy and special treats (such as free time)<br>Verbal praise<br>Smiles, hugs, high-fives, pat on the shoulder |
| Punishment | Verbal warnings<br>Removing student from group to regain control<br>"Paying back" wasted instructional time through the use of noninstructional time such as recess |
| Ignoring | Giving no verbal or nonverbal responses to a student engaged in an inappropriate attention-getting activity |

## Social Learning

A second approach to explaining the impact of the environment on human learning suggests that people acquire knowledge, skills, strategies, and attitudes by observing others. Social learning theory suggests that people gain knowledge of the world by watching others and how the environment reacts to their actions. Without actually engaging in these tasks at the time of learning, they are able to internalize the actions and perform them at some future time. Albert Bandura (1977) is generally credited with developing this theory of learning. He describes two essential elements to his model: vicarious learning and modeling (see Table 6.5).

Bandura (1986) suggests that much of human learning occurs indirectly through

*Social interactions can lead to quality learning.*

what he calls **vicarious learning** as the learner watches the behavior of others and how the environment responds to this action. Learning in this way is faster than having to perform the behavior in order to master it. Students can also gain understanding without having to suffer any negative consequences associated with certain behaviors. For example, watching a film about the negative effects of cocaine can help students avoid the harmful results of drug use. There are a number of different sources for vicarious learning, including *live people* such as parents, teachers, and peers; *electronic sources* such as television, computers, and videotapes; and *printed materials* including books and magazines.

The concept of **modeling** is the second critical component of Bandura's theory. Rather than being a more direct demonstration of a specific skill, modeling tends to be an informal expression of attitudes and skills that can be taken in by the observer only through repeated exposure to the model. Learning has taken place when the observer displays new behaviors that wouldn't occur without having been exposed to the model. So, for example, when you are consistently excited and enthusiastic about the subjects you teach, many of your students will observe this behavior and will demonstrate similar interests themselves. Also, the ways in which you deal with errors in logical thinking or the wrong answers students give to questions asked will be carefully observed and imitated by students as well.

Take a moment now to reflect on this concept of modeling. Think about your own life and a person who has had a strong influence on who you have become. How did you come in contact and what attracted you to him or her? What qualities does this person have that you like? Describe what this person said or did that was appealing to you. Can you describe the ways in which this person served as a role model for you?

**Reflective Journey 6.4**

| TABLE 6.5   Elements of Social Learning Theory | |
|---|---|
| **Element** | **Description** |
| Vicarious learning | Watching others and indirectly learning specific information and skills from their successes and failures |
| Modeling | Developing more general attitudes and skills through repeated observations of a role model |

## What is the role of assessment in learning?

How are you at test taking? If you study hard and have a good idea of the format and content of the exam, do you normally do well? Or are you one of those people that always seems to struggle through every test despite your level of preparedness? Tests are one form of **assessment** frequently used to evaluate student learning (see Figure 6.4). In your future classroom, you will construct and use many tests to assess student learning. Be aware as you do so that while tests have an important role to play in evaluating student progress, they are useful primarily in measuring knowledge of facts and other information retained by students. Some of the more important outcomes of schooling, such as "determination, idealism, wisdom, strategic reasoning, judgment, experience, persistence, stamina, creativity, and writing ability" (Haladyna, 1999, p. x) are not effectively evaluated by most tests. Many teachers are looking critically at the problems associated with tests and are working to use a greater variety of proven assessment techniques. Because some students do not test well, you should be aware of, and consider using, an assortment of strategies to evaluate student learning.

Assessments of student learning are important for two main reasons. First, they provide teachers with a progress report on student learning while they are still engaged in a particular unit of study. This type of evaluation is referred to as **formative evaluation** and serves as an in-

**Figure 6.4**    Types of Assessment

- *Tests.* Some tests are used to determine students' grades; others help teachers decide what concepts need to be retaught; and yet others measure levels of achievement or intelligence compared to other students.
- *Informal observations.* Informal observation strategies get used most often because they can be easily accommodated by the teaching day. The high school Spanish teacher who listens unobtrusively to the conversations of small groups is engaged in informal student observations.
- *Formal observations.* One example of a formal observation is the anecdotal record, consisting of brief written notes by the classroom teacher. It includes the date and time of the observation, a description of who was observed, what the students were doing, and the words spoken. A second technique that provides teachers with many insights about learning is the checklist. To use, the teacher merely places a check beside the items observed.
- *Written responses.* The most common assessments of student learning are in the form of written responses on tests, quizzes, homework, in-class assignments, papers, and projects. Most of these written assessments are developed and evaluated by the classroom teacher from options provided in school textbooks and other teacher resource materials.
- *Oral responses.* Throughout the school day, teachers evaluate the questions students ask and mentally critique the responses they give to questions posed by the teacher. These oral responses of students provide important information.
- *Self-reports.* When students rate their own learning, they are engaged in self-reporting. The most common form for these reports is a questionnaire that the teacher develops.
- *Portfolios.* A portfolio is a collection of student work (including such things as papers, tests, audio- and videotapes of student activities, pictures, and drawings) and teacher-generated assessments that collectively are used to evaluate student learning.

*Sources: Learning Theories: An Educational Perspective,* 3rd ed., by D. Schunk, Upper Saddle River, NJ: Merrill/Prentice Hall; and *Portfolio Assessment,* by A. DeFina, 1992, New York: Scholastic Professional Books.

formal spot-check of student progress that enables teachers to adjust, modify, and reteach content as they proceed through a particular unit of study (Linn & Gronlund, 2000). For example, a secondary history teacher who asks the class a series of questions following a discussion of World War I is engaging in formative evaluation. He will use the responses the students give to help him decide what modifications need to be made for the discussions on World War I planned for the next day. Also, the sixth-grade teacher giving a practice spelling test is using formative evaluation to gather information that will help her decide if further instruction is needed prior to the actual test next week.

The second main purpose for assessing student learning is to evaluate what

*Assessment strategies include the parent–teacher conference.*

students have learned or accomplished. This is called **summative evaluation** and is completed after instruction has ended (Linn & Gronlund, 2000). The physical education teacher observing student performance in a game of soccer is using a form of summative evaluation. She uses her observations to evaluate the soccer unit she has just completed. The secondary mathematics teacher who tests student knowledge of geometric proofs following instruction by administering an hour-long exam is also using summative evaluation. Both formative and summative evaluations are used extensively in school settings.

## views from the classroom

## Building the Future, Every Day

**Taryn Decker**
**South Plainfield High School**
**South Plainfield, New Jersey**

Learning is a continuous process that does not halt for me or for my students, and both teaching and learning must be approached with an open mind. As a teacher, are you willing to dive in and begin the journey or are you willing to wait until the student is ready to commit to learning? If you wait, it will be too late. These everyday moments define you as a teacher.

There are wonderful days when the lessons you slaved over work to perfection, and there are days when nothing works as planned. As teachers, we must improvise and take advantage of the teaching moment. Students are only so patient; we must motivate them to maintain attention as well as gain their respect.

As a career, teaching allows me to be a positive role model for all my students. I believe in what I do, and I believe my students know that I truly care about their learning. I can use my creativity to produce new and different lessons that appeal to the students' different learning styles. There is no greater compliment than having a student say, "I love the way you teach. You break things down so easily." I credit this to careful planning, with a focus on the needs of every learner within a diverse classroom, and to the patience, positive attitude, and organizational skills that I bring to the classroom. I aspire to continually improve the lives of students who share my day. I recognize I teach them more than just mathematics: I teach them life lessons.

## High-Stakes Testing

One test that has received considerable criticism over the years has been the **standardized test:**

> Standardized tests are used in psychology, as well as in everyday life, to measure intelligence, aptitude, achievement, personality, attitudes and interests. Attempts are made to standardize tests in order to eliminate biases that may result, consciously or unconsciously, from varied administration of the test. Standardized tests are used to produce norms—or statistical standards—that provide a basis for comparisons among individual members of the group of subjects. Tests must be standardized, reliable (give consistent results), and valid (reproducible) before they can be considered useful psychological tools. (*Gale Encyclopedia of Psychology,* 2001)

Despite the efforts at standardization, many people suggest that these tests are inaccurate and put various populations of students at a disadvantage in school:

> While African-Americans and most other minorities have shown both relative and absolute gains in standardized test scores over the past several decades, they still score much lower than whites as a group. Some educators believe that many standardized tests are culturally biased, drawing primarily upon the experiences of middle-class white students. (*Education Week Assessment,* 2002)

Yet these same tests are now being used by all states to measure student achievement. More significantly, many states have now implemented policies that make them **high-stakes tests:**

> Certain uses of achievement test results are termed "high stakes" if they carry serious consequences for students or for educators. Schools may be judged according to the school-wide average scores of their students. Low school-wide scores may bring public embarrassment or heavy sanctions. For individual students, high scores may bring a special diploma attesting to exceptional academic accomplishment; low scores may result in students being held back in grade or denied a high school diploma. (American Educational Research Association, 2000)

### Research the Issue

Research this topic online using the links provided in the *Engage in the Debate* module for Chapter 6 on the Companion Website. Link to the online source articles by *Education Week* (2002) and the American Educational Research Association (2000) and explore the information provided at the additional sites listed.

1. From your research, what are some of the assessment options available besides standardized tests to measure student progress? Why are standardized tests the most common assessment tool used?
2. What are the strengths and limitations cited of using standardized tests in high-stakes decision making?

### Explore Your Views

1. What is your opinion about the use of standardized tests in general? Do they have a place in schools?
2. Do you think that high-stakes testing is a good approach to educational reform? Why or why not?

 *To research this issue and submit your responses online, go to the Engage in the Debate module for Chapter 6 of the Companion Website for this text.*

Sources: *Gale Encyclopedia of Psychology,* 2nd ed., 2001, New York: The Gale Group; *Education Week Assessment,* 2002, retrieved August 6, 2002, from http://www.edweek.org/context/topics/issuespage.cfm?id=41; and *High Stakes Testing in Pre-K–12 Education,* by American Educational Research Association, 2000. Retrieved August 6, 2002, from http://www.aera.net/about/policy/stakes.htm

## Summary

In this chapter, four organizing questions were identified to assist you in developing a better understanding of student learning:

### Do student needs affect learning?

A number of student needs influence student learning:
- Basic human needs (Praxis II, topic Ic)
- Need for social acceptance (Praxis II, topic Ic)
- Self-esteem needs

### How does development influence learning?

Factors from within the individual help explain many aspects of learning:
- Developmental theories (Praxis II, topic Ia)
- Developmental norms and teaching (Praxis II, topic Ia)
- Learning styles (Praxis II, topic Ia)

### What is the impact of the environment on student learning?

Environmental factors explain many aspects of student learning:
- Behavioral learning
- Social learning

### What is the role of assessment in learning?

There are many different types of evaluation, each of which has value in teaching and learning:
- Types of assessment (Praxis II, topic IIc)
- Role in learning (Praxis II, topic IIc)

## Key Terms

assessment
behavioral learning theory
cognitive-developmental theory
developmental norms
developmental theories
formative evaluation
high-stakes tests
learning styles

learning theorists
modeling
psychosocial theory
self-esteem
social learning theory
standardized test
summative evaluation
vicarious learning

## Reflective Journey: Online Journal

Use the questions for thought and reflection highlighted throughout the chapter to help guide your personal journey of reflection and professional development as a teacher. To complete your journal entries online, go to the *Reflective Journey* module for this chapter of the Companion Website.

**PRAXIS**   Test Preparation Activities

 To review an online chapter case study, test your understanding of chapter topics and concepts, and begin preparing for the Praxis II: Principles of Learning and Teaching examination, go to the *Praxis Test Preparation* module for this chapter of the Companion Website.

**inTASC**   Becoming a Reflective Practitioner

To complete these activities and submit your responses online, go to the *Becoming a Reflective Practitioner* module for this chapter of the Companion Website.

## Do student needs affect learning?

**Review Questions**

1. What happens when students feel socially unaccepted by either peers or teachers?
2. How does self-esteem impact student learning?
3. What is your role as a teacher in responding to student needs?

**Building Your Portfolio: *Meeting Student Needs***

**INTASC Standard 2.** Choose one of the personal student needs described in this chapter. For this need, describe how you will plan to help students meet it for the age/grade you are interested in teaching. If you are aware of any school or community resources available to help meet this need, include that information as well.

## How does development influence learning?

**Review Questions**

1. What is a developmental theory?
2. Describe the usefulness of developmental norms to a classroom teacher.
3. In what ways should an understanding of learning styles influence the ways in which you teach?

**Building Your Portfolio: *Create a Developmental Profile***

**INTASC Standard 2.** For the age/grade you think you want to teach, create a developmental profile that outlines the typical abilities of students at that age. After referring to one or more child development texts, describe the key intellectual, social, emotional, and physical attributes of that age/grade.

## What is the impact of the environment on student learning?

**Review Questions**

1. How is behavioral learning theory different from developmental theory?
2. In what ways do teachers engage in modeling as they spend time in their classrooms?

**Field Experience**

Observe a teacher engaging students in learning experiences. As you watch students working to gain knowledge, which of the developmental or learning theories presented in this chapter best describes their efforts? What did you see or hear that makes you think this? Discuss your thoughts with others.

**Building Your Portfolio:** *Social Learning*

**INTASC Standard 2.** Remember back to your own K–12 learning experiences. Identify a situation in which you learned from observing someone else's behavior. Describe what happened and why you learned from this other person's actions. Based on what you remember from this situation and others, write a short essay describing what you see as both the strengths and weaknesses of social learning.

## What is the role of assessment in learning?

### Review Questions

1. What other forms of assessment besides tests are available?
2. Describe the differences between formative and summative evaluation.

### Field Experience

Spend some time in a classroom of your choice making several anecdotal record observations of a single student. It would be best if you could do this task with a partner so that you can compare notes about what is being observed. Refine your ability to see and record accurate details of what this student says and does. After completing your observations, write a summary in which you discuss your interpretation of what you observed.

### Building Your Portfolio: *Student Portfolios*

**INTASC Standard 8.** Do some reading about the use of portfolios with students. You may also wish to talk to a classroom teacher about the effectiveness of portfolios as an evaluative tool. Once you have done your research, describe both the strengths and limitations of portfolios for the age/grade you would like to teach.

## Suggested Readings

Linn, R., & Gronlund, N. (2000). *Measurement and assessment in teaching* (8th ed.). Upper Saddle River, NJ: Merrill/Prentice Hall. This text provides an excellent overview of the problems and benefits of measurement and assessment and gives information about the elements necessary for good teaching. It provides clear guidance in the development of different assessment instruments for use in the classroom.

Schickedanz, J., Schickedanz, D., Forsyth, P., & Forsyth, G. (2001). *Understanding children and adolescents* (4th ed.). Boston: Allyn and Bacon. In addition to describing developmental theories, the authors give detailed information about every component of child development for infants and toddlers, preschool children, school-age children, and adolescents.

Schunk, D. (2000). *Learning theories: An educational perspective* (3rd ed.). Upper Saddle River, NJ: Merrill/Prentice Hall. As the title implies, this text does a thorough job of describing the major theories of learning. There are separate chapters on the behavioral and social learning theories.

# chapter 7

## Developing Curriculum

One of the important tasks you will engage in as a future teacher is determining what should be taught. While it is possible to simply follow what is outlined in a textbook, the best teachers spend considerable time and energy tailoring the content and activities to meet the needs and interests of different groups of students. In this chapter, four organizing questions will help you better understand the excitement and challenges of this process.

## Focus Questions

◢ How is curriculum defined and developed?

◢ How has curriculum changed over time?

◢ What factors influence curriculum decisions?

◢ What are current curriculum trends?

*Sarah Hanson has just gotten the last of her fifth-grade students out the door and is relaxing for a few moments before tackling her next project. It is 3:30 on a beautiful Friday afternoon and she would love to be working in her garden or going for a leisurely walk. Before she can leave school, however, Sarah must spend some time planning for the coming week. Having just finished a unit on decimals, next week she will begin a discussion of problem-solving strategies in mathematics. After reviewing the relevant standards from the National Council of Teachers of Mathematics, her state's goals for problem solving, and the school's mathematics textbook, Sarah makes plans for the content she wants to present on this topic. In addition to her preparations for mathematics, Sarah will need to make similar plans for the writing, science, social studies, and reading content she will be addressing with her students. As usual, there will be no time for leisure this afternoon. Sarah is busy developing the curriculum for the coming week.*

Can you imagine yourself getting excited about teaching if all you had to do day after day was to simply pick up a textbook and follow the detailed plan described there? If you used this approach and strictly adhered to the content and sequence of topics listed in the text, the end result might well be a series of uninteresting teaching experiences for both you and your students. "For today's science lesson, students, please begin by reading pages forty-three through forty-eight. We will then discuss questions one through five listed on page forty-eight, and near the end of the hour I will assign homework problems from those listed on page forty-nine." This approach leads to a very mechanical approach to teaching that requires little imagination or thought. It would also be considerably less likely to meet students' needs and interests or excite them about learning in general.

A more creative approach to teaching and learning occurs when you take the time to develop your own **curriculum** from a variety of resources and with the needs and interests of your students in mind. When compared to the "teaching from the textbook" method, this approach is far more difficult. It requires greater amounts of time and mental effort to do well. Working to create your own curriculum, however, is one of the many exciting intellectual endeavors that make teaching such a rewarding experience. Furthermore, your involvement in detailed curriculum planning will do much to motivate your students to learn the meaningful content you have organized.

## How is curriculum defined and developed?

The curriculum is all that is taught, both knowingly and unknowingly in the schools. It is a multifaceted and complex aspect of schooling. Teachers typically spend a major portion of their planning time working on developing curricula for their classrooms. They are influenced as they engage in this process by various school, district, state, and national guidelines that are in place for each subject taught.

### Curriculum Defined

Although curriculum has been described as having many different elements, in this chapter it will be defined as having four main components: the formal curriculum, an informal curriculum, the hidden curriculum, and the null curriculum (see Table 7.1). Teachers are primarily responsible for helping develop and implement the first element. They may also influence, either directly or indirectly, the other three components of the curriculum.

**Formal curriculum.** The **formal curriculum** consists of every subject that the schools intend to teach their students. It includes more traditional subject matter content in areas like mathematics, reading, science, social studies, music, art, and physical education. In addition, the for-

| **TABLE 7.1** Components of Curriculum | |
|---|---|
| **Component** | **Description** |
| Formal curriculum | Every subject that the schools intend to teach their students |
| Informal curriculum | Activities, interest groups, clubs, and sports programs offered within the schools |
| Hidden curriculum | Everything that the schools indirectly teach students through the attitudes and behaviors of teachers and staff |
| Null curriculum | All the potential subjects and topics that are *not included* in the curriculum |

mal curriculum includes such things as learning about different cultures, drug and alcohol awareness, sex education, and violence prevention. This formal curriculum is often identified at the national level, defined more specifically within individual states, and further refined at the district, school, and classroom levels. For example, the No Child Left Behind Act of 2001 is a recent piece of federal legislation that has important implications for public education. One portion of this act identifies reading as an essential element of the primary grades by stating that all children should learn to read by the end of the third grade. Based on legislation such as this and other sources of national information, individual states then determine somewhat more specific goals for the reading curriculum. For example, the

*Curriculum may include social and relational issues.*

Nebraska Department of Education has defined beginning reading, word identification, comprehension, vocabulary, and work/study skills expected from all children in the state. A sample of the expectations for fourth-grade students reads: "Students will demonstrate the use of multiple strategies in reading unfamiliar words and phrases" (Nebraska Department of Education, 2002). School districts, schools, and finally individual classroom teachers then work to make these broad statements into more specific curriculum plans for students.

**Informal curriculum.** Ramona Zarelli teaches high school social studies. In addition to her regular teaching load, she has taken on coaching responsibilities for the girls' volleyball team. Ramona receives extra pay for this voluntary assignment. Two other teachers in her department also have taken on additional responsibilities. Jeremy Black is involved in driver's education classes after school, and Vanessa Williamson works with the chess club. Each of these teachers is participating in the **informal curriculum** of the school.

Every school has an informal curriculum that supplements the formal classes and content taught. At the elementary level, for example, students may choose to come to school early or stay late for supplemental studies in learning a foreign language, mathematics enrichment, or refining writing skills. These activities are viewed as enjoyable enrichment times for children with special interests and talents in these areas. Often structured as clubs for students, they may include competitions or special events that serve as culminating experiences. In addition to these and other more varied enrichment activities, middle schools and high schools offer students the opportunity to participate in a number of organized sports (see Table 7.2). These, too, have important curricular benefits for students. Working as part of a team, meeting challenges, and physical fitness are among the many benefits that can come from organized sports.

**Hidden curriculum.** Bill Hornberger is in his 27th year of teaching middle school mathematics. Although he was enthusiastic and effective as a teacher for many of those years, Bill is tired of working with the high-energy students in his classes. He plans on retiring at the end of this year and he is basically "going through the motions" as he finishes up his career. He tends to be abrupt and aloof in his interactions with students and spends a minimum of time in planning and evaluating his curriculum. Bill's attitude is having an impact on his students' attitudes about mathematics and middle school life in general. He is influencing the **hidden curriculum** of his classroom and school.

**TABLE 7.2**   Middle School and High School Activities and Sports

| Level | Activities | Sports |
|---|---|---|
| Middle school | Art<br>Chess<br>Spirit<br>Math<br>Yearbook staff<br>Student government<br>Student mentors<br>Photography | Football<br>Soccer<br>Baseball<br>Track<br>Swimming |
| High school | Intramurals<br>Drama<br>Debate<br>Honor Society<br>Science team<br>Math team<br>Dance team<br>Multicultural club<br>Community service<br>Chess club<br>Leadership | Football<br>Tennis<br>Soccer<br>Cross country<br>Swimming<br>Volleyball<br>Basketball<br>Gymnastics<br>Wrestling<br>Golf<br>Baseball<br>Track |

The hidden curriculum is generally described as everything that the schools indirectly teach students through the attitudes and behaviors of teachers and staff (Parkay & Haas, 2000). As a future teacher, you will strongly influence what is learned in the hidden curriculum. Attitudes toward learning, values, ways of interacting with students, and feelings about diversity issues are just a few of the many things that students learn indirectly from their teachers.

Although the hidden curriculum engages students in indirect learning and may seem to have limited influence, it actually has a significant impact. Think back to your own K–12 learning experiences and identify one teacher who you remember as particularly outstanding. What do you recall learning from this person that could be considered part of the hidden curriculum? How did this teacher share this part of the curriculum with you? Most people find that they remember attitudes, ways of thinking, and perspectives more often than the actual content taught. The potential for having a long-term impact on students' lives through the hidden curriculum is great.

**Reflective Journey 7.1**

**Null curriculum.** Elliot Eisner (1994) identifies the **null curriculum** as all potential curriculum topics that are *not included* in the classroom. These topics tend to be avoided for two main reasons: They are either too controversial or the perceived value to students is low. Topics such as religion, homosexuality, creationism, and abortion rights are all examples of controversial issues typically avoided by the schools. For these topics and others, it is difficult for schools and individual teachers to engage students in impartial learning experiences that add to their understandings while being sensitive to the diversity of attitudes that students and their families have regarding them.

The second set of topics contained in the null curriculum consists of those not addressed because they are seen as less important to students. An example of this type at the elementary level is art education. Most school districts support the value of art education, but few actually hire full-time art educators for elementary schools. At the same time, many elementary teachers find that they are consumed by the demands of what they and others consider the core curriculum and consequently have little time for the teaching of art. By default, then, art instruction becomes a part of the null curriculum.

## Approaches to the Curriculum

As you develop curricula for your classroom, you will manage the task in one of two distinct ways. The more traditional approach at most educational levels is typically referred to as the **subject-centered curriculum.** Teachers using this strategy see the curriculum as best organized around the logical order of the discipline. In the elementary mathematics curriculum, addition is taught before subtraction, followed by multiplication and then division. From this perspective, the discipline itself determines the order of the curriculum. Other planners engage in a **student-centered curriculum.** Teachers who use this methodology first determine student needs and interests before identifying content to be taught. Instead of determining curriculum content and then seeing how this information can best be taught to students (the subject-centered approach), the student-centered curriculum planner looks at the developmental abilities and interests of a particular class of students and then matches that with relevant content.

**Subject-centered approach.** Marv Kinsley teaches seventh- and eighth-grade science and mathematics at Compton Middle School. Today, he is planning for the coming week's science activities. Having just completed Chapter 7 in the science text, the class will be starting a new unit on chemical changes as an introduction to the study of chemistry. Chapter 8 in the text for science suggests a sequence of activities that Marv modifies to better match his own thinking about how the activities should be sequenced. Next, he plans strategies that he can use to make this content interesting and exciting for his students. Marv is using a subject-centered approach to curriculum planning.

**Student-centered approach.** In the above example, if Marv Kinsley were teaching using a child-centered curriculum approach, he would begin by determining his students' needs and interests regarding science. He can gather this information through observations of the class, asking them directly, or by knowing what typical seventh- and eighth-grade students are interested in learning about science. Once this information is determined, Marv then begins to identify what will be taught in the coming week. He collects information from a variety of sources, including the school text for science, and begins to develop more specific curriculum plans. Although this approach is more responsive to student needs and interests, it should be clear that using this strategy for curriculum development is also more time consuming and challenging for teachers.

Take a moment to consider both the subject-centered and the student-centered curriculum. Both approaches can be effectively used by teachers, but one will probably be more attractive to you. Which do you think sounds most appealing at the present time? What is it about this approach that you like? Can you identify personality characteristics that may make one approach a better "fit" for you than the other? Think about the implications of this preferred approach for teaching and learning in your future classroom.

**Reflective Journey 7.2**

## National, State, and District Influences on Curriculum

Curriculum development is a complex process that includes input from a great many sources. You will need to make decisions about what should be taught after examining information from a variety of levels. National curriculum standards, state curriculum goals, and school district curriculum materials all directly influence what you will actually teach in the classroom.

**TABLE 7.3** *Sample National Curriculum Standards*

| Organization | Sample Standard | Subcomponents of Standard |
|---|---|---|
| National Council of Teachers of Mathematics (NCTM) | Number and operations | • Understand numbers.<br>• Understand meanings of operations.<br>• Compute fluently. |
| National Council for the Social Studies (NCSS) | Culture and cultural diversity | • Human beings create, learn, and adapt culture.<br>• Culture helps us understand ourselves as individuals and as members of groups.<br>• Cultures exhibit both similarities and differences. |
| Music Educators National Conference (MENC) | Singing, alone and with others (grades 9–12) | • Sing with expression and technical accuracy.<br>• Sing music written in four parts.<br>• Demonstrate well-developed ensemble skills. |

**National curriculum standards.** Many national professional organizations (see Chapter 5 for more information on these organizations) help shape the curriculum by developing standards that describe in broad terms the content these groups feel is important for K–12 students to know. While these **curriculum standards** do not identify specific content for K–12 classrooms, they create a conceptual framework on which this curriculum can be based. Sample standards are listed in Table 7.3.

**State curriculum standards.** Every state has a centralized office that deals with issues associated with K–12 education. Often called the office of the superintendent for public instruction or simply the state department of education, these state organizations play a significant role in the development of a framework for conceptualizing the curriculum that is taught in the schools. Although the curriculum standards developed by states are generally broad and nonspecific, they define the parameters that schools use in developing curricula. Sample state curriculum standards are shown in Table 7.4.

**District influences on curriculum.** While national and state standards create the framework on which curriculum is based, local school districts have primary responsibilities for developing and/or adopting more specific curriculum plans and activities. School boards, administrators, and teachers all have important roles to play in this activity (see Table 7.5). Typically, school boards serve as approval-giving bodies for curricula that are adopted district-wide. School board members generally listen to the concerns voiced by others regarding the existing curricula and then empower groups within the district to develop or review alternative programs for potential approval by the board. For example, a new mathematics curriculum for grades K–12 that has been carefully studied by teachers, administrators, and community members would be implemented only after receiving the approval of members of the school board.

Depending on their leadership styles, superintendents, assistant superintendents responsible for curriculum, and building principals may either take leadership in developing new curricula (top-down curriculum development) or empower teachers and community members serving on curriculum committees to create their own curriculum plans and materials (grassroots curricular

**TABLE 7.4 Sample State Curriculum Standards**

| State | Standard | Sample Content Standard | Sample Benchmarks |
|---|---|---|---|
| Michigan | Mathematics: geometry and measurement | Shape and shape relationships | High school:<br>1. Use shape to identify plane and solid figures, graphs, loci, functions, and data distributions.<br>2. Determine necessary and sufficient conditions for the existence of a particular shape and apply those conditions to analyze shapes. |
| Washington | Reading: understands and uses different skills and strategies to read. | Use word recognition and word meaning skills to read and comprehend text. | Grade 4:<br>1. Apply phonetic principles to read including sounding out, using initial letters, and using common letter patterns to make sense of whole words.<br>2. Use meaning, context, and pictures to comprehend story. |

reform). The former administrative style is exemplified by a building principal who chairs a high school curriculum committee charged with developing a new music program and uses the position of chair to carefully guide the committee's work in the development of curricular programs. An example of the latter administrative style would be an assistant superintendent for curriculum calling together a group of teachers and community members to develop a drug awareness and

**TABLE 7.5 District Influences on the Curriculum**

| Group | Roles |
|---|---|
| School boards | Serve as approval-giving bodies for curricula that are adopted district-wide. |
| Administrators | Administrators either take leadership in developing new curricula in the school or district or empower teachers and community members serving on curriculum committees to create their own curriculum plans and materials. |
| Teachers | Teachers serve on curriculum development and review committees both within their own school buildings and for similar groups meeting on district-wide projects. |

prevention curriculum. After clarifying the task and providing the group with resources, the administrator then gives the committee the time and resources needed to develop the curriculum.

### Your Role as a Teacher in Curriculum Development

In addition to serving on curriculum committees within your school building and district, you will be expected to make specific long- and short-term plans for the curriculum of your classroom. Working within the established curricula for your school and district, and taking into consideration state and national guidelines, you will plan an organized and motivating curriculum for your classroom. When you engage students in meaningful interactions with relevant content, they are much more likely to become motivated learners.

As you begin the curriculum development process for your own students, two key elements are essential to your success. The first is *meeting the needs of individual students*. After reading Chapter 6, you should be aware that every student has unique abilities and needs. A major task you will face in planning curriculum, then, is including strategies that will allow you to vary such things as content emphasized, skills to be mastered, and learning materials used to meet individual student needs (Glatthorn, 1994).

The second key to your success in curriculum planning is *helping students recognize the connections between disciplines*. Learning outside the classroom is seldom organized into neat little boxes that carry labels such as "mathematics knowledge" or "reading skills." It is much more likely to be integrated around a topic of interest to the learner. Yet, this "compartmentalization of learning" is often the way in which we teach these subjects in school settings. You will need to work hard to help students make the connections between disciplines through your organization and presentation of content, the use of real-world applications, or clear explanations of the connections that exist among disciplines.

## How has curriculum changed over time?

The curriculum taught in American schools has changed dramatically since colonial times. For much of the 17th and 18th centuries, most of the decisions about content were made locally by teachers based on an understanding of what was important for students to know. The 19th and 20th centuries saw growing involvement on the part of national figures and professional organizations as a more uniform curriculum began to evolve (see Table 7.6).

During the 20th century, five major reform efforts shaped the curricula offered in America's schools (see Table 7.7). In general, these efforts can be seen as focusing on either a student-oriented approach to curriculum planning or a subject-oriented one. The pendulum has swung from one extreme to the other in an attempt to create either relevant or rigorous content for students at all levels within the K–12 system. Hopefully, curriculum planners for the 21st century can avoid the "either/or" mentality demonstrated in the efforts described next and instead create new options that are both rigorous *and* relevant.

### Progressive Education

One of the early efforts of this century to change the content of curricula came to be known as the **progressive education** movement. Growing primarily from the philosophy of education promoted by John Dewey (see Chapter 11), the progressive movement sought to develop curricula that were based on the needs and interests of students. Students were seen as experiencing beings who learned the most when they were engaged in "learning by doing." They were encouraged to spend classroom time manipulating real-world materials and learning from their conversations with teachers and peers. In 1919, this child-centered approach became a formal organization called the Progressive Education Association (PEA).

**TABLE 7.6   Historical Trends Influencing Curriculum**

| Trend | Dates | Key Aspects |
|---|---|---|
| Religious emphasis | 1620–1780 | • Emphasized religious training<br>• Mostly private schools<br>• Primarily available to upper class families |
| Citizenship emphasis | 1780–1820 | • Help students become productive citizens<br>• More public school options<br>• Developing a sense of American identity |
| Common school revival | 1812–1865 | • Equal opportunity led to more public schools<br>• Primary growth was in elementary school options<br>• Broad, general curriculum began to emerge |
| Public high schools | 1880–1920 | • Free public high schools became available<br>• Shift to a more comprehensive curriculum seen |
| Meaningful curriculum content | 1890–1930 | • Public begins to question content of curriculum<br>• Growing desire to make curriculum meaningful surfaces. |

## *Sputnik* and Curricular Excellence

In the 1950s, advances in Russian technology caused a panicked American public to call for change in American schooling. The 1957 launch of the *Sputnik* satellite, apparently placing Russia ahead of the United States in the international competition to conquer space, caused many Americans to be concerned about the curricula being taught in the schools. Admiral Hyman Rickover (1959) was one of the vocal proponents of a renewed emphasis on strong academic curricula. In particular, the science and mathematics curricula were seen as weak and in need of more rigorous content. With the support of federal monies, many new curriculum packages were developed, teachers were trained in the new approaches, and research was conducted to determine the effectiveness of these new options. Every effort was made to strengthen curricular offerings in an attempt to get American education back on track so that we could compete with the Russians in the "race into space."

## Inquiry-Based Curriculum

At the same time that Admiral Rickover was publishing his concerns about American education, Jerome Bruner was summarizing the results of an important conference of scientists and educators held in 1959. His summary of this event formed the basis for the influential book *The Process of Education* (Bruner, 1960). Bruner suggested that instead of learning facts about specific disciplines such as mathematics, students should learn about the "methods of inquiry" used by mathematicians. Using an **inquiry-based curriculum** allows students to understand the structure and methods of disciplines as they begin to think like mathematicians, scientists, and others. Bruner's perspective suggested to those planning curricula that the content could be made more rigorous for all students.

**TABLE 7.7**    More Recent Curriculum Reform

| Reform Movement | Dates | Key Perspectives |
|---|---|---|
| Progressive education | 1919–1955 | • Curriculum based on student needs and interests<br>• Students should be self-motivated<br>• Teachers serve as guides to learning |
| *Sputnik* and curricular excellence | 1957–1969 | • America seen as falling behind Russia in education<br>• Need seen to strengthen mathematics and science curricula in particular |
| Inquiry-based curriculum | 1960–1975 | • Emphasis on "methods of inquiry" used in disciplines<br>• Any subject can be appropriately taught at any age |
| Questioning curriculum options | 1964–1980 | • Curriculum content criticized<br>• Development of curriculum relevant to individual students |
| Back-to-the-basics movement | 1980–present | • Criticized student-centered curriculum<br>• Suggested elimination of extraneous parts of the curriculum<br>• Emphasized excellence in curriculum basics |

One of the most well-known statements Bruner (1960) made in this book is that "Any subject can be taught effectively in some intellectually honest form to any child at any stage of development" (p. 33). This was interpreted to mean that subjects like physics that were typically taught to advanced students in high school settings could be appropriately addressed by teachers working with children as young as 3 or 4 years of age. By discussing physics principles in terms that young children can understand, preschoolers playing with blocks and manipulatives, for example, can develop fundamental understandings that can be built on in later schooling. While controversial, this perspective on teaching and learning has had a significant impact on curriculum development at all grade levels.

### Questioning Curriculum Options

The 1960s and 1970s were decades of social and political unrest in the United States. With the passage of the Civil Rights Act in 1964 and the concurrent involvement of America in the Vietnam war, many began to question the directions being taken in virtually all aspects of society. Education was no exception, and schools received considerable scrutiny in terms of the curriculum being taught. Many felt that what was being taught in the schools was both frivolous and irrelevant. In his 1970 book *Crisis in the Classroom,* Charles Silberman wrote: "Much of what is taught [in the schools] is not worth knowing as a child, let alone as an adult, and little will be remembered. The banality and triviality of the curriculum in most schools has to be experienced to be believed" (p. 173). Two other influential books that were published during this same period and which criticized the curriculum of the schools were John Holt's *How Children Fail* (1964) and *Teaching as a Subversive Activity* by Neil Postman and Charles Weingartner (1969).

Many different curriculum options were experimented with during this period in attempts to correct this perception of crisis in the schools. Individual teachers were encouraged to think

## Arts Education

At all levels, when budgets get tight or a more "basic" curriculum is emphasized, one of the first parts of the school curriculum to be scrutinized for cuts is the arts. The National Endowment for the Arts (1988) has warned that the arts are in "triple jeopardy" in American schools because they are not viewed as serious areas of study, knowledge in the arts is not viewed as a prime educational objective, and curriculum developers cannot agree as to the content of arts education. When the arts are considered less important, they tend to receive a smaller portion of the budget, especially in difficult financial times.

This rather poor status, however, appears to be changing. Within the last few years there has been a renewed interest in making the arts more valued components of the curriculum. In 1998, Hillary Rodham Clinton hosted a White House special event titled "Recognizing the Power of the Arts in Education." The arts were applauded as unique means of expression that are essential to include in K–12 education (Boss, 1999).

Recent research has also supported the importance of arts education to the K–12 curriculum. In a review of more than 400 studies in dance, music, theatre, and art, the Association for the Advancement of Arts Education (Ashton, 1996) found that the arts contribute to students' educations in four major ways:

**Building basic skills.** Particularly in the elementary school years, the arts help develop basic mental and physical capacities.

**Developing "habits of the mind."** The arts help students develop creativity, critical thinking, problem-solving strategies, self-discipline, and self-confidence.

**Gaining knowledge of the arts themselves.** The arts surround us everyday. Understanding them enriches and adds new meaning to lives.

**Becoming better communicators.** The arts are effective means of communication with others. Knowledge of the arts strengthens interpersonal skills, the ability to work in teams, and leadership skills.

### Research the Issue

Research this topic online using the links provided in the *Engage in the Debate* module for this chapter of the Companion Website.

1. From your research, what reasons are cited for including arts education in the K–12 curriculum?
2. What strategies can be employed to help maintain an arts education curriculum in the schools?

### Explore Your Views

1. How well were the arts supported financially and conceptually in your K–12 education? Did your schools have full-time arts education instructors?
2. Do you think that arts education is as important as the more standard components of the curriculum such as mathematics, science, and social studies? Why or why not?
3. Should arts education have a higher priority in K–12 education? What is your rationale for the position you take?

 *To research this issue and submit your responses online, go to the Engage in the Debate module for Chapter 7 of the Companion Website for this text.*

*Sources: Toward Civilization, by National Endowment for the Arts, 1988, Washington, DC: Author; "Applauding the Arts," by S. Boss, 1999, in Arts Education: Basic to Learning, Portland, OR: Northwest Regional Educational Laboratory; and How the Arts Contribute to Education: An Evaluation of Research, by J. Ashton, 1996, Cincinnati, OH: Association for the Advancement of Arts Education.*

more carefully about what was being taught and why. Attempts were made to create a curriculum that was relevant to the needs and interests of individual students. In addition, more comprehensive reform efforts such as the **open classroom** (Kohl, 1969) were initiated during this period. The open classroom was an attempt to use small-group activities, freedom of movement, more informal interactions between students and teachers, and a more relevant curriculum with more options for students in an attempt to reshape the American educational system.

### Back-to-the-Basics Movement

While some aspects of the curriculum reform efforts of the 1960s and 1970s have had a long-lasting impact on education, criticisms of these student-centered options led to what came to be known as the **back-to-the-basics movement** of the 1980s. As the name implies, many people felt that the curriculum of the schools was becoming too fragmented and that what was needed was a return to a core curriculum consisting primarily of reading, writing, mathematics, science, and social studies. Admiral Rickover (1983) was again a leading proponent of this approach:

> Some curricula involve expensive gimmicks, trivial courses and quick fixes of dubious value. . . . Many students have settled for easy, so-called relevant and entertaining courses. They and their parents are deceived by grade inflation. And the lack of national standards of performance blinds everyone to how poor our education system is. (p. 8)

Although the term *back-to-the-basics* became less popular in the later 1980s and into the 1990s, the key elements of this reform effort have remained. In the late 1980s, for example, then U.S. Secretary of Education William Bennett proposed a more rigorous academic curriculum for America's high schools in his 1987 book titled *James Madison High School: A Curriculum for American Students*. Ernest Boyer published *High School: A Report on Secondary Education in America* in 1983 with a similar focus and published a follow-up book in 1995 titled *The Basic School: A Community for Learning*.

## What factors influence curriculum decisions?

The reform efforts just described have had a significant impact on curriculum planning for America's schools. In addition, other less obvious factors have influenced the curriculum of American schools. The textbooks used in K–12 schools, the technology found in classrooms, diversity issues, and parent and community influences have also been important factors that have shaped the content taught in the schools.

### Textbook Selection

The textbook selection process varies between states. In Texas and California, for example, the state governing body for K–12 education selects the textbook options from which school districts can choose. After receiving input from interested citizens, these states determine the best textbooks for all subjects at all grade levels. In other states, however, textbook decisions are left to individual school districts after input from parents and interested community members.

Regardless of the methods of adoption, textbooks play a significant role in curriculum planning. For example, in 1999, one of the textbooks approved for use by California in the eighth-grade social studies curriculum was *The American Nation,* published by Prentice Hall (Davidson & Staff, 1998). Teachers who use this book are influenced in several ways as they develop curricula for their classrooms. First, the organization of the text may well determine the order and organization for many eighth-grade social studies classrooms. The content presented in the text, chapter objectives, learning activities, and evaluation strategies are other components of the textbook package that may influence the curriculum of many classrooms.

## Technology in the Classroom

When you think about the word **technology,** what is the first thing that comes to mind? If you are like most people, your thoughts probably focus on computers. Although computers are one of the more recent and important technological advances, technology actually includes much more than this. The International Technology Education Association (2001) states:

> Broadly speaking, technology is how people modify the natural world to suit their own purposes. From the Greek word *techne,* meaning art or artifice or craft, technology literally means the act of making or crafting, but more generally refers to the diverse collection of processes and knowledge that people use to extend human abilities and to satisfy human needs and wants. (p. 1)

*Technology has significantly influenced curriculum.*

When first introduced to the schools, technological innovations as diverse as chalkboards (early 1800s) and educational television (1950s) were promoted as having the potential to radically change teaching and learning in the K–12 classroom. Yet, time has demonstrated that these important and useful technologies have failed to truly revolutionize education.

Similar claims have been made about the potential of computers to completely change the content and process of education. Seymour Papert (1980), in his classic book *Mindstorms,* stated:

> This book is about how computers can be carriers of powerful ideas and of the seeds of cultural change, how they can help people form new relationships with knowledge that cut across the traditional lines separating humanities from sciences and knowledge of the self from both of these. It is about using computers to challenge current beliefs about who can understand what and at what age. (p. 4)

Thirteen years later, in *The Children's Machine* (1993), Papert was still optimistic that computers would change the educational landscape in new and dramatic ways.

It is still too early to determine the long-term impact that computers will have on reshaping American education, but it is becoming clear that teachers who use computers regularly are changing the content of their classroom curricula (Herr, 2000). The increased availability of high-quality software programs, CD-ROM materials in all subject areas, and Internet access for growing numbers of schools (*Education Week,* 2001) are changing both the quantity and quality of information that teachers and students can use in the classroom.

Take a moment now to reflect on your personal attitudes toward using computers and other technology in learning. Do you see yourself as a person who embraces these options and gets excited about using them yourself? Or, are you a little more resistant to trying out new alternatives? Will your personal attitudes toward technology influence your willingness to incorporate it into your future classroom? Why or why not?

**Reflective
Journey 7.3**

## Diversity Issues

Another factor influencing the direction of curriculum planning in the United States is the increased emphasis on diversity issues. As you develop curricula for your future classroom, you will need to ensure that you emphasize the contributions of diverse people to academic disciplines. For example, most science textbooks now include information about how men and women, people with handicapping conditions, and people from different cultures have all helped shape the content and direction of the sciences. As a future teacher you will be encouraged by your school, district, and state to be more sensitive about including this information in your classroom.

Another way in which diversity issues are influencing the curriculum is through the recognition that the diverse learners in today's classrooms require more individualized and personalized curricula. An obvious example of this type is that non-English-speaking students need instruction in English as a second language. Similarly, when students with special needs are included in the regular classroom, curriculum modifications are often needed. Perhaps not so obvious, however, is the need to structure the curriculum and classroom experiences so that girls have more equitable opportunities to learn mathematics (Levi, 2000). In each of these instances, and more, the needs of diverse learners have led to a richer, more diversified curriculum.

## reflect on diversity

## Multicultural Education

Because of the growing diversity that exists in the classroom, part of what you will be doing as you create a curriculum for your future classroom is developing strategies for multicultural education. Before you can begin this process, however, you will need to know more about what it is. Actually defining the content of multicultural education, however, is not easy. Gorski (2000) states that since its beginnings in the 1960s, "multicultural education has been transformed, refocused, reconceptualized, and in a constant state of evolution both in theory and in practice. It is rare that any two classroom teachers or education scholars will have the same definition for multicultural education."

What is clear from many sources is that multicultural education is a complex process that will have a significant impact on the future of teaching and learning. It should be viewed as a transformational element that will significantly change the educational landscape. Gorski (2000) identifies three strands to multicultural education. The first is the *transformation of self*. Every teacher must begin by identifying the prejudices he or she brings to teaching and learning.

Becoming aware of one's own biases and then working to overcome them is a critical ingredient in multicultural education. A second strand is the *transformation of schools and schooling*. A multicultural curriculum is student centered and one in which all subjects are studied from diverse perspectives. Banks et al. (2001) have identified 12 essential principles of multicultural education that can lead to this transformation in schools. The third strand in multicultural education is the *transformation of society*. The ultimate goal of a multicultural curriculum is to promote social justice and equity and fundamentally change the nature of American society.

It should be clear from even this brief introduction that multicultural education will require considerable effort on your part as a classroom teacher. You will need to learn more about cultures different from yours, examine your own biases and their roots, take care to plan a curriculum that includes a diversity of perspectives, and support the goal of transforming American society. This will require a deep commitment on your part.

### Explore and Reflect

Learn more about multicultural education by reading the online source articles by Gorski (2000) and Banks et al. (2001) and reviewing other online resources provided in the *Reflect on Diversity* module for Chapter 7 of the Companion Website.

1. How much "transformation of self" will you need to do in order to be ready to effectively deal with the diversity in your future classroom? What evidence do you have to support your response?

2. Will you be committed to the time and effort it will take to engage in quality multicultural education? Why or why not?

 *To explore this topic further and submit your responses online, go to the Reflect on Diversity module for Chapter 7 of the Companion Website for this text.*

*Sources:* "The Challenge of Defining a Single 'Multicultural Education,'" by P. Gorski, 2000. Retrieved April 2, 2003, from http://www.mhhe.com/socscience/education/multi/define.html; and "Diversity Within Unity: Essential Principles for Teaching and Learning in a Multicultural Society," by J. Banks et al., 2001. Retrieved April 2, 2003, from http://depts.washington.edu/centerme/cenpub.htm

# EDUCATION IN THE NEWS

## God and Evolution in Kansas Classrooms

John Scopes went on trial in Tennessee for teaching the theory of evolution to his students some 75 years ago. He was found guilty and fined $100, a verdict later overturned on appeal. In the summer of 2000, in response to creationists, the Kansas Board of Education decided to drop the teaching of evolution in the state schools, or to at least to drop the testing of it. Many Fundamentalist Christians praised the decision, but many educators and scientists expressed their dismay at the decisions. Several Supreme Court decisions have made it clear that it is unconstitutional to try to teach the book of Genesis in a public school science class. Still the debate lingers. Evolution can be taught in science classrooms. Religion can be taught in religion classes. The controversy between the two often goes on without debate.

### Critical Thinking Questions

1. What parts of these curriculum issues do you think should be part of the formal curriculum of public schools? Why? How does this issue become part of the formal curriculum or is it part of the informal, hidden, or null curriculum?

2. If you had to write a policy to address this issue, what would it say and why?

3. With respect to the theory of evolution, what are your state and local standards and/or guidelines? What are your beliefs? What, if any, difficulty will you have in teaching with these standards and/or guidelines in mind?

 *To submit your responses online, go to the Education in the News module for Chapter 7 of the Companion Website.*

## Parent and Community Influences

Public schools, by definition, exist to meet the educational needs of children as identified by individual states and local communities. It should come as no surprise, then, that both parents' and community members' opinions about the content of the curriculum influences what you will teach. Particularly at the local level, parents and community members discuss their views of curriculum content with individual teachers, participate in curriculum planning efforts in the schools, and attend school board meetings to share their opinions about curriculum matters.

Parents and community members often want to have the things they value emphasized in the school curriculum. For example, parents with strong religious beliefs often work hard to have certain textbooks either included or excluded from the curriculum because they are in agreement with, or in opposition to, their religious views. Other community members, with strong commitments to having children learn content in such areas as art, music, the "basics," care for the environment, drug prevention education, sex education, and AIDS education work to communicate their beliefs to teachers and schools so that this content can also be addressed in the curriculum.

## What are current curriculum trends?

The significant shifts in curriculum described above and the opinions of parents and community members have led to constantly changing notions about what should be taught in America's schools. Despite these past swings, current curriculum planners at the national, state, and local levels seem to be drawing closer to agreement on the content that students should be encountering in the classroom. In this section, an overview of current trends for eight curriculum areas is given.

## Language Arts and English

Certainly one of the most basic and important skills that all students must have in order to be productive members of society is the development of strong expertise in reading and writing. And while the content for these basic skills may seem easy to define, there actually has been considerable controversy about what should be taught.

In reading, for example, a long-standing debate concerns the relative values of teaching phonics versus what is called a whole-language approach. For the last several decades, literacy experts have debated the relative merits of **phonics instruction** (teaching the relationships between sounds and sound combinations to their written counterparts) and **whole-language learning** (helping children construct reading and writing understandings from meaningful literacy activities). More recently, many researchers and writers have began to suggest that reading instruction must integrate both phonics and the whole-language approach to be successful (National Association for the Education of Young Children, 1998; Snow, Burns, & Griffin, 1998).

Similarly, the writing curriculum has changed to a more integrated approach. The traditional emphasis on teaching grammar and spelling has been combined with a more natural emphasis on meaningful writing experiences to create a stronger overall curriculum for students at all grade levels. An example of a popular approach to teaching writing that follows this more integrated approach is the **six-trait writing process** (see Table 7.8) (Spandel, 2001). By identifying six qualities or characteristics of successful writers and helping students develop proficiency in using them as they engage in meaningful writing experiences, better writing from more motivated students is obtained.

## Mathematics

Historically, the K–12 mathematics curriculum consisted of two main components. First, students were expected to memorize facts related to the mathematical content being learned. In elementary schools, for example, addition, subtraction, multiplication, and division facts were memorized. Secondly, students were taught the computational skills they would need to solve

### TABLE 7.8   6-Trait Writing Process

| Trait | Description |
|---|---|
| Ideas | Quality writing begins with a clear point, a theme, or story line that is backed up with good details. |
| Organization | The structure and order of the writing are important. |
| Voice | The writer's personal style combined with concern for the needs and interests of the audience helps create good writing. |
| Word choice | Carefully chosen words and phrases make for more interesting reading. |
| Sentence fluency | How sentences sound and "fit together" when read aloud is important. |
| Conventions | The importance of such things as spelling, grammar, capitalization, and punctuation is emphasized. |

*Source: Dear Parent: A Handbook for Parents of 6-Trait Writing Students,* by Northwest Regional Education Laboratory, 1998, Portland, OR: Author.

mathematical problems. So, at the secondary level, learning the procedures involved in solving quadratic equations was a typical task.

Although these facts and procedures are needed and should be taught, they are not enough for students to truly understand mathematics. They fail to help students understand the structure and broad concepts that are essential to the discipline. Beginning in the 1960s, with Bruner's inquiry-based approach (1960) to the curriculum, more effort has been made to help students better understand the structure of the discipline. The National Council of Teachers of Mathematics (2001) makes it clear that the "basics" in mathematics education today, while including the learning of computation facts and procedures, should also include applications of computation to real life, an understanding of what computation means, a deeper knowledge of computational procedures, and topics that prepare students for success in the 21st century.

## Science

The elementary science curriculum has typically focused on helping children understand the world around them. The natural world of plants and animals is often addressed first and then followed by the study of such things as electricity, simple machines, and magnetism. Middle school science tends to address these same topics in greater depth and is followed by a high school curriculum that typically includes multiterm courses in general science, biology, chemistry, and physics.

Trends in the science curriculum parallel those described above for mathematics. Science educators, criticized for their emphasis on the learning of facts and isolating science from other disciplines and the real world, have begun to make changes in the curriculum to include more emphasis on understanding science concepts in the context of meaningful learning experiences. The American Association for the Advancement of Science (2001) has published *Project 2061* (the expected year of return for Halley's comet) in order to identify the common knowledge that all K–12 students must possess in order to understand the nature of science.

*Science provides many opportunities for "learning through doing."*

## Social Studies

The social studies curriculum includes a broad variety of disciplines whose main purpose is to understand people and their interactions with one another. While history is often viewed as a cornerstone of the social studies curriculum, geography, political science, sociology, psychology, economics, and anthropology are also important elements. Portions of the content of each of these disciplines can be effectively taught at all levels within the K–12 educational system.

An issue that is having significant impact on current directions in social studies education is the inclusion of diverse perspectives in the content being addressed. In history courses, for example, educators are working hard to make sure that a variety of cultural perspectives are included when discussing historical events. When addressing early colonial times in America, it is appropriate to go beyond the perspectives of the European people who immigrated to this country and include discussions about the attitudes and feelings of the Native American people and the African men, women, and children who were brought to America as slaves. Rather than approaching history using a strictly **eurocentric curriculum**, educators

## Character Education

An issue that is having significant impact on the social studies curriculum is the extent to which values should be taught in relation to the topics being addressed. Over the years, two opposing views have emerged. One view, based largely on the theory and writings of Lawrence Kohlberg (1981), suggests that there are values common to all people and they should be directly taught to students in K–12 classrooms. People taking this view feel that in this complex world it is simply too difficult for students to absorb these values from the world around them. The most common title for this approach today is *character education* and there is considerable support for its inclusion in the K–12 curriculum.

A second perspective, influenced by the writing of Syd Simon and others in the book *Values Clarification* (Simon, Howe, & Kirschenbaum, 1972) strongly discourages the teaching of specific values in the schools. This point of view sees the development of values as a personal decision in which teachers and the schools must remain neutral. Values are seen to vary among subgroups within society and can only be internalized through personal efforts at clarification. This *values clarification* perspective predominated through much of the latter decades of the 20th century.

The interest in including character education in the K–12 curriculum is particularly strong in the social studies. The National Council for the Social Studies has taken the following stand:

> In the primary grades, teachers must focus on basic social skills and the development in children of habits such as civility and self-discipline that are necessary for working successfully with others. At the secondary level, there should be an increasing emphasis on the development of a mature understanding of the fundamental principles of our shared civic life and their history, as well as on the dispositions and skills needed to engage in the public debate over the practice of these principles. (2001)

### React and Reflect

1. Do you think schools should offer programs in character education? Why or why not?

2. Is character education a topic that you would like to address in some way in your future classroom?

 *To explore this topic further and submit your reactions and reflections online, go to the Explore Your Beliefs module for Chapter 7 of the Companion Website for this text.*

*Sources: Essays on Moral Development,* by L. Kohlberg, 1981, New York: Harper and Row; *Values Clarification,* by S. Simon, L. Howe, and H. Kirschenbaum, 1972, New York: Hart Publishing Company; and *Fostering Civic Virtue: Character Education in the Social Studies,* by National Council for the Social Studies, 2001, Washington, DC: Author. Retrieved April 27, 2001, from http://www.socialstudies.org/standards/positions/character.html

are adding insights from the diverse peoples around the world who have had a major influence on American society.

### The Arts

The arts are generally thought of as including art, music, dance, and theatre. While there are exceptions, most K–12 schools have demonstrated a low level of commitment to a strong arts curriculum. In most elementary schools, for example, the regular classroom teacher is expected to teach most of the arts curriculum, with help from either volunteers or specialists who travel between schools offering limited additional instruction. At the middle school and high school levels, students have more access to specialists who teach a variety of courses in art, music, drama, and dance. Unfortunately, most of these courses are considered electives by the schools and students take fewer of them or none at all.

Often considered "frills" during hard economic times, the arts have typically been the first components of the curriculum to be cut. In addition, when educators emphasize a back-to-the-

| TABLE 7.9   Overweight Children | | | | |
|---|---|---|---|---|
| **Age Range** | **All (%)** | **White (%)** | **Black (%)** | **Hispanic (%)** |
| 2–5 | 10.4 | 10.1 | 8.4 | 11.1 |
| 6–11 | 15.3 | 11.8 | 19.5 | 23.7 |
| 12–19 | 15.5 | 12.7 | 23.6 | 23.4 |

*Source:* "Prevalence and Trends in Overweight Among U.S. Children and Adolescents, 1999–2000," by C. Ogden, K. Flegal, M. Carroll, and C. Johnson, 2002, *Journal of the American Medical Association, 288*(14), pp. 1728–1732.

basics curriculum, the arts are often overlooked. Finally, if you compare the number of faculty hired to teach the arts in K–12 classrooms with those engaged in mathematics, language arts, science, and social studies instruction, it is clear that the schools have placed most of their teaching resources in areas other than the arts.

## Physical Education

The physical education curriculum in the K–12 schools has many components, all of which are growing in importance as Americans become increasingly more sedentary. Recent national statistics indicate that the percentage of overweight children has increased from approximately 4% in the 1960s to more than 15% in 2000 (see Table 7.9) (Ogden, Flegal, Carroll, & Johnson, 2002). The physical education curriculum includes physical fitness, physical skills development, health, recreation, and dance. Organized sports and recreation programs are also offered as extracurricular activities. At the elementary school level, specialists in physical education work with individual classes of students once or twice each week for approximately 30 minutes each session on aspects of this broad curriculum. Classroom teachers are then expected to supplement this instruction with additional content in physical education. Physical education specialists teach the entire curriculum at the middle school and high school levels. Most secondary schools offer both elective and required courses in physical education.

## Vocational-Technical Education

Historically, the emphasis in **vocational-technical education** had been on the preparation of students for entry-level work in jobs that required less than a 4-year college degree. The back-to-the-basics reform movement and the growing complexity of most entry-level occupations have led to more comprehensive vocational-technical preparation programs. Students now take a balanced curriculum that includes a combination of academic, vocational, and technical course work (Levesque, Lauen, Teitelbaum, Alt, & Librera, 2000). In addition, more students who complete high school vocational-technical programs go on to complete postsecondary programs as well.

*Vocational-technical education takes many forms.*

### Foreign Languages

While students in America's schools are increasingly involved in foreign language learning, they lag far behind their peers from around the world who frequently engage in learning additional languages from the beginning of their schooling experiences. The push to increase academic standards for graduation from high school has nearly doubled the number of courses in foreign language study that students take (National Center for Education Statistics, 2001). Still, only about 40% of all American students are involved in foreign language course work. Comparatively, in many other countries, students are required to learn their native language(s) *and* English.

As the world becomes increasingly more interconnected, the need to have American students trained in foreign languages will continue to grow. The American Council on the Teaching of Foreign Languages (1996) stated the issue as follows:

> Language and communication are at the heart of the human experience. The United States must educate students who are linguistically and culturally equipped to communicate successfully in a pluralistic American society and abroad. This imperative envisions a future in which ALL students will develop and maintain proficiency in English and at least one other language, modern or classical. Children who come to school from non-English backgrounds should also have opportunities to develop further proficiencies in their first language. (p. 2)

## Summary

In this chapter, four organizing questions were presented to help you develop a better understanding of developing curriculum:

### How is curriculum defined and developed?

Curriculum takes a variety of forms and is influenced by a number of different groups:
- Curriculum defined
- Approaches to the curriculum
- National, state, and district influences (Praxis II, topic IIb)
- Your role as a teacher in curriculum development (Praxis II, topic IIb)

### How has curriculum changed over time?

Throughout American history, the curriculum has continued to change based on various social influences:
- Progressive education
- *Sputnik* and curricular excellence (Praxis II, topic IIIa)
- The inquiry-based curriculum
- Questioning curriculum options
- Back-to-the-basics movement

### What factors influence curriculum decisions?

Four factors have a significant influence on curriculum decisions:
- Textbook selection (Praxis II, topic IIa)
- Technology in the classroom (Praxis II, topic IIa)
- Diversity issues (Praxis II, topic Ib)
- Parent and community influences (Praxis II, topic IVb)

## What are current curriculum trends?

All of the factors identified above have influenced the current status of curriculum:

- Language arts and English (Praxis II, topics Ib, d, e)
- Mathematics (Praxis II, topic IIb)
- Science (Praxis II, topic IIb)
- Social studies (Praxis II, topic IIb)
- The arts (Praxis II, topic IIb)
- Physical education (Praxis II, topic IIb)
- Vocational-technical education (Praxis II, topic IIb)
- Foreign languages (Praxis II, topic IIb)

## Key Terms

back-to-the-basics movement
curriculum
curriculum standards
eurocentric curriculum
formal curriculum
hidden curriculum
informal curriculum
inquiry-based curriculum
null curriculum

open classroom
phonics instruction
progressive education
six-trait writing process
student-centered curriculum
subject-centered curriculum
technology
vocational-technical education
whole-language learning

## Reflective Journey: Online Journal

Use the questions for thought and reflection highlighted throughout the chapter to help guide your personal journey of reflection and professional development as a teacher. To complete your journal entries online, go to the *Reflective Journey* module for this chapter of the Companion Website.

## PRAXIS Test Preparation Activities

To review an online chapter case study, test your understanding of chapter topics and concepts, and begin preparing for the Praxis II: Principles of Learning and Teaching examination, go to the *Praxis Test Preparation* module for this chapter of the Companion Website.

## INTASC Becoming a Reflective Practitioner

To complete these activities and submit your responses online, go to the *Becoming a Reflective Practitioner* module for this chapter of the Companion Website.

## How is curriculum defined and developed?

### Review Questions

1. How important are the informal, hidden, and null curricula when compared with the formal curriculum of the schools?

2. What are the differences between the subject-centered and student-centered curricula?

3. Describe the national, state, and district influences on the curriculum.

### Field Experience

Spend some time talking to an administrator in a school of your choice. Seek information from this person about the informal curriculum. What options are available at that school? How many students participate in the various activities? Who serves as instructors for these programs? Which are paid positions and which are assignments for adult volunteers? Discuss what you found with others.

### Building Your Portfolio: *State Curriculum Guidelines*

**INTASC Standard 7.** For the state in which you currently live, or the one where you plan to eventually teach, locate and study the state curriculum guidelines that have been developed for all students. In many instances, this information is available on state department of education websites. If possible, make a hardcopy of these documents for inclusion in your portfolio. After reviewing the available materials, summarize their contents and include this information in your portfolio.

## How has curriculum changed over time?

### Review Questions

1. How did the subject-centered and student-centered approaches to curriculum development influence curriculum reform in the 20th century?
2. What is the inquiry-based curriculum?
3. How did the social and political unrest of the 1960s and 1970s influence curriculum change?

### Building Your Portfolio: *Curriculum Reform Effort*

**INTASC Standard 1.** Choose one of the five major curriculum reform efforts described in this chapter and research it in more depth. What were the forces that led to the reform? How was the proposed reform different from what already was happening in the schools? Are there aspects of this reform effort that are still evident today? Write up your findings for a portfolio entry.

## What factors influence curriculum decisions?

### Review Questions

1. In what ways do textbooks influence curricula in the schools?
2. How has an increased emphasis on diversity issues impacted school curricula?

### Field Experience

Review the textbook(s) used in a classroom of your choice. Critique the content being presented. What is included and what has been omitted? Also analyze the directions provided for teachers to help them present this content to students. Are there specific directions or more general guidelines for teachers to consider? Look at things like pictures, boxed features, and special interest getting tools used to help motivate students to read and use the text. Share your findings with others.

### Building Your Portfolio: *Parent and Community Influences on Curriculum*

**INTASC Standard 10.** Attend a school board meeting with the purpose of observing how parents and community members influence the curriculum of the schools. You may also want to talk to a school board member, principal, or district administrator to find out additional information. From your observations and discussions, what impact do parents and community members have on the curriculum? Give specific examples where possible.

## What are current curriculum trends?

### Review Questions

1. Describe the current debate over literacy learning in America's schools.

2. What have been the major criticisms of mathematics and science instruction during the last several decades?

3. What disciplines are associated with social studies?

### Building Your Portfolio: *Subject Area Curricular Trend*

**INTASC Standard 1.** Choose one of the curriculum areas discussed in this chapter and spend some time studying in more detail the emerging trends for this discipline. You may wish to locate one of the appropriate national curriculum organizations (such as the National Council of Teachers of Mathematics) and review information on this organization's website to obtain the needed information. For the grade level of your choice, summarize the implications of these curriculum trends for your portfolio.

## Suggested Readings

Bennett, W. (1987). *James Madison High School: A curriculum for American students.* Washington, DC: U.S. Department of Education. Bennett argues for a stronger emphasis on the basics in American high schools and proposes a core curriculum that all students should complete.

Bruner, J. (1960). *The process of education.* New York: Random House. In this classic book, Bruner identifies the inquiry-based curriculum and presents a rationale for this approach to curriculum planning.

Neill, A. (1960). *Summerhill: A radical approach to child rearing.* New York: Hart Publishing Company. As the title implies, this book documents a radical approach to schooling. It is one in which the students themselves define the curriculum.

Silberman, C. (1970). *Crisis in the classroom.* New York: Random House. Silberman is often considered a spokesperson for those who were dissatisfied during the 1970s and 1980s with the unimaginative and lackluster curriculum of the schools. He outlines the perceived problems and presents suggestions for improvement.

# chapter 8

## Using Effective Teaching Strategies

Excellent teachers have a variety of different styles and use a diverse array of strategies to motivate students to learn. Despite the differences, however, good teaching has a common core that all good teachers know and use. In this chapter, four organizing questions will help you better understand both the similarities and differences that exist among good teachers.

## Focus Questions

◢ Why are strong relationships with students and other adults important?

◢ What does research tell us about effective instructional strategies?

◢ What instructional models can I use?

◢ What skills will I need in management and discipline?

"The rewards I find in teaching are rooted in the joy of not only watching but also being part of my students' learning and development," stated Michele Forman, the National Teacher of the Year for 2001. "A good teacher needs not only a good understanding of what he or she teaches, but also a sense of excitement in learning and a clear vision of how the key elements of a subject can be conveyed to students."

With this philosophy Forman emphasizes an incredibly strong teacher and learner relationship. "Without mutual trust, students are wary of accepting the risk and vulnerability of learning," she said. "For them, the threat of feeling or appearing inept or incompetent is best overcome with the support of a teacher in a caring, accepting and respectful relationship."

Among Forman's many beliefs about education, she is especially passionate about classes that include students with varied backgrounds and ability levels. "Education is enriched for all students when learners bring their different experiences, perspectives and skills to the group," she said. (Council of Chief State School Officers, 2001)

Michele Forman, who teaches social studies at Middlebury Union High School in Middlebury, Vermont, has been honored as an outstanding educator by being named the National Teacher of the Year for 2001 by the Council of Chief State School Officers. But what makes her such an excellent teacher? While she is a unique individual with a teaching style that is hers alone, she shares many elements in common with other outstanding educators. This chapter is designed to build on Ms. Forman's insights regarding the elements of effective teaching and help provide you with a better understanding of both the similarities and differences that exist between all good teachers. Please realize, however, that the information presented here is only a brief overview of these important topics. You will need to learn a great deal more before you truly understand the complex task of teaching.

## Why are strong relationships with students and other adults important?

Teaching can be successful only when several key ingredients are present. Many would suggest that the most fundamental of these is the ability to establish and maintain effective working relationships with students and other adults. It is the humanity of the teacher, the ability to be real and make connections with students and others, that often determines whether or not learning takes place in the classroom. Greenberg (1969) states it this way: "The human, emotional qualities of the teacher are the very heart of teaching. No matter how much emphasis is placed on such other qualities in teaching as educational technique, technology, equipment, or buildings, *the humanity of the teacher is the vital ingredient if children are to learn*" (p. 20).

### Developing Positive Relationships with Students

**Reflective Journey 8.1**

Think back to your K–12 schooling experiences. Do you remember a teacher who was well-loved by her or his students? What was it that this teacher did to attract students to him or her? Can you remember aspects of this teacher's personality that were attractive to you? How did she or he interact with students? Try to remember some specific things this teacher did that made it enjoyable to be nearby. Most people have fond memories of one or more teachers that fit this category. These remarkable educators always seem to have time to spend listening and responding to both the joys and sorrows of their students' lives while approaching teaching and learning with an enthusiasm that is infectious. The strong relationships these teachers develop are at the heart of good teaching.

One writer who emphasized the importance of effective teacher–student relationships was Thomas Gordon (1974). He identified several characteristics of successful interactions between teachers and students:

The relationship between a teacher and a student is good when it has (1) *Openness or Transparency,* so each is able to risk directness and honesty with the other; (2) *Caring,* when each knows that he is valued by the other; (3) *Interdependence* (as opposed to dependency) of one on the other; (4) *Separateness,* to allow each to grow and to develop his uniqueness, creativity, and individuality; (5) *Mutual Needs Meeting,* so that neither's needs are met at the expense of the other's needs. (p. 24)

*Having fun with students can help build relationships.*

Nel Noddings (1992) is another educator who, more recently, has emphasized the importance of caring in relationships with students. She identified four components to this caring process. The first component she calls *modeling*. Teachers' interactions with students provide examples of the caring relationships students should have with each other and with adults. Secondly, teachers and students need to engage in *dialogues* that are open-ended discussions with no predetermined outcome. Caring relationships also require *practice*. Students need opportunities to practice caring in their relationships with others. Community service projects are one example of this type. The final component of caring relationships is *confirmation*. Teachers need to find ways to validate student progress in developing caring relationships.

Teachers build strong relationships with students in one of two main ways. First, they take the time and effort needed to have authentic, meaningful interactions with students. When teachers engage in the simple act of greeting students warmly as they arrive at the classroom door, they are engaged in this process of relationship building. A second option for strengthening teacher–student relationships is to engage students in planned activities that can systematically provide for more positive interactions (see Table 8.1). By actually including these activities during the school day or after hours, teachers can become more purposeful in building relationships with students. This is particularly important for those students who are quiet and unassuming or for those who are more difficult for the teacher to like.

# MASTER TEACHER SERIES

## Segment III: The Pressure of the Big Test: Never Give Up

In this segment of the *Master Teacher Series*, Ms. Jones continues to work on the test-taking abilities of the students in her challenging task at PC 27 in Red Hook, Brooklyn. She is feeling more in control of her class but worries about how the students are coping with her tough assignments and about whether or not she has prepared them adequately. One student continues to be a problem as both the teacher and parent struggle to identify a successful way to handle him. Effective teaching strategies seem to have been abandoned for test prep because, as always, the test looms over their heads. When the test is over, more problems arise.

### For Deeper Understanding

1. How can you tell that Ms. Jones is committed to teaching? Can you recall how your teachers demonstrated they were committed to teaching? How will you demonstrate your commitment to teaching to your students?

2. Keith's mom and Ms. Jones both struggle with what to do with Keith. What do you think the problem is and how it might best be solved?

3. Recall the chapter discussion that teachers build relationships with students in two ways: by taking the time and effort needed to have authentic, meaningful interactions with students and by engaging students in planned activities that can systematically provide for more positive interactions. From watching the first three segments of the *Master Teacher Series*, provide examples that indicate that Ms. Jones has built positive relationships with her students.

4. Several different instruction techniques have been identified that have been proven successful in boosting student academic achievement. What are some of those that Ms. Jones has employed? What would you do?

5. From the video segments about Ms. Jones and her students, what ways can you identify that tell you that sometimes teaching is emotional and stressful?

6. Students seem to have developed test phobia. How has that happened? Who is at fault?

*To submit your responses online, go to the Master Teacher Series module for Chapter 8 of the Companion Website.*

**TABLE 8.1   Planned Activities for Building Relationships**

| Activity | Description |
|---|---|
| Eating lunch with students | Particularly at the elementary level, teachers can schedule times to visit informally with individual students over lunch. |
| Arranging interviews | Students interview teachers to learn more about them as individuals. |
| Sending letters and notes to students | Letters of introduction and positive notes to individual students help build relationships. |
| Using a suggestion box | Teachers can show their interest in student ideas by having a suggestion box where students can anonymously share their thoughts. |
| Participating in school and community events | Events such as carnivals, musical and dramatic productions, sporting events, and debates are opportunities for teachers to relate to students outside the classroom. |
| Getting involved in playground time | At the elementary level, teachers can spend some enjoyable time with students on the playground. |
| Sending birthday cards | Knowing student birthdays and sending a card is a good way to build relationships. |

*Source: Comprehensive Classroom Management: Creating Communities of Support and Solving Problems,*
by V. Jones and L. Jones, 2001. Boston: Allyn & Bacon.

## Working with Parents

Linnea Wilson, who teaches middle school language arts, is preparing for **parent–teacher conferences** in 2 weeks. She has sent home information with her students about the content and format of these meetings and made personal telephone calls to the parents she particularly wants to see. Next week she will prepare an agenda for each of the scheduled appointments so that the conference time can be as productive as possible. Linnea is in her fourth year of teaching and has found that parent conferences are an excellent format for sharing information about schooling with parents. Like Linnea, you will want to build strong working relationships with parents and families through the use of parent conferences and other involvement strategies.

There has been a growing emphasis in America's schools on the importance of establishing good working relationships with students' parents and guardians. A topic that was seldom mentioned 30 years ago, working with parents has become a significant research issue and an important component of many teacher preparation programs (Berger, 2000). Teachers, parents, and children all benefit when positive communication and interaction take place between the home and school (Gestwicki, 2000). Table 8.2 suggests some ways in which current technology can help with communication. Teachers benefit from increased support in the classroom and at home. Parents develop a better understanding of their own children and strengthen their own parenting skills. In addition, good home–school relationships increase student performance and enhance student self-concept.

Take a moment to think about this aspect of your future teaching. How do you think you will feel about taking the time to communicate and interact with parents in positive ways? Do you think you will be comfortable in talking and working with them? Can you see some of the benefits of these interactions? Are there some parents you may be more comfortable with than others?

**Reflective Journey 8.2**

## His Name Is Michael

The following is excerpted from a 2002 *Education Week* article:

> He appeared at my classroom door in the middle of a busy morning gripping the hand of a harried school secretary. He was a tiny child with carefully combed hair, wearing a crisply pressed shirt, tightly clutching his lunch money. The secretary handed this child to me and rattled off the institutional essentials: "His name is Michael. He is a bus rider. He doesn't speak English." Not much of an introduction, but that's how it happens in schools. . . .
>
> We did all the usual new-kid things that day. We played the name game. The kid of the day gave him the grand tour of our room. He got to sit on the couch even though it really wasn't his turn. The children insisted that Michael have a buddy for absolutely everything—learning buddy, lunch buddy, cubby buddy, line buddy, water buddy, rug buddy, bus buddy. . . .
>
> Michael existed marginally on the outside of the group. Sometimes he was on the outside looking in;
>
> sometimes he was on the outside looking out. I often saw him with his eyes closed—looking somewhere hidden. He was well-mannered, punctual, respectful, cute-as-a-button—but completely detached from me, from the children, and from the learning.
>
> I met with the bilingual resource teacher to chat about concerns and possibilities. She told me she could come to an informal observation "a week from tomorrow." It was a long wait, but that's how it is in schools. She came. She watched. She listened. On her way out she said, "You might have better results, dear, if you call him Miguel." . . .
>
> Miguel didn't stay with us for long. His family moved on to follow their own calendar of opportunities. We didn't get to say goodbye, but that's how it happens in schools.
>
> Miguel's paperwork arrived about three weeks after he had moved away. I was going through the folder, updating it for his next teacher, when I noticed something that made me catch my breath. His name wasn't Michael. It wasn't Miguel. His name was David. (Marriott, 2002, p. 35)

### Explore and Reflect

Learn more about non-English-speaking students by reading the online source article by Marriott (2002) and reviewing other online resources provided in the *Reflect on Diversity* module for Chapter 8 of the Companion Website.

1. What steps can you take as a future teacher to develop better working relationships with non-English-speaking students like David?

2. In the busyness of life in the classroom, even the best teachers find that students like David who are quiet and respectful get "lost in the shuffle." What can you do as a future teacher to keep this from happening?

 *To explore this topic further and submit your reflections online, go to the Reflect on Diversity module for Chapter 8 of the Companion Website for this text.*

*Sources:* "His Name Is Michael," by D. Marriott, 2002, *Education Week*, October 9, 2002, p. 35. Retrieved from http://www.edweek.org/ew/ewstory.cfm?slug=06marriott.h22&keywords=His%20Name%20is%20Michael. Reprinted with permission.

## Other Collaborative Relationships

You might have assumed from past educational experiences that you would be relatively independent as you planned for and taught your future students. That is, once the school day began, you would be the primary person responsible for educating those under your care. Although there is considerable truth to this assumption, teaching is becoming an increasingly collaborative profession. For example, some of your students may require assistance with their oral speech development. If so, you will need to plan and implement appropriate strategies with a *speech therapist*. The principal and vice principal are other school personnel who are actively involved in working with teachers to implement effective management and discipline procedures and assist in curriculum

| TABLE 8.2 Using Technology to Communicate with Parents | |
|---|---|
| **Communication Tool** | **Description** |
| Electronic mail | For the growing number of parents who have computers and Internet access, sending a quick e-mail message is a very convenient and easy way to communicate with parents. |
| Video/audiotapes | Many parents can't come visit the classroom as often as they would like, but would still like to see/hear what is going on there. Making a video/audiotape of classroom activities that can be then checked out by parents can help keep them involved. |
| Websites | Many schools and some teachers now have their own websites that parents can use to access a great deal of information about school/classroom activities. Technology options have made this a relatively easy option for schools and teachers to consider using. |
| Homework hotline | Hardware and software are now available that allow individual teachers to record a daily message for parents and students regarding homework for the next day. Parents can call the school and find out what assignments are due and details regarding their completion. |

planning. You will want to collaborate with them as well. A third example of an important collaborative relationship is with the *special education teacher.* Because students with special needs are included in the regular classroom, you will need to work closely with the special education teacher assigned to students in your classroom.

It should be clear from the above sampling that you will need to establish good working relationships with a variety of different colleagues in order to be successful in your work with students. As with any relationship, taking the time to build rapport, engaging in regular and effective communications, and respecting differences are all essential in working with these individuals.

## What does research tell us about effective instructional strategies?

You may be surprised to learn that the area of systematic, scientific study of effective teaching strategies is only about 30 years old. In the early 1970s, researchers began to study the effects of different instructional skills on student learning. During the last three decades of the 20th century, research evidence slowly began to mount and a clear pattern has developed regarding the strategies individual teachers use to positively influence student learning. The Mid-continent Research for Education and Learning (McREL) group recently completed a review of this research (Marzano, Pickering, & Pollock, 2001) and identified instructional techniques that have proven successful in boosting academic performance (see Table 8.3).

### Identifying Similarities and Differences

The ability to **identify similarities and differences** is a broad skill that enables students of all ages to engage in problem solving and information processing that is basic to all aspects of learn-

**TABLE 8.3    Instructional Strategies Influencing Student Achievement**

| Category | Description |
|---|---|
| Identifying similarities and differences | Effective teachers help students identify similarities and differences. Researchers have found these mental operations to be basic to human thought. |
| Summarizing and note taking | Effective teachers explicitly teach students how to summarize the information being learned and strategies for effective note taking. |
| Reinforcing effort | Good teachers help students understand the importance of effort and guide them in seeing its impact on individual performance. |
| Homework and practice | The assignment of an appropriate amount of homework (increasing with age) and opportunities to practice new and developing skills are necessary for effective learning. |
| Nonlinguistic representations | Good teachers help students generate mental pictures and provide graphic representations of the information being learned. |
| Goal setting and providing feedback | Effective teachers establish a direction for learning and give students feedback about how well they are doing. |
| Generating and testing hypotheses | Good teachers help students apply knowledge by guiding them in generating and testing hypotheses. |
| Activating prior knowledge | Teachers need to help students remember and use what they already know through the use of cues or hints, effective questioning strategies, and advance organizers. |

*Source: Classroom Instruction That Works: Research-Based Strategies for Increasing Student Achievement,* by R. Marzano, D. Pickering, and J. Pollock, 2001, Alexandria, VA: Association for Supervision and Curriculum Development.

ing (Medin, Goldstone, & Markman, 1995). Take, for example, Mrs. Jackson's American history class (Marzano et al., 2001). As a part of their study of the 1960s, her students were reading and discussing Martin Luther King, Jr.'s "I Have a Dream" speech. Knowing that her students had been exposed to this speech several times in the past, Mrs. Jackson wanted to help her students understand it in a different way, so she presented them with an incomplete analogy:

> "I Have a Dream" was to the Civil Rights Movement as _____ was to _____.
>
> In small groups, students were to complete the analogy using another historical event or document in the first blank and a movement or event in the second blank. The students were asked to be ready to explain their completed analogy to the entire class.
>
> To Mrs. Jackson's surprise, students were quite adept in designing and explaining their analogies. To the students' surprise, this activity deepened their understanding of the effect the "I Have a Dream" speech had on the Civil Rights Movement. (Marzano et al., 2001, p. 13)

Through the use of analogies, Mrs. Jackson enabled her students to engage in a complex process of identifying similarities and differences that helped them deepen their understanding of American history.

### Summarizing and Note-Taking

A second category of research-based strategies that effective teachers use is assisting students in **summarizing** what they have learned and engaging in effective **note-taking**. To effectively summarize or take good notes, students must first decide what information is worth knowing and what should be omitted and then determine a method of organization. Teachers at all levels can help their students develop effective summarizing and note-taking strategies. You can assist in this process by providing an organizational framework to assist students in summarizing or by periodically providing your students with teacher-prepared notes.

### Reinforcing Effort

Rather than attempting to directly enhance students' cognitive skills, **reinforcing effort** focuses on students' attitudes and beliefs (Marzano et al., 2001). Good teachers work to strengthen posi-

## engage in the debate

## Drill and Practice Software

One way in which students today receive opportunities to practice what they are learning is through the use of what has been called *drill and practice software*. As the name implies, these software programs give students who have learned content the opportunity to practice what they have studied so that it can be internalized. Drill and practice software is available for virtually every subject and grade.

> The majority of educational software available today is designed to complement other forms of instruction. This is often referred to as "drill and practice" software (or "drill and kill" software, as instructional designers facetiously call it). For applications in which the subject mat-

ter needs to be mastered through memorization of facts or replicable patterns, this type of software can be useful in reinforcing knowledge." (Brogan, 2001, p. 1)

Despite its availability, many are suggesting that drill and practice software has only limited applicability in the classroom and schools should locate and use more software that allows for open-ended exploration. "The best stuff is the stuff that's experiential, exploratory . . . promoting inquiry-based learning. . . . The best software takes more problem-solving, more thinking skills for the activities . . . The students become engaged with doing something with the information presented" (Zehr, 1999, p. 14).

### Research the Issue

Research this topic online using the links provided in the *Engage in the Debate* module for this chapter of the Companion Website. Link to the online source articles by Brogan (2001) and Zehr (1999) and explore the information provided at the additional sites listed.

1. From your research, what are the strengths and weaknesses of drill and practice software?
2. What other software options are available and what are their benefits?

### Explore Your Views

1. Is drill and practice software a better option for students to use in practicing skills than the paper and pencil tasks often assigned by teachers?
2. Do you think schools should spend their technology resources to purchase drill and practice software? Why or why not?

*To research this issue and submit your responses online, go to the Engage in the Debate module for Chapter 8 of the Companion Website for this text.*

*Sources:* "The Good, the Bad, and the Useless: Recognizing the Signs of Quality in Educational Software," by P. Brogan, 2001, *Electronic School*. Retrieved August 21, 2002, from http://www.electronic-school.com; and "Screening for the Best," by M. Zehr, 1999, in *Technology Counts 1999*, Bethesda, MD: *Education Week*, pp. 13–22.

tive attitudes about effort by talking about its effects and helping students to see its impact. Teaching about effort can include such things as personal stories about times when perseverance paid off for you, having students share their own examples of effort and its impact on their lives, or reading and discussing stories that demonstrate the value of effort (e.g., *The Little Engine That Could* for primary children). By periodically providing students with scoring guides that help them rate their own effort and corresponding level of achievement, you can also help students see that their efforts do result in higher levels of achievement.

## Homework and Practice

**Homework** has become a common component of American education that begins for most students in the early elementary school years. Because a relatively small portion of a student's waking life is actually spent in school, homework provides an opportunity to extend learning experiences beyond the classroom. Research conducted on the benefits of homework suggests that academic gains are smaller in the early years and gradually grow in significance throughout the high school experience (Cooper, 1989). In addition to the potential academic benefits, proponents indicate that homework helps students develop good study habits, promotes positive attitudes toward school, and encourages the realization that learning takes place in a variety of settings.

Most of the skills being learned in schools need considerable **practice** for them to be perfected. That may seem most obvious with a physical skill such as handwriting or keyboarding. It is equally true, however, with cognitive skills such as reading, written communications, mathematics, and the scientific method. These are all complex skills that require many repetitions in order to master. The old adage "practice makes perfect" contains a great deal of truth. The challenge for teachers is to provide opportunities to practice developing skills in ways that are both interesting and meaningful to students. It takes a surprisingly large number of repetitions to achieve a relatively modest level of competence in using new skills (Anderson, 1995), so teachers need to be sure to provide a variety of interesting practice experiences. Playful activities and ones that allow students to apply their developing skills in meaningful situations are examples of ways in which teachers allow for more interesting practice.

## Nonlinguistic Representations

Paivio (1990) suggests that when people acquire new information, it is coded and stored in both a linguistic and an imagery mode. We create "mental word strings" and either mental pictures or actual physical sensations to store new information. These latter two categories are referred to as **nonlinguistic representations.** An example of this type would be the mental imagery readers engage in as they create "pictures" of the actions and settings described in print. Using both linguistic and nonlinguistic representations enables students to better process and remember what they are learning.

You will have a variety of strategies to choose from to help students use nonlinguistic representations in their learning (Marzano et al., 2001). One example would be the use of *physical models.* They represent in concrete terms the concepts being studied. For example, rectangular sticks of varying lengths known as Cuisenaire rods are used in many elementary school mathematics classrooms

*Charts and diagrams help organize student understandings.*

to represent arithmetic operations. Another nonlinguistic representation is the use of *pictures and pictographs.* Drawing a picture of a flower and its major parts or using symbols and symbolic pictures to describe the process of photosynthesis helps students understand and remember what they are studying. A third example of a nonlinguistic representation is *physical movement.* Young children learning to write the letters of the alphabet can trace sandpaper representations of each letter and thereby create a "physical memory" that helps them remember the motions needed to write them.

## Goal Setting and Providing Feedback

Setting broad goals for learning and giving students regular feedback about how well they are attaining these goals are two additional strategies that effective teachers use to enhance instruction. Educational research supports the many benefits associated with both strategies (Walberg, 1999). The process of **goal setting** is like consulting a road map before starting a trip in the car. It provides opportunities for teachers and students to set directions for the learning process. And while there are many possible pathways to the same end result, knowing the chosen direction helps both students and teachers prepare for and achieve the desired goal. When students know where they are going, it makes it much more likely that they will reach both their short-term and long-term objectives.

After analyzing literally thousands of studies on teaching, Hattie (1992) found that providing students with **feedback** on their performances was a powerful strategy that effective teachers use to enhance achievement. This feedback should tell students both what they are doing well and what needs to be done differently. Corrective feedback, when shared in a timely way, provides the greatest opportunities for student improvement (Marzano et al., 2001). One effective strategy for providing feedback is through the use of a **rubric.** Rubrics, such as the one shown in Figure 8.1, provide students with specific feedback on their individual levels of knowledge and skill development.

**Figure 8.1**   Rubric for Fourth-Grade Science Experiment

| | 4 | 3 | 2 | 1 | 0 |
|---|---|---|---|---|---|
| **Content**<br>Is there a clear description of the science content learned? | | | | | |
| **Process**<br>Was the scientific process followed as described in class? | | | | | |
| **Written Description**<br>Is the report easy to read? Does it have clear sentences, good spelling, and appropriate grammar? | | | | | |
| **Points Earned** | | | | | |

*Key:* 4 = excellent; 3 = good; 2 = needs improvement; 1 = unacceptable; 0 = no judgment possible.

**Comments:**

## Generating and Testing Hypotheses

While **generating and testing hypotheses** is often associated with scientific investigations, it is actually a part of most fields of study. For example, an historian looking at Native American cultures in the years prior to the 1400s would need to generate hypotheses about what life was like and then seek to verify them through careful study of existing artifacts and the writings of others. Or a political scientist studying colonial governments in America would first generate hypotheses about what factors influenced the structure of government in each of the colonies and then read various accounts of this period to test these hypotheses.

## Activating Prior Knowledge

When teachers help their students remember what they already know regarding a specific topic, they are **activating prior knowledge.** Teachers typically use cues, questions, and advance organizers to accomplish this task. While these strategies have much in common, each is useful in helping students call to mind what they already know. *Cues* are hints from the teacher about what is to be experienced and how it relates to what has already been learned. Marsha Harvey cues her second-grade class as they prepare for their upcoming field trip to the seashore by reminding them that they have studied local sea life and will be seeing some forms they investigated while discovering new ones as they explore the tide pools and beach area. *Questioning* is another strategy teachers use frequently to activate prior knowledge. Questioning accounts for a high percentage of the time teachers spend interacting with students. Research would indicate that teachers use between 45 and 150 questions for every half hour of teaching in the classroom (Nash & Shiman, 1974). *Advance organizers* were originally identified as an important educational strategy by David Ausubel (1968). He viewed them as introductory materials that were presented prior to the actual learning experience to "bridge the gap between what the learner already knows and what he needs to know before he can successfully learn the task at hand" (p. 148).

# What instructional models can I use?

In addition to the more specific instructional strategies described above, researchers and writers have worked to identify the different styles teachers use to interact with their students. For more than 40 years, Bruce Joyce and Marsha Weil (2000) have been influential educators engaged in this process of studying promising approaches to teaching. They have found many different models and organized them into four broad groups: the behavioral systems model of instruction, the personal model, the information processing model, and the social model of instruction (see Table 8.4). As you go through your teacher preparation program, you will learn more about these models and begin making decisions about which approaches you will want to use in your work with students.

## Behavioral Systems Model of Instruction

The basic premise behind the **behavioral systems model of instruction** is that human beings of all ages learn from the ways in which the environment around them responds to their behaviors. For example, a student chooses to work on difficult geometric proofs because she has received praise for her past efforts from both the classroom teacher and her parents. A second example of behavioral systems learning would be when a student observes a classmate receiving some free time on the computer after having completed his math assignment and decides to complete her own work in the hope of earning a similar reward. In both examples students are engaging in behaviors because of the perceived benefits received from those around them for these actions.

The theoretical basis for this approach is often referred to as *behavior modification* and is rooted in the work of Thorndike (1913), Pavlov (1927), Watson (1924), and B. F. Skinner

| TABLE 8.4 | Models of Instruction | |
|---|---|---|
| **Model** | **Description** | **Example(s)** |
| Behavioral systems model | Students learn as they modify behavior in response to environmental feedback. | Direct instruction Mastery learning |
| Personal model | Each individual must take responsibility for his or her own learning while striving to reach full potential. | Nondirective teaching |
| Information processing model | Students make sense of their world as they are assisted in organizing the information around them. | Constructivist education |
| Social model | Students learn as they interact with peers and teachers in learning communities. | Cooperative learning |

*Source: Models of Teaching,* 6th ed., by B. Joyce and M. Weil, Boston: Allyn and Bacon.

(1953). These behaviorists and others have developed an approach to teaching that relies on observable behaviors, carefully crafted learning tasks, and highly organized systems for reinforcing appropriate student behavior and discouraging inappropriate ones. The behavior systems model has been viewed as an attempt to develop a more scientific approach to teaching and learning.

One important example of the behavioral systems approach to instruction is referred to as **direct instruction.** It is generally viewed as a highly organized, carefully planned teaching methodology. Teachers using direct instruction tend to place a strong emphasis on academics, engage in considerable direction and control over student learning, have high expectations for student progress, and have developed an organized system for managing instructional time (Joyce & Weil, 2000).

## Personal Model of Instruction

When most people think of teaching, the first thing to come to mind is the major role teachers have in sharing knowledge in one form or another with their students. The study of mathematics, investigating the social studies, science learning, an appreciation for the arts, and developing skills in reading are among the many things that effective teachers address. Yet, teaching is much more than this. It also includes helping students develop physically, emotionally, and socially so that they can become productive members of society.

The **personal model of instruction** emphasizes the development of the selfhood of each individual student. In its purest form, this approach de-emphasizes the importance of the teacher's role in intellectual development and instead promotes each student's self-understanding and social/emotional well-being. Teachers using the personal model of instruction believe that as students grow in self-understanding, they will be able to engage more effectively in academic learning. The emphasis, therefore, is on assisting students in their personal growth.

The theoretical underpinnings of this approach come from the work of people such as Stanley Coopersmith (1967) who wrote about student self-esteem, Abraham Maslow's (1968) work on needs and growth toward self-actualization, and most specifically from the writings of Carl Rogers (1969), whose work on nondirective counseling was applied to teaching. In the prologue to his book *Freedom to Learn,* Rogers gives the following rationale for **nondirective teaching,** the best example of the personal model of instruction:

> I want to speak to them (educators) about *learning.* But *not* the lifeless, sterile, futile, quickly forgotten stuff which is crammed into the mind of the poor helpless individual tied into his seat by ironclad bonds of conformity! I am talking about LEARNING—the insatiable curiosity which drives the adolescent boy to absorb everything he can see or hear or read about gasoline engines in order to improve the efficiency and speed of his "hot-rod." I am talking about the student who says, "I am discovering, drawing in from the outside, and making that which is drawn in a real part of *me.*" (1969, p. 3)

Personal models of instruction, in their purest form, are infrequent in classrooms today. But many teachers use the core concepts to create a learning environment that is more responsive to student needs, that involves students in determining what should be learned, and that encourages self-understanding. In other words, many teachers use the personal model as a framework for their instructional efforts and then incorporate other instructional strategies to meet the needs of students.

*Teachers find many ways to personalize instruction.*

## Information Processing Model of Instruction

Each of us is bombarded daily with a wealth of information that must be understood and categorized. The basic job of teachers using the **information processing model of instruction** is to give students the tools they need to make sense of these data. In this model students are seen as innately motivated to seek out information from the world around them and make sense of it. Joyce and Weil (2000) describe several different examples of this type.

One example of the information processing model of instruction is referred to as **constructivist education.** Grounded in the developmental theories of Jean Piaget (1950) and Lev Vygotsky (1978), this approach to education is based on the notion that students process information differently depending on their stage of intellectual development. Teachers using the constructivist approach promote the idea that students build or construct their own understanding of the world through activities based on personal interests. As they manipulate real-world objects and interact with the people around them, students create for themselves an understanding of the world. Perkins (1999) describes three main types of learning that take place in constructivist education. The first of these is *active learning.* Rather than passively taking in information, students engage in discussion, research topics, and get involved in tasks that involve them physically and intellectually. Secondly, constructivist education engages students in *social learning.* Students learn through their social interactions with peers, teachers, and other adults. Finally, students engage in *creative learning.* Rather than simply taking in new information, students actually create or recreate knowledge for themselves.

Veronica Morris teaches third grade and uses constructivist teaching in her classroom. Just this past fall, she organized her room into five centers, each with a separate emphasis on mathematics, science, literacy, the arts, and technology. During much of the school day, students are allowed to move freely between centers and engage in projects that Veronica has planned for their consideration. She also encourages students to actively pursue issues that are of interest to them and often finds that many projects that students design last for several months. They frequently work in teams to research their special interests, write reports, and create physical artifacts that demonstrate what they have learned.

### Social Model of Instruction

In the **social model of instruction,** it is assumed that students learn best when they engage in social interactions with their peers and with teachers. Although many theorists have promoted social interactions as essential to effective learning, the writings of John Dewey (1929) have had the most significant impact on current educational thinking. Through the communications that take place in social interactions, Dewey stated:

> Not only is social life identical with communication, but all communication (and hence all genuine social life) is educative. To be a recipient of a communication is to have an enlarged and changed experience. One shares in what another has thought and felt and in so far, meagerly or amply, has his own attitude modified. (1929, p. 6)

Teachers who want to develop a climate conducive to social learning must create **learning communities** in which students work cooperatively in small and large groups to grow in knowledge through their interactions. These learning communities require effort on the part of the teacher to establish. Students must be provided with strategies that enable them to communicate effectively with each other, be given opportunities to build good working relationships, and have clearly defined educational tasks before they can be successful as a community of learners.

The best known example of a social learning model is **cooperative learning.** Students engaged in cooperative learning work in small groups organized by the teacher to complete tasks that require them to learn as a team. The 1970s and 1980s showed a growing interest in cooperative learning, with considerable research and writing being done during these years (i.e., Johnson & Johnson, 1975; Slavin, 1983). For cooperative learning to be successful, teachers must first make sure they monitor student behavior during small-group times. This helps keep students engaged and gives the teacher important information for future activities and evaluation. In addition, as groups work to complete their tasks, the teacher needs to give students feedback on ineffective and effective use of social skills. When needed, activities designed to teach additional social skills are taught to ensure smooth functioning of the groups (Ellis & Whalen, 1990).

After reading about the behavioral systems, personal, information processing, and social models of instruction, take a few minutes to think carefully about each of them. Which do you find appealing and why? Can you see yourself using them in the classroom someday? Are there one or more options that you think you may not be comfortable with? What makes you feel this way? Can you identify personality characteristics in yourself that may make it easier or more productive to use one or more of the models identified?

**Reflective Journey 8.3**

## What skills will I need in management and discipline?

Part of any good teacher's repertoire of skills is the ability to deal with the routines of teaching. Such things as passing out papers, moving students physically and psychologically from one activity to the next, and making sure the lesson moves at a rate that keeps students interested in what is going on are referred to as **management** skills. This ability to organize and coordinate learning experiences is an essential talent you will need to possess. Equally important is the teacher's ability to respond positively to the problem behaviors that students produce. When students talk out of turn, fail to complete their work, or demean fellow students, you will need to be prepared with effective **discipline** strategies. Management and discipline skills are frequently discussed together because they share much in common and both are necessary to create an environment that is conducive to learning. Both new and experienced teachers will tell

**TABLE 8.5   Components of Effective Management and Discipline**

| Component | Description |
|---|---|
| Understanding current research and theory | Research and theory have grown extensively during the last several decades and are useful for understanding and responding to both positive and negative student behaviors. |
| Recognizing and responding to students' personal and psychological needs | Teachers who are aware of unmet student needs can provide understanding, assistance, and/or resources that in turn help eliminate problem behaviors. |
| Developing strong teacher–student and peer relationships | When teachers work to create classrooms that are "caring communities," learning is enhanced and problem behaviors diminish. |
| Implementing effective instructional strategies | When students are engaged in quality educational experiences, they are less likely to misbehave. |
| Using proven classroom organization and management skills | The physical organization of the classroom indirectly tells students a great deal about teacher expectations. When combined with effective management of classroom routines, student misbehavior declines. |
| Dealing effectively with inappropriate student behavior | Because of the characteristics of individual students and each unique situation, teachers need a variety of strategies to deal with misbehaving students. |

*Source: Comprehensive Classroom Management: Creating Communities of Support and Solving Problems,*
by V. Jones and L. Jones, 2001, Boston: Allyn & Bacon.

you that successful management and discipline make a very big difference in teacher effectiveness (Long & Morse, 1996). Table 8.5 lists some important components of effective management and discipline.

## Problem Prevention Strategies

Many of the management strategies that teachers use are designed to prevent problems from occurring in the first place. In fact, the best overall strategy for classroom management and discipline is to engage first and foremost in **problem prevention strategies** (Sergiovanni, 1994). An example of this type discussed earlier in the chapter is the importance of building strong teacher–student relationships. The careful preparation of the classroom environment and developing clear rules for students are other important problem prevention strategies.

Meredith Jacobsen, a teacher of seventh- and eighth-grade English at Eisenhower Middle School, provides an example of the importance of preparing the classroom environment. Prior to beginning her fifth year of teaching, Meredith spends some time organizing her classroom space. Every classroom in the building is equipped with individual student desks. Meredith wants a wider aisle down the middle of these desks so that she can move easily through the room. She plans for an even number of desks on each side of this aisle so that students can work in pairs during parts of each class period. A note to the custodian will help her maintain this desired arrangement.

*Clear expectations help prevent problems.*

Meredith has two computers and wants to have them both easily available to students during class time without being disruptive to others. A collection of novels used in several of her classes will also need to be shelved in such a way that students can have ready access to them. Meredith has several posters and numerous quotes that she will want to display around the classroom as well. These elements, and more, must be organized prior to the first day of school.

Another important problem prevention strategy is the development of clear rules for student behavior (Good & Brophy, 2000). When students understand the value of behavior standards and agree to follow them, many misunderstandings and problems between teachers and students can be avoided. How rules are developed may differ depending on the level at which you teach. Elementary teachers often find that engaging students in the rule-making process is helpful in promoting ownership (Evertson, Emmer, Clements, & Worsham, 1997). Secondary teachers generally don't want to develop a separate list of rules for five or six classes and prefer instead to create their own rules and ask each class for additional ideas that may be helpful (Jones & Jones, 2001). Table 8.6 suggests some useful ways to develop classroom rules.

| TABLE 8.6 Developing Classroom Rules | |
|---|---|
| **Guideline** | **Description** |
| Keep the list short. | Four to six rules are all that are necessary. Too many rules make the list difficult to remember and create an unwanted feeling of rigidity. |
| Make rules broad in focus. | Rules should identify broad categories of behavior that you expect in the classroom, rather than specific ones. Listing all of your behavioral expectations is both difficult and unnecessary. |
| State rules positively. | Rather than saying, "don't hurt others," it is more appropriate to state your rules more positively: "Treat each other with respect." Positive rules tell students what *to do*, rather than what *not to do*. |
| Identify rules the first day of class. | Rather than waiting for problems to present themselves, expectations should be clarified the first day of school. |
| Develop rules consistent with your school/district. | Make sure that the rules are in agreement with written policies of the school and district in which you teach. |
| Create rules that apply to you as well. | Classroom rules are meant primarily for students but should also apply to you as the teacher. |

## Managing Instruction

Adam Barclay, in his second year of teaching high school mathematics, is struggling with group instruction. Getting students' attentions before beginning the lesson, setting a good pace for his instruction, and making sure a variety of students participate in discussions are examples of the problems he faces. It is discouraging to prepare interesting lessons for his classes and have only modest success in presenting them. After observing Adam during two separate lessons, his principal has suggested that in addition to the interesting lessons, focusing on improving the management of his teacher-led activities will enhance his instruction. Adam's **classroom management skills** need work.

The importance of strong skills in the management of instruction was first researched by Kounin (1970). After identifying two groups of classroom teachers, one acknowledged as highly effective and the other as struggling with their teaching, Kounin collected several thousand hours of videotapes of their interactions with students. Careful analysis of these tapes led to the finding that successful teachers were able to prevent many problems from occurring through the use of strong management skills. These skills (see Table 8.7) allowed effective teachers to manage teacher-led activities smoothly and without getting off-track.

## Options for Discipline

Although every teacher works to avoid student misbehavior through the implementation of problem prevention and classroom management strategies, issues still arise. Unmet student

**TABLE 8.7   Management Strategies**

| Type | Strategy | Description |
|---|---|---|
| Preventing misbehavior | Withitness | Dealing with small misbehaviors before they escalate into bigger ones by recognizing and dealing quickly with them |
| | Overlapping | Addressing two or more events at the same time rather than dropping one and focusing entirely on the other |
| Managing movement | Momentum | Speeding up and slowing down the rate of instruction to maintain the right pace for learning |
| | Smoothness | Staying focused rather than wandering through instruction, which can confuse and frustrate many students |
| Maintaining group focus | Group alerting | Making sure that students in the group are paying attention to, and are ready to engage in, the discussion and interactions |
| | Encouraging accountability | Letting students know that their participation will be noticed and evaluated in some manner |
| | High participation formats | Finding ways to keep students actively involved even when they are not responding directly to a teacher's questions |

*Source: Discipline and Group Management in Classrooms,* by J. Kounin, 1970, New York: Holt, Rinehart, and Winston.

**TABLE 8.8    Discipline Options**

| Option | Key Elements |
|---|---|
| Glasser's problem-solving approach | Teacher-guided problem-solving approach |
| Teacher effectiveness training | I-message<br>"No lose" method of problem solving |
| Dreikurs' approach | Importance of social acceptance<br>Natural consequences<br>Logical consequences |
| Behavior modification | Positive reinforcement<br>Punishment<br>Ignoring |

needs, poor self-image, and testing behaviors are just some of the reasons why even the best prepared teachers still have misbehaving students. Teachers need a variety of strategies that they can use to respond to these problems. Although many more discipline approaches are available than can be discussed here, four options are introduced briefly in the paragraphs that follow (see Table 8.8).

**Glasser's problem-solving approach.** More than 30 years ago, William Glasser (1969) described an approach to discipline that has become an important option used by many teachers. Based on his own theory for treating behavior problems (called *reality therapy*), Glasser's problem-solving approach to discipline actively involves students in planning for better behavior. When a problem occurs, the teacher sits down and guides the student through a seven-step process culminating in a plan for better behavior. This same approach can also be used with the entire class. More recently, Glasser (1986, 1990) has refined his initial thinking to include the importance of instructional strategies and classroom climate in dealing with discipline issues.

**Teacher effectiveness training.** A second program to have a significant impact on classroom management and discipline was developed by Thomas Gordon (1974). His approach was first developed to assist parents and was called *parent effectiveness training* (Gordon, 1970). Using the same basic techniques, *teacher effectiveness training* promotes the idea that teachers must create an atmosphere in which shared decision making is used to solve classroom problems. Gordon encourages teachers to give up their authoritarian power over students in favor of a more equitable approach to classroom management and discipline. He believes that when students and teachers work together to resolve conflicts, the end result is more satisfying and effective for all parties.

Gordon (1974) suggests two strategies to use in working through conflicts. The first he calls an **I-message.** An effective I-message consists of three parts: (1) the personal pronoun *I*, (2) the feelings experienced by the adult, and (3) the effect the student behavior has on the teacher. For example, Rachelle, a second-grade child in your classroom, interrupted the math instruction three times today with inappropriate comments. Following the lesson, you take her aside and respond using an I-message: "I get frustrated when you interrupt my teaching with comments that aren't related to the lesson." Gordon's second strategy for dealing with problem behaviors is his *no lose method* of problem solving. In situations in which I-messages haven't worked or are inadequate, this problem-solving strategy is implemented in much the same way as Glasser's approach discussed earlier.

**Dreikurs on discipline.**  Another major contributor to the field of classroom management and discipline is Rudolf Dreikurs. His approach, like that of Gordon, was first applied to parenting and later to teaching (Dreikurs, Grunwald, & Pepper, 1971). Dreikurs believes that when students feel unacceptable to either their peers or teachers, they become behavior problems in the classroom (Charles, 2002). They mistakenly choose undesirable behaviors in an attempt to gain social acceptance. Dreikurs identifies a downward spiral of misbehaviors on the part of students: (1) attention seeking, (2) power over others, (3) seeking revenge, and (4) displays of inadequacy (giving up).

Dreikurs et al. (1971) identify two important discipline strategies for teachers to use in their work with students. They are both designed to help students recognize the fact that their inappropriate classroom behaviors have related consequences. **Natural consequences** follow automatically from the student's behavior and require no adult intervention. For example, Alicia has been warned several times that tipping her chair back on two legs may lead to her falling down. Rather than punishing her for this behavior, the teacher decides to allow the natural consequence to occur. While Alicia may be slightly hurt or embarrassed, this natural consequence may help her choose to eliminate the behavior in the future. **Logical consequences** are teacher-determined outcomes that are directly related to the student's behavior. For example, Angela has been drawing patterns on her desk during eighth-grade English class. You have decided that she will need to come back during her free time and scrub her desk clean. The consequence for Angela's behavior is directly related to the behavior itself and is a logical consequence.

**Behavior modification.**  The final discipline approach discussed here is called *behavior modification*. Based primarily on the theory of operant conditioning developed by B. F. Skinner (Skinner, 1953), this approach is based on the premise that human behavior is either encouraged or discouraged by the responses from the environment that immediately follow it. Behavior modification consists of three strategies that teachers can use to manage student behavior. The first of these is referred to as **positive reinforcement.** Typically, this is defined as anything that immediately follows a behavior and increases the likelihood that the behavior will occur in the future (Kameenui & Darch, 1995). A smile, a pat on the back, spending time with a child, and positive comments about student work are all examples of potentially reinforcing actions. A second behavior modification technique is called **punishment** and can be defined as anything that follows a behavior and decreases the likelihood that it will occur again in the future. For example, Julian has just interrupted you for the third time during the math lesson to ask an unrelated question. Having reminded him about the importance of appropriate questions the first two times he disturbed your teaching, you now implement a mild punisher by telling Julian that he "owes" you 5 minutes from the upcoming recess. During this time owed, Julian will sit at his desk and work on assignments not yet completed. The final behavior modification technique is usually referred to as **ignoring** (Sprick, Sprick, & Garrison, 1992). Ignoring occurs when no response is given to a student behavior. While this may sound easy, it is actually a skill that requires practice. To truly ignore a behavior, you must give no verbal or nonverbal feedback. Eye contact, sighing, and moving closer to a student who is engaged in an undesirable behavior are all responses that must be avoided when ignoring is used.

## Developing Your Own Management and Discipline Style

For much of American educational history, the decision on which discipline approach to use was a simple one. The praise and punishment strategies associated with behavior modification were the most commonly applied. It wasn't until the late 1960s that other options

## Consequences or Punishment?

Dreikurs, Grunwald, and Pepper (1971) make a clear distinction between consequences and punishment. While both are intended to help students change their behavior, consequences are directly linked with student misbehavior whereas punishments are not. Dreikurs et al. view punishment as an outdated method of discipline that causes children to rebel because they see no relationship between the punishment and the "crime." Instead of punishment, they feel that natural and logical consequences are a much better alternative.

Those who use punishment feel differently. They believe that anything which follows an unwanted behavior and decreases the likelihood that the misbehavior will occur in the future is an acceptable alternative to modify student behavior. In their minds, there is no need to make a connection between student misbehavior and the consequences that follow it. All that matters is that student behavior changes and moves in a positive direction. From their perspective, natural and logical consequences are simply a smaller set of all possible punishments that might be used to modify a student's behavior.

Here is an example that highlights these different perspectives: Janice Overstreet and April Williams both teach fifth grade at Briar Elementary School. Janice uses mostly natural and logical consequences for student misbehaviors while April feels that behavior modification is more effective. On the playground today, both encounter students who are running while playing on the asphalt. The school rules indicate that this is unacceptable behavior because several students have fallen and gotten significant scrapes and bruises from running in the past. Janice feels that a logical consequence is the best alternative in dealing with this problem. When she notices a child running, she restates the rule and then has the student return to the point at which he or she began to run and walk back to the destination. April, seeing the same misbehavior, uses a punishment. The offending child "owes" her 2 minutes out of the recess period when the child is required to sit and do nothing until the allotted time is up.

### React and Reflect

1. Do you believe it is possible to create such an exciting classroom learning environment that there is no need for the teacher to use either consequences or punishment? Similarly, can large doses of praise and positive interactions eliminate the need for consequences or punishment? What makes you feel this way?

2. If you were forced to choose between consequences and punishment as discipline tools, which would you select and why?

 *To explore this topic further and submit your reactions and reflections online, go to the Explore Your Beliefs module for Chapter 8 of the Companion Website for this text.*

*Source: Maintaining Sanity in the Classroom, by R. Dreikurs, B. Grunwald, and F. Pepper, 1971, New York: Harper and Row.*

become available for use in the classroom (Jones & Jones, 2001). The variety of approaches available today is both a blessing and a potential problem. The problem comes from needing to identify which discipline options to use. As you grow in your understanding of teaching styles and student learning, you will also want to increase your understanding of discipline options and begin to identify strategies that you feel good about using and that will be effective with students.

You will want to know about and be able to use a variety of discipline techniques because every student and situation is unique. The distinctiveness of each child and situation will make it necessary for you to think carefully about the problem and implement an appropriate solution. Students will come to your classroom with their own set of experiences, attitudes, abilities, and personalities. It shouldn't be a surprise, then, that a discipline strategy that works for one student may not help a second. Similarly, every discipline situation

## Rediscovering Delight in Poetry and Teaching

**Janice McClain**
**Leon High School**
**Tallahassee, Florida**

For me, teaching has been a relationship of the most intense variety—one that is exhausting and frustrating, but one that I cannot bring myself to leave. A few years ago, I figured out why. I was teaching a Wordsworth poem to my senior AP students. In this work, Wordsworth introduces a familiar scene of great natural beauty to his beloved sister. She responds with awe and joy, just as he had once done. Watching her, Wordsworth rediscovers his own initial delight. As my students discussed their own similar moments, I suddenly understood why teaching is a necessary part of my life. Everyday, I have the privilege of rediscovering a piece of the world through at least one of my students' eyes. This keeps renewed joy in my heart and allows me to see the world again with an innocence untainted by routine and complacence.

has its own unique set of players and circumstances, thus making it difficult to use a single approach.

To develop your own management and discipline approach, you will also need to know yourself. Each of the discipline options identified in this chapter has the enthusiastic support of many good teachers around the country. For example, some very good teachers find that behavior modification techniques are their primary discipline strategies, whereas others select Glasser's method as their major approach. These successful teachers have studied the available discipline options, looked at their own personal strengths, weaknesses, and preferences, and then selected approaches that best fit their personality and teaching style. Your challenge will be to do the same analysis for yourself. What personal strengths and weaknesses do you have that will influence the ways in which you discipline students? Which of the approaches discussed in this chapter are most interesting to you? At some point within the next few years, you will want to select discipline techniques that fit you and use them to deal with students' problem behaviors.

**Reflective Journey 8.4**

## Summary

In this chapter, four organizing questions were identified to clarify your thinking about effective teaching strategies:

### Why are strong relationships with students and other adults important?

Effective relationships are essential to good learning. They can be encouraged by:
- Developing positive relationships with students (Praxis II, topics Ic, IIIa)
- Working with parents (Praxis II, topic IVb)
- Encouraging other collaborative relationships (Praxis II, topic IVa)

### What does research tell us about effective instructional strategies?

Research has identified several strategies that effective teachers use in their work with students:
- Identifying similarities and differences (Praxis II, topic IIa)
- Summarizing and note-taking (Praxis II, topic IIa)
- Reinforcing effort (Praxis II, topic IIa)
- Homework and practice
- Nonlinguistic representations (Praxis II, topic IIa)
- Goal setting and providing feedback (Praxis II, topic IIa)
- Generating and testing hypotheses
- Activating prior knowledge (Praxis II, topic IIa)

### What instructional models can I use?

Four broad models of instruction are used in classrooms:
- Behavioral systems model of instruction (Praxis II, topic IIa)
- Personal model of instruction (Praxis II, topics IIa, IIIc)
- Information processing model of instruction (Praxis II, topic IIa)
- Social model of instruction (Praxis II, topic IIa)

### What skills will I need in management and discipline?

Effective teachers need both management and discipline skills to create a positive atmosphere for learning:
- Problem prevention strategies (Praxis II, topic Ic)
- Managing instruction (Praxis II, topic Ic)
- Options for discipline (Praxis II, topic Ic)

## Key Terms

activating prior knowledge
behavioral systems model of instruction
classroom management skills
constructivist education
cooperative learning
direct instruction
discipline
feedback
generating and testing hypotheses
goal setting
homework
identify similarities and differences
ignoring
I-message
information processing model of instruction
learning communities

logical consequences
management
natural consequences
nondirective teaching
nonlinguistic representations
note taking
parent–teacher conference
personal model of instruction
positive reinforcement
practice
problem prevention strategies
punishment
reinforcing effort
rubric
social model of instruction
summarizing

## Reflective Journey: Online Journal

 Use the questions for thought and reflection highlighted throughout the chapter to help guide your personal journey of reflection and professional development as a teacher. To complete your journal entries online, go to the *Reflective Journey* module for this chapter of the Companion Website.

## PRAXIS  Test Preparation Activities

 To review an online chapter case study, test your understanding of chapter topics and concepts, and begin preparing for the Praxis II: Principles of Learning and Teaching examination, go to the *Praxis Test Preparation* module for this chapter of the Companion Website.

## inTASC  Becoming a Reflective Practitioner

To complete these activities and submit your responses online, go to the *Becoming a Reflective Practitioner* module for this chapter of the Companion Website.

### Why are strong relationships with students and other adults important?

**Review Questions**

1. What are some of the characteristics of effective teacher–student relationships?
2. How do teachers, parents, and children benefit from positive home–school relations?
3. Give some examples of the collaborative relationships with other adults that will be important to you as a future teacher.

**Field Experience**

After spending some time observing in a classroom of your choice, pick out a student with whom you would like to develop a good working relationship. Try to select someone who you aren't drawn to naturally. Develop a list of strategies that you could use to build your relationship. If possible, try them out to see how they work. Discuss your experiences with others.

**Building Your Portfolio: *Working with Parents***

**INTASC Standard 10.** One of your future roles as a teacher will be to develop good working relationships with the parents and guardians of your students and work to get them involved in the educational process. After having reviewed a book on parent involvement in education (see Suggested Readings for an example), describe five strategies that you would use to communicate more effectively with parents and five strategies for involving parents for your portfolio.

### What does research tell us about effective instructional strategies?

**Review Questions**

1. What are the keys to good note-taking?
2. What benefits are often associated with homework?
3. What is a rubric and how is it used?

### Field Experience

Spend some time observing a teacher at work in the classroom. What strategies did you observe from the list of research-based techniques described in this chapter? How would you assess their effectiveness? Did you observe strategies that you felt were ineffective?

### Building Your Portfolio: *Developing a Rubric*

**INTASC Standard 5.** Identify a specific writing project that would be appropriate for the grade and subject you are considering as a future teacher. For that writing project, develop a scoring rubric that would give students completing the assignment clear feedback on the criteria being used for evaluation. Place a copy of the rubric in your portfolio.

## What instructional models can I use?

### Review Questions

1. How does a teacher use direct instruction in the classroom?
2. What is the primary emphasis of the personal model of instruction?
3. What types of learning are attributed to constructivist education?
4. What is the primary mode of learning in the social model of instruction?

### Building Your Portfolio: *Investigate an Instructional Model*

**INTASC Standard 5.** Choose one of the instructional models that is of interest to you and spend some time researching this option further. Use the references found in the text, do an Internet search using key names, and spend some time in the library to gather information on the model you chose. Write a summary of the strengths and limitations of the instructional model for inclusion in your portfolio.

## What skills will I need in management and discipline?

### Review Questions

1. Describe examples of the management skills needed by teachers.
2. What are the key ingredients for developing effective rules?
3. What is an I-message and how is it used?

### Field Experience

Talk to a classroom teacher about her or his discipline procedures. What does the teacher do or say to deal with inappropriate student behavior? Discuss with the teacher the ingredients needed for effective discipline in the classroom. Share your findings with classmates.

### Building Your Portfolio: *Classroom Rules*

**INTASC Standard 5.** For an age/grade of your choosing, develop a list of classroom rules that you would use for that age group. Why did you include the rules you did? How would you introduce these rules to the class? Do any of the rules need clarification for students? If so, how would you go about doing this?

## Suggested Readings

Berger, E. (2000). *Parents as partners in education* (5th ed.). Upper Saddle River, NJ: Merrill/Prentice Hall. This book presents an excellent overview of the steps needed to build effective relationships with parents. The principles presented apply to all relationships in the classroom.

Jones, V., & Jones, L. (2001). *Comprehensive classroom management: Creating communities of support and solving problems* (6th ed.). Boston: Allyn & Bacon. This book provides strong content and an excellent framework for creating a comprehensive program for classroom management and discipline.

Joyce, B., & Weil, M. (2000). *Models of teaching* (6th ed.). Boston: Allyn & Bacon. Joyce and Weil share their extensive knowledge about different models of instruction. This book is generally considered the best overview of the subject.

Marzano, R., Pickering, D., & Pollock, J. (2001). *Classroom instruction that works: Research-based strategies for increasing student achievement.* Alexandria, VA: Association for Supervision and Curriculum Development. This book provides a thorough overview of the research that has been done on effective teaching strategies. Many good examples illustrate the strategies being discussed.

# chapter 9

## Integrating Technology

As a future teacher, you will have many opportunities to use computers and the Internet in support of teaching and learning. You will need to understand technology's potential and be able to effectively use it in the classroom. Four organizing questions will help you more fully understand the changing relationships between education and technology.

## Focus Questions

◢ How has technology been used in the classroom?

◢ What are schools doing to enhance technology use in the curriculum?

◢ What is the impact of computers on teaching and learning?

◢ What issues must be resolved to strengthen technology's impact?

*Mrs. Simpson's
fifth-period social
studies class has just
begun and Kelly, Angie, and
Megan have gathered in a small
group to talk about their upcoming
presentation to the class about ancient Greek
architecture. These seventh-grade students have spent time searching the Internet, reading appropriate
information from the class CD-ROM encyclopedia, and finding books from the school library on their chosen
topic. Kelly located some interesting digital images on the Internet that the group wants to share with the class.
Angie used the school's digital camera to photograph local architectural designs for comparison with those
from ancient Greece, and the group is now thinking about a PowerPoint® multimedia presentation that will
allow them to share what they have learned with their classmates. With Mrs. Simpson's assistance, the girls
excitedly plan the next steps as they prepare for the class presentation.*

Although the scenario just described is not common in all classrooms, it is becoming more prevalent in most schools. Teachers are working to develop the skills they need to integrate technology into their instruction at the same time that students are engaged in using these options at school and in the home to learn more about the world around them. As computers and the Internet become increasingly more available in school settings, these technologies and others are strongly influencing teaching and learning in America's schools.

## How has technology been used in the classroom?

In Chapter 7, **technology** was broadly defined as any device or tool that can be used to extend human abilities. Using that definition, can openers, paper clips, hammers, and telephones are all examples of technology. Similarly, in education, the overhead projector, video camera, and the ruler are all technology tools commonly found in many classrooms. While we tend to think of the computer as being synonymous with technology in the classroom, many other tools have in fact been used over the years to assist teachers and students in the learning process.

As you read this section, think about technological innovations you remember from your own schooling. What made them either successful or unsuccessful? Were computers a part of your educational experience? If so, how were they used? What changes have occurred in the ways computers have been used during the last 10 years? Reflect on the changes you might expect to see in the next decade.

**Reflective Journey 9.1**

### Early Technology Options

The introduction of new technology in the classroom has often been viewed as a quick and easy solution to very complex problems. Near the beginning of the 20th century, for example, the radio was seen as an important new technology that would allow teachers to supplement classroom teaching, update the information found in school textbooks, and expose students to a wider array of topics and information than the classroom teacher could do on his or her own (Trotter, 1999).

Some technological advances have had little impact on schooling, but others have been very successful in transforming teaching and learning (Trotter, 1999). For example, the radio, telephone, and television are among the many technologies that were initially seen as tools that would dramatically change education but never lived up to that potential. On the other hand, the mimeograph machine, videocassette recorder, and overhead projector have all had a significant influence on America's classrooms. Tyack and Cuban (2000) suggest that new technologies are successful when they are flexible tools that assist the teacher in managing the traditional aspects of their classroom lives, but that they are relatively ineffective when they require teachers to change dramatically their interactions with students.

### Television

When educators began experimenting with television for the delivery of courses in the 1940s, many predicted that this technology would revolutionize schooling (Trotter,

*Overhead projectors have had a significant impact on education.*

1999). Administrators saw television as an option that would allow the schools to deliver courses to a growing student population without hiring large numbers of new teachers. Others felt that with a few top quality teachers developing courses for delivery via television, more students would receive the best possible instruction. In addition, many teachers were enthralled by the glamour of television broadcasting.

Not everyone, however, was enthusiastic about the use of the television in the classroom (Trotter, 1999). Some teachers were concerned about the implications for their jobs, whereas others felt that the impersonal nature of television viewing detracted from the educational experience. Before the advent of the VCR, the coordination of class schedules needed to allow students the opportunities to view live broadcasts left still other teachers and administrators frustrated. Hardware breakdowns and insufficient numbers of television sets were additional administrative hurdles that caused many to react negatively to the proposed addition of this new technology (Tyack & Cuban, 2000).

## Computers

The most recent technology to gain momentum as a tool to reform teaching and learning is the computer. From the 1980s to the present, the numbers and quality of computers and software available to students have continued to grow. The number of students per computer, a long-standing measure of computer access, decreased from 125 in 1981 (Tyack & Cuban, 2000) to 4.9 in 2000 (Meyer, 2001) (see Table 9.1). Similarly, virtually all schools in the country now have Internet access and 63% of all classrooms are wired for this service (Meyer, 2001).

Because computers have been a relatively new addition to America's schools, it is still unclear whether or not they will have a major influence on teaching and learning. On the one hand, most teachers have moved beyond a minimum level of competence with computers and are beginning to use them more regularly in their classrooms (Meyer, 2001). At the same time, only a small minority has the advanced skills necessary to effectively integrate computer technology into the classroom day. Time will tell whether computers will follow educational television as a short-lived educational technology phenomenon or become as invaluable as the photocopier in assisting teachers in the delivery of instruction.

**TABLE 9.1  Computer and Internet Availability**

|  | 1992 | 1993 | 1994 | 1995 | 1996 | 1997 | 1998 | 1999 | 2000 |
|---|---|---|---|---|---|---|---|---|---|
| **Students per instructional computer** | 19.2 | 12.0 | 10.8 | 9.1 | 9.0 | 7.3 | 6.3 | 5.7 | 4.9 |
| **Students per Internet-connected computers** |  |  |  |  |  |  | 19.7 | 13.6 | 7.9 |
| **Schools with Internet access (%)** |  |  | 35 | 50 | 65 | 78 | 89 | 95 |  |
| **Classrooms with Internet access (%)** |  |  | 3 | 8 | 14 | 27 | 51 | 63 |  |

*Source:* From "New Challenges," by L. Meyer, in *Technology Counts 2001: The New Divide,* pp. 49–64. Access Chart (p. 51): Education Week/Market Data Retrieval, "Technology Education 2000" and other MDR surveys. Reprinted with permission from *Education Week,* Vol. 20, Issue No. 35, May 10, 2001.

**Teacher uses.** Regardless of their long-term impact on instruction, teachers and students are putting computers to use in a variety of important ways. The most common option for teachers is *word processing*. They create handouts for students, write letters to parents, and respond to administrators' requests for information. Another common use is for *record keeping*. Grade files for students, standardized test results, and lesson planning are among the many options for record keeping. Most teachers also use computer technology for *communicating* via e-mail with other teachers, administrators, and parents. Finally, teachers are using technology for *assessment*. Some teachers, for example, are using test generating software to create their own exams to use with students.

**Instructional uses.** In addition to the teacher productivity tools mentioned above, the number of instructional uses for the computer is growing. A wealth of software options provide students with a variety of learning experiences on the computer (see Table 9.2). One available option is called **drill and practice software** and is used by students to practice what they have already

**TABLE 9.2  Software Options**

| Type | Example | Description | Publisher |
|------|---------|-------------|-----------|
| Drill and practice | Mighty Math Astro Algebra | Teaches students in grades 7–9 basic concepts and problem-solving strategies for algebra. | Edmark Software (800) 362-2890 |
| Simulation | The Oregon Trail | Students lead a wagon train through the many challenges facing the early American pioneers. | The Learning Company (800) 395-0277 |
| Word processing | Imagination Express | Allows elementary and middle school students to create interactive electronic books. | Edmark Software (800) 362-2890 |
| Encyclopedia software | Compton's Encyclopedia | The CD-ROM equivalent of paper encyclopedias with a wealth of information, charts, data, and pictures. | The Learning Company (800) 395-0277 |
| Creativity software | Make a Simulation: AgentSheets | Allows students at the middle school and high school levels to engage in entry-level computer programming as they create their own simulations, models, and games. | Sunburst Corporation (800) 321-7511 |

learned. Another option found in many classrooms is **simulation software.** Students using this type of software assume roles and reenact events as they manipulate scenarios created by the software. A third software program being used by students is **word processing software.** Used for writing tasks such as papers, reports, and creative writing assignments, good word processing software is available for all grade levels. **Encyclopedia software,** generally available on CD-ROM, is another common option. Several excellent programs serve as the electronic equivalents of encyclopedias. Students can use these sources to gather information for class projects and report writing. A final software type that is available in limited quantity is **creativity software.** While many software products falsely advertise their creative potential, some pieces actually are available that allow students to actively engage in creative thinking.

## The Internet

Are you a regular Internet user? If so, you are aware of the vast quantities of information available from the Internet. Although some Internet sites are either of low quality or contain information that is inappropriate for student use, a great deal of information is available on the Internet that both students and teachers can productively use to facilitate teaching and learning. As a future teacher, you will want to be aware of both the strengths and limitations of Internet use in the classroom.

Just as computers are beginning to have an impact on schools in America, the rapid growth in Internet use is also influencing teaching and learning. In simple terms, the **Internet** is a worldwide collection of interconnected computers. Using technology referred to as the **World Wide Web,** Internet users are able to quickly and easily move between sites using a simple visual format (Provenzo, Brett, & McCloskey, 1999). Growth in worldwide Internet use has been very rapid, with 20 million users in 1993 and over 400 million in 2000 (Petska, 2001), with the United States having the largest number of users (see Table 9.3).

The Internet has opened up a huge world of new information to both teachers and students. Teachers, for example, are using it to create at least a portion of their lesson plans. Becker (1999) found that 28% use the Internet weekly to gather resources for lessons and 40% occasionally do so.

**TABLE 9.3   Top Ten Countries in Internet Use**

| Rank | Country | Users (millions) |
| --- | --- | --- |
| 1 | United States | 160.7 |
| 2 | Japan | 64.8 |
| 3 | China | 54.5 |
| 4 | Germany | 30.4 |
| 5 | United Kingdom | 27.2 |
| 6 | South Korea | 26.9 |
| 7 | Italy | 20.9 |
| 8 | Canada | 17.8 |
| 9 | France | 16.7 |
| 10 | India | 16.6 |

*Source:* From "USA Tops 160M Internet Users," by Computer Industry Almanac, 2002. Retrieved March 26, 2003, from http://www.c-i-a.com/pr1202.htm. Reprinted with permission.

**TABLE 9.4**   Percentage of Public School Classrooms with Internet Access

|  | 1994 | 1996 | 1998 | 1999 |
|---|---|---|---|---|
| **Elementary schools** | 3 | 13 | 51 | 62 |
| **Secondary schools** | 4 | 16 | 52 | 67 |
| **All public schools** | 3 | 14 | 51 | 63 |

*Source:* "Internet Access in U.S. Public Schools and Classrooms, 1994–99," in *Stats in Brief* (NCES 2000-8086), by National Center for Education Statistics, February 2000, Washington, DC: Author.

Most teachers are also engaged in sending e-mail and some are creating their own websites to share positive teaching experiences and student work with others. Students are also very involved in Internet use. Most use it at least occasionally as an information-gathering tool for school assignments. More than 70% of students have been given classroom instruction in using an Internet search engine to find information for their work at school (Meyer, 2001). Many students are also using the Internet to communicate with others via e-mail. Table 9.4 shows Internet access percentages in public schools.

## What are schools doing to enhance technology use in the curriculum?

If computers and Internet use are to be more than just another marginalized technology option, they must be carefully integrated into the everyday life of the schools. Rather than being employed only sporadically, computers need to be used daily in all subject matter areas as important tools for teaching and learning. This complex task requires the schools to carefully plan and implement strategies that can make increased computer use a reality.

# EDUCATION IN THE NEWS

## Computers in the Classroom

Will spending $50 billion for computers in classrooms produce results, transform education, and raise achievement? The Internet connects people around the world, but will computers in classrooms really make a difference in our education?

### Critical Thinking Questions

1. Think about how technology is a part of your life at home and as a student. Some say that there is a digital disconnect between home and schools. What do you think this means? How is it true in your life? How would education have to change in order for technology to really make a difference in classrooms?

2. Todd Oppenheimer notes that "Just because they're excited doesn't necessarily mean they're learning, especially learning the art of discipline and study, synthesis of concepts, discussion, how to stay with something when it gets frustrating, which is one of the main lessons in life." How might you counter that argument with regard to computers and other technologies?

3. If you could equip a classroom (equipment, materials, supplies, people) with just exactly what is needed for learning in the area of your chosen teaching field, what would you select and why? Remember to consider the national (and maybe your state) technology standards for students in your decisions.

 *To submit your responses online, go to the Education in the News module for Chapter 9 of the Companion Website.*

# Computer Labs or Classroom Computers?

Greenwood Elementary is typical of many elementary schools around the country in terms of computer access and use. The dedicated faculty and staff are working hard to incorporate technology into their teaching and learning where possible. Currently, the school has a computer lab set up in a portion of the library area. With a block of 28 networked computers, all of which are connected to the Internet, teachers can use the lab at scheduled times to conduct a number of tasks. Most frequently, lab times are used to teach the whole class skills in computer use. Today, for example, the school's technology expert is working with Angelina Lopez's third-grade class to help them be more productive as they search for information on the Internet. Later in the day, Devon Martin's fifth-grade class will be using the computer lab to refine their keyboarding skills. The lab is busy throughout the school day with different groups of students engaged in a variety of learning experiences. In addition, the lab is periodically used for in-service teacher training on computer use. Because the lab was installed several years ago, the computers found there are older than the newer options being purchased for classroom use.

In addition to the computer lab described above, Greenwood Elementary has continued to add computers to individual classrooms based on the availability of funding and teacher demand. Every teacher has access to a computer for personal use and all but two classrooms have at least one computer available for student projects. In addition, five classrooms have clusters of four computers that teachers are using for individual or small-group work. Because the building is old, it has been more difficult to add classroom Internet access, but currently more than 80% have been connected.

Carolyn Jacobson is a new fourth-grade teacher in the school. As the most recent addition to the staff, her classroom has just one computer available for students to use. She has requested three more, but doesn't expect to receive them until next academic year. It will be more difficult for Carolyn to fully integrate technology into her teaching this year.

In an ideal world, schools like Greenwood Elementary would have the resources to fully support both a modern computer lab and individual classroom computers. Unfortunately, most schools find that they must make difficult choices about which of the two options to fund.

## Research the Issue

Research this topic online using the links provided in the *Engage in the Debate* module for this chapter of the Companion Website.

1. Spend some time talking to a technology specialist about the computer lab at her or his school. How is it equipped? What equipment and software would be needed to make it more effective? How do teachers and students use the lab? Could the lab be used more productively?

2. Talk to a classroom teacher about his or her use of computers in the classroom. How many computers are available in the classroom? Are they connected to the Internet? How does this teacher use the computers in instruction? What is needed to more productively use computers in the classroom?

## Explore Your Views

1. What do you see as both the strengths and limitations of computer labs in the schools? Similarly, what are the strengths and limitations of computers in individual classrooms?

2. Are computer labs or individual classroom computers more important to teaching and learning in America's schools? What is your rationale for this perspective?

 *To research this issue and submit your responses online, go to the Engage in the Debate module for Chapter 9 of the Companion Website for this text.*

**Reflective Journey 9.2**

The integration of computer technology into the classroom will require extended effort on the part of teachers. As you read this section, reflect on the relative merits of this task. Is it worth doing? In addition, think about your willingness as a future teacher to commit the time and energy needed on your part to integrate technology into your teaching. How do you think you will feel about engaging in this task? Do you think you will enjoy it or is it something you may struggle to fit into an already busy schedule?

*Many classrooms have computers for small-group student use.*

## Classroom Computers with Internet Access

When computers were first introduced into the schools, they were generally grouped together in a computer lab. Because only a few machines were available, creating a lab allowed for better access by students throughout the school. It also made it possible for the one or two trained computer "experts" to teach others how to use the equipment and software. Unfortunately, this setup also meant that students typically only had access to computers for a few minutes each week.

As computers became more commonly available and a growing number of teachers started to use them on a regular basis in their teaching, this technology has increasingly been placed in individual classrooms. Currently, over 60% of all U.S. classrooms have at least one computer with Internet access. On the other hand, even though more computers are being placed directly in classrooms, the ratio of students to classroom computers still remains high at 11.3 students per computer (Meyer, 2001).

Despite the huge increases in Internet access during the last several years, many teachers and their students still find they have fewer opportunities for Internet use than they would like (Meyer, 2001). For example, Janice Beatty wants to incorporate the use of technology into her teaching of high school social studies. Janice knows that there is a great wealth of information on the Internet that would be of interest to her students and would help motivate them in class. Her problem is that she currently has only two computers in the room (both connected to the Internet) and an average of 24 students in each of her classes. To be equitable, she can only allow students a few minutes each week for computer use. Janice needs three or four more computers (all connected to the Internet) before she can effectively integrate computers into her curriculum.

## Quality Software

Another issue that schools must face if they are to effectively increase computer use is to have quality software available for students and teachers to use in their work. Many school districts and some states provide teachers with preapproved lists of software that may be purchased with school funds (Zehr, 1999). Even in these circumstances, however, you will be faced with a bewildering array of options and little guidance in making appropriate selections for students' individual needs.

Take, for example, Tom Harding. He is interested in finding some new software to use on the five computers that were recently purchased for his fifth-grade classroom. Tom is particularly interested in locating some software for mathematics instruction. But after reviewing the software catalogs in the school office, Tom is unsure how to proceed. He found 22 pieces of software from different publishers that look good in the catalogs and seem to meet his requirements. Tom needs some assistance in making good selections from the many options available to him. Table 9.5 provides suggestions for evaluating software.

| **TABLE 9.5   Evaluating Software** | |
|---|---|
| **Characteristic** | **Criteria** |
| Content | Does the software meet your instructional objectives? Review the software itself to make sure it has content that is developmentally appropriate for your students and follows a logical learning sequence. |
| Methodology | Are the methods of instruction used in the software consistent with sound learning theory? Are you comfortable with the approach used and does it fit with your own instructional methodologies? |
| Utilization | Determine the ease of use of the software. Can students operate it with minimal adult assistance? Is the software easy to enter, exit, and use? Can the teacher have some control over the program (i.e., turn off the sound if desired)? |

*Source: Computers, Curriculum, and Cultural Change,* by E. Provenzo, A. Brett, and G. McCloskey, 1999, Mahwah, NJ: Lawrence Erlbaum.

## What is the impact of computers on teaching and learning?

Robert Schank (2000), from the Institute for the Learning Sciences at Northwestern University, has a vision for the role of technology in education during the 21st century:

> Technology is on the verge of fundamentally reshaping the American education system. In particular, the technology to deliver full-length courses online is rapidly becoming a reality. . . . The teaching of traditional academic subjects, first in high school and later in elementary school, will be increasingly done via online courses. . . . Teachers will be left to provide things that technology cannot: personal one-on-one tutoring; teaching kids how to work in a group to accomplish something; and teaching crucial interpersonal relationship skills. (p. 43)

Similarly, Seymour Papert (2000), the developer of a computer programming language for children called LOGO, believes computers have this same potential for completely re-forming education.

Neil Postman (2000) argues for a more cautious approach to the use of computers in the classroom. He sees other issues as being more important to address:

> I am not arguing against using computers in school. I am arguing against our sleepwalking attitudes toward it, against allowing it to distract us from more important things, against making a god of it. This is what Theodore Roszak (1986) warned against in *The Cult of Information:* "Like all cults," he wrote, "this one has the intention of enlisting mindless allegiance and acquiescence. People who have no clear idea of what

*Instructional strategies often change with computers in the classroom.*

they mean by information, or why they should want so much of it, are nonetheless prepared to believe that we live in an Information Age, which makes every computer around us what the relics of the True Cross were in the Age of Faith: emblems of salvation (p. x)." To this I would add the sage observation of Alan Kay of Apple Computer. Kay is widely associated with the invention of the personal computer, and certainly has an interest in the use of computers in schools. Nonetheless, he has repeatedly said that any problem the schools cannot solve without computers, they cannot solve with them. (p. 294)

## Impact on Teaching

While it is difficult to predict the future impact of computers, it appears that many teachers are changing what they do in the classroom as they increase their reliance on technology. Rather than continuing to use the strategies they found effective in the past, these teachers are rethinking the ways in which they teach. Some are blending technology use into their current teaching strategies while others are using computers and Internet access to fundamentally change the ways in which they teach (see Table 9.6).

Reflect on Schank's (2000) vision for education quoted earlier as you read this section of the chapter. Do you think computers will truly reshape teaching and learning in American schools?

**TABLE 9.6    The Computer's Impact on Teaching and Learning**

| Impact on Teaching | Description | Influence on Learning | Description |
|---|---|---|---|
| Blending technology and teaching | Many teachers are incorporating computers and Internet use into their current teaching methods to strengthen their instructional efforts. | Digital age literacy | Students need to learn how to effectively use the many new technological advances surrounding them. |
| Teacher as facilitator of learning | Some teachers are completely changing the ways in which they teach with the assistance of computers, becoming facilitators of learning rather than imparting knowledge. | How students learn | Computers provide real-world contexts for learning, help students make connections with outside experts, provide visualization and analysis tools, create scaffolds for problem solving, and provide opportunities for feedback, reflection, and revision. |
| | | Distance learning | Distance learning allows students in diverse locations to take courses from home or in other settings rather than coming to the site where the course is actually being taught. |

How would you feel if this became a reality? Would the role of the teacher as we currently know it cease to exist? There are strong feelings both for and against this possibility.

**Reflective
Journey 9.3**

**Blending technology and teaching.**  Most teachers are increasingly willing and able to combine their current methods of classroom instruction with computer use. While they are not dramatically changing the teaching that takes place in their classrooms, they are taking advantage of the computer's strengths to supplement what they are already doing. Recent surveys indicate that many teachers are at least beginning this blending of technology and teaching (*Education Week,* 2001). In 2000, 28% of a representative sample of teachers was rated as having beginning level skills in their use of computers, 46% were at an intermediate level, and an additional 8% were classified as advanced users. So, a large majority of teachers are engaging in at least some instruction via the computer and providing students with a variety of opportunities to use technology during the school day. Students also report, as shown in Table 9.7, that most of their teachers have used computers to show them how to do research, write papers, search for information on the Internet, create presentations, use spreadsheets, visualize new concepts, and find help with homework.

**Teacher as facilitator of learning.**  If most teachers continue to use technology as one of many teaching strategies, the computer will have an important, but limited, impact on the overall directions of schooling. Fundamental changes, like those described by Schank (2000), will come about only if teachers reconfigure their roles and interact differently with students. Rather than dispensing information to students, the teacher who makes extensive use of computers can become more of a guide and work with individuals or small groups to facilitate their learning. This is a major shift in emphasis for most teachers and often takes place over several years, if at all. Pat Herr (2000), an elementary teacher in Leesburg, Virginia, describes her multiyear effort to integrate technology into her teaching. As Pat's school district spent more money on computers and technology training, she began to see a change in her teaching:

> With the spending of so much taxpayer money on technology, teachers were expected to start integrating technology into the curriculum. During the year, we attended seven full-day in-services at the county's computer training center. We learned to use a wide array of technology tools and resources, and, more importantly, began to learn how to integrate them into our teaching.

**TABLE 9.7   Teacher and Student Use of Computers**

| Teachers Used Computer to Show Students How to: | Percent | Students Use Computers to: | Percent |
|---|---|---|---|
| Do research | 89 | Do research | 96 |
| Write papers | 86 | Write papers | 91 |
| Use an Internet search engine | 71 | Do homework | 62 |
| Create presentations | 69 | Practice things learned in class | 57 |
| Use spreadsheets | 64 | Get homework help | 44 |
| Visualize new concepts | 51 | Study for tests | 39 |
| Find homework help | 43 | | |

*Source:* From "New Challenges," by L. Meyer, in *Technology Counts 2001: The New Divide,* pp. 49–64. Use Chart (p. 54). Education Week/MDR/Harris Interactive Poll of Students and Technology, 2001. Reprinted with permission from *Education Week,* Vol. 20, Issue No. 35, May 10, 2001.

Technology integration began to become an everyday occurrence in my classroom. Projects included using the computer to teach students how to organize information using a database, researching a project on the Internet, and using electronic encyclopedias. I saw my students becoming more excited about learning. My teaching style also took a drastic change, as my role became more of a facilitator and less of a dispenser of knowledge. (p. 30)

## Influence on Learners

Without question, the computer has become a major change agent in the world of work. Every occupation from grocery clerk to orthopedic surgeon has been significantly changed through a growing reliance on technology as a tool for everything from the mundane to the extremely complex. Computers have become so essential to all walks of life that every student today will need to develop confidence and competence in using these tools as part of future work efforts in the 21st century. Data from the worlds of business and industry are clear: New workers will need competence in technology (U.S. Department of Labor, 2000).

**Digital age literacy.** This strong need for a technologically literate citizenry has led many schools to change their curricula to include time spent teaching students how to use the many new technological advances surrounding them. Computer labs have been one setting used by schools to help students develop such things as keyboarding skills, effective use of software tools (word processing, data management, etc.), and methods for finding information on the Internet. Many students are learning these skills at home, but others need schools to provide the opportunity to familiarize themselves with the many tools needed for success in our digital world.

**How students learn.** In addition to changing the curricula of the schools, computers are also having an impact on how students learn. Current researchers and writers are looking at ways in which technology can facilitate the best kinds of learning in students. Bransford (1999) identifies five ways in which the computer helps facilitate the best learning:

- *Real-world contexts for learning.* Communicating with a survivor of World War II on an Internet list serve, for example, allows students to get authentic feedback on the causes and effects of this major historical event.

- *Connections with outside experts.* Although classroom teachers have expertise in several areas, the computer allows students to tap into a deep pool of talent on very specialized topics.

- *Visualization and analysis tools.* Software programs including Sunburst's *Everything Weather* help students visualize such things as the destruction caused by a tornado.

- *Scaffolds for problem solving.* For elementary students, Edmark's *Thinkin' Things* software helps students use their different learning styles to solve problems as they play a variety of enjoyable learning games.

- *Opportunities for feedback, reflection, and revision.* For example, students can post their work on the school or class website to get feedback from peers, parents, teachers, and others.

**Distance learning.** The evidence above suggests that technology is beginning to have a significant impact on the format and content of instruction. In a similar way, computers and the Internet are also influencing where learning takes place. **Distance learning** allows students in diverse locations to take courses from home or in other settings rather than coming to the site where the course is actually being taught. It may surprise you to learn that distance education actually came into existence long before computers became prominent in education. For example, the Independent Study High School (ISHS) under the management of the University of Nebraska–Lincoln

**TABLE 9.8   Sample Virtual High School Participants, 2000–2001**

| School | Description and Location | Course(s) Offered |
|--------|--------------------------|-------------------|
| Forks High School | A small rural high school located 4 hours west of Seattle, Washington, in the Olympic Rain Forest. | Aeronautics and Space Travel<br><br>WebQuest: A Literary Odyssey |
| Faubian Middle School | Serving 1,200 students in grades 6–8 in a community 30 miles north of Dallas, Texas. | Math in the Real World: Measuring the Earth |
| Liverpool High School | Liverpool, New York, is located just northwest of Syracuse. | Aquaculture Science<br><br>Artists and the 20th Century |
| John F. Kennedy High School | A diverse suburban high school of 1,450 students located in the "Silicon Valley" in Fremont, California. | Discovering Algebra I |

*Source: Introduction to VHS,* by Virtual High School, 2001. Retrieved July 16, 2001, from http://vhs.concord.org/content

(University of Nebraska–Lincoln, 2001) began in 1929. While the ISHS currently offers its courses primarily via the Internet, in its early years courses were taught by sending written assignments back and forth through the mail. Learning through correspondence has been a fairly common educational practice for many years.

Distance learning is a rapidly growing alternative for many school districts trying to meet the needs of increasingly diverse groups of students. Some districts are creating their own courses and offering them over the Internet for students in different schools. For example, a rural school district may not need an advanced calculus course taught in every high school, but rather may find that one class for the entire district can be offered through distance education. Or, another district may decide to teach Russian through distance learning to meet the needs of the limited number of high school students that may want to take this course for a language elective. Another alternative for distance learning is for school districts to find courses being offered by "virtual schools" and have interested students sign up for appropriate courses through one of these organizations. Table 9.8 lists some of these types of schools.

## What issues must be resolved to strengthen technology's impact?

While many influential groups such as the U.S. Department of Education (2000), the Web-Based Education Commission (2000), and the David and Lucile Packard Foundation (Lemke & Martin, 2001) are promoting computer technology as an important agent for change in America's schools, each of these groups also identifies goals to be met and challenges that must be overcome if technology is to become truly effective in improving education (see Table 9.9). As you read this section, think about how these changes can take place. The costs of having quality hardware and

| **TABLE 9.9** Strengthening Technology's Impact | |
|---|---|
| **Group** | **Issues to Be Resolved** |
| Web-Based Education Commission | 1. Making broadband access widely available for quick Internet use<br>2. Providing continuous and relevant training and support for school personnel<br>3. Obtaining new research on how people learn in the Internet age<br>4. Developing high-quality online educational content<br>5. Revising school regulations that impede innovation<br>6. Protecting online learners and ensure their privacy<br>7. Sustaining funding for technology |
| David and Lucile Packard Foundation | 1. Supporting effective use of computers in the classroom<br>2. Ensuring equal access for all<br>3. Protecting children from harm and improving content |

*Sources: Children and Computer Technology: Issues and Ideas,* by C. Lemke and C. Martin, 2001, Los Altos, CA: David and Lucile Packard Foundation; and *The Power of the Internet for Learning: Moving from Promise to Practice,* by Web-Based Education Commission, 2000. Retrieved June 3, 2002, from http://www.hpcnet.org/webcommission

**Reflective Journey 9.4**

software that is accessible to all are high. Who should pay for these costs? What role should teachers have in resolving the issues presented here? How can administrators, school districts, and state departments of education be involved?

## Technology Costs: Initial and Continuing

One issue that must be resolved if computer technology is to become more integrated into teaching and learning is the initial and continuing costs of the hardware, software, and maintenance that this technology brings to schools. While many districts are just now reaching the point where they have adequate numbers of computers combined in networks and connected to the Internet, the problems have just begun. Getting computers into classrooms is only the first step in making sure that the technology can be used properly. In 1999, the Consortium for School Networking began to educate schools about the actual costs of computers and networks through an initiative called "Taking TCO to the Classroom". TCO is a business world concept that refers to the *total cost of ownership.* These costs include not only the initial money required for hardware and software, but also the costs of training, maintenance, and technology support needed to keep the computers and software operating properly.

To meet the budget demands required when schools add computer technology and Internet access, many districts are seeking grant money from large corporations such as IBM, Apple Computers, Dell Computers, and Microsoft. These companies and others have a vested interest in providing schools with computers and software for use in teaching and learning. They make it relatively easy for teachers to receive equipment and materials to assist them in instruction. Consequently, you may find yourself writing a grant proposal to a technology corporation in an effort to add needed technology to your classroom.

## Equitable Access

One issue that is being carefully studied by many researchers and writers is the problem of students having equal access to computer technology. Unfortunately, girls, students in low-income schools, minority students, low-performing students, and students with special needs are receiving fewer opportunities to use computers and the Internet. This is often referred to in the literature as the **digital divide** to emphasize the inequities that separate the "haves" from the "have-nots" in terms of access to technology. This split has been brought about partly as a result of the high costs of equipment and maintenence and partly through the attitudes of teachers and others about who should have access to technology.

**Inequities due to funding.** As you might expect, schools in poorer areas tend to have students who are less able to use technology in their school and home life. In the state of Maryland, for example, significantly higher percentages of classrooms in wealthy schools are connected to the Internet, while considerably lower percentages of high-poverty classrooms have this same option (see Table 9.10) (Maryland State Department of Education, 2000). Johnston (2001) makes it clear that the issue of inequitable access to computer technology due to poverty is a national one and not simply a problem for Maryland educators. America's schools that serve primarily low-income students tend to have fewer computers connected to the Internet and those machines are older. Teachers in these schools also provide students with fewer opportunities to use computers in their work (Lemke & Martin, 2001).

*Girls need equitable access to computers.*

**Racial disparities.** Because greater percentages of African American, Hispanic, and Native American students come from situations of poverty, they are less likely to be using computer technology in schools and at home. But even when income is taken into account, White students tend to use the computer more than other racial and ethnic groups. For example, in a recent survey only 15% of African American students and just 12% of Hispanic students indicated having used the Internet in school as compared to 21% of White students (Reid, 2001).

Although there are no clear reasons for these differences, some claim it is due to covert racism. Others cite the lack of racially and ethnically diverse content and fewer teachers of color as role models for technology use as reasons for these differences (Reid, 2001). Although there are signs that this inequity is being addressed in many schools and the gap may be narrowing, racial disparities remain a problem that educators must continue efforts to solve.

**Gender differences and equity.** There is a growing concern by many educators and others that girls are not getting as deeply involved in using computer technology as are boys. A statistic

| TABLE 9.10    Maryland's Digital Divide | | | | |
|---|---|---|---|---|
| **Level of Classroom Technology Use** | **Schools with Less than 11% Free and Reduced Lunch** | **Schools with 11% to 30% Free and Reduced Lunch** | **Schools with 31% to 70% Free and Reduced Lunch** | **Schools with More than 70% Free and Reduced Lunch** |
| Regular technology use | 70% | 62% | 46% | 32% |
| No use | 1% | 2% | 4% | 12% |

*Source:* From *Digital Divide Results,* by Maryland State Department of Education, 2000. Retrieved July 18, 2001, from http://msde.aws.com/digitaldivide.asp. Reprinted with permission.

## Girls and the Digital Divide

This is a story about a fourth-grade girl named Tanya, who changed from an eager learner in all areas (including science, mathematics, and technology) to one who started to narrow her horizons (Wood, 2001). Rather than being an excited user of technology with a keen interest in mathematics and science, Tanya began to withdraw into areas more traditionally of interest to girls.

This change occurred rather rapidly during Tanya's fourth-grade year. Up until that point, she was as eager as the boys in learning about technology and finding success in mathematics and science. In first grade, for example, when the class put on the play *Peter Pan,* Tanya suggested and then took leadership in designing invitations on the computer to send home to parents. During her third-grade year, Tanya and her class studied ecosystems. She and her classmates got excited about publishing their findings on the Internet so that other students could benefit from their study.

> But then something happened. In fourth grade, Tanya's interest in science and computers plummeted. She stopped going to the after-school Computer Club. She told her mother she thought science was for geeks and her teacher that she felt uninterested in the computer games the boys in her classroom played—games that usually featured male action heroes, battles, and destruction. (Wood, 2001)

In addition to science and technology, Tanya also lost interest in mathematics. While the boys began to take more leadership for class discussions and problem solving, Tanya didn't participate and seldom contributed to the discussion. She had changed from an eager and excited mathematics learner to one who saw herself as a student who disliked and wasn't very good at mathematics learning.

> Although Tanya still used technology as a tool to find information or write reports, she no longer showed a desire to become skilled in the use of computer graphics, digital cameras, or programming languages. That is, she did not aspire to become a "power user"—someone who has developed an intuitive sense of how to use computers and who can quickly, and independently, learn new programs, according to Cornelia Brunner, researcher at the Center for Children and Technology at the Education Development Center in New York City. (Wood, 2001)

Unfortunately, there are many girls like Tanya in America's schools. Considerable evidence shows that boys stay involved in technology, mathematics, and the sciences while girls are permitted by parents and their teachers to phase out of these important subjects as they move into early adolescence.

### Explore and Reflect

Learn more about girls and the digital divide by reading the source article by Wood (2001) and reviewing other online resources provided in the *Reflect on Diversity* module for Chapter 9 of the Companion Website.

1. Talk to a girl of middle school or high school age. Ask her about her comfort level with technology and how she uses it. What is her current career choice? Does she see herself using technology as part of that career? In what ways?

2. Do you think teachers can help girls be more interested in computer use? Should they (and you) actively pursue this option?

 *To explore this topic further and submit your responses online, go to the Reflect on Diversity module for Chapter 9 of the Companion Website for this text.*

*Source:* "The Girls Have It!" by M. Wood, 2001, *Instructor.* Retrieved July 24, 2001, from http://teacher.scholastic.com/professional/todayschild/thegirlshaveit.htm.

that supports this concern is the number of girls taking the advanced placement exam for computer science. In 2000, only 15% of the test takers were girls. Similarly, the percentage of women receiving undergraduate degrees in computer science dropped from 37% in 1984 to 27% in 1998 (Gehring, 2001). One reason cited for this lack of involvement is the greater number of girls who opt out of advanced-level science and mathematics courses. The consequence of this is that the scientific, engineering, and technological fields responsible for designing new technologies remain dominated by men. These men then design products that appeal more to other males and are used less often by girls (Brunner, Bennett, & Honey, 2000).

**Inequities due to academic performance.** Evidence suggests that teachers who have high-achieving classes tend to use more complex computer applications such as graphics and presentation software than teachers of low-achieving classes (Manzo, 2001). On the other hand, teachers with low-achieving students tend to use considerably more drill and practice software. Because teachers are still struggling to figure out how to effectively use computers with low-achieving students, their higher achieving peers end up with more and better quality time with technology. This continues to accentuate the digital divide that exists between students based on academic performance.

**Inequities due to special needs.** Most students with special needs spend at least a part of their school day within the regular classroom. Through inclusion, they are provided with the most effective environment for academic and social learning. Computers and related technologies can provide these students and their teachers with the tools they need to adapt classroom activities to individual needs. Provenzo et al. (1999) identify two broad categories of technology for students with special needs. The first is referred to as **assistive technology** and consists of all technology options that help students do something they could not do by themselves. For example, digitized speech devices are available to help students who are otherwise unable to speak clearly to communicate with peers and teachers. The second category of support for students with special needs is called **adaptive technology.** This is the computer hardware and software used to help students with special needs overcome a limiting condition. For example, Braille printers are available to assist blind students in creating documents that they can read.

Despite the growing efforts of educators to meet the requirements of students with special needs, several hurdles remain to be negotiated before equitable access for this group can be achieved. These include lack of funds to purchase the needed hardware and software, the training of students and teachers to use the technology properly (Provenzo et al., 1999), and software that is incompatible with adaptive technology used by students with special needs (Fine, 2001). Continued work will need to be done in the future to ensure this group's access to appropriate technology options.

**Language barriers.** Many limited English-proficient (LEP) students, in addition to frequently encountering the racial disparities associated with technology use described above, also find that they have problems because of language differences. Zehr (2001) identifies four issues that make it difficult for LEP students to effectively use computer technology:

- *Lack of teacher training.* Most bilingual and English as a Second Language (ESL) teachers lack the computer skills needed to select and use appropriate software and to assist students as they use technology in the classroom.

- *Limited hardware.* Most bilingual and ESL programs have limited access to computers and related technology in their classrooms.

- *Lack of quality software and appropriate websites.* Programs for LEP students suffer because of the limited number of software options available to them and the lack of good websites designed to accommodate students with limited English proficiency.

## Technology Standards

Because computer technology has only recently become available in the schools, its history as an area of study to be regulated by national and state agencies is short. Unlike other curriculum areas such as mathematics and social studies, national standards for technology use are a very recent addition (International Technology Education Association, 2000). These standards are only slowly having an impact on state guidelines for instruction. In 2001, just 35 of the 50 states had standards for students that included technology and only 4 of those had any measures in place to assess students' abilities in technology (*Education Week,* 2001). As standards for technology become more available in individual states and administrators at that level develop ways of promoting technology in K–12 classrooms, the potential influence of computers on instruction and learning should be enhanced. Classroom teachers will be encouraged, personally and by their administrators, to use technology as an important tool for learning. Table 9.11 lists some representative standards from the International Society for Technology in Education.

## Guiding Internet Use

Most people who use the Internet regularly find it to be a wonderful source of information and services that enriches both their personal and professional lives. At the same time, however, the huge growth in websites and the lack of regulations regarding its use have created several problems for educators and students. These issues must be resolved before the Internet can be fully integrated into the daily life of the classroom.

**Protecting students from inappropriate sites.**  One problem created by the Internet is the accessibility of inappropriate websites. Unfortunately, a considerable amount of information is available on the Internet that should not be viewed or read by students. Inappropriate language, hate group propaganda, and sites with strong sexual themes are just some of the problems that teachers and students may encounter. Unsuitable sites for students may also include adult chat rooms where people communicate online about personal issues. There have been several well-publicized incidents during the last several years in which children have been befriended by adults with serious mental or emotional problems and been lured away from school or home and into very difficult circumstances. Although software is available to block students from gaining access to most of these sites (Provenzo et al., 1999), teachers must still be vigilant in monitoring students so that they can be sure they are visiting appropriate Internet sites.

**Internet plagiarism.**  Another significant problem associated with Internet use has been student plagiarism. As use of the Internet has grown, a corresponding increase has been seen in this inappropriate activity. In a recent survey of 4,500 high school students at 25 schools around the country, more than half of the students admitted to either copying a few sentences or downloading an entire document from a website for use in their schoolwork (Hafner, 2001). This problem appears to be greatest at the high school level where the penalties for such activity are often less severe than for students in colleges and universities.

While the Internet has made it easier for some students to use the work of others, it has also provided new services to catch those who plagiarize. For example, Turnitin.com is an Internet business that allows both students and teachers to submit work for electronic assessment. By comparing the material with its database of websites and previously submitted papers, the company can detect plagiarism with a good level of accuracy. High schools pay approximately $1,000 per year for an unlimited number of submissions to this service (Hafner, 2001).

## Teacher Training and In-Service

One of the major issues that must be resolved in order to integrate technology more effectively into everyday classroom life is to ensure that all teacher preparation programs include a strong

**TABLE 9.11   Student Technology Standards**

| Category | Standards |
|---|---|
| Basic operations and concepts | • Students demonstrate a sound understanding of the nature and operation of technology systems.<br>• Students are proficient in the use of technology. |
| Social, ethical, and human issues | • Students understand the ethical, cultural, and societal issues related to technology.<br>• Students practice responsible use of technology systems, information, and software.<br>• Students develop positive attitudes toward technology uses that support lifelong learning, collaboration, personal pursuits, and productivity. |
| Technology productivity tools | • Students use technology tools to enhance learning, increase productivity, and promote creativity.<br>• Students use productivity tools to collaborate in constructing technology-enhanced models, preparing publications, and producing other creative works. |
| Technology communications tools | • Students use telecommunications to collaborate, publish, and interact with peers, experts, and other audiences.<br>• Students use a variety of media and formats to communicate information and ideas effectively to multiple audiences. |
| Technology research tools | • Students use technology to locate, evaluate, and collect information from a variety of sources.<br>• Students use technology tools to process data and report results.<br>• Students evaluate and select new information resources and technological innovations based on the appropriateness to specific tasks. |
| Technology problem-solving and decision-making tools | • Students use technology resources for solving problems and making informed decisions.<br>• Students employ technology in the development of strategies for solving problems in the real world. |

Source: From *National Technology Standards for Students,* by International Society for Technology in Education (ISTE) NETS Project, June 1998. Copyright, 1998, ISTE 800-336-5191, iste@iste.org, www.iste.org. All rights reserved. Reprinted with permission. Reprint permission does not constitute endorsement by ISTE.

component of technology education. In addition, once teachers enter the classroom, they need extensive and ongoing in-service training so that they can effectively integrate technology into their teaching and learning experiences. While the level of training is continuing to improve, many teachers still fail to receive the initial and ongoing training they need to be successful in using technology in the classroom.

**Initial teacher preparation.** Take a few moments to review the teacher preparation program for your present college or university. Is course work required in educational technology? If so, what is the content of the course or courses you will take? Currently, state teacher preparation

## Internet Plagiarism

Steve Gardiner (2001), a high school English teacher, writes about his first encounter with what he calls cybercheating:

> In the middle of grading a stack of some 90 essays analyzing Shakespeare's *Macbeth*, I was interrupted. When I returned to grading, the words on the page seemed too familiar. I thought for sure I had made marginal comments on this paper and given it an A. Must have been the interruption, I thought. But as I read on, I knew I had marked this one already. I reached over to the face-down papers on the edge of my desk and turned over the top one. Sure enough, the writing was identical. (p. 172)

Steve assumed that one of the students had written the paper and the other had simply turned it in as his own work. When he confronted the students, however, he learned that both had downloaded the paper off the Internet. It had been pure chance that both students had copied the same paper and that they had ended up together in Steve's stack to grade.

After talking to a computer education colleague at the high school and spending some time searching the Internet, Steve began to realize how easy it was to get papers from the Internet and decided he needed to confront his classes:

> Since it was the first time I had knowingly dealt with cybercheating, I made my students an offer. "If you downloaded your paper from the Internet and you give it to me today with a note telling me what you did, I'll work with you on a solution. If, after today, I find out you downloaded your paper, you will get a zero on a required paper, which means a failure in senior English and no graduation." (p. 173)

By the end of the day, Steve had six additional papers on his desk.

### React and Reflect

1. In your opinion, how widespread is the issue of cybercheating and how do you think students and other teachers view the problem?
2. As a future teacher, what will you do to prevent and confront this issue?

 *To explore this topic further and submit your reactions and reflections online, go to the Explore Your Beliefs module for Chapter 9 of the Companion Website for this text.*

*Source:* "Cybercheating: A New Twist on an Old Problem," by S. Gardiner, 2001, *Phi Delta Kappan, 82*(3), pp. 172–174.

programs are inconsistent in what they require for technology competencies. As shown in Figure 9.1, only 26 states have standards that must be met before candidates can receive initial certification (*Education Week,* 2001), and these criteria vary considerably in breadth and scope. While some states list requirements for what teachers should learn and know, others simply state the number of technology courses that teachers must complete for graduation. Consequently, many teachers are entering the profession with limited skills in using computer technology effectively in the classroom.

**In-service technology training.** Although most school districts are doing the best they can to provide teachers with adequate in-service instruction in technology by spending a larger percentage of their technology budget on teacher training (*Education Week,* 2001), educators often feel that more needs to be done. In a recent survey, 82% of teachers polled felt that the number one barrier to their use of technology was lack of release time to learn about technology, practice using it, and plan to implement technology into daily classroom activities (Smerdon et al., 2001).

**Figure 9.1**    States Requiring Technology Training for Certification

Require technology training
for certification

Assessment in technology
for certification

*Source: Technology Counts 2001: The New Divide,* by *Education Week,* 2001, Washington, DC: Author.

## Summary

In this chapter, four questions were presented to help you learn more about the issues surrounding integrating technology into classroom teaching and learning activities:

### How has technology been used in the classroom?

Technology has been an important component of American education from its earliest days and continues to influence classroom life today:
- Early technology options
- Television
- Computers (Praxis II, topic IIa)
- The Internet (Praxis II, topic IIa)

### What are schools doing to enhance technology use in the curriculum?

The K–12 schools are making many changes that are helping increase computer use:
- Classroom computers with Internet access (Praxis II, topic IIa)
- Quality software (Praxis II, topic IIa)

## What is the impact of computers on teaching and learning?

In many schools, computer technology is having a significant effect on what happens in the classroom:

- Impact on teaching (Praxis II, topic IIa)
- Influence on learners (Praxis II, topic Ia)

## What issues must be resolved to strengthen technology's impact?

Several significant issues must be addressed before technology can have a stronger impact on teaching and learning:

- Technology costs: initial and continuing
- Equitable access (Praxis II, topics Ib, IIIb)
- Technology standards
- Guiding Internet use (Praxis II, topic Ic)
- Teacher training and in-service (Praxis II, topic IVa)

## Key Terms

| | |
|---|---|
| adaptive technology | encyclopedia software |
| assistive technology | Internet |
| creativity software | simulation software |
| digital divide | technology |
| distance learning | word processing software |
| drill and practice software | World Wide Web |

## Reflective Journey: Online Journal

 Use the questions for thought and reflection highlighted throughout the chapter to help guide your personal journey of reflection and professional development as a teacher. To complete your journal entries online, go to the *Reflective Journey* module for this chapter of the Companion Website.

## PRAXIS   Test Preparation Activities

 To review an online chapter case study, test your understanding of chapter topics and concepts, and begin preparing for the Praxis II: Principles of Learning and Teaching examination, go to the *Praxis Test Preparation* module for this chapter of the Companion Website.

## inTASC   Becoming a Reflective Practitioner

To complete these activities and submit your responses online, go to the *Becoming a Reflective Practitioner* module for this chapter of the Companion Website.

## How has technology been used in the classroom?

### Review Questions

1. Broadly defined, what is technology?
2. Name an early technology option used in the schools (prior to the 1980s) and discuss its impact.
3. What is simulation software and how is it used?

## Field Experiences

Find a classroom that has computers in it for students to use. Observe how the teacher incorporates technology in her or his teaching. What kinds of software are available and how are students using it? Does the teacher appear comfortable when using computers in teaching? Do students seem to benefit from their use?

## Building Your Portfolio: *Software Evaluations*

**INTASC Standard 3.** For a grade and/or subject of your choice, review two or three pieces of software that students are using. Place yourself in the role of a student and evaluate the actual content being taught, the methods used to develop student understanding, and the ease of use (see Table 9.5). Do you think these software programs would be effective learning tools for students? Include these reviews in your portfolio.

## What are schools doing to enhance technology use in the curriculum?

### Review Questions

1. What must occur so that computers don't become another marginalized technology option?
2. What are the negative aspects of having only computer labs (rather than classroom computers) in schools?

### Field Experiences

Spend some time in a school of your choice observing how the computer lab is used. Who instructs students during lab time and what is being learned? What do you see as the benefits and drawbacks of computer labs?

### Building Your Portfolio: *Internet Resources*

**INTASC Standard 3.** Select a topic that you think could be effectively researched using the Internet for a grade and subject of your choice. Spend time researching the topic using the World Wide Web. Describe the topic selected, the methods used in searching the Internet, and the results for inclusion in your portfolio. Discuss the usefulness of the Internet for teaching the subject and grade of your choice.

## What is the impact of computers on teaching and learning?

### Review Questions

1. What are the arguments for computers having the potential to completely reform teaching and learning?
2. What are the reasons given by some for proceeding with caution when using computers in the classroom?
3. How have computers influenced students as learners?

### Field Experiences

Talk to a teacher of your choice about technology use in the classroom. Have the teacher identify for you both the benefits and problems associated with its use. Does this teacher see the computer as a valuable addition to classroom activities or a tool with limited use?

### Building Your Portfolio: *Technology in Teaching*

**INTASC Standard 3.** Create two or three scenarios in which you describe how you would use technology in teaching the grade/subject of your choice. In each scenario, describe as specifically as you can how you would use technology as you teach and the ways in which students would learn as they interact with technology. Include these scenarios in your portfolio.

## What issues must be resolved to strengthen technology's impact?

**Review Questions**

1. What is the digital divide?

2. What inequities exist in technology use?

3. How significant is the issue of Internet plagiarism?

**Building Your Portfolio:** *Technology Skills*

**INTASC Standard 9.** As you develop your technology skills, keep examples of the work you do for your portfolio. Clip art used to make your documents more professional, figures and tables created, color documents, spreadsheets, materials located through an Internet search, and digital pictures added to files are just some examples of the types of options you could consider including. Continue to update this component of your portfolio as new skills are learned.

## Suggested Readings

*Education Week.* (2002). *Technology counts '02: E-learning education.* Washington, DC: Author. Available on the World Wide Web at http://www.edweek.org/sreports/tc01/. This and earlier editions of *Technology Counts* discuss a wealth of issues related to technology use. Much of this issue deals with how electronic learning is changing how students learn.

Jossey-Bass (Ed.). (2000). *The Jossey-Bass reader on technology and learning.* San Francisco: Jossey-Bass. This book contains several very thought-provoking articles from other sources about the potential of computers and the Internet to dramatically change how schools operate.

Lemke, C., & Martin, C. (2001). *Children and computer technology: Issues and ideas.* Los Altos, CA: The David and Lucile Packard Foundation. Available on the World Wide Web at http://www.futureofchildren.org. This document presents many interesting issues about children and technology use and provides many excellent resources for further study.

U.S. Department of Education. (2000). *E-learning: Putting a world-class education at the fingertips of all children.* Washington, DC: Author. Available on the World Wide Web at http://www.ed.gov/Technology/elearning/index.html. This document is a revised plan for technology use in America's schools developed by the U.S. Department of Education. It provides a list of five ambitious goals for technology use.

# part 3

## What Are the Foundations for Reflective Teaching?

# chapter 10

## Historical Influences

History can provide you with many important insights into current educational thinking and practice. By learning from the successes and failures of the educators who preceded you, you are more likely to engage in effective educational decision making. In this chapter, four key questions will help you clarify the values of studying history.

## Focus Questions

◢ How does history affect my future teaching?

◢ What is the history of education for young children?

◢ What has influenced modern secondary education?

◢ How has history shaped current educational issues?

Let us look at the
general status of the
pupil (in southern Negro
schools). In the first place
approximately 1,000,000, or
30 per cent, of the 3,048,289 children of
public school age never entered a school of any
kind last year [1930]. Of the 2,165,147 who did enroll, 2,038,991, or 94 per cent, were in the elementary
grades; 107,156, or 5 per cent, in high schools; and 19,000, slightly less than 1 per cent, in college. . . .

[Of the south's Negro teaching force in 1931], 18,130 [38.7 per cent] . . . have less than high school
training; 27,561 (58 per cent) have less than two years beyond high school, which is usually considered
minimum for elementary teachers.

From facts and estimates given later in this study it appears that the typical rural Negro teacher of the
South is a woman of rural heritage about 27 years of age. She has completed high school and had ten weeks in
summer schools. She teaches 47 children through six grades for a term of six months, remaining about two
years in the same school. Her annual salary is $360, or $1 a day, and she teaches for about five years.
(McCuistion, 1932, pp. 16–17)

The study of history is a subject that evokes a negative reaction in many people. Memorizing facts about people and events from the past without making connections to current events makes history appear irrelevant, dry, and dull. If you experienced history from this perspective, you may be wondering about its value in understanding education today. In actuality, however, history provides many important insights into current educational thinking and practice. As can be seen from the article quoted at the beginning of this chapter, many of the issues faced by teachers and schools today are not new. Concerns about adequate teacher preparation, salaries, large class size, high school graduation rates, and teacher turnover are just as real today as they were in 1932. By studying these issues from a historical viewpoint and benefiting from the insights presented, educators can avoid the mistakes and build on the successes experienced by others. History also gives perspective on the progress that educators have made over time. As you can see from the earlier example, very real improvements have occurred in each of the areas mentioned.

## How does history affect my future teaching?

When studied through the lens of current events, history can provide a wealth of important insights (see Table 10.1). First, it allows you to identify forces that have affected and continue to impact education today. A study of history also helps you learn from past successes and failures so that future progress is enhanced. Finally, learning about past people and events that have influenced education can provide you with useful information about the current status and future directions of educational issues.

### Forces Affecting Education

Looking back at the past often allows us to see clearly what was difficult to understand as the events themselves took place. From a personal perspective, most of us can identify actions we have taken that led to problems in our lives. At the time, these actions seemed reasonable. Looking back, however, we can see more clearly the potential pitfalls. The passage of time, combined with the opportunity to reflect on what we did or didn't do, gives us important insights into the factors that caused our behavior to have negative consequences. In much the same way, a look at historical figures and events provides you with a better understanding of the forces that influence education today.

Take, for example, the life of Martin Luther (1483–1546). Although he is best known for his efforts in religious reformation, Luther had a significant impact on educational thinking as well.

**TABLE 10.1    Studying the History of Education**

| Benefit | Description |
|---|---|
| Understanding the forces affecting education | Studying history helps you understand social, political, and religious forces and their impact on education. |
| Learning from the past | You can learn from both the successes and failures of past educational efforts. |
| Clarifying history's impact on current issues | It is important for you to understand the impact of historical figures and events on current educational issues. |

Because of his conviction that the Bible was the key to Christian reform, Luther began to promote improved education, particularly the ability to read, as an essential in German society. To establish a personal relationship with God, he felt everyone needed to be able to read the Bible. Among other things, his influence led to both boys and girls being educated in Germany's schools (Cubberley, 1934). This was an early step that led, after several centuries, to more equitable educational opportunities for girls in this country.

## Learning from the Past

We can also learn a great deal from both the successes and failures of past educational efforts. By studying historical figures and events, we can avoid the pitfalls and build on the successes of others. As an example, consider the work of John Dewey (1859–1952). During the early part of the 20th century, Dewey's ideas formed the basis for a major reform movement known as **progressive education** (Butts & Cremin, 1953). Emphasizing educational relevance and learning through social interactions, this movement added many exciting elements to an American educational climate that many critics found dull and uninteresting (see Chapters 7 and 11 for more information on progressivism as an educational philosophy). Despite its promise, however, progressive education gradually lost much of its momentum as an educational movement.

Today, many educators still believe strongly in the principles Dewey proposed and are attempting to implement his philosophy in new and creative ways. For example, cooperative learning (see Chapter 8) is based in large part on concepts presented by Dewey. Those attempting to implement these teaching strategies in the classroom can learn much from studying progressive education to understand the reasons for its decreased influence.

## History's Impact on Current Issues

A third way in which historical figures and events affect your future teaching is through their influence in shaping current educational issues. By understanding the factors that led to the development of current ideas and approaches to education, you will have a better perspective from which to deal with these issues. For example, one current issue facing teachers today is the impact that equitable educational opportunities have on students' abilities to learn. Studying how others have dealt with this issue historically adds further insights into this complex topic. In the early part of the 20th century, Maria Montessori (1870–1952) worked with what were then called "idiot" children in the slums of Rome (Lillard, 1972). Her efforts provide an early example of an attempt to offer more equitable educational opportunities for students with special needs. Montessori's early students came from institutional settings and were viewed by Italian society as very low-functioning individuals with little chance to be successful in life. Following careful observations of these children, however, Montessori felt differently and designed materials and educational experiences to enhance their learning. Within a few short years, these castoffs from society were able to take and complete the examinations for the primary certificate, typically the highest level of education attained by most students (Lillard, 1972).

*The Civil Rights Movement has had a major impact on schooling.*

# What is the history of education for young children?

In Chapter 4, the first two age-related levels of education were defined as early childhood education and elementary education. Early childhood education today is typically defined as birth through age 8 (third grade), while elementary education generally includes children from 5 to 12 years of age. The history of schooling at both levels provides important insights into the current theory and practice found in these settings.

## Early Childhood Education

A study of the historical roots of early childhood education provides a better understanding of the similarities and differences between early childhood and traditional public elementary school education. Beginning with three European educators and continuing into 20th-century America, several key people and events have strongly influenced current directions in early childhood education, as listed in Table 10.2.

**European influences.** Although many European educators have had a significant impact on early childhood education, three are discussed here as having made perhaps the most noteworthy contributions to the field. Johann Pestalozzi (1746–1847) was a gifted Swiss educator who, without formal training, quickly established himself as a caring, creative teacher. Basing his method primarily on the theories of Rousseau (1979), Pestalozzi took charge of an orphanage in Stanz, Switzerland, and was able to make remarkable progress with children who were considered incapable of learning. Characteristics of his teaching included careful observation of children, recognizing the potential in each child, understanding the importance of teacher–student relationships, strengthening peer relations, and learning through the use of the senses. All of these attributes of teaching are seen as essential to early childhood educators today.

Another European educator to significantly influence early education was Friedrich Froebel (1782–1852). Much of Froebel's educational training came from time spent carefully observing

**TABLE 10.2    History of Early Childhood Education**

| Influences | Key Person/Event | Description |
|---|---|---|
| European influences | Pestalozzi | Gifted teacher who based his method on the theories of Rousseau. |
| | Froebel | Emphasized the importance of childhood play; started kindergarten. |
| | Montessori | Developed quality educational materials for use in the early childhood classroom. |
| American efforts | Kindergarten movement | Early kindergarten programs designed to help low-income children become successful in school. |
| | Child study movement | Effort to better understand child growth and development. |
| | Cooperative nursery schools | Parents assist teacher in implementing preschool program. |
| | Head Start | Begun in 1960s to help low-income preschool children be more successful in school. |

Pestalozzi teaching young children. While agreeing with much of what he saw, Froebel developed his own teaching method (Froebel, 1886). One of his major contributions to early education was the emphasis he placed on **play** as an important method of learning for young children. He said this about play:

> It gives, therefore, joy, freedom, contentment, inner and outer rest, peace with the world. It holds the sources of all that is good. A child that plays thoroughly, with self-active determination, perseveringly until physical fatigue forbids, will surely be a thorough, determined man, capable of self-sacrifice for the promotion of the welfare of himself and others. (cited in Braun & Edwards, 1972, p. 67)

Froebel focused initially on working with 5-year-old children and named his program the **kindergarten** (meaning "children's garden" in German). His approach gradually spread throughout Germany and later to the United States. Froebel is often referred to as the father of the modern kindergarten, and his ideas about play, the values of singing with children, and circle time experiences are all considered important parts of kindergarten and early childhood education today.

Maria Montessori (1870–1952) is the third European educator who had a significant impact on the theory and practice of early childhood education. One example of her influence is the educational materials she developed (see Table 10.3). Montessori felt very strongly that these materials should be beautiful (Lillard, 1996). They were constructed with care from only the finest woods and other materials and carefully finished to look and feel good to children. Since most of her students were from low-income families, this equipment provided one of the very few opportunities they had to interact with truly beautiful objects.

**Early American efforts.**  The kindergarten movement in the United States marked the beginnings of early childhood education in this country. In 1855, after having studied under Froebel in Germany, Mrs. Carl Schutz opened the first kindergarten classroom in Watertown, Wisconsin (Braun & Edwards, 1972). Throughout the remainder of the 19th century, most kindergarten programs were privately operated and funded through grants from philanthropic organizations to help low-income children become more successful in school (Braun & Edwards, 1972).

In addition to kindergarten education, near the beginning of the 20th century the **child study movement** provided the momentum for new programs for 3- and 4-year-old children (Weber, 1984). This movement grew out of an attempt to better understand children and their development. One setting that became increasingly more common across America for studying child growth and development was the *laboratory nursery school*. Initially funded through federal

**TABLE 10.3   Montessori Materials**

| Characteristic | Description |
| --- | --- |
| Careful attention to concept development | Each piece of equipment was designed to teach specific concepts to children. |
| Graduated difficulty/complexity | As children develop, they need increasingly challenging materials to stimulate continued intellectual growth. |
| Self-correcting | Whenever possible, materials were designed to be self-correcting so that students could use them without adult guidance. |
| Sensory oriented | Materials were designed to stimulate all the senses as an aid to learning. |

*Source: Maria Montessori: Her Life and Work,* by E. Standing, 1962, Fresno, CA: Academy Guild Press.

grants and private foundations, these nursery school and kindergarten programs provided researchers with children to observe and study in a controlled environment.

At about the same time that laboratory nursery schools became more common, **cooperative nursery schools** were also being implemented. For this option, parents of 3- and 4-year-old children hired a nursery school teacher and then agreed to assist her for a portion of the school week so that a low adult–child ratio could be maintained at a minimal cost (Braun & Edwards, 1972). In addition to the quality educational experiences available to children, the parents who spent time in the classroom had many opportunities to see and use good toys and equipment and learn parenting skills as they observed teachers interacting with children.

**Project Head Start.** During the presidencies of John F. Kennedy and Lyndon B. Johnson, a concerted effort was made to help low-income families break free from the grip of poverty. A cornerstone of this "War on Poverty" was federal support for early childhood programs designed to assist young disadvantaged children (Hymes, 1978). The thinking of policy makers was that the cycle of poverty could only be broken by providing young children from low-income families with quality educational experiences. These children would then do better in school, find higher paying jobs, and break free from poverty's grip. Beginning in 1964, the federal government provided money to local sites for preschool-aged children from low-income families.

The most famous of the programs begun during this period is **Head Start.** Started in 1964 to help low-income 4-year-olds catch up academically with their more advantaged peers, Head Start has stood the test of time as an important program for young children. It currently serves more than 905,000 3- and 4-year-old children across the United States (U.S. Department of Health and Human Services, 2002b). The Head Start program is considered comprehensive because of its emphasis on all aspects of the child's development. In addition to focusing on social, emotional, intellectual, language, and physical development, Head Start emphasizes good health and provides resources and assistance with medical, dental, nutritional, and mental health needs.

## Elementary Education

Although today virtually every child attends and completes an elementary school education, during early American history this was not the case. Children from less affluent homes often

*A 19th-century school in New Hampshire.*

**TABLE 10.4   History of Elementary Education**

| Time Period | Schooling Options | Description |
|---|---|---|
| Early colonial times | Dame schools | Informal programs were run by women from the community who had basic educational skills. |
| | Apprenticeship programs | Children were taught the skills needed in specific trades by others who had already mastered them. |
| | Charity schools | Funded by religious groups for poor children to learn basic academic skills along with religious training. |
| Mid-1600s | Town schools | Funded by tuition paid by parents of children within the local community. |
| | Moving schools | Teacher traveled between towns and taught children for several months before moving on. |
| | District schools | Townships were divided into districts, each with its own school. |
| Late 1700s | Common schools | The idea of universal education and compulsory attendance laws led people such as Horace Mann to promote the establishment of common schools. |

went to work at a very young age. The luxury of private schooling was beyond the means of most families. Boys from upper class families tended to be the only ones receiving formal educational training in either a private school setting or through tutoring experiences. Table 10.4 provides a snapshot of the history of elementary education; each topic listed there is discussed in more detail next.

**Colonial origins.** Although early American settlers placed a high value on education, the harsh realities of colonial life meant that many children in the 1600s failed to receive any formal educational experiences. Parents were the primary teachers of their own children, passing on their limited knowledge when possible. In addition to home learning, the three most common educational options available to children throughout the colonies were dame schools, apprenticeships, and charity schools. **Dame schools** were informal programs run by women from the community who had some basic skills in reading, writing, mathematics, and religion. They would take children into their homes and, for a small fee, teach them beginning academic and religious skills (Cubberley, 1934). Girls were also frequently given instruction in basic household skills such as cooking and sewing. Less privileged children throughout the colonies often found themselves in **apprenticeship programs** to learn a trade. In addition to the skills needed to be a blacksmith or carpenter, for example, some apprentices learned basic reading, writing, and arithmetic skills that would be helpful in their future occupations (Spring, 1986). Apprenticeship programs lasted from 3 to 10 years and typically ended when the students become young adults, ready to begin work on their own. Another schooling option occasionally available to children from low-income families was the **charity school**. Funded by contributions from religious groups, these programs offered poor children

**TABLE 10.5  Early Teaching Materials**

| Material | Description |
|---|---|
| *The Hornbook* | The most common colonial teaching material was the hornbook, which consisted of a piece of paddle-shaped wood covered with a sheet of paper containing the alphabet and possibly one or two religious writings (such as the Lord's Prayer). This paper was then covered by a thin coating of cow's horn for protection from the elements, hence the name. |
| *New England Primer* | The first real book used in the schools was the *New England Primer*. Small in size and having thin wooden covers, these early religiously oriented books of 50 to 100 pages contained the alphabet, lists of words, and verses with small pictures for children to read and study. |
| *McGuffey Readers* | During the 1800s, the most popular books were a six-volume series called the *McGuffey Readers*. Moving away from the heavy emphasis on religion, this series promoted morality and Americanism through the poetry and writings of various leaders of the time. |

*Sources: Early Schools and Schoolbooks of New England,* by G. Littlefield, 1965, New York: Russell and Russell; and *Public Education in the United States,* by E. Cubberley, 1934, Boston: Houghton Mifflin.

the opportunity to learn basic academic skills in a school setting while strengthening their religious beliefs. In addition to funding these schools, missionary groups were often responsible for providing the teachers as well (Cubberley, 1934).

While dame schools, apprenticeship programs, and charity schools were available throughout the colonies, other educational options tended to vary somewhat by region. The southern colonies relied heavily on private tutoring to meet the educational needs of children from well-to-do families. In the middle colonies, private venture schools and church-related school options were common. The New England area provided children with access to community-controlled schools with a religious emphasis (Butts & Cremin, 1953). Table 10.5 lists some of the early teaching materials used during colonial times.

The combination of a common religious heritage that valued learning and greater concentrations of children in towns and cities led to the development of a more organized system of schooling in the northern colonies. Religious leaders felt that it was important to educate all children so that they could read and interpret the Bible. This, combined with the demand for skilled and semiskilled workers in the towns and cities, led to the passage of laws emphasizing the importance of education. The most famous of these laws was the *Old Deluder Satan Act,* passed in 1647. This act was so named because Massachusetts Puritans felt that the devil was working hard to keep people from understanding the truths found in the Bible (Spring, 1986). To keep Satan from being successful in deluding people, this act required that every town with 50 or more families had to hire a teacher paid through parental tuition so that children could learn to read and write.

With the passage of similar laws in other New England colonies, the colonial governments for the first time began taking responsibility for the education of children. In towns and cities, these schools were first called **town schools** and were funded by tuition paid by the parents of children (primarily boys) within the local community (Butts & Cremin, 1953). As settlers began to move west in search of good farmland, smaller communities helped fund **moving schools,** where a teacher traveled from one small town to the next and taught children for several months

# MASTER TEACHER SERIES

## Segment IV: When Teaching Is Only Part of the Job

In this segment of the *Master Teacher Series,* Ms. Jones continues to work with the students and parents in difficult situations. Two children argue, and one threatens to kill the other. A student, along with her mother, accuses Ms. Jones of calling the child an idiot. Despite all of these incidents, there are good days and successes. Her students are speaking in whole sentences, and a few are reading close to sixth-grade level. The science materials have finally come in. Outside of the classroom, Ms. Jones also focuses her attention on a student who has excessive absences due to her needing to baby-sit at home.

### For Deeper Understanding

1. What are the difficulties of teaching a classroom full of students with special (academic, personal, social) needs?

2. Consider state efforts to systematize and unify the training required of teachers and the content of the school curricula, often as a result state-funded financial support of public education. How is this evident in the *Master Teacher Series?* How is it evident in your college or university? How is it evident in your state?

3. Ms. Jones has a meeting with the principal, the child who accused the teacher of calling her an idiot, and the child's parents to determine if the allegations are true and whether the child should stay in Ms. Jones's classroom. Analyze the incident. What might have been done differently?

4. If you had a child who wasn't doing well in school, how would you like to hear about it from the teacher?

 *To submit your responses online, go to the Master Teacher Series module for Chapter 10 of the Companion Website.*

before moving on. Gradually, the **district school** became more common in the northern colonies (Butts & Cremin, 1953). In this system, townships (36 square miles) were divided into districts, each with its own school. Schools were funded by local district revenues (primarily from parents) and provided more consistent schooling options for children within a region.

**Establishment of common schools.** Beginning with the American Revolution and the unification of the 13 original colonies under a common federal government, ideas about schooling in the United States started to change. First, the earlier laws in the northern colonies requiring towns and districts to have schools under the authority of the local government set a precedence for the rest of the union. In addition, there was a growing consensus that not only should these schools exist, but that they should be paid for by the public so that a free basic education would be available to all (Cubberley, 1934). This notion of **universal education** was slowly implemented during the next century through the passage of state and federal laws and the tireless efforts of a leading proponent, Horace Mann.

One significant contribution to the implementation of common schools throughout the United States was the passage of the *Northwest Ordinances of 1785 and 1787* by the federal government. These acts divided the Northwest territories (currently the states of Illinois, Indiana, Michigan, Ohio, Wisconsin, and part of Minnesota) into townships of 36 square miles. One section of each township was set aside for public schools. In addition to promoting the establishment of common schools in the Northwest territories, these acts provided a model for other future states for the creation of common schools.

The second set of legal mandates that had a major impact on universal public education was the implementation of **compulsory attendance laws** in individual states. Massachusetts was the first state to pass such legislation in 1852 and make public school attendance mandatory. Other states followed suit, and by the start of the 20th century, most had passed similar legislation (Cremin, 1980). These laws slowly pushed communities and districts to offer common school options to children, and attendance grew rapidly through this period (Snyder, 1993).

Although many people can be credited with advancing the cause of common schools in the United States, Horace Mann (1796–1859) is unquestionably the most significant contributor. Trained as a lawyer, he became a well-known Massachusetts politician and educational spokesman (Gibbon, 2002). Mann believed strongly in the provision of common schools for all and tirelessly

## engage in the debate

### Alternatives to Compulsory Attendance

Horace Mann was an early proponent of an education for all. In 1846 he wrote:

> I believe in the existence of a great, immutable principle of natural law, or natural ethics,—a principle antecedent to all human institutions and incapable of being abrogated by any ordinances of man,—a principle of divine origin, clearly legible in the ways of Providence as those ways are manifested in the order of nature and in the history of the race,—which proves the *absolute right* of every human being that comes into the world to an education; and which, of course, proves the correlative duty of every government to see that the means of that education are provided for all. (Noll, 2003, p. 74)

Mann not only believed that schools should be universally available but also that governments assume the responsibility for making sure that all children were receiving an education.

Daniel Pink, on the other hand, sees compulsory school attendance as a concept that has outlived its purpose: "Compared to the rest of the world, America is a remarkably hands-off land. We don't force people to vote, or to work, or to serve in the military. But we do compel parents to relinquish their kids to this institution (school) for a dozen years, and threaten to jail those who resist" (Noll, 2003, p. 79). The work world, according to Pink, is changing as a large number of workers are becoming what he calls "free agents" in the sense that they are self-employed, freelancers, and telecommuters in their jobs. Pink suggests that education must adjust to these changing demands of the workplace. In fact, he sees the growing numbers of home-schooled children as one indicator that this process has already begun. Pink believes that home schooling and electronic learning will eventually replace much of what has traditionally been accomplished under the guise of compulsory education.

#### Research the Issue

Research this topic online using the links provided in the *Engage in the Debate* module for this chapter of the Companion Website.

1. From your research, what strengths and limitations are cited for home schooling?
2. Is electronic learning a good option for some students and their families to consider? Why or why not?

#### Explore Your Views

1. Should parents and students be able to choose between home schooling, electronic learning, and school attendance?
2. Do you think states should continue to require some form of compulsory education? Why or why not?

 *To research this issue and submit your responses online, go to the Engage in the Debate module for Chapter 10 of the Companion Website.*

*Source: Taking Sides: Clashing Views on Controversial Education Issue,* 12th ed., by J. Noll, 2003, Guilford, CT: McGraw-Hill/Dushkin.

advocated their implementation throughout his career (Butts & Cremin, 1953). In his role as secretary of the Massachusetts State Board of Education and as the editor and founder of *The Common School Journal*, Mann wrote and spoke convincingly about the values of common schools. His writings were distributed throughout the country and had a major impact on the expansion of educational opportunities in the United States.

Stop for a moment to reflect on your own educational experiences through elementary school. How do they compare to those described above? Did you attend a preschool or kindergarten program? In what ways were they similar to, and different from, the historical programs identified? For much of American history, many American children did not have access to a free, public elementary education. Can you imagine what your life would be like without this most basic educational opportunity?

**Reflective Journey 10.1**

## What has influenced modern secondary education?

Although early forms of secondary education began in colonial times, the availability of this option lagged behind those at the elementary level. The first programs were designed to prepare students for a college education, were funded privately, and only gradually became a part of the public educational system starting in the early 1800s (see Table 10.6). Access to public high school experiences remained sporadic well into the 20th century, especially in poor and rural areas.

### Early Options

Three secondary school options were available to students in the American colonies and through the early years of the new nation. The **Latin grammar school** prepared students for the college experience and was the first program available in the colonies. **English grammar schools** were designed for those who needed formal education beyond the elementary level for business and

**TABLE 10.6 History of Secondary Education**

| Time Period | Schooling Option | Description |
|---|---|---|
| Colonial America | Latin grammar school | Prepared students for college through the study of Latin and Greek. |
| | English grammar school | Prepared students who needed formal education beyond the elementary level, but weren't planning to attend college. |
| | American Academy | Prepared students for either college or the business world. |
| Late 1800s | Public high school | Publicly funded high schools for both boys and girls were made available. |
| Early 1900s | Junior high school | Because young adolescents were seen as having different needs, they were separated from high school students for grades 7–9. |
| 1960s | Middle school | The onset of puberty in many sixth-grade students led to the growth of schools for grades 6–8. |

commerce, but weren't planning to attend college. The **American Academy** was a combination of the other two options and served the dual purposes of preparing students for college and life in the business world.

**Latin grammar schools.** Students in the American colonies initially had two choices for a college experience. They could travel to Europe and attend college there or enroll at what is now Harvard University (founded in 1636) in Cambridge, Massachusetts, near Boston (Cubberley, 1934). In both instances, these institutions demanded that students be trained in Latin and Greek before they could be admitted. The curriculum of the Latin grammar school, whose sole purpose was the preparation of students for the college experience, was thus centered on this classical preparation. Students typically spent 7 years learning both Latin and Greek and then studying classical texts in both languages (Cubberley, 1934). The first Latin grammar school began in Boston in 1635, with others opening soon thereafter in the northern colonies. Gradually, this option spread to the middle colonies. Students in the South were typically tutored at home or traveled to England for training if they were planning on attending college. Latin grammar schools were for young men only. It was some time before women had similar educational opportunities.

**English grammar schools.** During the 1700s, the rapid growth of middle-class businesses (particularly in the northern and middle colonies) created the need for a new educational option. The English grammar school was designed to prepare students for work in the business world, with diverse course work to prepare students in such things as bookkeeping, letter writing, marine and military engineering, navigation, and foreign languages (Butts & Cremin, 1953). These programs tended to have more flexible admission policies than the Latin grammar school and some women were able to participate as students.

**The American Academy.** During the second half of the 18th century, the American academy became a third secondary school option available to students. It combined the college preparatory experiences found in the Latin grammar school with the more practical and business-oriented education of the English grammar school (Marr, 1959). Over time, the academy began to replace both of its predecessors as the primary form of secondary education found in America. It served as the forerunner for today's modern high school. Benjamin Franklin is credited with starting one of the first American academies in Philadelphia in 1751. Like other similar programs, the academy provided instruction in English, rather than Latin. While including course work that was designed to prepare students for college, the academy offered a curriculum designed to prepare young people for employment. Subjects taught included writing, geography, history, mental and moral philosophy, music, scientific agriculture, and mechanical arts (Marr, 1959).

## Public Secondary Schools

Although most academies were public in the sense that young men with families able to pay the required tuition could attend, publicly funded high schools for both boys and girls became a more common option during the last quarter of the 19th century. The demand for this option grew in the aftermath of the Civil War with the increasing urbanization and industrialization of American life.

**Legal support.** The growth of public high schools was slow prior to the Civil War. In 1860, there were only 300 nationwide, compared to approximately 6,000 private academies (Binder, 1974). Three legal activities, however, helped speed the implementation of publicly supported options. The first of these was the famous *Kalamazoo case* (Cubberley, 1934). Those opposing a publicly funded high school in Kalamazoo, Michigan, argued that while elementary education should be provided at public expense, a secondary education was a luxury and thus should be funded privately. The Michigan courts, however, disagreed and ruled that school districts could legally tax its citizens for the support of both elementary and secondary schools. The pas-

## Spare the Rod, Spoil the Child

The original European settlers who came to America did so in large measure to avoid religious persecution. They brought with them strong views on parenting and human relations that were based in large part on their Christian beliefs as defined in the Bible. It shouldn't surprise you to learn, then, that early colonial schools were strongly influenced by these religious beliefs. One outcome was the common acceptance of what has come to be known as corporal punishment. Physical punishment, primarily in the form of spanking, was the chief means of discipline in colonial schools. The rationale for this approach comes from Proverbs 13:24, which states: "He who spares his rod hates his son, But he who loves him disciplines him diligently."

Corporal punishment has a long tradition in American schools. While many states and individual districts have banned its use, 22 states currently still allow it to take place in the schools:

In some cases, children are forced to grab their ankles and then are struck three or more times on their backsides with a half-inch-thick board 2 1/2 feet long, according to a *USA Today* review of local spanking rules. Most spanking is done by teachers in classrooms, though some schools require administrators to do the paddling. Spanking usually occurs in elementary and middle schools, but it is legal in high school in some states. (*USA Today*, 2002)

Many national organizations such as the American Academy of Pediatrics, the National Association of Elementary School Principals, the National Education Association, and the National Parent Teacher Association have spoken out against corporal punishment. Despite the concerns of highly respected organizations, many parents, and numerous citizens, corporal punishment remains a viable discipline strategy in many states.

### React and Reflect

1. Were you or someone you knew ever spanked in a school setting? Think back to your reactions. What do you remember about the situation? What does this tell you about the impact of spanking?

2. If you are in a state in which corporal punishment is allowed, can you see yourself using it as a discipline strategy? Why or why not?

3. Do you think that corporal punishment should be allowed or abolished in all classrooms? Give your reasoning for the position you take.

 *To explore this topic further and submit your reactions and reflections online, go to the Explore Your Beliefs module for Chapter 10 of the Companion Website for this text.*

*Source:* "Our View: Many School Districts Wisely Ban Denounced Corporal Punishment," *USA Today*, August 22, 2002. Available at http://www.nospank.net/usa-2.htm

sage of **child labor laws** in the latter part of the 19th century, coupled with compulsory attendance laws passed by individual states during the late 19th and early 20th centuries, also led to increased numbers of public high schools around the country (Butts & Cremin, 1953).

**Public school growth.** Statistics indicate that only a small number of public high schools existed around the country prior to the Civil War. However, conditions in the late 1800s and early 1900s led to a rapid growth in programs. With a change in public attitudes about the value of a high school education and a period of economic growth that provided a larger tax base to support secondary schools, public high schools grew to 2,526 in 1890 as compared to 1,632 private academies (Gutek, 1991). By the end of World War I, most communities and school districts within the United States were providing high school education options to all who wanted them.

## Junior High and Middle School Programs

In the early 1900s, elementary schools tended to be for students in grades 1 through 8 and secondary schools were set up to accommodate students in grades 9 through 12. This format was gradually modified to include junior high programs for students in grades 7, 8, and 9. More recently, middle schools options for grades 6, 7, and 8 have become popular. Junior high schools were first established in Columbus, Ohio, in 1909 and were common after 1930 (Pulliam & Van Patten, 1999). Middle schools, on the other hand, are a more recent development, having become popular since the 1960s.

*Junior high schools became popular in the 1930s.*

**Junior high school.** This schooling option became popular largely due to the recommendations of a national curriculum review committee looking at what should be taught at the secondary level. In 1892, the National Education Association, in an effort to identify the essential components of the secondary curriculum, convened what came to be known as the *Committee of Ten* (Gutek, 1991). Composed of mostly higher education personnel, this committee recommended that schools begin at earlier ages to teach subjects such as science, mathematics, history, and English in greater depth. Rather than focus on the basic skills taught in traditional elementary school programs, the Committee of Ten recommended that schools provide an earlier introduction to more specific academic content. This became part of the rationale for separating grades 7 and 8 from elementary school programs.

With the increased popularity of the junior high school option came a new configuration of public education. Elementary schools were redefined as including grades 1 through 6 (with the gradual addition of kindergarten classes), the junior high school consisted of grades 7 through 9, and high school programs were shortened to 3 years. This 6–3–3 configuration eventually became the most common pattern for public school systems (Gruhn & Douglass, 1971).

**Middle school options.** The junior high school option grew in popularity until the 1960s when it began to compete with new middle school programs designed for students in grades 6 through 8. A major reason given by educators for this new middle school configuration was the attempt to create an educational climate that better matched the developmental needs of young adolescents (Wavering, 1995). At this age, students are struggling to understand the world in which they live and how they will become a productive part of it. They are transitioning from childhood to adulthood and require both freedom to explore and firm guidance from caring adults. While children in early adolescence have outgrown the traditional format of elementary education, they are not yet ready for the compartmentalized academic emphasis of the high school curriculum. Middle school programs are designed to help students grow personally and intellectually as they prepare for the high school experience.

Reflect for a moment on the reasons cited above for the creation of junior high and middle school programs. Which rationale makes the most sense to you at this point? Do middle schools or junior high schools seem to better meet the needs of young adolescents? If you had had a choice, which option do you think would have been better for you at that age? Why do you think both options continue to exist?

**Reflective Journey 10.2**

## How has history shaped current educational issues?

One of the lessons we learn from studying historical figures and events is that positive changes in education often take much longer than initially anticipated. At the same time, however, a historical perspective demonstrates that much progress can be made with patience and perseverance. Rather than having big changes occurring rather quickly, history suggests that it is more likely that you will see small incremental growth over longer periods of time. By looking at current educational issues and seeing the growth that has taken place with each, you can better understand the forces that have shaped these issues and have more realistic expectations for future progress. In this section, you will read about a sampling of current educational issues and their historical roots.

### Equitable Educational Opportunities for Girls

Historically, girls have had far fewer opportunities for schooling than their male counterparts. In colonial America, only a small number of girls received beginning academic instruction in dame schools and through home training. Most had very little opportunity for formal instruction of any kind. Few expectations were placed on girls beyond learning how to be good mothers and wives (Sadker & Sadker, 1994). It wasn't until the beginning of the common school movement in the 1800s that girls had more consistent opportunities to participate in what today would be called elementary education (Cremin, 1970).

Girls experienced similar difficulties at the secondary level. They were typically excluded from the Latin grammar schools available in colonial times and only gradually were able to enroll in the English grammar schools that followed. Girls from poor families, particularly in the South, were the least likely to have secondary education available to them. It wasn't until academies were opened specifically for young women in the early 1800s that slow growth began to take place in the secondary education opportunities for girls:

> By the first half of the nineteenth century, some communities in Massachusetts began to experiment with the radical concept of high school education for girls. A high school for boys had already been established in Boston, and in the late 1820s the public demanded one for girls, too. But city leaders underestimated the interest, and there were far more applicants than spaces available. Three out of four girls were turned away. (Sadker & Sadker, 1994, p. 17)

In the 20th century, as educational opportunities became more readily available for young women, the concern shifted to more equitable experiences. With the passage of the *Nineteenth Amendment* to the U.S. Constitution in 1920, women were given the right to vote for the first time. Although this didn't directly change the educational opportunities available to girls, it began to set the expectation that women should be treated equitably. The Civil Rights Movement of the 1960s and 1970s added further expectations regarding equal opportunities for women in all aspects of life. With the passage of **Title IX** of the Education Amendments Act in 1972, equitable schooling for girls received a major boost. This amendment prohibited discrimination on the basis of sex in any educational program receiving federal assistance for either academics or athletics (Sadker & Sadker, 1994). Table 10.7 shows the progress made since 1972 toward gender equity in high school sports.

### Educating Minorities

For much of early American history, educational opportunities for minority children were virtually nonexistent. Religious organizations concerned about the spiritual well-being of all people developed the earliest programs. Gradually, however, educational options became available and minority children became more integrated into American educational life.

| Year | Boys (thousands) | Girls (thousands) |
|------|------------------|-------------------|
| 1971 | 3,700 | 290 |
| 1978 | 4,500 | 2,000 |
| 1985 | 3,400 | 1,750 |
| 1993 | 3,500 | 2,000 |
| 2000 | 3,900 | 2,800 |

**TABLE 10.7   Gender Equity in High School Sports**

*Source:* From *Title IX at 30: Report Card on Gender Equity,* by National Coalition for Women and Girls in Education, 2002, Washington, DC: Author. Reprinted with permission.

A brief review of the histories of African American and Native American children identifies the general trends experienced by minority groups.

**African American education.** The first schooling opportunities for African American children were established in the northern states in the mid-1700s (West, 1972). These options were segregated, with White students attending separate schools. While the North was providing limited options for African American students, the South actually prohibited by law the establishment of schools for them.

Following the Civil War, the federal government and private philanthropies began promoting schooling options for African American students and increasing numbers of children began attending school. As might be expected, the Southern states were the most reluctant to fund and establish schools for African American students and only gradually developed segregated schools for them. Enrollments slowly increased so that by the end of the 19th century approximately 35% of African American children were enrolled in mostly segregated schools (U.S. Department of Commerce, 1975). The programs provided were poorly funded by both the federal and state governments, making it difficult for these schools to provide the same quality of experiences found in the better funded schools for White students (West, 1972).

The problems of inequitable funding and segregated schools continued into the mid-1950s when the Supreme Court ruled in *Brown v. Board of Education of Topeka* (1955) that separate schools for African American students were unfair and must be eliminated. This decision, often viewed as the start of the Civil Rights Movement, was met with strong legal resistance and considerable violence around the country (Ravitch, 1983). Only gradually have segregated schools been replaced by more equitable educational opportunities for African American students. And today, in 21st-century America, although the inequities have decreased, they have yet to be eliminated. This issue continues as a distressing reminder of the slowness with which deeply rooted attitudes change over time.

If you are a member of the majority culture, it is probably difficult to understand what it truly feels like to be discriminated against because of your skin color. In an effort to better understand the frustrations, try to imagine an educational system in which students who are blue-eyed receive discriminatory treatment. Many of these blue-eyed students have no opportunities at all for schooling. Those who do are all housed together in older, poorly equipped school buildings, with fewer well-qualified teachers and very limited numbers of current books and materials. You are blue-eyed and find yourself experiencing these inequities. How would all this make you feel? Do you think you would be able to excel academically under these circumstances?

 **Reflective Journey 10.3**

**Native American education.** Through early statehood and the westward expansion of America, Native American children received virtually no organized educational experiences. As tribes were gradually placed on reservations by the federal government, the earliest schools were established by missionaries intent on providing education as an essential tool for religious

# The School Days of an Indian Girl

The following are excerpts from the story written by a Native American woman who is reflecting back on her early school experiences. She was one of eight who left their homes and traveled by train to the East to live with and be taught by missionaries in a boarding school:

> The first day in the land of apples was a bitter-cold one; for the snow still covered the ground, and the trees were bare. . . . A paleface woman, with white hair came up after us. We were placed in a line of girls who were marching into the dining room. These were Indian girls, in stiff shoes and closely clinging dresses. The small girls wore sleeved aprons and shingled hair. As I walked noiselessly in my soft moccasins, I felt like sinking to the floor, for my blanket had been stripped from my shoulders. I looked hard at the Indian girls, who seemed not to care that they were even more immodestly dressed than I, in their tightly fitting clothes.
>
> A small bell was tapped, and each of the pupils drew a chair from under the table. Supposing this act meant they were to be seated, I pulled out mine and at once slipped into it from one side. But when I turned my head, I saw that I was the only one seated, and all the rest at our table remained standing. Just as I began to rise, looking shyly around to see how chairs were to be used, a second bell was sounded. All were seated at last, and I had to crawl back into my chair again. I heard a man's voice at one end of the hall, and I looked around to see him. But all the others hung their heads over their plates. As I glanced at the long chain of tables, I caught the eyes of a paleface woman upon me. Immediately I dropped my eyes, wondering why I was so keenly watched by the strange woman. The man ceased his mutterings, and then a third bell was tapped. Every one picked up his knife and fork and began eating. I began crying instead, for by this time I was afraid to venture anything more.
>
> But this eating by formula was not the hardest trial in that first day. Late in the morning, my friend Judewin gave me a terrible warning. Judewin knew a few words of English; and she had overheard the paleface woman talk about cutting our long, heavy hair. Our mothers had taught us that only unskilled warriors who were captured had their hair shingled by the enemy. Among our people, short hair was worn by mourners, and shingled hair by cowards!
>
> A short time after our arrival we three Dakotas were playing in the snowdrifts. We were all still deaf to the English language, excepting Judewin, who always heard such puzzling things. One morning we learned through her ears that we were forbidden to fall lengthwise in the snow, as we had been doing, to see our own impressions. However, before many hours we had forgotten the order, and were having great sport in the snow, when a shrill voice called us . . . Judewin said: "Now the paleface is angry with us. She is going to punish us for falling into the snow. If she looks straight into your eyes and talks loudly, you must wait until she stops. Then, after a tiny pause, say 'No.'" . . . As it happened, Thowin was summoned to judgment first. . . . Just then I heard Thowin's tremulous answer (to the woman's question), "No." . . . With an angry exclamation, the woman gave her a hard spanking. Then she stopped to say something. Judewin said it was this: "Are you going to obey my word the next time?" Thowin answered again with the only word at her command, "No." (Zitkala-Sa, 1900, pp. 186–188)

## Explore and Reflect

Learn more about Native American education by reviewing the online resources provided in the *Reflect on Diversity* module for Chapter 10 of the Companion Website.

1. Have you ever been in circumstances where everyone else knew and was speaking a language you didn't understand? What do you remember of the experience and how did it make you feel?

2. Have you experienced differences between yourself and others that left you confused about how you should act? It might be something as simple as not understanding the order and form of worship in a church different from your own or the appropriate response to an unusual greeting from someone else. How did you feel in these circumstances? Does this give you any insights about what it would be like to be a part of a minority culture?

3. As a teacher, you will encounter many linguistic, cultural, and social differences among the students you teach. What are some small things that you can do to decrease the tension and stress that is associated with these differences?

 *To explore this topic further and submit your responses online, go to the Reflect on Diversity module for Chapter 10 of the Companion Website for this text.*

*Source:* From "The School Days of an Indian Girl," by Zitkala-Sa, 1900, *Atlantic Monthly, 85*(508), pp. 185–194.

conversion (Szasz, 1977). In the late 1800s, the federal government slowly began to provide new options in the form of boarding schools and day schools for Native American children. Under the direction of the Bureau of Indian Affairs (BIA), these schools remained the primary options until the 1970s.

The Civil Rights Movement, led by the African American community, created a climate in which it gradually became possible for Native Americans to reclaim more control over the schooling experiences offered to their children. Limited federal money became available for model tribal school programs that were designed to demonstrate new directions for Native American education. Rather than emphasizing assimilation into the mainstream of American culture as was the aim of the BIA schools, these tribal schools sought to revive a sense of pride in Native American traditions and included study of such traditions as part of the curriculum (American Indian Education Foundation, 2002).

During the last three decades of the 20th century, the federal government slowly transferred responsibility for most of Native American education from the BIA to the public schools. Today, the vast majority of these students are integrated into the K–12 system, with only about 10% remaining in BIA schools (Joyner, 1997). This has reduced the former isolation of Native American students and helped motivate schools to include their unique cultural heritage as part of the curriculum.

## Students with Special Needs

"There have always been exceptional learners, but there have not always been special educational services to address their needs" (Hallahan & Kauffman, 2000, p. 24). Most historians suggest that special education can trace its roots to Europe during the mid-1800s. Primarily through the efforts of Jean-Marc-Gaspard Itard, a French physician, and Edouard Seguin, special education was born (Kanner, 1964). Both men worked with children who were labeled by those around them as "idiots" and were successful in dramatically improving their levels of knowledge.

It wasn't until the mid-1800s that America also began to seriously engage in the process of educating children with special needs. For example, Samuel Howe, a physician by training, was the driving force behind the founding of the Perkins School for the Blind in Watertown, Massachusetts. Similarly, Thomas Gallaudet opened the first school for the deaf in Hartford, Connecticut, in 1817. Other similar programs gradually became available across the country as efforts were made to assist students with special needs (Cubberley, 1934). In all cases, however, these early educational options for children with special needs were separate from those offered to "normal" children and were found in no more than one or two cities in each state.

During the first half of the 20th century, more opportunities for children with special needs were made available in communities across the country. This was followed in the latter half of the century with federal legislation that mandated the integration of regular and special education efforts whenever possible. The passage of the *Education for All Handicapped Children Act* in 1975 was an

*Educating students with special needs has changed significantly during the last 30 years.*

important turning point for this movement (see Chapter 13 for more information on this and other legal mandates). The act guaranteed all students with special needs a free and appropriate public education. Whenever possible, their educational experiences were to occur within the regular education classroom. Gradually, then, students with special needs were included in regular instructional settings and special education became an integral part of America's educational efforts (Hallahan & Kauffman, 2000).

## The Professionalization of Teaching

By today's standards, teachers in colonial America were very poorly prepared for their roles (Cubberley, 1934). In almost every case, teachers received no special training at all. If they had been students themselves, knew the content to be taught, saw themselves as teachers, and were accepted by the local community, they were able to teach. Perhaps the biggest reasons for this lack of preparation were the poor pay and lack of prestige afforded the teaching role. Unfortunately, teachers today still suffer from these same two problems as they continue to professionalize teaching. Stop and reflect on this issue for a moment. Why do you think teachers have tended to be poorly paid in this country? Do you have any thoughts about why teaching has been viewed as a low-status profession?

**Reflective Journey 10.4**

**Teacher preparation institutions.** As was the case with early secondary programs in the United States, the first schools to train teachers were modeled after their European counterparts. The French and German educational systems both had teacher training components that Americans studied and gradually implemented as **normal schools.** The word *normal* has Latin roots and means "model" or "rule." Thus, normal schools were to provide teachers with the "rules for teaching" (Butts & Cremin, 1953). The earliest public normal school in this country was established in 1839 in Lexington, Massachusetts.

Students entered the normal school following the completion of their elementary education and typically spent 2 years taking general knowledge courses similar to those offered in the high schools of the time. A course in pedagogy (teaching) and some practice teaching were also included. It wasn't until the beginning of the 20th century that students were required to complete a high school education before being admitted into a normal school. Expectations gradually increased, partly because high school teachers needed expertise in subject matter areas. The length of teacher training gradually expanded to 3 and then 4 years as the demands for better training continued. With the granting of baccalaureate degrees, normal schools changed their names and began to call themselves **state teachers' colleges.** Most states today have several colleges and universities that can trace their roots to the normal school and state teachers' college programs described here.

**State control of education.** As states gradually increased their financial support for public education, a corresponding effort was made to systematize and unify the training required of teachers and the content of the school curricula. States began developing offices within their governments whose primary responsibility was the education available to students (see Chapter 14 for more information). The offices of state superintendent of education or commissioner of education were created (Butts & Cremin, 1953). Similarly, people from around the state were elected or appointed to state boards of education. These groups were given supervisory responsibilities for education within the state. Following the Civil War, most states had governmental offices and boards to monitor the directions of education. These state offices and boards gradually began to define the requirements for teacher preparation and worked to identify the content that should be taught in elementary and secondary schools. Initially, the powers of these groups were mostly supervisory, but they have gradually come to have primary responsibilities for teacher qualifications and state curriculum guidelines (Lunenburg & Ornstein, 2000).

## Looking Back; Looking Ahead

**Barbara Inforzato**
**Saint Monica School**
**Philadelphia, Pennsylvania**

I have been teaching for 35 years. My career began at age 17 when I was entrusted with a class of 65 third graders in a parochial school—for a salary of $2,000 per year! When I started to teach in 1965, there were so many children and not enough teachers. To accommodate these large numbers of students, special teacher programs were instituted in which we were able to teach and go to college. I attended college classes in the evening, on Saturday, and in the summer. I earned my degree in 5 years from St. Joseph University, Philadelphia, PA. I have taught in first, second, third and sixth grades, but enjoy the primary grades the best: I am presently teaching second grade.

Through the years, many things in education may have changed; some have even gone full circle. We are always adapting to new methods and curriculum, but the basic principle remains that we have the awesome responsibility to form and to lead children to become good thinkers and people of integrity. It certainly has always been a challenge to face a classroom full of young people so eager to learn and so willing to please. Children remain much the same, although their situations may be more complex. Trying to meet the needs of today's children—even with only a class of 24 students—can be more difficult than meeting the needs of a class of 65 some 30 years ago.

I am happy that I have chosen this vocation. Being with children every day adds a dimension to my life that I know I could not have experienced anywhere else. I consider it a privilege to be a part of so many lives.

## Summary

In this chapter, four organizing questions were used to help you understand the value of knowing and studying historical events in education:

### How does history affect my future teaching?

History can have a direct impact on your classroom teaching:

- Forces affecting education
- Learning from the past
- History's impact on current issues

### What is the history of education for young children?

Teaching children from birth through age 12 has a rich historical tradition:

- Early childhood education
- Elementary education (Praxis II, topic Ic)

### What has influenced modern secondary education?

The availability of secondary school education has lagged behind that of elementary education:

- Early options (Praxis II, topic Ic)
- Public secondary schools (Praxis II, topic Ic)
- Junior high and middle school programs (Praxis II, topic Ic)

## How has history shaped current educational issues?

Although taking many decades, progress has been made in many important areas:
- Equitable educational opportunities for girls (Praxis II, topic Ib)
- Educating minorities (Praxis II, topic Ib)
- Students with special needs (Praxis II, topic Ib)
- The professionalization of teaching (Praxis II, topic IVa)

## Key Terms

| | |
|---|---|
| American Academy | kindergarten |
| apprenticeship programs | Latin grammar schools |
| charity school | moving schools |
| child labor laws | normal schools |
| child study movement | play |
| compulsory attendance laws | progressive education |
| cooperative nursery schools | state teachers' colleges |
| Dame schools | Title IX |
| district school | town schools |
| English grammar school | universal education |
| Head Start | |

## Reflective Journey: Online Journal

  Use the questions for thought and reflection highlighted throughout the chapter to help guide your personal journey of reflection and professional development as a teacher. To complete your journal entries online, go to the *Reflective Journey* module for this chapter of the Companion Website.

## PRAXIS  Test Preparation Activities

  To review an online chapter case study, test your understanding of chapter topics and concepts, and begin preparing for the Praxis II: Principles of Learning and Teaching examination, go to the *Praxis Test Preparation* module for this chapter of the Companion Website.

## INTASC  Becoming a Reflective Practitioner

To complete these activities and submit your responses online, go to the *Becoming a Reflective Practitioner* module for this chapter of the Companion Website.

## How does history affect my future teaching?

### Review Questions

1. Give some examples of how teachers can learn from educational history.
2. How do past educational figures and events impact current issues?

### Building Your Portfolio: *Key Historical Figure*

**INTASC Standard 9.** Choose one historical person that had a significant influence on the age/grade you want to teach and spend some time further researching the contributions that this person made to education today. Write a one- or two-page summary of your findings for inclusion in your portfolio.

## What is the history of education for young children?

### Review Questions

1. What are Froebel's contributions to early childhood education?
2. What were cooperative nursery schools?
3. What was elementary education like in colonial America?
4. What role did Horace Mann play in the implementation of common schools?

### Field Experience

Talk to a retired or senior school district administrator or teacher about the addition of kindergarten education to the public school offerings of that district. When did it occur and what did classes look like then as compared to now? Did parents pay part of the costs? Check to see if prekindergarten programs are offered in this same school district. What is available? When did these programs begin and how are they funded?

### Building Your Portfolio: *Living History Interview*

**INTASC Standard 9.** Search for an older American (70+ would be best) and talk to that person about his or her own personal educational history. Did this person participate in preschool or kindergarten education? What were his or her teachers like? What subjects were taught? Did any world events influence this person's education? Write up your findings for inclusion in your portfolio.

## What has influenced modern secondary education?

### Review Questions

1. What were the differences between Latin and English grammar schools?
2. What was the American Academy?
3. Describe the differences between junior high and middle school programs.

### Field Experience

See if you can find an older administrator or teacher who can describe for you the changes that have occurred in middle school/junior high school programs during the last few decades. Were the junior high schools followed by middle schools? What reasons were given for the format of schooling available to students during their early adolescent years?

### Building Your Portfolio: *Legal Foundations for Secondary Education*

**INTASC Standard 9.** Choose one of the three legal activities discussed in this chapter that helped promote public secondary education. Research this issue in greater depth. For your portfolio, describe how this legal action provided momentum for the growing number of public secondary schools in America.

## How has history shaped current educational issues?

### Review Questions

1. What key 20th-century events helped girls receive more equitable educational opportunities?
2. Describe some of the general characteristics of segregated schools for African American students following the Civil War.
3. What role did normal schools play in professionalizing teaching?

**Building Your Portfolio:** *History of Current Issue*

**INTASC Standard 9.** Choose a current educational issue that interests you and study further its historical roots. How did this investigation help you to better understand the current status of the educational issue? Write up your findings.

## Suggested Readings

Braun, S., & Edwards, E. (1972). *History and theory of early childhood education.* Belmont, CA: Wadsworth Publishing. This classic text provides a detailed description of the history of early childhood education.

Cubberley, E. (1934). *Public education in the United States.* Boston: Houghton Mifflin. This is a classic text on the history of American education. Easy to read, and providing its own history, this text gives a strong overview of educational events through the beginning of the 20th century.

Herbst, J. (1996). *The once and future school: Three hundred and fifty years of American secondary education.* New York: Routledge. Herbst provides a comprehensive discussion of the history of American high schools and the social and political forces that shaped them.

Wavering, M. (Ed.). (1995). *Educating young adolescents: Life in the middle.* New York: Garland. This edited book deals with a variety of middle school issues. It also includes a strong chapter on the history and rationale for middle schools.

# chapter 11

## Philosophical Foundations

Although philosophy conjures up images of esoteric discussions with little relevance to real life, developing a philosophy of education is a fairly straightforward task that is important for you to accomplish. In this chapter, you will begin to investigate philosophical foundations of education as you address four organizing questions.

## Focus Questions

◢ What is philosophy and why is it important to me as a future teacher?

◢ What key beliefs are associated with different educational philosophies?

◢ How does your choice of educational philosophy impact what you do in the classroom?

◢ How do I develop an educational philosophy?

As part of the lesson on sensory details, Ms. Hyman takes out a small bag of potato chips and says, "After today no more food, I promise." With slight melodrama, she holds the bag up and demonstrates. "I have an ordinary brand of potato chips." The students laugh enthusiastically, as they appreciate the reference to television commercials. "Let's see if we can describe potato chips using sensory details. . . . Juan, how would you describe by sight this potato chip?" "It is brown, round, yellow, with a brown burn spot on it," responds Juan. "Maria, touch it, feel it . . . what can you tell me about the feel?" Maria reaches for the chip and describes it as "a little hard, rough . . . I can feel the grains of salt." From the back of the room Roberto calls out, "Hey, over here, I'll try the taste." The class erupts in laughter as the teacher responds to Roberto's offer. The class quiets immediately when Ms. Hyman says, "Listen, boys and girls," and in the silence breaks a single potato chip. "Crunch," says one volunteer; "snap," says another as they try to match the correct word to the sound.

Up at the blackboard, the teacher writes three words on the board and demonstrates their meaning by crushing a potato chip in her hand, letting the pieces fall to the floor, and by shaking the bag. Together they identify "crunchy" (to crush noisily), "crumble" (to break into little pieces), and "rustle" (one thing rubbing softly against the other). (Lawrence-Lightfoot, 1983, pp. 80–81)

In the example presented above, Sara Lawrence-Lightfoot (1983) describes a creative high school teacher by the name of Ms. Hyman who is working with a group of 28 Hispanics, 3 Asians, and 1 Russian student to help them increase their sensory word vocabulary. Clearly, Ms. Hyman didn't just grab a bag of potato chips and begin an extemporaneous lesson. She thought carefully about what she wanted to accomplish and why it was important. After determining her purposes for the activity and its value, she engaged in planning that included thinking about interesting visuals, motivating demonstrations, and appropriate questions to stimulate the discussion she wanted from her students. In every instance, Ms. Hyman was using her own philosophy of education to make the choices that led to this very creative and captivating lesson. Hyman's beliefs about teaching and learning (her educational philosophy) led to the engaging teaching activity described above.

Although some people enjoy the intellectual challenges that philosophy presents, many see it as an exercise in deep thinking that, while interesting, has little practical value. **Philosophy,** which can be defined as a seeking after, and love of, wisdom, is in actuality a basic fundamental that is essential for every educator to possess. Robert Heslep (1997), in his book *Philosophical Thinking in Educational Practice,* argues that every teacher must attain a "practical wisdom" as he or she works to prepare the most effective educational experiences for students. Teachers who question and reflect on their selection of goals for teaching and learning and the actions they take in attaining those goals are, in fact, engaging in philosophical thinking and continuing to refine their own philosophy of education.

## What is philosophy and why is it important to me as a future teacher?

In a general sense, each of us has a philosophy of life that consists of a set of beliefs and values that consciously and unconsciously govern our actions. Hopefully, we have thought carefully about why we do most of the things we do, and have a clear rationale for the beliefs and values we hold. In a similar way, those who choose to enter the field of teaching have a responsibility to students and their families to spend considerable time and energy in developing a reasoned set of beliefs and values about teaching and learning. This philosophy of education should be grounded in an understanding of philosophy in general, a more specific knowledge of educational philosophy, and a clear grasp of the importance of engaging in the development of this belief system.

**Reflective Journey 11.1**

As you read this section, reflect on what you expect of other professionals in terms of a belief and value system. Should other professionals such as accountants, sales representatives, lawyers, and doctors have specific values and beliefs that help make them better at what they do? What would you expect, for example, the beliefs and values of a competent lawyer to be? Now apply this same thinking to teaching. Should teachers have a well-defined belief system/ educational philosophy to strengthen what they do in the classroom?

### Philosophy Defined

Although philosophy was briefly defined in the introduction to this chapter, it is important to understand the discipline itself in more depth before looking at its applications to education. As with any field of study, philosophy has its own set of commonly used terms that help people dealing with ideas and problems related to the discipline discuss them with one another. This section identifies some of the terms that help people talk about philosophy.

Philosophy is often conceptualized as consisting of four main branches (Ozman & Craver, 1999), as shown in Table 11.1. Each branch emphasizes a different focus of attention for philosophical thought. The first such branch is generally referred to as **metaphysics.** Philosophers who are engaging in metaphysical analysis are busy trying to determine what is real. It is an attempt to understand the true nature of existence. The philosopher in this realm struggles with tough meta-

| TABLE 11.1 | Branches of Philosophy | |
|---|---|---|
| **Branch** | **Description** | **Key Questions** |
| Metaphysics | An attempt to determine what is real | • What is the meaning of life?<br>• Does life have a purpose?<br>• Are people born good or evil?<br>• Does the universe have a design or purpose? |
| Epistemology | Questions about knowledge and knowing | • What are the limits of knowledge?<br>• Where do we find the sources of knowledge?<br>• How do we acquire knowledge?<br>• Are there ways of determining the validity of knowledge?<br>• What is the truth? |
| Logic | Procedures for arguing that bring people to valid conclusions | • What is the validity of ideas and how can this be determined?<br>• How can we communicate with others without contradicting ourselves?<br>• What do our arguments mean? |
| Axiology | Seeking wisdom about the nature of ethical and aesthetic values | *Ethical:*<br>• What are values and why are they important?<br>• How should we live our lives? What is right and what is wrong?<br>*Aesthetic:*<br>• How do we judge what we see, touch, and hear?<br>• What is beauty? |

physical questions such as these: What is the meaning of life? Does life have a purpose? Are people born good or evil? Does the universe have a design or purpose? Because of the nature of the questions being asked, this branch of philosophy is often considered the most vague and abstract.

Teachers need to be aware of their own metaphysical perspectives so that they can be shared with students as an important part of the teaching/learning process. In addition, the teacher's views on reality help determine the curriculum. For example, Matt Burns, a seventh-grade social studies teacher, believes that a major reality for his students in this ghetto community is the daily encounters with drugs and violence. Because these issues are a fact of life for his students, Matt has invited guest speakers from the community to come in and help students develop effective coping strategies.

A second branch of philosophy is referred to as **epistemology.** This branch is concerned with issues relating to knowledge and knowing. The epistemologist studies the methods, structure, and validity of knowledge. Some key questions asked by those engaged in epistemological study include the following: What are the limits of knowledge? Where do we find the sources of knowledge? How do we acquire knowledge? Are there ways of determining the validity of knowledge? What is the truth?

Clearly, questions of knowledge and knowing are of central importance to teachers. For example, Kendra Hendrickson is a second-grade teacher who has come to the conclusion that it is

## Perspectives on Teaching and Learning

It is hopefully clear to you at this point that just as there are significant differences among students, there are also many fine examples of excellent teaching that come from teachers who have varying opinions about what should be taught and how. The following examples of two very different teachers will give you the opportunity to begin developing your own perspectives on teaching and learning.

Jim Barnes (Fenstermacher & Soltis, 1998) is a well-liked elementary teacher with 12 years of experience in the classroom. Using a more traditional approach, he has been very successful with students and their families.

> He is always firm and in command, but also kind and gentle. Jim believes that his contribution to the education of these youngsters is to give them both a set of basic skills that will be useful to them all their lives and a knowledge of specific subject matter that will allow them to successfully progress through their schooling and eventually become well-informed citizens in a democratic society.
>
> He has experimented with a lot of different curriculum materials, but the ones he likes best and finds to be most effective share a number of common characteristics. They are highly organized and systematic, so the children can follow them easily . . . [T]he children are able to quickly develop useful patterns and strategies for dealing with them. They are progressive; that is, the children need what they learn today to be able to do the work tomorrow. Each new learning builds on the last and leads to the next. Jim also relies on numerous nonthreatening evaluations so he can know exactly how each child is doing, what each needs help with, and when each is ready to move on. He prides himself on being a very efficient and effective teacher. (Fenstermacher & Soltis, 1998, pp. 1–2)

Another successful educator with a different approach to teaching and learning is Ms. Dickerson (Lawrence-Lightfoot, 1983). Among her several classroom assignments, she teaches American literature at the high school level. The students, many of whom have learning disabilities, often have difficulty staying focused on the material being studied. Ms. Dickerson is observed leading a discussion of the book *Death of a Salesman* and, from the comments made, several students appear to be confused by what they have read. The teacher seeks to help the class members clarify their thinking. The central topic being discussed is the decision to commit suicide by the book's central character, Willie Loman. Ms. Dickerson wants the class to share their thoughts with one another, rather than using her as the focal point for discussion. She quietly directs one girl who is struggling to be more assertive to share her thoughts with the rest of the class.

At one point, the conversation becomes unfocused and the teacher enters the discussion and reminds the class that a variety of separate ideas have been discussed and need to be sorted through. She suggests a few minutes of silent reflection so that students can begin to make sense of what they have been discussing. "I have heard at least fifteen explanations for Willie's suicide. . . . See if you can reconstruct it" (Lawrence-Lightfoot, 1983, p. 206). As the class quietly engages in writing down their thoughts, Ms. Dickerson walks around the room to assist individual students who are still struggling. She then gives the class an important clue to assist their thinking, reminding them of a question posed by a student earlier in the discussion and referring to it as a turning point in the class conversation. Students engage in several minutes of individual work before the teacher asks the class to combine the thinking they have been doing on their own. There is an immediate response from the class, with many good reasons given for Willie's suicide.

### React and Reflect

1. Intuitively, which of the two teachers described above comes closest to the kind of teacher you think you would like to be? What is it that you like about this approach to teaching and learning?

2. What characteristics of the two teachers described here mesh with your perceptions of effective teaching? Are there aspects of either teaching style that you don't like?

3. As you go through this chapter, work to identify the philosophies of education represented by each of these teachers so that you can begin to identify the perspective that most closely matches your current beliefs.

 *To explore this topic further and submit your reactions and reflections online, go to the Explore Your Beliefs module for Chapter 11 of the Companion Website for this text.*

*Sources: Approaches to Teaching,* by G. Fenstermacher and J. Soltis, 1998, New York: Teachers College Press; and *The Good High School,* by S. Lightfoot, 1983, New York: Basic Books.

more important to know how to find information than it is to have that knowledge memorized. So, even though she spends considerable time helping students memorize their addition and subtraction facts, she also allows her students to use calculators in class and on tests. Kendra also believes that students develop mathematical knowledge best when they are actively engaged in learning by doing. She has many manipulative materials available in the room that students can use as they develop conceptual understandings of addition and subtraction. Kendra's understanding of knowledge and knowing strongly influence the ways in which she teaches her students.

The third main branch of philosophy is referred to as **logic.** The emphasis of philosophers engaged in this line of thinking is on understanding the rules and techniques of reasoning. It is an ordered way of thinking that attempts to avoid vagueness and contradictions. Typical questions asked by those in this branch of philosophy are as follows: What is the validity of ideas and how can this be determined? How can we communicate with others without contradicting ourselves? What do our arguments mean?

A major goal of education is to help students communicate and think clearly. Teachers can model logical thinking and communicating as they interact with their students. In addition, they can teach logic informally as they share reasoning strategies with students. Two types of reasoning are typically taught in America's schools (see Table 11.2). **Deductive reasoning** proceeds from a generalization to the learning of new specific facts and applications. Conversely, **inductive reasoning** proceeds from specific facts to a more generalized conclusion.

A final branch of philosophy is called **axiology.** This philosophical perspective looks at values. Values can be divided into two main categories. One is called **ethics** and represents an attempt to know the correct way to live our lives, to deal with issues of right and wrong, to understand the differences between good and evil, and to internalize principles of right conduct. A second set of values, called **aesthetics,** deals with issues of beauty. Those taking an axiological perspective work to answer the following types of ethical questions: What are values and why are they important? How should we live our lives? What is right and what is wrong? They also consider issues of aesthetics: How do we judge what we see, touch and hear? What is beauty?

**TABLE 11.2   Types of Reasoning**

| Type of Reasoning | Description | Example |
| --- | --- | --- |
| Deductive → | Reasoning from general to specific → | *Generalization:* All students at this school wear uniforms. <br> ↓ <br><br> *Specifics:* <br> • Uniforms help students feel part of the group. <br> • Uniforms discourage labeling due to economic status. |
| Inductive → | Reasoning from specific to general → | *Specifics:* <br> • Students benefit from clear expectations for their conduct. <br> • School policies help identify uniform procedures for all teachers and staff. <br> ↓ <br><br> *Generalization:* <br> Because of the benefits, the school should develop a handbook that clearly states expectations for students. |

Teachers regularly deal with issues of ethics and aesthetics in the classroom. In addition to understanding their own perspectives on these issues, they are responsible for helping students develop their own ability to engage in ethical behavior. For example, Cassandra Hastings is dealing with ethics in her kindergarten classroom as she helps children understand after a related incident that stealing the personal belongings of others is wrong. Denise Black focuses on aesthetic issues with her high school social studies classes when she engages the class in discussions regarding ethnic beauty and perceived differences in beauty across cultures.

## The Importance of Educational Philosophy

While philosophy in a larger sense attempts to answer the most fundamental questions of human existence, **educational philosophy** looks more specifically at questioning the essentials of good teaching. Because education has always been a central element of every society, fundamental questions about effective teaching and learning have been addressed from the earliest of times. Philosophies of education attempt to clarify issues surrounding four essential elements of education, as shown in Figure 11.1. The first of these is our *perceptions of students*. Educational philosophies work to explain what students are like. Are there differences due to age? What motivates students to learn? Are there identifiable strategies that students use to effectively learn? What differences exist between learners? Secondly, educational philosophies address *beliefs about teaching and learning*. What does it mean to really teach someone? How do you know when teaching has been effective? What does it truly mean to learn? An *understanding of knowledge* is another important issue addressed by philosophies of education. Questions about the nature of knowledge, where it comes from, and how it is acquired are all considered. Finally, educational philosophies are helpful in *determining what is worth knowing*. Because there is so much that could be known about our world, it is important to have some mechanisms for deciding what information has the most value. For example, is it more important to know and be able to describe the parts of a plant or know where to find this information if it is needed?

It should be clear to you at this point that a well-defined perspective on all four of the above elements is needed for good teaching. Take a moment to reflect on these essentials. Can you imagine teaching without first having an understanding of what students are like and how they learn? Is it possible to be an effective teacher if you haven't first determined what is worth knowing and how this information should be taught and learned?

**Reflective Journey 11.2**

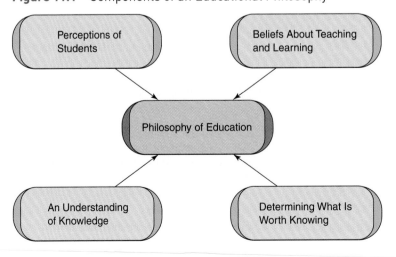

**Figure 11.1**    Components of an Educational Philosophy

Perceptions of Students

Beliefs About Teaching and Learning

Philosophy of Education

An Understanding of Knowledge

Determining What Is Worth Knowing

# What key beliefs are associated with different educational philosophies?

Throughout history, educational philosophers have worked to define what good teaching and learning should look like. Many different perspectives emerged and have been influential with educators at various times. Currently, five distinct philosophies of education are considered of importance to those working in the classroom. Each has its group of devotees and others who disagree with its basic tenets.

## Perennialism

**Perennialism** is an educational philosophy in which the world is seen as unchanging and permanent (see Table 11.3). What was true and right for teachers and students in the past is still the same today. Those who take this perspective feel that education should be geared toward helping students learn about those things that are eternally important. Consequently, classical thought, as expressed through traditional subjects such as history, mathematics, music, science, and art, is the core of the perennialist curriculum. The great works of literature, philosophy, history, science, and the arts are the main texts used for this approach (Kneller, 1971).

An effective perennialist teacher has had a strong education in the liberal arts, a clear understanding of the classical works to be used in the classroom, and the skills needed to engage students in effective dialogue regarding the truths being discussed. Teachers using this educational philosophy see themselves as traditionalists in terms of teaching methodologies. They are "in control" as they share with students the truths to be learned. Students become the receivers of these truths. Metaphors used to describe the perennialist teacher include "director of mental calisthenics" and "intellectual coach" (Webb, Metha, & Jordan, 2000).

Some recent proponents of perennialism include Mortimer Adler (1982), Allan Bloom (1987), and E. D. Hirsch (1996). All three writers have echoed similar concerns in separate books on education. In his book *The Paideia Proposal,* Adler (1982) promotes a curriculum based on the great books that would be appropriate for all students. He emphasizes high-quality course work in mathematics, literature, the sciences, the arts, and social studies. Hirsch (1996) discusses the importance of schools transmitting to students a body of knowledge that must be understood by them if they are to be considered literate Americans. This knowledge, necessary to understand and function as part of our national culture, has been called **cultural literacy.** Bloom's (1987) book *The Closing of the American Mind* suggests that more and more Americans are becoming culturally illiterate and that this is a major crisis of our time. He feels that a return to a more traditional curriculum is needed to reverse this trend.

### TABLE 11.3  Perennialist Perspectives on Education

| Perceptions of Students | Beliefs About Teaching and Learning | Understanding of Knowledge | What Is Worth Knowing |
|---|---|---|---|
| Human nature is constant. All students learn and grow in similar ways. | Teaching is orderly and carefully articulated. Traditional subjects of study emphasized. | Internalize wisdom of the ages. Teacher dispenses knowledge, students absorb. | Eternal truths are learned through studying great books. |

| | | | |
|---|---|---|---|
| **TABLE 11.4**   Progressivist Perspectives on Education | | | |
| **Perceptions of Students** | **Beliefs About Teaching and Learning** | **Understanding of Knowledge** | **What Is Worth Knowing** |
| Learners are active, self-motivated.<br><br>Every student has unique needs and interests. | Teacher serves as facilitator.<br><br>Students learn best from active involvement. | Knowledge is obtained by students as they interact with people and things.<br><br>Students construct knowledge from what they see, hear, and do. | Information and skills are of interest to the student.<br><br>Process of knowing is more important than product. |

## Progressivism

A second educational philosophy that has had a major impact on teaching and learning is called **progressivism** (see Table 11.4). The progressive perspective is quite different from the perennialist philosophy just presented. Drawing primarily on the writings of John Dewey (1929, 1938, 1939), the progressive educator believes that education should be considered a part of life itself, rather than a preparation for life in the future. Learning, from a progressive perspective, should be centered on activities that are of interest to the child and are frequently selected by children themselves. Teachers using this philosophy act more as guides to learning rather than as dispensers of knowledge. Students frequently engage in problem-solving activities that they do in cooperation with their peers.

The progressive teacher feels that the curriculum should be experience centered. Students learn best when they are engaged in conversations with peers or as they manipulate real-world materials that are relevant to their lives. For example, a teacher using the progressive philosophy in a ninth-grade art class would include considerable opportunities for students to talk with each other regarding the art and artists being studied. A trip to an art museum would add other opportunities for real interactions with materials to make the learning meaningful.

As indicated in Chapter 10, the progressive education movement was most influential from the early 1900s to about the mid-1950s. While less prominent today, many educators continue to center their approach to teaching on the progressive philosophy. The student-centered curriculum and the integrated curriculum discussed in Chapter 7 have strong ties to the progressive philosophy. One additional approach to teaching and learning that has been given considerable emphasis in schools is **constructivism.** Grounded in the philosophy of Dewey and the theories of Piaget (1950) and Vygotsky (1978), constructivism is based on the premise that students learn best when they are able to construct their knowledge, often from hands-on interactions with materials or people in their environment.

*John Dewey is a key figure in the progressive education movement.*

# Constructivist Learning

Constructivism takes many forms. During the preschool and primary years, similar approaches to constructivism have been described by Kamii and DeVries (1978), Forman and Hill (1984), and Gandini (1993). In each case, students are engaged in learning with real-world materials that are chosen because they are meaningful to them at the time. For example, preschool children may select blocks from the block center to construct buildings and roads as they informally learn with their peers about the spatial and mathematical concepts that are inherently a part of these playful interactions.

With older students, constructivism is often called *project learning* (Katz & Chard, 2000) or *problem-based learning* (Perkins, 1999), and teachers engage students in long-term projects (generally of the students' own choosing) that integrate learning across disciplines. A high school science teacher who allows a small group of students to choose a topic such as black holes and spend a regular part of class times during the course of a school term to research the scientific and mathematical implications of this special interest and then write a paper on this phenomenon is engaging in project learning.

In constructivism, the small group is the major structural vehicle. The prevailing classical educational approach used so widely, particularly in junior high and high schools (and beyond), of rows of kids, who primarily listen to teachers, is replaced by small groups of students who interact to solve problems, work on projects, or themselves deal with issues. . . . In constructivist classrooms, students' interests and needs become major factors in establishing the program, that is, students participate in establishing the goals; students' interests and needs are factored into the process of teaching and learning; students are given increasing opportunity to make choices. (Shapiro, 2000, pp. 3–4)

Constructivist education leads to increased involvement of students in their own schooling as they help choose topics, plan educational experiences, and engage in learning. While this approach may seem to free teachers up from some of their traditional roles, it also adds new ones. In fact, most teachers find that it requires more preparation and planning on their part than a more traditional approach.

## Research the Issue

Research this topic online using the links provided in the *Engage in the Debate* module for this chapter of the Companion Website.

1. In what ways is constructivist learning being used in pre-K through 12 classrooms?
2. What are the strengths and limitations given in the literature for constructivist learning?

## Explore Your Views

1. Do you think constructivist teaching is more difficult or easier for the teacher to prepare for? What makes you think this?
2. Is constructivist teaching something you will consider using as a future teacher? Why or why not?

 *To research this issue and submit your responses online, go to the Engage in the Debate module for Chapter 11 of the Companion Website for this text.*

Sources: *Physical Knowledge in Preschool Education*, by C. Kamii and R. DeVries, 1978, Upper Saddle River, NJ: Prentice Hall; *Constructive Play: Applying Piaget in the Preschool*, by G. Forman and F. Hill, 1984, Menlo Park, CA: Addison-Wesley; "Fundamentals of the Reggio Emilia Approach to Early Childhood Education," by L. Gandini, 1993, *Young Children*, 49(1), pp. 4–8; *Engaging Children's Minds*, 2nd ed., by L. G. Katz and S. C. Chard, 2000, Westport, CT: Ablex Publishing; and *Leadership for Constructivist Schools*, by A. Shapiro, 2000, Lanham, MD: The Scarecrow Press.

## Essentialism

A third educational philosophy that influences teaching and learning is called **essentialism** (see Table 11.5). Essentialists believe that every educated person must have developed vital under-standings in core areas of the curriculum: reading, writing, mathematics, social studies, the sci-ences, and foreign language training. Although this sounds much like the perennialist perspective described earlier, there are differences between the two philosophies. Essentialists, for example, find themselves less concerned with teaching from the great books of the past. Unlike perennialists, the essentialist philosopher is considered an eclectic in terms of teaching methodologies. The essen-tialist is mainly interested in having an organized, rigorous curriculum that challenges students to do their best and learn as much as possible while in school. Essentialists also are ready to change their core curriculum as needed to keep pace with societal change. For example, the addition of computer literacy to the curriculum would be a sensible option for the essentialist educator.

Essentialism began as an effort to reverse the perceived trend by many of the continued de-cline in the academic standards of America's schools (Webb et al., 2000). People currently hold-ing this perspective believe that schools have gotten too involved in nonacademic services to students and thus lost sight of their primary purpose, which is training of the intellect. Such things as vocational education, career counseling, and psychological services have taken schools away from their true calling and led to a steady devaluation of scholastic performance. Essen-tialists believe that the educational system has geared the curriculum to the average student, leaving the brightest and most capable with fewer options for a quality education. In addition, the essentialist believes that the curriculum in many schools is weakened by the introduction of "life adjustment" courses (Webb et al., 2000). The teaching of lessons about self-esteem to chil-dren at the elementary level and courses in vocational education at the high school level are both examples that the essentialist would point to as proof of this "watering down" of the curriculum.

Although essentialism has deep historical roots going back to the time of Plato and Aristotle, its growth in popularity in the 20th century can be traced to reactions against the progressive edu-cation movement. Admiral Hyman Rickover (1959) was an early spokesperson for this perspec-tive. He wrote:

> Our schools have done a fine job making Americans out of motley groups of foreigners from all
> corners of the globe and doing it in record time. This job is finished. The schools must now
> tackle a different job. They must concentrate on bringing the intellectual powers of each child to
> the highest possible level. Even the average child now needs almost as good an education as the
> average middle- and upper-class child used to get in the college-preparatory schools. The
> talented child needs special schooling to move him rapidly through the period of absorbing

**TABLE 11.5  Essentialist Perspectives on Education**

| Perceptions of Students | Beliefs About Teaching and Learning | Understanding of Knowledge | What Is Worth Knowing |
|---|---|---|---|
| Student motivation frequently comes from teacher. Students need to be disciplined and work hard to learn. | Teacher is responsible for motivating students. Teacher dispenses knowledge of traditional subjects, students absorb. | Knowledge comes from memorizing content and internalizing skills of traditional subjects. Knowledge comes from hard work. | Traditional academic subjects, plus technology, are seen as valuable. Vocational education not encouraged. |

knowledge into the period when his fine mind can turn this knowledge into new ideas, new discoveries, new ways of life. (p. 31)

More recently, the educational reform movements of the 1980s have tended to support the essentialist perspective. For example, the National Commission on Excellence in Education's (1983) report titled *A Nation at Risk: The Imperative for Educational Reform* emphasized the need to move back to a more basic core curriculum that was rigorous and espoused high academic standards for all.

## Existentialism

A fourth philosophy of education that gained popularity in the last half of the 20th century is **existentialism** (see Table 11.6). Rather than viewing human beings as having an essential core or some set of universal characteristics, the essentialist views each person as an individual with the freedom and responsibility for her or his own actions (Wingo, 1974). From the existentialist perspective, if students are to have authentic learning experiences they must be allowed to make choices regarding their goals and the educational curriculum pursued. At the same time, students must learn to make mature decisions and take responsibility for their actions.

Several key principles are associated with the existentialist philosophy of education (Webb et al., 2000). First, students are expected to *take responsibility for their own actions.* They should be given the freedom of choosing much of what they learn and how they learn it, but then be responsible for the results of their actions. Group learning experiences are considered less meaningful by the existentialist philosopher, whereas individualized educational experiences are promoted as the primary vehicle for learning. Another key principle is that *the teacher's role is to demonstrate the value of discipline in pursuing academic goals* rather than trying to force that discipline on students. Unlike the essentialist, existential philosophers believe that discipline must come from within the student and the teacher can merely encourage and model this discipline. Students must voluntarily choose to be disciplined in their studies. Finally, the purpose of education from the existentialist perspective is to *help students discover who they are as individuals* and support their growing awareness of the importance of making responsible choices in life. This process of self-discovery and self-motivation is a lifelong quest in which each person is expected to live each day to its fullest, growing and learning to the best of his or her abilities.

There have been several proponents of the existentialist philosophy of education during the latter part of the 20th century. Perhaps the best known educational program based on existential

**TABLE 11.6    Existentialist Perspectives on Education**

| Perceptions of Students | Beliefs About Teaching and Learning | Understanding of Knowledge | What Is Worth Knowing |
|---|---|---|---|
| Every student is an individual. Students should have freedom to choose, take responsibility for actions. | Teacher's role is to demonstrate importance of discipline in pursuing academic goals. Individualized educational experiences are promoted. | Knowledge is discovering who we are as individuals. Personalized information is needed to make responsible choices in life. | Individually determined learning is based on life experiences and understanding of the world. Knowledge that leads to self-discovery and responsible choice is sought. |

principles is A. S. Neill's Summerhill school. Neill (1960) gave students complete freedom to choose when they participated in school activities while encouraging responsibility for the choices made. Another well-known author with an existential perspective is Carl Rogers, who states in his book *Freedom to Learn* (1969):

> I have come to feel that the only learning which significantly influences behavior is self-discovered, self-appropriated learning. Such self-discovered learning, truth that has been personally appropriated and assimilated in experience, cannot be directly communicated to another. As soon as an individual tries to communicate such experience directly, often with a quite natural enthusiasm, it becomes teaching, and its results are inconsequential. It was some relief recently to discover that Soren Kierkegaard, the Danish philosopher, had found this too, in his own experience, and stated it very clearly a century ago. (p. 153)

A third current proponent of the existentialist perspective in education is Nel Noddings (1992, 1995). She promotes the development of schools in which students are encouraged to make their own choices about educational experiences that are personally meaningful while taking responsibility for the options selected. Noddings also describes an alternative model for education that emphasizes the importance of caring relationships in the classroom.

## Social Reconstructionism

The final philosophy of education discussed here is called **social reconstructionism** (see Table 11.7). Educators with this perspective believe that society must make significant changes in how it operates and that the schools are one of the best agents for implementing the transformations needed (Webb et al., 2000). Feminist concerns, racial equality, and gay/lesbian issues are examples of some of the topics that social reconstructionists feel schools should address in order to change societal attitudes. Schools have a significant role to play in helping society free itself from all forms of discrimination, seeing the world as a global village, and working to reconstruct society for the betterment of all.

Although social reconstructionism can be traced back to early Greek times and the writings of Plato, its more modern version is seen as having its roots in the writings of Karl Marx (Jacobsen, 1999). Marx believed that capitalism and the competition that is inherent in it were wrong and that

### TABLE 11.7    Social Reconstructionist Perspectives on Education

| Perceptions of Students | Beliefs About Teaching and Learning | Understanding of Knowledge | What Is Worth Knowing |
|---|---|---|---|
| Students are the hope for future growth and change in society. Students are capable of changing society if given necessary knowledge and skills. | Teachers lead by modeling democratic actions and exciting students about the needs for social change. Much of true learning occurs outside the classroom as students work to change society. | The information and skills needed to be a part of society while working to implement positive change are important. | Life skills necessary for serving as successful change agents in society are sought. |

# MASTER TEACHER SERIES

## Segment V: The Master Teacher and Her Classroom Full of Trouble

Politicians are firmly fixed on the importance of a first-class education. "It's all well and good for the politicians to rail about poor schools and raising standards. It's encouraging, even uplifting to believe in the sincerity of Governor Bush's memorable phrase denouncing 'the soft bigotry of low expectations,' but reality does not easily give way to elegant phrases alone" (Ted Koppel, ABC News—*Master Teachers Series*, 8/22/00). Ms. Jones, however, shows us what's happening in the classrooms with glimpses into the lives of today's students. Some pass. Some fail. What is the solution?

### For Deeper Understanding

1. Both the teacher and the students tried hard on a daunting journey to pass the state tests. What hurdles did the students have to overcome? What have they done to increase their opportunities to pass the test?

2. Ms. Jones tires of the negativity in the classroom and wants to start to live, dream, eat, sleep and demonstrate love so that things will change. With which educational philosophy does this ideal most align? How?

3. Students have to make it in the 21st century. Will high-stakes tests assure that they will? Why or why not?

4. How does the stress of high-stakes testing affect students? What are alternatives to the high-stakes testing of students (preK–12 students, preservice teachers, and teachers) to show competence?

5. Several students failed the test. Would you say it was the test, the students, or Ms. Jones? Why?

 *To submit your responses online, go to the Master Teacher Series module for Chapter 11 of the Companion Website.*

---

a social revolution was called for in which the working class should rise up and overthrow the ruling class to create a more equitable society. Gradually, the ideas of Marx were blended with those of people such as Kant, Hegel, and Freud to create a philosophy that has focused on social justice issues and the importance of schooling in fundamentally changing attitudes about these matters.

The social reconstructionist teacher places a high value on democracy and sees the classroom as an important place to model democratic ideals. Students explore their own histories and cultures as they work to become more sensitive to, and accepting of, the histories and cultures of others. Reconstructionists emphasize the importance of human relationships and understanding how to make them work. A problem-solving approach to issues is the preferred mode of addressing concerns in the social reconstructionist classroom (Webb et al., 2000).

Two well-known advocates of social reconstructionism are Ivan Illich and Paulo Freire. In Illich's (1972) book titled *Deschooling Society*, he states that schools are failing in their efforts to help children from poor families break out of the cycle of poverty and lead productive lives. Illich believes that since most true learning actually takes place casually outside of the formal classroom, schools should be "disestablished" or done away with and in their place more appropriate societal structures should be created to assist all students in becoming creative, thoughtful adults. Paulo Freire lived and taught in Latin America and had firsthand experience teaching and working with illiterate peasants. Like Illich, he was primarily concerned with the problems schools created in dealing with the poor (Freire,

1970). Rather than helping them in their efforts to move out of poverty, Freire saw schools as creating mechanisms for keeping the oppressed in their place and the ruling classes in theirs.

Stop for a moment and reflect on which of these five educational philosophies makes the most sense to you at this point in your teacher preparation program. Is there one approach that is particularly appealing to you? Do you find yourself agreeing with some aspects of several philosophies while disagreeing with others? What else will you need to know before you can begin determining your own educational philosophy? Remember that this is just a starting point for the development of an educational philosophy, but begin "trying them on for size" so that you can get going now with this important process.

Reflective Journey 11.3

## How does your choice of educational philosophy impact what you do in the classroom?

In this section, we take a more detailed look at three fundamental components of good teaching and read about how each of the educational philosophies discussed earlier would address them. By describing each philosophy's perspectives on the content of the curriculum, methods of instruction, and classroom management and discipline, you should develop a better understanding of each one and continue to refine your own beliefs about teaching and learning.

### Content of the Curriculum

As discussed in Chapter 7, the curriculum taught in American schools is largely determined by local, state, and national guidelines. Yet, every teacher has the opportunity to take the basic curriculum as defined by others and present it to students in a way that reflects his or her personal views of what is valuable to know. Each of the five educational philosophies provides different perspectives on how this part of the curriculum should unfold (see Table 11.8).

**Perennialist view of curriculum.**  The driving force in the perennialist curriculum is the training of the mind in traditional subject matter areas. Every student is expected to complete a core curriculum in social studies, mathematics, the sciences, music, and art. These subjects allow students to develop the intellectual skills needed for success in later life (Adler, 1982). The great books from the past serve as the main vehicle for delivering this classic curriculum. A perennialist high school English teacher, for example, would teach from such literary giants as Shakespeare, Chaucer, and

**TABLE 11.8    Philosophical Perspectives on Curriculum Content**

| Perennialism | Progressivism | Essentialism | Existentialism | Social Reconstructionism |
|---|---|---|---|---|
| Train the mind in traditional subjects. Core curriculum consists of social studies, mathematics, the sciences, music, and art. | Individual topics are learned through meaningful experiences. Integrated curriculum includes topics of interest to students. | Rigorous common core of traditional courses is taught. Computer literacy is also considered important. | Individual curriculum is designed to help students understand selves and life's meanings. | Understanding of social justice and equity issues are important. Strategies are needed to implement social change. |

Thoreau to help develop mental abilities in students. In addition to these core subjects, the perennialist educator also believes that character education and issues related to moral development should be included in the curriculum (Webb et al., 2000). The fundamental truths that can be learned from the past also include key values such as honesty, caring about others, and freedom.

**Progressivism's perspectives on curriculum.** Unlike the perennialists, whose curriculum is well defined, the progressivist philosophy would suggest a curriculum that is considerably more individualized. Rather than emphasizing a set of universal truths to be learned through carefully crafted core subjects, the progressive teacher emphasizes the importance of learning through experiences that are meaningful to the individual. These teachers also integrate academic subjects into these experiences, rather than separately studying subjects such as mathematics, reading, and social studies. So, for example, Matt and Christie are two fifth-grade students who are interested in the upcoming local elections. They have been given some time each day during the last 2 weeks to work on a report to their peers on the preparations for, and results of, the elections. They are incorporating reading, writing, mathematics, and social studies into this short-term project.

**Curriculum from an essentialist perspective.** The essentialist teacher, like the perennialists, believes that the curriculum should focus on a rigorous common core of subjects that all students should complete. Rather than relying solely on the great books from the past, however, the essentialist believes that a variety of materials can be used to teach students this core. The inclusion of more modern curriculum content, such as computer literacy, is also considered valuable to the essentialist. In addition, more recent proponents of essentialism feel that moral/character education is an important part of the core curriculum, and support its inclusion (Bennett, 1993).

Essentialists are primarily concerned with academic rigor. They want the curriculum to be challenging to all students so that they can develop the mental skills needed for success in later life. By holding to high academic standards, the essentialist believes that students can rise to the challenges encountered. Because of these beliefs, these teachers feel comfortable in testing students to make sure they are measuring up to the high standards set by the schools for passage through the system (Webb et al., 2000).

**Existentialist curriculum.** Existential educators believe that learning is personal and different for each student. Even more so than the progressives, these teachers develop a highly individualized curriculum whose purpose is to help students become more aware of themselves and the meanings surrounding their lives. Existentialists engage their students in dialogues that help them gain insights into the fundamental questions we all face: What is the meaning of life? Is it possible to love and be loved? How should an understanding of death influence the way I live? These questions and others are obviously subjective and are designed to help students come to an understanding that is personally meaningful (Greene, 1988). The results of learning from this curriculum cannot be measured by standardized tests, which would be discouraged by the existentialist.

Literature, biographies, art, music, and film tend to be favored options for discussing the existentialist perspective. A middle school social studies teacher wanting to discuss humankind's struggle between good and evil might consider showing the movie *Schindler's List*. In this film, a German industrialist grapples with his own materialism and the moral dilemma of knowing that most of his Jewish workers will end up facing the Nazi gas chambers. He finally works to save as many workers as he can from this terrible fate. By showing and then discussing this film, students can develop new insights into the human condition.

**Social reconstructionist's perspective on curriculum.** The focus of the social reconstructionist curriculum is on understanding the democratic ideals of social justice and equity and helping students develop strategies for implementing social change. Topics of concern to the social reconstructionist, such as poverty, discrimination due to race, sexual preference, or religious affiliation, and world peace, would be addressed at every opportunity in the classroom. For example,

**TABLE 11.9    Philosophical Perspectives on Instructional Methods**

| Perennialism | Progressivism | Essentialism | Existentialism | Social Reconstructionism |
|---|---|---|---|---|
| Direct instruction, Socratic method used. Traditional methods of instruction are used. | Constructive and cooperative learning is preferred. | Traditional methods such as direct instruction and Socratic method are used. Other methods are used when they can be effective. | Methods model decision making and choosing between alternatives such as story telling and discussions of existential questions. | Methods vary, with their intent being to guide students to an understanding of social issues and constructive methods of dealing with them. |

an elementary teacher with this perspective could spend time helping students become aware of the problems associated with poverty and get students involved in a project to collect food and clothing to give to local charities involved in assisting low-income families.

### Methods of Instruction

A second component of teaching strongly influenced by your choice of educational philosophy is the instructional methods you will use in the classroom. Decisions, for example, about whether to use small- or large-group instructional strategies, direct instruction, cooperative learning, or project learning are all made based on your choice of philosophy. Each of the five perspectives suggests somewhat different techniques to be used in helping students learn (see Table 11.9).

**Perennialist perspectives on methods of instruction.** The perennialist teacher tends toward more traditional methods of instruction. Direct instruction, in which the teacher shares information in an organized and motivating manner with groups of students, is often the preferred instructional strategy (see Chapter 7 for more information). The Socratic method, in which the teacher uses a series of questions to lead students to an understanding of the chosen topic, is also promoted by perennialists (Adler, 1982).

**Progressive methods of instruction.** Because the progressivist teacher promotes a more personalized curriculum in which students are actively engaged in their learning, constructivist and cooperative learning (see Chapter 8) are preferred methods of instruction. In constructivist education, the teacher helps students select activities or projects in which they learn from real-world interactions with materials and people that are meaningful to them. Cooperative learning engages students in interactions with others in small groups. The learning that takes place through either option is personally meaningful to students and is seen by the progressive educator as the foundation for lifelong learning.

*Your educational philosophy will directly influence your instructional strategies.*

**Essentialist perspectives on teaching methods.** Much like the perennialists, the essentialist educator tends to emphasize traditional methods of instruction such as direct instruction and the Socratic method. Other techniques are used when they can be justified within an ordered and carefully sequenced curriculum. Students need to be made aware of the purposes and organization of the curriculum through detailed course syllabi and clearly articulated lesson plans. According to the essentialist, this high level of organization in instruction helps make it clear to students what needs to be learned and makes the actual learning experience more effective.

**Existentialist methods of instruction.** The existentialist's desire to help students decide the major issues of life leads the existentialist to choose methods of instruction that model decision making and choosing between alternatives. Nel Noddings (1993) states it this way:

> In the discussion of religious, metaphysical, and existential questions, teachers and students are both seekers. Teachers tell stories, guide the logic of discussion, point to further readings, model both critical thinking and kindness, and show by their openness what it means to seek intelligent belief or unbelief. (p. 135)

An existentialist middle school science teacher, for example, in a series of discussions on the human life cycle, might address the topic of euthanasia by telling a story about a dying man kept alive solely through the use of medical machines. After seeking feedback from the class on the family's rights to end life and discussing the options with students, the teacher could then provide time for students to individually reflect on their feelings about euthanasia before discussing the issue again as a large group.

**Social reconstructionist views on methods.** The social reconstructionist teacher wants to make students aware of the key social issues facing America and the world. The method of sharing may vary, but the passionate need to change how things operate would not. The social reconstructionist would first want to convince students through facts, logic, and emotion that these issues cannot be overlooked and that every individual has a role to play in creating a better world for us all. Having convinced students of the rightness of these causes, the social reconstructionist teacher would then work to get students involved in real-world activities that lead to change. For example, a fifth-grade elementary teacher might choose to convince students that cutting down trees and vegetation creates an imbalance in our ecological system that could eventually lead to a poorer quality of life for us all. Once students are convinced of the problems associated with deforestation, the class can spend some time planting and caring for new trees in a field near the school as a tangible way of improving the situation.

## Classroom Management and Discipline

A third component of successful teaching that is strongly influenced by your choice of educational philosophy is classroom management and discipline (see Table 11.10). This collection of strategies, used to create an environment that is conducive to effective learning, is based on your understanding of what students are like and what they need to be successful in learning. In turn, your views of students determine the educational philosophy you choose.

**Perennialist classroom management and discipline.** The traditional views of the perennialist educator extend to the management and discipline areas as well. These teachers see themselves as in control and expect students to respect them as educational leaders in the classroom. In addition to training the mind through the great works from the past, the perennialist believes that the teacher's role is to mold the spirit of each student. Students are expected to work hard, obey classroom rules, and respect the authority of adults. It is the responsibility of the teacher to make sure that an orderly and calm environment is available to all who enter the classroom.

## Religious Diversity and Schooling

It may surprise you to know that despite the fact that approximately 80% of Americans claim Christianity as their religious affiliation (Weiss, 2001), there is a small but growing population of other religious groups throughout the country. In the state of Michigan, for example, Baha'i, Buddist, Hindu, Islamic, Jewish, and Sikh religious centers can be found among their Christian neighbors (The Pluralism Project, 2003). In addition, Detroit, Michigan, is the site for the oldest Islamic religious center in the United States, which currently serves approximately 10,000 members (The Pluralism Project, 2003).

Diana Eck (2002) suggests that this change in the American landscape came about primarily as a result of the passage of the 1965 Immigration and Nationalities Act, which eliminated many of the earlier discriminatory practices toward those with non-Christian beliefs. She goes on to state that this religious diversity is now so extensive that everyone is impacted by it: "The map of the world in which we live cannot be color coded as to its Christian, Muslim, Hindu identity, but each part of the world is marbled with the colors and textures of the whole. People of different religious traditions live together all over the world—as majorities in one place, as minorities in another" (Eck, 2002, p. 1).

American schools are recognizing this religious diversity and struggling to find ways of helping students understand and respond positively to these changes. In some instances, these religious diversity lessons are being called into question. "Earlier this year, a number of communities in California were in an uproar about 'role-playing' Islamic practices in the classroom" (Haynes, 2002, p. 1). In another instance, a middle school in Michigan was criticized for holding a "mini powwow" in the gym which included prayers, songs, and Native American dances (Haynes, 2002).

### Explore and Reflect

Learn more about religious diversity and the schools by reading the online source articles by Weiss (2001), the Pluralism Project (2003), Eck (2002), and Haynes (2002) and reviewing other online resources provided in the *Reflect on Diversity* module for Chapter 11 of the Companion Website.

1. Choose a community of interest to you and find out what you can about the religious diversity to be found there. What religious groups are represented in the community?

2. Is it important for the schools to be more involved in helping students understand and respond favorably to the religious diversity found in most communities? Make a case for the position you take.

3. Describe some strategies that you could use to deal with religious diversity in your future classroom.

 *To explore this topic further and submit your reflections online, go to the Reflect on Diversity module for Chapter 11 of the Companion Website for this text.*

*Sources:* "Mostly Christian and Most Diverse," by J. Weiss, *The Dallas Morning News*, June 2, 2001. Retrieved April 10, 2003, from http://www.racematters.org/religiousdiversitydeck.htm; "The Pluralism Project," by Harvard University, 2003. Retrieved April 11, 2003, from http://www.fas.harvard.edu/~pluralism; "A New Religious America: Managing Religious Diversity in a Democracy," by D. Eck, 2002. Retrieved April 11, 2003, from http://www.usembassymalaysia.org.my/eck.html; "Religious-Diversity Lessons Can Go Too Far," by C. Haynes, *The Morning Sun*, July 21, 2002. Retrieved April 10, 2003, from http://www.morningsun.net/stories/072102/opE_0721020024.shtml

**Progressive views on management and discipline.** The progressive stance on classroom management and discipline is rooted in the belief that students should actively participate in all aspects of classroom life. Students, for example, would be expected to work with the teacher to develop classroom rules and the consequences associated with breaking the rules. Management and discipline problems that had an impact on the entire class would be discussed and resolved with the whole class participating. The teacher would then work to guide individual students who are engaging in inappropriate behaviors in more positive directions. William Glasser's (1969) problem-solving approach (discussed in Chapter 8) is one example of a discipline style that engages students as participants in the management and discipline process.

| | TABLE 11.10 | Philosophical Perspectives on Management and Discipline | | |
|---|---|---|---|---|
| **Perennialism** | **Progressivism** | **Essentialism** | **Existentialism** | **Social Reconstructionism** |
| Traditional methods that emphasize control and student respect for the teacher as educational leader are used. | Students actively participate in planning for and implementing classroom management and discipline. | Students are expected to follow the rules, work hard, and allow others to engage in learning. Character training is also emphasized. | Open approach to management and discipline in which students are given equal responsibility with teacher for dealing with problems and conflict. | Stresses importance of community building. Students need skills for effective group action. |

**Essentialist management and discipline.**  Traditional methods of management and discipline are considered the most valuable strategies to the essentialist. Students are expected to understand and follow the rules as defined by the teacher, work hard to master the content being presented, and allow others to engage in quality learning experiences. Firm management and control are seen as important to the essentialist teacher. In addition, modern essentialists feel strongly about character education and take time as part of their management and discipline efforts to help students understand the reasons for engaging in appropriate classroom behaviors. The academic literacy required of all students is thus supplemented with moral literacy (Bennett, 1993).

**Existentialist views on management and discipline.**  Of all the philosophical perspectives presented here, existentialism has the most "open" approach to management and discipline. Because considerable responsibility is placed on students for their own learning, freedom of choice and a more student-centered approach are used. Existentialists generally view students as partners in the decision-making processes surrounding management and discipline. Educators using this philosophy would work to understand students' perspectives on areas of conflict within the classroom and interact with them more as equals in determining solutions to the problems encountered. The teacher effectiveness training program of Thomas Gordon (1974) discussed in Chapter 8 is an example of management and discipline that most closely matches this philosophy.

**Social reconstructionist perspectives.**  The social reconstructionist emphasis on working together to positively influence society's directions on major social issues leads these educators to emphasize the importance of community building. Because everyone needs to understand the problems facing society and work cooperatively to make the necessary changes, it is important for students and teachers to develop a sense of togetherness that leads to effective group action. Considerable time is spent in these classrooms on getting to know one another and understanding the similarities and differences that exist among racial and ethnic groups, males and females, religious affiliations, and people of different sexual orientations. Both planned and naturally occurring team building activities are used to create a stronger community of learners and social change agents.

Now that you have read through the information in this section, think about the choices you would currently make regarding what is relevant content, methodology, and management and

discipline for a classroom of your choice. How did you come to believe what you now do about content, methodology, and management and discipline? Who or what influenced you in these beliefs? What would you need to know or do before you could change what you hold to be true?

## How do I develop an educational philosophy?

As you begin to develop an educational philosophy that will guide your future teaching, an initial step you can take is to decide whether you want to be an "eclectic" philosopher, choosing bits and pieces from several educational philosophies to create your own unique perspectives, or a "purist" who finds one of the defined philosophies clearly representing your beliefs about students, teaching, and learning. In addition, there are several steps you can take now to begin developing your philosophy of education.

### Eclectic or Purist

Many teachers develop their own eclectic educational philosophy. Their reasoning for this approach stems from a deeply held belief that both teachers and students are unique individuals. Because of their uniqueness, no one philosophy can adequately describe the specific teaching and learning strategies needed for all. It makes more sense to the eclectic to create a philosophy of education that takes into consideration the uniqueness of the teacher and the continually changing array of students that enter the classroom each year. There is a danger, however, in using this line of thinking. Without careful thought, it becomes easy for teachers to be less concerned about creating a consistent rationale for what they believe and do in the classroom. Eclecticism becomes an excuse for not taking the time and effort it requires to conceptualize a framework for teaching and learning that makes sense and can be articulated to others.

Just as there are many teachers who develop an eclectic educational philosophy, there are large numbers of educators who find one existing philosophy that meshes well with their own way of thinking. After careful study, they adopt it as their own. The major advantage of this approach is that it provides a consistent and logical perspective that has been developed after care-

*Your educational philosophy may include attending students' sporting events.*

ful analysis by educational leaders both past and present. Each of the five educational philosophies presented in this chapter was developed and refined over many years by bright, articulate writers who have worked to create a systematic, reasoned approach to the education of students of all ages. Teachers who choose one of these five philosophies have ready access to written information that will assist them in understanding the philosophical position and its implications for teaching.

## Creating Your Own Educational Philosophy

There are several steps you can take now and in the coming years to develop and refine your own philosophy of education. The first is to *learn more about students and teaching.* The more you know, the better able you will be to make good decisions about a philosophy of education. Secondly, you should *study educational philosophy.* Either in course work during your initial teacher preparation program or later, you should take additional opportunities to study educational philosophy in more depth. Use these experiences to add to your existing knowledge of philosophy as you continue to define what seems right to you. A third step you should take is to *discuss educational philosophy with others.* Don't let the term *educational philosophy* scare you. Remember that it is simply "practical wisdom" (Heslep, 1997) about the teaching and learning process. You should take the time to talk to other teachers and future teachers so that you can refine your own thinking about philosophical issues. Finally, take the time you need to *reflect on your own teaching practices.* One of the best ways to refine your thinking is to thoughtfully consider your own teaching practices to determine what is working and what needs to change. As you make decisions about these real-world experiences, your educational philosophy is also being refined.

Stop for a moment and reflect once again on the five educational philosophies presented in this chapter. At this point do you see yourself as a "purist" or an "eclectic"? Does one of the philosophies seem to fit your way of thinking so well that you could see yourself selecting it to represent your views on students, teaching, and learning? Or do you think you will choose parts of several philosophies to use in your work with students?

Reflective
Journey 11.5

## views from the classroom

## Sharing the Love of Learning

**Jordan Adair**
**Durham Academy–High School**
**Durham, North Carolina**

Upon walking into my classroom you will see a multitude of images that reflect my eclectic interests and send a signal to my students—here's a person who loves learning, loves exploring new ideas, loves to share with others the infinite variety of life. From posters of John Coltrane, Robert Johnson, and Albert Einstein to reproductions of Edward Hopper and Georgia O'Keefe paintings and Frank Lloyd Wright houses, I surround myself with the images that fascinate me and will hopefully stimulate my students. If I can bring enthusiasm and an intellectual rigor to my classes, if I can convince my students that learning is both challenging and rewarding, and if I can make them better writers and better thinkers by the time they've left my classroom, then I have succeeded in doing my job. To do this, I have to be an active

learner every day of my life. So I read, write, explore, watch films, listen to music, and pay attention to what is going on in the world around me. I want my students to cultivate these same habits in their lives. In the end, I have to convince my students of the validity of what I am trying to do. I treat them as the young adults they are. I don't patronize them; instead, I listen to and respect them. I value what they have to say and genuinely care about the lives they live. I share some of the stories from my life as well, stories of my own adolescence and adulthood, with the intention of humanizing myself. High school students are going through many drastic and transcendent changes year in and year out, and to share in that transformation has to be one of the most gratifying experiences I could ask for.

## Summary

Four organizing questions were used in this chapter to help you develop better understandings of educational philosophies and their importance:

### What is philosophy and why is it important to me as a future teacher?

Philosophy is often seen as consisting of four main branches:
- Metaphysics—determining what is real
- Epistemology—issues related to knowledge and knowing (Praxis II, topic Ia)
- Logic—the rules and techniques of reasoning
- Axiology—issues related to ethics and aesthetics

### What key beliefs are associated with different educational philosophies?

Five educational philosophies were discussed:
- Perennialism (Praxis II, topic IVa)
- Progressivism (Praxis II, topic IVa)
- Essentialism (Praxis II, topic IVa)
- Existentialism (Praxis II, topic IVa)
- Social reconstructionism (Praxis II, topics IVa, IIIb)

### How does your choice of educational philosophy impact what you do in the classroom?

Educational philosophy influences three major elements of classroom life:
- Content of the curriculum (Praxis II, topic IIb)
- Methods of instruction (Praxis II, topics IIb, IIIc)
- Classroom management and discipline (Praxis II, topic IIa)

### How do I develop an educational philosophy?

You can begin to take steps now to develop an educational philosophy by:
- Deciding to choose either an eclectic or a specific educational philosophy
- Taking steps to create your own educational philosophy (Praxis II, topic IVa)

## Key Terms

aesthetics

axiology

constructivism

cultural literacy

deductive reasoning

educational philosophy

epistemology

essentialism

ethics

existentialism

inductive reasoning

logic

metaphysics

perennialism

philosophy

progressivism

social reconstructionism

## Reflective Journey: Online Journal

Use the questions for thought and reflection highlighted throughout the chapter to help guide your personal journey of reflection and professional development as a teacher. To complete your journal entries online, go to the *Reflective Journey* module for this chapter of the Companion Website.

# PRAXIS Test Preparation Activities

To review an online chapter case study, test your understanding of chapter topics and concepts, and begin preparing for the Praxis II: Principles of Learning and Teaching examination, go to the *Praxis Test Preparation* module for this chapter of the Companion Website.

# inTASC Becoming a Reflective Practitioner

To complete these activities and submit your responses online, go to the *Becoming a Reflective Practitioner* module for this chapter of the Companion Website.

## What is philosophy and why is it important to me as a future teacher?

### Review Questions

1. What are the four branches of philosophical thought?
2. Why is epistemology an important branch of philosophy for educators?
3. Which branch of philosophy deals with ethics and aesthetics?
4. What four essential elements of education are addressed by educational philosophies?

### Building Your Portfolio: *Content of the Curriculum*

**INTASC Standard 7.** Although your thoughts will probably change over time, what do you *currently believe* should be the content of the curriculum for the grade or subject of your choice? Describe in a few paragraphs what you think is important for students to know and be able to do.

## What key beliefs are associated with different educational philosophies?

### Review Questions

1. Why do perennialists feel that studying the classics is important?
2. Which educational philosophy is associated with constructivism?
3. Identify one key principle associated with the existentialist philosophy of education.

### Field Experience

Observe a teacher in a classroom of your choice. Note what is done and said. See if you can determine the educational philosophy that this teacher is using as the basis for his or her actions. What did you see or hear that helped you make a decision about the philosophy being used?

### Building Your Portfolio: *Educational Philosophy Critique*

**INTASC Standard 4.** Choose one of the educational philosophies in this chapter that is appealing to you at this point and spend more time reading about it. Once you have developed a deeper understanding of this perspective, summarize what you see to be the strengths and limitations of this philosophy of education. Include this critique in your portfolio.

## How does your choice of educational philosophy impact what you do in the classroom?

### Review Questions

1. What is the perennialist view of curriculum?
2. Which methods of instruction would be associated with the social reconstructionist philosophy of education?
3. What are the existentialist views on management and discipline?

### Field Experience

Talk to a teacher about the perceived importance of developing your own educational philosophy. Is it seen as important or unimportant by this teacher? Does this teacher have a personal philosophy that can be shared? How does this person's philosophy impact his or her teaching?

### Building Your Portfolio: *Classroom Management and Discipline*

**INTASC Standard 5.** Describe in a few paragraphs what you *currently believe* will be the classroom management and discipline strategies you will use in your future teaching. Rather than getting too specific, work on identifying general methods that seem to make sense to you. Refer to Chapter 8 for more information on specific options. Which of the educational philosophies in this chapter most closely aligns with your views?

## How do I develop an educational philosophy?

### Review Questions

1. What is an eclectic educational philosophy?
2. How can you begin to develop your own educational philosophy?

### Building Your Portfolio: *Philosophy of Education*

**INTASC Standard 9.** Review your responses to the earlier portfolio activities for this chapter. Use this information to begin identifying a framework for your philosophy of education. If your *current beliefs* match one of the educational philosophies presented in this chapter, describe in your own words what that philosophy means to you. If you are more eclectic in your current thinking, describe the components of your personal philosophy of education.

## Suggested Readings

Kneller, G. (1971). *Introduction to the philosophy of education.* New York: John Wiley & Sons. This classic text provides a clear description of the educational philosophies described in this chapter.

Noddings, N. (1995). *Philosophy of education.* Boulder, CO: Westview Press. The author presents a strong overview of several philosophies, with a particularly good overview of existentialism.

Ozman, H., & Craver, S. (1999). *Philosophical foundations of education* (6th ed.). Upper Saddle River, NJ: Merrill/Prentice Hall. This book is a good resource for philosophies not addressed in this textbook, giving detailed descriptions of them.

# chapter 12

## Societal Influences

Students' attitudes, values, and beliefs are shaped in many ways by the society in which they live. In addition, society determines the purposes and directions for institutions such as the public schools. In this chapter, several key questions will help you better understand these influences.

## Focus Questions

◢ What are the key socializing agents influencing students?

◢ Are there social issues that affect student behavior?

◢ How should teachers and schools respond to social issues?

◢ How does society influence schooling?

*Amber, a shy student in your eighth-grade social studies class, has you concerned. Although her classroom comments and writing assignments indicate that she is a very capable student, Amber often disengages herself from classroom activities and stares blankly out the window. You learned from a brief conversation with her seventh-grade language arts teacher that her dad left the family last year to be with another woman and Amber's mom is struggling financially and emotionally to deal with this loss. Having seen Amber's permanent folder, you are aware that she is very bright and has done excellent work in the past. Part of your concern, however, stems from Amber's growing involvement with a group of students who are known to be experimenting with drugs. There have been several times lately when you noticed her talking animatedly with this group before class. You would really like to be able to build a better relationship with Amber and help get her back on track educationally. But you are unsure about where to begin or what to do.*

You are planning to enter a profession filled with complex human interactions with people like Amber. Every day you will be challenged to make decisions about each student you teach based on an understanding of that person's background, experiences, and personality. The more you know about what influences human behavior and how that applies to individuals within your classroom, the better able you will be to respond thoughtfully to students' needs.

In addition to influencing individuals' lives, society imparts purpose and value to its institutions. You need to know what those purposes are for American educational institutions and why they are valued by society. This understanding then forms a framework on which all of your teaching experiences are built. For example, one of the purposes for education is the preparation of students for participation in the workforce. Our society needs competent new workers to replace those who retire. Knowing about this purpose and its value helps you as a future teacher to plan learning experiences that can support this objective.

## What are the key socializing agents influencing students?

As a nation, the United States is a diverse collection of people consisting of numerous subgroups. Each of these groups has its own set of beliefs, traditions, and lifestyles. At the same time, the American people share common institutions, similar governmental structures, and a core set of values. This combination of diversity and shared elements identifies the **society** in which we live. Institutions within society such as the family, peer group, television, religion, and the schools are all considered socializing agents (Cushner, McClelland, & Safford, 2000) that have a significant impact on students' lives (see Table 12.1).

### The Family

Literally from the day of birth, families are either directly or indirectly shaping every aspect of a child's life (Berger, 2000). For example, parents who positively respond to their infant's needs for food, shelter, and loving attention are also developing the young child's ability to trust in others (Erikson, 1963). Or, later in a young person's life, parents who discuss and model responsi-

**TABLE 12.1**  Socializing Agents

| Socializing Agent | Description |
|---|---|
| The family | Either directly or indirectly, family life influences every aspect of a child's development. It is the most significant socializing agent for the majority of students through their elementary school years. |
| Peer group | By adolescence, many young people question the values and attitudes of family members while embracing the habits, language, and rituals of their peers. |
| Television | Because of the high number of hours spent viewing television, this media has a significant impact on attitudes toward violence, sex roles, consumerism, and sexuality. |
| Religion | Nearly 80% of all families report that religion has a significant influence on their lives. |
| Schools | Schools prepare students for the workforce, assist them to become effective citizens, and help them reach their full potential as individuals. |

ble consumption of alcohol are influencing that student's attitudes about drinking. Although the family's socializing influences are the greatest during childhood, this process continues throughout life.

Take a moment to reflect on your own family history. Can you identify ways in which your attitudes, values, and thinking have been influenced by family members? In some instances, you probably recognize where you have accepted the values held by others in your family as personally meaningful. On the other hand, you may remember having consciously chosen to value some things differently than certain members of your family. In either case, your family unit had (and continues to have) a powerful influence on how you view the world.

**Reflective Journey 12.1**

## Peer Group Influences

While the family's role as a socializing agent is the greatest in the early years and gradually decreases over time, **peer group** influences become readily apparent when children enter elementary school and continue to grow stronger (Gandara, 2001). By adolescence, many young people question the values and attitudes of family members while embracing the habits, language, and rituals of the peer group. Like the family, peer groups can have a significant impact on every aspect of students' lives. For example, many young people choose clothing, speech patterns, hair styles and colors, and jewelry options that distinguish themselves from parents and other adults. These relatively unimportant lifestyle choices are strongly influenced by a student's peer group. More significantly, the peer group often affects student decisions about such things as using drugs and alcohol, engaging in sexual activity, involvement in gangs, and employing violence in relating to others. Furthermore, peer groups influence students' attitudes toward diverse people, sex role expectations, and feelings about education.

Spend a few moments thinking about the influence of peers on your life to date. Try to remember your own middle school and high school years. How did peers impact your decisions and actions? Did they have more or less influence during this period than your family? Try to identify at least two or three specific examples of peer group influence.

**Reflective Journey 12.2**

## Television

While popular magazines, newspapers, music, and radio broadcasts are all media that influence students' lives, television viewing consumes the most time and also has the greatest impact. Children in the United States watch an average of 3 to 5 hours of television daily (Wiecha, Sobol, Peterson, & Gortmaker, 2001). Because of these high levels of viewing, television is often seen as rivaling the home and school as a major socializing agent.

But how does television programming influence student attitudes and values? Many people are suggesting that high levels of viewing are influencing *attitudes toward violence*. Statistics indicate that by the end of the elementary school years children will have viewed approximately 8,000 murders and 100,000 acts of violence on television (Federman, 1998). Others are concerned about *stereotypic sex roles*. Men, for example, are more often portrayed as active, outgoing, and confident while women are typically cast as passive and dependent (Bryant & Bryant,

*Television viewing may lead to several problem behaviors.*

2001). Television has also been criticized for its *advertising to promote consumerism.* Children are bombarded with thousands of television advertisements designed to develop brand name recognition and promote consumerism. It is estimated that children watch approximately 20,000 commercials each year (Clearinghouse on Elementary and Early Childhood Education, 1990). *Sexual content* of television programs is yet another concern. As with televised violence, children are repeatedly exposed to sexual content that may negatively influence attitudes toward sexuality ( Jordan, 1996).

## Religion

Religion plays an important role in the socialization process for many young people, with 78% of families reporting in a recent survey that religion is becoming an increasingly more significant aspect of their lives (Pew Research Center, 2001). Religion influences such things as people's attitudes about sex roles, discipline, child-rearing practices, the role of the family, and ways of relating to others. For example, traditional Christian teachings would encourage such positive actions as sexual abstinence before marriage and an attitude of respect toward those in authority. On the other hand, strongly held religious beliefs can cause tension and separation between people with divergent perspectives or life experiences. For example, a Christian who believes in the importance of strong family units with both a mother and father may have a difficult time accepting and relating to other family constellations.

## Schools and Socialization

Education serves three main roles in socializing students. First is the *preparation of capable workers* to meet the demands of the American economy. This preparation has taken two major directions. One is an education that leads students more directly to work following graduation from high school, while the other has been to prepare students for the college experience. In both instances, the goal is to prepare students for success in later life. The recent passage of the *No Child Left Behind Act of 2001,* has specified that this goal should include all children regardless of race, ethnicity, or economic status (see Table 12.2). The act states: "The purpose of this title [act] is to ensure that all children have a fair, equal, and significant opportunity to obtain a high-quality education and reach, at a minimum, proficiency on challenging state academic achievement standards and state academic assessments" (No Child Left Behind Act, 2002).

A second role of the schools is to help prepare students for *effective citizenship.* Being a good citizen means many different things. It includes understanding and valuing the structure of the U.S. political system, making a commitment to democracy, embracing the diversity within American society, and working to promote positive social change. Schools help prepare good citizens in two ways. First, students can learn a great deal through lessons and course work. At the elementary level, for example, students can study diversity and grow in their understanding and acceptance of people different from themselves. Secondly, schools prepare good citizens through a variety of informal learning opportunities. A spontaneous discussion of political corruption following a related news story is an example of this type of learning opportunity.

The third socializing role of the schools is to assist students in *personal growth.* In our society, individuality and personal growth are prized. For this reason, schools are engaged in the task of helping students reach their full potential as individuals. Building self-concept, developing lifelong learning skills, valuing student interests (sports, music, art, hobbies, etc.), and encouraging positive attitudes are some of the ways in which schools assist in this aspect of socialization. Much of the school's ability to influence personal growth occurs informally through interactions between students and school staff. Taking the time to listen to students talk about their interests and giving positive feedback about extracurricular activities are examples of this type.

**TABLE 12.2   Provisions of the No Child Left Behind Act**

| Provision | Description |
|---|---|
| Accountability for results | Each state must use assessments to measure what students know and learn in grades 3 through 8. |
| Reduce federal, state, and local "red tape" | To allow states and local school districts to have greater flexibility in the use of federal money, the "red tape" will be reduced. |
| Options for parents whose children are located in failing schools | Public school choice, supplemental services, and charter schools will be made available for children and families whose schools are failing. |
| Ensuring that every child can read | The federal government has tripled its funding of reading instruction to help ensure that all children learn to read. |
| Strengthen teacher quality | States are being asked to put a highly qualified teacher in every public school classroom by 2005. |
| Promoting English proficiency | The act consolidates federal agencies assisting limited English-proficient (LEP) students to learn English quickly and effectively. |

Source: *No Child Left Behind Act,* (2002). Retrieved September 26, 2002, from http://www.ed.gov/legislation/ESEA02/pg1.html#sec101

## Are there social issues that affect student behavior?

In today's fast-paced society, students encounter a great many social pressures that influence their attitudes and behavior both in and out of school (see Table 12.3). Take, for example, 11-year-old Martin, a student in your elementary classroom. It is amazing how "normal" he appears despite the situations he has faced during the past 2 years. From his former teachers you have learned that Martin is currently living with his mother after a long and bitter custody fight stemming from his parents' divorce. His mother has been unable to find employment and the family has been living on welfare for the past year. To complicate matters, Martin's older brother was seriously injured in a car accident 3 weeks ago. Despite all of these challenges, Martin appears happy, is doing above-average schoolwork, and is well liked by others in the class. Martin's response is unusual. His resilience under very stressful circumstances is remarkable.

### The Changing Family

One social institution that has undergone significant change during the past several decades is the American family. Two-parent families in which dad works and mom stays home to raise the children now account for a much smaller percentage of all families (see Table 12.4), with other configurations taking their place (Berger, 2000). One of the most common of these is the single-parent family. A little more than a quarter of all children live in families with only one parent (Annie E. Casey Foundation, 2002). Approximately 85% of single-parent households are

| TABLE 12.3 | Social Issues Affecting Students |
|---|---|
| **Social Issue** | **Description** |
| The changing family | Growing numbers of single-parent, dual-career, blended, homeless, and gay and lesbian families are influencing the lives of students. |
| Poverty | Approximately one family in five lives in poverty, which has a significant negative impact on schooling. |
| Teen pregnancy | America continues to lead all industrialized nations in the number of teen pregnancies. |
| AIDS | AIDS is a significant health issue that influences the lives of families and schools. |
| Child abuse and neglect | Students who are abused or neglected experience deep emotional trauma that influences their school performance. |
| Alcohol and drugs | Young people may experiment with alcohol and drugs as early as the elementary school years, with many potential social and school-related problems resulting. |
| Suicide | Suicide is the second leading cause of death among young people between the ages of 15 and 19. |
| Violence | Violence among students and directed toward teachers is a growing concern to educators and others. |
| School dropouts | Although school dropout rates have decreased, those who do drop out are even less likely than before to find productive work. |

headed by women, with many of these families living at or below the poverty level. From necessity, most single parents work and consequently have more limited opportunities to communicate and interact with teachers (Berger, 2000). Students from single-parent families may have a variety of feelings that cause them stress and can lead to potential problems in the classroom (Gestwicki, 2000). For example, feelings of guilt stemming from an unreasonable belief that they have caused the divorce are common among younger students.

During the past decade, there has also been a dramatic increase in the number of homeless families in the United States (Gollnick & Chinn, 2002). Estimates of numbers vary from about

| TABLE 12.4 | Two-Parent Families |
|---|---|
| **Racial Group** | **Percentage** |
| African American | 38 |
| Hispanic | 65 |
| White | 78 |
| All Families | 69 |

*Source: America's Children: Key National Indicators of Well-Being,* by Forum on Child and Family Statistics, 2002, Vienna, VA: National Maternal Child Health Clearinghouse.

150,000 to 1.5 million families, depending on who reports the figures. Approximately 40% of all people in homeless shelters today are families with children (National Coalition for the Homeless, 1999). Clearly, homeless families are struggling and need a great deal of support from the school and community in order to manage the day-to-day challenges of living. While teachers and schools can't be expected to meet all of the needs of homeless families, providing information, support, and understanding can extend an important lifeline to both parents and children in these circumstances. Without this assistance, homeless students may well be one of the most at-risk groups for school failure (Sandham, 2000).

The National Center for Lesbian Rights (cited in Berger, 2000) estimates that 2 million children in the United States are being raised in gay or lesbian families. Students and parents in these families face many different challenges (Springate & Stegelin, 1999). Most obvious, perhaps, is that the prejudices of the general public toward gay and lesbian people are often very strong, with social alienation and negative interactions the common result. Many teachers also find these circumstances difficult to accept and consequently relate less positively to both the children and parents in gay and lesbian families. In addition, there is currently no legal status for gay and lesbian

## reflect on diversity

## America's Fifth Child

Imagine a very wealthy family with five young children under the age of three. Four have enough to eat and comfortable warm rooms in which to sleep. One does not. She is often hungry and lives in a cold room. Sometimes she has to sleep on the streets, in a shelter, and even be taken away from her family and be placed in foster care with strangers.

Imagine this family giving four of their very young children nourishing meals everyday, but letting the fifth child go hungry.

Imagine this very wealthy family making sure four of their young children get all their shots and regular check-ups before they get sick, but ignoring the fifth child who is plagued by chronic infections and respiratory diseases like asthma. (Children's Defense Fund, 2002, p. 3)

While none of us can imagine a wealthy family that would engage in the behaviors described above, American society is in fact allowing approximately one in five children to not have enough to eat, live in substandard housing, and grow up without adequate health care. The richest nation in the world is doing less than it could to combat poverty and assist children as they struggle to deal with its negative consequences.

Poverty is pervasive throughout American society and can be found in small towns as well as large urban areas. It often has a permanent and negative impact on the lives of children and their families. Students from low-income homes frequently find that their life circumstances make it very difficult for them to be successful in school. Consequently, many grow up and live their adult lives in poverty. Eventually, they often become the parents of the next generation of poor children and the cycle of poverty continues.

### Explore and Reflect

Learn more about America's fifth child by reading the source article by the Children's Defense Fund (2002) and reviewing other online resources provided in the *Reflect on Diversity* module for Chapter 12 of the Companion Website of this text.

1. Do you know one of America's fifth children? If not, talk to a classroom teacher who could describe one for you. What are the circumstances this student faces and how is he or she coping with the stresses of life?

2. If you were the teacher of the student you described above, what are some of the little things you could do to assist in helping this person cope?

 *To explore this topic further and submit your responses online, go to the Reflect on Diversity module for Chapter 12 of the Companion Website for this text.*

*Source: The State of Children in America's Union,* by Children's Defense Fund, 2002, Washington, DC: Author. Reprinted with permission.

| TABLE 12.5 Family Income Levels* | | |
|---|---|---|
| **Income Category** | **Income** | **Percentage** |
| Extreme poverty | Less than $8,800 | 7 |
| Poverty | $8,800–17,600 | 8 |
| Low income | $17,600–35,200 | 21 |
| Medium income | $35,200–70,400 | 34 |
| High income | Above $70,400 | 30 |

*Family of four, in 2000.

*Source: America's Children: Key National Indicators of Well-Being,* by Forum on Child and Family Statistics, 2002, Vienna, VA: National Maternal Child Health Clearinghouse.

families comparable to that for heterosexual families, so many either hide their lifestyle from others or avoid contact with the schools and other families (Springate & Stegelin, 1999).

Take a moment to reflect on your own attitudes about the diverse families you will encounter in your classroom. How will you feel about working with single-parent, homeless, and gay/lesbian families, for example? Do you think you can work with them in positive ways, or will you bring personal convictions to these interactions that may well get in the way of your relationships? Will your ability to work with all types of families potentially impact your relationships with some of your students?

**Reflective Journey 12.3**

## Poverty

Another major social problem facing many students and their families is **poverty.** Despite numerous governmental and private efforts over the years, the percentage of families living in poverty has remained fairly constant at about one in five (Berger, 2000) (see Table 12.5). The problems associated with poverty are many. Parents frequently feel alienated and powerless and often pass these feelings on to their children (Springate & Stegelin, 1999). Low levels of parent involvement in the schools and poor school performance from children may well be the result (Sherman, 1997). Other common problems associated with poverty are poor health, inadequate health care, increased levels of violence, and higher drug usage (Berger, 2000; Springate & Stegelin, 1999).

## Teen Pregnancy

Statistics indicate that while the birth rate for teenagers between the ages of 15 and 17 dropped somewhat from 1991 to 1997, America still leads all industrialized nations in the numbers of teen pregnancies at over 32 per 1,000 (Annie E. Casey Foundation, 2002). Stated another way, each day in the United States 1,403 babies are born to teen mothers (Children's Defense Fund, 2002). Although the stigma associated with teen pregnancy has lessened somewhat, the problems associated with children bearing and raising children are many. In a large majority of cases, teen pregnancies occur outside of

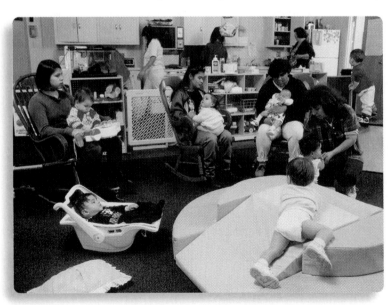
*Many high schools provide child care for teen parents.*

marriage and leave the mother with a more limited support system. Teen mothers are more likely to have low-birth-weight babies with greater health care needs (Annie E. Casey Foundation, 2002). At the same time, teen mothers are far more likely to be living in poverty and drop out of high school at higher rates than their peers.

## Acquired Immunodeficiency Syndrome (AIDS)

**AIDS** is a significant health issue that influences the lives of more than 850,000 people in the United States. While only a small percentage of this total are young people, through June 1999, 1,924 children between the ages of 5 and 12 had contracted the disease and another 3,564 children ages 13 through 19 were reported with AIDS (U.S. Department of Health and Human Services, 1999b). Statistics indicate that the HIV virus that causes AIDS is most often spread in the teen years through homosexual activity (U.S. Department of Health and Human Services, 1999b). Other significant issues such as heterosexual contact with an HIV carrier, common needles for drug injection, and being born to an AIDS/HIV parent also are factors in contracting this disease. Controlling the spread of the AIDS epidemic requires a continued educational emphasis on eliminating these high-risk behaviors whenever possible.

## Child Abuse and Neglect

Four main types of child abuse and neglect are defined by the National Clearinghouse on Child Abuse and Neglect (2002). **Physical abuse** is the infliction of physical injury through the punching, beating, kicking, biting, burning, or shaking of a child. **Child neglect** can take three forms: *physical neglect* (e.g., refusal of health care, abandonment, expulsion from the home), *educational neglect* (e.g., allowing chronic truancy, failure to enroll a child in school), and *emotional neglect* (e.g., inattention to the child's need for affection, failure to provide psychological care, allowing alcohol or drug use by the child). **Sexual abuse** includes fondling a child's genitals, intercourse, incest, rape, sodomy, exhibitionism, and commercial exploitation through prostitution. **Emotional abuse** occurs when parents or caregivers engage in behavior that causes or could cause serious behavioral, cognitive, emotional, or mental disorders (e.g., extreme forms of punishment or habitual belittling). Table 12.6 gives a breakdown of incidences of child abuse and neglect.

## Alcohol and Drugs

Student alcohol and drug use is another serious issue facing teachers and schools (National Center for Education Statistics, 2001). Consumption negatively influences academic achievement,

| TABLE 12.6   Incidence of Child Abuse and Neglect* | |
| --- | --- |
| **Category** | **Percent of Total** |
| Neglect | 63 |
| Physical abuse | 19 |
| Sexual abuse | 10 |
| Psychological abuse | 8 |

*In 2000, 879,000 children were found to be victims of child abuse and neglect.

*Source: National Child Abuse and Neglect Data System (NCANDS) Summary of Key Findings from Calendar Year 2000, by Administration on Children, Youth and Families. Retrieved April 16, 2002, from http://www.calib.com/nccanch/prevmnth/scope/ncands.cfm*

impairs interactions with other students and school staff, and increases the chances of a child dropping out of school. When students engage in alcohol and drug use, the immediate and long-term costs to society are high. Beginning as early as the elementary school years, students place themselves at risk of addiction. Jalil (1996) suggests that addiction becomes a problem for many teens for three main reasons. First, *drug use accelerates over time.* Gradually, students take larger quantities of drugs at more frequent intervals to get the same "high." Secondly, *adolescents tend to use more than one drug at a time.* Students experiment with different drugs during a short time period because their friends are trying new options and encourage others to do the same. Finally, *adolescents underestimate the power of drugs.* Thinking that they are in control of the drugs rather than the other way around, students fail to see the addictive power of drugs.

**Reflective Journey 12.4**

Take a moment to reflect back on your own K–12 experiences. Do you remember times when friends or acquaintances experimented with drugs or alcohol? When did you become aware of this activity? How did these experiences influence the students' lives? Based on these remembrances, do you think it will be important for you as a future teacher to be aware of and work to help students who engage in drug and alcohol use?

### Suicide

For a variety of reasons, young people experience strong feelings of confusion, self-doubt, pressure to succeed, and general stress that can lead to attempted or actual suicide. Suicide is the sec-

## EDUCATION IN THE NEWS

### Action, Reaction, and Zero Tolerance

As a reaction to continued violence in society and schools, zero tolerance policies against drugs, alcohol, weapons, and threats of violence have emerged in many of today's schools. When implemented to the letter of the policy, young children in innocent play are suspended from school and criminally charged. Knowing when students are playing or being real is difficult to assess on the spot. Immediate responses required by adults may not allow time to determine whether it is an honest mishap or a true violation.

When zero tolerance policies are implemented, some indicate that incidents of violence are reduced. Research, however, does not yet indicate that zero tolerance has made an impact on improving student behavior or ensured the safety of schools. Professionals ask the question, though—How many incidents have we stopped?

#### Critical Thinking Questions

1. What is an adult sensible solution to the problems identified in this documentary on zero tolerance? How can schools calibrate the zero tolerance policies?

2. The Columbine shootings have influenced much of what is going on in schools today with regard to zero tolerance. What influence do you think the tragic events of terrorist activities of September 11, 2001, have had on schools? What types of policies might schools design in response to activities such as September 11 or other homeland violence?

3. What are some effective methods of conflict resolution? How might skills in conflict resolution help you as a prospective teacher? How might these skills help today's students?

*To submit your responses online, go to the Education in the News module for Chapter 12 of the Companion Website.*

ond leading cause of death among young people ages 15 to 19 years (American Psychiatric Association, 2002). The symptoms of young people considering suicide are similar to those of depression. Parents and teachers who become aware of several of the following signs should seek professional assistance to prevent the possibility of suicide:

- Change in eating and sleeping habits
- Withdrawal from friends, family, and regular activities
- Violent actions, rebellious behavior, or running away
- Drug and alcohol use
- Unusual neglect of personal appearance
- Marked personality change (American Academy of Child and Adolescent Psychiatry, 2002)

## Violence

Violence in schools is a growing concern that in recent years has received wide media attention. Although it is definitely a problem that must be addressed, the federal government states in a recent report on the nature and scope of school violence: "From an overall perspective, our schools have been successful in keeping most of their students and employees safe from harm. The perception of risk at these schools is often greater than the actual risk incurred" (U.S. Departments of Education and Justice, 2000, p. 6). At the same time, however, youth violence, once thought to be a problem associated primarily with large urban schools, is now a concern in suburban and rural schools as well. **Gang activity,** for example, is more common today and can lead to severe violence. While less than 1% of students are gang members and this percentage has remained relatively constant for larger cities, numbers appear to be growing in the suburbs and smaller cities (Howell & Lynch, 2000).

## School Dropouts

The good news about school dropout rates is that they are decreasing (see Table 12.7). Unfortunately, the bad news is that those who do drop out of school are less likely than ever before to be financially successful. The chances of falling into poverty are roughly three times higher for high school dropouts than for those who have finished their secondary education (Annie E. Casey Foundation, 2002). Between 1973 and 1995, the average hourly wage (adjusted for inflation) of high school dropouts fell by 23%. As we continue to move further into the 21st century, the increasing demand for workers with advanced skills and technical knowledge will mean that those not completing a high school degree will likely face a dismal future.

**TABLE 12.7   Percentage of School Dropouts, 1970–1999**

| Year | Total | White | Black | Hispanic |
|------|-------|-------|-------|----------|
| 1970 | 15 | 13.2 | 27.9 | |
| 1980 | 14.1 | 11.4 | 19.1 | 35.2 |
| 1990 | 12.1 | 9 | 13.2 | 32.4 |
| 1999 | 11.2 | 7.3 | 12.6 | 28.6 |

*Source: Fast Facts,* by National Center for Education Statistics, 2002. Retrieved October 9, 2002, from http://nces.ed.gov/fastfacts/display.asp?id=16

# How should teachers and schools respond to social issues?

Not so many years ago, the issues discussed on pages 281–287 were considered somehow separate from the work of the schools and were frequently left to others for resolution. During the last 30 or 40 years, however, teachers and schools have gradually become more involved in supporting students and their families as they work through these difficult social situations. While there is great variability in their responses, both teachers and schools today feel responsible for providing support and assistance in dealing with these complex issues.

## Your Response as a Future Teacher

Responding to the societal pressures faced by your future students can lead you in two very different directions. One approach that some teachers use is to simply ignore these problems and concentrate on teaching the school curriculum. While this method allows you to be successful with those students whose problems are relatively minor, it leaves a significant number without adequate support. Your other option is to broaden your role in working with students and families by getting involved at some level in helping resolve the social issues students face. Table 12.8 lists some suggestions for getting involved, each of which is discussed in more detail in the subsections below.

Take, for example, 6-year-old Kara who is a student in your second-grade classroom. While she comes from an intact two-parent family, you know from Kara's first-grade teacher that they are struggling financially. Neither parent holds a steady job and you were told at a recent parent–teacher conference that they may be evicted from their apartment at the end of the month because they can't afford to pay the rent. Kara has been doing low-average work in your class, but it seems entirely possible that if she were homeless, her academic pursuits would be overshadowed by the family's financial and housing concerns. Being aware of your community's resources for homeless families, you recommend two community agencies that may be able to help.

**TABLE 12.8   Your Responses to Social Issues**

| Response | Description |
|---|---|
| Take time for relationship building | Building trust and rapport with students and their families is a key to assisting them. |
| Accommodate family differences | You will need to be aware of, and responsive to, differences in family circumstances. |
| Know the warning signs | Knowing the warning signs for child abuse and neglect, alcohol and drug abuse, and suicide will allow you to refer students for the help they will need. |
| Understand your legal and school-mandated responsibilities | Knowing your legal and school-mandated responsibilities will help you know how and when to respond to student and family needs. |
| Be aware of resources | An awareness of school, community, state, and national resources will allow you to direct students and families to the help they need. |
| Identify your personal limits | You will need to decide how personally involved you can be in the issues students and families face. |

**Take time for relationship building.**   Relationships are the key to any helping profession, including teaching. If you take the time to build trust and rapport with your students and their families, it is much more likely that they will come to you for assistance with their problems and listen to your suggestions. Without these strong working relationships, you can do little to help your students with the stresses they face. The challenges of creating good rapport, however, are many. The students and families who need your support and concern the most are often the most difficult to reach. It may be that they have sought out others in the past and been hurt because of it, or their struggles may be so painful and difficult that the situation appears hopeless.

**Accommodate family differences.**   One way in which you can respond effectively to the pressures students face is to be aware of family circumstances and make modifications in your teaching and interactions where possible. If, for example, you know that Amanda's parents are divorced and do not communicate well, it may be necessary to offer them separate parent–teacher conference times. Or, being aware of Bruce's family financial situation, you work to find money to pay for his ticket to the zoo for the upcoming field trip. Finally, knowing that Juanita's parents speak and read only Spanish at home, you could find an adult to translate your written communications into Spanish before sending them to this family. Each of these accommodations requires extra effort on your part, but will pay big dividends in your relationships with both students and families.

**Know the warning signs.**   Child abuse and neglect, alcohol and drug use, and suicide are serious problems that you cannot manage on your own as a teacher. However, if you know the warning signs that indicate these problems may exist, you can refer students and their families to professionals who have the skills needed to deal with them. It is beyond the scope of this text to adequately prepare you to recognize the warning signs for these problems. While some were provided earlier in this chapter as samples, you should expect to take additional course work or workshops during your teacher preparation program or as a future teacher to get the more detailed information you will need.

**Understand your legal and school-mandated responsibilities.**   As a teacher, you are legally responsible in all 50 states to report suspected cases of child abuse and neglect. Should you identify clear physical or behavioral indicators, suspected abuse and neglect must be reported to the appropriate state agency. In addition to understanding your legal responsibilities, it is important to be aware of and to adhere to school-mandated procedures for dealing with inappropriate student behaviors. Depending on the grade level you teach and the setting of your school, you may be responsible for knowing and following rules for dealing with student alcohol and drug use, procedures for violent student behaviors, and policies on handling students who bring weapons into the school setting. Although these are not commonly occurring events, it is clearly best to be prepared to deal with them if needed.

**Be aware of resources.**   Many times, students' problems go well beyond the abilities of most teachers to resolve. For example, a pregnant student who confides her recently confirmed condition to you is definitely in need of assistance. Without proper counselor training, however, it may be very difficult to provide her with adequate help. Knowing where to go for specialized support, on the other hand, is a more manageable role that most teachers can assume. Resources to assist students can be found in the school setting itself or within the local community. School options may include other teachers with specialized training in dealing with social issues, counselors, specialists (such as a school nurse or psychologist), and administrators. Community resources are often more extensive and include options such as monetary assistance through churches and other organizations, counseling services, support groups (e.g., Alcoholics Anonymous), crisis hotlines, low-cost medical and dental care, and job training/counseling programs.

**Identify your personal limits.** Think back to your own schooling experiences for a moment. Can you recall one or more teachers that always seemed to have students "hanging out" in their classrooms before or after school to get assistance with nonacademic matters? Most schools have a few teachers that attract students in this way. They consistently help students in need by being a sympathetic listener, serving as a ready resource for good advice, or by providing a few words of encouragement. By taking the time to develop close working relationships with these students and then finding additional opportunities to informally counsel them, these teachers often have a major influence on students' lives.

You are going to need to decide for yourself how much of a helping person you can be in your teaching career. While it is essential that everyone get involved to some extent in this aspect of teaching, your level of student support may be different from that of the teachers described above. Take a few minutes to think about your feelings on this topic. Can you see yourself being a support and encouragement to students who face the kinds of problems identified in this chapter? Is this something you will feel good about or a part of the job you will resent?

**Reflective Journey 12.5**

## The School's Response to Social Issues

Do you remember times when the schools you attended responded in some way to the many different social issues students face? What programs or people were available to help with these challenges? Try to recall two or three different examples of this type. As you spend more time in the classroom, you will probably find that schools today are continuing to add new options to help students resolve these complex social concerns (see Table 12.9). Although considerable debate surrounds the appropriateness of these actions, there is a growing awareness that these are critical issues that must be addressed by someone if students are to be successful in the school setting.

**Student and family support.** For quite some time, part of the business of schools has been the support of students and their families. Take, for example, the free and reduced-cost breakfasts and

---

**TABLE 12.9   The School's Response to Social Issues**

| Response | Description |
|---|---|
| Student and family support | Free and reduced-cost breakfasts and lunches, vocational counseling, before and after school care, interpreters, community services coordinators, and medical and dental services are all being offered in school settings. |
| Educational awareness programs | Schools are taking greater responsibility for educating students about the dangers associated with such things as violence, early sexual activity, and drug use. |
| Implementing rules and procedures | Schools are identifying rules and procedures for students and staff in response to violence and drug use. |
| Counseling | Guidance counselors, a tradition at middle schools and high schools, are now more often available for elementary schools as well. |
| Alternative education | For students who are unable to work within the traditional school system, alternate educational opportunities are being provided. |

lunches funded by the federal government. The free and reduced-price lunch component began in 1946 and currently serves more than 27 million children each school day (U.S. Department of Agriculture, 2001). Another example of the school's long-standing support of students is the vocational counseling opportunities that have been available to many high school students for much of the 20th century (Baker, 2000).

More recently, schools have become involved in many other strategies to assist students and their families. One example of this type is *before- and after-school care* (Dryfoos, 1994). While schools seldom fund these programs, just having them in the elementary school building is a convenience and service to many families. Schools are also providing *interpreters and translators* for activities such as parent–teacher conferences. This allows families to more fully participate in school activities. More schools are now providing *home/school/community coordinators*. These coordinators serve families in a variety of ways, such as locating and recommending community services. Finally, *full-service schools* are more common today. Particularly in low-income urban areas, some schools are providing educational, medical, dental, social, and human services on-site to meet the needs of students and their families (Hurst, 2003).

**Educational awareness programs.**  For many of the issues that young people face, schools are taking greater responsibility for educating students about their dangers. These efforts may include an informal discussion in class, a more formalized lesson or activity, or a long-term educational awareness program. Particularly for violence prevention, sex education, and alcohol and drug use prevention, schools are finding it necessary to implement programs that span several years in an attempt to convince students to avoid these problem behaviors.

Many schools are implementing **violence prevention programs** as early as the elementary school years to help deter youth violence (Indiana Education Policy Center, 2002). These programs often include strategies for anger management, impulse control, appreciating diversity, and developing conflict resolution skills (Children's Defense Fund, 2002). Discussions about the problems associated with gang membership are another important component of many programs. Other attempts to decrease violence in the schools focus on encouraging positive behavior. Teachers and schools work to recognize positive interactions and reward good school citizenship. Rather than discussing what students should avoid, these programs emphasize the importance of creating a school climate in which students and staff get along with one another (Indiana Education Policy Center, 2002).

Despite high teen pregnancy levels and the growing concerns over the AIDS epidemic, the issue of **sex education programs** in the schools remains a controversial one. Some people argue that the family and church should be responsible for dealing with all aspects of sex education. Others feel that while factual information about human reproduction is appropriate content for the school curriculum, issues related to the morality of sexual activity should be dealt with elsewhere. Despite these and other controversies, the courts have ruled that schools have the right to offer sex education as a part of the curriculum.

A third effort being made by many schools is the implementation of **alcohol and drug awareness programs.** The efforts to prevent student use of alcohol and drugs have been promoted by a variety of state and

*Law enforcement officials provide important educational opportunities.*

# Sex Education in the Schools

A long-standing dispute in many schools centers on the issue of including sex education as a part of the curriculum. Initially, there was much heated discussion between parents and school personnel about the appropriateness of addressing this topic in a school setting. Many people felt that sex education was best done at home where parents and guardians could share their own beliefs and attitudes toward sexuality. These parents and others were suggesting that schools should simply avoid addressing this topic. Those who wanted sex education taught in school settings argued that many families were not talking about issues related to sex and students were either getting no information or inaccurate data on this important subject.

While there are still those who argue that sex education should not be included in the curriculum, the current debate focuses more often on the perspective the schools should take in discussing sexuality. On one end of the continuum are those who support what has come to be known as *comprehensive sex education* (Kaiser Family Foundation, 2002). As the name implies, this approach seeks to educate young people about all aspects of sex and sexuality, including the use of birth control to prevent pregnancy and protect against sexually transmitted diseases. In a recent survey, parents and guardians strongly supported the comprehensive sex education approach (Kaiser Family Foundation, 2002). By a margin of five to one, they felt that this approach would be most useful in helping their children concerning issues of sexuality.

A growing movement in sexuality education during the past few years has been the *abstinence education* option. Programs aligned with this option emphasize the social, psychological, and health benefits that come from abstaining from sexual activity until marriage (Parker, 2001). This movement has received the support of the federal government, with Congress appropriating $50 million dollars annually to promote abstinence until marriage.

## Research the Issue

Research this topic online using the links provided in the *Engage in the Debate* module for this chapter of the Companion Website. Link to the online source articles by Parker (2001) and the Kaiser Family Foundation (2002) and explore the information provided at the additional sites listed.

1. From your readings, what do you see as the advantages and disadvantages of comprehensive sex education?

2. Identify the advantages and disadvantages of abstinence education.

## Explore Your Views

1. Should schools be involved in sex education issues? Why or why not?

2. If you were required to teach either comprehensive sex education or abstinence education, which would you choose? Give a rationale for the position you take.

 *To research this issue and submit your responses online, go to the Engage in the Debate module for Chapter 12 of the Companion Website for this text.*

*Sources: Sex Education in the U.S.: Policy and Politics,* by Kaiser Family Foundation, 2002. Retrieved April 28, 2003, from http://www.kff.org/content/2002/3224/policyandpoliticsissueupdate2002.pdf; *School-Based Sex Education: A New Millenium Update. ERIC Digest,* by T. Parker, 2001. Retrieved April 28, 2003, from http://www.ed.gov/databases/ERIC_Digests/ed460130.html

national groups. The U.S. Department of Education, for example, has sponsored the Safe and Drug-Free Schools Program. As the federal government's primary vehicle for promoting alcohol and drug abuse education and prevention activities, it provides funding to states for these activities and coordinates information development and dissemination at the national level (U.S. Department of Education, 2002).

**Implementing rules and procedures.** As schools struggle to respond to the many social issues presented by modern society, one important step they have taken is to clearly identify rules and procedures that both students and staff should follow in responding to these concerns. When these rules and procedures are seen as fair and consistently applied, the impact of social issues is reduced. Some examples help highlight how schools have responded:

- *Gang attire.* Many schools have implemented rules concerning the wearing of clothing associated with gang membership. By identifying and banning this attire, gang activity in the schools is discouraged.

- *Weapons ban.* The Children's Defense Fund (2002) estimates that more than 135,000 guns are brought into U.S. schools each day. Based on a federal mandate, schools have implemented a policy of zero tolerance for guns and knives in the school setting and have created heavy penalties for their presence.

- *School safety policies.* Rules and procedures for dealing with violent acts have been implemented by most schools to help curb problem behaviors (Indiana Education Policy Center, 2002). The development of a code of conduct demonstrates a commitment on the part of schools to violence prevention.

- *Monitoring students.* Many schools are committing resources to overseeing students as they congregate in hallways, restrooms, and cafeterias. While school staff have traditionally served in this role, some schools are hiring security guards or seeking parent volunteers to patrol their buildings (*Education Week,* 2002).

- *Closed campuses.* On many high school campuses the option of leaving the school grounds during normal hours of operation is severely limited. In particular, these closed campuses hope to decrease student opportunities for drug and alcohol use.

**Counseling.** Guidance counselors are a vital component of American schooling. Many of the problems facing students today are too complex for teacher assistance. Trained counselors who can talk with students, listen to their concerns, and refer them to appropriate community resources are needed. Guidance personnel can often detect the early warning signs of potential problems and work with families to develop solutions. Working in partnership with teachers and families, counselors can help troubled students receive the assistance they need before it is too late. Traditionally, counseling has been available primarily at the junior high/middle school and secondary levels. More recently, however, elementary schools have begun hiring guidance personnel (Holmgren, 1996).

**Alternative education.** For some students, the regular school classroom proves ineffective in meeting their needs. Without specialized programs, they often drop out of school and create further problems for themselves and society. In response to this issue, school districts have developed **alternative education programs** to meet the needs of these at-risk students. Some of these alternative options are housed within existing schools, while others are located in separate school or community settings. Increasing the number of these programs is being promoted by some as a way to reduce violence in schools in addition to decreasing dropout rates (DeBlois, 2000).

Alternative education programs are often designed to serve a variety of purposes, including assistance to teen mothers, dropout prevention, and violence education/prevention. With smaller class sizes, specialized curricula, and teachers committed to helping at-risk students, alternative programs are often successful in preventing school dropouts. An example of this type is the McAlester Alternative High School in McAlester, Oklahoma (Texas Youth Commission, 2000). The school provides on-site child care for teen parents; a counselor for personal, crisis, and career issues; and a flexible program with small class sizes. Class attendance is optional and is determined by the students themselves. Four teachers and one counselor work to meet the needs of 70 to 80 students. This program has received national recognition for efforts to help troubled youth.

| TABLE 12.10 | Society's Influence on Schooling |
|---|---|
| **Influence** | **Description** |
| Determining purposes | Society identifies the three main purposes of education as preparing students for the workforce, creating effective citizens, and facilitating personal growth. |
| Establishing values | Society is the driving force behind the values placed on different aspects of the curriculum (art, music, educating the gifted, etc.), the value placed on diversity, and the perceived importance of equal educational opportunity. |

## How does society influence schooling?

In addition to significantly influencing the lives of your future students, society also has a major impact on schools. Both the content of your future classroom curriculum and the strategies you use in instruction will be in large part determined by society. Because schools are institutions created by society to serve its purposes, this statement shouldn't surprise you. While schools do help shape and refine the directions of society, they primarily reflect the purposes and values assigned it by the larger group (see Table 12.10).

### Determining Purposes

Earlier in this chapter, schools were described as socializing students in three ways: by preparing them for the workforce, creating effective citizens, and facilitating personal growth. Each of these socializing tasks identifies a major purpose for education. And while schools vary in the emphasis placed on each, these core purposes chart a clear course for American education.

It is important to realize that these purposes are not static, but are often redefined as the needs and interests of society vary. For example, in 1957, the launching of Russia's first satellite into space caused great concern in America. We were losing the "race into space" and it was assumed that our schools were the main culprit. American students were thought to need stronger mathematics and science skills. Consequently, a major push was made by the schools to improve instruction in these areas (Webb, Metha, & Jordan, 2000). The goal of preparing students for the workforce was modified to accommodate this perceived need by society.

In addition to the broad purposes cited above, society also helps determine other more specific components of American educational efforts, such as the schools' involvement in drug and alcohol awareness, suicide prevention, sex education, and violence prevention programs. For example, the high U.S. teen suicide rates have led many schools to train staff members to identify students at risk of suicide and refer them to appropriate agencies (American Psychiatric Association, 2002). While these directions for education are often controversial, most schools are engaged in efforts to assist and educate students in this way.

*Corporate America has a vested interest in quality education.*

## Establishing Values

In addition to determining the major purposes and directions for education, society is the driving force behind the values placed on certain aspects of schooling. If, for example, American society greatly valued educating the "best and brightest" students, schools would allocate more of their resources to gifted education. Or, if music, drama, and art were highly prized, more teachers of the arts would be found in American schools. Similarly, society also determines how schools value less tangible things such as diversity and equal educational opportunity. While they are more difficult to assess, these values play an important role in the directions of American education.

**Diversity.**  In chapter 2 we established that diversity is a fact of life in American schools. Different family lifestyles, cultures, religions, and abilities comingle in educational settings across the country. Urban areas, the suburbs, and rural America are all becoming increasingly diverse. What is not so clear, however, is the value placed on this diversity. Part of the reason for this lack

## explore your beliefs

# Oppression

How would you define oppression? Do you understand the complexities and impact that it has on various groups of people? In simplified terms, oppression is the cruel use of power by those in authority to subdue those who are in less powerful positions. If you are not a part of a group that is consistently oppressed, you may find it difficult to understand what it is like for many people in this country who are oppressed.

The image of a birdcage has been used to explain how oppression works. Cohen (1998) states it this way:

> It isn't possible to understand the nature of oppressive systems by studying any one aspect of discrimination; that would be like trying to understand how a birdcage constrains by examining only one wire in its structure. In order to understand a cage, it is necessary to step back and see all the wires and the webbed pattern they form. Similarly, in order to understand sexism, for instance, one must look at patterns of discrimination in employment, education, family roles, athletics, corporate styles of communication and decision-making, etc. (p. 58)

Oppression can take many forms and affects a variety of groups. For example, racial oppression can take place when the authority and power of the majority are used to control the lives of people from minority groups. Overt forms of oppression are less common today due to legal and moral constraints. More subtle expressions, however, such as the messages being sent through the media regarding minority groups and women and the failure to include the contributions made by different racial groups among the topics taught in the schools, have a significant impact on self-concept and motivation. Similarly, lower pay and less prestigious positions in business and industry are examples of gender oppression.

### React and Reflect

1. Most of us have experienced times in which others tried to use their power and authority to control us unfairly. Try to remember an incident in your past for which this was the case for you. How did you react to this situation? Does this give you any insight into what it must feel like to experience oppression on a regular basis?

2. Do you think oppression is something that should be of concern to teachers? Why or why not?

3. Are there things you could do in your future classroom to educate others about oppression?

 *To explore this topic further and submit your reactions and reflections online, go to the Explore Your Beliefs module for Chapter 12 of the Companion Website for this text.*

*Source:* "The True Colors of the New Jim Toomey: Transformation, Integrity, Trust, in Educating Teachers About Oppression," by C. Cohen. In E. Lee, D. Menhart, and M. Okazawa-Rey (Eds.), *Beyond Heroes and Holidays: A Practical Guide to K–12 Anti-Racist, Multicultural Education and Staff Development*, 1998, Washington, DC: Network of Educators of the Americas.

of clarity may be the fact that attitudes are in the process of changing. For much of American history, the United States was viewed as a **cultural melting pot,** where people from diverse backgrounds came together and were assimilated into the dominant culture (Campbell, 2000). By setting aside their traditions, languages, and beliefs these people were "Americanized." More recently, society has begun to recognize the strengths of diverse people while striving to create a new mix that is uniquely American. In what is often described as **cultural pluralism,** each group of diverse people adds its own unique traditions and experiences to that of the larger society. This shift to valuing cultural pluralism is far from universally held and will require much effort and time to accomplish. Over the next several decades, schools will play an important role in making this a reality.

**Equal educational opportunity.** A long-standing belief about American education is that it should provide every student with an equal opportunity to develop the knowledge and skills needed to succeed in life. For everyone willing to work hard and spend the time required, success would be assured. On the surface, at least, it would appear that society values equal educational opportunities for all.

It would be naïve, however, to suggest that this is, in fact, a reality. Among other things, the quality of teachers, the quantity and currency of textbooks and curriculum materials, and the home lives of students all vary dramatically from one school to the next. Can a student who takes calculus from a teacher trained in social studies education do as well as one taking the same course from a teacher with a degree in mathematics? Probably not. Does a child from a low-income family with no health care and little money to spend on books and toys have the same chances to learn as her more privileged peers? Clearly, the answer is no. So, while society's heart may be in the right place, the realities of life mean that many students do not have an equal opportunity to be successful in school.

## views from the classroom

## Meeting the Needs of Your Students and Yourself

**Kate Walker**
**Parkview Elementary School**
**Bellingham, Washington**

Being a teacher isn't quite what I expected. It's extremely hard work. It's impossible to do what is expected of you in the hours given, and there are so many other things to take care of before you can actually teach. Have your students had breakfast that day? Do they have a safe place to sleep tonight? Is the excuse for that bruise acceptable or should I further investigate? When a third grader says, "I want to kill my stupid teacher," is this a serious threat, a cry for help, or both? I didn't realize I would have to meet basic needs of my students before I could teach them. And it's not that I work in an inner city school or low-income area. While it is true that the school in which I work is schoolwide Title 1, meaning over 40% of our students live at or below the poverty level, these same concerns are in every school. Once you are able to move past all this and actually teach, that's where it all becomes worthwhile.

I will never be able to accomplish in a day what I need to accomplish, and I had to learn to balance my life with my career. I make a conscious effort to turn the teacher off when I go home and try my hardest to go home on time. I have worked very hard to set boundaries and to learn how to let go—something many teachers struggle with—and I am a better teacher and a happier person because of it.

What keeps me going through all the paperwork and meetings and state standards and student issues is that flash of understanding I see in a student's eyes when they finally "get it." It is the note from my most behaviorally challenged student that says, "You're the best teacher ever." It is knowing that I am making a difference in a child's life, and that I am helping to shape the future.

## Summary

In this chapter, four organizing questions were presented to help you better understand the social issues affecting students and learning:

### What are the key socializing agents influencing students?

Five key socializing agents were presented as having a major impact on student development:

- The family (Praxis II, topic Ia)
- Peer group (Praxis II, topic Ia)
- Television (Praxis II, topic Ia)
- Religion (Praxis II, topic Ia)
- Schools (Praxis II, topic Ia)

### Are there social issues that affect student behavior?

A variety of social issues influence student learning and development:

- The changing family (Praxis II, topic Ia)
- Poverty (Praxis II, topic Ia)
- Teen pregnancy (Praxis II, topic Ia)
- Acquired immunodeficiency syndrome (AIDS)
- Child abuse and neglect (Praxis II, topic Ia)
- Alcohol and drugs (Praxis II, topic Ia)
- Suicide (Praxis II, topic Ia)
- Violence (Praxis II, topic Ia)
- School dropouts

### How should teachers and schools respond to social issues?

Both teachers and schools have responsibilities in responding to societal influences on students:

- Your response as a future teacher (Praxis II, topic IVa)
- The school's response to social issues (Praxis II, topic IVb)

### How does society influence schooling?

Society influences schooling in two major ways:

- Determining purposes (Praxis II, topic Ib)
- Establishing values (Praxis II, topic IVb)

## Key Terms

AIDS
alcohol and drug awareness programs
alternative education programs
child neglect
cultural melting pot
cultural pluralism
emotional abuse
gang activity

peer group
physical abuse
poverty
sex education programs
sexual abuse
society
violence prevention programs

## Reflective Journey: Online Journal

Use the questions for thought and reflection highlighted throughout the chapter to help guide your personal journey of reflection and professional development as a teacher. To complete your journal entries online, go to the *Reflective Journey* module for this chapter of the Companion Website.

## Test Preparation Activities

To review an online chapter case study, test your understanding of chapter topics and concepts, and begin preparing for the Praxis II: Principles of Learning and Teaching examination, go to the *Praxis Test Preparation* module for this chapter of the Companion Website.

## Becoming a Reflective Practitioner

To complete these activities and submit your responses online, go to the *Becoming a Reflective Practitioner* module for this chapter of the Companion Website.

### What are the key socializing agents influencing students?

**Review Questions**

1. How does family life influence the students you will teach?
2. In what ways does television affect students?
3. What are the roles of schools in socializing students?

**Field Experience**

Talk to a classroom teacher about the social forces that impact students. What issues are identified and how significantly do they influence student behavior? How does the teacher try to help students with these problems?

**Building Your Portfolio: *Course Work or Seminars That Deal with Social Issues***

**INTASC Standard 2.** Keep a careful record of the courses you take or the seminars you attend that give you more detailed information about the social issues students face. This content knowledge should better prepare you to deal with the many issues your future students will encounter.

### Are there social issues that affect student behavior?

**Review Questions**

1. How does poverty impact students' lives?
2. What are the four main types of child abuse and neglect?
3. What signs might indicate that a student is considering suicide?

**Field Experience**

With the help of a classroom teacher, identify a student who is dealing with a social issue discussed in this chapter. Spend some time observing this student. How does the stress being faced seem to influence performance in class? Also observe this student's social interactions with peers. With the teacher's help, see if you can identify some strategies to help the student work through at least some aspects of the social issue faced.

**Building Your Portfolio:** *Document Experience in Dealing with Social Issues*

**INTASC Standard 2.** Perhaps you have already had experience in your own educational career in helping peers deal with various life stressors. If not, you should have opportunities to do so as you begin working with students. Summarize these experiences for your portfolio.

## How should teachers and schools respond to social issues?

**Review Questions**

1. How can you respond to the social issues you will face as a future teacher?
2. What are some of the ways in which schools are responding to the social issues faced by students?

**Field Experience**

Make an appointment with a school counselor. How does she or he develop good working relationships with students? What types of problems does this person deal with the most in his or her work with students? How are these problems handled? What interactions does the counselor have with regular classroom teachers?

**Building Your Portfolio:** *Identify Key Community Resources*

**INTASC Standard 10.** While you will probably move to a new location to begin your teaching career, knowing the resources available in your current community and summarizing them for your portfolio will demonstrate your ability to find and use these options in your future work with students and families.

## How does society influence schooling?

**Review Questions**

1. Why do the purposes for education, as defined by the larger society, change?
2. Compare and contrast the concepts of *cultural melting pot* and *cultural pluralism*.

**Building Your Portfolio:** *Purposes of Education*

**INTASC Standard 9.** Review the broad purposes of education identified in this chapter. Write a position statement in which you make a case for the relative importance of each of these purposes. Identify which you see as the most important through the least important. Include your statement in your portfolio.

## Suggested Readings

Campbell, D. (2000). *Choosing democracy* (2nd ed.). Upper Saddle River, NJ: Merrill/Prentice Hall. This text discusses several of the social issues discussed in this chapter and includes a separate chapter on the impact of culture on the schools.

Children's Defense Fund. (2002). *The state of children in America's union: A 2002 action guide to leave no child behind.* Washington, DC: Author. U.S. government agencies publish reports on various aspects of children's well-being: health and health care, educational achievement, economic status, family structure, and others. This document organizes this information and provides a complete picture of how children fare in this country.

Cushner, K., McClelland, A., & Safford, P. (2000). *Human diversity in education: An integrative approach* (3rd ed.). New York: McGraw-Hill. This book provides a broad treatment of the various forms of human diversity found in today's schools including nationality, ethnicity, race, religion, gender, class, language, sexual orientation, and ability levels.

# chapter

## Legal Issues

Every day in the classroom teachers are faced with
decisions that have legal implications. To effectively
resolve the many dilemmas they encounter, teachers
need to have a clear understanding of their rights and
responsibilities under the law. Three organizing
questions will be used in this chapter to assist you in
developing your understandings of these aspects of
teaching.

## Focus Questions

◢ What are your legal rights and
responsibilities as a teacher?

◢ Which legal issues will affect your
teaching?

◢ What legal issues impact students?

Janice has just
excused her
sophomore English class
and they are noisily leaving
the room at the end of another
busy day at Lincoln High School. As she
is sorting through the papers on her desk, Janice
notices that Kimberly has remained behind and is shyly approaching her desk. Over the past 3 months, Janice
has been spending extra time working with Kimberly to strengthen her writing skills. The response has been
positive and Kimberly has made significant progress.

As Kimberly approaches, Janice notices tears streaming down Kimberly's face as she glances warily around
to be sure no one else is near. She is unprepared to hear what spills forth as Kimberly shares with her the
troubles she faces. Kimberly tearfully relates her story of being beaten and sexually assaulted by a former
boyfriend following a football game 3 weeks ago. She is fearful of the repercussions if her story is told, but also
worries that she may be pregnant.

After comforting her as best she can, Janice promises to give Kimberly's situation more thought and get
back to her the next day with some possible suggestions. Janice realizes that this is a difficult set of
circumstances that may have legal implications. While maintaining confidentiality, she will need to get some
help from the school counselor and others so that she can assist Kimberly in the best ways possible.

No teacher wants to hear the kind of story outlined above, but at times these and other less sensational social issues present themselves to teachers in the classroom. This chapter was written to assist you in "doing the right thing" both legally and ethically in these and other situations. Your responses will be influenced by the system of state and national laws that address issues related to schooling. **Educational law** creates a framework that teachers must use in determining appropriate and inappropriate behaviors for both themselves and their students.

## What are your legal rights and responsibilities as a teacher?

There are two main sources for the legal guidelines that will have an impact on you as a future teacher: **legislation** and **case law.** Your legal rights and responsibilities (see Table 13.1) are determined in the first instance by either federal or state legislatures empowered to enact laws regarding all aspects of people's lives, including education. In addition, the specific decisions made by federal and state courts on issues relating to education have a major influence on schooling. Referred to as case law, these decisions help schools understand and interpret the educational laws passed by state and federal legislatures.

### Right of Due Process

Legislation and case law have identified many rights that teachers have in their roles as educators. One that is guaranteed to every person, including teachers and students, is the **right to due process** under the law. Basically, due process means that teachers must be treated fairly and that their rights as individuals shall be protected. Both the Fifth and Fourteenth Amendments to our nation's Constitution guarantee every person this right to due process. Various potential situations could arise in which the teacher's right to due process may become an issue. For example, a teacher who discusses creationism as well as evolution as part of the science curriculum and is fired by the school district has the right to due process under the law. Or a nontenured teacher who has received a low performance evaluation by the school principal and is not rehired at the end of the

**TABLE 13.1   Your Legal Rights**

| Right | Legal Foundation | Summary |
|---|---|---|
| Due process | Fifth and Fourteenth Amendments to the U.S. Constitution | Every teacher is guaranteed the right to due process when personnel issues such as nonrenewal of contracts and firing are raised. |
| Nondiscrimination | Civil Rights Act of 1964<br>Section 504 of the Rehabilitation Act of 1990<br>Americans with Disabilities Act of 1990 | Employers cannot discriminate in the hiring of teachers because of race, color, religion, sex, national origin, or disability. |
| Freedom of expression | *Pickering v. Board of Education* (1968) | Freedom to express opinions about actions of administrators and school board when this does not impact the smooth functioning of schools. |
| | *Parducci v. Rutland* (1970) | Right of teachers to speak freely about the subjects they teach (academic freedom). |

**Figure 13.1**   Ensuring Due Process

To ensure due process, teachers must be given:
1. Notification of the charges
2. An opportunity for a hearing
3. Time to prepare a response to the charges
4. The names of witnesses and time to review the evidence
5. An impartial hearing
6. The option of being represented by an attorney
7. The chance to provide their own evidence and to cross-examine witnesses
8. A summary of the procedures and results of the hearing
9. The right to appeal any decisions of the hearing

*Source: Public School Law: Teachers' and Students' Rights,* 4th ed., by M. McCarthy, N. Cambron-McCabe, and S. Thomas, 1998, Boston: Allyn and Bacon.

academic year also can expect the opportunity for due process. A final example in which due process can be expected would be an openly gay teacher being asked to resign his position because of sexual orientation. Figure 13.1 lists some of the elements required to ensure due process.

## Right to Nondiscrimination

Another broad right guaranteed to teachers is the **right to nondiscrimination** in employment and retention. The Civil Rights Act of 1964 protects teachers and others from discrimination when it states:

> It shall be an unlawful employment practice for an employer (1) to fail or refuse to hire or to discharge any individual, or otherwise to discriminate against any individual with respect to his compensation, terms, conditions, or privileges of employment, because of such individual's race, color, religion, sex, or national origin; or (2) to limit, segregate, or classify his employees or applicants for employment in any way which would deprive or tend to deprive any individual of employment opportunities or otherwise adversely affect his status as an employee, because of such individual's race, color, religion, sex, or national origin.

Section 504 of the Rehabilitation Act of 1973 and the Americans with Disabilities Act of 1990 extend the legal mandate against discrimination in hiring and retention to individuals with disabilities.

Although these laws have greatly reduced discrimination in the areas defined by law, other potentially discriminatory practices are less well protected. An example of this latter type is discrimination against openly homosexual or bisexual teachers. In Washington State, for example, a high school teacher who admitted being homosexual to the school's assistant principal was dismissed from his teaching position. Upon appeal, the court upheld this dismissal on the grounds that the teacher's presence would interfere with the smooth operation of the school (*Gaylord v. Tacoma School District No. 10,* 1977). Other courts, however, have overruled the firing of homosexual and bisexual teachers when no laws have been broken and sexual conduct has remained private (Fischer, Schimmel, & Kelly, 2003).

## Right to Freedom of Expression

On the issue of **freedom of expression,** teachers find themselves struggling to balance their individual right to freedom of speech and writing with the impact that these communications may have on the smooth functioning of the school. While the U.S. Constitution guarantees individuals freedom of expression, it is important that teachers realize they cannot simply say or write anything they wish in the school environment. Up until the last three decades of the 20th century, teachers who openly criticized their administrators or school board members would likely find themselves

## Affirmative Action Policies

Until the passage of the Civil Rights Act of 1964, legal barriers and the actions of many people in positions of power prevented qualified minority candidates from entering colleges and universities and later securing good jobs. Although this act prohibited these discriminatory practices, many believed that this wasn't enough. They felt that affirmative (proactive) actions were needed to make up for the inequities of the past. From the mid-1960s until very recently, a variety of affirmative action policies have been used in an attempt to increase the number of minority students on college campuses.

Although some view these policies as unfair because they give preferential treatment to minority students, others see them as an important step needed to correct past problems. Arguments for both sides have been made to the U.S. Supreme Court on different occasions. In 1978 (*Regents of the University of California v. Bakke*), the justices struck down strict racial quotas for college and university admissions, but left intact the option of using race as a factor in admis-

sions. More recently, the Supreme Court again heard arguments on whether race can be one of several factors used in making college admissions decisions (Walsh, 2003).

Because some people believe that affirmative action policies are themselves discriminatory, some alternatives to traditional affirmative action policies are being tried. For example, in the state of Texas, high school students can guarantee themselves a spot in any state university by having a high school ranking in the top 10% (Cavanagh, 2003). This plan is heralded by many as a colorblind admissions standard that still provides opportunities for students from low-income and less prestigious high schools to have ready access to a quality public education. Other race-neutral approaches that are being implemented "seek to improve the educational performance of our nation's students, particularly those who attend traditionally low performing schools, to such an extent that the admissions process will naturally produce a diverse student body" (U.S. Department of Education, 2003, p. 8).

### Explore and Reflect

Learn more about affirmative action by reading the online source articles by Walsh (2003), Cavanagh (2003), and the U.S. Department of Education (2003) and reviewing other resources provided in the *Reflect on Diversity* module for Chapter 13 of the Companion Website.

1. Where do you stand on affirmative action policies for admission to colleges and universities? Should race be considered as a factor for admissions?

2. Are there affirmative action policies in place at your college or university for admission into teacher education? What is the policy and how do you feel about it? If a policy exists, do you think it is helping to increase the number of minority teacher candidates?

 *To explore this topic further and submit your responses online, go to the Reflect on Diversity module for Chapter 13 of the Companion Website for this text.*

*Sources:* "Supreme Court Hears Arguments in Key Affirmative Action Case" by M. Walsh, *Education Week*, April 1, 2003, p. 29; *Regents of the University of California v. Bakke*, 438 U.S. 265 (1978); "Affirmative Action: Texas Alternative Gets Mixed Reviews" by S. Cavanagh, *Education Week*, March 26, 2003, pp. 1, 14, 15; "Race-Neutral Alternatives in Postsecondary Education: Innovative Approaches to Diversity" by U.S. Department of Education, 2003. Retrieved April 22, 2003, from http://www.ed.gov/ocr/raceneutralreport.html

dismissed without any opportunity for recourse. An important court case in the late 1960s, however, helped give teachers greater freedom of expression. Marvin Pickering, a high school teacher in Illinois, was fired from his teaching position after a letter he wrote was published in the local newspaper criticizing several actions of the superintendent and members of the school board. Pickering appealed his dismissal, and the U.S. Supreme Court eventually forced the school district to reinstate him and pay his back salary. The court ruled that teachers do have the right as members of American society to be publicly critical of school concerns as long as it doesn't impact the smooth functioning of the schools (*Pickering v. Board of Education*, 1968; *Stroman v. Colleton County School District*, 1992). Table 13.2 lists the *Pickering* case and others that have dealt with freedom of expression.

## TABLE 13.2   Freedom of Expression

| Type | Legal Basis | Description |
|---|---|---|
| Freedom of speech | *Pickering v. Board of Education* (1968) | Teachers have the right to be publicly critical of schools as long as they do not disrupt the smooth functioning of the schools. |
| Freedom of symbolic expression | *Guzick v. Debras* (1971) | Posters, buttons worn on clothing, and styles of clothing that express specific opinions about societal issues are allowed as long as they do not significantly disrupt schooling. |
| Academic freedom | *Parducci v. Rutland* (1970) *Cary v. Board of Education* (1979) | Teachers may speak freely about the subjects they teach and select materials and methods they feel are appropriate as long as their activity does not disrupt school functioning or conflict with district or government policy. |

# EDUCATION IN THE NEWS

## Transgender Teacher

David Warfield, a devoted father, devoted son, loving husband, sports fan, and enthusiastic outdoorsman, was an award-winning teacher. Tormented for years knowing something was wrong, trying to fit himself to the "boy" he was, David finally realized in psychotherapy that he really wasn't that "boy" he was. Deciding to make the transition to being a woman was not easy for David. His family supported him as he became Dana; however, at least four families in the school where she wished to return to teach and the school board felt she was unfit to return to the classroom. She continued with the process to make the change, losing her job in the meantime. Dana, along with many of her students and peers, believe that an excellent teacher is lost to the many students who would have reaped the benefits of her teaching.

### Critical Thinking Questions

1. What do you think were some of the specific reasons or concerns that caused the board of education to decide they would not allow Dana to return to the classroom? Do you agree or disagree with their decision? Why or why not?

2. Many school district policies do not allow the teaching of sex education in the classroom without parental consent. Do you agree or disagree with this? Knowing that most districts have policies like these, how will you handle the questions that arise from the very youngest students (How/where do the baby kittens come out of the mom?) to the older ones (How does Viagra actually affect the male body during sex?)?

3. Think back to the teachers you have had in school. How much did you know about the teacher's "real" lives? How much of a teacher's life is commonly known by the students and families in that teacher's classroom? How much do you feel should be known?

 *To explore this topic further and to submit your responses online, go to the Education in the News module for Chapter 13 of the Companion Website.*

*Wearing campaign buttons is one form of freedom of expression.*

**Symbolic expression.** In addition to freedom of speech and writing, it is important for you to be aware of teachers' rights and limits regarding **symbolic expression.** Such things as posters displayed in rooms, buttons worn on clothing to express specific opinions about societal issues, and styles of clothing worn in school settings are all examples of symbolic expression. In general, the courts have supported both teachers and students in their freedom of symbolic self-expression. The exceptions are in situations in which these expressions are sexually suggestive, encourage drug use, or defame a particular group of people (Fischer et al., 2003). For example, it would be inappropriate for a teacher or student to wear a T-shirt emblazoned with the message "Co-Ed Naked Band: Do It with Rhythm" because of its sexual theme.

**Academic freedom.** Another form of freedom of expression is referred to as **academic freedom.** This includes:

> the right of teachers to speak freely about their subjects, to experiment with new ideas, and to select appropriate teaching materials and methods. Courts have held that academic freedom is based on the First Amendment and is fundamental to our democratic society. It protects a teacher's right to evaluate and criticize existing values and practices in order to allow for political, social, economic, and scientific progress. (Fischer et al., 2003, p. 168)

In *Parducci v. Rutland* (1970), for example, a teacher was fired for presenting her eleventh-grade class with course content that included a satire by Kurt Vonnegut, Jr., titled "Welcome to the Monkey House." The principal and associate superintendent determined that the story encouraged promiscuous sexual activity and the killing of the elderly to make room for younger generations. When the teacher appealed her dismissal to a federal court, she was reinstated when the judge hearing the case decided that the content of the satire did not significantly interfere with school discipline or morale and that the school administration had infringed on the teacher's academic freedom in choosing curricular content.

At the same time, however, the teacher's right to academic freedom must be balanced against other factors within the school and district. For example, if a school board has approved or prohibited a list of books for use in the classroom, teachers must use this list to select materials for instruction. In *Cary v. Board of Education* (1979), for example, a Colorado school board banned 10 books from a list being used by high school teachers in their literature courses. While the teachers felt that this violated their academic freedom, the court disagreed. Teachers were told they could mention the banned books and discuss them briefly in class, but the school board had the right to select and ban the use of specific books from the school district curriculum.

Take a moment to reflect on the issue of freedom of expression. Are you the type of person who feels strongly about your right to express yourself in whatever ways you feel are appropriate? Do you think that you will find it difficult to accept the decisions that will be made by your school board that influence your freedom of expression? How will you deal with these issues in your future teaching career?

**Reflective Journey 13.1**

## Avoiding Liability Due to Negligence or Malpractice

Along with the broad legal rights described above come significant responsibilities that teachers need to accept as part of their teaching role (see Table 13.3). One such responsibility is avoiding liability due to negligence or malpractice. **Negligence** occurs when a teacher fails to do what a reasonable and careful person would have done in the same circumstances. For example, Margaret Sheehan, an eighth-grade student, was injured on the playground when her teacher left the class unattended for a few moments and a rock tossed by one of a group of boys struck her in the eye and caused serious injury (*Sheehan v. St. Peter's Catholic Church,* 1971). The court found the teacher guilty of negligence because a reasonable person in similar circumstances would have realized that there was a significant potential for student injury and would not have left the students unattended. While teachers cannot be expected to anticipate and prevent all injuries to their students, they are responsible for taking reasonable care to avoid potential mental or physical harm to any of their students.

In addition to negligent behavior in and around the classroom, teachers must avoid educational **malpractice.** Just as lawyers and doctors can engage in inappropriate behaviors that are harmful to their clients, educators can also use strategies and options that can be viewed as harmful to their students. For example, the parents of a student who graduated from high school with fifth-grade reading skills sued the school for educational malpractice (*Peter W. v. San Francisco Unified School District,* 1976). While the court supported the school district and denied the claim of educational malpractice, in at least one other case a school was held liable for its inappropriate placement of a student in a special education classroom (*B.M. by Berger v. State of Montana,* 1982).

### TABLE 13.3  Teachers' Legal Responsibilities

| Responsibility | Legal Foundation | Summary |
|---|---|---|
| Avoiding liability due to negligence or malpractice | *Sheehan v. St. Peter's Catholic Church* (1971) | Teachers are negligent when they fail to do what a reasonable person would have done in the same circumstances and students are injured. |
| | *B.M. by Berger v. State of Montana* (1982) | Teachers and schools engage in malpractice when students are inappropriately placed in special education classes. |
| Reporting child abuse and neglect | Child Abuse Prevention and Treatment Act of 1974 Legal mandates from each of the 50 states | Teachers are required to report suspected cases of child abuse or neglect. |
| | *McDonald v. State of Oregon* (1985) | Teachers cannot be sued for libel when they act in good faith to report suspected abuse or neglect. |
| Observing copyright laws | Copyright Act of 1976 | Teachers can make one copy of materials for personal use in preparing for instruction, but must limit the copies they provide to students in their classes. |

## Reporting Child Abuse and Neglect

Teachers are also legally responsible for reporting any suspected cases of **child abuse** and **neglect** to the proper authorities. While this problem is ageless, educators began to consistently address the issue when the federal government passed the Child Abuse Prevention and Treatment Act (PL 93-147) in 1974. This law provided financial assistance to states for the creation of programs focusing on the prevention of child abuse. All 50 states have since created their own legal mandates that require teachers to report abuse or suspected cases of abuse (Kelly, 1998). Failure to do so can result in criminal charges of negligence, make the teacher and/or school liable for damages, and may result in a prison term or disciplinary actions by the local school board.

**Reflective Journey 13.2**

Reflect for a moment on your reactions to child abuse and neglect. If you were to suspect that a student in your class was being subjected to abuse or neglect, would you willingly report it? How do you think you would feel toward the abusing adult or family member? Could you remain professional in your interactions with both the student and the abuser?

## Observing Copyright Laws

Another significant legal responsibility that teachers must face is the observance of **copyright laws.** These laws protect authors' intellectual work from unfair use by others that may result in a loss of income. On a daily basis, most teachers use copyrighted materials in a variety of forms and need to be aware of what constitutes **fair use** of these items. The most common area in which copyright laws affect teachers is in the making of photocopies of books or magazines for instructional use. In addition, videotapes, computer software, and materials published on the Internet are also subject to copyright restrictions.

Good teachers are always on the lookout for new materials to use in the classroom. As they read poignant stories, humorous anecdotes, and exciting new information on topics of interest to their students, there is a strong temptation to photocopy the material and share it with them. Although this is an admirable quality, you must temper this inclination with a clear understanding of fair use based on copyright law. The basic federal legislation dealing with this issue is the Copyright Act, first enacted in 1906 and later updated in 1976. This act and other more recent guidelines state that teachers can make one copy of a book chapter, an article from a magazine or newspaper, short stories, and poems when this copy is to be used for the teacher's own personal use in preparing for instruction. Specific guidelines are also in place for the fair use of copyrighted materials in classes (see Table 13.4).

### TABLE 13.4   Photocopying Copyrighted Materials for Classes

| Item | Length |
| --- | --- |
| Complete poem | If less than 250 words |
| Excerpt from longer poem | Excerpt must be less than 250 words |
| Complete article, story, or essay | If less than 2,500 words |
| Longer article, story, essay, or book | Excerpt must be less than 1,000 words |
| Chart, diagram, or cartoon | No more than one from a book or magazine |

*Source: Teachers and the Law,* 6th ed., by L. Fischer, D. Schimmel, and C. Kelly, 2003, New York: Longman.

# Which legal issues will affect your teaching?

The broad legal rights and responsibilities described above help define the ways in which you will teach. In addition, many school-related concerns have been resolved through the courts that will impact your work in the classroom. These legal matters frequently guide what you can and cannot do in your interactions with students, colleagues, and others. In this section, you will learn about several of these legal issues and the impact they are going to have on your life as a teacher.

## Certification, Contracts, and Tenure

State laws and court cases have much to say about who can be hired to teach in public school classrooms and what must be done to maintain a contract with a school district. Every state has defined these issues in slightly different ways, so certification issues, teaching contracts, and tenure decisions are all important legal concerns that you should understand before committing to a long-term program of teacher preparation.

**Certification.** Lupe Perez has just finished her sophomore year at her local university and is interested in completing the teacher certification program there and becoming a fifth-grade teacher. She is surprised to learn of the many requirements that must be met before being admitted and the breadth of course work that students complete for teacher certification. What Lupe may not know is that the initial teacher certification program is in large part determined by the state in which she lives and varies little from one college or university to the next. Every state has developed a set of legally binding criteria that students must meet before being certified to teach all subjects in an elementary classroom or specialized subjects such as mathematics or English at the middle school and high school levels. (Table 13.5 shows a sample set of certification requirements.) These state ex-

| TABLE 13.5 | Wisconsin Elementary Teacher Certification Requirements, Grades 1–6 |
|---|---|
| **Category** | **Description** |
| All teacher education candidates | 1. Three semester credits in special education<br>2. Preparation in human relations<br>3. Preparation in working with children at risk<br>4. Study of the history, philosophy, and social foundations of education<br>5. Course work addressing legal, political, economic, and governmental foundations of education<br>6. Study of gifted and talented students<br>7. Preparation in conflict resolution |
| Elementary education candidates | 1. At least 12 semester credits of course work in teaching reading and the language arts<br>2. At least 12 semester credits in teaching mathematics, social studies, and science education<br>3. Course work in environmental education<br>4. Course work in educational psychology or the psychology of learning<br>5. Study in the methods of teaching<br>6. Student teaching<br>7. A minor approved by the state superintendent of instruction |

*Source: Teacher Education and Licensing,* by Wisconsin Department of Public Instruction, 2001. Retrieved April 21, 2003, from http://www.dpi.state.wi.us

| TABLE 13.6 | The Praxis Series Exams |
|---|---|
| **Exam** | **Description** |
| Praxis I | Approximately 70% of the states currently require teacher education students to take a basic skills test like the Praxis I as a requirement for entrance into teacher education. The Praxis I measures basic reading, writing, and mathematics skills. These assessments are available in either a paper-based or computer-based format. |
| Praxis II | States that use the Praxis II exam typically use it as an exit examination. When students have completed their college course work and are preparing to enter the profession, this exam measures their knowledge of the subjects they will teach, principles of teaching, and how students learn. |

pectations continue to expand as the teaching role itself grows increasingly more complex. For example, a test of basic academic skills is often used as one factor in determining who can enter teacher education programs. A second test used to measure an understanding of the subjects being taught and knowledge of students, learning, and teaching is more frequently being required of students completing their certification programs. The Praxis I exam is frequently being used as a test of basic skills, and the Praxis II is a common exam of the latter type (Educational Testing Service, 2002) (see Table 13.6).

In addition to initial teacher certification, many states also require teachers to take more course work or engage in further professional development before they receive a permanent teaching credential. For example, the state of Washington now requires new teachers to complete 15 credits of additional course work beyond their initial teaching certificate. The purpose of this experience is to plan for and complete an individualized professional growth plan designed to assist them in gaining the skills and knowledge needed to be a professional educator (Washington Office of the Superintendent for Public Instruction, 2002).

**Teaching contracts.** When you seek employment in a school or district, you will be interviewed and initially selected by personnel within the schools. Ultimately, however, local school boards have been given the legal responsibility for hiring new teachers. Because they are the final authority in determining who should receive a contract, these school officials must be careful to avoid violating individual teachers' rights of nondiscrimination described above (Fischer et al., 2003).

In general, school boards typically issue one of two types of contracts to teachers: term contracts and tenure contracts (McCarthy, Cambron-McCabe, & Thomas, 1998). **Term teaching contracts** are good for a fixed period of time, usually one academic year. At the end of the contract term, the school board can either issue a new contract or decide to end contractual arrangements with the teacher. New teachers are almost always hired on a term contract until such time as they have met the requirements for a more permanent one. This permanent contract is referred to as a **tenure contract** and can only be terminated when the school board can provide evidence that there has been a serious breach of professional conduct. Teachers whose tenure contracts are ended must be granted a fair hearing regarding the charges against them to protect their rights to due process.

**Tenure.** When you begin your career as a teacher, you will be given a term contract good for one academic year and renewable at the discretion of the school board. During this time, you will be observed and evaluated regarding your teaching effectiveness. While every attempt will be made to ensure your future success, you are viewed at this point as a probationary employee and as such you will need to prove yourself to fellow teachers and administrators. This probationary period varies between states and districts, but typically extends from 1 to 3 years. Once you are granted **tenure** and receive a permanent contract, you are fully launched into your teaching career. At this point, a teacher can expect a continuing commitment from the school district for employment. Being tenured gives teachers more flexibility to express their feelings on important issues and to teach in ways they feel are most appropriate for student learning without fear of reprisal from others who may disagree. Although there are clearly limits to this freedom, tenure allows more autonomous and creative teaching to take place.

Teacher tenure definitely has benefits, but many have criticized its effectiveness. The primary concern frequently voiced is that tenure makes it very difficult to remove poor teachers from the classroom. Take, for example, Matt LeBlanc. He has taught social studies at the middle school and high school levels for the past 7 years. He did an adequate job during his probationary period, but he has now taken a position as a part-time financial consultant and spends very little time preparing for his classes and participates only minimally in the life of the school. Matt gives few assignments and does a very cursory job in his grading to save time for his part-time position. He seems to be marking time until he can build up his consulting job to the point where he can quit teaching. Students have complained to the administration, but as a tenured teacher, Matt is protected from having his contract terminated because it would be difficult to dismiss him with good cause.

Take a moment now to reflect on teacher tenure. Is tenure a concept you find attractive or do you think of it as an unnecessary facet of teaching? Do you think you will use teacher tenure in the positive ways for which it is intended? How will you feel if you have to work with a tenured teacher who is abusing the system and not really giving his or her all to the profession?

**Reflective Journey 13.3**

## Unions, Collective Bargaining, and Strikes

Beginning in the latter part of the 20th century, teachers have increasingly organized into unions for the purpose of collectively seeking better working conditions and improved professional development (see Chapter 5 for more details). One important task these teacher unions perform for many educators is to engage in **collective bargaining.** In approximately two thirds of the states, legislation has been passed to allow unions to negotiate with school districts regarding salary and benefits for their teachers (Fischer et al., 2003). Table 13.7 shows an example of one such union and how it benefits teachers. Working together with union officials, teachers in these states have engaged in collective bargaining efforts leading to improved salary and benefit packages.

| TABLE 13.7 | What Does the National Education Association Do? |
|---|---|
| **Level** | **Actions** |
| Local | Conducts professional workshops. <br> Supports collective bargaining and strike efforts (where legal). |
| State | Lobbies legislators for school resources. <br> Campaigns for higher professional standards for teaching. <br> Files legal actions to protect academic freedom. |
| National | Coordinates innovative projects in education. <br> Fights or supports congressional efforts related to education. |

*Source: National Education Association Frequently Asked Questions,* by National Education Association, 2001. Retrieved September 10, 2001, from http://www.nea.org/aboutnea/faq.html

*Striking teachers make a strong political statement.*

In about half the states, laws have been passed that allow teachers a limited opportunity to **strike.** In these states, when good-faith negotiations between the union and school district do not lead to an agreement on salary and benefits, teachers are allowed to protest by engaging in a work stoppage until a contract agreement has been reached (Fischer et al., 2003). In many states that do not allow teachers to strike, the law defines specific penalties that can be imposed if teachers engage in an illegal strike. It should be clear that it is important to understand the laws regarding collective bargaining and strikes for the state in which you plan to teach.

### Corporal Punishment

**Corporal punishment** or spanking has been a traditional method of discipline in schools throughout much of American history. Despite its past usage, spanking has become a very controversial issue, with some claiming that it is a form of child abuse and others suggesting that it is an effective discipline strategy when used appropriately. During the last several decades, many states have passed laws to ban this approach. In 1971 one state had banned its use. By the year 2000, that number had grown to 27 (Riak, 2000) (see Figure 13.2). Although many individual court cases have clearly identified teachers and administrators that have used excessive force in the administration of corporal punishment, the U.S. Supreme Court has ruled that it does not violate a student's constitutional rights (*Ingraham v. Wright*, 1977).

Those opposing corporal punishment have been lobbying state governments for many years to have it abolished. Their rationale is that more recent innovations in discipline are superior in the results they receive and provide better models of how we should interact with one another. Despite a concerted effort on the part of many individuals and groups, the list of states in which corporal punishment is banned has grown slowly over time. The support of groups such as the National Education Association, the American Medical Association, the American Academy of Pediatrics, and the National PTA has failed to motivate the school districts and states that still use spanking as a form of discipline to abolish its use in the classroom.

**Reflective Journey 13.4**

What are your thoughts on corporal punishment? Take a few moments to reflect on the issues surrounding this topic. If it is legal in your state to use corporal punishment, do you see yourself doing so? If it is banned in your state, do you think this is a mistake? What do you see as the possible strengths and limitations of corporal punishment?

### Sexual Harassment

Under Title VII of the 1964 Civil Rights act, both students and teachers are protected against sexual harassment and a hostile work environment. **Sexual harassment** has been defined as "repeated and unwelcomed sexual advances, derogatory statements based on . . . sex, or sexually demeaning gestures or acts" (Nolan, 1982, p. 227). A **hostile work environment** exists when "abusive language, physical aggression, and other demeaning behavior" repeatedly occurs in the work place (McCarthy et al., 1998, p. 346). It is important to know that sexual harassment and hostile work environments do exist in school settings. Although not a common occurrence, the day-to-day interactions of school staff may lead to either of these two conditions. Teachers need to know their legal rights and take steps to eliminate these problem behaviors.

**Figure 13.2**    Corporal Punishment

☐ States that allow corporal punishment

■ States in which more than half of the students are in districts with no corporal punishment

☐ States that have banned corporal punishment

*Source: Facts About Corporal Punishment,* by National Coalition for Abolishing Corporal Punishment in the Schools, 2002. Retrieved October 18, 2002, from http://www.stophitting.com/disatschool/ facts.php#U.S.%20States%20Banning%20Corporal%20Punishment

## Religion and Schooling

Until the latter half of the 20th century, religious experiences such as Bible readings and prayer were a common part of school life. During the last several decades, however, the relationship between religious experiences and schooling has become one of the most controversial issues facing teachers and schools. Many people believe that religious experiences and even intellectual discussions about religion have no place in the schools. Those taking this position feel, for example, that prayer in schools, teaching creationism, singing Christmas carols, and celebrating religious holidays should be excluded. This viewpoint is often labeled as **secular humanism.** At the other end of the continuum, those with strong religious beliefs often feel that when all references to religion are eliminated an antireligious bias is created that in some ways becomes its own religion/philosophy. Those taking this position feel that such things as prayer in schools ought to be allowed on a voluntary basis and schools should provide space in their buildings for religious clubs that meet before and after the school day. Table 13.8 lists some of the important religion and schooling issues and their related court cases.

## Schooling Choices

During the last decade of the 20th century, a nationwide effort to give parents and students more options for schooling gained momentum. State and federal legislation has allowed three options

| TABLE 13.8 | Religion and Schooling | |
|---|---|---|
| **Issue** | **Legal Foundation** | **Summary** |
| Separation of church and state | First Amendment, U.S. Constitution | Laws cannot promote or prohibit religious expression. |
| School-sponsored prayer and Bible study | *Engel v. Vitale* (1962) | Schools may not sponsor prayer or Bible study because of students' First Amendment rights. |
| Prayer at public school functions | *Lee v. Weisman* (1992) | Prayer at public school functions is unconstitutional. |
| Religious clubs | *Board of Education of Westside Community Schools v. Mergens* (1990) | Religious clubs can have access to school buildings when other non-curriculum-related student groups are also allowed space. |

to emerge. **Charter schools** "are public schools that have been created under state law but are exempt from many local and state regulations in exchange for greater accountability for student performance" (Holloway, 2001b, p. 81). **Vouchers** allow parents and students to select schools other than the ones they would normally attend, with the home district transferring to the new school the financial allotment from the state for educating each transferred student. **Home schooling** is an option in which the parents choose to educate their own children in the home environment.

**Charter schools.** Charter schools (see Chapter 4 for more information) have become a relatively popular option in many states. Between 1992 and 2002, the number of states approving legislation that allowed for the development of charter schools grew from 1 to 38 and the number of schools operating with charters has grow to 2,500 (Nathan, 2002). Although these growing numbers are impressive, results on the movement are still unclear. The evidence so far would indicate that most students, parents, and teachers who participate in charter schools are generally pleased with the option (Manno & Finn, 1998). The research on student academic performance in charter schools has been less conclusive, however, with most studies finding little difference between charter schools and other public schools (National School Board Association, 2000).

**Vouchers.** The idea of school vouchers has been around since at least the 1950s. At that time, economist Milton Friedman proposed that competition among public schools would have a positive impact on school quality and student performance. He reasoned that if the public schools were more like the free-market system in place for business, teachers would rise to the challenges and provide better instruction and students would consequently engage in higher levels of learning. Friedman advocated for vouchers that parents could use to pay for tuition at the schools of their choice (Latham, 1998). In spite of the efforts of Friedman and many other more recent proponents such as former President Bill Clinton, voucher programs have been considerably more controversial than the charter school movement. Consequently, only Florida has thus far passed legislation providing for a statewide voucher system (Sandham, 1999). Others such as Texas, New Mexico, Washington, California, Colorado, and Pennsylvania have debated the possibility of voucher plans, but thus far have not passed legislation enabling their creation.

# School Vouchers

Considerable controversy surrounds the use of vouchers as a method of giving parents and their children choices in the schools attended. Those who support voucher plans see them as a means of returning to families the tax monies authorized for each student and allowing the family to "spend" this allotment for tuition at public and private schools of their choice. They believe that parents, given this ability to choose, would seek out the best schools for their children and support them financially with their vouchers. These schools would in turn attract the best teachers by rewarding them both financially and by creating even stronger environments for teaching and learning. By having schools compete for voucher money, the best schools would become stronger, while the weak would either be required to improve or close their doors. Voucher proponents also see it as a way to equalize educational opportunities for low-income families. Vouchers would give these families the financial ability to choose the best schools for their children while continuing to meet other basic family needs. Kevin Walthers (2001) summarizes what he sees as the benefits of voucher programs when he states: "By implementing a true choice plan, educators would elevate the stature of their field, allow for specialized, relevant academic standards, and intimately involve parents in the education of their children" (p. 199).

Those who oppose school choice through vouchers have equally strong opinions about the problems associated with such a plan. They suggest that the free-market system in business and what could be created in education with the use of vouchers are worlds apart. Money and the profit motive in business are very different from the motivations associated with education: "But money is not the primary motivator in education. Motivations come in soft packages: Self-satisfaction? Seeing your students succeed? Intellectual stimulation? Indeed, a principle motivation that undergirds 'choice' is fear, the threat of losing students. And students may be lost whether or not you are delivering the 'best' educational product you can deliver" (Lewis, 2001, p. 203).

Another argument often cited against school vouchers concerns the support of private schools with public money. Because many of these schools have a religious affiliation, the legality and "rightness" of this move has been questioned. In a recent Supreme Court case, however, the court ruled that "publicly financed tuition vouchers to be used at religious schools does not violate the First Amendment's prohibition against a government establishment of religion. The 5–4 ruling, which upheld the state-enacted voucher program in Cleveland, was a landmark victory for the private-school-choice movement" (*Education Week*, 2002, p. 43).

## Research the Issue

Research this topic online using the links provided in the *Engage in the Debate* module for this chapter of the Companion Website. Link to the online *Education Week* (2002) source article and explore the information provided at the additional sites listed.

1. From the research you conducted, what do you see as the benefits of school vouchers?
2. What have others indicated are the problems associated with vouchers?

## Explore Your Views

1. Do you think vouchers should be used to fund student tuition at private, religious schools?
2. Do you think states and local school districts should be promoting the use of school vouchers? Why or why not?

 *To research this issue and submit your responses online, go to the Engage in the Debate module for Chapter 13 of the Companion Website for this text.*

*Sources:* "Saying No to Vouchers: What Is the Price of Democracy?" by J. Lewis. In J. Noll (Ed.), *Taking Sides: Clashing Views on Controversial Educational Issues*, 11th ed., 2001, Guilford, CT: Dushkin/McGraw-Hill; "Saying Yes to Vouchers: Perception, Choice, and the Educational Response," by K. Walthers. In J. Noll (Ed.), *Taking Sides: Clashing Views on Controversial Educational Issues*, 11th ed., 2001, Guilford, CT: Dushkin/McGraw-Hill; "Education and the Supreme Court: The 2001–2002 Term," *Education Week*, July 10, 2002, p. 43.

**Home schooling.** The issue of religion in the schools (or lack thereof) is one of the four main reasons often cited for the growth of the home schooling movement. Although the percentage of parents participating in this option is still small, home schooling has grown in acceptance and popularity during the last few decades with the number reaching approximately 1.2 to 1.8 million families at the turn of the century (Archer, 1999). While home schooling is now legal in all 50 states, there is considerable variation in the level of regulation. For example, only a handful of states have established minimum academic requirements for parents who home school, while home-schooled students in about half of the states are required to participate in standardized testing (LaMorte, 2002).

There are four statutes regarding home schooling that tend to be common among most states:

- *Equivalent instruction.* Most states emphasize the importance of including subjects and instruction in home schooling that parallel what is done in public school classrooms.
- *Qualified parent instructors.* While few states require parents to be certified, most require that they be qualified to teach the needed subjects.
- *Systematic reporting.* Parents who home school are expected in most states to keep school authorities apprised of what they are doing.
- *Minimum hours of instruction.* Parents and students are expected to engage in a state-mandated minimum hours of teaching/learning experiences each day (Klicka, 1996).

## What legal issues impact students?

Like you, your students will also have important rights guaranteed by law and through decisions reached by various state and federal courts. You will need to understand these legal issues so that you can advocate on behalf of students whose rights are being violated and conduct yourself in ways that promote these rights. The issues of sexual harassment, search and seizure, student records, suspension and expulsion, and freedom of expression are addressed here.

### Sexual Harassment

It has been clear for many years that sexual harassment of students by their teachers or other school staff is morally indefensible and grounds for dismissal. What may not be clear, however, is the extent of the problem among students themselves. In a recent report by the American Association of University Women (2001), students surveyed indicated that the problem is a significant one for both boys and girls. The AAUW reports that harassment by peers can begin as early as the elementary school years, it occurs regularly in virtually all schools, and is upsetting to both boys and girls. In its survey of more than 2,000 students in the 8th through 11th grades, 83% of the girls and 79% of the boys reported having experienced harassment.

Teachers need to address student sexual harassment in two primary ways. First, they need to be aware of the impact of recent court rulings on this issue. In a 1999 U.S. Supreme Court case (*Davis v. Monroe County Board of Education*), it was determined that teachers could be held liable if they failed to implement strategies to end known cases of sexual harassment. It is therefore essential that teachers take the time to work through instances of sexual harassment as they are encountered. Secondly, teachers can work to stamp out harassment by helping students understand the legal and ethical problems with this behavior and suggesting more appropriate ways of interacting with each other. By discussing relevant problems as they occur, teachers can help students break out of this inappropriate and harmful mode of interaction. Table 13.9 suggests some ways in which teachers can respond to situations of sexual harassment among students.

**TABLE 13.9   Responding to Sexual Harassment Among Students**

| Strategy | Description |
|---|---|
| Student education on harassment | This should begin in elementary school, be age appropriate, and describe what constitutes harassment without creating a climate of fear. |
| Antiharassment policy | Every school should have a well-publicized policy that prohibits all forms of verbal and physical harassment. |
| Responding to harassment | Everyone involved (including witnesses) should be given the opportunity to describe the harassment in their own words. The targets should be asked about solutions to the problem. |
| Professional development | Schools should provide regular training to staff in how to deal with harassment. |
| Family involvement | Families should be educated about harassment and their support solicited in dealing with problems as they arise. |

## Search and Seizure

Under the Fourth Amendment to the U.S. Constitution, all of America's citizens are protected from having their personal belongings and spaces examined without a formal search warrant. This protection from **search and seizure** extends to students as well. Searches are only allowed if there is a strong suspicion that an illegal substance or a dangerous object may be present. So, if school officials have a strong reason to believe that students have drugs, alcohol, or dangerous weapons in their locker, desk, or backpack and use reasonable methods of investigating their suspicions, a legal search can be conducted. For example, two girls in a New Jersey high school were caught smoking in the bathroom and taken to the school office. One girl denied that she was smoking, whereupon the assistant vice principal opened her purse and found not only cigarettes, but also marijuana and related paraphernalia (*New Jersey v. T.L.O.,* 1985). The girl filed suit, claiming that the search of her purse violated her rights, but the court disagreed because of the reasonableness of the investigation under the circumstances.

## Student Records

American schools have historically kept all sorts of educational records of student progress. Over the years, the list of items included has grown successively longer. Grades on assignments, test scores, records of discipline problems, psychologists' reports, counseling sessions, results of standardized tests, and attendance records are all examples of the items typically collected. Until the mid-1970s, these records were considered private and neither parents nor students were able to review what was kept in these files. With the passage of the Family Educational Rights

*Searching for drugs can be done without violating student rights.*

## Fairness Requires That All Students Be Treated the Same

There is considerable talk in educational circles today about the importance of equity. That is, all students should have equal opportunities to learn and grow in the classroom. For example, students should have equal access to technology, the same opportunity for a safe classroom environment, and equitable interactions with the classroom teacher. This would seem to imply that all students should be treated the same. But, fairness in interactions with students doesn't always mean that teachers always treat them in identical ways. In many circumstances, treating students fairly means that we need to interact with them in somewhat different ways. Here are some examples of situations in which students are treated fairly, but are not treated exactly the same as other students.

Fatima is a gifted student in Danielle Brown's fifth-grade classroom. She performs at the tenth-grade level in reading. While most of the other students are using the fifth-grade reading text for their reading curriculum, Danielle has developed a separate reading list based on Fatima's interests and ability levels. She is being treated differently in order to meet her academic needs and interests.

Jon is a low-performing student in Max Davis's middle school science classroom. He is doing barely passing work and Max has found it necessary to spend extra time with him during independent work periods. While it seems to be helping Jon grasp the science concepts involved, he is getting more teacher time than some of his more independent peers.

Shawn has chosen the vocational/technical option at his high school and is taking mathematics and science courses that will help prepare him for the technical college he plans to enter next fall. His friend Lateesha, however, is enrolled in precalculus and physics in preparation for her college course work next year. These two students are being treated differently by their school through the curriculum choices they have voluntarily made.

Erik is a second-grade student who has a hard time controlling his anger in Pat Murphy's classroom. Pat has tried several approaches that have worked well with others in the class, but were unsuccessful with Erik. With the input of Erik's parents, a strict behavior management plan has been developed to assist Erik in dealing with his temper.

### React and Reflect

1. Revisit the title statement: "Fairness requires that all students be treated the same." What is your reaction to this statement? In what ways do you think all students should be treated exactly the same? You may want to brainstorm a list of possibilities and then discuss your options with others.

2. For what categories of behavior do you think students should be treated fairly but differently? How will you make decisions about when and how to vary your interactions with students?

3. When you decide to treat students fairly but differently, is it important to communicate this to your students?

 *To explore this topic further and submit your reactions and reflections online, go to the Explore Your Beliefs module for Chapter 13 of the Companion Website for this text.*

and Privacy Act (FRPA) in 1974, this policy was changed. Parents with children under 18 years of age and students themselves who were 18 or older were given access to these records under what has now come to be known as the **Buckley Amendment** (see Table 13.10).

Although this act has clearly benefited both students and their parents, many teachers and administrators have reservations about some aspects of the law. One concern stems from the rights of eligible students and their parents to review letters of recommendation written by faculty and staff. Because they can no longer be considered confidential, many teachers and staff are writing more general and "safe" recommendations, rather than opening themselves up to criti-

| TABLE 13.10    The Buckley Amendment | |
| --- | --- |
| **Feature** | **Description** |
| Written policy | School districts must have a written policy that deals with student records and inform parents annually of their rights under the act. |
| Reviewing student files | School personnel, parents, and eligible students can review their files, but others may not. |
| Challenging contents of files | Procedures are in place for parents and eligible students to challenge the contents of the files. |
| Meeting terms of the act | Parents can contact the Family Right to Privacy Act Office when they feel the school has failed to meet the terms of the act. |

Source: *Teachers and the Law,* 6th ed., by L. Fischer, D. Schimmel, and C. Kelly, 2003, New York: Longman.

cism from parents and students. In similar ways, teachers and school staff may be more guarded in the assessments that end up as part of permanent student records because of parental and student access to these materials.

Have you thought about these issues of student confidentiality? Take a few moments now to reflect on this aspect of your role as a teacher. Do you feel it is important to protect the privacy of student records? In what circumstances would you need to exercise the most care to avoid violating this right? Can you anticipate situations in which this right may get in the way of your efforts to effectively work with students and their families?

**Reflective Journey 13.5**

## Suspension and Expulsion

Not so many years ago, life was simpler in American schools. The serious offenses that led to suspension or expulsion consisted mostly of things like a fistfight in the school parking lot, smoking on school grounds, and swearing at the classroom teacher. During the last three or four decades, however, the level of problems encountered has escalated. Teachers and administrators today must deal with drugs and alcohol in and around the school, incidents of physical attacks on both students and teachers, and dangerous weapons being carried by students or stored in school facilities.

Despite efforts at prevention, problems continue to occur in schools that require teachers and administrators to consider suspension and/or expulsion for students. The most common options used by schools are to remove problem students from regular classes and place them in a special in-school suspension, temporarily remove students from the school for a set number of days (regular suspension), or deny students permanent access to school for an extended period of time (expulsion). In-school suspension is used for the least serious offenses, while expulsion is a last resort when all other options have failed.

Court cases over the years have helped define student and school rights when suspension and expulsion are being considered. In the most serious cases in which longer term suspension or expulsion is being considered, students should receive a written notice specifying the charges and a description of the procedures to be used at the hearing. Furthermore, they should be told what evidence has been collected, the names of any witnesses being called, and know that they can question witnesses and present their own evidence (*Dixon v. Alabama State Board of Education*, 1961).

**TABLE 13.11    Effective Zero-Tolerance Policies**

The following elements are considered necessary for an effective zero-tolerance policy:
- Specify clear consequences for misbehavior, with consistency of application.
- Allow flexibility and consider expulsion alternatives.
- Clearly define what constitutes a weapon, a drug, or an act of misbehavior.
- Comply with state due process laws and allow for student hearings.
- Develop the policy collaboratively with all stake-holding agencies (for example, state departments of education, juvenile justice, and health and human services).
- Learn from the experiences educators have had with zero tolerance in other states, schools, and districts.
- Integrate comprehensive health education programs that include drug and alcohol curricula.
- Tailor the policy to local needs.
- Review the policy each year.

*Source: Zero Tolerance Policies* (ERIC Digest No. 146), by T. McAndrews, 2001. Retrieved April 21, 2003, from http://www.ed.gov/databases/ERIC_Digests/ed451579.html

In a recent attempt to take a firm stance against violence and drug use within the schools, many districts are implementing **zero-tolerance policies** to clarify for students the behaviors that are unacceptable within the schools. Loosely modeled after the strict sentencing laws that have gained popularity within the criminal justice system, zero-tolerance policies for schools clearly state that when students are found with weapons or drugs they face automatic suspension or expulsion (see Table 13.11). Although this attempt by the schools to get tough against violence and drugs has many positive aspects, there have been repeated examples in national and state news in which students have been suspended for rather inconsequential behaviors such as carrying a squirt gun to school or using mouthwash after lunch.

## Freedom of Expression

Freedom of expression is considered an important right available to all Americans. This right has been tested in the courts by students and, while not absolute, is available to them in school settings as well. The classic case defining this right was *Tinker v. Des Moines Independent Community School District* (1969). In 1965, as debate over American involvement in the Vietnam War heated up, several students in Des Moines, Iowa, wore black armbands to school to signify their opposition to the war. Some students refused to remove them even though they knew that the bands were specifically banned by district policy. They were suspended and took their case to the courts. The Supreme Court eventually ruled in favor of the students, stating that they didn't "shed their constitutional rights to freedom of speech or expression at the schoolhouse gate."

At the same time, however, schools can legally limit student expression if there is a reasonable expectation that these communications will be disruptive to life in the schools. For example, a federal appeals court supported a Cleveland high school's rule to ban all buttons and badges because they had led to racial friction between Black and White students (*Guzick v. Debras*, 1971). The evidence presented suggested that an escalation of racial tensions and a deterioration of the educational climate would have occurred if the buttons and badges had been allowed.

# Summary

In this chapter, three organizing questions were presented to help you develop insights about legal issues in education:

## What are your legal rights and responsibilities as a teacher?

State and federal laws and court cases have determined several legal rights and responsibilities for teachers:

- Right of due process (Praxis II, topic IVb)
- Right to nondiscrimination (Praxis II, topic IVb)
- Right to freedom of expression (Praxis II, topic IVb)
- Avoiding liability due to negligence or malpractice (Praxis II, topic IVb)
- Reporting child abuse and neglect (Praxis II, topic IVb)
- Observing copyright laws (Praxis II, topic IVb)

## Which legal issues will affect your teaching?

A number of legal issues will directly impact your role as a teacher:

- Certification, contracts, and tenure (Praxis II, topic IVb)
- Unions, collective bargaining, and strikes (Praxis II, topic IVb)
- Corporal punishment (Praxis II, topic Ic)
- Sexual harassment (Praxis II, topic IVb)
- Religion and schooling (Praxis II, topic IVb)
- Home schooling (Praxis II, topic Ic)

## What legal issues impact students?

Students also have rights and responsibilities under the law, providing protections and opportunities to all:

- Sexual harassment (Praxis II, topic Ic)
- Search and seizure (Praxis II, topic Ic)
- Student records (Praxis II, topic IIc)
- Suspension and expulsion (Praxis II, topic Ic)
- Freedom of expression (Praxis II, topic Ic)

# Key Terms

| | |
|---|---|
| academic freedom | malpractice |
| Buckley Amendment | neglect |
| case law | negligence |
| charter schools | right to due process |
| child abuse | right to nondiscrimination |
| code of professional ethics | search and seizure |
| collective bargaining | secular humanism |
| copyright laws | sexual harassment |
| corporal punishment | strike |
| educational law | symbolic expression |
| fair use | tenure |
| freedom of expression | tenure contract |
| home schooling | term teaching contracts |
| hostile work environment | vouchers |
| legislation | zero-tolerance policies |

## Reflective Journey: Online Journal

 Use the questions for thought and reflection highlighted throughout the chapter to help guide your personal journey of reflection and professional development as a teacher. To complete your journal entries online, go to the *Reflective Journey* module for this chapter of the Companion Website.

**PRAXIS** ## Test Preparation Activities

 To review an online chapter case study, test your understanding of chapter topics and concepts, and begin preparing for the Praxis II: Principles of Learning and Teaching examination, go to the *Praxis Test Preparation* module for this chapter of the Companion Website.

 ## Becoming a Reflective Practitioner

 To complete these activities and submit your responses online, go to the *Becoming a Reflective Practitioner* module for this chapter of the Companion Website.

### What are your legal rights and responsibilities as a teacher?

**Review Questions**
1. What are the two main sources for the legal guidelines that will have an impact on your future teaching?
2. What are the different types of freedom of expression?
3. What can happen to you as a teacher if you fail to report a suspected case of child abuse or neglect?

**Field Experience**
Talk to a classroom teacher of your choice regarding legal issues he or she has either dealt with in the classroom or is concerned about for the future. Summarize your discussion and share it with your peers.

**Building Your Portfolio: *A Teacher's Legal Rights***
**INTASC Standard 10.** Identify a legal right that is of importance to you as a classroom teacher. Spend some time reading about the laws and court cases that are relevant to this issue. Summarize your findings, including the most important court cases, for inclusion in your portfolio.

### Which legal issues will affect your teaching?

**Review Questions**
1. How have requirements for teacher certification changed over time?
2. What is a hostile work environment and how is it related to sexual harassment?
3. How is a charter school different from a more traditional K–12 school?

**Field Experience**
Research the policies for teacher tenure in a school district of your choice. For how many years is a teacher given a term contract? What criteria are used in determining whether or not a teacher should be tenured? What are the strengths and limitations of teacher tenure?

**Building Your Portfolio:** *Signs of Child Abuse and Neglect*

**INTASC Standard 10.** Search for information about indicators of child abuse and neglect. You may choose to contact a school district, mental health agency, or search the Internet for information. Develop a one- or two-page handout for your portfolio that describes symptoms of child abuse and neglect that you should be aware of as a future teacher.

## What legal issues impact students?

### Review Questions

1. Under what circumstances can a school search the personal belongings of students?
2. What issues are addressed by the Buckley Amendment?
3. What is a zero-tolerance policy?

### Field Experience

Talk to a school administrator of your choice and find out the procedures used by the school to address sexual harassment, searching for and dealing with drugs/alcohol/weapons, or suspending students from the school. If there are written policies, ask for a copy. Share your finding with others in your class.

**Building Your Portfolio:** *A Student's Legal Rights*

**INTASC Standard 10.** Choose one of the student's legal rights described in this chapter and spend some time reading about the laws and court cases that are relevant to this issue. Summarize your findings, including the most important court cases, for inclusion in your portfolio.

## Suggested Readings

Fischer, L., Schimmel, D., & Kelly, C. (2003). *Teachers and the law* (6th ed.). New York: Longman. This book provides a well-organized and thorough description of legal issues that are of importance to teachers and their students.

McCarthy, M., Cambron-McCabe, N., & Thomas, S. (1998). *Public school law: Teachers' and students' rights* (4th ed.). Boston: Allyn and Bacon. The authors present a strong overview of legal mandates and court decisions that impact teaching and learning within America's schools.

# chapter 14

## School Governance and Finance

The rules and regulations that impact how schools operate and are funded come from local, state, and federal sources. Knowing how schools are governed and financed will help you be more effective in your future classroom. In this chapter, three organizing questions will be used to strengthen your understanding of school governance and finance.

## Focus Questions

◢ Who sets school directions?

◢ What other groups shape educational policies?

◢ What sources of funds exist for education?

*Katy Carmichael has just returned to her second-grade classroom following a meeting with her school principal. Katy requested new curriculum materials on behalf of the primary teaching team in her school to help students learn mathematics. The Montessori manipulative materials the team wants to purchase are considered by many early childhood educators to be some of the finest available to help students visualize and understand mathematical concepts. Katy and her teaching team feel they would be well worth the nearly $1,000 price tag that comes with their purchase. Her principal has explained, however, that because of the cost, this decision would need to first be reviewed by the school curriculum committee. This group consists of three teachers, the principal, and two parents. If approved by the curriculum committee, the local school board could then be approached for final endorsement prior to purchase. Katy has been asked to write a clear rationale for the purchase of these mathematics materials and include examples of how they would be used in the classroom. If the school board is unwilling or unable to fund these materials, the principal has also indicated that another option for funding could be to write a small grant proposal to a regional business that supports educational efforts in mathematics and science.*

Katy's request for new materials highlights the importance of understanding how schools are run and financed. In many practical ways, a working knowledge of these aspects of schooling helps teachers be more effective in their classrooms. By knowing how decisions are made, teachers can take the steps needed to discuss issues of importance with appropriate governing bodies. An understanding of financial matters helps teachers find funding sources for the innovative ideas they want to implement. So, what may at first appear to be merely an academic exercise becomes important information for conducting business within the schools.

## Who sets school directions?

Schools are governed by a complex array of local, state, and federal laws, regulations, and agencies. At each level, there are numerous people who individually and collectively help determine the directions taken by schools. While every district and state is somewhat different, the information shared here should help you develop a much clearer understanding of the people and organizations that will influence the schools in which you teach.

### Local Control

In the public schools, most of the day-to-day decision making that occurs regarding such things as curriculum, instruction, financial expenditures, and personnel issues is dealt with at the local school district level. The specific "nuts and bolts" decisions about textbooks to use, curriculum packages to adopt, money to spend, and teachers to hire are ultimately made by the local school board. But other groups, including parents and community members, teachers, and administrators, all have a significant impact on the decisions that are made. Figure 14.1 summarizes the relationships that exist in local school district governance.

*Important decisions are often made at school board meetings.*

**Reflective Journey 14.1**

**Parents and community members.** Think back to your own time in the schools. Do you remember parents and/or community members who publicly stated their views about teachers and schools? Your own parents or relatives may be helpful in remembering people and situations. What were the issues that these parents and/or community members raised and how did they share their views with others? Do you remember how the schools responded to the positive and negative issues that were presented? Did parents and community members actually have an impact on teachers and schools? What specific examples come to mind?

While parents and community members typically have no legal authority in school governance, they have had a significant, and growing, influence on educational decisions. One option open to parents and community members is participation in any of the organizations that exist to support and influence educational efforts. For example, parents who have children in band and orchestra programs may form a booster club to engage in fund-raising activities with monies generated from these efforts used to buy new uniforms and pay for travel to performances in the region. Parents and community members also influence educational decisions as they participate in special projects related to the schools. Some examples of this type include volunteering to serve on a curriculum review board for an individual school or the entire school district, being elected to the school board, lobbying the school board for the inclusion or deletion of books and curriculum materials used in the schools, supporting or speaking out against local taxes

**Figure 14.1**  Local School District Governance

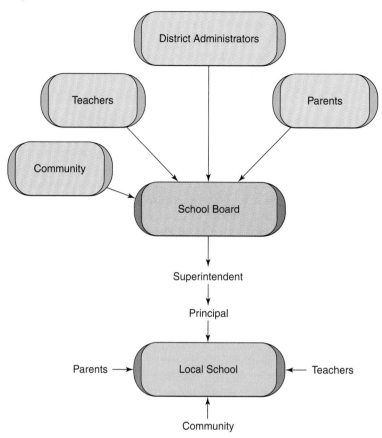

used to support school activities, and engaging in discussions with others about the importance of quality schools.

**Teachers' roles.**  Traditionally, teachers in the United States have been involved in making important decisions that affect schooling at the local level in a variety of ways. For example, Dianne VanderVelde is a high school mathematics teacher who is currently serving on a special task force to identify a textbook series to be used for the teaching of mathematics. Along with three other teachers, two administrators, two parents, and a school board member, she is making an important decision that will influence both teachers and students within the district. Other options for teacher involvement in governance activities have included such things as serving on school or district-wide committees, participating on search committees to select school administrators, working individually or collectively to influence the decisions made by local school boards, and getting involved in union activities to have an impact on the salaries and working conditions for all teachers. In addition, teachers clearly have a very significant role to play in determining the curriculum and instructional methods used in their own classrooms.

More recently, teachers have been participating in a relatively new approach to school governance called **site-based management.** In close collaboration with the school principal, parents, and community members, teachers are actively engaging in making many of the decisions that were formerly the responsibility of district administrators and school boards. Rather than using the older "top-down" model, site-based management teams engage in shared decision making that is seen by many as being a more effective approach (Holloway, 2000).

How do you think you will feel about working to influence the directions of education in your school and district? Take a moment to reflect on this issue. Do you see yourself as a person who will be willing to serve on committees, speak out to parents and others, and attend school board meetings for the purpose of influencing decisions being made? How important is this role for you as a future teacher?

**Reflective Journey 14.2**

**Administrator roles.** Traditionally, school administrators have been almost exclusively white and male. During the last two or three decades, the number of women and minority administrators has been growing slowly. Figure 14.2 shows a breakdown of school administrators by gender and race.

The role of the school **principal** has changed dramatically over the years. From a part-time job assumed along with other teaching duties, the principalship has evolved into a complex mix of administrative and instructional leadership tasks (Sergiovanni, 2001). Today's principals have primary responsibility for managing all of the day-to-day operations of their schools. Meetings with parents, teachers, and district administrators, paperwork, student discipline, and facilities maintenance are some of the many management tasks they face on a daily basis.

Despite the obvious importance of these administrative tasks, more and more educators are looking to the school principal as an instructional leader as well (Fink & Resnick, 2001). Principals are being asked to spend time in classrooms helping teachers identify areas of strength and those that need improvement, determining and implementing effective assessment strategies, assisting with the selection of curriculum materials, and taking leadership in the development of a school-wide management and discipline program. The use of site-based management further complicates these tasks as principals work to involve teachers, parents, and community members in meaningful decision making within their schools.

Although being a principal is a complex administrative assignment, it is still less taxing than the position of **superintendent of schools.** The superintendent serves as chief executive officer of the school system and must manage a complex array of planning, staffing, budgeting, evaluating, and reporting tasks. Imagine for a moment a relatively small school district that

**Figure 14.2    Race and Gender of School Administrators**

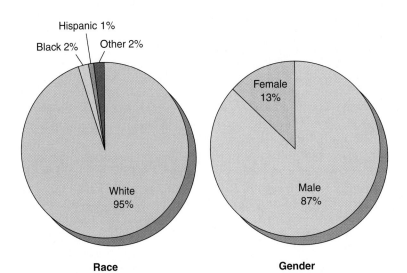

Race                                                Gender

*Source:* Data from "The Changing Face of Education," by K. Vail, 2001, *American School Board Journal, 188*(12), pp. 39–42. Reprinted with permission from *Education Vital Signs 2001.* Copyright 2001 National School Boards Association. All rights reserved.

consists of seven elementary schools, two middle schools, an alternative high school, and a traditional high school. The superintendent in this setting is responsible for the education of more than 4,000 students and serves as instructional leader for approximately 350 teachers and paraprofessionals. He or she oversees the efforts of 12 principals, a custodial and maintenance staff of more than 50, and dozens of secretarial employees. Acting on behalf of the school board, the superintendent is responsible for the hiring and firing of faculty and staff, maintaining school buildings and equipment, managing the school district budget, and making decisions about curriculum and instruction.

**School board roles.** Each state has provisions in its statutes for the selection of community members to serve on **school boards** for local districts. In some states, board membership is determined through public election, while others have an appointment system. Figure 14.3 provides a description of school board members by gender and race. School board members come from diverse professional backgrounds and typically have little or no training in the field of education. In fact, the only qualification board members must generally meet in order to serve is that they live within the school district.

Regardless of their public school knowledge, local school board members have the legal authority to determine educational policy within their districts. Acting on behalf of the community they represent, school board members assume ultimate responsibility for the education of students within the district. This commitment to placing community members in roles

# EDUCATION IN THE NEWS

## One Last Chance

Vouchers and charter schools offer students and families an alternative to public education. Charter schools are nonsectarian public schools that operate without all of the regulations that apply to traditional public schools. The length of time a charter school may operate varies, but in the end, the charter is continued only if positive results are demonstrated. Schools for Educational Evolution and Development (SEED) is a charter school in Washington, DC, and as with other charter schools, students are selected by a locally mandated lottery system. However, this school is unique: It is an urban boarding school for students in grades 7–12. Started in 1997 by two entrepreneurs, SEED provides students with what their communities often do not: esteem for education, adult supervision, plenty of extra assistance, three meals a day, and a clean, safe place to live. The expectations are high, and students must pass a series of gateway tests before being admitted into the high school section. In 2004, SEED will graduate its first class of students.

### Critical Thinking Questions

1. Students who attend SEED (Schools for Educational Evolution and Development) begin in the 7th grade by attending a boarding school Think back to when you were in 7th grade. What would it have been like for you to attend a boarding school? How would you have felt? How would your parents have felt? What about your thoughts and the thoughts of the SEED students might be the same? Different? Why?

2. If you could start a charter school in your home area to increase student achievement, what would its vision, mission, and outcomes be? What would you change about your own education to make it different (better) for more students? Why?

3. Who do you think makes the decisions about what is taught in your college classrooms? How do you think those decisions are or should be made? How is this different from high schools? Who do you think makes the decisions about what is taught in high schools? How do you think those decisions are or should be made?

   *To explore this topic further and to submit your responses online, go to the Education in the News module for Chapter 14 of the Companion Website.*

**Figure 14.3**   Race and Gender of School Boards

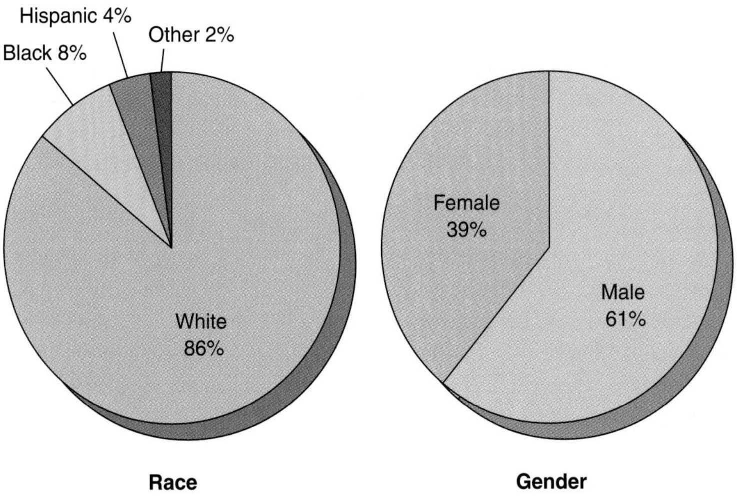

Race                                    Gender

of authority regarding all aspects of local educational programming is unique to the American educational system.

## State Authority

Although local school districts make most of the practical decisions that impact teaching and learning within classrooms, states are responsible for enacting the laws and regulations that determine the framework for them. The Tenth Amendment to the U.S. Constitution empowers the states to take responsibility for education and each state has responded by creating extensive legal requirements and state agencies to assist with their implementation (see Figure 14.4). In recent years, states have increasingly used their "policy muscle" to influence the directions taken by local school districts (Johnston & Sandham, 1999). As states have increased their share of financial support for K–12 education, there has been a corresponding interest on the part of state governments to make sure that this money is well spent. "When we control the money, it's hard to get out of the details," indicates California State Senator Deirdre Alpert (Johnston & Sandham, 1999, p. 24).

The following are examples of ways in which states have increased their involvement in the decision making of local schools:

- *Statewide academic standards.* Forty-eight states now have statewide academic standards that all schools are expected to meet. Although these standards have been in place in most states for several years, they are now being taken far more seriously due to the mandated testing that frequently accompanies them.

- *Mandated testing.* In 39 states, the academic standards are aligned with mandated tests that schools are expected to administer. Typically, this is done at the 4th-, 8th-, and 12th-grade levels. Scores on these tests are carefully reviewed by the state, and pressure is being placed on schools to be more accountable for the academic success of their students.

- *Failing school districts.* Twenty-three states have passed legislation that allows them to take control of school districts (and, in some cases, individual schools) where students are failing to meet academic standards.

**Figure 14.4**   State Governance of Schools

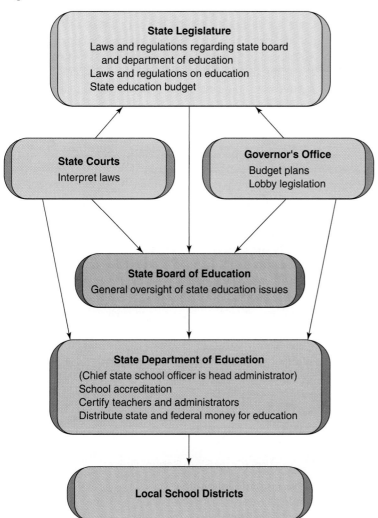

- *Increased regulation.* Virtually every state has greatly expanded the laws and regulations that impact public education. From the 1960s to the present, these regulations have increased from a relatively simple document to several volumes. States are now seen as regulating virtually every aspect of schooling (Johnston & Sandham, 1999).

**State board of education.**   There are five governmental agencies within states that have a major impact on schools. The first of these is called the **state board of education.** Legislatures grant to state boards of education the authority to engage in general oversight of schools. Every state but Wisconsin has a board of education (Lunenburg & Ornstein, 2000). They are considered the highest level education agency within each state. In most instances, it is the governor's responsibility to appoint members to the board of education. In many respects, the state board of education operates with similar personnel and in much the same way as local school boards. Lay leaders who have agreed to serve on the state board commit time on a regular basis to meeting, discussing broad issues influencing state public education, and engaging in policy-making activities that impact the schools. Because of the voluntary nature of service on state boards of education, members tend to be older and have the time that it takes to commit to regular meetings during normal working hours.

One common function of the state board of education is the selection of the **chief state school officer.** Sometimes called the *state superintendent* or *commissioner of education*, the chief state school officer usually serves both as head of the state board of education and as chief executive of the state department of education (discussed below). This full-time position is funded by the individual states and usually is assumed by a professional educator. In some states, the chief state school officer is an elected position.

**State department of education.** Although state boards of education are made up of fairly small groups of part-time volunteers, the **state department of education** is a large state agency that consists of numerous full-time staff operating under the direction of the chief state school officer. While state departments of education generally report to the state board of education, they tend to be the most influential of the two groups. The full-time nature of the staff, combined with generally better connections to the governor's office and the legislative branches of state government, make state departments of education a powerful player in relation to state education issues. Figure 14.5 shows the key staff of one state's department of education.

Traditionally, the main task of the department of education was to collect and share statistics about education within the state. As states increased the level of regulation over schools, however, departments of education grew in both size and authority. They now typically engage in the following functions: (1) deciding on school accreditation, (2) certifying teachers, (3) distributing state funds for education, (4) dealing with student transportation and safety issues, (5) checking to make sure state regulations are implemented, (6) engaging in research and program evaluation, and (7) overseeing the distribution and proper use of federal funding given to local school districts (Lunenburg & Ornstein, 2000).

**Figure 14.5**    Key Staff, Texas Department of Education

**Commissioner of Education (Chief State School Officer)**

**Deputy Commissioner for Initiative and Administration**
Assistant Commissioner, Statewide Initiatives
Assistant Commissioner, Governmental Relations
Managing Director, Charter Schools
Chief of Operations
Managing Director, Fiscal Management

**Deputy Commissioner for Finance and Accountability**
Associate Commissioner, Quality, Compliance, and Accountability Reviews
Associate Commissioner, Finance and Support Systems
Managing Director, Information Systems
Associate Commissioner, Accountability Reporting and Research

**Deputy Commissioner for Programs and Instruction**
Associate Commissioner, Curriculum, Assessment, & Technology
Managing Director, Curriculum and Professional Development
Associate Commissioner, Continuing Education & School Improvement
Managing Director, Continuing Education
Associate Commissioner, Special Populations

*Source:* Retrieved November 8, 2001, from http://www.tea.state.tx.us/hr/chart.html

**State government.** Three other groups with considerable influence over educational issues are all housed within the state government itself. To varying degrees, the governor, branches of the legislature, and the state court system are involved in setting directions for public school education. Due to either their visibility within the state, the passing of regulations regarding schooling, or by interpreting the legal requirements affecting education, each has an impact on teaching and learning.

While the actual influence of state governors varies depending on their interest in and commitment to education, their potential impact is great. For example, in many states the governor appoints both the chief state school officer and members of the state board of education. Governors also are responsible for making budget recommendations to their legislatures on issues such as teacher salaries and overall state funding for education (see Figure 14.6). Depending on the quality of their relationships with state legislatures, governors can often successfully lobby for or against laws being considered that have an impact on public education. They may also choose to use their veto powers to strike down other measures that may adversely affect education. Furthermore, governors can use their public offices to champion education causes. Their support of a specific issue can often influence the thoughts and actions of the general public.

State legislatures are given the power to pass laws and regulations that have a far-reaching impact on the schools. These commonly fall into three broad categories (Lunenburg & Ornstein, 2000). The first deals with *issues impacting state education agencies.* For example, legislatures

**Figure 14.6**   State Budget (Percent) Allocated to Education

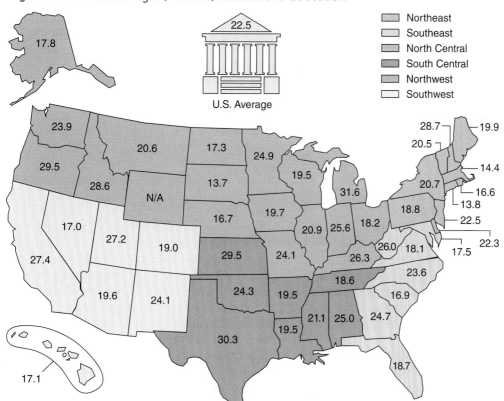

*Source:* Data from "State of the States: A Statistical Portrait of U.S. Schools," 2001, *American School Board Journal, 188*(12), pp. 43–49. Reprinted with permission from *Education Vital Signs 2001.* Copyright 2001 National School Boards Association. All rights reserved.

usually are responsible for laws that determine such things as how chief state school officers and state boards of education are selected, others that address the organization and responsibilities of the state department of education, and laws that define the types of local and regional school districts that will exist within the state. A second type of legislation addresses *issues related to the financing of public education.* Legislatures determine the annual amount of financial support the state will provide to fund such things as teacher salaries and benefits, district administration, and school building maintenance and construction. In many cases, they also pass laws and provide guidelines that assist cities and counties in raising additional money to support local schools. The third set of laws passed by legislatures addresses *broad educational issues* such as the length of compulsory education within the state, the general content of the curriculum, the length of the school year, and standards for the construction of school buildings.

The laws passed by state legislatures are of necessity broad and open to interpretation. Parents, teachers, schools, and communities often differ in their understandings of the laws relating to education. When various opinions come into conflict, the state court system becomes the arbitrator and assists schools and others in clarifying the actual intent of the laws passed by legislatures. There is no one uniform organization to state court systems across the nation. Typically, however, there are three levels (Lunenburg & Ornstein, 2000). The first is usually referred to as the **municipal** or **superior court.** Most medium-sized cities have municipal/superior courts and they serve as the initial arbitrator in settling disputes regarding educational law. Parties that disagree with the decisions reached at this level can appeal to the **appellate court.** Appellate courts review the trial record from the lower court and allow both sides in the dispute to provide additional information in support of their positions. The highest level of appeal in most states is referred to as the **state supreme court.** Once arguments are heard from both parties, the decision of this court is final unless an issue relating to the U.S. Constitution is raised. In these situations, the U.S. Supreme Court may choose to hear the case when either party in the dispute seeks further clarification of lower court decisions.

## Federal Influence

Despite the fact that the U.S. Constitution delegates most of the responsibilities for public education to the states, several agencies of the federal government have significant roles to play in public school governance (see Figure 14.7). Throughout American history, these roles have continued to expand (Razik & Swanson, 2001). For example, in the 150 years between 1787 and 1937, the U.S. Congress passed only 14 significant laws related to education. Since that time, more than 160 pieces of important legislation have been enacted (National Center for Education Statistics, 1997).

**Federal agencies.** Approximately $650 billion is spent annually on education in the United States. Of that amount, only 9%, or roughly $58.5 billion, comes from the federal government (U.S. Department of Education, 2003). Three federal agencies share responsibilities for overseeing and distributing these funds. The U.S. Department of Education is the most influential, because its sole function is to address issues related to schools. The Department of Health and Human Services and the Department of Agriculture have less prominent, yet important roles.

The original Department of Education became a part of the federal government in 1867 and had as its primary purpose the collection of information on schools and teaching that would assist states in creating effective school systems. Since that time, the department has grown in size and influence. Currently, the department has nearly 5,000 federal employees and a budget of roughly $42 billion dollars. This accounts for approximately two thirds of the total expenditures of the federal government for state and local education programs (U.S. Department of Education, 2003). In 1980, the U.S. Department of Education was established as a cabinet-level agency. Since that time, several prominent individuals such as William Bennett, Lamar Alexander, and Richard Riley have served as secretary. Because of the visibility and influence of this position, these individuals have had a significant impact on the reform efforts that have occurred since the 1980s.

**Figure 14.7**   Federal Government Involvement in Education

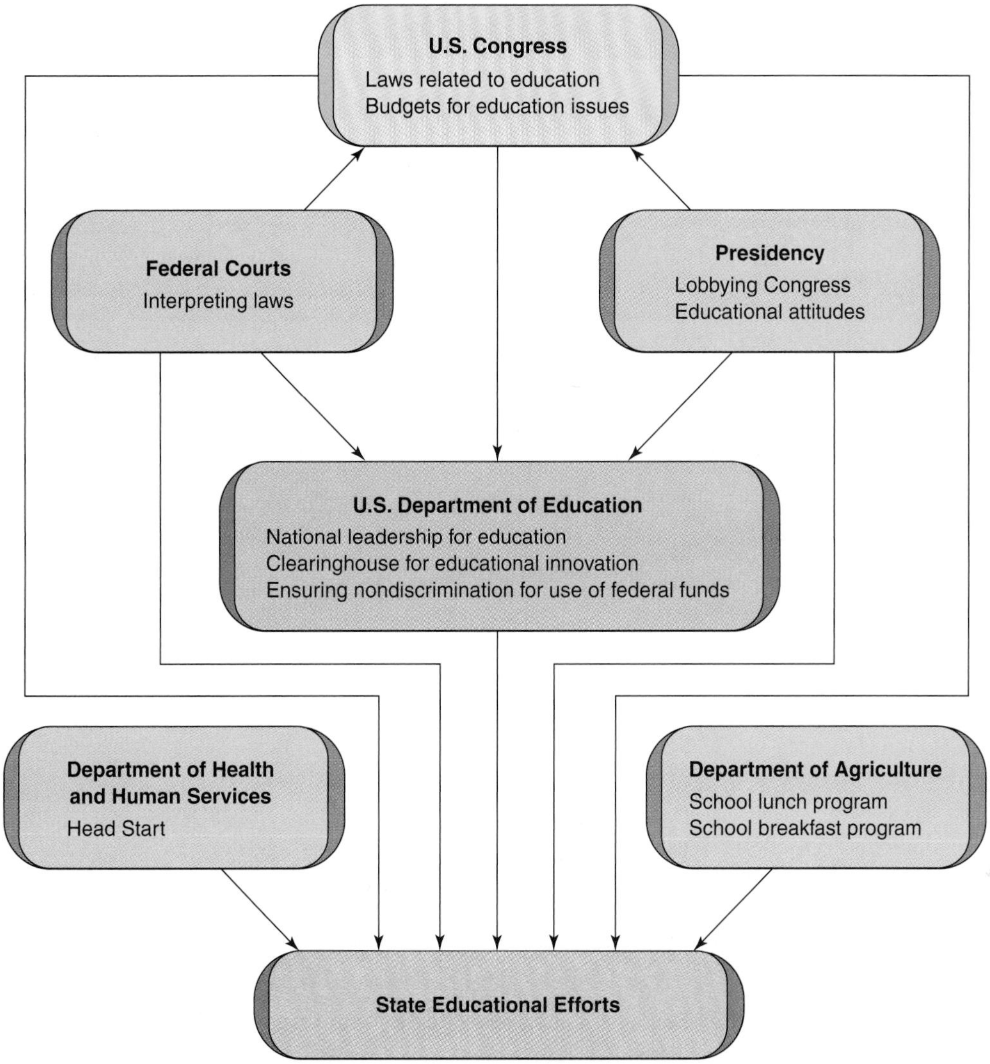

The Administration for Children and Families, under the direction of the Department of Health and Human Services, is responsible for overseeing the Head Start program (see Chapter 4 for more information). Serving approximately 800,000 low-income preschool children nationally, this program is viewed as an important federal program aimed at assisting children in "catching up" with their more advantaged peers. At an annual cost of approximately $5,000 per child, Head Start programs offer high-quality, low-cost options that have proven to be effective in assisting young children to develop the skills they need to be successful in their later school experiences.

The U.S. Department of Agriculture administers several food programs that assist low-income children and their families. The longest running option is the National School Lunch Program, which began in 1946. It currently serves low-cost or free lunches to nearly 27 million children each school day (U.S. Department of Agriculture, 2001). Other options include the School Breakfast Program, which serves approximately 7.7 million children daily, and the Special Milk Program, which provides milk to children in schools and child care settings that do not participate in other federal meal programs.

## The No Child Left Behind Act

On January 8, 2002, President Bush signed a piece of federal legislation called the "No Child Left Behind Act." This act is designed to help low-income and minority students perform at the same achievement levels as their peers. The law requires states and school districts to test students annually to assess their academic skills in grades 3 through 8. This powerful piece of legislation couples requirements for testing with a push for higher teacher qualifications and strict sanctions when schools fail to improve test scores for all students.

While no one questions the intent of the No Child Left Behind legislation, many do argue with its methods. The whole notion of testing and its impact on minority students is hotly debated: "While African-Americans and most other minorities have shown both relative and absolute gains in standardized test scores over the past several decades, they still score much lower than whites as a group. Some educators believe that many standardized tests are culturally biased, drawing primarily upon the experiences of middle-class white students" (*Education Week*, 2002).

The Center on Education Policy (Jennings, 2002), while fully supporting the intent of the No Child Left Behind legislation, describes other potential challenges:

It is not enough, however, for federal policymakers to simply insist that educators be held accountable and that states and local districts take stronger actions. If the president and the Congress truly expect all students to learn more, all teachers to teach better, and all schools to provide a high-quality education, then all levels of government—including the federal government—must deliver much more. School districts, states, and the federal government must provide additional funding and other meaningful assistance to improve classroom instruction and raise academic achievement. (p. 8)

### Research the Issue

Research this topic online using the links provided in the *Engage the Debate* module for this chapter of the Companion Website. Link to the online source articles by Jennings (2002) and *Education Week* (2002) and explore the information provided at the additional sites listed.

1. From your research, what are the major provisions of the No Child Left Behind Act?
2. How will this act work to improve the academic performance of low income and minority students?
3. What are the stated strengths and weaknesses of this act?

### Explore Your Views

1. As a future teacher, how might the No Child Left Behind Act positively influence your teaching? What may be possible negative consequences?
2. Should you be striving in your teaching to leave no child behind? Is it possible to achieve this goal?

 *To research this issue and submit your responses online, go to the Engage in the Debate module for Chapter 14 of the Companion Website for this text.*

*Sources:* "Hot Topics: Assessment," by *Education Week*, 2002. Retrieved April 28, 2003, from http://www.edweek.org/context/topics/issuespage.cfm?id=41; "New Leadership for New Standards," by J. Jennings, 2002, *The State Education Standard, 3*(2), pp. 7–18. Retrieved April 28, 2003, from http://www.ctredpol.org/standardsbasededucationreform/stricterfederaldemandsbiggerstaterolejune2002.pdf

**The federal government.** In addition to the federal agencies described above, the legislative, judicial, and executive branches of the federal government all influence the directions of American education. The U.S. Congress, for example, has passed numerous laws that have had a major impact on what happens in local schools. A sampling of some of the more significant laws that impact different aspects of K–12 education includes the Perkins Vocational Education Act of

1984, the Bilingual Education Act of 1968 (amended in 1974), the Education for All Handicapped Children Act of 1975, and the No Child Left Behind Act of 2001.

The federal courts are another aspect of American government to strongly influence schooling. This system consists of three main divisions: district courts, courts of appeal, and the Supreme Court (Kowalski & Reitzug, 1993). These courts, particularly the U.S. Supreme Court, have had a major impact on the directions of K–12 education. They have repeatedly heard and

## reflect on diversity

## School Desegregation

For much of American history, students of different races seldom mixed in school settings. Most often, schools were established for Black students while their White agemates received their education in separate locations. It wasn't until 1954 that the U.S. Supreme Court, in a landmark decision (*Brown v. Board of Education of Topeka*) unanimously outlawed segregation of students by race. Prior to that date, states were allowed to have "separate but equal" facilities for different groups of students. Beginning in the mid-1950s, then, school districts that had all-White and all-Black schools were ordered to integrate their buildings. The two main methods of compliance were for districts to redraw school boundary lines so that mixed groups of students were in attendance or to bus students (usually black) to other schools or districts (*Education Week*, 2003). More recently, magnet schools (see Chapter 4) have been viewed as an important option for desegregation.

A half-century later, after the courts eased the restrictions on school districts for desegregation (*Freeman v. Pitts*, 1992), the issue is receiving renewed debate. Proponents and critics are taking very different perspectives on

what can and should be done regarding this controversial topic. Critics claim that "other factors are more important than racial balance; that trying to desegregate schools in overwhelmingly segregated environments is a waste of energy; that schools are desegregated enough; and that perhaps separate can be equal after all" (*Education Week*, 2003, p. 1). Those supporting desegregation feel that relaxing standards is a major step backward. They argue that as our nation becomes even more multicultural, integrating students in school settings is an even more important goal.

Recent studies indicate that segregation is in fact growing rather than decreasing in America's schools. For example, segregation in the southern states is approaching the levels found in the 1950s (Richard, 2002). The growing numbers of Hispanic families and residential segregation have been cited as the main reasons for this growth. Another indicator of the growth in segregation comes from recent research on private schools (Zehr, 2002). Students who attend private schools are more likely to find themselves in racially segregated classrooms than others who attend public schools.

### Explore and Reflect

Learn more about desegregation by reading the online source articles by *Education Week* (2003), Richard (2002), and Zehr (2002) and reviewing other online resources provided in the *Reflect on Diversity* module for Chapter 14 of the Companion Website.

1. Reflect back on your own schooling experiences. How much diversity existed and what was the impact on you as a student? Would you have preferred more or less diversity?

2. Do you think schools should continue to work toward the goal of desegregation? Why or why not?

3. How would increased desegregation influence the ways in which you teach? What makes you feel this way?

 *To explore this topic further and submit your reflections online, go to the Reflect on Diversity module for Chapter 14 of the Companion Website for this text.*

*Sources:* "Desegregation" by *Education Week*. Retrieved April 23, 2003, from http://www.edweek.org/context/topics/issuespage.cfm?id=27; "Researchers: School Segregation Rising in South" by A. Richard, 2002, *Education Week*, September 11, p. 5; "Studies Cite Segregation in Private Schools" by M. Zehr, 2002, *Education Week*, July 10, p. 14.

ruled on a variety of significant issues. Their most influential decisions may well be in the area of protecting teachers and students from too much governmental intervention. A variety of civil rights suits have been reviewed over the years on topics such as the states' authority to compel public school attendance (*Pierce v. Society of Sisters,* 1925), the school's ability to require students to salute the flag (*Minersville School District v. Gobitis,* 1940), teachers' freedom of expression (*Pickering v. Board of Education,* 1968), and students' rights to due process for suspensions and expulsions (*Goss v. Lopez,* 1975).

The office of president of the United States has also had a strong impact on educational issues as well. For example, Ronald Reagan's two terms in office (1980–1988) saw a scaling back of the government's involvement in education. Federal funding and intervention in the affairs of schools decreased during these years. Other presidents, such as Bill Clinton, have emphasized the importance of excellence in education and provided support for moving toward this goal. Although these efforts only indirectly affect what happens in classrooms, they help influence the attitudes of others who do impact educational practices.

## What other groups shape educational policies?

Although local, state, and federal governmental bodies all have significant roles in educational decision making, other groups also influence what takes place in America's classrooms. Businesses, special interest groups, college and university faculty, and professional education associations provide money, research, and political influence that impact teaching and learning (see Table 14.1).

### Business Organizations

Businesses have been involved in supporting schools since the late 1800s, with more formalized partnerships in existence since the 1970s (Lankard, 1995). The demand for educational reform that began in the 1980s coupled with the need for highly skilled workers entering the workforce led to increased numbers of business/education partnerships. Traditionally, businesses provided such things as grant money for innovative school projects, materials and up-to-date equipment for teaching, and scholarships for students with high academic performance. More recently, businesses also expect to be more directly involved in school reform efforts to make sure that their goals are being addressed.

### Special Interest Groups

**Special interest groups** are organizations that have a common interest and work collectively to influence the directions of education locally and nationally. These can be as informal as a group

| TABLE 14.1    Other Groups Shaping Educational Policies | |
|---|---|
| **Group** | **Description** |
| Business | The need for highly skilled workers entering the workforce has led to increased numbers of business/education partnerships. |
| Special interest groups | These organizations have an interest in education and work to influence its direction both locally and nationally. |
| College and university faculty | College and university faculty associated with teacher education programs shape the profession through their role in the preparation of future teachers. |
| Professional education associations | Professional education associations lobby for better schooling and also help identify best practices for the profession. |

of parents working together to raise money for playground equipment or lobbying the local school board regarding specific curriculum materials. Special interest groups can also be national organizations that have greater resources and a broader influence on the direction of education in America. One example of a national special interest group is the National Alliance of Black School Educators (NABSE, 2001). The NABSE, founded in 1970 by Dr. Charles Moody and other prominent black educators, was established to improve the achievement levels of African American youth. The group promotes professional development programs that are designed to enhance the skills of school staff in working with African American students, serves as a forum for the exchange of successful ideas and strategies on diversity topics, and advocates for policies that impact quality education in our schools.

## College and University Faculty

College and university faculty in teacher education programs are another group that influences activities in the public schools in many ways. Perhaps the most significant of these is their role in the preparation of future teachers. Most college professors who instruct teacher education students have completed a doctoral degree in a discipline related to education and have had experience teaching in public or private schools. The Association of Teacher Educators (ATE), a national professional organization that addresses all aspects of teacher preparation, has identified standards that college and university faculty should meet in order to successfully prepare new teachers. They include (1) modeling excellent teaching in their instruction of college students, (2) engaging in scholarly activity that is related to teaching or learning, (3) reflecting on their teaching and demonstrating a commitment to lifelong learning, (4) providing leadership in the development of quality teacher education programs, (5) collaborating in significant ways with the public schools and others in education-related positions, and (6) advocating for high-quality education for all students (ATE, 2001).

*Teacher education faculty have a significant impact on schooling.*

## Professional Education Associations

A large number of **professional education associations** influence the activities that take place in the K–12 schools. These organizations can be loosely categorized into two broad groups (see Chapter 5 for more information): (1) national teachers' unions (For example, the National Education Association and the American Federation of Teachers) and (2) specialty organizations that address specific aspects of teaching and learning (such as the International Reading Association). The teachers' unions have had a significant impact on education at all levels. At the local level, for example, these organizations often serve as bargaining agents for such things as teacher salaries and benefits, special contracts for additional services (such as driver's education and coaching), and teacher workshop days. Teachers' unions also offer workshops for teachers on current issues at state and national meetings and develop publications on current topics in education (Arizona Education Association, 2001).

Specialty organizations also influence the directions of teaching in many ways. For example, art educators often participate in the National Art Education Association (NAEA), which publishes a long list of pamphlets and books on topics related to art education. A sampling includes books titled *Creating Curriculum in Art, Aesthetics for Young People, The Visual Arts and Early Childhood Learning,* and *Student Behavior in Art Classrooms: The Dynamics of Discipline* (NAEA, 2001). In addition to an annual conference in which art educators learn more about recent issues in their field, 29 states have organizations affiliated with the NAEA and also conduct state meetings on topics of interest to their members.

## What sources of funds exist for education?

The three primary sources of money used to support public education are local, state, and federal funds (see Table 14.2). Until fairly recently, property taxes assessed at the local level were used to pay the major portion of these expenses. Currently, however, state funds provide the largest share at approximately 48%, while local sources account for nearly 45%, and federal spending is just under 7% of the total (National Center for Education Statistics, 2001).

### Private School Funding

Before looking at the funding sources for public education in more depth, it is important to remember that a significant number of students attend private schools in America and that this attendance directly impacts funding for public schools. As indicated in Chapter 4, approximately 11% of all school-aged children are currently enrolled in private schools (National Association of Independent Schools, 2001). Most of the funds used to support these students' educational expenses come from the tuition fees paid by their parents. If they were enrolled in local schools that were publicly funded, the increased expenses for school districts would be significant. State and local revenues would need to be increased in order to simply maintain the levels of service currently provided to public school students.

### State and Local Support

As mentioned earlier, the primary source of funding for schools at the local level comes from *property taxes*. In most instances, these taxes are collected based on the value of the real estate within the school district. All property holders are assessed an annual tax based on the value of the land and buildings they own. So, for example, the elderly couple next door, the couple across the street who have chosen to forego children, and the family with three school-aged children are all homeowners who are assessed an annual tax based on the values of their homes and land as determined by a local assessor. It is quite possible that these homeowners would have differing opinions about using property taxes as a significant source of funding for local schools.

### TABLE 14.2    Financial Support for K–12 Education

| School Year | Federal (%) | State (%) | Local (%) |
|-------------|-------------|-----------|-----------|
| 1919–1920 | 0.3 | 16.5 | 83.2 |
| 1941–1942 | 1.4 | 31.4 | 67.1 |
| 1951–1952 | 3.5 | 38.6 | 57.9 |
| 1961–1962 | 4.3 | 38.7 | 56.9 |
| 1971–1972 | 8.9 | 38.3 | 52.8 |
| 1981–1982 | 7.4 | 47.6 | 45.0 |
| 1991–1992 | 6.6 | 46.4 | 47.0 |
| 1997–1998 | 6.8 | 48.4 | 44.8 |

*Source: Digest of Education Statistics,* by National Center for Education Statistics, 2000, Washington, DC: U.S. Government Printing Office.

Reflective
Journey 14.3

Take a moment to reflect on each of the families mentioned above. How do you think the childless couple would feel about paying a significant portion of their property taxes for schooling? What attitude would be most likely from the elderly couple, especially if they are living on a small fixed income? Would you expect the parents with three school-aged children to support the use of property taxes for schooling? What other factors besides having school-aged children may determine homeowners' attitudes toward funding schooling through property taxes?

Property taxes have been criticized for creating inequities in school funding. A school located in a low-income area could potentially receive far less tax revenue than a similar sized school in a well-to-do neighborhood. These disparities in funding tend to accentuate the differences that already exist between low-income families and others in the community. With fewer resources, poorer schools tend to have students who score lower on standardized tests of achievement and who take fewer higher level courses in subjects such as mathematics, science, and English. These students are more likely than their more advantaged peers to perpetuate the cycle of poverty by opting out of school at an early age and taking employment in low-paying jobs (Greenwald, Hedges, & Laine, 1996).

While local support for schools comes primarily from property taxes, state assistance tends to be from either *sales taxes* on goods and services or a *state income tax*. In the former situation, when a state resident buys a new shirt or an upgraded computer, he or she pays a sales tax that is used to support a variety of state programs, including the public schools. States that have income taxes typically assess residents a tax based on their adjusted gross income from federal income tax forms, with a portion of that money being used to support the public schools. In some states, residents pay both a sales tax on goods and services and a state tax on their annual income. Figure 14.8 compares states' per-pupil education funding.

## Federal Funding

As indicated earlier, the level of federal support for public education is rather small. With under 7% of the total currently coming from this source, it would appear that the federal government has a minimal impact on the funding for public education. In reality, however, the tight budgeting situations faced by most school districts have made even these relatively small amounts of money a necessity. These funds are used to implement a variety of valuable programs promoted by the federal government. For example, the federal government budgeted $354 million in 1998 to support bilingual and migrant education programs (Sack, 1998). Another example of this type is the commitment of the federal government to financially support vocational education. In 1994, approximately 10% of the funding for these programs was provided by the federal government (Sack, 1998).

## Recent Funding Options

Despite the acknowledged importance of educating America's youth, many citizens have begun to rebel against traditional forms of support for public education. By rejecting efforts by states and local districts to increase taxes and speaking through the power of their votes to elect politicians who promise lower levels of taxation, the American public has made it more difficult to raise the money necessary to fund education. In response to this shrinking pool of traditional support, a variety of newer funding options have been tried (see Table 14.3).

**Schools for profit.**  One recent trend in education funding is the **schools for profit** movement. Beginning in the mid-1990s, states such as Michigan and Pennsylvania have allowed private enterprise to take over schools that are failing academically as a last-ditch effort to improve the teaching and learning in these settings (Cook, 2001). These schools for profit, operated by companies known as **education management organizations** or EMOs, have struggled to be both profitable and academically successful in very difficult situations. One example is the Pulaski-Edison Junior Academy in Chester, Pennsylvania. Rated by the state of Pennsylvania as the lowest performing

**Figure 14.8**   State Per-Pupil Funding for Education[*]

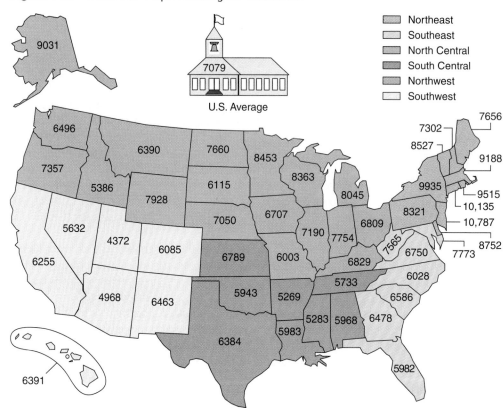

[*]Estimate for 2000–2001.
*Source:* Data from "State of the States: A Statistical Portrait of U.S. Schools," 2001, *American School Board Journal, 188*(12), pp. 43–49. Reprinted with permission from *Education Vital Signs* 2001. Copyright 2001 National School Boards Association. All rights reserved.

school in the lowest performing district in the state, the academy was recently taken over by Edison Schools, the largest education management organization in the country. "Edison is banking on its belief that it can turn around the district with its longer class day, structured curriculum, teacher training, enhanced technology, and overall improved school atmosphere" (Cook, 2001, p. 10).

**School district foundations.**  An increasing number of school districts are creating their own nonprofit **school district foundations** for the purpose of receiving donations from individuals and corporations. Although it is difficult to get reliable figures on numbers, an estimated 4,000 public school foundations exist in the United States (Addonizio, 1999). Some examples of this type include the Martinez Education Foundation of Martinez, California. Created in 1984 to supplement the dwindling state funding, the foundation has contributed more than $500,000 to help support teachers and learning in the district (Martinez Educational Foundation, 2001). The Harlem Foundation (2001) is another example of this type. The Harlem School District, with approximately 7,000 students, is located in Illinois about 90 miles northwest of Chicago. In addition to providing monetary support to schools within the district, the foundation has created a scholarship program to assist needy students in attaining their higher education goals.

**Booster clubs.**  Another option for school funding that has been available in many districts for some time and is gaining in nationwide popularity is the **booster club.** Typically, these clubs are

| TABLE 14.3 Recent Funding Options | |
| --- | --- |
| **Option** | **Description** |
| Schools for profit | Private enterprise takes over failing schools in a last-ditch effort to improve teaching and learning. |
| School district foundations | School districts are creating nonprofit foundations to receive gifts from individuals and corporations. |
| Booster clubs | Parents and interested community members create a club to provide assistance to a single school and focus their energy and fund-raising efforts on a specific aspect of school activity. |
| User fees | Certain services such as driver education programs, swimming instruction, certain types of school supplies, participation in athletics, and bus use are being paid for in some schools through fees charged to those using the service. |
| Leasing facilities and services | Some schools are leasing unused facilities to community organizations or local businesses to generate revenue. |
| Advertising on school property | Some schools are allowing advertising on school buses, on homework handouts, and on educational television programming broadcast in the schools as a method of fund-raising. |

created to provide assistance to a single school and focus their energy and fund-raising efforts on a specific aspect of school activity. Most commonly, these booster clubs have supported pursuits such as athletics, band, orchestra, chorus, debate, and drama (Addonizio, 1999). Parents and other booster club members contribute money, solicit financial support and equipment donations from community members, and engage in work tasks that enable these important aspects of schooling to operate successfully with less local and state funding.

**User fees.** In a growing number of circumstances, users of specific school-provided services are being required by local school districts to pay for them. For example, driver education programs, swimming instruction, certain types of school supplies, participation in athletics, and bus use are being supported by user fees in some districts. As the number of user fees has grown, their legality has been challenged in both state and federal courts (Dayton & McCarthy, 1992). Typically, the courts have looked at relevant state laws to determine the appropriateness of these fees. A survey of state departments of education indicated, for example, that only 8 states allowed the charging of fees for required textbooks, while 29 permitted equipment fees and 20 allowed fees for field trips (Addonizio, 1999).

**Leasing of facilities and services.** Some local school boards are also authorizing schools to lease portions of their facilities to community organizations or local businesses as an additional method of generating revenue or providing services for the district.

*Bake sales are used to generate additional money for schools.*

## explore your beliefs

# Community Partnerships

In an effort to improve teaching and learning, schools are taking a hard look at different ways in which they can bring about positive change. One option that is growing in popularity is to build partnerships with community groups.

Recognizing that there is no single solution to school improvement, many schools increasingly rely on collaborative efforts. Collaborations with local businesses, universities, medical and religious centers, foundations, and other community-based organizations are intended to enhance both academic and nonacademic skills for schoolchildren.

The challenge is ensuring that teachers, neighbors, parents, and guardians are working together to set and reinforce consistent messages and standards for children. This uneasy marriage between schools and communities, growing numbers of experts agree, must be strengthened. Only by working together, the theory goes, can these lifelong partners hope to salvage young lives and fulfill education's promise of literacy and opportunity. Admittedly, it's a tall order. (*Education Week,* 2002)

One example of this growing connection between schools and local communities comes from New Orleans, where newly certified teachers are being offered signing bonuses to teach there. Local businesses are helping by donating money to help pay for these incentives (Hoff, 2002). The Hillsboro, Oregon, schools have made different, but equally valuable, connections with their community to help immigrant families from Mexico transition to life in America (Zehr, 2002). School district personnel help guide students and their families to community resources that provide food, shelter, medical care, and other necessities so that basic needs can be met.

### React and Reflect

1. Do you see community involvement as an important direction for schools? What do you see as the potential strengths and limitations?

2. Can you see yourself working as a future teacher to involve your local community in the activities of your classroom or school? Why or why not?

3. Are there special skills you would need to develop to be successful in involving the community in your class or school?

 *To explore this topic further and submit your reactions and reflections online, go to the Explore Your Beliefs module for Chapter 14 of the Companion Website for this text.*

*Sources:* "Hot Topics: Community Partnerships," by *Education Week,* 2002. Retrieved September 12, 2002, from http://www.edweek.org/context/topics/issuespage.cfm?id=46; "New Orleans Soliciting Businesses for Bonuses," by D. Hoff, 2002, *Education Week,* May 1. Retrieved April 16, 2003, from http://www.edweek.org/ew/ew_printstory.cfm?slug=33recruit.h21; "Oregon School District Reaches Out to New Arrivals from Mexico," by M. Zehr, 2002, *Education Week,* March 27. Retrieved April 22, 2003, from http://www.edweek.org/ew/ew_printstory.cfm?slug=28hillsboro.h21

So, for example, an elementary school with unused classroom space could consider leasing that space to a Head Start program to allow for better connections with this early childhood option while generating additional revenue for the district. Or a school might lease space to a counseling service in exchange for a contracted number of hours of free counseling for students. Some schools also lease portions of school services such as food preparation or transportation to private schools and community organizations as another method of generating income (Pijanowski & Monk, 1996).

**Advertising on school property.** One final option for increasing revenue available to the schools is the use of advertising on school property. A variety of options have been tried, including the sale of advertising on school buses in New York City and space for advertising on homework handouts in California (Pijanowski & Monk, 1996). Undoubtedly the best known example of revenues generated from advertising on school property is the Whittle Communications Channel One television broadcasts. Local school districts that contract with Whittle Communications receive about $50,000 worth of programming and equipment (including a satellite dish, recorders, and television sets) and then have access to daily news broadcasts that include some advertisements. In 1995, approximately 8 million students in 12,000 schools nationwide received these daily broadcasts from Channel One. Stated another way, approximately 40% of U.S. students in grades 6 through 12 received these news programs and accompanying advertisements (Johnston, 1995).

## Summary

To help you understand the ways in which American schools are governed and financed, this chapter was organized around three central questions:

### Who sets school directions?

A number of different groups influence the governance of public schools:
- At the local level, parents and community members, teachers, administrators, and school boards influence schooling (Praxis II, topic IVb)
- State authority for schools rests with the board of education, department of education, and state government (Praxis II, topic IVb)
- Federal agencies and the three branches of the federal government all influence schooling (Praxis II, topic IVb)

### What other groups shape educational policies?

A number of other groups at the local, state, and national levels also influence educational policy:
- Business organizations
- Special interest groups
- College and university faculty (Praxis II, topic IVb)
- Professional education associations (Praxis II, topic IVb)

### What sources of funds exist for education?

There are three primary sources for school funding, with some newer options gaining in popularity:
- Private school funding
- State and local support (property taxes, state income taxes, and/or sales taxes) (Praxis II, topic IVb)
- Federal funding (Praxis II, topic IVb)
- Recent developments (schools for profit, school district foundations, booster clubs, user fees, leasing of facilities and services, advertising on school property) (Praxis II, topic IVb)

## Key Terms

appellate court
booster club
chief state school officer
education management organizations
municipal/superior court
principal
professional education associations
school boards

school district foundation
schools for profit
site-based management
special interest groups
state board of education
state department of education
state supreme court
superintendent of schools

## Reflective Journey: Online Journal

 Use the questions for thought and reflection highlighted throughout the chapter to help guide your personal journey of reflection and professional development as a teacher. To complete your journal entries online, go to the *Reflective Journey* module for this chapter of the Companion Website.

## PRAXIS    Test Preparation Activities

 To review an online chapter case study, test your understanding of chapter topics and concepts, and begin preparing for the Praxis II: Principles of Learning and Teaching examination, go to the *Praxis Test Preparation* module for this chapter of the Companion Website.

## inTASC    Becoming a Reflective Practitioner

To complete these activities and submit your responses online, go to the *Becoming a Reflective Practitioner* module for this chapter of the Companion Website.

### Who sets school directions?

**Review Questions**

1. What roles will you play as a future teacher in school governance?

2. In what ways does a state legislature influence schooling in that state?

3. How does the U.S. Supreme Court help determine directions for schooling?

**Field Experience**

Attend a school board meeting for a local district. Who participated in the meeting? What topics were addressed? Collect an agenda and any handouts distributed. Discuss what you learned with your peers.

**Building Your Portfolio: *State Education Agencies***

**INTASC Standard 10.** Take some time to get to know the structure and organization of your state education agencies. Library and Internet resources should give you a good idea of their make-up. Summarize each of the major agencies by developing an organizational flow chart for each. Add these documents to your portfolio.

## What other groups shape educational policies?

### Review Questions

1. In what ways do special interest groups influence the directions of education?
2. How do teachers' unions impact schooling?

### Building Your Portfolio: *Professional Education Organizations*

**INTASC Standard 9.** Talk to your college instructors or teachers you know about professional education organizations that you might want to join in the future. Once you have identified several possibilities, spend some time on the Internet collecting more information. Select three professional organizations that you think may be of future interest and write brief summaries of the services offered by each group. Include these summaries in your portfolio.

## What sources of funds exist for education?

### Review Questions

1. How do private schools influence funding needs for public education?
2. What are the two main methods of school funding at the state level?
3. What is the purpose of a school district foundation?

### Field Experience

Schedule and conduct an interview with a principal or assistant principal of a school of your choice. Talk to this person about school finances. What does this administrator see as the major financial needs and resources of the school? Which of the newer funding options described in this chapter are being used in this school?

### Building Your Portfolio: *Funding for Local Education*

**INTASC Standard 9.** Seek additional information about property taxes and other local school fund-raising activities for a district of your choice. You may want to talk to a financial officer for that district. City or county offices may have additional information about taxes and their use. Describe your findings in a two- or three-page paper that you include in your portfolio.

## Suggested Readings

Addonizio, M. (1999). New revenues for public schools: Alternatives to broad-based taxes. In *Selected papers in school finance.* Washington, DC: U.S. Department of Education. Retrieved April 22, 2003, from http://nces.ed.gov/pubs99/1999334/text4.html. This Internet resource provides an excellent discussion of alternative funding sources for schools.

Lunenburg, F., & Ornstein, A. (2000). *Educational administration: Concepts and practices.* (3rd ed.). Belmont, CA: Wadsworth. This text is one used by principal candidates as they prepare for their administrative roles. It provides a clear discussion of school governance issues.

Razik, T., & Swanson, A. (2001). *Fundamental concepts of educational leadership* (2nd ed.). Upper Saddle River, NJ: Merrill/Prentice Hall. Another textbook for principals, this book has good information on administrators' roles, school governance, and school finance.

# part 4

## How Do I Grow as a Reflective Practitioner?

**Chapter 15:** **The First Years and Beyond**

# chapter 15

## The First Years and Beyond

This chapter is designed to give you a glimpse of what is yet to come in your future career. What will it be like to close the classroom door for the first time and begin your adventure in teaching? You should come away from this chapter with additional understandings of those initial classroom experiences and gain insights into your long-term teaching career. Four organizing questions will be used to guide you through this process.

## Focus Questions

◢ What will I need to do to get a teaching position?

◢ What can I expect as a first-year teacher?

◢ What must I do to be successful as a beginning teacher?

◢ How can I continue to grow personally and professionally?

*Though I think I learned a lot from my preteaching seminars, nothing that was said or done in education classes could have prepared me for the gut-level aspects of day-to-day teaching. You can talk about it and do everything in your power to psych yourself up for the real thing, but the feeling of having complete control of a classroom full of students has to be a unique experience for someone just starting out. Managing your own classroom is totally different from helping in another teacher's class. I couldn't avoid feeling like a guest during my aiding and student teaching semesters. Now I'm feeling the full force of the responsibility for my own classroom. It isn't that my knowledge of teaching has increased that much, it's just that overnight I'm having to behave like a real teacher. Up to this point I've been a student. (MacDonald & Healy, 1999, p. 2)*

In addition to the changes that occur when moving from the role of student to teacher, there is much "on-the-job training" that begins that first day in the classroom and hopefully continues throughout your teaching career. Teaching is simply too complex to be summed up in neat little boxes that can be easily dispensed to those wishing to enter the profession. Even the best beginning teachers find that there is a great deal more that needs to be understood and practiced. Although you will have learned a great deal and practiced many different teaching techniques as you complete your teacher preparation program, the road to mature teaching is a long one that requires even more thought, observation, discussion, and practice.

## What will I need to do to get a teaching position?

Somewhere in the not-too-distant future you will be finishing your teacher preparation program. After reaching this important milestone, an obvious next step will be to locate a job in your chosen profession. You will want to take what you have learned and apply it in the real world of the classroom. Finding the best possible match between your interests and skills and the available teaching positions can be made easier if you understand the steps that are needed to successfully find a good job. The typical procedures used to find a position are outlined on Table 15.1 and discussed in the following subsections.

### Know the Job Market

The job market for teachers across the country continues to improve (see Table 15.2). In 1999, the U.S.Department of Education estimated that more than 2 million new teachers will be needed in the first decade of the 21st century (Bradley, 1999). Two main reasons are cited for these opportunities (Bureau of Labor Statistics, 2001). The first is that large numbers of teachers are expected to retire within the next decade, creating vacancies at all levels. In addition, the number of students entering school systems is expected to rise gradually. These two factors have already led to shortages in certain teaching specialties and in many geographic regions.

Some subject areas and certain specialty positions currently have the greatest need for teachers, while others provide fewer opportunities. Well-qualified teachers in mathematics and science (especially chemistry and physics) are in the greatest demand. Educators with expertise in foreign languages and computer science are also highly recruited. Specialty positions in special education and bilingual education are additional areas of high need (Recruiting New Teachers, 2000). Physical education and social studies, on the other hand, are two areas in which the current supply of qualified teachers meets or exceeds the demand (Bureau of Labor Statistics, 2001).

| **TABLE 15.1    Steps in Finding a Teaching Position** ||
| **Step** | **Description** |
|---|---|
| Know the job market | Although there are variations between locations and for different subjects and levels taught, the job market for teachers continues to improve. |
| Locate openings | College placement services, Internet sites, and direct contact with schools and districts are all possible sources for locating job openings. |
| Submit applications | Most job openings require the submission of a cover letter, résumé, a completed job application form, and letters of reference. |
| Participate in interviews | You will participate in interviews conducted by a team of school personnel that may include teachers, administrators, and school board members who will quiz you about specific aspects of teaching and learning. |

**TABLE 15.2   Job Openings in Education, 2000–2010 (in thousands)**

| Occupation | Number Employed 2000 | Projected Number Employed 2010 | Total Job Openings Due to Growth and Replacements |
|---|---|---|---|
| Preschool and kindergarten teachers | 597 | 707 | 184 |
| Elementary teachers | 1,532 | 1,734 | 551 |
| Middle school teachers | 570 | 625 | 184 |
| Secondary school teachers | 1,113 | 1,314 | 540 |
| Special education teachers | 453 | 592 | 197 |

*Source: Occupational Employment: Projections to 2010,* by D. Hecker, 2001, Washington, DC: Bureau of Labor Statistics. Retrieved April 24, 2003, from http://stats.bls.gov/opub/mlr/2001/11/art4full.pdf

While the overall number of pre-K through 12 teaching openings has grown steadily during the past several years, some settings are affected more than others. For example, urban schools are currently experiencing severe shortages at nearly every level and for most specialties (Recruiting New Teachers, 2000). While the highest demands are in the areas of special education, science, mathematics, and bilingual education, teachers at all levels and for nearly every subject are needed. In addition, rural areas, because of their remote locations and typically lower teacher salaries, also have difficulty attracting enough teachers (Bureau of Labor Statistics, 2001).

## Locate Openings

Once you understand the general job market for teaching, you may wish to consider several options in locating openings of interest to you. Before actually selecting the best strategies, however, consider the level of flexibility you bring to the search process. Are you willing to move anywhere in the state or even across the nation in an effort to find a good position? Or are you "place bound" and only seeking a teaching job in a specific community or area? If you had a choice, would your want to work in an urban, suburban, or rural setting? Do you have thoughts at this point about the characteristics of the students with which you would most like to work? Your answers to these questions will help you begin to decide which strategies you may want to use in seeking a teaching position. Take a few moments now to reflect on your responses to these questions at this point in your teacher preparation program.

**Reflective Journey 15.1**

For new teachers willing to consider a variety of community settings, an effective job location strategy is to visit and consult with a college or university **placement service.** Designed to help all students at that institution find employment, these offices typically have up-to-date postings of state and national jobs in education that can be reviewed on a regular basis. With the growth of Internet access, most placement services also allow you to review these options on their websites. Normally, the basic services of the placement center are available to students or recent graduates at no cost.

Those who are targeting specific communities in their job search may be more successful in locating a position if they take a more direct and personal approach. By calling, writing, and taking every opportunity to make yourself known to teachers and administrators in districts of interest, the chances of getting hired are increased. Take the time needed to meet school administrators and teachers. If possible, consider volunteering time in the classroom as a way of gaining experience with students while making yourself known to school personnel. Make sure you know of the teaching openings that become available. Most districts post job openings in a centralized location and many provide this service on their websites.

## Submit Applications

Once you have located teaching positions that are of interest to you, the next step is to submit an application. Most applications have four main components:

- *Cover letter.* Also called a **letter of application,** this brief, one-page letter indicates that you are applying for a particular teaching position and states your qualifications for the job. Although each letter has much in common, you should individualize each of them for the specific job for which you are applying.

- *Résumé.* A **résumé** is generally a one- or two-page summary of your life as it relates to teaching and includes such things as your formal education (including teaching certificates earned), experiences related to teaching, awards, memberships in professional organizations, and special interests and skills that make you a strong candidate for a teaching position. College and university placement services often provide guidance in creating an effective résumé. A sample résumé is shown in Figure 15.1.

- *Application.* The **job application** itself is typically a standardized, multipage document from the local school district that asks for detailed information regarding your teacher preparation and skills in teaching. It often includes an essay question to assess both your writing skills and attitudes toward teaching. A separate application is completed for each teaching position of interest to you.

- *References.* Letters of recommendation from people who have seen you in the classroom working with students or who can speak to your academic preparation are another important element of the application process. To save everyone time and effort, most new teachers create a **placement file** with their college or university placement service that includes letters of recommendation. On request, this file is mailed to school districts of your choosing for a small fee.

## Participate in Interviews

Once school districts have reviewed all of the written applications submitted for a job vacancy, they select a small number of applicants for face-to-face interviews. Although commonly held in school district buildings, they may also take place at college and university job fairs or as part of professional education meetings. Depending on the circumstances, these interviews can be as short as half an hour or as long as several hours. Teachers, principals, school board members, and district administrators are all potential participants in these interviews.

Job interviews are a critical part of the search process and require careful preparation. Make sure you think about your attire so that you convey the right professional image and consider materials that you might bring to the interview to highlight your knowledge and skills. You should expect the interviewers to ask several challenging questions about teaching and learning as they seek to gain specific information about your

*Interviewing is an important part of the job search process.*

**Figure 15.1**   Sample Résumé

**MICHAEL J. HANSEN**
1453 Stevens Boulevard
Amherst, MA 01002
Phone: (555) 474-1800

**Personal Information**
Married Lisa M. Gibbons, June 7, 2001
No children
Age: 23; Health: excellent

**Education**
B.A. in mathematics, Gettysburg College, 2000
M.I.T. with elementary certification, University of Massachusetts at Lowell, 2002

**Experience with Students**
Volunteer, Springhill Elementary, Gettysburg, PA, grades 4 and 6, 1999–2000
Tutor in mathematics, elementary through middle school students, Lowell, MA
   2001–2002
Student teaching internship, fourth grade, Middleton Elementary, Lowell, MA,
   spring 2002

**Special Interests**
Trombone player through high school and undergraduate degree
High school wrestling and football
Math Olympics coach, 2000–2002

**Awards**
Dean's List, Gettysburg College, six of eight semesters
Pemberton Scholarship recipient, 2000–2002

**References**
Placement file available on request, Career Planning and Placement Center,
   University of Massachusetts at Lowell, 800 Tower Place, Lowell, MA 02894

qualifications and skills. Taking the time to think through the possible questions and your answers to them is an effective strategy to use in preparing for the interview. Most interviews also include time for you to ask questions of the district representatives. It is important that you be prepared to ask good questions about the school district and teaching position so that you can make an informed decision if a position is offered. Interviewers also gain important insights about you from the questions asked.

## Closing the Achievement Gap

As you think ahead to your future as an educator, it is important to understand that one of the key issues you will face relates to the many challenges associated with closing the achievement gap that exists between White middle-class students and the many other diverse groups of students who tend to be less successful in the classroom. Students from low-income families, African American students, Hispanic students, students with special needs, and students learning English as a second language are among the many that will need your assistance to perform well in the classroom. The national educational agenda, as evidenced in the No Child Left Behind Act of 2002 (see Chapter 14), clearly emphasizes the importance of helping every student learn. Individual states and school districts are also working hard to close this achievement gap.

Your role in this effort will be pivotal. It is clear that quality teaching is the essential ingredient needed to leave no child behind (*Education Week*, 2003). No matter where you choose to teach, your interactions with struggling students are critical to their success. You should begin now to develop the attitudes and skills needed to help every child learn.

In addition to developing the skills needed to be successful with all students, you may want to consider taking at least some time during your teaching career to work in a school that has a high percentage of low-performing students. Having quality teachers who can engage all students in effective learning experiences is even more critical for "high-poverty, high-minority, and low-achieving schools" (Olson, 2003, p. 10). Very few schools that fit this profile have been successful in attracting large numbers of well-qualified teachers to join their ranks. This has led to a "teacher gap" in which middle-class schools with mostly White students are able to hire a larger percentage of quality candidates than other less desirable schools. This gap can be effectively closed only when well-prepared teachers commit to working in these settings.

### Explore and Reflect

Learn more about closing the achievement gap by reading the online source articles by *Education Week* (2003) and Olson (2003) and reviewing other online resources provided in the *Reflect on Diversity* module for Chapter 15 of the Companion Website.

1. What skills and attitudes do you have that will help you be successful in helping every student learn? What do you need to do or learn in order to strengthen your ability to leave no child behind?

2. Can you envision yourself teaching in a low-income, highly diverse school setting? Why or why not? What would be needed for you to actively consider this type of assignment?

 *To explore this topic further and submit your responses online, go to the Reflect on Diversity module for Chapter 15 of the Companion Website for this text.*

*Sources:* "To Close the Gap, Quality Counts" by *Education Week. Quality Counts 2003*, p. 7. Retrieved April 23, 2003 from the World Wide Web at http://www.edweek.org/sreports/qc03/templates/article.cfm?slug=17exec.h22; "Quality Counts Reveals National 'Teacher Gap' " by L. Olson, 2003, *Education Week*, January 8, p. 10. Retrieved April 23, 2003, from http://www.edweek.org/ew/ew_printstory.cfm?slug=16qc.h22

## What can I expect as a first-year teacher?

No two teachers or classroom settings are ever exactly alike, so it is difficult to predict with certainty what your first year of teaching will be like. With that said, however, new teachers' reflections on this experience suggest some common responses to the first year of teaching (see Figure 15.2). Four specific elements of beginning teaching will be addressed in more detail here. The physical setting of your classroom and school, the students themselves, parents and families, and colleagues and administrators in your school district will all have a significant impact on your first year of teaching.

**Figure 15.2**   Comments from First-Year Teachers

Here are some typical comments made by first-year teachers:

At the beginning, I just wanted to get through my first year of teaching. . . . And I've changed in my perspective from that kind of survival mode to now where I want to focus on refining everything, and really honing my skills, and trying to do everything a little better every time. (Archer, 2001, p. 52)

The greatest difference between my expectations and actual classroom experiences has been the arduous task of balancing lessons that target the high achievers and low achievers in the same classroom. . . . During the first six weeks of teaching pre-algebra, I altered my teaching strategies to reach those students who counted on their fingers, those who multiplied and divided on a beginner level, and those who have surpassed all eighth grade objectives. (DePaul, 1998, p. 2)

My first year of teaching has been full of many wonderful surprises. I never knew the average teenage girl's voice could hit such octaves. I never expected to reach a point in my life where I would yearn for my bed at 9:30 every night. I was not prepared for the moment I first heard myself ask, "Does anyone in class not think that spitting on the floor is inappropriate behavior?" But most of all, I never thought that teaching would be such an exhilarating and rewarding career, continually pushing me in my quest to be a master educator. (DePaul, 1998, p. 26).

*Sources:* First Impressions by J. Archer, *Education Week,* September 5, 2001, pp. 48–54; *What to Expect Your First Year of Teaching,* by A. DePaul, 1998, Washington, DC: U.S. Department of Education.

## The Physical Setting

Have you ever taken the time to look carefully at the condition of school buildings in your local community? If you have, it should be clear from these observations that schools tend to be older, overcrowded, and often in need of significant updating. Recent surveys indicate that the average public school was built more than 40 years ago, with approximately one third not having been renovated since 1980 (see Table 15.3) (National Center for Education Statistics, 2001). A report

**TABLE 15.3   Age of School Buildings**

| School Characteristic | Built Before 1950 | Built 1950–1969 | Built 1970–1984 | Built 1985 or Later |
|---|---|---|---|---|
| Elementary | 29% | 46% | 15% | 11% |
| Secondary | 24 | 46 | 23 | 8 |
| Northeastern schools | 30 | 49 | 15 | 6 |
| Southeastern schools | 23 | 43 | 20 | 14 |
| Central U.S. schools | 33 | 46 | 14 | 8 |
| Western schools | 25 | 44 | 19 | 13 |

*Source: The Condition of Education,* by National Center for Education Statistics, 2000, Washington, DC: U.S. Government Printing Office.

from the U.S. General Accounting Office (2000) estimates that it would cost about $112 billion to bring existing American schools into good overall condition. And while increasing numbers of new schools are being built to accommodate rising student enrollments, the problems of overcrowding are still significant in many areas.

It is also important to realize that the physical setting you will inherit as a new teacher will probably be one of the less desirable classrooms containing fewer pieces of new equipment and more materials that other veteran teachers have left behind. While this "natural pecking order" can be found in every work situation and may be viewed as negative, it need not hinder your ability to teach effectively. What is important is that you are aware that it is likely to occur and work to compensate for it. Take a moment now to reflect on this aspect of teaching. How do you think you will feel about getting desks, chairs, teaching supplies, and classroom space that have been passed over by others? Do you think that the physical setting you inherit will affect the ways in which you will teach and your students will learn?

**Reflective Journey 15.2**

## The Students

Most new teachers indicate that students are both their biggest frustration and greatest reward in the first years of teaching. On the one hand, it is frustrating when teachers give all that they have in an effort to stimulate learning and some students just don't seem to care. Conversely, most teachers report that there is no greater satisfaction than seeing the light dawn as a student grasps a concept you have worked hard to teach. Susan Palmer was a beginning teacher during the 2000–2001 school year. Susan's story, like many others, is full of many ups and downs. Through it all, however, she found that her relationships with students brought both the greatest joys and the biggest headaches. Susan's experiences are common to many first-year teachers:

> Palmer kept an apple-shaped book on her desk all year long to record the high points of teaching: the day a student gave her an apple; the time one of her most difficult classes really got into a discussion on dreams; the occasions when a struggling student finally engaged in learning.
>
> "That's my favorite part," Palmer says. "It's cool when a student writes a note and says, 'Thanks.' It's even better to show me by working, by showing improvements."
>
> But by year's end, about half of the apple-shaped notebook was still blank. And the lows of teaching outnumbered the highs.
>
> Palmer found herself irritated, even incensed, by student apathy. At the start of the year, she had not realized how tough it would be to motivate them. (May, 2001, p. 2)

## Parents and Families

As with students, most beginning teachers find that working with parents and families can be both challenging and rewarding. It is difficult when parents either don't get involved in the educational process or question every move the teacher makes. Sometimes, for example, parents push their own children too hard and expect them to earn all A's. If that doesn't happen, the teacher may receive the blame. Other parents are just too busy or too stressed to participate in their child's education. On the other hand,

*Parent conferences are an excellent communication tool.*

many parents can be important allies in the educational process and provide much-needed support to you as a beginning teacher. When good relationships with parents have been established, they will work with you to make sure their children are learning and growing. This will make your job as teacher both easier and more rewarding. In addition, having supportive parents can be a big boost to your self-esteem during those periods of uncertainty and doubt that will come your way during those early years of teaching.

## Mentoring Opportunities

As a student in a teacher education program, you now have many opportunities to talk with your professors and other students both in and out of class as you encounter questions or problems related to teaching. Many new teachers are surprised to find that these same opportunities for help and support are not as readily available in most schools (Grubb, 2000). Teachers and administrators won't try to avoid you and they will certainly provide support when it is asked for. The realities of school life, however, are that each day you will walk into your classroom, close the door, and spend your teaching day mostly isolated from others who work next door or down the hall (Goodlad, 1984). The few times during the day when you are free from students (lunch periods, planning times, and after school hours) are crowded with other activities that make it difficult for you and others to commit the extra time and energy needed to get together and discuss concerns and successes.

Numerous efforts have been made in recent years to deal with these feelings of isolation. For example, many states and school districts are implementing **mentoring programs** in which new teachers are paired with veteran educators who serve as guides through the struggles and successes of the beginning years. (See Figure 15.3 and the section on mentoring later in this chapter.) New teachers are also creating their own informal support systems by seeking out more experienced teachers and other beginning teachers to help them understand and respond to the many problems they encounter in the classroom. In either case, these interactions are proving invaluable:

> Mentors are very important. Every new teacher should have a mentor teacher who can help her or him to break in. It would also be helpful to connect first- and second-year teachers. The second-year teachers would have fresh memories of experiences that first-year teachers would encounter and would be able to give them some forewarning and suggestions regarding how to best handle those experiences. (DePaul, 1998, p. 15)

**Figure 15.3**  Mentoring Program Goals

There are three major goals that a quality mentoring program should be working to accomplish:

1. *Orientation to the district, school, and classroom.* New teachers need to learn the job expectations, the organizational structure and climate, key people, and educational philosophy of others in the district.

2. *Induction to the profession.* Mentors work with new teachers to help them refine their skills in teaching as they move from novice to more experienced educators.

3. *Creating a climate for lifelong learning.* New teachers need to view their profession as a continuing journey of refinement as they strive to become master teachers in their work with students. A quality mentoring program assists teachers in this effort.

*Source:* "Ask the Mentor of Mentors: A Collection of Answers to Frequently Asked Questions," by B. Sweeny, 2001. Retrieved April 24, 2003, from http://teachermentors.com/RSOD%20Site/AskMOM.html

# What must I do to be successful as a beginning teacher?

You can take several steps during your early years in the classroom to increase your chances of success. You should plan to continually refine and strengthen your personal teaching style, create a community of learners in your classroom, maintain a healthy lifestyle, and understand why some teachers leave the profession (see Table 15.4). Begin now to develop the skills and attitudes you will need to be successful during your beginning years in the classroom and beyond.

## Refine Your Teaching Style

One message that has been repeated several times throughout this text is that there is no one "right" way of teaching. There are many different styles of good teaching that are based largely on the personality and strengths of individual teachers. As you identify personal strengths and limitations and grow in your understanding of teaching and learning, your personal style will begin to emerge. This process of refinement should start now and continue for most, if not all, of your teaching career.

You will need to take several steps as you hone your personal style. The first is to *continue to grow in your understanding of students*. Your perceptions of students and how they learn (see Chapter 6) should always be an essential foundation for your curriculum planning, teaching strategies, and discipline options. A second step in the development of your personal teaching style is to *clarify your beliefs about good teaching* (MacDonald & Healy, 1999). As you read the theory and research of others regarding teaching, work to identify those attitudes and teaching strategies that make the most sense to you. A third component needed to refine your teaching style is to *develop a teaching plan*. After you have identified the elements of teaching that you want to implement, it is then necessary to create from them an overall strategy for how you will approach teaching. A final step is to *monitor the development of your own teaching skills*. MacDonald and Healy (1999) identify three good strategies that you can use to become a better teacher. The first is to obtain direct feedback from your students. You can seek this information through class discussions or simple evaluations following instruction. Two other options are to audiotape or videotape classroom instruction and then use these recordings to critique and improve your teaching. One final strategy for monitoring your own teaching is to regularly reflect on the little things you are doing in the classroom and ask yourself how you can improve them.

Take a few moments now to reflect on what you know and what you need to know about your personal teaching style. What do you feel you know about students? What do you think you still need to know? Can you identify basic beliefs you have about teaching at this point in your

| TABLE 15.4 Becoming a Successful Teacher | |
|---|---|
| **Step** | **Description** |
| Refine your teaching style | You will need to continue to grow in your understanding of students, clarify your beliefs about good teaching, develop a teaching plan, and monitor the development of your own teaching. |
| Create a community of learners | By being a caring person who takes advantage of naturally occurring opportunities for community building and using teacher-created situations, you can build a community of learners in your future classroom. |
| Maintain a healthy lifestyle | You will need to make time and energy to maintain good physical and mental health so that you can be successful in working with others. |
| Understand why teachers leave the profession | It is important for you to understand why some educators leave the profession so that you can better determine if you would be happy working as a teacher. |

development? What teaching strategies have you identified as important to you? If you are currently working with students in some capacity, how could you seek feedback about the strengths and areas for growth in your work with these students?

## Create a Community of Learners

Another factor that will help ensure your success as a classroom teacher is the creation of what is often called a community of learners (Kohn, 1996). When there are strong relationships among students and between students and teachers, the opportunities for learning are greatly enhanced (see Chapter 8 for more information). From the first day of your teaching career, you should work to build good relationships. Creating a learning community where respect and cooperation predominate is not easy, but it is well worth the effort needed to implement.

In a study of 24 elementary schools from around the country, students were asked to what extent they felt their classrooms and schools were supportive communities (Battistich, Solomon, Kim, Watson, & Schaps, 1995). Those students who experienced a positive learning community reported liking school more than those who did not have the advantages of this setting. They were better able to resolve conflicts with others and tended to be more supportive of their peers. In addition, these students were more likely to see learning as valuable and actively engaged in classroom activities. Furthermore, these findings were strongest in schools with high percentages of low-income students.

The fundamental starting point for building a community of learners is for you to *be a caring person* in your communications with students. As you treat students with the dignity and respect they deserve, they in turn will interact with each other and you more positively. As described in Kohn (1996), a classroom community is a place where:

> . . . care and trust are emphasized above restrictions and threats, where unity and pride (of accomplishment and in purpose) replace winning and losing, and where each person is asked, helped, and inspired to live up to such ideals and values as kindness, fairness, and responsibility. [Such] a classroom community seeks to meet each student's need to feel competent, connected to others, and autonomous. . . . Students are not only exposed to basic human values, they also have many opportunities to think about, discuss, and act on those values, while gaining experiences that promote empathy and understanding of others. (p. 102)

A community of learners also requires strong working relationships with colleagues. Other teachers and administrators can provide you with much-needed support, encouragement, and guidance as you begin your teaching career. You, in turn, can provide colleagues with insights that will strengthen their classroom interactions as well. As teachers, administrators, and staff exchange ideas about teaching, learning, and dealing with student behaviors, a school-wide learning community is created. The professional interactions at this level provide opportunities for all the adults involved to grow both personally and professionally. This growth will continue to strengthen the learning communities within individual classrooms (Kohn, 1996). Table 15.5 suggests some ways to build communities of learners.

## Maintain a Healthy Lifestyle

Being successful in the classroom also means that you must take the time needed to maintain your own personal health. You will need to be physically, mentally, and emotionally fit in order to manage the many challenges you will face as a teacher. The first year of teaching can be especially difficult for many teachers and every effort must be made to counterbalance the stresses with a healthy lifestyle. Each person has unique ways of taking care of his or her own physical and mental health. It may be a good idea to write down a list of options that work for you and keep it handy for those times when it will be

*Exercise helps in maintaining a healthy lifestyle.*

| TABLE 15.5 | Examples of Community Building |
|---|---|

| Example | Description |
|---|---|
| Getting acquainted through interviews | At the beginning of each school year, many teachers take the time to get students better acquainted by having them interview each other. It is often helpful to begin by asking students to develop the list of questions they would like to ask. Suggest that students pair up with a classmate that they don't know as well and have each pair interview their partner. The information learned can then be shared with the rest of the class. |
| Class spirit (elementary) | To help elementary students develop a better sense of identity and cohesiveness, work with them in developing a list of class favorites. You could have a class animal, name, song, cheer, cartoon character, or other markers that help students see themselves as a cohesive group. Once these class attributes are identified, they can be reinforced throughout the year. For example, a class song could be practiced and sung for parents at an open house or characteristics of the class animal could be researched for a science project and written about as part of a language arts task. |
| Tower building (secondary) | Give groups of four or five students straws and paper clips. Tell them that they have 10 minutes to construct the highest tower possible. Once time is completed, have each group identify and share one factor that facilitated their work. Record these responses. Then ask each group to share one thing that blocked the group's effectiveness and list them as well. Use these positives and negatives to have a group discussion of how groups function and the implications for their work together in class. |

*Source: Comprehensive Classroom Management: Creating Communities of Support and Solving Problems,* 6th ed., by V. Jones and L. Jones, 2001, Boston: Allyn and Bacon.

**Reflective Journey 15.4**

needed. What do you do to maintain your own physical well-being? Do you engage in exercise, find time for extra sleep, and vacation to stay physically healthy? Are there other strategies you use? Similarly, how do you maintain your mental health? Figure 15.4 provides further suggestions for your consideration.

## Understand Why Teachers Leave the Profession

While most teachers are satisfied with their career choice (see Table 15.6), approximately 8% are not. Typically, those who end up leaving the profession are those who are dissatisfied with teaching. (See Table 15.7 for some of the more common reasons for leaving.) In addition, much of this attrition occurs within the first 5 years. In a time of increasing personnel shortages, it is of considerable concern to many in education that fairly large numbers of new teachers choose to leave education after only a few years in the classroom. Statistics indicate that nationally approximately 30% of all new teachers and nearly 50% of new educators in urban districts leave the field in the first 5 years (Markow, Fauth, & Gravitch, 2001).

One frequently cited reason for the relatively high turnover rate for new teachers is the *stress of the job.* It takes considerable time and effort to engage in quality instruction. During the first few years of teaching, it can take far longer than many expect to develop the creative lessons needed to motivate and excite students (Kronowitz, 1999). Sam Fisher, who was observed during his first year of teaching in Estacada, Oregon, experienced this problem during an earth science lesson (Boss, 2001b). Standing in front of his fourth-grade class a month into the new school year, Fisher realized that the unit on erosion from the textbook was not working out well:

**Figure 15.4**   Maintaining a Healthy Lifestyle

- Plan a weekend away (or stay home and hibernate).
- Buy yourself flowers.
- Read a book you "don't have time for."
- Play with your pet.
- Buy a new article of clothing.
- Spend some time alone.
- Take a walk.
- Bake or cook.
- Listen to music.
- Go to the gym.
- Give yourself a facial.
- Have your house or apartment cleaned.
- Get a babysitter.
- Keep a journal.
- Play a board game.

*Source: Your First-Year of Teaching and Beyond,* 3rd ed. (pp. 176–177), by E. Kronowitz, 1999, New York: Longman.

He snaps his book shut and asks the class, "Is it just me, or is this boring?" That gets their attention. "Tomorrow," he promises, "we'll start a new unit." Then he asks the class to suggest ways that the Earth changes. That's the larger lesson that fourth-graders are supposed to master in science. What do they wonder about? What intrigues them? In the lively discussion that ensues, several students bring up questions about volcanoes. Fisher feels his own curiosity heating up. "Tomorrow," he promises, "we'll start on volcanoes." (Boss, 2001b, p. 23)

**TABLE 15.6   Reasons for Satisfaction with Teaching**

| Reason | Percentage Citing |
|---|---|
| Enjoy working with students | 22 |
| Rewarding profession | 19 |
| Feel good knowing a child has learned | 16 |
| Making a difference in a student's life | 16 |
| Get to see child's growth | 15 |
| Love teaching (general) | 14 |

*Source:* From Markow, D., Fauth, S. and Gravitch, D. *The MetLife Survey of the American Teacher 2001: Key Elements of Quality Schools.* N.Y.: MetLife, Inc. Reprinted with permission.

**TABLE 15.7**    Reasons for Teacher Dissatisfaction

| Reason | Percentage Citing |
|---|---|
| Low salary | 18 |
| Lack of administrative support | 17 |
| Too much administration | 15 |
| Discipline problems | 14 |
| Lack of resources | 14 |
| Lack of support | 14 |
| Large class size | 14 |

*Source:* From Markow, D., Faith, S. and Gravitch, D. *The MetLife Survey of the American Teacher 2001: Key Elements of Quality Schools.* N.Y.: MetLife, Inc. Reprinted with permission.

This promise to his students meant that Fisher was up all night, surfing the Internet to locate materials he could use to teach the promised unit on volcanoes. Not only that, but inventing this new unit required several weeks of additional evening and weekend work.

Another common stressor for teachers is the challenge of *helping students deal with social pressures.* Each situation is complex and typically beyond the teacher's ability to fully resolve. Yet, when teachers commit their time and energy in an attempt to help students deal with these situations, the resulting stress can be significant. Interactions with family members, counselors, law enforcement personnel, and students themselves can be emotionally draining.

The issue of *low teacher salaries* is often identified as a significant negative factor associated with teaching. (See Figure 15.5 for average 2000–2001 salaries.) It is the most frequently cited reason teachers give for dissatisfaction with their jobs (Markow et al., 2001). A recent survey of young college graduates also found that nearly 80% of the respondents felt that teachers were seriously underpaid (Farkas, Johnson, & Foleno, 2000). Finally, the *33rd Annual Phi Delta Kappa/Gallup Poll of the Public's Attitudes Toward the Public Schools* (Rose & Gallup, 2001) determined that 88% of the general public felt that raising teacher salaries would be an important strategy to use in addressing teacher shortages.

Despite these consistent perceptions that low teacher salaries contribute to people either avoiding education or leaving the profession, there is at least some evidence that other issues may be more significant in both attracting and keeping good people in the classroom. While 75% of teachers who had taught for 5 years or less felt they were underpaid, given the hypothetical choice between a significantly higher salary or better student behavior and parental support, 86% chose the latter option. Similarly, 82% hypothetically chose stronger administrative backing over a significantly higher salary (Farkas et al., 2000). While improved salaries would undoubtedly make a difference in attracting and retaining teachers, these other factors just mentioned appear to be much more significant to teachers (Hanushek, Kain, & Rivkin, 2001).

A final reason that some teachers give for leaving teaching is *frustration with the system.* Teachers enter the profession committed to helping students become well-educated, productive citizens. These good intentions can get derailed, however, by the schooling system in which these dedicated individuals find themselves working. The need to follow a curriculum determined by others, the mounds of paperwork to meet local, state, and national mandates, the low levels of financial support, the difficulty of bringing about effective change, and the differing opinions about the goals and directions of education are just some of the many irritants that teachers encounter. Most teachers find ways to cope with these frus-

**Figure 15.5**   Average Teacher Salaries, 2000–2001

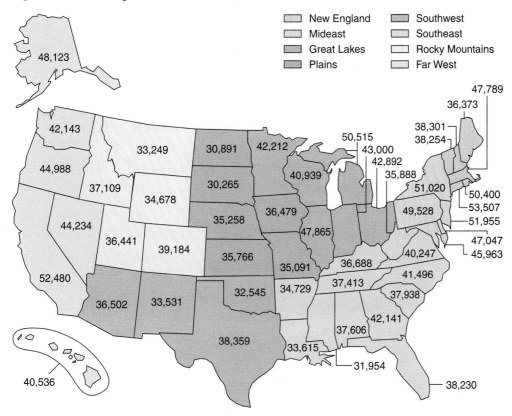

*Source:* From *Survey Analysis of Teacher Salary Trends 2001,* by Nelson, F. H., Drown, R., and Gould, J. (2002). Washington, DC: American Federation of Teachers, AFL-CIO. Reprinted with permission.

trations while continuing to focus on the positive aspects of teaching. For some, however, these annoying elements build to the point that they overshadow all of the good things that are happening in the classroom. Table 15.8 provides some suggestions for dealing with teachers' frustrations with the system.

**TABLE 15.8   Dealing with System Frustrations**

| Strategy | Description |
|---|---|
| Avoid trouble areas when possible | If, for example, you find that attending school board meetings is disturbing, try to avoid attending and spend the time you save in activities that are more productive for you. |
| Pick your battles carefully | Sometimes it is better to set aside your dissatisfaction over little things so that you can save your energy for those that really matter. By focusing on trying to change a fewer number of these problem areas, you will be more likely to succeed without creating undue personal stress. |
| Focus on what really matters | Every profession, including teaching, has its frustrations. But if you spend the majority of your time thinking about the problems, it means there is less opportunity to focus on the positives. Shifting mentally to an emphasis on things that can help make things better in your classroom and school will make the problem areas seem less troublesome. |

# MASTER TEACHER SERIES

## Segment VI: When the Test Seems to Be All That Matters

The children in Lesley-Diann Jones's class in Red Hook, Brooklyn, have had a hard time passing the standardized tests imposed by New York State and New York City. Her challenge, and theirs, was to prepare themselves for another round of tests. Measured by the results in the most recent round of tests, it wasn't a great year. None of Ms. Jones 10 fifth graders had a passing score and only 4 of the 10 fourth-grade students passed. Ms. Jones faces questions from herself and others about the decisions she made, the methods she used, and how much time she devoted to test preparation versus social skills and focusing on students' home lives. She must break difficult news to many of her students and face comparisons with the outcomes realized by other teachers in similar classrooms.

### For Deeper Understanding

1. "I have to fight for them. Fight for them to have the right—the privilege—to walk across that stage on June 26th and graduate" (Lesley-Diann Jones, ABC News—Master Teacher Series, 8/23/00). Why does Ms. Jones say she has to fight for her students? Do you agree with her position?

2. Most opponents of high-stakes testing suggest that multiple measures should be used to make high-stakes decisions. What are other measures that might be used?

3. What do you feel were Ms. Jones's strengths as a teacher? Her weaknesses? If you had to write her a short note, what would it say?

4. If students are different, schools are different, and teachers are different, should we have the same expectations for all students? Why or why not?

5. As Lesley-Diann Jones looks back on this year, what successes will she remember?

 *To submit your responses online, go to the Master Teacher Series module for Chapter 15 of the Companion Website.*

## How can I continue to grow personally and professionally?

Once you have successfully navigated through those first few years of teaching, there is still much to be done as you continue to mature as an educator. You will have both good days and bad ones. There will be many successes and some failures. The challenges and victories lead to both personal and professional growth and make teaching a career unlike most others. Good teachers experience these highs and lows throughout their careers and use them as the basis for continued growth in their chosen profession. This process of professional development occurs through personal reflection, reflections with others, additional formal learning experiences, and advanced certification options (see Table 15.9).

### Personal Reflections on Teaching and Learning

One way in which experienced teachers continue to grow both personally and professionally is through **reflection.** Conducted individually or with others, these thoughtful considerations of the teaching/learning process help teachers refine their knowledge and skills. The importance of reflection has been emphasized throughout this book as an essential tool in understanding the content and processes of education.

**TABLE 15.9   Growing as a Professional Educator**

| Strategy | Options |
|---|---|
| Personal reflections | • Journaling<br>• Teaching portfolio |
| Reflections with others | • Mentoring<br>• Informal collaborations with colleagues |
| Additional formal learning experiences | • In-service programs<br>• Workshops<br>• Graduate degree programs |
| Advanced certification options | • Second-stage teacher certification<br>• National Board for Professional Teaching Standards certification |

Two tools have been integrated into this text to assist you in personal reflection. The first is the use of a **journal.** Keeping a journal is an excellent method of continuing to grow as an educator. When you write down both the positive and negative things you learned from an experience and include reminders of factors to consider in similar future experiences, this journaling of events becomes a very personal and useful tool in refining your teaching.

Another personal reflection tool emphasized throughout this text has been the **teaching portfolio.** These samples of student work and teacher activities are another way in which teachers can learn to improve their instruction. But, collecting these artifacts as a future teacher is not enough. You will need to stop and reflect on the materials you have placed in the portfolio (Lyons, 1999). Take a few moments now to think about the portfolio materials you have collected for this text. What do they tell you about the teaching techniques you will probably use? Are these techniques consistent with your developing philosophy of education? What do you need to know and be able to do to improve your teaching and student learning? As you reflect on your answers to these and other questions, continued growth as an educator will take place.

**Reflective Journey 15.5**

## Reflections with Others

For many years, professions such as medicine have required new inductees to complete an apprenticeship period in a real-world setting before becoming fully endorsed to work more independently in their chosen career. This gives the new graduate an opportunity to work in the field while reflecting on effective practice with other more experienced professionals. Recently, educators have grown interested in having new teachers serve a similar apprenticeship under the guidance of experienced teachers. For example, the National Commission on Teaching and America's Future (1996) recommended that the first few years of teaching be restructured so that new teachers can work more closely with master teachers to hone their knowledge and skills.

*Teachers benefit from reflection with colleagues.*

## Using Portfolios to Assess Student Progress

Throughout this text you have been provided with opportunities to develop your own portfolio of materials to demonstrate what you know and can do as a future teacher. As mentioned in Chapter 6, it is also important to realize that portfolios are growing in importance as a student assessment tool. Rather than relying solely on test results to measure student learning, many teachers are working with students to assist them in thoughtfully constructing a portfolio to demonstrate their growth as learners.

> A portfolio at the K–12 education level is a collection of a student's work which can be used to demonstrate his or her skills and accomplishments. An educational portfolio is more than just a group of projects and papers stored in a file folder. It includes other features such as teachers' evaluations, rubrics and student self-reflections.... A portfolio may be used to demonstrate a student's achievements in specific subject areas such as mathematics and science or it may be used across the curriculum to assess abilities in all subject areas. (Lankers, 1998, p. 1)

Not everyone, however, believes that portfolios can be an effective assessment tool. Berger (1998) emphasizes the difficulties in measuring what students are learning through the use of portfolios. He suggests that "boosters today promote portfolios as 'accurate measures of educational performance,' offering 'credible,' 'standardized' data. Unfortunately, portfolio scoring simply doesn't work" (p. 1).

### Research the Issue

Research this topic online using the links provided in the *Engage in the Debate* module for this chapter of the Companion Website. Link to the online source articles by Lankers (1998) and Berger (1998) and explore the information provided at the additional sites listed.

1. From your research, what do others say are the values of using student portfolios as an assessment tool?
2. What are the current problems associated with student portfolios?

### Explore Your Views

1. Do you think portfolios should replace or supplement standardized tests? Why or why not?
2. Can you see yourself using student portfolios as an assessment strategy in your future classroom? What are your reasons for the position you take?

*To research this issue and submit your responses online, go to the Engage in the Debate module for Chapter 15 of the Companion Website for this text.*

*Sources:* "Portfolios: A New Wave in Assessment," by A. M. D. Lankers, 1998, *T.H.E. Journal.* Retrieved April 28, 2003, from http://www.thejournal.com/magazine/vault/A3380.cfm; "Portfolio Folly," by P. Berger, 1998, *Education Week,* January 14. Retrieved April 28, 2003, from http://www.edweek.com/ew/ew_printstory.cfm?slug+18berger.h1

The first 1 to 3 years of teaching is often referred to as a period of **teacher induction**, during which you will become acclimated to life in the schools. During this period, you will receive informal and/or formal assistance from other educators so that you can refine the knowledge and skills needed to be successful in the classroom. Informal support includes things like getting advice from the teacher next door on the best ways to manage the paperwork associated with teaching or sitting down with an experienced teacher to discuss ideas for presenting a specific concept to students. Because teachers lead very busy lives, you will probably need to take the initiative in seeking out this assistance from others.

In many school districts today, new teachers also receive more formalized assistance from an expert teacher who serves as a mentor. Mentoring, which emerged in the 1980s as an effort to help novice educators develop the skills they needed to be successful in the classroom, has become an essential component of teacher induction in many schools. Mentors are often either paid additional salary for serving in this role or are given release time from teaching so that they can dedicate more of their energy to providing meaningful assistance to new teachers.

A review of research on mentoring programs (Holloway, 2001a) indicates that this activity benefits both novice teachers and those who serve as mentors. In one survey, 96% and 98% of all new teachers and mentors, respectively, believed that they benefited from the experience. In addition, other research shows that new teachers who engage in reflective activities with their mentors both improve their skills in teaching and are less likely to leave the profession. Mentors find that their role allows them to help others while also benefiting from the new teachers' fresh ideas and enthusiasm.

As you collaborate both informally and formally with more experienced colleagues, numerous opportunities will arise to think through with them the many intricacies of the teaching/learning process. This practice of reflection has the potential to lead to significant growth as an educator. These thoughtful considerations of your teaching and student learning will lay the groundwork for a successful career in education. It is also important to remember that this attitude of learning and growing as a teacher will keep you excited and challenged throughout your years in the classroom.

## Additional Formal Learning Experiences

While you will learn a great deal from conversations with other teachers, there are also many opportunities for professional growth that come from additional formal learning experiences. Through in-service programs, workshops, and course work leading to a graduate degree, you will have many options to grow in your understanding of teaching and learning.

**In-service programs.**   Each year, schools and school districts identify specific issues that they feel are important topics for teachers and administrators to study in more depth. For example, a school may choose to review the use of portfolios as an assessment strategy. Or, a district may wish to look at new materials and methods for use in the science curriculum. For the issues selected, schools and districts set aside time for **in-service education** opportunities. In some instances, school district personnel serve as leaders for these training sessions. For other experiences, state or national experts are called on to conduct the in-service education.

**Workshops.**   Many teachers continue their education by periodically taking additional courses through colleges and universities that are designed to give teachers a deeper understanding of topics that are of interest to them. Many institutions offer courses each term that provide teachers with new learning opportunities. For example, the University of Missouri at Kansas City offered courses in understanding autism, legal issues related to teaching, science education, storytelling, teaching students with special needs, and math education as options for interested teachers during winter semester 2002 (University of Missouri at Kansas City, 2002). In addition to the more traditional workshop courses where students and instructors meet face to face, many colleges and universities (including the University of Missouri at Kansas City) also offer distance learning courses that are either conducted through written correspondence or via the Internet. While these workshop courses typically cannot be used as part of a graduate degree program, they provide teachers with greater depth of understanding on a wide variety of topics.

**Graduate degree programs.**   Once educators have met the initial challenges of teaching, many find that completing a graduate degree program is another important way in which they can grow as professionals. Approximately 45% of current teachers hold a master's degree, while another 1% possess a doctorate (Parsad, Lewis, & Farris, 2001). Graduate degree programs in education are numerous and include specialties in such things as early childhood education, literacy, mathematics education, science education, instructional technology, multicultural education, and special education. In most districts, teachers who receive an advanced degree are usually rewarded with an increase in their annual salary. While this shouldn't be the primary reason for completing a graduate program, this financial incentive does make the additional study more attractive to many teachers.

### Advanced Certification Options

Because of the complex nature of teaching, more and more states are recognizing the need for teachers to continue their learning throughout their careers. Rather than following an older model in which educators were given a permanent teaching credential that required no further education or development, many states now require teachers to complete a program that leads to an advanced level of teacher certification. The National Association of State Directors of Teacher Education and Certification (2001) refers to advanced teacher preparation as **second-stage teacher certification** and indicates that 44 states currently offer educators this option and, of that number, 27 require that all teachers eventually complete advanced certification programs (see Table 15.10).

**TABLE 15.10    Second-Stage Teacher Certification**

| State | Second-Stage Certificate Required? | Second-Stage Certificate Offered? | State | Second-Stage Certificate Required? | Second-Stage Certificate Offered? |
|---|---|---|---|---|---|
| Alabama | N | Y | Montana | N | Y |
| Alaska | N | N | Nebraska | N | Y |
| Arizona | Y | Y | Nevada | N | Y |
| Arkansas | N | N | New Hampshire | Y | Y |
| California | Y | Y | New Jersey | Y | Y |
| Colorado | N | Y | New Mexico | Y | Y |
| Connecticut | Y | Y | New York | Y | Y |
| Delaware | N | Y | North Carolina | Y | Y |
| Florida | N | N | North Dakota | Y | Y |
| Georgia | N | N | Ohio | N | Y |
| Hawaii | N | N | Oklahoma | Y | Y |
| Idaho | N | Y | Oregon | Y | Y |
| Illinois | Y | Y | Pennsylvania | Y | Y |
| Indiana | N | Y | Rhode Island | Y | Y |
| Iowa | Y | Y | South Carolina | Y | Y |
| Kansas | N | Y | South Dakota | N | N |
| Kentucky | Y | Y | Tennessee | Y | Y |
| Louisiana | N | Y | Texas | N | Y |
| Maine | Y | Y | Utah | Y | Y |
| Maryland | Y | Y | Vermont | Y | Y |
| Massachusetts | Y | Y | Virginia | N | Y |
| Michigan | Y | Y | Washington | Y | Y |
| Minnesota | Y | Y | West Virginia | N | Y |
| Mississippi | N | N | Wisconsin | N | N |
| Missouri | Y | Y | Wyoming | N | N |

*Source:* From *The NASDTEC Manual on the Preparation and Certification of Educational Personnel,* by National Association of State Directors of Teacher Education and Certification, 2001, Dubuque, IA: Kendall/Hunt. Reprinted with permission.

In addition to state options for advanced teacher certification, the National Board for Professional Teaching Standards (NBPTS) offers a nationally recognized opportunity for teachers to demonstrate competence as master teachers. Created in 1987, the NBPTS has as its mission to enhance teaching and learning by these means:

- Maintaining high and rigorous standards for what accomplished teachers should know and be able to do

- Providing a national voluntary system certifying teachers who meet these standards

- Advocating related education reforms to integrate national board certification in American education and to capitalize on the expertise of national board certified teachers (National Board for Professional Teaching Standards, 2002).

Teachers who seek national board certification work closely with a mentor who helps them complete a rigorous portfolio demonstrating their teaching skills. Thirty-one states currently give teachers with national board certification either one-time or permanent salary increases of several thousand dollars for their demonstrated competence as master teachers.

## explore your beliefs

### National Board Certified Teachers

The National Board for Professional Teaching Standards (NBPTS) was established in 1987 to provide a voluntary process that teachers can use to demonstrate advanced teaching skills. Similar to the system medical doctors have for their profession, experienced teachers spend an entire year developing portfolios of their work, providing videotapes of their teaching, and taking an exam to assess their knowledge of subject matter and teaching (Archer, 2002). Many states are rewarding those who successfully complete the certification process with a raise in salary.

Although most educators support the concept of advanced teacher certification, some concerns are being voiced. One major criticism of the NBPTS system is that it certifies a low percentage of minority teachers (Viadero, 2002). Despite the fact that minority teachers account for more than 15% of the workforce, only about 7% are national board certified. The causes for this discrepancy are currently under investigation. Because teachers seeking national board certification spend more than $2,000 in fees and put forth a great deal of personal effort to complete the process, another question being asked is whether it is worth all the effort. Although an initial study found that national board certified teachers are better on a number of measures than those who tried to meet the standards and failed (Blair, 2000), further research must be conducted to determine the effectiveness of this process. The key question that needs to be answered is "Does it bring about improvements in student achievement?" (Viadero, 2002, p. 7). Several studies are currently under way to answer this and other related questions.

#### React and Reflect

1. Do you think national board certification strengthens teaching as a profession? Why or why not?

2. Can you see yourself completing the process for national board certification at some future point in your career as an educator? What makes you think this way?

3. Should all teachers become national board certified?

 *To explore this topic further and submit your reactions and reflections online, go to the Explore Your Beliefs module for Chapter 15 of the Companion Website for this text.*

*Sources:* "National Board Is Pressed to Prove Certified Teachers Make a Difference," by J. Archer, 2002, *Education Week,* January 30, pp. 1, 11. Retrieved April 29, 2003, from http://www.edweek.org/ew/ew_printstory.cfm?slug=20board.h21; "AFT Urges New Tests, Expanded Training for Teachers," by J. Blair, 2000, *Education Week,* April 19, p. 11; "Standards Board Identifies Research to Examine Effects," by D. Viadero, 2002, *Education Week,* September 18, p. 7. Retrieved April 20, 2003, from http://www.edweek.org/ew/ew_printstory.cfm?slug=03nbpts.h22

## Small Gestures Can Change Lives

**Leslie J. Reed**
**Guiderland Central School District**
**Guiderland, New York**

Even after finishing my Master's degree, I still thought teaching was mostly organizing lesson plans and regurgitating them back to the students. I thought that I would touch the students' lives by teaching them how to sound out words or multiply . . . but I soon found out that I could touch lives in different ways.

I had a parent come to me and tell me that her son *hated* to read. His teacher had given up on him because he failed to succeed at "sustained individual reading." However, he *loved* nonfiction, especially history books. I gave her a list of books from the Scholastic, Inc. series *My Name Is America*. I wondered what would happen, and if I would get the chance to speak with her again. About a month later, I saw her again. She came up to me and hugged me, saying, "He has read them all!" She hugged me again before leaving.

After the parent left the room, I had to sit down and process what had taken place. Here I am, a substitute teacher . . . waiting for my own classroom to "touch lives". . . and I was afforded the opportunity without even realizing it. I realized that I wouldn't change students' lives by simply imparting to them a new skill or concept. Sometimes, the smallest gesture has the greatest impact on both the education and the life of a student.

## Summary

In this chapter, four organizing questions were used to guide your thinking about the first years of teaching and beyond:

### What will I need to do to get a teaching position?

You will need to follow several key steps in securing your first teaching job:

- Knowing the job market
- Locating job openings
- Submitting applications
- Participating in interviews

### What can I expect as a first-year teacher?

Although no two teachers experience exactly the same things as beginning teachers, they will have several elements in common:

- The physical setting of the classroom
- The students
- Parents and families
- Mentoring opportunities

## What must I do to be successful as a beginning teacher?

Several steps are available that you can take to be more successful as a beginning teacher:
- Refine your teaching style
- Create a community of learners (Praxis II, topic Ic)
- Maintain a healthy lifestyle
- Understand why teachers leave the profession

## How can I continue to grow personally and professionally?

Teaching should be viewed as a lifelong learning experience that can be facilitated by the following:
- Personal reflections on teaching and learning (Praxis II, topic IVa)
- Reflection with others (Praxis II, topic IVa)
- Additional formal learning experiences
- Advanced certification

## Key Terms

| | |
|---|---|
| in-service education | placement service |
| job application | reflection |
| journal | résumé |
| letter of application | second-stage teacher certification |
| mentoring programs | teacher induction |
| placement file | teaching portfolio |

## Reflective Journey: Online Journal

Use the questions for thought and reflection highlighted throughout the chapter to help guide your personal journey of reflection and professional development as a teacher. To complete your journal entries online, go to the *Reflective Journey* module for this chapter of the Companion Website.

## PRAXIS   Test Preparation Activities

To review an online chapter case study, test your understanding of chapter topics and concepts, and begin preparing for the Praxis II: Principles of Learning and Teaching examination, go to the *Praxis Test Preparation* module for this chapter of the Companion Website.

## InTASC   Becoming a Reflective Practitioner

To complete these activities and submit your responses online, go to the *Becoming a Reflective Practitioner* module for this chapter of the Companion Website.

## What will I need to do to get a teaching position?

### Review Questions

1. What categories of teachers are in greatest and least demand nationally?
2. What are the typical ingredients of a résumé?

### Field Experience

Find a teacher or administrator who has participated in interviewing teachers seeking jobs. Discuss with this person what you can expect to take place in the interview process. Based on your discussion, develop a list of tips for making the interview a positive experience.

### Building Your Portfolio: *Constructing a Résumé*

**INTASC Standard 9.** One of the things you will need to do when you begin your future search for a teaching job is to create a résumé summarizing your education, work experience, and personal interests to date. While you will add many experiences between now and then, constructing a résumé at this point will help you consider engaging in actions that will help you be more competitive in the job market. Consider working with the career planning and placement center at your college or university as you develop an initial draft of your résumé. Include a copy of the results as part of your portfolio.

## What can I expect as a first-year teacher?

### Review Questions

1. What are some common characteristics of school buildings in the United States?
2. What are the goals of mentoring programs?

### Field Experience

Talk to a first-year teacher about the start of his or her teaching career. What does this teacher find to be both the joys and frustrations of the teaching experience? What suggestions does this person have for being successful during the first year? How can you adapt the strategies presented to make your first year more productive?

### Building Your Portfolio: *Teacher Mentoring*

**INTASC Standard 10.** In preparation for your first year of teaching, take some time to learn more about teacher mentoring programs. Search the Internet and your college library for articles on teacher mentoring and then write a short paper describing the types of activities typically available and the reasons cited for the importance of mentoring. Include your paper in your portfolio.

## What must I do to be successful as a beginning teacher?

### Review Questions

1. What steps can you take to refine your personal teaching style?
2. Describe strategies you could use to create a community of learners within your future classroom.
3. Why do teachers leave the profession?

### Building Your Portfolio: *Maintaining a Healthy Lifestyle*

**INTASC Standard 9.** One of the keys to your initial success as a future teacher is to find ways to stay physically and emotionally healthy despite the regular stress you will face. Develop a list of strategies that you will use to maintain a healthy lifestyle. Include a copy of this list in your portfolio.

## How can I continue to grow personally and professionally?

### Review Questions

1. What are some strategies you can use to engage in personal reflection about your own teaching?
2. What strategies are schools using to assist with teacher induction?
3. Describe some of the additional formal learning experiences that teachers have throughout their careers.

## Field Experience

Find an experienced teacher with 15 or more years of teaching and discuss with that person the keys to success as a teacher. What has helped this person be successful with students and manage the stress of teaching? Ask for tips that would help you be successful as a first-year teacher.

## Building Your Portfolio: *A Case for Teaching*

**INTASC Standard 9.** A portfolio assignment made for Chapter 1 was to create the most persuasive argument you can for teaching as a career. Now that you have completed reading this text and gained additional insights on teaching and learning, go back and review the essay you developed earlier. Revise it so that it reflects your current view on the values of a career in education. Include your revised essay as a component of your portfolio.

## Suggested Readings

Codell, E. (1999). *Educating Esmé.* Chapel Hill, NC: Algonquin Books. This book presents the raw and powerful diary of a beginning teacher's first year in an inner city school. Esmé Codell shares her successes, failures, joys, and sorrows in an engaging format that makes it a difficult book to put down. This unconventional teacher has much to say to all teachers.

DePaul, A. (1998). *What to expect your first year of teaching.* Washington, DC: U.S. Department of Education. Available at http://www.ed.gov/pubs/FirstYear/. This publication gives numerous anecdotes from first-year teachers and advice from more experienced teachers and administrators that paint a vivid picture of what that year will be like.

Kronowitz, E. (1999). *Your first year of teaching and beyond* (3rd ed.). New York: Addison Wesley Longman. This book provides a strong overview of the challenges of the first few years of teaching and provides good suggestions for strategies that can help new teachers be successful in their chosen career.

MacDonald, R., & Healy, S. (1999). *A handbook for beginning teachers* (2nd ed.). New York: Addison Wesley Longman. This text has separate chapters on how to work creatively within the educational system and strategies for continuing growth as an educator. It has many good suggestions for the beginning teacher.

# References

Abbott, G. (1994). ALPHA: A survivor. *Educational Leadership, 52*(1), 23–26.

Addonizio, M. (1999). New revenues for public schools: Alternatives to broad-based taxes. In *Selected papers in school finance.* Washington, DC: U.S. Department of Education. Retrieved from http://nces.ed.gov/pubs99/1999334/h3

Adler, M. (1982). *The Paideia proposal: An educational manifesto.* New York: Macmillan.

Aguero, K. (Ed.) (1993). *Daily fare: Essays from the multicultural experience.* Athens: University of Georgia Press.

Albert, L. (1996). *Cooperative discipline.* Circle Pines, MN: American Guidance Service.

American Academy of Child and Adolescent Psychiatry. (2000). *Teen suicide.* Retrieved February 7, 2000, from www.aacap.org/publications/factsfam/suicide.htm

American Academy of Child and Adolescent Psychiatry. (2002). *Teen suicide.* Retrieved February 10, 2002, from www.aacap.org/publications/factsfam/suicide.htm

American Association for the Advancement of Science. (2001). *Project 2061.* Washington, DC: Author. Retrieved April 27, 2001, from http://www.project2061.org

American Association of University Women. (1992). *How schools shortchange girls: The AAUW report.* Washington, DC: The AAUW Educational Foundation.

American Association of University Women. (2001). *Hostile hallways: Bullying, teaching, and sexual harassment in school.* Washington, DC: The AAUW Educational Foundation.

American Council on the Teaching of Foreign Languages. (1996). *Standards for foreign language learning: Preparing for the 21st century.* Yonkers, NY: Author.

American Federation of Teachers. (2001). *PreK–12 educational issues department.* Retrieved November 21, 2001, from http://www.aft.org/edissues/index.htm

American Federation of Teachers. (2002). *About AFT.* Retrieved July 26, 2002, from http://www.aft.org/about/index.html

American Indian Education Foundation. (2002). *History of Indian education in the U.S.* Retrieved August 27, 2002, from http://www.aiefprograms.org/history_facts/history.html#1960

American Psychiatric Association. (2002). *Teen suicide.* Retrieved September 9, 2002, from http://www.psych.org/public_info/teen.cfm

American Psychological Association. (2002). *Healthy lesbian, gay, and bisexual students project.* Retrieved July 2, 2002, from http://www.apa.org/ed/hlgbschclim.html

Anderson, J. (1995). *Learning and memory: An integrated approach.* New York: Wiley.

Annie E. Casey Foundation. (2002). *2002 Kids count data book.* Baltimore, MD: Author.

Archer, J. (1999, December 8). Home schooling is growing, but many researchers shy away from the topic. *Education Week,* pp. 22–25.

Archer, J. (2000, January 26). Teacher recruitment harder in urban areas, report says. *Education Week,* p. 7.

Archer, J. (2001, September 5). First impressions. *Education Week,* pp. 48–54.

Arizona Education Association. (2001). *AEA Regional Leadership Conference.* Retrieved November 21, 2001, from http://www.arizonaea.org/frame.html

Ashton-Warner, S. (1963). *Teacher.* New York: Bantam Books.

Association of Teacher Educators. (2001). *Standards for teacher educators.* Retrieved November 16, 2001, from http://www.siu.edu/departments/coe/ate/standards/Testandards.htm

Ausubel, D. (1968). *Educational psychology: A cognitive view.* New York: Holt, Rinehart & Winston.

Ayers, W. (2001). *To teach: The journey of a teacher.* (2nd ed.). New York: Teachers College Press.

Bailey, R., Magpantay, G., & Rosenblum, D. (2001). *Redistricting and the gay, lesbian, bisexual, and transgender community: A strategy memo.* New York: The Policy Institute of the National Gay and Lesbian Task Force.

Baker, K. (1998). Structured English immersion: Breakthrough in teaching limited English-proficient students. *Phi Delta Kappan, 80*(3), 199–204.

Baker, S. (2000). *School counseling for the twenty-first century* (3rd ed.). Upper Saddle River, NJ: Merrill/Prentice Hall.

Bandura, A. (1977). *Social learning theory.* Upper Saddle River, NJ: Prentice Hall.

Bandura, A. (1986). *Social foundations of thought and action: A social cognitive theory.* Upper Saddle River, NJ: Prentice Hall.

Banks, J. (1993). Multicultural education for young children: Racial and ethnic attitudes and their modification. In B. Spodek (Ed.), *Handbook of research on the education of young children.* Upper Saddle River, NJ: Prentice Hall.

Banks, J. (2002). *An introduction to multicultural education* (3rd ed.). Boston: Allyn and Bacon.

Banner, J., & Cannon, H. (1997). *The elements of teaching.* New Haven, CT: Yale University Press.

Battistich, V., Solomon, D., Kim, D., Watson, M., & Schaps, E. (1995). Schools as communities, poverty levels of student populations, and students' attitudes, motives, and performance: A multilevel analysis. *American Education Research Journal, 32*(4), 627–658.

Becker, H. (1999). *Internet use by teachers.* Center for Research on Information Technology and Organizations. Retrieved from http://www.crito.uci.edu/frameset-ie.htm

Bennett, W. (1987). *James Madison High School: A curriculum for American students.* Washington, DC: U.S. Department of Education.

Bennett, W. (1992). Bilingual education: A failed path. In J. Crawford (Ed.), *Language loyalties.* Chicago: University of Chicago Press.

Bennett, W. (1993). *The book of virtues: A treasury of great moral stories.* New York: Simon & Schuster.

Berger, E. (2000). *Parents as partners in education* (5th edition). Upper Saddle River, NJ: Merrill/Prentice Hall.

Biber, B. (1964). Preschool education. In R. Ulich (Ed.), *Education and the idea of mankind.* New York: Harcourt Brace.

Binder, F. (1974). *The age of the common school.* New York: John Wiley & Sons.

Black, S. (1996, September). The pull of magnets. *The American School Board Journal,* pp. 34–35.

Blair, J. (2000, April 19). AFT urges new tests, expanded training for teachers. *Education Week,* p. 11.

Block, J. (Ed.). (1971). *Mastery learning: Theory and practice.* New York: Holt, Rinehart & Winston.

Bloom, A. (1987). *The closing of the American mind.* New York: Simon & Schuster.

Bloom, B. (1971). Mastery learning. In J. H. Block (Ed.), *Mastery learning: Theory and practice.* New York: Holt, Rinehart & Winston.

*B.M. by Berger v. State of Montana,* 649 P.2d 425 (Mont. 1982).

*Board of Education of Westside Community Schools v. Mergens,* 110 S. Ct. 2356 (1990).

Boss, S. (2001a). Facing the future. *Northwest Education, 7*(2), 3–9, 41.

Boss, S. (2001b). Mr. Fisher finds his calling. *Northwest Education, 7*(2), 20–23, 36–40.

Boyer, E. (1983). *High school: A report on secondary education in America.* New York: Harper.

Boyer, E. (1995). *The basic school: A community for learning.* Princeton, NJ: Carnegie Foundation for the Advancement of Teaching.

Bracey, G. (1999). The ninth Bracey report on the condition of public education. *Phi Delta Kappan, 81*(2), 147–168.

Bradley, A. (1998, September 9). New teachers are hot commodity. *Education Week,* pp. 1, 20.

Bradley, A. (1999, March 10). States' uneven teacher supply complicates staffing of schools. *Education Week,* p. 18.

Bransford, J. (Ed.). (1999). *How people learn: Brain, mind, experience, and school.* Washington, DC: National Research Council.

Braun, S., & Edwards, E. (1972). *History and theory of early childhood education.* Belmont, CA: Wadsworth Publishing.

Bredekamp, S., & Copple, C. (Eds.). (1997). *Developmentally appropriate practice in early childhood programs* (rev. ed.). Washington, DC: National Association for the Education of Young Children.

Bronfenbrenner, U. (1979). *The ecology of human development.* Cambridge, MA: Harvard University Press.

Brophy, J. (1983). Research on the self-fulfilling prophecy and teacher expectations. *Journal of Educational Psychology, 75,* 631–661.

Brown, A., Campione, J., & Day, J. (1981). Learning to learn: On training students to learn from texts. *Educational Researcher 10,* 14–24.

*Brown v. Board of Education of Topeka,* 349 U.S. 294 (1955).

Bruner, J. (1960). *The process of education.* New York: Random House.

Bruner, J. (1966). *Toward a theory of instruction.* Cambridge, MA: Harvard University Press.

Brunner, C., Bennett, D., & Honey, M. (2000). Girl games and technological desire. In *The Jossey-Bass reader on technology and learning.* San Francisco: Jossey-Bass.

Bryant, J., & Bryant, A. (Eds.). (2001). *Television and the American family* (2nd ed.). Mahwah, NJ: Lawrence Erlbaum.

Bureau of Labor Statistics. (2001). *Occupational outlook handbook.* Retrieved from http://stats.bls.gov/oco/ocos069.htm

Butts, R., & Cremin, L. (1953). *A history of education in American culture.* New York: Henry Holt.

Campbell, D. (2000). *Choosing democracy* (2nd ed.). Upper Saddle River, NJ: Merrill/Prentice Hall.

Canter, L., & Canter, M. (1992). *Assertive discipline: Positive behavior management for today's classrooms* (2nd ed.). Santa Monica, CA: Lee Canter & Associates.

*Cary v. Board of Education,* Adams-Arapahoe School District, 598 F.2d 535 (10th Cir. 1979).

Catri, D. (1998). *Vocational education's image for the 21st century.* Columbus, OH: ERIC Clearinghouse on Adult Career and Vocational Education.

Center for Education Reform. (2001). *Charter law scorecard ranks states.* Retrieved from http://www.edreform.com/press/2001/cslaws.htm

Center on National Education Policy. (2000). *Do you know . . . The good news about American education.* Washington, DC: Author.

Charles, C. (2002). *Building classroom discipline* (7th ed.). New York: Longman.

Children's Defense Fund. (2002). *The state of children in America's union.* Washington, DC: Author.

Clearinghouse on Elementary and Early Childhood Education. (1990). Guidelines for family television viewing. *ERIC Digest* (EDO-PS-90-3). Urbana, IL: ERIC Author.

Codell, E. (1999). *Educating Esmé. Diary of a teacher's first year.* Chapel Hill, NC: Algonquin Books.

Coloroso, B. (1994). *Kids are worth it! Giving your child the gift of inner discipline.* New York: William Morrow.

Consortium for School Networking. (2001). Taking TCO to the classroom. Retrieved July 17, 2001, from http://www.cosn.org

Cook, G. (2001). Searching for miracles. *American School Board Journal 188*(12), 18–23.

Cooper, H. (1989). Synthesis of research on homework. *Educational Leadership, 47*(3), 85–91.

Coopersmith, S. (1967). *The antecedents of self-esteem.* San Francisco: W. H. Freeman.

Council for Exceptional Children. (2002). *About CEC.* Retrieved July 26, 2002, from http://www.cec.sped.org/ab

Council of Chief State School Officers. (1999). *Early childhood and family education.* Washington, DC: Author.

Council of Chief State School Officers. (2001). *Vermont social studies teacher named National Teacher of the Year at White House ceremony.* Retrieved October 13, 2001, from http://www.ccsso.org/ntoy/2001/ntoy01.html

Council of Chief State School Officers. (2002). *Voices for the future.* Retrieved April 17, 2002, from http://www.ccsso.org/ntoyletters.html

Cremin, L. (1970). *American education: The colonial experience 1607–1783.* New York: Harper & Row.

Cremin, L. (1980). *American education: The national experience.* New York: Harper & Row.

Crosby, E. (1993). The at-risk decade. *Phi Delta Kappan, 74*(8), 598–604.

Cubberley, E. (1934). *Public education in the United States.* Boston: Houghton Mifflin.

Cummins, J. (1984). *Bilingualism and special education: Issues in assessment and pedagogy.* San Diego: College-Hill Press.

Curwin, R., & Mendler, A. (1988). *Discipline with dignity.* Alexandria, VA: Association for Supervision and Curriculum Development.

Cushner, K., McClelland, A., & Safford, P. (2000). *Human diversity in education: An integrative approach* (3rd ed.). New York: McGraw-Hill.

Dalaker, J. (2001). *Poverty in the United States: 2000.* Washington, DC: U.S. Census Bureau.

Danielson, C. (1996). *Enhancing professional practice: A framework for teaching.* Alexandria, VA: Association for Supervision and Curriculum Development.

Darling-Hammond, L., & Wise, A. (1992). Teacher professionalism. In *Encyclopedia of educational research* (pp. 1359–1366). Upper Saddle River, NJ: Merrill/Prentice Hall.

Davidson, J., & Stoff, M. (1998). *The American nation.* Upper Saddle River, NJ: Prentice Hall.

*Davis v. Meek,* 344 F.Supp. 298 N.D.Ohio (1972).

*Davis v. Monroe County Board of Education,* 526 U.S. 629 (1999).

Dayton, J., & McCarthy, M. 1992. User fees in public schools: Are they legal? *Journal of Education Finance, 18*(2), 127–141.

DeBlois, R. (2000, February 23). The need for more alternative schools. *Education Week,* pp. 40, 45.

DeFina, A. (1992). *Portfolio assessment.* New York: Scholastic Professional Books.

DePaul, A. (1998). *What to expect your first year of teaching.* Washington, DC: U.S. Department of Education.

Derman-Sparks, L., & Phillips, C. (1997). *Teaching/ learning anti-racism—A developmental approach.* New York: Teachers College Press.

DeVries, R., & Kohlberg, L. (1987). *Constructivist early education: Overview and comparison with other programs.* Washington, DC: National Association for the Education of Young Children.

Dewey, J. (1929). *Democracy and education.* New York: Macmillan.

Dewey, J. (1933). *How we think: A restatement of the relationship of reflective thinking to the educative process.* Boston: D.C. Heath and Company.

Dewey, J. (1938). *Experience and education.* New York: Collier Books.

Dewey, J. (1939). *Freedom and culture.* New York: G. P. Putnam's Sons.

Dickinson, T. (Ed.). (2001). *Reinventing the middle school.* New York: Routledge Falmer.

Disney Learning Partnership. (2002). *American Teacher Award honorees.* Retrieved July 16, 2002, from http://disney.go.com/disneylearning/ata

*Dixon v. Alabama State Board of Education,* 294 F.2d. 150 (5th Cir. 1961).

Dreikurs, R., Grunwald, B., & Pepper, F. (1971). *Maintaining sanity in the classroom.* New York: Harper and Row.

Dryfoos, J. G. (1994). *Full-service schools: A revolution in health and social services.* San Francisco: Jossey-Bass.

Early, P. (1994). *Goals 2000: Educate America Act: Implications for teacher educators.* Washington, DC: American Association of Colleges for Teacher Education.

Eck, D. (2001). *A new religious America: How a "Christian country" has become the world's most religiously diverse nation.* San Francisco: Harper.

Education Week. (2000, November 29). A rising tide of disabilities. *Education Week,* p. 25.

Education Week. (2001). *Technology counts 2001: The new divide.* Washington, DC: Author.

Education Week. (2002). *Hot topics: School-based management.* Retrieved from http://www.edweek.org/context/topics/issuespage.cfm?id=18

Education Week. (2003). *Hot topics: Charter schools.* Retrieved May 5, 2003, from http://www.edweek.org/context/topics/issuespage.cfm?id=42

Educational Testing Service. (2002). *The Praxis series: Professional assessments for beginning teachers.* Princeton, NJ: Author. Retrieved December 23, 2002, from http://www.ets.org/prxsets.html

Edwards, C. (1997). *Classroom discipline and management* (2nd ed.). Upper Saddle River, NJ: Merrill/Prentice Hall.

Eisner, E. (1994). *The educational imagination: On the design and evaluation of school programs* (3rd ed.). Upper Saddle River, NJ: Merrill/Prentice Hall.

Ellis, S., & Whalen, S. (1990). *Cooperative learning: Getting started.* New York: Scholastic.

*Engel v. Vitale,* 370 U.S. 421 (1962).

Erikson, E. (1963). *Childhood and society* (2nd ed.). New York: W. W. Norton.

Etzioni, A. (1969). *The semi-professions and their organization: Teachers, nurses, social workers.* New York: Free Press.

Evertson, C., Emmer, E., Clements, B., & Worsham, M. (1997). *Classroom management for elementary teachers* (4th ed.). Boston: Allyn and Bacon.

Farkas, S., Johnson, J., & Foleno, T. (2000). *A sense of calling: Who teaches and why.* New York: Public Agenda.

Federman, J. (Ed.). (1998). *National television violence study* (Vol. 3). Santa Barbara: University of California, Santa Barbara.

Feiman-Nemser, S. (1999). *From preparation to practice: Designing a continuum to strengthen and sustain teaching.* New York: Supporting and Strengthening Teaching Project.

Fenstermacher, G., & Soltis, J. (1998). *Approaches to teaching.* New York: Teachers College Press.

Fine, L. (2001). Special-needs gaps. In *Technology counts 2001: The new divide* (pp. 26–27). Washington, DC: Education Week.

Fink, E., & Resnick, L. (2001). Developing principals as instructional leaders. *Phi Delta Kappan, 82*(8), 598–606.

Fischer, L., Schimmel, D., & Kelly, C. (2003). *Teachers and the law* (6th ed.). New York: Longman.

Flavell, J. (1963). *The developmental psychology of Jean Piaget.* New York: D. Van Nostrand.

Fleischman, H., & Hopstock, P. (1993). *Descriptive study of services to limited English proficient students* (Vol. 1). Arlington, VA: Development Associates, Inc.

Forum on Child and Family Statistics. (2002). *America's children: Key national indicators of well-being, 2002.* Vienna, VA: National Maternal Child Health Clearinghouse.

Freire, P. (1970). *The pedagogy of the oppressed.* New York: Herder and Herder.

Freud, S. (1920). *A general introduction to psychoanalysis.* (Joan Riviere, Trans.). New York: Liveright.

Froebel, F. (1886). *Education of man* (J. Jarvis, Trans.). New York: Appleton-Century-Crofts.

Frye, M. (1983). *The politics of reality: Essays in feminist theory.* Trumansburg, NY: Crossing Press.

Gandara, P. (2001). *Peer group influence and academic aspirations across cultural/ethnic groups of high school students.* Santa Cruz: Center for Research on Education, Diversity, and Excellence, The University of California, Santa Cruz.

Garcia, G. (2000). Lessons from research: What is the length of time it takes limited English proficient students to acquire English and succeed in an all-English classroom? *Issue and Brief* (No. 5). Washington, DC: National Clearinghouse for Bilingual Education.

Gardner, H. (1983). *Frames of mind: The theory of multiple intelligences.* New York: Basic Books.

Gathercoal, F. (1991). *Judicious discipline.* Davis, CA: Caddo Gap Press.

*Gaylord v. Tacoma School District No. 10,* 559 P.2d 1340 (Wash. 1977).

Gehring, J. (2001). Not enough girls. In *Technology counts 2001: The new divide* (pp. 18–19). Washington, DC: Education Week.

Gesell, A., and Ilg, F. (1949). *Child development: An introduction to the study of human growth.* New York: Harper & Brothers.

Gestwicki, C. (2000). *Home, school, and community relations* (4th ed.). Albany, NY: Delmar.

Gibbon, P. (2002, May 29). A hero of education. *Education Week,* pp. 33, 36.

Glasser, W. (1965). *Reality therapy.* New York: Harper and Row.

Glasser, W. (1969). *Schools without failure.* New York: Harper and Row.

Glasser, W. (1986). *Control theory in the classroom.* New York: Harper and Row.

Glasser, W. (1990). *The quality school: Managing students without coercion.* New York: Harper and Row.

Glatthorn, A. (1994). *Developing quality curriculum.* Alexandria, VA: Association for Supervision and Curriculum Development.

Gollnick, D., & Chinn, P. (2002). *Multicultural education in a pluralistic society* (6th ed.). Upper Saddle River, NJ: Merrill/Prentice Hall.

Good, T., & Brophy, J. (2000). *Looking in classrooms* (8th ed.). New York: Harper and Row.

Goodlad, J. (1984). *A place called school.* New York: Macmillan.

Goodlad, J. (1990). *Teachers for our nation's schools.* San Francisco: Jossey-Bass.

Goodlad, J., Soder, R., & Sirotnik, K. (1990). *The moral dimensions of teaching.* San Francisco: Jossey-Bass.

Gordon, T. (1970). *Parent effectiveness training.* New York: New American Library.

Gordon, T. (1974). *Teacher effectiveness training.* New York: Wyden.

Gordon, T. (1976). *P.E.T. in action.* New York: Random House.

*Goss v. Lopez,* 419 U.S. 565 (1975).

Greenberg, H. (1969). *Teaching with feeling.* Indianapolis, IN: Pegasus.

Greene, J. (1998). *A meta-analysis of the effectiveness of bilingual education.* Claremont, CA: Tomas Rivera Center.

Greene, M. (1988). *The dialectic of freedom.* New York: Teachers College Press.

Greenwald, R., Hedges, L., & Laine, R. (1996). The effect of school resources on student achievement. *Review of Educational Research, 66*(3), 361–396.

Grubb, W. (2000). Opening classrooms and improving teaching: Lessons from school inspections in England. *Teachers College Record, 102*(4), 696–723.

Gruhn, W., & Douglass, H. (1971). *The modern junior high school* (3rd ed.). New York: Ronald Press.

Guild, P., & Garger, S. (1998). *Marching to different drummers* (2nd ed.). Alexandria, VA: Association for Supervision and Curriculum Development.

Gutek, G. (1991). *Education in the United States: An historical perspective.* Upper Saddle River, NJ: Prentice Hall.

*Guzick v. Debras,* 401 U.S. 948 (1971).

Hafner, K. (2001, June 28). Lessons in Internet plagiarism. *New York Times.* Retrieved from http://www.nytimes.com

Haladyna, T. (1999). *Developing and validating multiple-choice test items.* Mahwah, NJ: Lawrence Erlbaum.

Hallahan, D., & Kauffman, J. (2000). *Exceptional learners: Introduction to special education* (8th ed.). Boston: Allyn and Bacon.

Hansen, D. (1995). *The call to teach.* New York: Teachers College Press.

Hansen, D. (2001). *Exploring the moral heart of teaching.* New York: Teachers College Press.

Hanushek, E., Kain, J., & Rivkin, S. (2001). *Why public schools lose teachers.* Cambridge, MA: National Bureau of Economic Research. Retrieved from http://www.nber.org/papers/w8599

Harlem Foundation. (2001). *Harlem Consolidated Schools District #122.* Retrieved November 28, 2001, from http://www.harlem122.org/Foundations/main.htm

Hattie, J. (1992). Measuring the effects of schooling. *Australian Journal of Education, 36*(1), 5–13.

Hefner-Packer, R. (1991). Alternative education programs: A prescription for success. *Monographs in Education.* Athens: The University of Georgia.

Henniger, M. (2001). *Teaching young children: An introduction.* (2nd ed.). Upper Saddle River, NJ: Merrill/Prentice Hall.

Herbst, J. (1996). *The once and future school: Three hundred and fifty years of American secondary education.* New York: Routledge.

Herr, P. (2000). The changing role of the teacher. *Technological Horizons in Education, 28*(4), 28–34.

Heslep, R. (1997). *Philosophical thinking in educational practice.* Westport, CT: Praeger.

Heward, W. (1996). *Exceptional children* (5th ed.). Upper Saddle River, NJ: Prentice Hall.

Hillabrant, W., Romano, M., Strang, D., & Charleston, M. (1992). Native American education at a turning point: Current demographics and trends. In P. Cahape & C. Howley (Eds.), *Indian nations at risk.* Charleston, WV: Clearinghouse on Rural Education and Small Schools.

Hirsch, E. (1996). *The schools we need and why we don't have them.* New York: Doubleday.

Hoff, D. (1999, May 19). The race to space rocketed NSF into classrooms. *Education Week,* pp. 34–35.

Hoff, D. (2000, May 17). International report finds U.S. teacher salaries lagging. *Education Week,* p. 5.

Hole, S., & McEntee, G. (1999). Supporting beginning teachers: Reflection is at the heart of practice. *Educational Leadership, 56*(8), pp. 34–37.

Holloway, J. (2000). The promise and pitfalls of site-based management. *Educational Leadership, 57*(7), 77–80. Also available at: http://www.ascd.org/readingroom/edlead/0004/holloway.html

Holloway, J. (2001a). The benefits of mentoring. *Educational Leadership, 58*(8), 85–86.

Holloway, J. (2001b). School choice and lessons learned. *Educational Leadership, 58*(4), 81–83.

Holmgren, V. (1996). *Elementary school counseling: An expanding role.* Boston: Allyn and Bacon.

Holt, J. (1964). *How children fail.* New York: Dell.

Hostetler, K. (1997). *Ethical judgment in teaching.* Boston: Allyn and Bacon.

Howe, K., Eisenhart, M., & Betebenner, D. (2001). School choice crucible: A case study of Boulder Valley. *Phi Delta Kappan, 83*(2), 137–146.

Howell, J., & Lynch, J. (2000). *Youth gangs in the schools.* Washington, DC: U.S. Department of Justice.

Howsam, R., Corrigan, D., Denemark, G., & Nash, R. (1976). *Educating a profession.* Washington, DC: American Association of Colleges for Teacher Education.

Hurst, M. (2003, January 8). Dental dilemma. *Education Week,* pp. 27–29.

Hymes, J. (1978). *Living history interviews.* Carmel, CA: Hacienda Press.

Illich, I. (1972). *Deschooling society.* New York: Harrow Books.

Indiana Education Policy Center. (2002). *Preventing school violence: A practical guide to comprehensive planning.* Retrieved September 9, 2002, from http://www.indiana.edu/~safeschl/psv.pdf

*Ingraham v. Wright,* 430 U.S. 651 (1977).

International Technology Education Association. (2000). *Standards for technological literacy: Content for the study of technology.* Reston, VA: Author.

International Technology Education Association. (2001). *What is technology?* Retrieved May 1, 2001, from http://www.iteawww.org/TAA/Whatis.htm

Jackson, A., & Davis, G. (2000). *Turning points 2000: Educating adolescents in the 21st century.* New York: Teachers College Press.

Jacobsen, D. (1999). *Philosophy in classroom teaching: Bridging the gap.* Upper Saddle River, NJ: Merrill/Prentice Hall.

Jacobson, L. (1998, August 5). Hispanic children outnumber young blacks for 1st time. *Education Week,* p. 6.

Jalil, G. (1996). *Street-wise drug prevention. A realistic approach to prevent and intervene in adolescent drug use.* Reading, PA: No More Drugs, Inc.

Jersild, A. (1955). *When teachers face themselves.* New York: Teachers College Press.

Jeub, C. (1994). Why parents choose home schooling. *Educational Leadership, 52*(1), 50–52.

Johnson, D., & Johnson, R. (1975). *Circles of learning.* Upper Saddle River, NJ: Prentice Hall.

Johnston, J. (1995). Channel One: The dilemma of teaching and selling. *Phi Delta Kappan, 77*(2), 437–442.

Johnston, R. (2001). Money matters. In *Technology counts 2001: The new divide* (pp. 14–15). Washington, DC: Education Week.

Johnston, R., & Sandham, J. (1999, April 14). States increasingly flexing their policy muscle. *Education Week,* pp. 23–25.

Jones, F. (1987). *Positive classroom discipline.* New York: McGraw-Hill.

Jones, V., & Jones, L. (2001). *Comprehensive classroom management: Creating communities of support and solving problems* (6th ed.). Boston: Allyn and Bacon.

Jordan, A. (1996). *The state of children's television: An examination of quantity, quality, and industry beliefs.* Philadelphia: Annenburg Public Policy Center, University of Pennsylvania.

Joyce, B., & Weil, M. (2000). *Models of teaching* (6th ed.). Boston: Allyn and Bacon.

Joyner, C. (1997). *School facilities. Reported condition and costs to repair schools funded by Bureau of Indian Affairs.* Washington, DC: General Accounting Office.

Kameenui, E., & Darch, C. (1995). *Instructional classroom management.* White Plains, NY: Longman.

Kanner, L. (1964). *A history of the care and study of the mentally retarded.* Springfield, IL: Charles C. Thomas.

Karnes, F., & Marquardt, R. (1997). Know your legal rights in gifted education. *ERIC Digest No. E541.* Washington, DC: Office of Educational Research and Improvement.

Kelly, E. (1998). *Legal basics: A handbook for educators.* Bloomington, IN: Phi Delta Kappa Educational Foundation.

Klicka, C. (1996). *Home schooling in the United States: A legal analysis.* Paeonian Springs, VA: Home School Legal Defense Association.

Kneller, G. (1971). *Introduction to the philosophy of education.* New York: John Wiley & Sons.

Kohl, H. (1969). *The open classroom.* New York: Random House.

Kohn, A. (1993). *Punished by rewards: The trouble with gold stars, incentive plans, A's, praise, and other bribes.* Boston: Houghton Mifflin.

Kohn, A. (1996). *Beyond discipline: From compliance to community.* Alexandria, VA: Association for Supervision and Curriculum Development.

Kohn, A. (2000, September 27). Standardized testing and its victims. *Education Week,* pp. 60, 46–47.

Kostelnik, M., Stein, L., Whiren, A., & Soderman, A. (1998). *Guiding children's social development.* Albany, NY: Delmar.

Kounin, J. (1970). *Discipline and group management in classrooms.* New York: Holt, Rinehart, and Winston.

Kowalski, T., & Reitzug, U. (1993). *Contemporary school administration: An introduction.* New York: Longman.

Kronowitz, E. (1999). *Your first year of teaching and beyond* (3rd ed.). New York: Longman.

Lally, R. (1995). The impact of child care policies and practices on infant/toddler identity formation. *Young Children, 51*(1), 58–67.

LaMorte, M. (2002). *School law: Cases and concepts* (7th ed.). Boston: Allyn and Bacon.

Lankard, B. (1995). *Business/education partnerships.* ERIC Digest #156. Washington, DC: ERIC Clearinghouse for Adult, Career, and Vocational Education.

Latham, A. (1999). School vouchers: Much debate, little research. *Educational Leadership, 56*(2), 28–30.

Latham, A., Gitamer, D., & Ziomek, R. (1999). What the tests tell us about new teachers. *Educational Leadership, 56*(8), 23–26.

Lawrence-Lightfoot, S. (1983). *The good high school.* New York: Basic Books.

Lee, E., Menkart, D., & Okazawa-Rey, M. (1998). *Beyond heroes and holidays: A practical guide to K–12 anti-racist, multicultural education and staff development.* Washington, DC: Network of Educators on the Americas.

*Lee v. Weisman,* 505 U.S. 577 (1992).

Lemke, C., & Martin, C. (2001). *Children and computer technology: Issues and ideas.* Los Altos, CA: The David and Lucile Packard Foundation.

Levesque, K., Lauen, D., Teitelbaum, P., Alt, M., & Librera, S. (2000). *Vocational education in the United States: Toward the year 2000.* Washington, DC: National Center for Education Statistics.

Levi, L. (2000). Gender equity in mathematics education. *Research into practice: Teaching children mathematics.* Reston, VA: National Council for Teachers of Mathematics.

Levine, S. (Ed.) (1999). *A passion for teaching.* Alexandria, VA: Association for Supervision and Curriculum Development.

Lewis, J. (2001). Saying no to vouchers: What is the price of democracy? In J. Noll (Ed.) *Taking sides: Clashing views on controversial educational issues* (11th ed.). Guilford, CT: Dushkin/McGraw-Hill.

Lillard, P. (1972). *Montessori—A modern approach.* New York: Schocken Books.

Lillard, P. (1996). *Montessori today: A comprehensive approach to education from birth to adulthood.* New York: Schocken Books.

Lines, P. (1996). Home schooling comes of age. *Educational Leadership, 54*(2), 63–67.

Linn, R., & Gronlund, N. (2000). *Measurement and assessment in teaching* (8th ed.). Upper Saddle River, NJ: Merrill/Prentice Hall.

Littlefield, G. (1965). *Early schools and school-books of New England.* New York: Russell & Russell, Inc.

Long, N., & Morse, W. (1996). *Conflict in the classroom: The education of at-risk and troubled students.* Austin, TX: Pro-Ed.

Lunenburg, F., & Ornstein, A. (2000). *Educational administration: Concepts and practices* (3rd ed.). Belmont, CA: Wadsworth.

Lyons, N. (1999). How portfolios can shape emerging practice. *Educational Leadership, 56*(8), 37–39.

MacDonald, R., & Healy, S. (1999). *A handbook for beginning teachers* (2nd ed.). New York: Longman.

Manno, B., & Finn, C. (1998). Charter schools: Accomplishments and dilemmas. *Teachers College Record, 99*(3), 537–552.

Manzo, K. (2000, October 4). Missed opportunities. *Education Week,* pp. 15–19.

Manzo, K. (2001). Academic record. In *Technology counts 2001: The new divide* (pp. 22–23). Washington, DC: Education Week.

Markow, D., Fauth, S., & Gravitch, D. (2001). *The MetLife survey of the American teacher.* New York: Metropolitan Life Insurance Company.

Marr, H. (1959). *The old New England academies.* New York: Comet Press.

Marsh, H., & Shavelson, R. (1985). Self-concept: Its multifaceted, hierarchical structure. *Educational Psychologist, 20,* 107–123.

Martinez Educational Foundation. (2001). *Mission statement and history.* Retrieved November 28, 2001, from http://www.martinezedfoundation.com

Maryland State Department of Education. (2000). *Digital divide results.* Retrieved from http://msde.aws.com/digitaldivide.asp

Marzano, R. (1998). What are the general skills of thinking and reasoning and how do you teach them? *Clearinghouse, 71*(5), 268–273.

Marzano, R., Pickering, D., & Pollock, J. (2001). *Classroom instruction that works: Research-based strategies for increasing student achievement.* Alexandria, VA: Association for Supervision and Curriculum Development.

Maslow, A. (1968). *Toward a psychology of being.* Princeton, NJ: Van Nostrand Reinhold.

May, H. (2001, June 11). *Highs, lows mark teacher's first year. Salt Lake Tribune.* Retrieved from http://www.sltrib.com/2001/Jun/06112001/utah/10894.htm

McCarthy, M., Cambron-McCabe, N., & Thomas, S. (1998). *Public school law: Teachers' and students' rights* (4th ed.). Boston: Allyn and Bacon.

McCuistion, F. (1932). The South's Negro teaching force. *Journal of Negro Education, 1*(1), 16–24.

Medin, D., Goldstone, R., & Markman, A. (1995). Comparison and choice: Relations between similarity

processes and decision processes. *Psychonomic Bulletin & Review, 2*(1), 1–19.

Meyer, L. (2001). New challenges. In *Technology counts 2001: The new divide* (pp. 49–64). Washington, DC: Education Week.

Michigan Department of Education. (2001). *Michigan Curriculum Framework.* Retrieved April 16, 2001, from http://cdp.mde.state.mi.us/MCF/MichiganCurriculumFramework.pdf

*Minersville School District v. Gobitis,* 310 U.S. 586 (1940).

Montecel, M., & Cortez, J. (2002). Successful bilingual education programs: Development and the dissemination of criteria to identify promising and exemplary practices in bilingual education at the national level. *Bilingual Research Journal, 26*(1), 1–21.

Music Educators National Conference. (1994). *National standards for arts education.* Reston, VA: Author.

Nash, R. (1996). *Real world ethics: Frameworks for educators and human service professionals.* New York: Teachers College Press.

Nash, R., & Shiman, D. (1974) The English teacher as questioner. *English Journal, 63,* 42–45.

Nathan, J. (2002, May 29). A charter school decade. *Education Week,* pp. 32, 35.

National Alliance of Black School Educators. (2001). *About NABSE.* Retrieved November 15, 2001, from http://www.nabse.org/about.htm

National Art Education Association. (2001). *NAEA publications list.* Retrieved November 21, 2001, from http://www.naea-reston.org/publications-list.html

National Association for the Education of Young Children. (1998). Learning to read and write: Developmentally appropriate practices for young children. *Young Children, 53*(4), 30–46.

National Association for the Education of Young Children. (2002). *About NAEYC.* Retrieved July 26, 2002, from http://www.naeyc.org/about/default.asp

National Association for Sport and Physical Education. (1992). *Outcomes of quality physical education programs.* Reston, VA: Author.

National Association for Sport and Physical Education. (1995). *Moving into the future: National physical education standards: A guide to content and assessment.* Reston, VA: Author.

National Association for Year-Round Education. (2001). *What is year-round education?* Retrieved March 23, 2001, from http://www.nayre.org/about.html

National Association for Year-Round Education. (2002). *Growth of public year-round education in the United*

*States over a 15-year period.* Retrieved July 24, 2002, from http://www.nayre.org/statistics.html

National Association of Independent Schools. (2001). *NAIS fact sheet.* Retrieved January 31, 2001, from http://www.nais-schools.org/nais/nafact.html

National Association of State Boards of Education. (2001). *Associate profile.* Retrieved from http://www.nasbe.org/Organization_Information/Association.html

National Association of State Directors of Teacher Education and Certification. (2001). *The NASDTEC manual on the preparation and certification of educational personnel.* Dubuque, IA: Kendall/Hunt.

National Board for Professional Teaching Standards. (2002). *History of the National Board.* Retrieved January 31, 2002, from http://www.nbpts.org

National Catholic Educational Association. (2002). *A statistical report on Catholic elementary and secondary schools.* Washington, DC: Author.

National Center for Children in Poverty. (2002). *Early childhood poverty—A statistical profile.* New York: Mailman School of Public Health, Columbia University. Retrieved from http://www.nccp.org

National Center for Education Statistics. (1993). *Language characteristics and schooling in the United States, a changing picture: 1979 and 1989.* Washington, DC: Government Printing Office.

National Center for Education Statistics. (1995). Approaching kindergarten: A look at preschoolers in the United States. In *National household education survey.* Washington, DC: Government Printing Office.

National Center for Education Statistics. (1997). *NAEP 1996 trends in academic progress.* Washington, DC: Government Printing Office.

National Center for Education Statistics. (2000, February). Internet access in U.S. public schools and classrooms, 1994–99 (NCES 2000-086). *Stats in Brief.*

National Center for Education Statistics. (2001). *Digest of education statistics.* Washington, DC: Government Printing Office.

National Clearinghouse on Child Abuse and Neglect Information. (2002). *What is child maltreatment?* Retrieved from www.calib.com/nccanch/pubs/factsheets/whatis.htm

National Coalition for the Homeless. (1999). *Homeless families with children.* Retrieved from http://www.qvctc.commnet.edu/student/GaryOkeefe/homeless/frame.html

National Commission on Excellence in Education. (1983). *A nation at risk: The imperative for educational reform.* Washington, DC: Government Printing Office.

National Commission on Teaching and America's Future. (1996). *What matters most: Teaching for America's future.* New York: Author.

National Council for Research on Women. (1998). *The girls report: What we know and need to know about growing up female.* New York: Author.

National Council for the Social Studies. (1994). *Expectations of excellence: Curriculum standards for social studies.* Washington, DC: Author.

National Council of Teachers of Mathematics. (2000). *Principles and standards for school mathematics.* Reston, VA: Author.

National Council of Teachers of Mathematics. (2001). *The basics: More than knowing computation facts and procedures.* Retrieved April 27, 2001, from http://www.nctm.org/news/speaksout/spksoutbasic.pdf

National Education Association. (1975). *Code of ethics of the education profession.* Washington, DC: Author.

National Education Association. (1997). *Status of the American public school teacher 1995–96.* Washington, DC: Author.

National Education Association. (2002). *NEA fact sheet.* Washington, DC: Author. Retrieved July 26, 2002, from http://www.nea.org

National Geographic Society. (1993). *The world of the American Indian.* Washington, DC: Author.

National School Board Association. (2000). *Charting a new course: Fact and fiction about charter schools.* Alexandria, VA: Author.

Nebraska Department of Education. (2002). *Nebraska reading/writing standards.* Retrieved August 14, 2002, from http://www.nde.state.ne.us/READ/Standards/ReadingWritingStandards.htm

Neill, A. (1960). *Summerhill: A radical approach to child rearing.* New York: Hart Publishing Company.

Nelson, J., Lott, L., & Glenn, S. (1997). *Positive discipline in the classroom.* (rev. ed.). Rocklin, CA: Prima.

*New Jersey v. T.L.O.*, 221 Cal. Rptr. 118, 105 S. Ct. 733 (1985).

Nieto, S. (1999). *The light in their eyes—Creating multicultural learning communities.* New York: Teachers College Press.

No Child Left Behind Act. (2002). Retrieved September 26, 2002, from http://www.ed.gov/legislation/ESEA02/pg1.html#sec101

Noddings, N. (1992). *The challenge to care in schools: An alternative approach to education.* New York: Teachers College Press.

Noddings, N. (1993). *Educating for intelligent belief or unbelief.* New York: Teachers College Press.

Noddings, N. (1995). *Philosophy of education.* Boulder, CO: Westview Press.

Nolan, D. (1982). Sexual harassment in public and private employment. *Education Law Reporter, 3,* 226–230.

Noll, J. (Ed.) (2001). *Taking sides: Clashing views on controversial educational issues* (11th ed.). Guilford, CT: Dushkin/McGraw-Hill.

Ogden, C., Flegal, K., Carroll, M., & Johnson, C. (2002). Prevalence and trends in overweight among U.S. children and adolescents, 1999–2000. *Journal of the American Medical Association, 288*(14), 1728–1732.

Olson, L. (2000, September 27). Children of change. *Education Week,* pp. 30–41.

Ozman, H., & Craver, S. (1999). *Philosophical foundations of education* (6th ed.). Upper Saddle River, NJ: Merrill/Prentice Hall.

Paintal, S. (1999). Banning corporal punishment of children. *Childhood Education, 76*(1), 36–39.

Paivio, A. (1990). *Mental representations: A dual coding approach.* New York: Oxford University Press.

Palmer, P. (1998). *The courage to teach.* San Francisco: Jossey-Bass.

Papert, S. (1980). *Mindstorms: Children, computers, and powerful ideas.* New York: Basic Books.

Papert, S. (1993). *The children's machine : Rethinking school in the age of the computer.* New York: Basic Books.

Papert, S. (2000). Computers and computer cultures. In *The Jossey-Bass reader on technology and learning.* San Francisco: Jossey-Bass.

*Parducci v. Rutland,* 316 F.Supp. 352 (N.D. Ala. 1970)

Parkay, F., & Haas, G. (2000). *Curriculum planning: A contemporary approach* (7th ed.). Boston: Allyn and Bacon.

Parsad, B., Lewis, L., & Farris, E. (2001). *Teacher preparation and professional development: 2000.* Fast Response Survey System. Washington, DC: U.S. Department of Education.

Pavlov, I. (1927). *Conditioned reflexes: An investigation of physiological activity of the cerebral cortex.* London: Oxford University Press.

Perelman, L. (1992). *School's out: Hyperlearning, the new technology, and the end of education.* New York: William Morrow.

Perkins, D. (1999). The many faces of constructivism. *Educational Leadership, 57*(3), 28–33.

*Peter W. v. San Francisco Unified School District,* 131 Cal. Rptr. 854 (Cal. App. 1976).

Petska, K. (2001). *U.S. has 33% share of Internet users worldwide year-end 2000 according to the Computer Industry Almanac.* Retrieved July 11, 2001, from http://www.c-i-a.com/200103iu.htm

Pew Research Center. (2001). *Post 9-11 attitudes: Religion more prominent, Muslim-Americans more accepted.* Washington, DC: Pew Forum on Religion and Public Life.

Piaget, J. (1950). *The psychology of intelligence* (M. Piercy & D. Berlyne, Trans.). New York: Harcourt, Brace.

*Pickering v. Board of Education,* 391 U.S. 563 (1968).

*Pierce v. Society of Sisters,* 268 U.S. 510 (1925).

Piirto, J. (1999). *Talented children and adults. Their development and education.* Upper Saddle River, NJ: Merrill/Prentice Hall.

Pijanowski, J. C., & Monk, D. H. (1996, July). Alternative school revenue sources: There are many fish in the sea. *School Business Affairs,* pp. 4–10.

Portner, J. (1998, February 25). Hispanic teenagers top black, white birthrate. *Education Week,* p. 5.

Postman, N. (2000). Some new gods that fail. In *The Jossey-Bass reader on technology and learning.* San Francisco: Jossey-Bass.

Postman, N., & Weingartner, C. (1969). *Teaching as a subversive activity.* New York: Delacorte Press.

Provenzo, E., Brett, A., & McCloskey, G. (1999). *Computers, curriculum, and cultural change.* Mahwah, NJ: Erlbaum.

Pulliam, J., & Van Patten, J. (1999). *History of education in America* (7th ed.). Upper Saddle River, NJ: Merrill/Prentice Hall.

Ravitch, D. (1983). *The troubled crusade: American education 1945–1980.* New York: Basic Books.

Ravitch, D. (1993, September 11). When school comes to you. *The Economist,* pp. 45–46.

Raywid, M. (1994). Alternative schools: The state of the art. *Educational Leadership, 52*(1), 26–31.

Razik, T., & Swanson, A. (2001). *Fundamental concepts of educational leadership* (2nd ed.). Upper Saddle River, NJ: Merrill/Prentice Hall.

Recruiting New Teachers. (2000). *The urban teacher challenge: Teacher demand and supply in the great city schools.* Belmont, MA: Author.

Reid, K. (2001). Racial disparities. In *Technology counts 2001: The new divide* (pp. 16–17). Washington, DC: Education Week.

Riak, J. (2000). *Danger zones: States in the U.S. that permit pupil-beating.* Retrieved from http://nospank. org/eddpts.htm

Rickover, H. (1959). *Education and freedom.* New York: E. P. Dutton.

Rickover, H. (1983, February 3). Educating for excellence. *Houston Chronicle,* p. 8.

Rogers, C. (1961). *On becoming a person.* Boston: Houghton Mifflin.

Rogers, C. (1969). *Freedom to learn.* Upper Saddle River, NJ: Merrill/Prentice Hall.

Rose, L., & Gallup, A. (2001). The 33rd annual Phi Delta Kappa/Gallup poll of the public's attitudes toward the public schools. *Phi Delta Kappan, 83*(1), 41–58.

Roszak, T. (1986). *The cult of information: The folklore of computers and the true art of teaching.* New York: Pantheon.

Rothstein, R. (1998). Bilingual education. The controversy. *Phi Delta Kappan, 79*(9), 672–678.

Rousseau, J. (1979). *Emile* (A. Bloom, Trans.). New York: Basic Books. (Original work published 1762.)

Rowan, B. (1994). Comparing teachers' work with work in other occupations: Notes on the professional status of teaching. *Educational Researcher, 23*(6), 4–17, 21.

Rubin, L. (1985). *Artistry in teaching.* New York: Random House.

Sack, J. (1998, February 11). Budget plan emphasizes new efforts. *Education Week,* pp. 1, 26.

Sack, J. (2000, December 6). Schools grapple with reality of ambitious law. *Education Week,* pp. 1, 27–29.

Sadker, M., & Sadker, D. (1994). *Failing at fairness: How America's schools cheat girls.* New York: Charles Scribner's Sons.

Sandham, J. (1999, May 5). Florida okays first statewide voucher plan. *Education Week,* pp. 1, 21.

Sandham, J. (2000, February 9). Barriers to the education of homeless cited. *Education Week,* p. 11.

Schank, R. (2000, January). A vision of education for the 21st century. *T.H.E. Journal,* pp. 43–45.

Schickedanz, J., Schickedanz, D., Forsyth, P., & Forsyth, G. (2001). *Understanding children and adolescents* (4th ed.). Boston: Allyn and Bacon.

Schunk, D. (2000). *Learning theories: An educational perspective* (3rd ed.). Upper Saddle River, NJ: Merrill/Prentice Hall.

Sergiovanni, T. (1994). *Building community in schools.* San Francisco: Jossey-Bass.

Sergiovanni, T. (2001). *The principalship: A reflective practice perspective* (4th ed.). Boston: Allyn and Bacon.

Shapiro, A. (2000). *Leadership for constructivist schools.* Lanham, MD: The Scarecrow Press.

*Sheehan v. St. Peter's Catholic School,* 188 N.W.2d 868 (Minn. 1971).

Sherman, A. (1997). *Poverty matters: The cost of child poverty in America.* Washington, DC: Children's Defense Fund.

Shulman, L. (1987). Knowledge and teaching: Foundations of the new reform. *Harvard Educational Review, 57*(1), 1–22.

Silberman, C. (1970). *Crisis in the classroom.* New York: Random House.

Sizer, T. (1984). *Horace's compromise: The dilemma of the American high school.* Boston: Houghton Mifflin.

Skinner, B. F. (1953). *Science and human behavior.* New York: Macmillan.

Slavin, R. (1983). *Cooperative learning.* New York: Longman.

Smerdon, B., Cronen, S., Lanahan, L., Anderson, J., Iannotti, N., & Angeles, J. (2001, Winter). Teachers' tools for the 21st century: A report on teachers' use of technology. *Education Statistics Quarterly.* Retrieved from http://nces.ed.gov/pubs2001/quarterly/winter/elementary

Snow, C., Burns, S., & Griffin, P. (1998). *Preventing reading difficulties in young children.* Washington, DC: National Academy Press.

Snyder, T. (Ed.). (1993). *120 years of American education: A statistical portrait.* Washington, DC: U.S. Department of Education.

Spandel, V. (2001). *Creating writers: Through 6-trait writing assessment and instruction* (3rd ed.). New York: Longman.

Sprick, R., Sprick, M., & Garrison, M. (1992). *Establishing positive discipline policies.* Longmont, CO: Sopris West.

Spring, J. (1986). *The American school 1642–1985.* New York: Longman.

Springate, K., & Stegelin, D. (1999). *Building school and community partnerships through parent involvement.* Upper Saddle River, NJ: Merrill/Prentice Hall.

Steel, L., & Levine, R. (1994). *Educational innovation in multiracial contexts: The growth of magnet schools in American education.* Palo Alto, CA: American Institutes for Research.

Strike, K., & Ternasky, P. (1993). *Ethics for professionals in education: Perspectives for preparation and practice.* New York: Teachers College Press.

*Stroman v. Colleton County School District,* 981 F.2d 152 (4th Cir. 1992).

Szasz, M. (1977). *Education and the American Indian.* Albuquerque, NM: University of New Mexico Press.

Taba, H. (1967). *Teachers handbook for elementary school social studies.* Reading, MA: Addison-Wesley.

Texas Youth Commission. (2000). *Dropout prevention programs.* Retrieved February 18, 2000, from http://www.tyc.state.tx.us/prevention

Thomas, R. (1985). *Comparing theories of child development* (2nd ed.). Belmont, CA: Wadsworth.

Thorndike, E. (1913). *The psychology of learning: Volume II. Educational psychology.* New York: Teachers College Press.

*Tinker v. Des Moines Independent Community School District,* 393 U.S. 503 (1969).

Trotter, A. (1999, May 19). Technology and its continual rise and fall. *Education Week,* pp. 30–31.

Tyack, D., & Cuban, L. (2000). Teaching by machine. In *The Jossey-Bass reader on technology and learning.* San Francisco: Jossey-Bass.

University of Missouri at Kansas City. (2002). *2002 Winter semester courses.* Retrieved January 31, 2002, from http://www.umkc.edu/ce4teachers/WS2002.htm

University of Nebraska–Lincoln. (2001). *Independent study high school.* Retrieved July 16, 2001, from http://www.unl.edu/ishs

U.S. Census Bureau. (2000). *Census 2000.* Washington, DC: Government Printing Office.

U.S. Department of Agriculture. (2001). *Child nutrition programs.* Retrieved from www.fns.usda.gov/cnd

U.S. Department of Commerce. (1975). *Historical statistics of the United States, colonial times to 1970.* Washington, DC: Author.

U.S. Department of Commerce. (1996). *Current population survey (October).* Washington, DC: Government Printing Office.

U.S. Department of Education. (2000). *E-learning: Putting a world-class education at the fingertips of all children.* Washington, DC: Author.

U.S. Department of Education. (2002). *Safe and drug-free schools program.* Retrieved September 9, 2002, from http://www.ed.gov/offices/OESE/SDFS/index.html

U.S. Department of Education (2003). *Overview of ED programs and services.* Retrieved January 10, 2003, from http://www.ed.gov/about/programs.jspon

U.S. Department of Health and Human Services. (1999a). *Child maltreatment 1997: Reports from the states to the National Child Abuse and Neglect Data System.* Washington, DC: Government Printing Office.

U.S. Department of Health and Human Services. (1999b). *HIV/AIDS surveillance report* (Vol. 11, No. 1). Washington, DC: Government Printing Office.

U.S. Department of Health and Human Services. (2002a). *A national strategy to prevent teen pregnancy.* Retrieved from http://aspe.hhs.gov/hsp/teenp/intro.htm on September 9, 2002.

U.S. Department of Health and Human Services. (2002b). *2002 Head Start fact sheet.* Retrieved August 28, 2002, from http://www2.acf.dhhs.gov/programs/hsb/research/02_hsfs.htm

U.S. Department of Justice. (1999). *1997 national youth gang survey.* Washington, DC: Government Printing Office.

U.S. Department of Labor. (1991). *The dictionary of occupational titles* (4th ed.). Washington, DC: Government Printing Office.

U.S. Department of Labor. (2000). *A nation of opportunity: Strategies for building tomorrow's 21st century workforce.* Washington, DC: Author.

U.S. Departments of Education and Justice. (2000). *2000 annual report on school safety.* Washington, DC: Authors.

U.S. General Accounting Office. (2000). *School facilities: Construction expenditures have grown significantly in recent years.* Washington, DC: Author.

Viadero, D. (1996, May 29). Middle school gains over 25 years chronicled. *Education Week,* p. 7.

Viadero, D. (1998, June 24). For better or worse, girls catching up to boys. *Education Week,* p. 5.

Virtual High School. (2001). *Introduction to VHS.* Retrieved July 16, 2001, from http://vhs.concord.org/content

Vygotsky, L. (1978). *Mind in society: The development of higher psychological processes.* Cambridge, MA: Harvard University Press.

Wagner, P. (1996). *Understanding professional ethics.* Bloomington, IN: Phi Delta Kappa Educational Foundation.

Walberg, H. (1999). Productive teaching. In H. C. Waxman & H. J. Walberg (Eds.) *New directions for teaching practice and research* (pp. 75–104). Berkeley, CA: McCutchen Publishing Corporation.

Walthers, K. (2001). Saying yes to vouchers: Perception, choice, and the educational response. In J. Noll (Ed.), *Taking sides: Clashing views on controversial educational issues* (11th ed.). Guilford, CT: Dushkin/McGraw-Hill.

Walther-Thomas, C., Korinek, L., McLaughlin, V., & Williams, B. (2000). *Collaboration for inclusive education.* Boston: Allyn and Bacon.

Washington Office of the Superintendent for Public Instruction. (2002). *New professional certificate.* Retrieved November 3, 2002, from http://www.k12.wa.us/ProfEd/Colleges/ProfCertInfo.asp

Watson, J. (1924). *Behaviorism.* New York: Norton.

Wavering, M. (Ed.) (1995). *Educating young adolescents: Life in the middle.* New York: Garland.

Webb, L., Metha, A., & Jordan, K. (2000). *Foundations of American education* (3rd ed.). Upper Saddle River, NJ: Merrill/Prentice Hall.

Weber, E. (1984). *Ideas influencing early childhood education.* New York: Teachers College Press.

Wenglinsky, H. (2000). *How teaching matters: Bringing the classroom back into discussions of teacher quality.* Princeton, NJ: Educational Testing Service.

West, E. (Ed.). (1972). *The black American and education.* Columbus, Ohio: Merrill.

White, K. (1999, October 27). Quietly, the school calendar evolves. *Education Week,* pp. 1, 12.

Wiecha, J., Sobol, A., Peterson, K., & Gortmaker, S. (2001). Household television access: Associations with screen time, reading, and homework among youth. *Ambulatory Pediatrics, 1*(5), 244–251.

Wingo, G. (1974). *Philosophies of education: An introduction.* Lexington, MA: D. C. Heath.

Wolfgang, C. (1999). *Solving discipline problems: Methods and models for today's teachers* (4th ed.). Boston: Allyn and Bacon.

Zehr, M. (1999). Reviewers play critical role in market for digital content. In *Technology Counts: 1999* (p. 28). Washington, DC: Education Week.

Zehr, M. (2001). Language barriers. In *The New Divides: Looking Beneath the Numbers to Reveal Digital Inequities* (pp. 28–29). Washington, DC: Education Week.

Zirpoli, T., & Mellow, K. (1997). *Behavior management: Applications for teachers and parents.* Upper Saddle River, NJ: Merrill/Prentice Hall.

# Name Index

# Subject Index

# Photo Credits

P. 317 by Jeff Atteberry, Indianapolis Star/SIPA Press; p. 117 by Peter Beck/Corbis; p. 312 by Shelley Boyd/PhotoEdit; p. 301 by Jeff Cadge/Getty Images Inc.–Hulton Archive Photos; p. 306 by Paul Conklin/Photo Edit; pp. 29, 30, 47, 89, 96, 140, 167, 183, 244 by Scott Cunningham/Merrill; p. 326 by Bob Daemmrich/Stock Boston; pp. 127, 153, 291 by Mary Kate Denny/PhotoEdit; p. 225 by H. Dratch/The Image Works; pp. 169, 270, 277 by Laima Druskis/PH College; p. 240 by Efield/Getty Images Inc.–Hulton Archive Photos; p. 132 by Anna Elias/Prentice Hall School Division; p. 95 by Buddy Endress/Silver Burdett Ginn; p. 354 by G & M David de Lossy/Getty Images Inc.–Image Bank; pp. 129, 367 by Will Hart/PhotoEdit; p. 9 by Chip Henderson/Getty Images Inc.–Stone Allstock; p. 106 by Michal Heron/PH College; p. 279 by Dorling Kindersley Media Library; p. 112 by Kathy Kirtland/Merrill; pp. 227, 232, 258 courtesy of the Library of Congress; pp. 3, 14, 16, 55, 63, 65, 79, 105, 143, 145, 151, 163, 175, 190, 201, 208, 209, 215, 251, 325, 351, 358 by Anthony Magnacca/Merrill; p. 58 by Karen Mancinelli/Pearson Learning; p. 339 by James Marshall/The Image Works; pp. 73, 176, 187 by Michael Newman/Photo Edit; p. 361 by Reuben Paris/Dorling Kindersley Media Library; p. 349 by Jose Pelaez/Corbis/Stock Market; p. 284 by A. Ramey/PhotoEdit; pp. 120, 343 by Mark Richards/PhotoEdit; p. 266 by Barbara Schwartz/Merrill; p. 294 by Silver Burdett Ginn; p. 229 by UPI/Corbis; p. 39 by ASAP/Sarit Uzieli/Photo Researchers; pp. 1, 202 by Todd Yarrington/Merrill; pp. 23, 45 by David Young-Wolff/PhotoEdit.